MW01626330

Stephen Shore

Stephen Shore

Quentin Bajac

With additional texts by David Campany, Kristen Gaylord, and Martino Stierli

The Museum of Modern Art, New York

Contents

As a partner of contemporary art at MoMA, Allianz is proud to sponsor the first exhibition in the United States to encompass the full range of photographer Stephen Shore's work, from the 1970s to the present day.

Allianz encourages people to explore new territories and to expand the boundaries they encounter, as we believe that there is no progress without risk-taking. Our engagement with the art of today reflects this belief, and we are honored to support exhibitions of contemporary artists who push the limits of their disciplines as they challenge expectations and conventions.

Throughout his career, Shore has been a true explorer of his medium, experimenting with a wide variety of photographic styles and formats: from the gritty black-and-white street photographs he made as a teenager, to the meticulously composed color images he shot with a view camera starting in the 1970s, to the iPhone pictures he has posted almost daily on his Instagram feed in recent years.

Stephen Shore's work reveals the uncommon in the ordinary and helps us to see the world differently, through the eyes of an artist. We hope viewers of this exhibition will gain inspiration from this extraordinary photographer's lifelong practice of reinvention and exploration in pursuit of his vision.

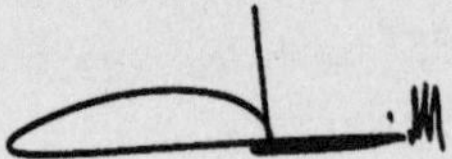

Jean-Marc Pailhol
Head of Group Market Management & Distribution
Allianz SE

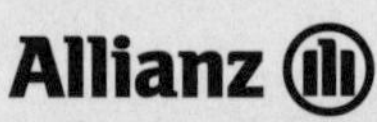

Director's Foreword

The Museum of Modern Art first acquired Stephen Shore's work in 1962, when Edward Steichen, the director of the Department of Photography, purchased three photographs from the artist, who was only fourteen at the time. Since then, Shore has become one of the most significant photographers of his generation, and central to the Museum's collecting and presenting of the photographic medium. In 1976 Shore had one of his first solo museum exhibitions here, and in 2013 MoMA organized a major acquisition of the photographer's work. Given his long history with the Museum, I am delighted to share this volume, published on the occasion of *Stephen Shore*, the most comprehensive exhibition of his work ever organized.

Quentin Bajac, The Joel and Anne Ehrenkranz Chief Curator of Photography, conceived of this important project, and his vision reveals the breadth and diversity of the artist's work. I offer thanks to him and to Kristen Gaylord, Beaumont and Nancy Newhall Curatorial Fellow, who assisted with all aspects of the exhibition and the publication. I am also grateful to author and curator David Campany and to Martino Stierli, The Philip Johnson Chief Curator of Architecture and Design, for their insightful contributions to this catalogue.

A project this ambitious is made possible only through the generosity of sponsors and lenders. We owe particular thanks to Allianz for its significant contribution to realizing this exhibition. Major support was also provided by The William Randolph Hearst Endowment Fund; The International Council of The Museum of Modern Art; our Committee Chairman, David Dechman, and Michel Mercure; and the Jo Carole Lauder Publications Fund. I am grateful to the Committee on Photography for its sustained commitment to building the Museum's collection of Shore's work.

And, finally, on behalf of the Board of Trustees, I am honored to salute Stephen Shore for his extraordinary career, and to thank him for entrusting its presentation to MoMA. It is always a privilege to work with contemporary artists, and the resourcefulness and good humor Shore brought to the project made the process all the more enjoyable.

Glenn D. Lowry
Director
The Museum of Modern Art, New York

[illegible] constantly changing nature of his work has sometimes been [illegible]

Rembrandt, for [illegible] is [illegible] for instance, how several ot[illegible]

Stephen Shore: Solving Pictures

Quentin Bajac

"Whenever I find myself copying myself—making pictures whose problems I've already solved—I give myself new issues to pursue."[1] Always moving forward, never locking into any single style, and seeing each image as a problem to solve: these practices have defined Stephen Shore's work for the past fifty years, regardless of his techniques or processes, whether shooting in color or black and white, using a view camera or posting images on Instagram. At the age of seventy, Shore is both one of the most influential and one of the most elusive American photographers of the twentieth and twenty-first centuries, a seeming paradox. After spearheading the movement known as the New Color Photography in the United States in the 1970s and directing the photography department at Bard College since 1982, Shore became a major catalyst in the renewal of documentary photography in the late 1990s, both in the United States and Europe—especially in Germany, where his work had struck a chord from the very beginning. Like the German photographers Bernd and Hilla Becher before him, Shore synthesized local photographic history (in his case, an American tradition spanning from Carleton Watkins to Walker Evans) with influences from various artistic movements, from Conceptual to Pop and even Photo-Realism.

The recognition of Shore's importance, however, is offset by the fact that the full range of his work remains unknown or misunderstood, too often reduced to his 1970s photographs of everyday American subjects. This can be explained by several factors, not the least of which is his lack of a clearly identifiable style. Shore's refusal to repeat himself has led him to seek out a new direction as soon as a style—that is, the combination of an approach and a subject—seems to be firmly in place, or when the visual solutions to a problem have become obvious to him and the pleasure of resolving the problem has vanished. His shifts between color and black and white, his use of both analog and digital, and his constant variation of scale and subject characterize a visually disparate body of work in which the prevailing rule seems to be the absence of rules. The black-and-white portraits taken at Warhol's Factory in the mid-1960s appear to be very unlike the large color landscapes of Montana from the 1980s, which in turn look quite different from the print-on-demand books he began in 2003.

The constantly changing nature of his work has sometimes been problematic for Shore; he has explained, for instance, how several of his galleries turned their backs on him when, after completing his series *Uncommon Places* in the early 1980s, he decided to open a new chapter. The variety of his output helps explain the unusual path his career has taken. Despite an extremely precocious beginning—selling three photographs to The Museum of Modern Art when he was a teenager and having his first solo exhibition at the Metropolitan Museum of Art at the age of twenty-three are part of his legendary backstory—Shore was largely overlooked in the 1980s and a good part of the 1990s. *American Surfaces*, now acknowledged as one of his most significant series, was not published until 1999, twenty-seven years after it was completed, and photography's wunderkind had to wait until the 2000s to see his photographs shown with any regularity. The true discovery of his work came only after he was fifty, largely through his admirers in Germany—and we might argue that he is still better known in Europe than in the United States.

The difficulty in grasping Shore's work as a whole has been heightened by the photographer's penchant for reinvention. In the past fifteen years, he has consistently revisited his own oeuvre, taking advantage of new technical possibilities, releasing ever more exhaustive publications of his best-known photographs, printing images from the 1970s in new sizes, and publishing print-on-demand books devoted to some of his past images. This constant reworking points to a photographer who has never been boxed in by a single approach and considers all of his work, whether current or past, to be alive and in flux. Although since 2000 a common misconception has arisen of Shore as a staunch defender of contact prints in the tradition of small-scale photography, he has repeatedly explained that, from the 1970s on, he has varied the dimensions of his prints and, more recently, has embraced new digital tools that he wishes he had had at his disposal thirty years earlier.

The somewhat inscrutable nature of his work is due to its level of detachment, which critics of *Uncommon Places* found unsettling from the start: Shore's images seemed to achieve a kind of perfect neutrality, both in their subject matter and their approach. Among the new American color photographers, he was undoubtedly the hardest to pin down and the most enigmatic, without the obsessiveness of William Christenberry, the picturesque qualities of Helen Levitt, the sensuality of Joel Meyerowitz, the baroque complexity of William Eggleston, or the narrative clarity of Joel Sternfeld. Even Shore's soft color tended toward the monochrome, staying true to a concept of photography as an art of transparency. It was this idea of "document as form" that John Szarkowski, head of the photography department at MoMA, was making the center of his program just as Shore was getting his start.[2] There are no heroics in Shore's images, but rather a poetics of the ordinary and the everyday and a refusal to create an effect for its own sake, echoing Walker Evans's desire to reveal the "deep beauty in things as they are."[3] His approach can be tied to a long American tradition of elevating the simple and the commonplace, in form as well as content, to a certain poetry and a way of life, from Ralph Waldo Emerson writing that "I embrace the common, I explore and sit at the feet of the familiar, the low,"[4] to Walt Whitman championing "a perfectly transparent, plate-glassy style, artless," characterized by "clearness, simplicity, no twistified or foggy sentences."[5] Despite its historical context, this enthusiasm for the vernacular, when expressed through photography, has been unsettling for some observers, and continues to be today.

The apparently unfathomable quality of Shore's photographs should not, however, obscure the fact that his work is founded on ideas that he uses to resolve the "problem" presented by each image. So, rather than trying to unify his oeuvre, we should accept it in all its diversity, seeing it as the result not of a style but simply of rules or practices. The first of these is his search for maximum clarity, which has been evident since the 1970s, when he began using an 8-by-10 camera, and is now furthered by the technical advances of digital cameras that allow for extreme precision but are much easier to handle than traditional view cameras. Shore abstains from retouching and reframing, showing the same kind of respect Henri Cartier-Bresson did for the shot as the key moment in the photographic act. Another guiding principle in the vast majority of his photographs is a respect—one might say a mystical respect—for natural light; his work does not include images taken at night, and, except in his early work, he very rarely uses artificial light or a flash. Shore has always had a preference for horizontal (or now, with Instagram, square) formats, which he considers better suited to his natural vision than vertical formats, of which there are very few examples in his work. But perhaps the most consistent of his practices is the discipline he exercises in limiting his number of shots as much as possible, a habit that owes a great deal to his use of the view camera: one shot of a given subject, and very little editing afterward. All in all, Shore's approach to photography is both transparent and contemplative, and marked by a willful economy of means. He likens the process of shooting photographs to one of his favorite activities: fishing. "I've found through experience that whenever—or so it seems—my attention wanders or I look away then surely a fish will rise to the fly and I will be too late setting the hook. I watch the fly calmly and attentively so that when the fish strikes—I strike. Then the line tightens, the playing of the fish begins, and time stands still. Fishing, like photography, is an art that calls forth intelligence, concentration, and delicacy."[6]

Shore has not yet been honored with a major retrospective in the United States, one that encompasses the diversity of his work, although a survey of his photographs recently traveled to several cities in Europe.[7] The current exhibition and catalogue aim to shed new light on his photography by presenting little-known and even never-reproduced pictures alongside deservedly famous series. The former include an exhibition of vernacular photography called *All the Meat You Can Eat*, which Shore organized in 1971, a true atlas of forms and ideas for his future work; editorial photographs that testify to the porous boundaries between his commissioned and personal images and illustrate the range of his work; stereoscopic images from 1974, which demonstrate his interest in constructing perspectival space; and landscapes, from natural, pared-down pictures of the American West to more domesticated views of the Hudson Valley to photographs taken outside the United States, as in his series of the Yucatán, Mexico, and Luzzara, Italy. The exhibition also features a number of images from Shore's Instagram posts, the latest expression of his longtime enthusiasm for popular forms of photography.

While the exhibition follows a chronological trajectory, the catalogue takes an intentionally different approach, one that sets it apart from other publications on or by Shore. Organized as an encyclopedia, the fifty-nine separate entries by four different authors bring together both overviews and details—discussions of the work overall, along with analyses of the specific images, people and places, publications and exhibitions, and themes and patterns that have constituted his career in photography. The structure of an encyclopedia allows the emphasis to be put on the leitmotifs that characterize his body of work, while its systematic and neutral perspective serves as a tribute to the descriptive, nonjudgmental approach of Shore himself. Rounding out the volume are research tools consisting of a detailed bibliography, a comprehensive list of Shore's exhibitions, and an extremely thorough photographic chronology compiled partially from travel logs the photographer kept during his trips. This publication aims to provide an image of Stephen Shore and his work with clarity, precision, and detail, like a photograph taken with an 8-by-10 view camera.

1. "Shifting Focus—The Decade Interview: Stephen Shore," Phaidon.com, February 4, 2011, www.phaidon.com/agenda/photography/picture-galleries/2011/february/04/shifting-focus-the-decade-interview-stephen-shore/.
2. Olivier Lugon, *Le Style documentaire* (Paris: Macula, 2001), 372.
3. James R. Mellow, "Walker Evans Captures the Unvarnished Truth," *New York Times*, December 1, 1974, D37.
4. Ralph Waldo Emerson, "The American Scholar," 1837, Digital Emerson: A Collective Archive, http://digitalemerson.wsulibs.wsu.edu/exhibits/show/text/the-american-scholar.
5. Walt Whitman, "Rules for Composition," early 1850s, The Walt Whitman Archive, http://whitmanarchive.org/manuscripts/transcriptions/duk.00130.html.
6. Stephen Shore, *Uncommon Places* (New York: Aperture, 1982), 63.
7. The traveling exhibition *Stephen Shore* was shown at Fundación MAPFRE, Madrid, and four other European venues, from September 2014 to September 2016. The last large exhibition of Shore's work in the United States was the Aperture Foundation's traveling exhibition *The Biographical Landscape: The Photography of Stephen Shore 1968–1993*, which focused primarily on his American photographs of the 1970s.

Encyclopedia

All the Meat You Can Eat

All the Meat You Can Eat took place November 8–20, 1971, at the 98 Greene Street Loft, a noncommercial alternative space in SoHo. The venue was started in 1969 by Holly and Horace Solomon, two art collectors who were also interested in theater, and the young Shore met them among Andy Warhol's entourage at the Factory. The Solomons hoped to break down barriers between disciplines by hosting not only exhibitions but also performances, theatrical productions, and poetry readings at the loft. Gordon Matta-Clark, Charles Simonds, Dennis Oppenheim, Bill Beckley, Bernadette Mayer, and Peter Schjeldahl all showed there—or showed up there—during the four years of the gallery's existence.

Embracing a century of photography, *All the Meat You Can Eat* was composed largely of found images collected by Shore and two friends, Weston Naef, then a curator at the Metropolitan Museum of Art, and Michael Marsh, an Amarillo native whom Shore met indirectly through Warhol's Factory. Featured in the exhibition were police photos of crime scenes; postcards; pages from interior design magazines; erotic and pornographic shots of various types (amateur, professional, reproduced on playing cards); ID photos; pictures of pets; commercial portraits; advertising images; press, fashion, and society photos (by Cecil Beaton and others); propaganda posters; and a photo of the American West by Eadweard Muybridge. The show also included images taken by Shore, such as shots taken with a Mick-a-Matic camera and color photos that would serve as the basis for the postcards in his series *Greetings from Amarillo, "Tall in Texas."*

With images framed or, most often, attached directly to the wall in grids or in sets and series, the presentation was deliberately dissonant; genres mixed and clashed with no apparent logic. *All the Meat You Can Eat* seemed emblematic of a new aesthetic marked by popular forms of photography, which Shore would embrace in *American Surfaces*, a series he undertook in March 1972, four months after the exhibition. As the photography critic Gene Thornton noted in the only published review, these images were selected not for their aesthetic appeal but for their contribution to the all-and-sundry nature of this production, a collection of pictures of a type rarely seen on the walls of galleries or museums. "Stephen Shore's fascinating selection is a healthy, if possibly somewhat unwelcome, reminder of the part that photography really plays in the world," Thornton wrote.[1] In 2004, Shore would reuse some of the postcards shown in *All the Meat* for one of his print-on-demand books, *Civic Architecture: Postcard Series.* (Quentin Bajac)

See also: *Amarillo, Texas*; *American Surfaces*

1. Gene Thornton, "From Fine Art to Plain Junk," *New York Times*, November 14, 1971, D38.

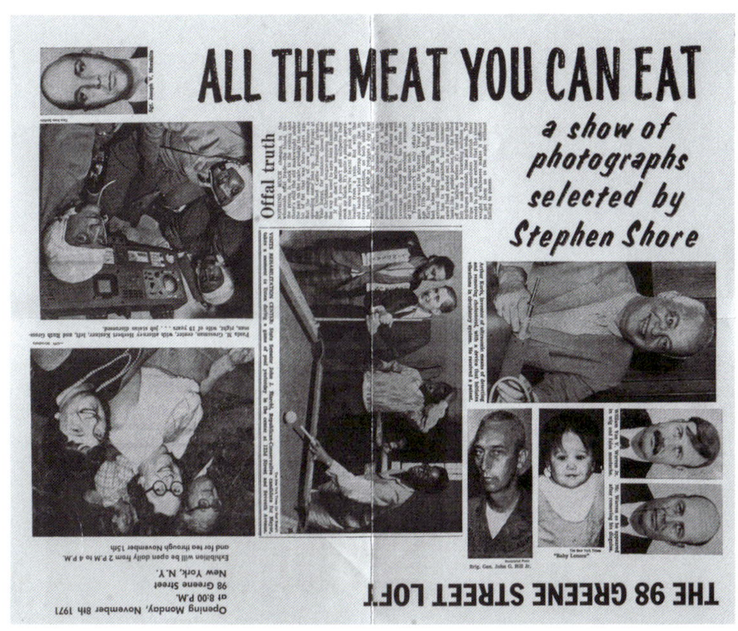

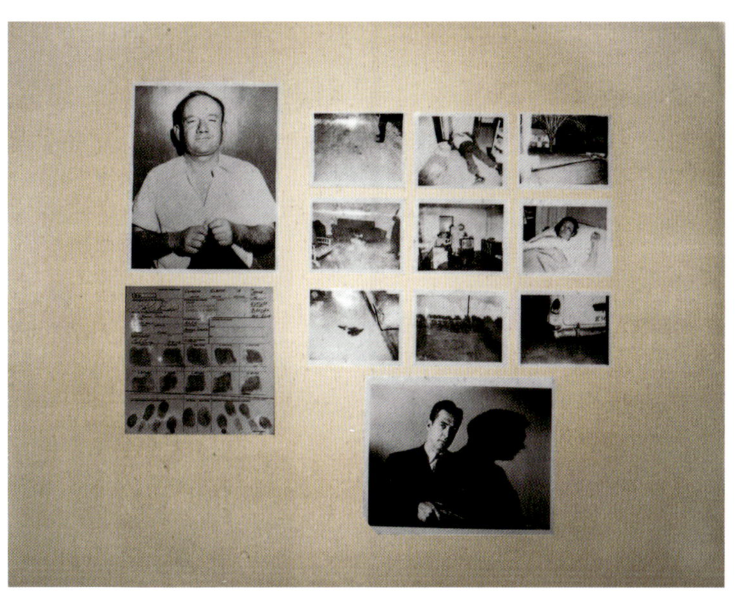

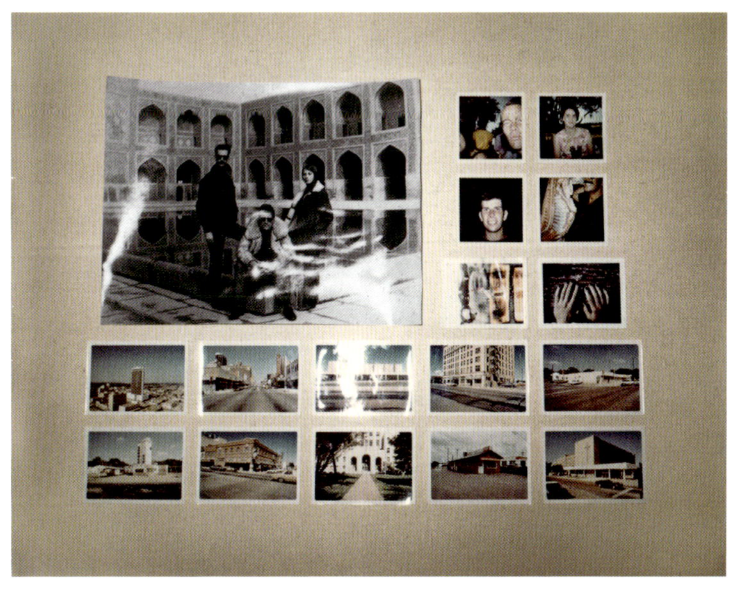

Poster for *All the Meat You Can Eat*, 98 Greene Street Loft, New York, November 8–20, 1971

Installation views of *All the Meat You Can Eat*, 98 Greene Street Loft, New York, November 8–20, 1971

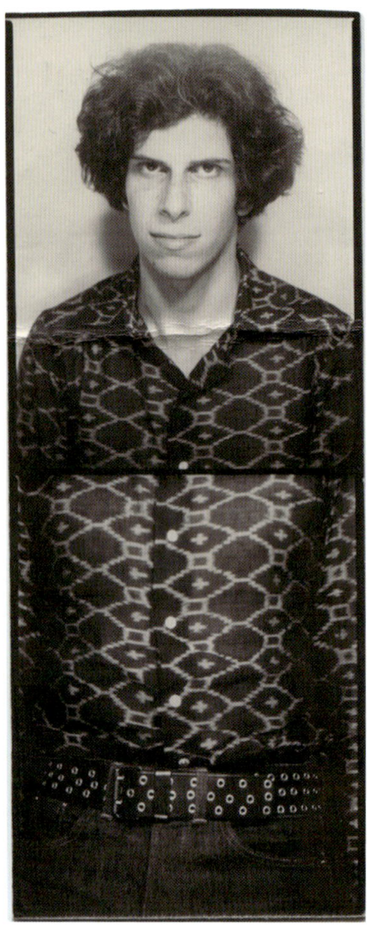

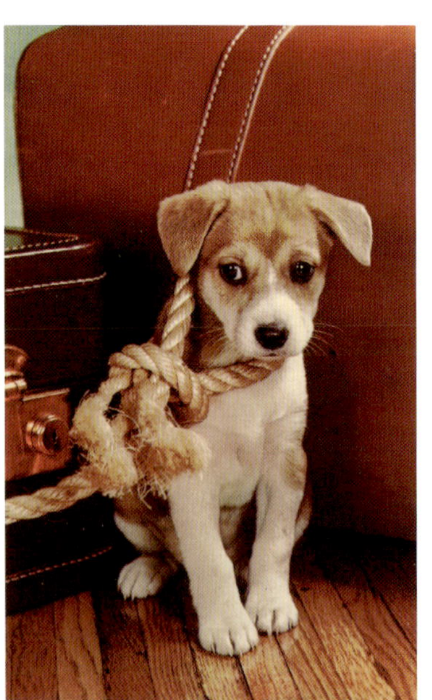

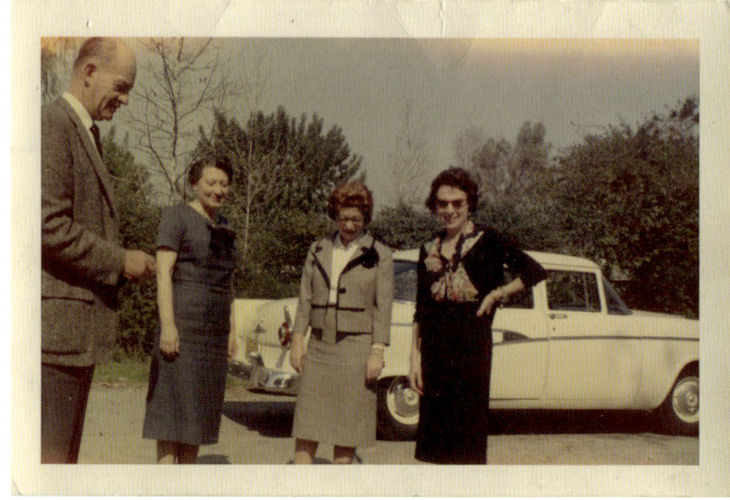

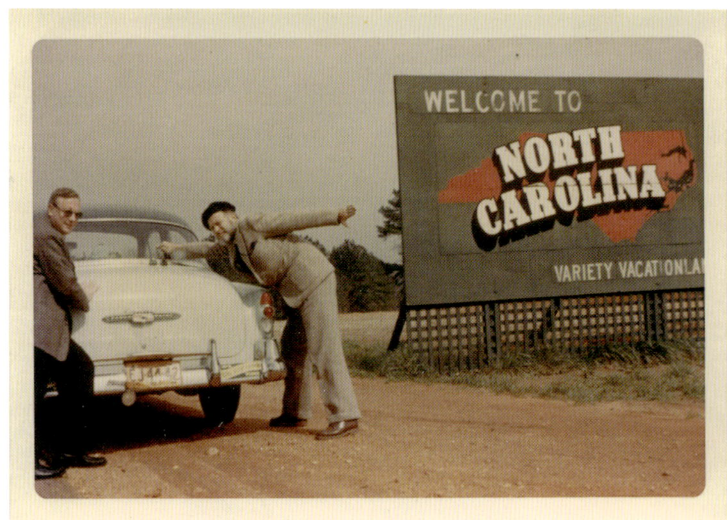

Material from *All the Meat You Can Eat*, 98 Greene Street Loft, New York, November 8–20, 1971

STAR
RESTAU
HALL TO RENT
BAR-B-Q

Greetings from
Oklahoma City
WEBERS
Jewelers

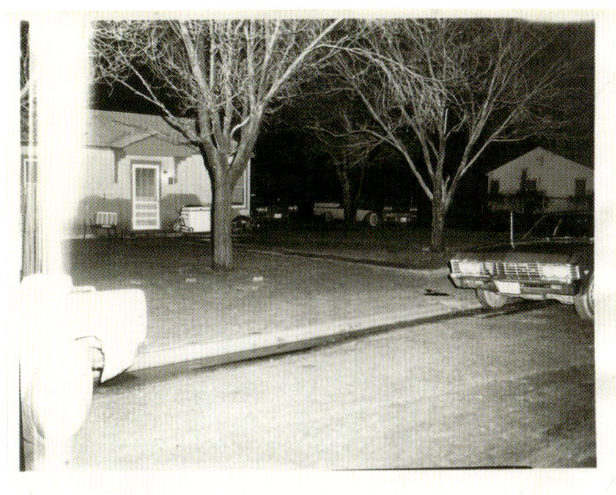

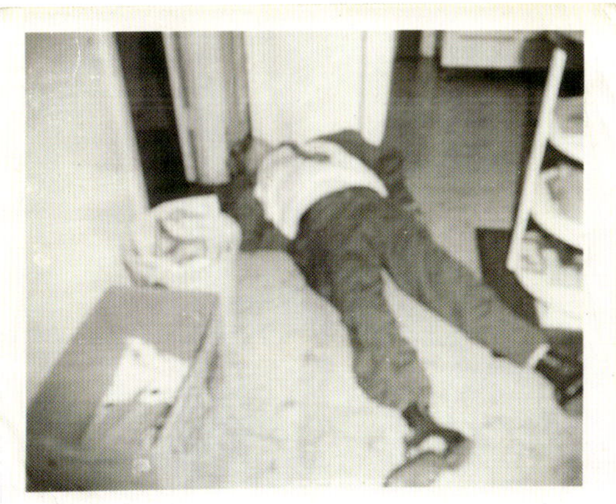

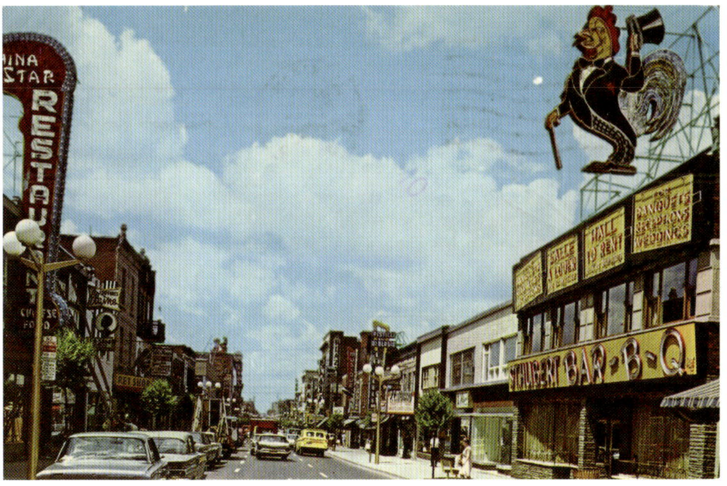

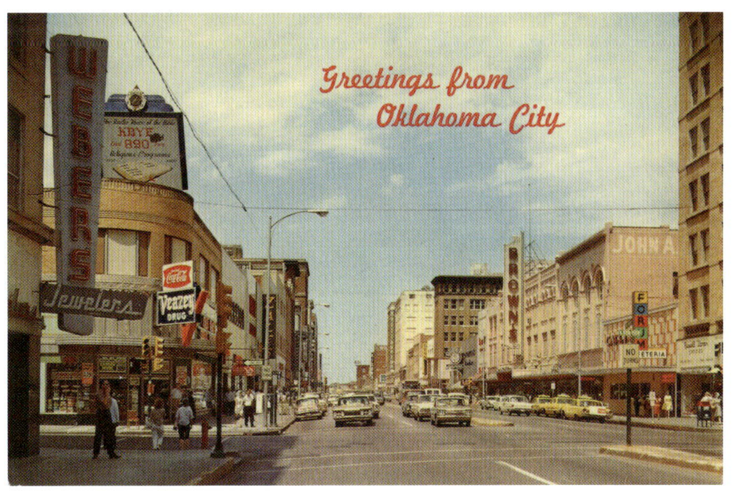

17.

Amarillo, Texas

Immortalized in the lyrics of "Route 66" by Bobby Troup, Amarillo, Texas, occupies a special place in the mythology of Shore's rural America. From 1969 to 1978, Amarillo was an essential stop in his summer travels through the southern and western United States. It was there that he stayed with his friend Michael Marsh, a native of Amarillo who spent the summer months at the family's ranch surrounded by friends and artists. Michael's brother, Stanley, a banker and heir to an oil and gas fortune, was an eccentric personality. Both an art collector and an artist in his leisure time, Stanley commissioned sculptures for the property from the Ant Farm collective, with whom he collaborated; from John Chamberlain, with whom Shore was friendly and traveled to England during this period; and from Robert Smithson (*Amarillo Ramp*, his last work).

Shore's first summers in Amarillo were crucial to his discovery of rural America and his decision to undertake a photographic exploration of it: "I loved Amarillo, not just what it looked like but the way people hung out—the pace of the life, the car culture, the barbecue joints."[1] Images made in Amarillo also appear in his two large color series from the 1970s, *American Surfaces* and *Uncommon Places*, including one of his best-known portraits, a photograph of Michael Marsh and his wife, Sandy (page 180).

During his third summer in Amarillo, in 1971, Shore created his first project in color, *Greetings from Amarillo, "Tall in Texas,"* a series of ten postcards of sites in the city, from public buildings to banal streetscapes, all photographed with a 35mm camera (pages 19–21). The identifications on the back of the cards include the name of the building or street but systematically omit the name of the city, thus creating a generic set of images representing the typical American town. Shore had 5,600 sets of the cards (packaged in their own case) manufactured at Dexter Press of West Nyack, New York, one of the country's best-known postcard printers.

Although *Greetings from Amarillo* was a commercial failure and was exhibited to relative indifference in 1972 at Thomas Gibson Fine Art in London (and at Light Gallery in New York the following year), the postcard sets were purchased by a number of Pop artists at the time, including David Hockney, R. B. Kitaj, and Eduardo Paolozzi. Later, Shore would reuse some of the unsold postcards, inserting them surreptitiously in postcard stands in cities he passed through during his travels, and he would occasionally receive them back in the mail, sent by friends. In 2007 Shore would devote one of his print-on-demand books, *11-1-07*, to Amarillo. (Quentin Bajac)

See also: *All the Meat You Can Eat*; *American Surfaces*; *Conceptual Sequences*; *Uncommon Places*

1. David Campany, "Ways of Making Pictures," in Marta Dahó, ed., *Stephen Shore* (Madrid: Fundación MAPFRE; New York: Aperture, 2014), 29.

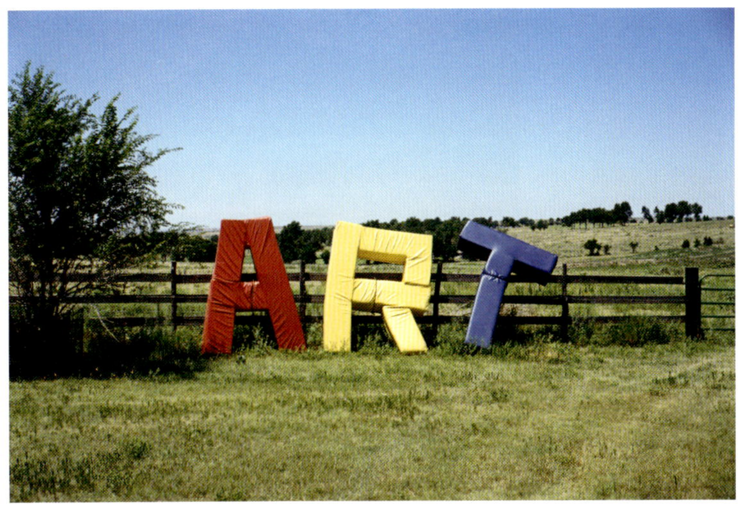

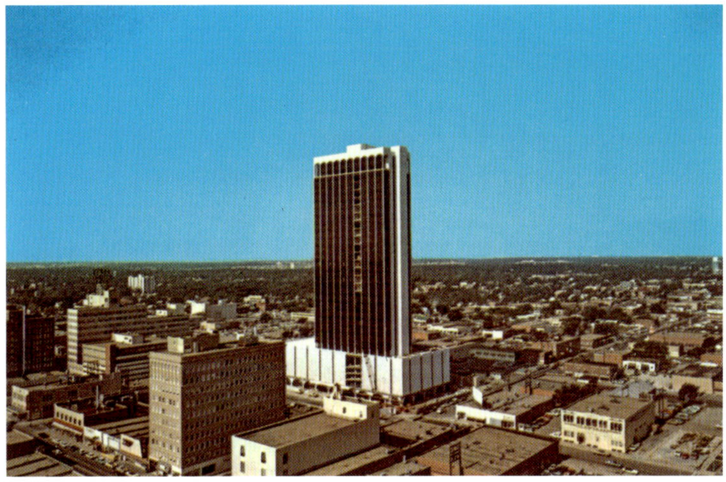

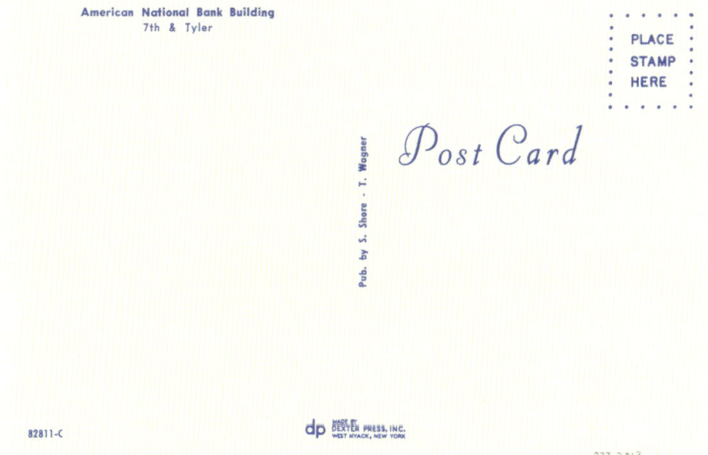

***Amarillo, Texas, July 1972.* 1972**

***American National Bank Building, 7th & Tyler.* 1971**

19.

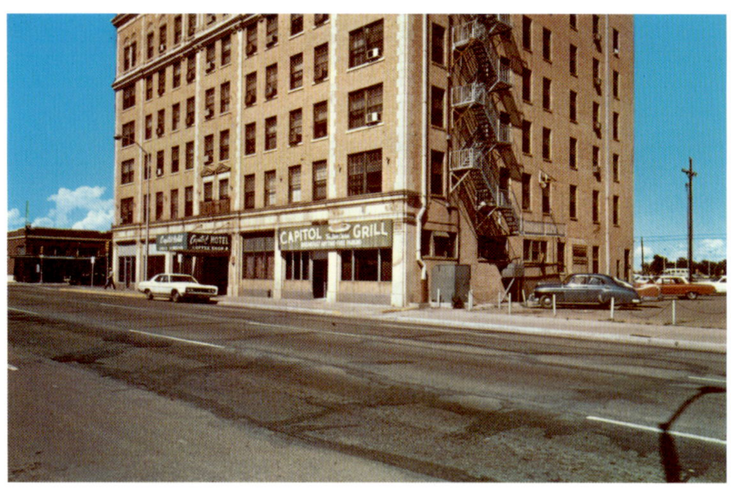

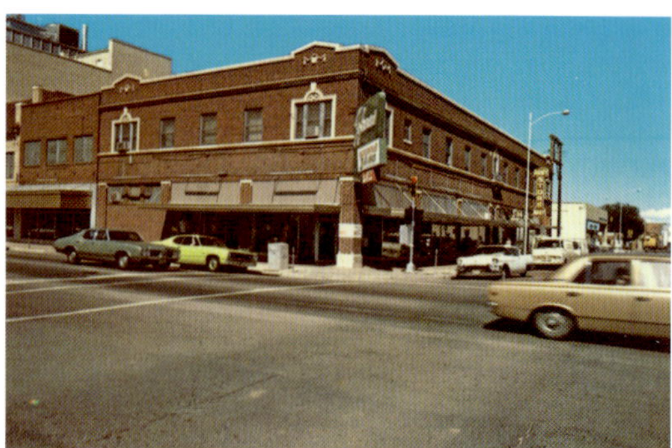

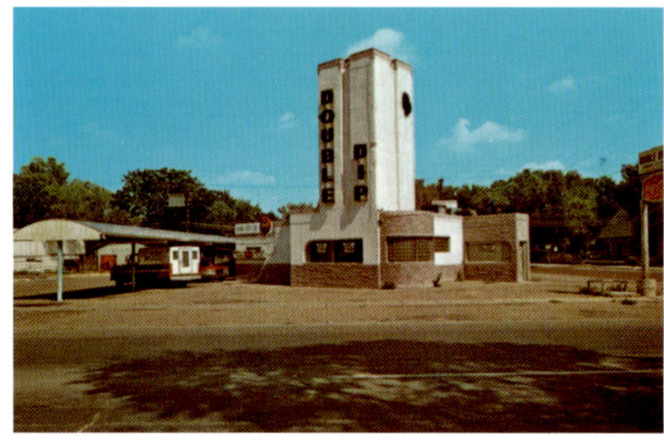

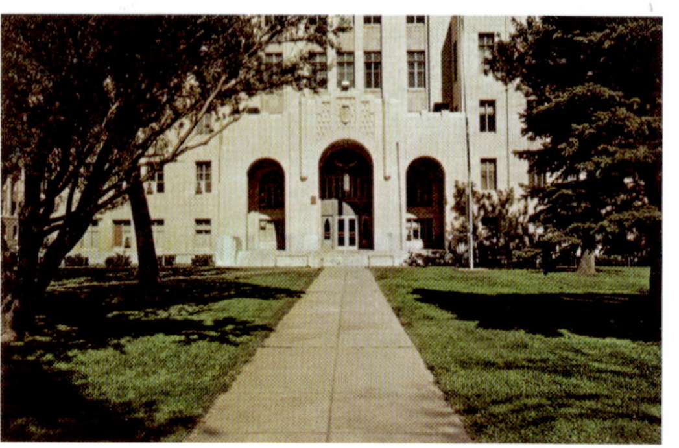

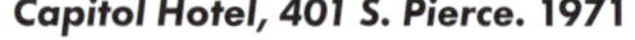

Capitol Hotel, 401 S. Pierce. 1971

Double Dip, 1323 S. Polk. 1971

Feferman's Army Navy Store, 201 E. 4th. 1971

Potter County Courthouse, Betw. 5th & 6th on Taylor. 1971

Fenley's Cafe, 322 W. 3rd. 1971

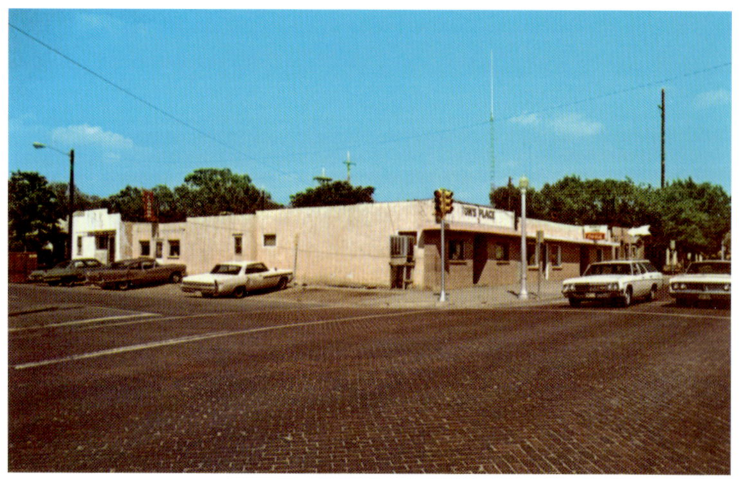

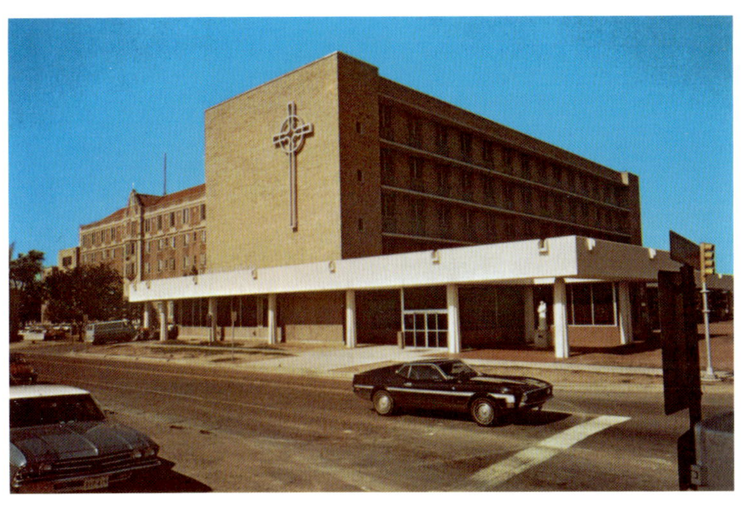

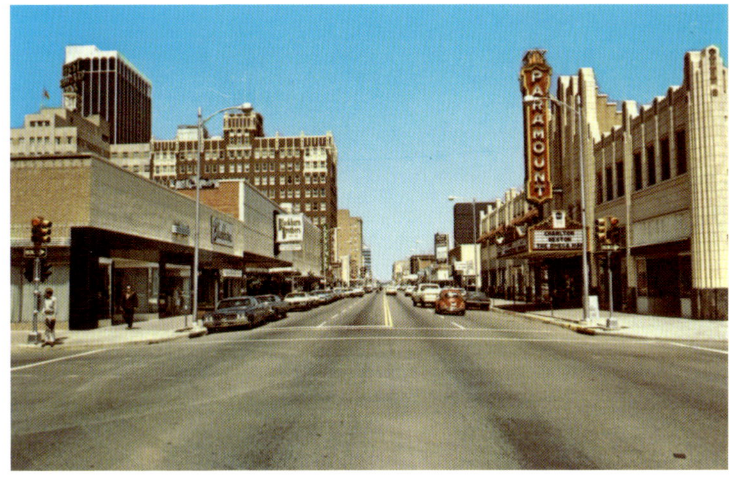

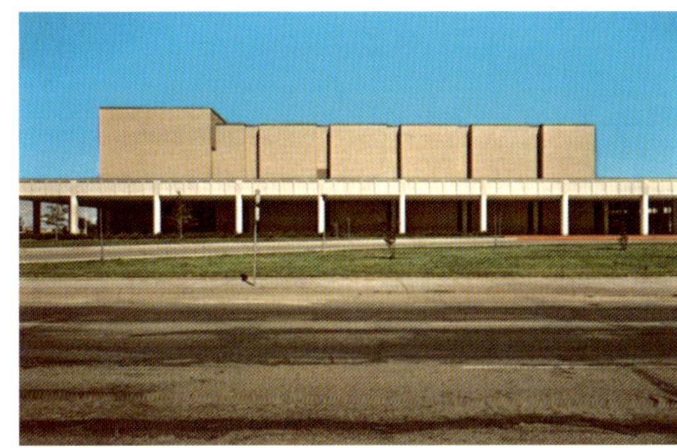

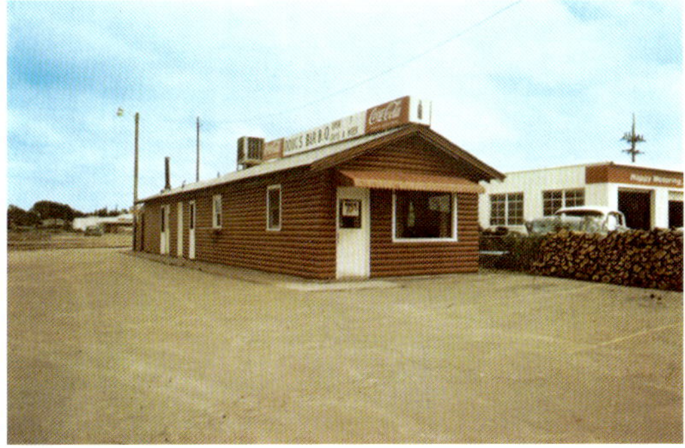

St. Anthony's Hospital, 735 N. Polk. 1971

Polk Street. 1971

Civic Center, 3rd & Buchanan. 1971

Doug's Bar B Q No. 1, 3313 S. Georgia. 1971

American Surfaces

American Surfaces is a series of color photographs that Shore began in March 1972, using a Rollei 35 equipped with a flash mounted beneath the camera. Initially focused on a trip from New York to the southern United States in June and July 1972, the series is often described as an American road trip, but it goes far beyond that. Continuing for more than a year and a half to the end of 1973, it also came to include a number of images made in New York and, over the course of subsequent travels, in the United States as well as in London and the Virgin Islands. The end of the series was marked by Shore's abandonment of the Rollei for a 4-by-5 camera, a change in device that would allow for more detailed negatives and larger prints.

Largely autobiographical, the series is presented as a photo-diary of Shore's daily life: "everyone I met, every meal, every toilet, every bed I slept in, the streets I walked on, the towns I visited," he explained in 2004.[1] This inventory reflects the repetitive nature of his subject matter—unremarkable buildings, main streets, highway intersections, hotel rooms, television screens, people's faces, toilet seats, unmade beds, a variety of ornamental details, plates of food, shopwindows, inscriptions, and commercial signs—as well as the intentionally simple and pedestrian photographic style Shore adopted, in the tradition of amateur snapshots.

Both a road movie in film stills and a private diary, *American Surfaces* exists at the juncture of several of Shore's preoccupations and influences at the time: a taste for repetitive patterns evident in his Conceptual practice, one that can be linked to both Andy Warhol's statement "I want to be a machine" and the systematic photographic series of Ed Ruscha, especially *Every Building on the Sunset Strip* (1966); a strong interest in amateur photography, evident in the almost constant presence of the halo of the flash, the classic amateur "mistake"; and, finally, a fascination with the aesthetics of kitsch and pop culture (particularly the postcard), but also with the vernacular, as seen in the work of Walker Evans, whose influence Shore readily acknowledges.

From September through October 1972, approximately 190 images from the series were shown at Light Gallery in New York, a selection that focused mainly on the trip Shore took earlier that year from New York through South Carolina, Alabama, and Texas to New Mexico and Arizona, returning via a northern route through Missouri, Illinois, and Ohio. The 3-by-5-inch Kodacolor prints, each with a thin white border, were displayed unframed, attached directly to the wall in a grid of three rows, across three walls in the back room of the gallery. The critic A. D. Coleman wrote a scathing review of the exhibition in the *Village Voice* (the only review published), in which he excoriated the photographer for the banality of the work and ridiculed the five-hundred-dollar price requested by the gallery for the set.[2] It was nevertheless purchased by Weston Naef, a friend of Shore's and a curator in the Department of Prints and Photographs at the Metropolitan Museum of Art, who, two years later, donated the entire set to the institution.

American Surfaces is sometimes credited with having a powerful influence on color photography over the next three decades, but it is necessary to put this claim in context: unpublished at the time, the series remained largely invisible for almost thirty years. It was rediscovered in 1999 by way of an exhibition in Cologne and Frankfurt and the accompanying catalogue (published by Schirmer/Mosel), followed in 2005 by an expanded English edition published by Phaidon. For both these editions Shore revisited his negatives, going beyond the trip of 1972 and extending the series to late 1973, adding a number of images and subtracting others. *American Surfaces* as it is known today, primarily through these publications, differs substantially from the series as it originally appeared in the 1972 exhibition. (Quentin Bajac)

See also: *Cameras*; *Color*; *Food*; *Germany*; *Light Gallery*; *Normal, Illinois*; *Portraiture*; *Road Trips*

1. "Stephen Shore in a Conversation with Lynne Tillman," in *Uncommon Places: The Complete Works* (New York: Aperture, 2004), 179.
2. A. D. Coleman, "Latent Image: American Yawn, Irish Wail," *Village Voice*, October 5, 1972, 31.

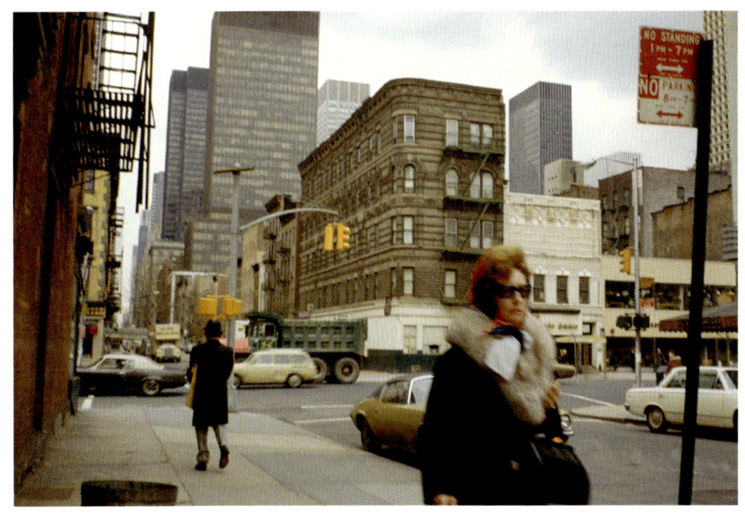

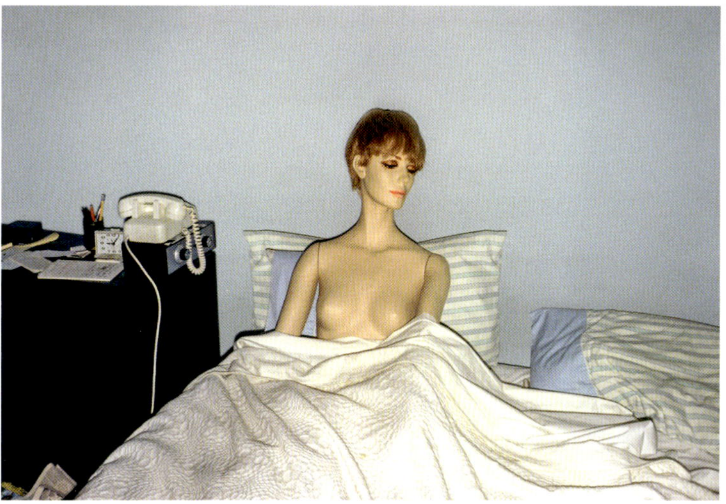

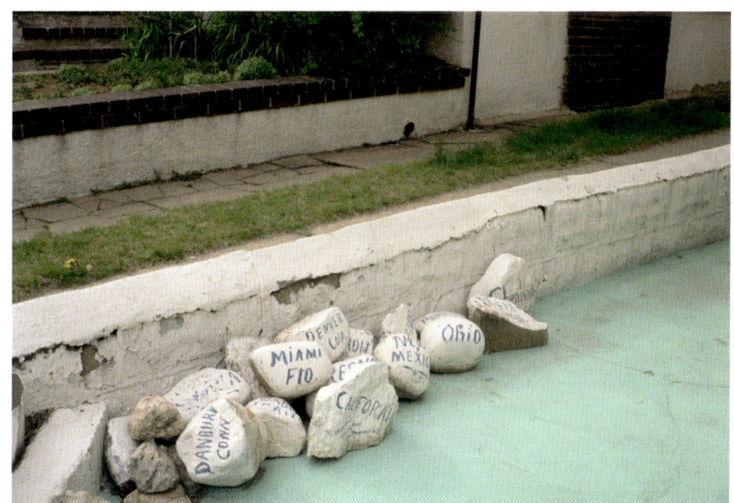

New York, New York, March 1972. 1972

New York, New York, April 1972. 1972

Queens, New York, April 1972. 1972

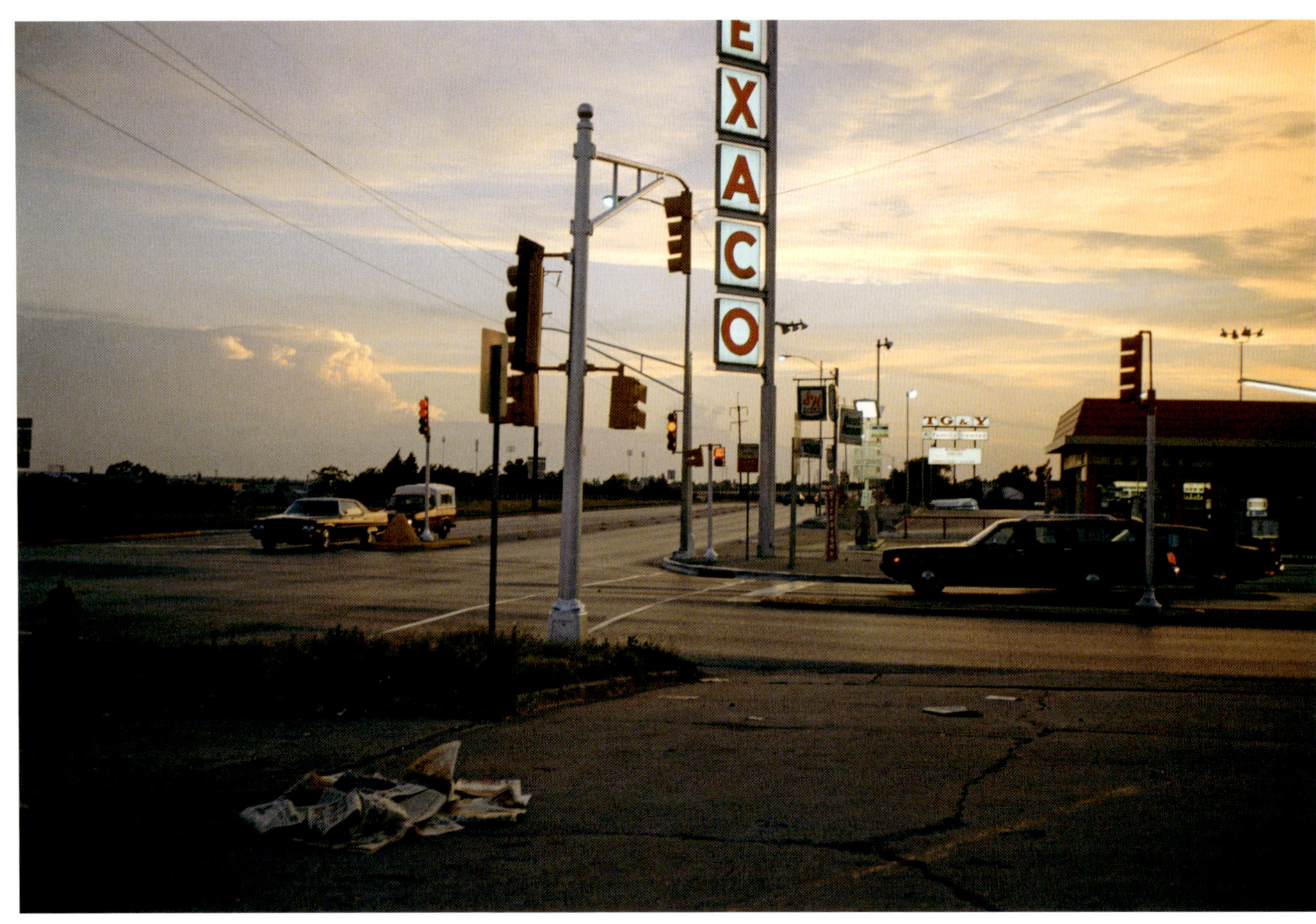

Oklahoma City, Oklahoma, July 1972. 1972

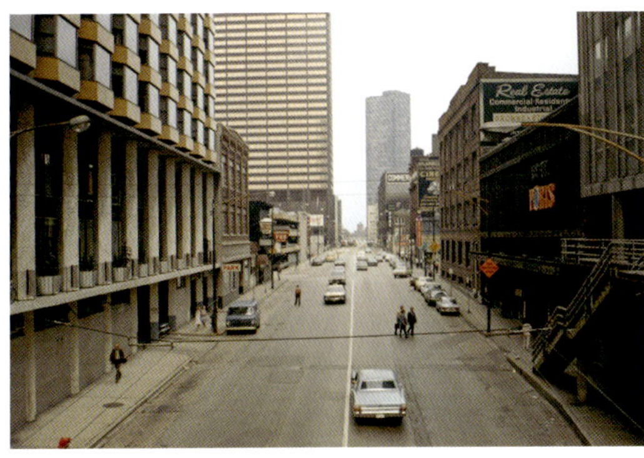

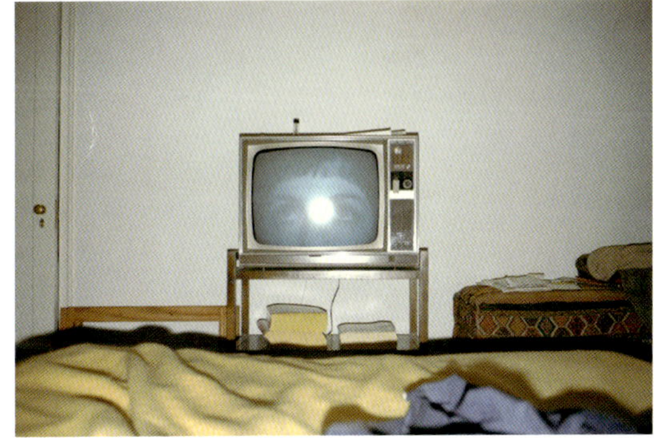

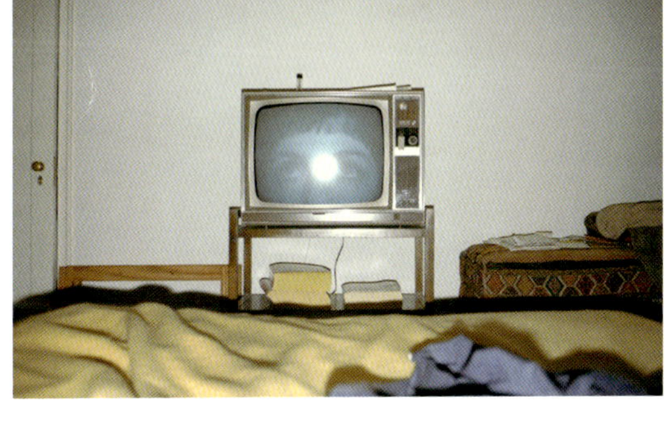

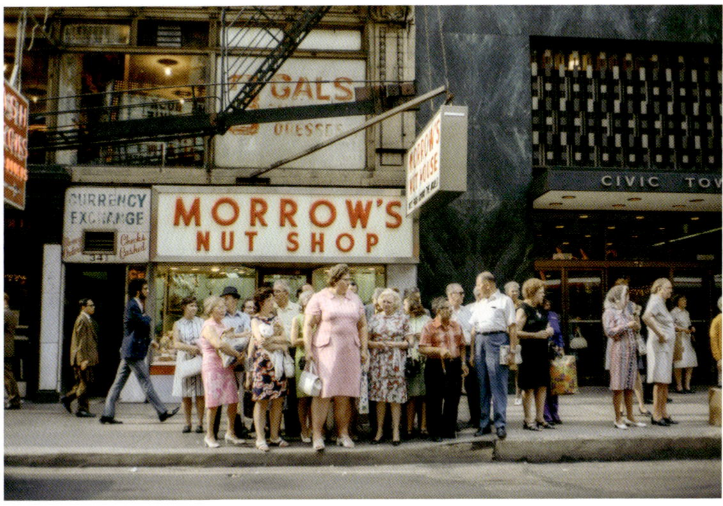

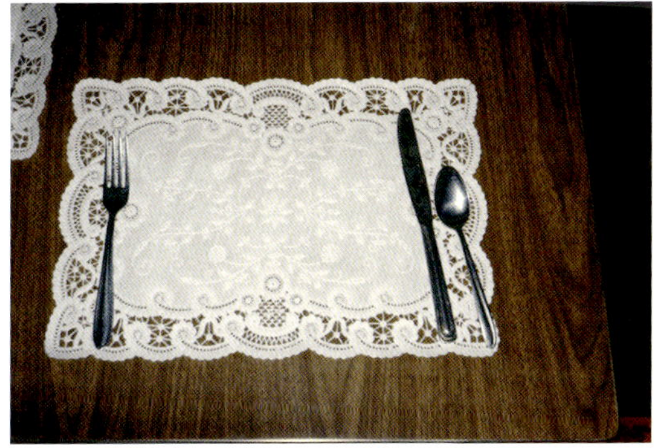

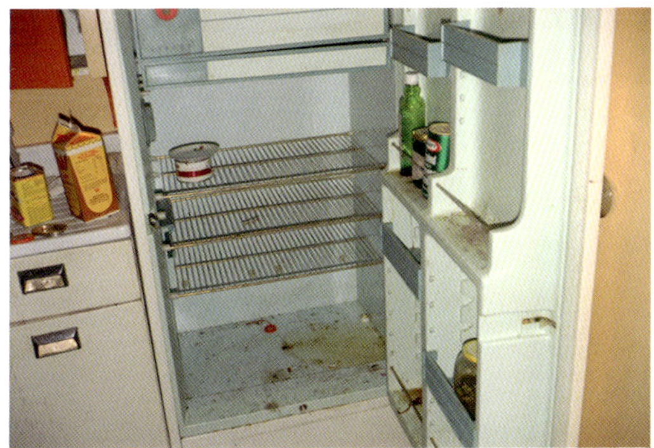

Chicago, Illinois, July 1972. 1972

New York, New York, March–April 1973. 1973

Chicago, Illinois, July 1972. 1972

Chicago, Illinois, July 1972. 1972

Pontiac, Michigan, July 1972. 1972

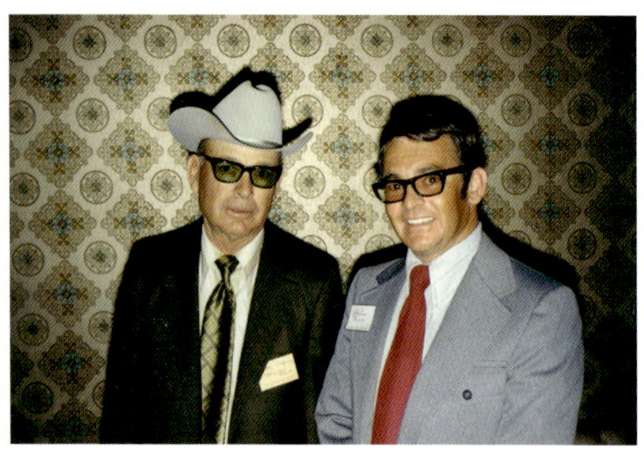

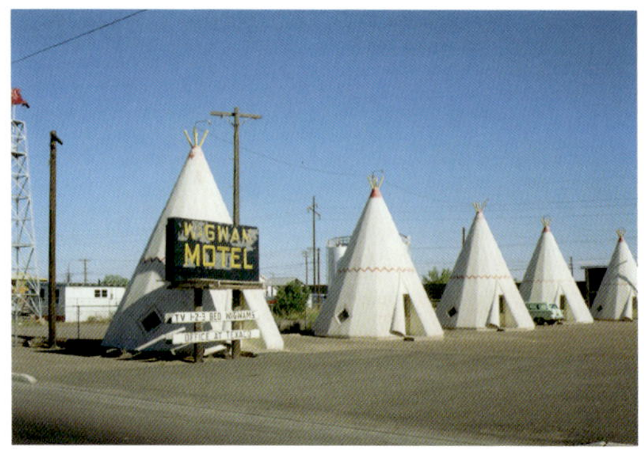

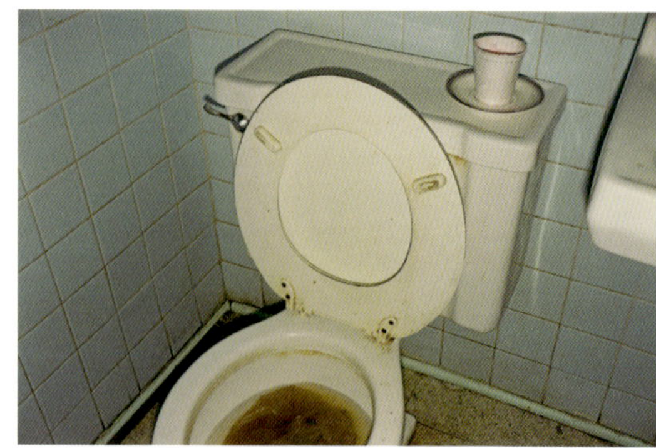

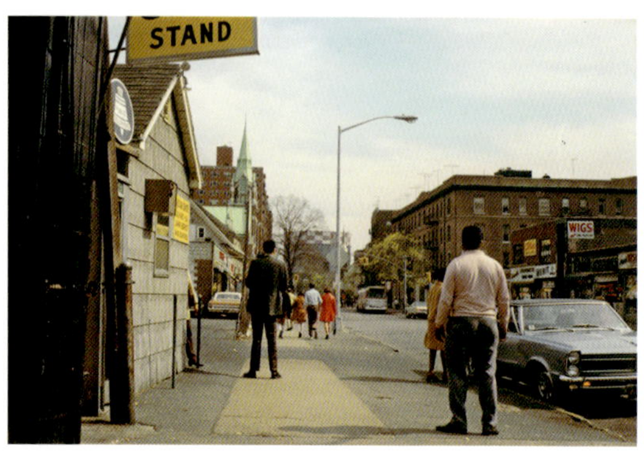

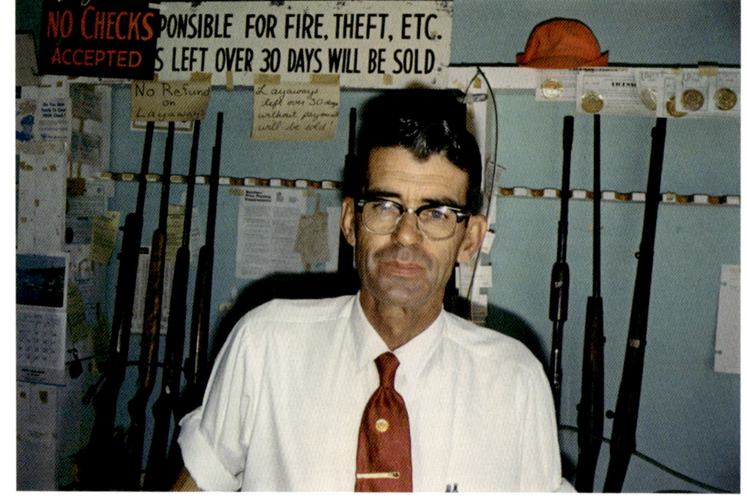

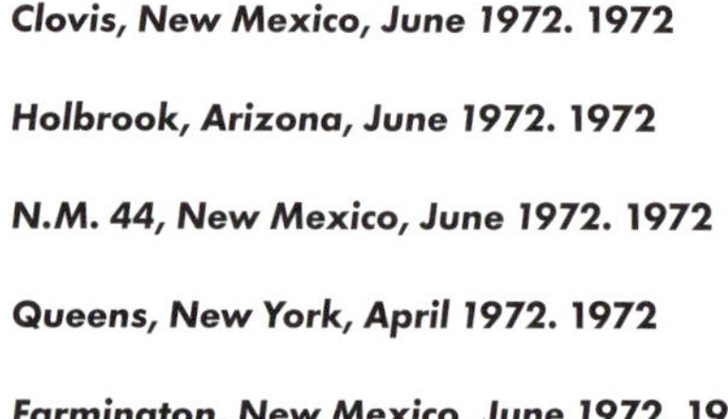

Clovis, New Mexico, June 1972. 1972

Holbrook, Arizona, June 1972. 1972

N.M. 44, New Mexico, June 1972. 1972

Queens, New York, April 1972. 1972

Farmington, New Mexico, June 1972. 1972

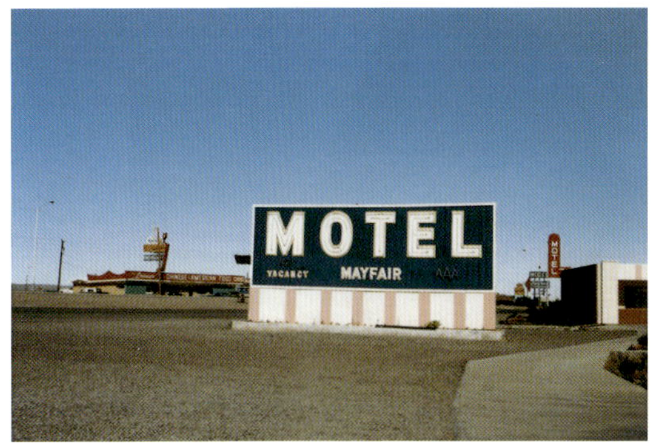

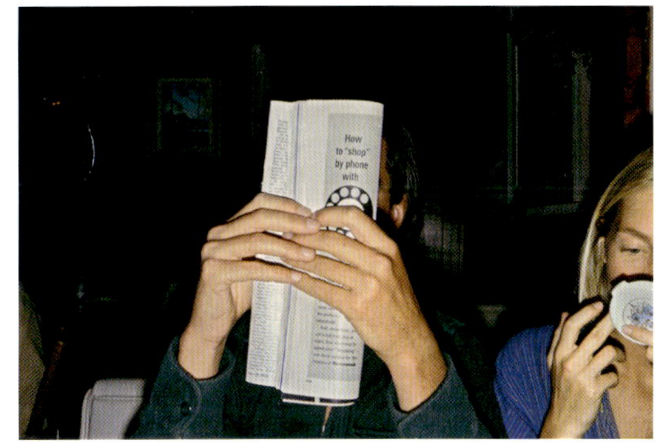

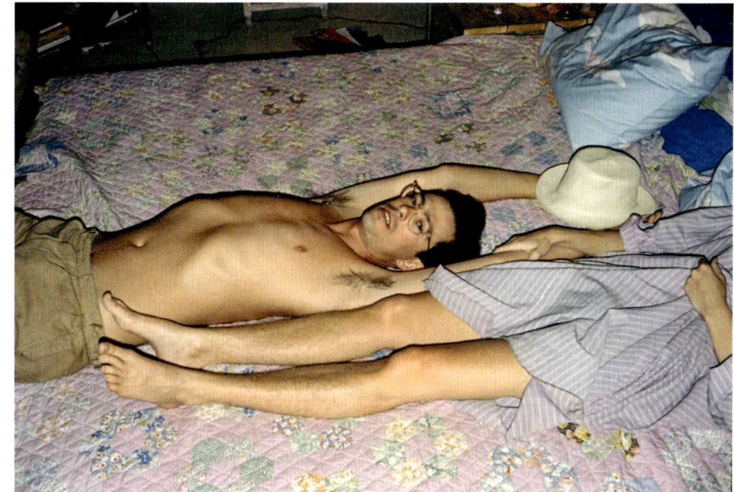

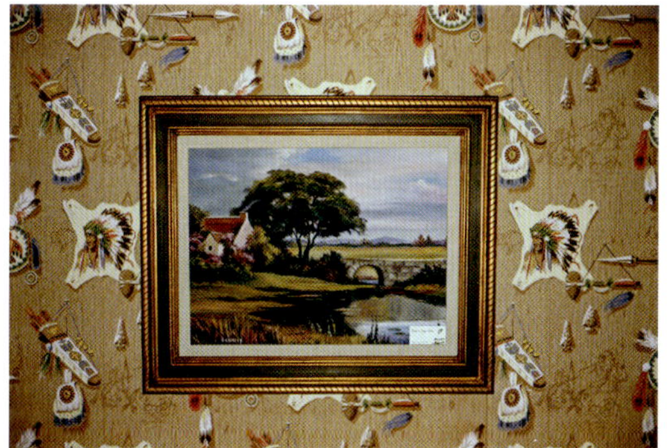

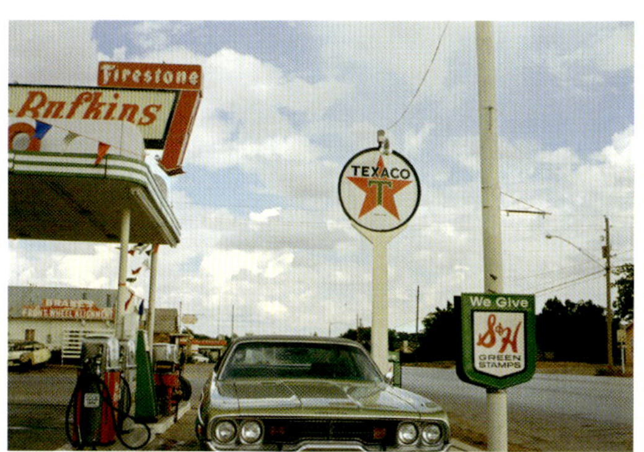

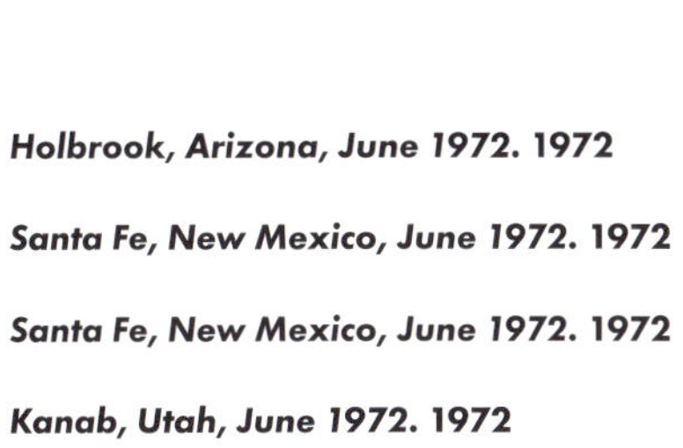

Holbrook, Arizona, June 1972. 1972

Santa Fe, New Mexico, June 1972. 1972

Santa Fe, New Mexico, June 1972. 1972

Kanab, Utah, June 1972. 1972

Mineral Wells, Texas, June 1972. 1972

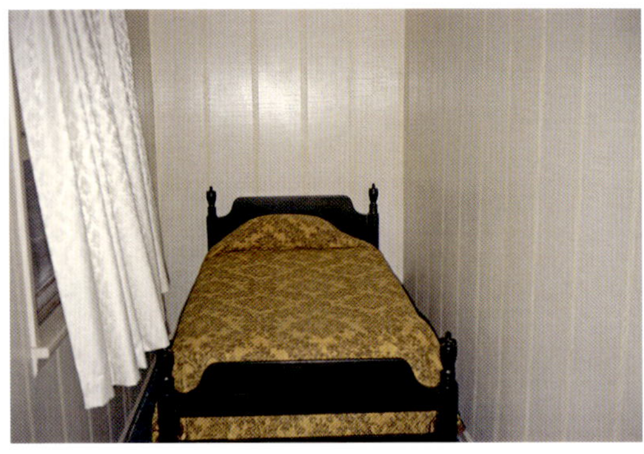

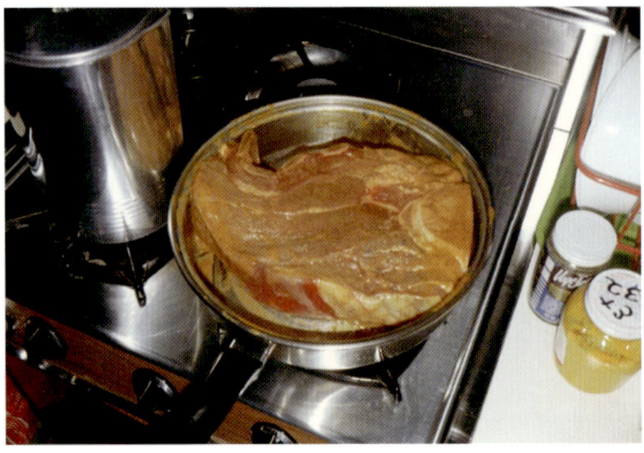

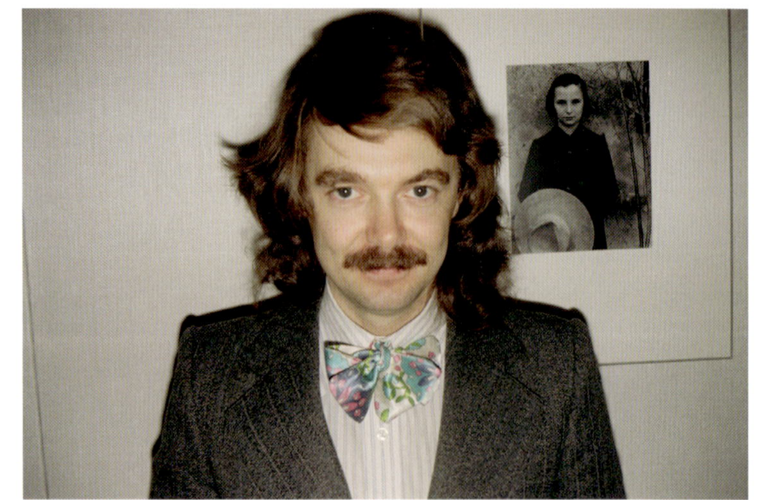

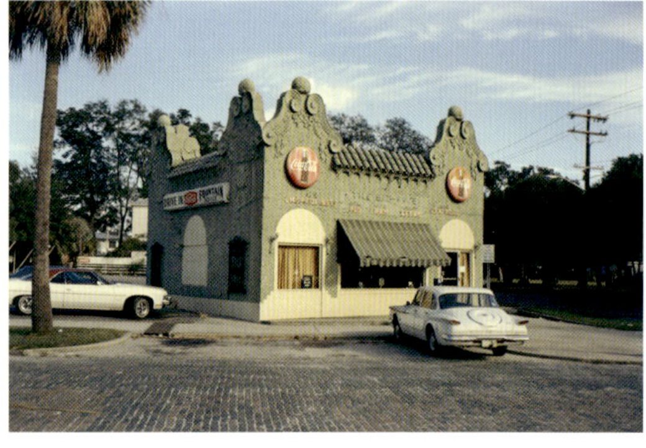

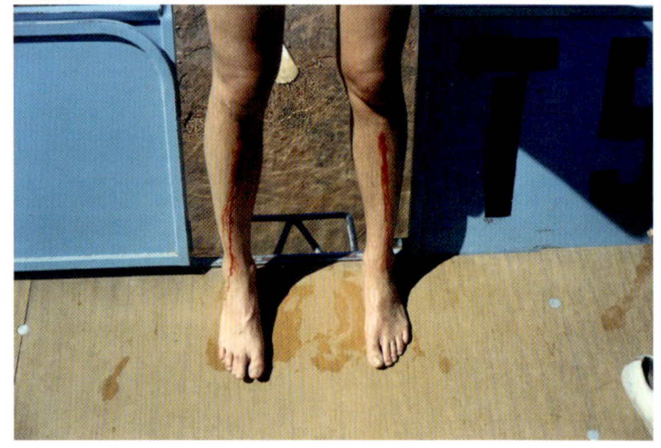

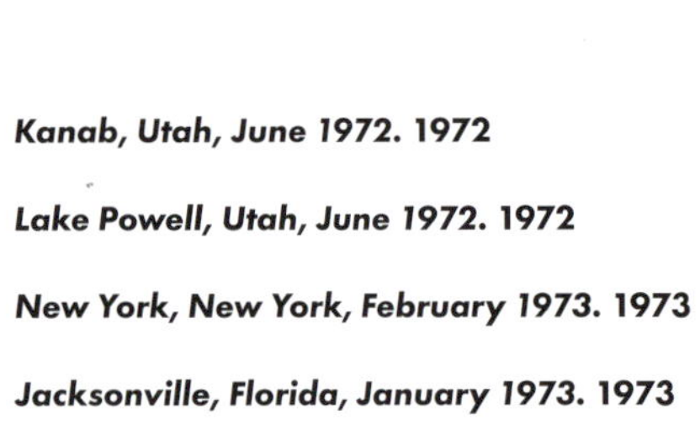

Kanab, Utah, June 1972. 1972

Lake Powell, Utah, June 1972. 1972

New York, New York, February 1973. 1973

Jacksonville, Florida, January 1973. 1973

Lake Powell, Utah, June 1972. 1972

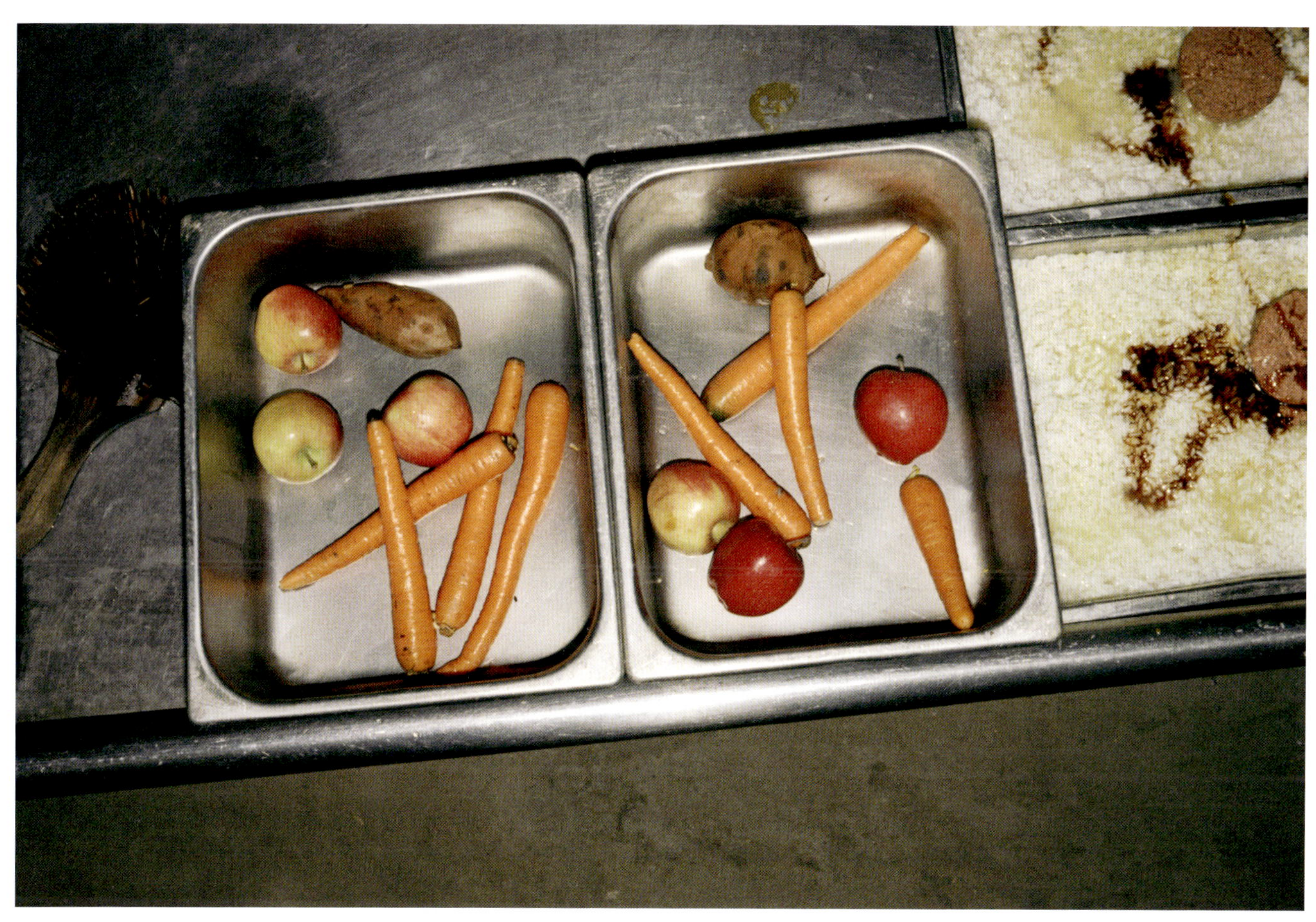

Washington, D.C., November 1972. **1972**

29.

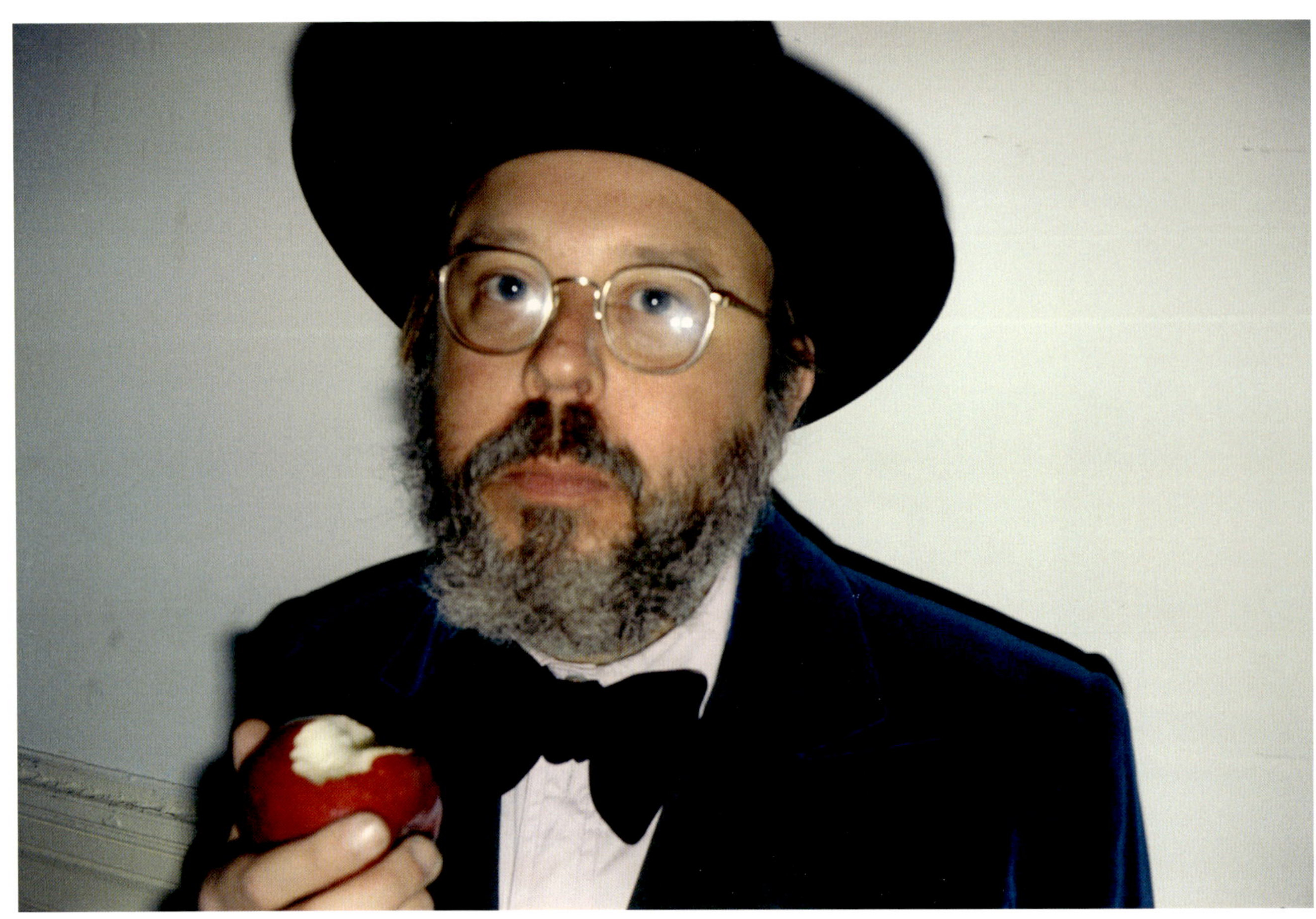

New York, New York, September–October 1972. 1972

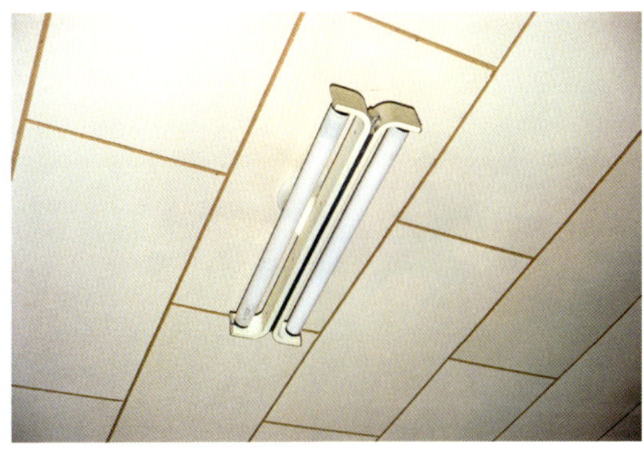

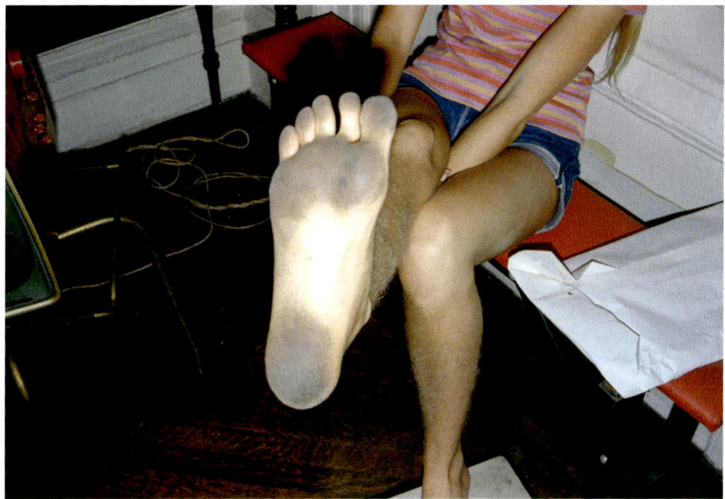

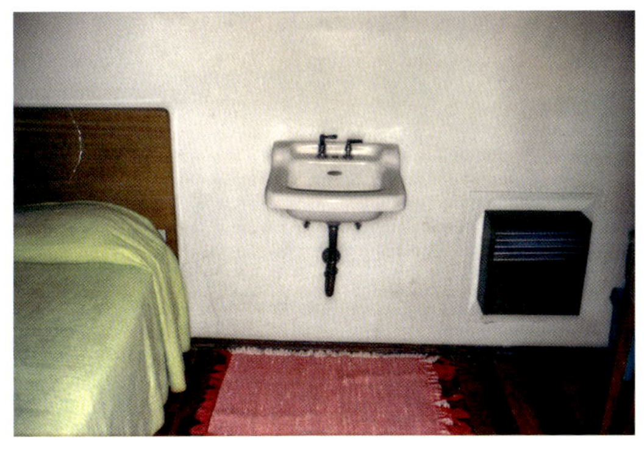

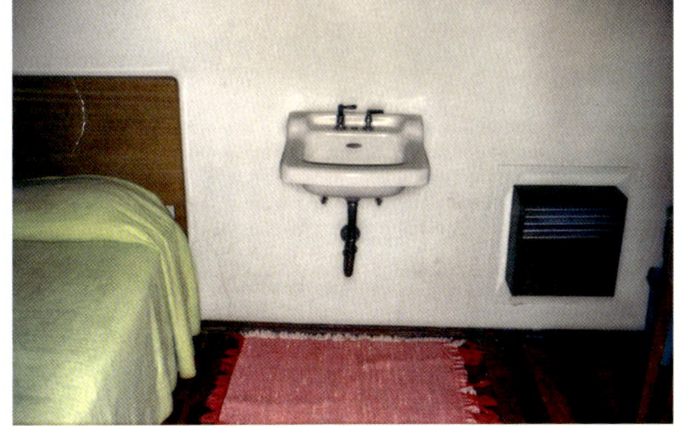

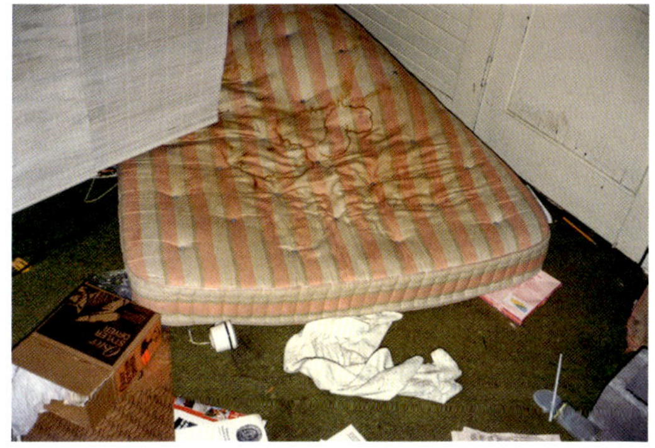

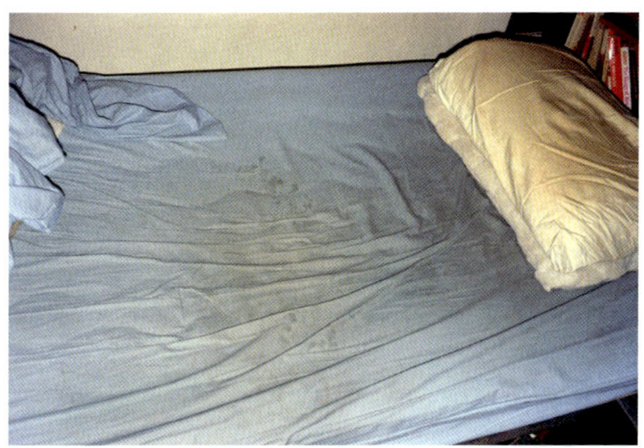

Granite, Oklahoma, July 1972. 1972

Granite, Oklahoma, July 1972. 1972

New York, New York, July 1972. 1972

Amarillo, Texas, August 1973. 1973

New York, New York, July 1972. 1972

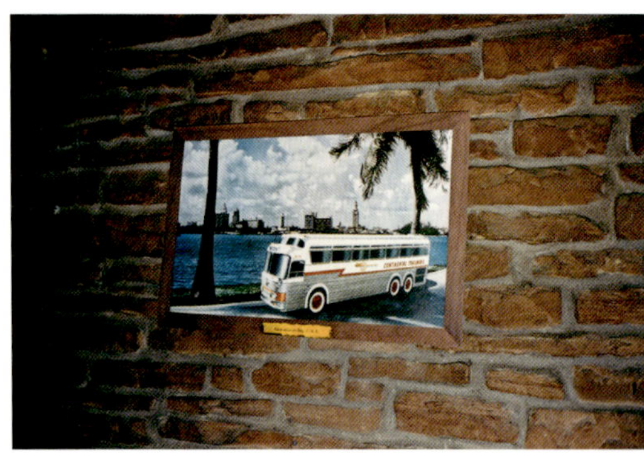

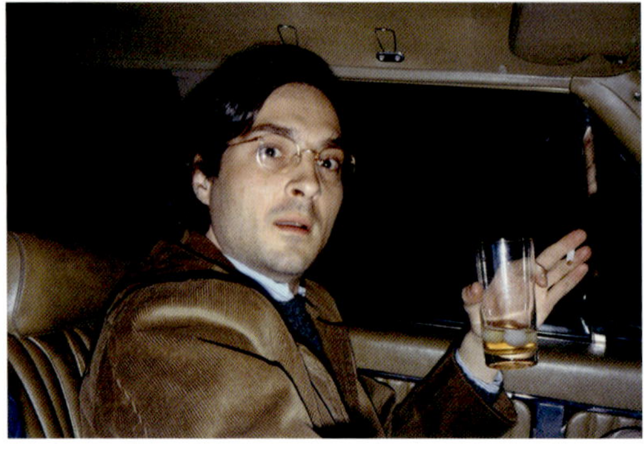

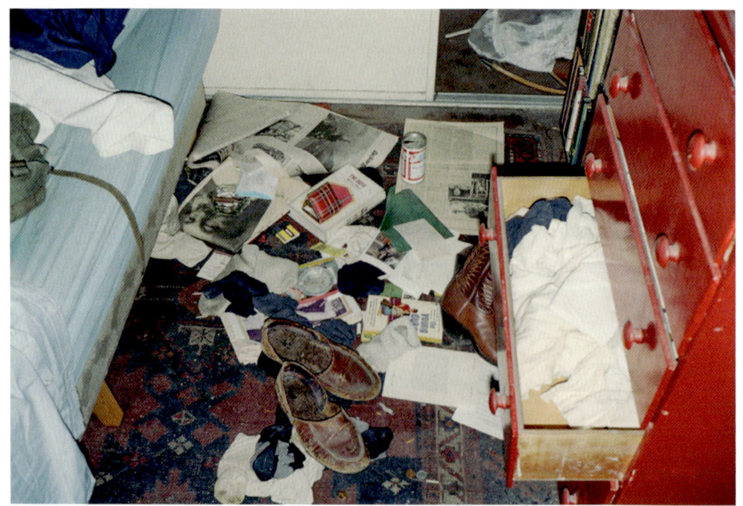

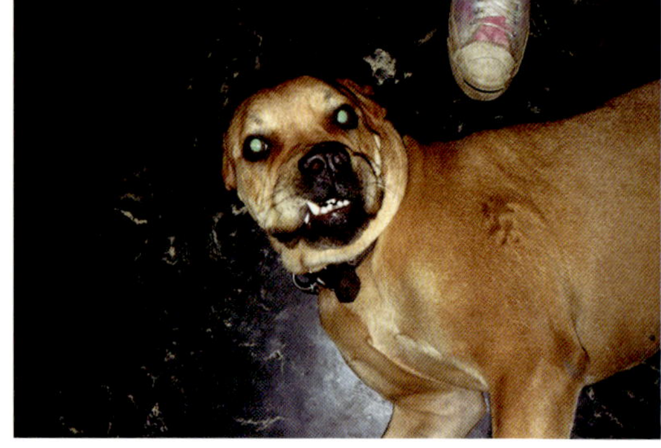

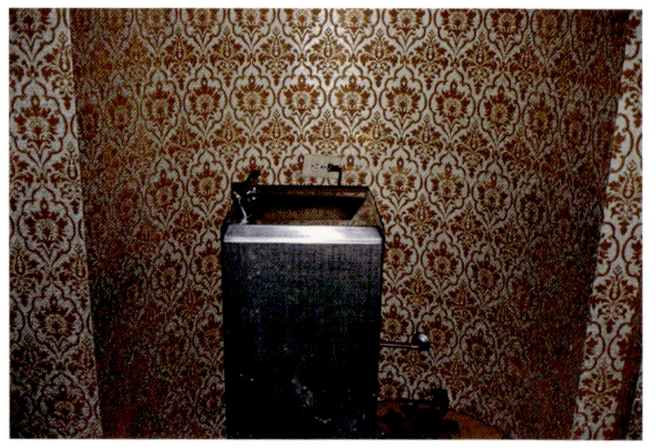

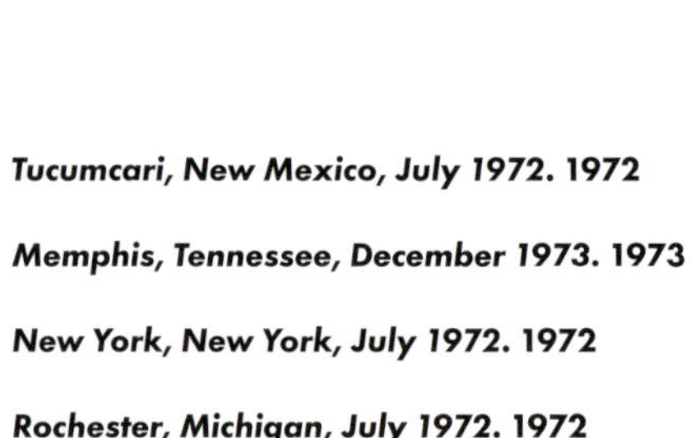

Tucumcari, New Mexico, July 1972. 1972

Memphis, Tennessee, December 1973. 1973

New York, New York, July 1972. 1972

Rochester, Michigan, July 1972. 1972

Rolla, Missouri, July 1972. 1972

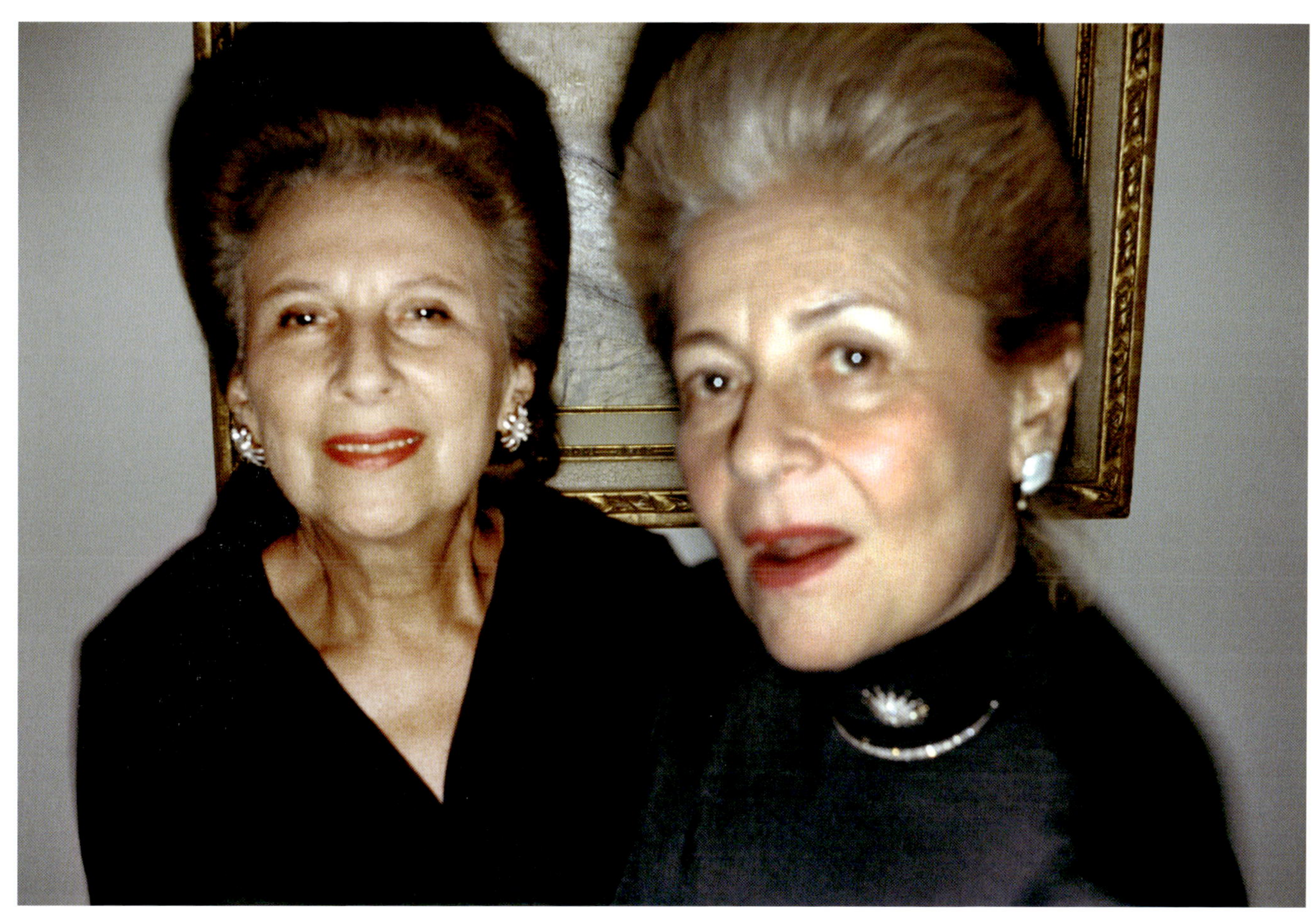

New York, New York, September–October 1972. 1972

33.

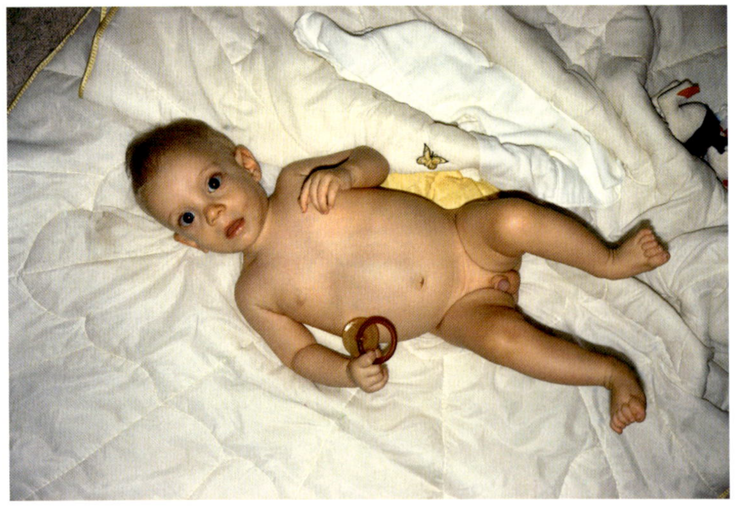

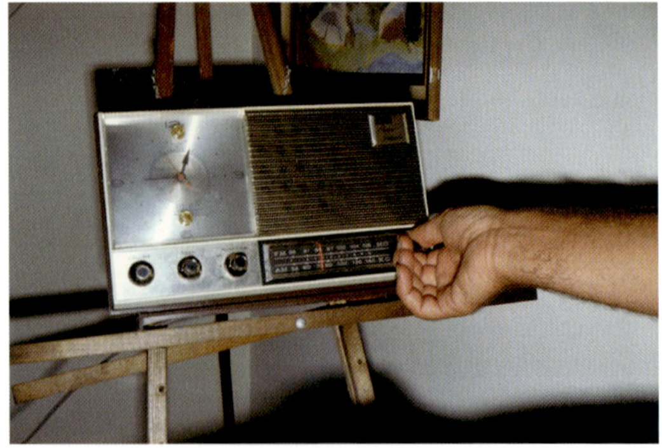

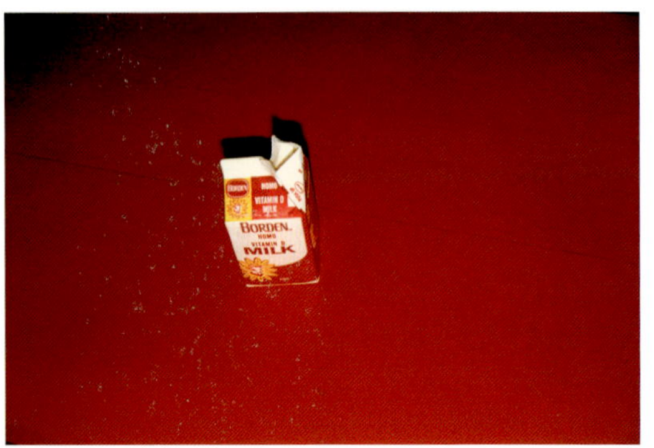

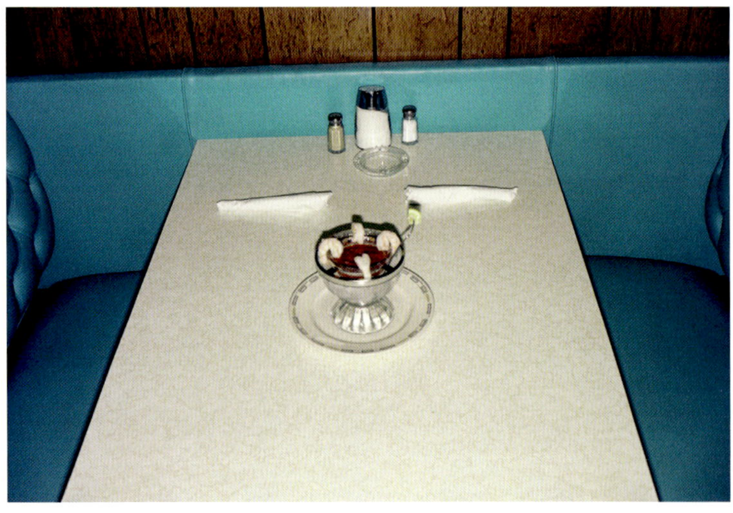

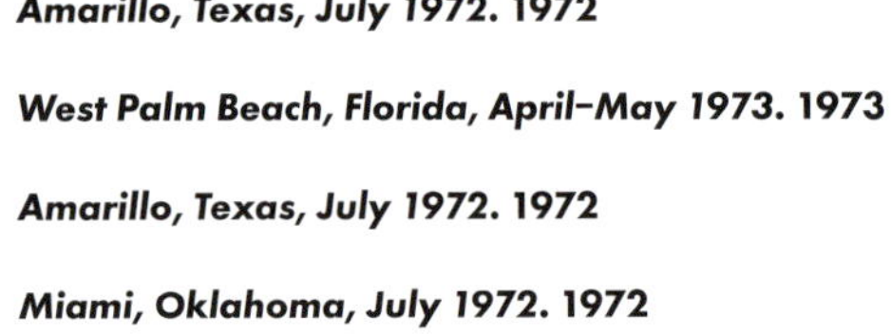

Amarillo, Texas, July 1972. 1972

West Palm Beach, Florida, April–May 1973. 1973

Amarillo, Texas, July 1972. 1972

Miami, Oklahoma, July 1972. 1972

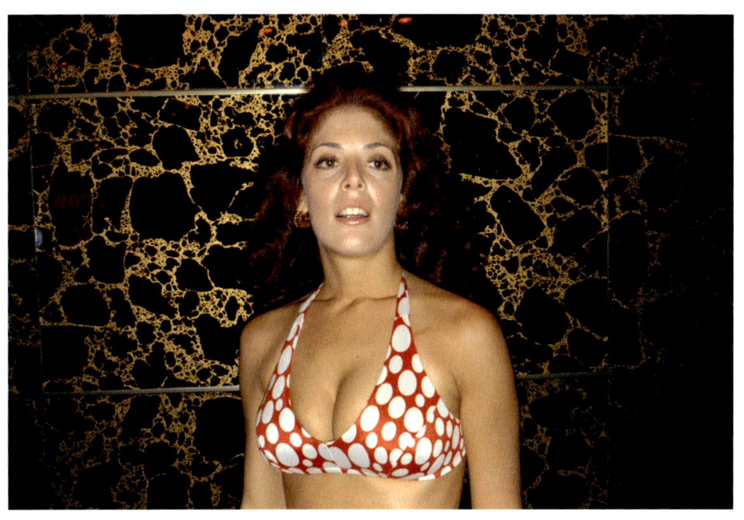

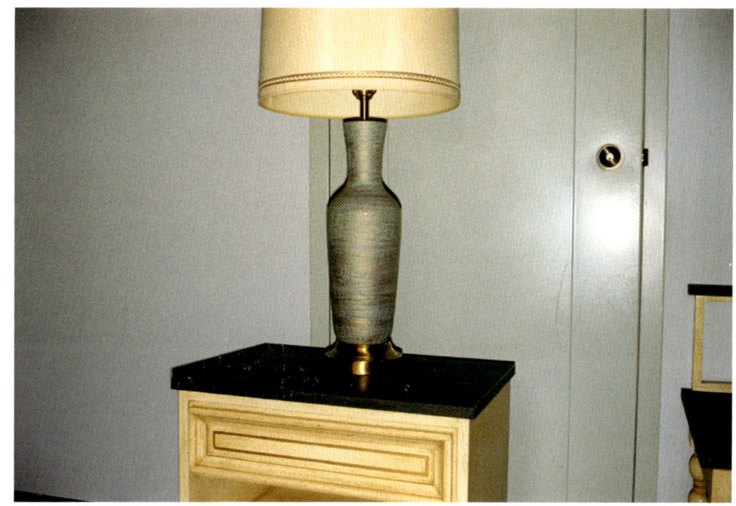

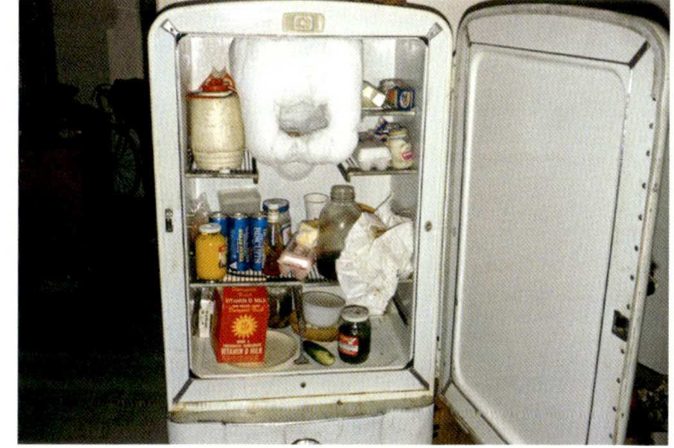

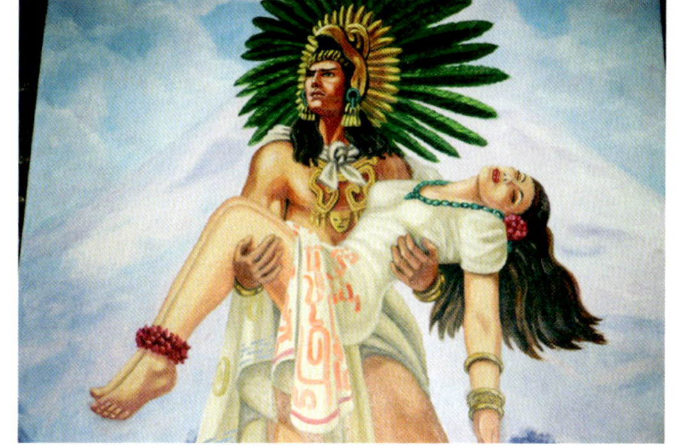

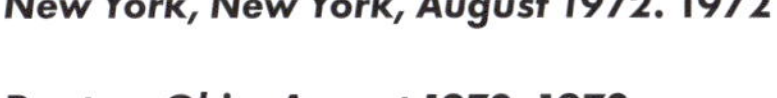

New York, New York, August 1972. 1972

Dayton, Ohio, August 1972. 1972

Amarillo, Texas, July 1972. 1972

New York, New York, November 1972. 1972

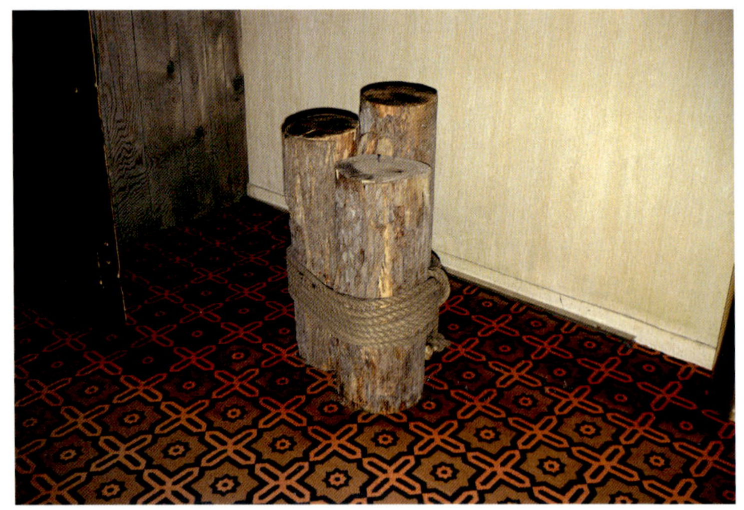

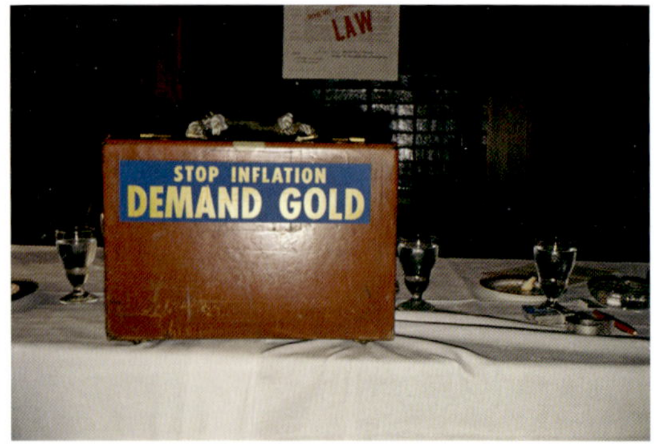

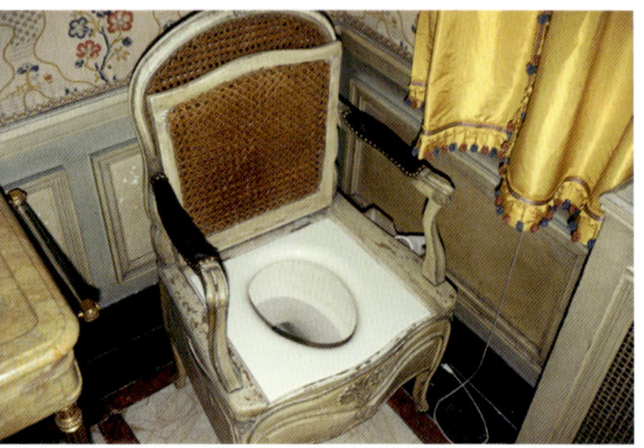

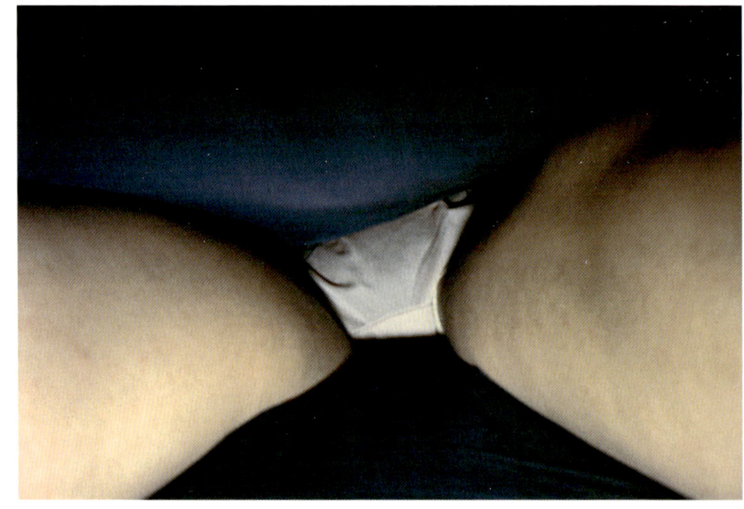

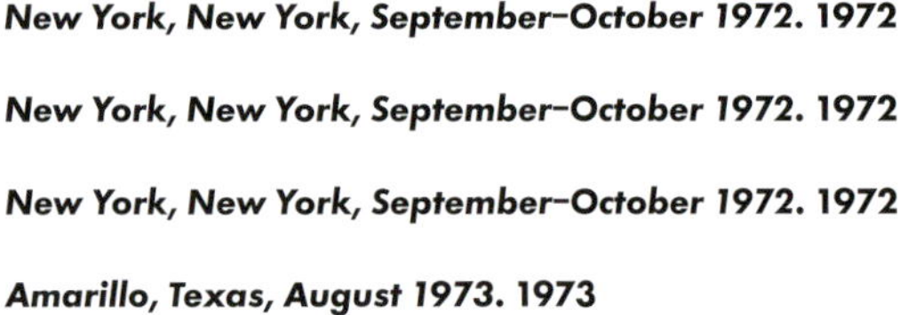

***New York, New York, September–October 1972.* 1972**

***New York, New York, September–October 1972.* 1972**

***New York, New York, September–October 1972.* 1972**

***Amarillo, Texas, August 1973.* 1973**

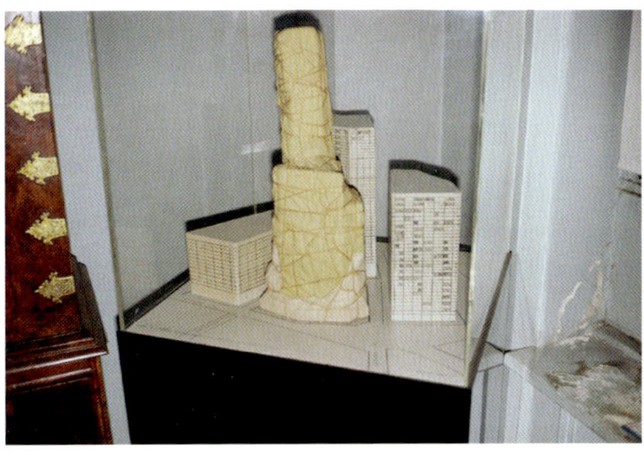

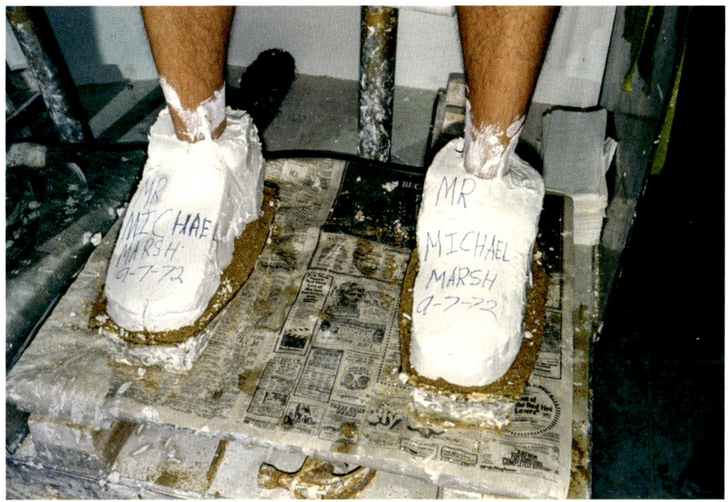

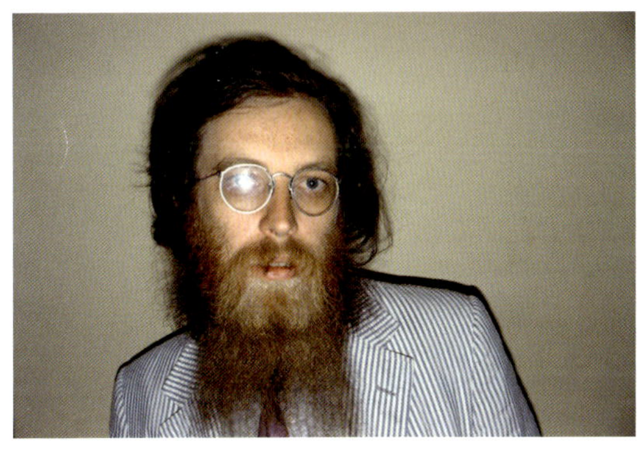

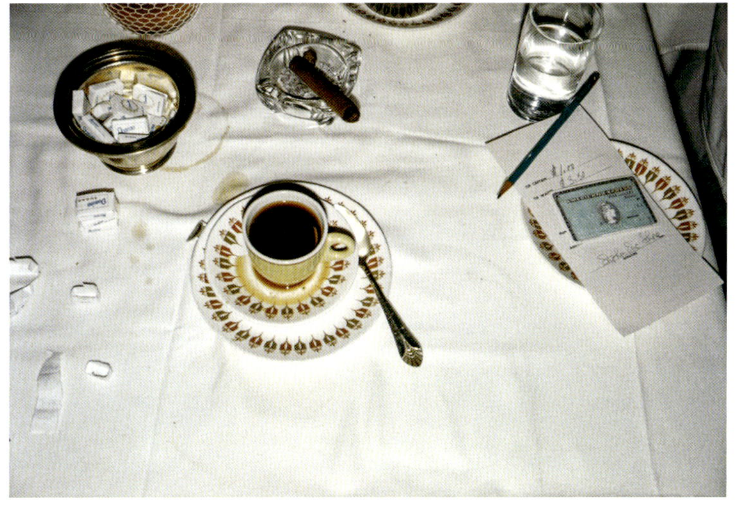

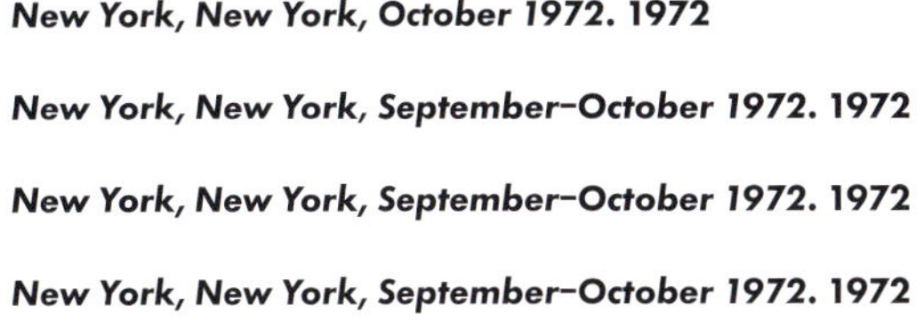

New York, New York, October 1972. 1972

New York, New York, September–October 1972. 1972

New York, New York, September–October 1972. 1972

New York, New York, September–October 1972. 1972

Archaeology

To the question "What could you imagine doing if you didn't do what you do?"—which *Frieze* magazine asked Shore in 2005—the photographer responded, "Archaeology."[1] In the 1990s, in particular, Shore was fascinated by the discipline, reading extensively on the subject in journals and books and undertaking various photographic projects around excavation sites. The first of these was in 1996, in Israel, mainly in Hatzor, a town north of the Sea of Galilee between Ramah and Qadesh, and in Ashkelon, an ancient port about thirty-five miles south of Tel Aviv. In 1997 he photographed in Aquileia, in the province of Udine, one of the most important excavation sites in northern Italy and a city that counted 100,000 inhabitants in the second century and now has a population of only 3,500. From these photographs, shot in black and white, Shore assembled portfolios composed of large-format Iris prints of impressive severity. In the excavation sites of these vanished cities, Shore was especially interested in the human dimension, domestic and secular, seen in bones, pottery, and vestiges of dwellings and shops.

In an interview with Shore published in 2014, David Campany pointed out how archaeology resonates with the language of photography: "digging in the ground and revealing a fragment has some kind of affinity with photography itself, understood as a medium of fragmentary traces of the past, fragments that cannot explain themselves."[2] In addition to his archaeological works of the 1990s, other images of Shore's can be seen to have an anthropological and even archaeological aspect. Capturing traces of everyday activity (store windows, signage, the remains of meals, discarded items), many of his photographs serve as a kind of archaeological survey. Though often devoid of human presence, most of Shore's images focus on humanity—our habits, movements, and meals; the places where we live, work, and play—a veritable archaeology of the contemporary world, in the making. (Quentin Bajac)

See also: *Black and White*; *Israel and the West Bank*

1. "Questionnaire: Stephen Shore," *Frieze* 95 (November–December 2005): 148.
2. David Campany, "Ways of Making Pictures," in Marta Dahó, ed., *Stephen Shore* (Madrid: Fundación MAPFRE; New York: Aperture, 2014), 52.

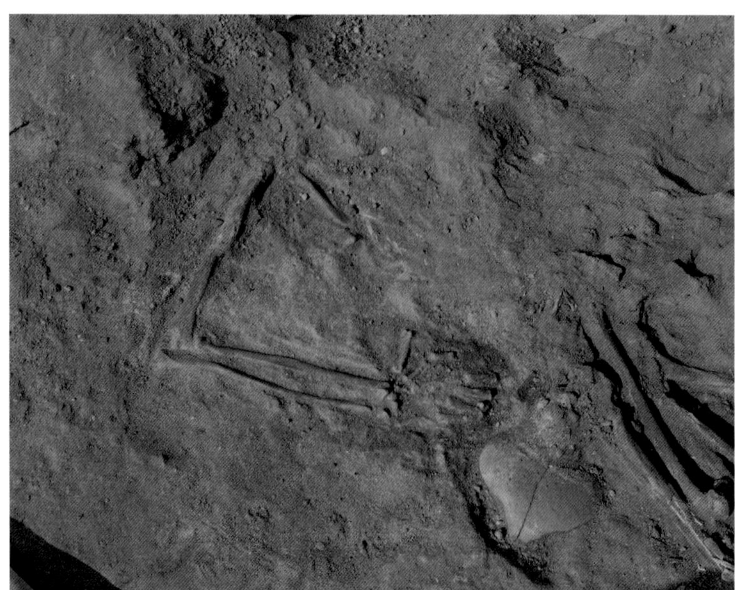

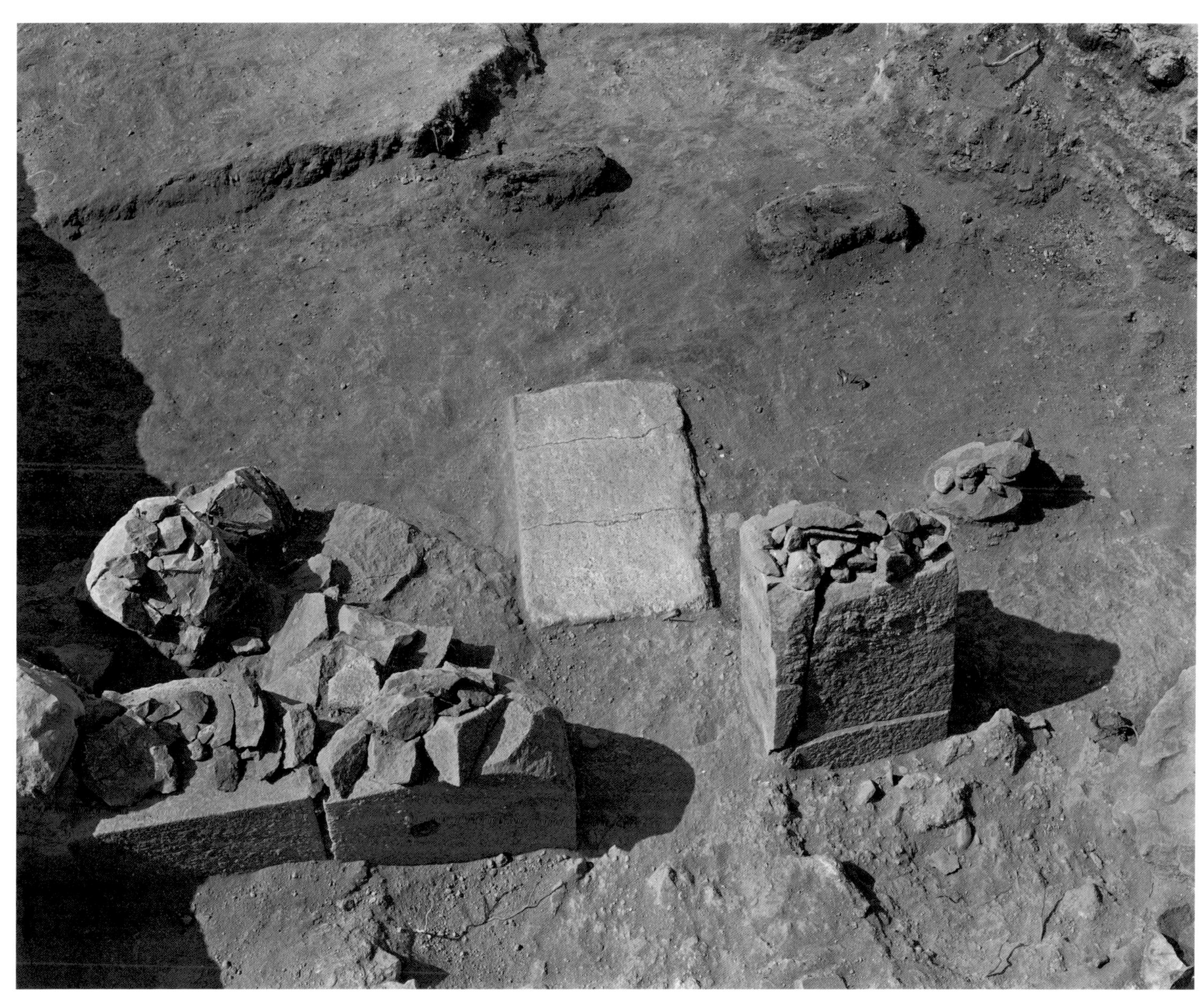

Ashkelon, Israel, 1996. 1996

Hatzor, Israel, 1996. 1996

39.

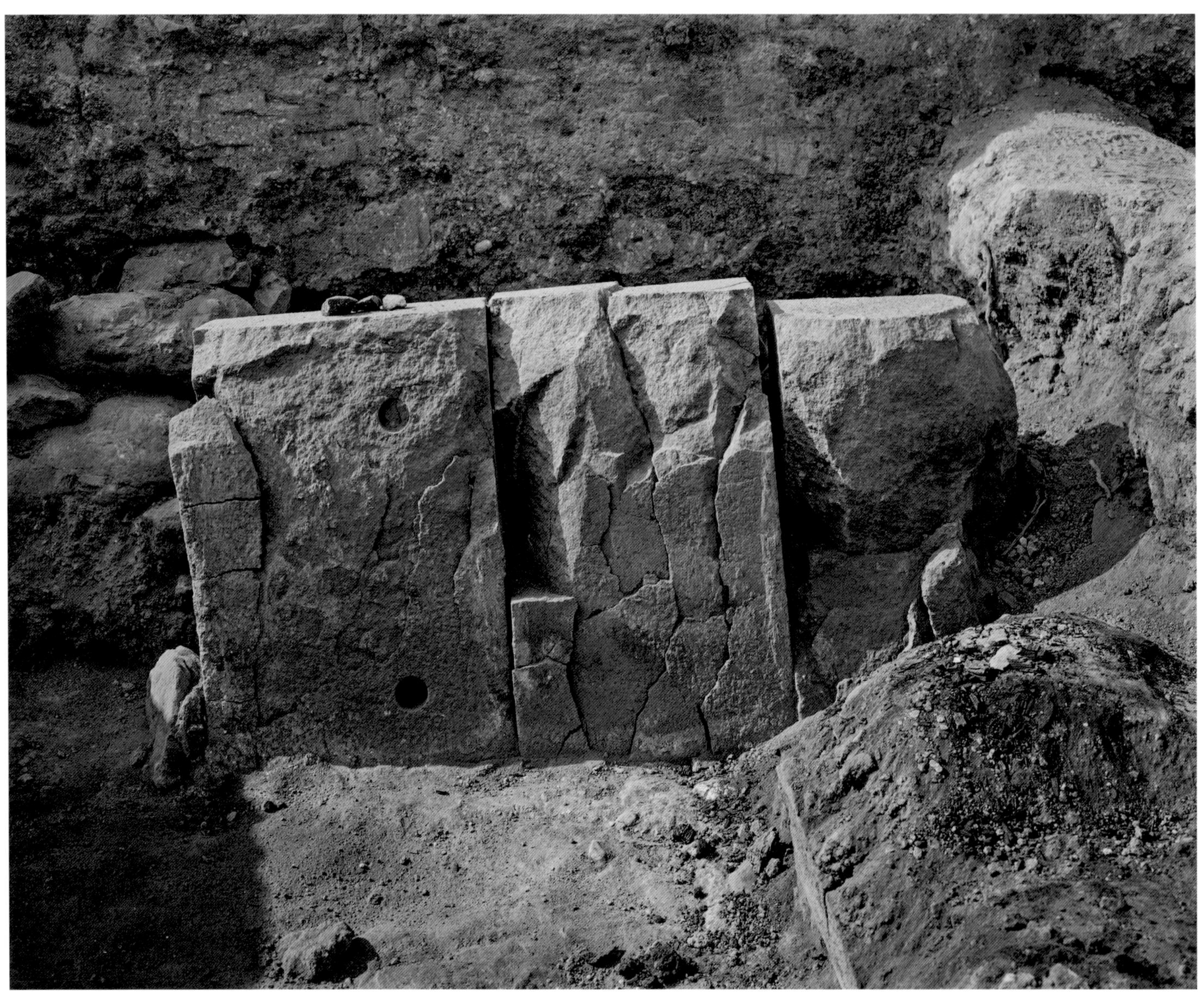

***Hatzor, Israel, 1996.* 1996**

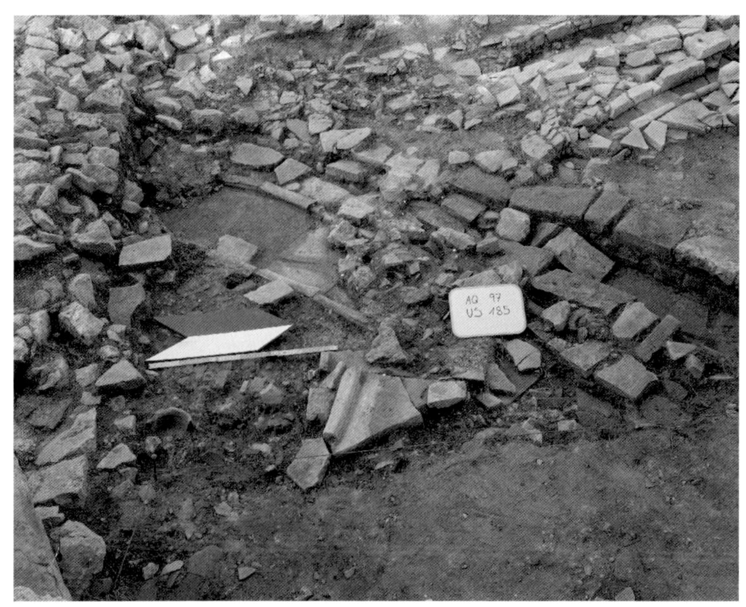

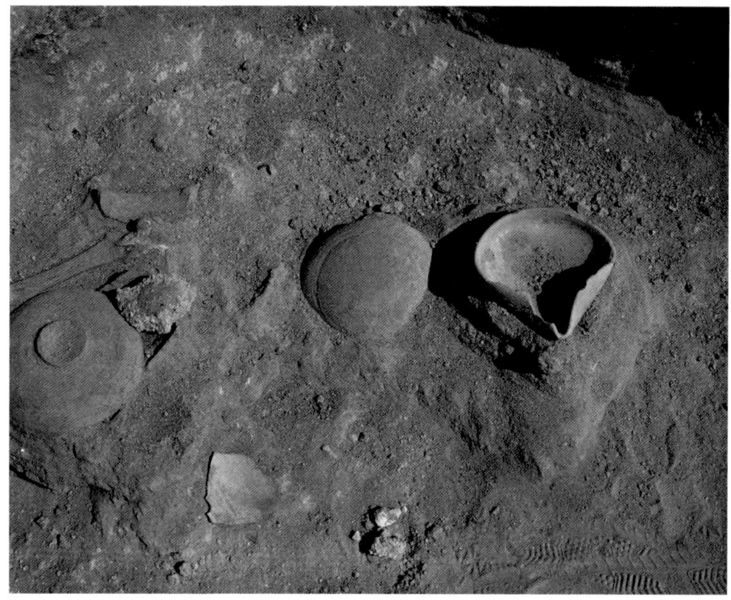

Aquileia, Italy, 1997. **1997**

Ashkelon, Israel, 1996. **1996**

Architecture

Shore is not an architectural photographer in the conventional sense, but architecture features prominently in many pictures throughout his oeuvre, both as subject matter and structuring principle. Architecture has been a preferred topic for photography from the early days of the medium's inception, and many contemporary photographers have addressed the subject in one way or another throughout their careers. In Shore's case, however, architecture seems to be much more than merely a passing interest of temporary character, but rather the starting point for continuous investigation into the physical manifestations of the forces underlying American culture.

Shore's interest revolves not so much around Architecture with a capital "A," but around "unconscious," unplanned, vernacular, and commercial buildings found mainly (but not exclusively) along U.S. highways and in the American West. This interest distinguishes him from an architectural photographer, whose main objective usually lies in deciphering and visualizing, from the appearance of a building, the architect's formal intentions and spatial imaginary, and translating them into compelling two-dimensional representations of those concepts. The translation from three-dimensional space to two-dimensional surface is fundamental for Shore's work as well; but for him, these representations—whether domestic or urban in character—are signifiers less of an individual's will to form than of a specific cultural condition. Paradoxically, it is only through a clear formal assertion on the photographer's part and through devices such as framing, point of view, exposure, and so on that his images take on a symbolic, almost metaphysical dimension that points to a truth beyond the apparent surface. Shore has stated in this regard: "There is an old Arab saying, 'The apparent is the bridge to the real.' For many photographers, architecture serves this function."[1] It is no coincidence, then, that Shore is regularly considered an attentive interpreter of everyday American culture.

If architectural photography privileges the single monument over the urban fabric and the exceptional over the ordinary, Shore's photographic approach to the built environment may be characterized as "topographic" in that it explores the visual quality of specific places. For this reason, it is fitting that his work was included in the groundbreaking 1975 exhibition *New Topographics: Photographs of a Man-Altered Landscape*, organized by William Jenkins for George Eastman House, which featured a group of photographers with similar interests in the aesthetic of the American human-made environment, among them Robert Adams, Lewis Baltz, and Joe Deal. (The German photographers Bernd and Hilla Becher were also included, contributing a non-American—and by now canonical—perspective on the postindustrial architecture of western Germany.) In Shore's oeuvre, we find the topographic approach most clearly pronounced in his *Uncommon Places* series, which was shot in 1973–81 on various road trips across the United States. The series addresses a variety of subjects Shore encountered en route—parking lots, commercial roadside structures, motel interiors, billboards along highways, main streets, breakfast pancakes, small-town street intersections, and even people—and while architectural objects are far from the only focus, they take a prominent place in the project. Contrary to the series title, the locations are for the most part rather common, ordinary places, archetypal sites/sights of contemporary civilization that combine to create a quintessential portrait of small-town America. These places become "uncommon" through Shore's careful framing of the ordinary, and through his ability to make visible what to his contemporaries appeared so inconspicuous that it never crossed the threshold of conscious perception.

Shore's topographic approach manifests itself even in cases where he was commissioned to photograph a monument. On the occasion of the 1979 designation of the New York State Capitol as a National Historic Landmark and the subsequent restoration of the building, Shore was invited, along with three other photographers, to capture the building in images. (A similar commission from Seagram in 1976 had led to a documentation of American courthouses, and another in 1977 by *Fortune* magazine to a portrait of decaying American steel towns, indicative of Shore's interest in architectural typologies.) Rather than focusing on the composition of the historicist facade or the intricacies of the beautiful stonework, Shore visualizes the building embedded in the landscape and partly hidden behind trees, stressing the topology of the terrain and the interaction of the monument with mundane elements of the streetscape such as cars and road signs.

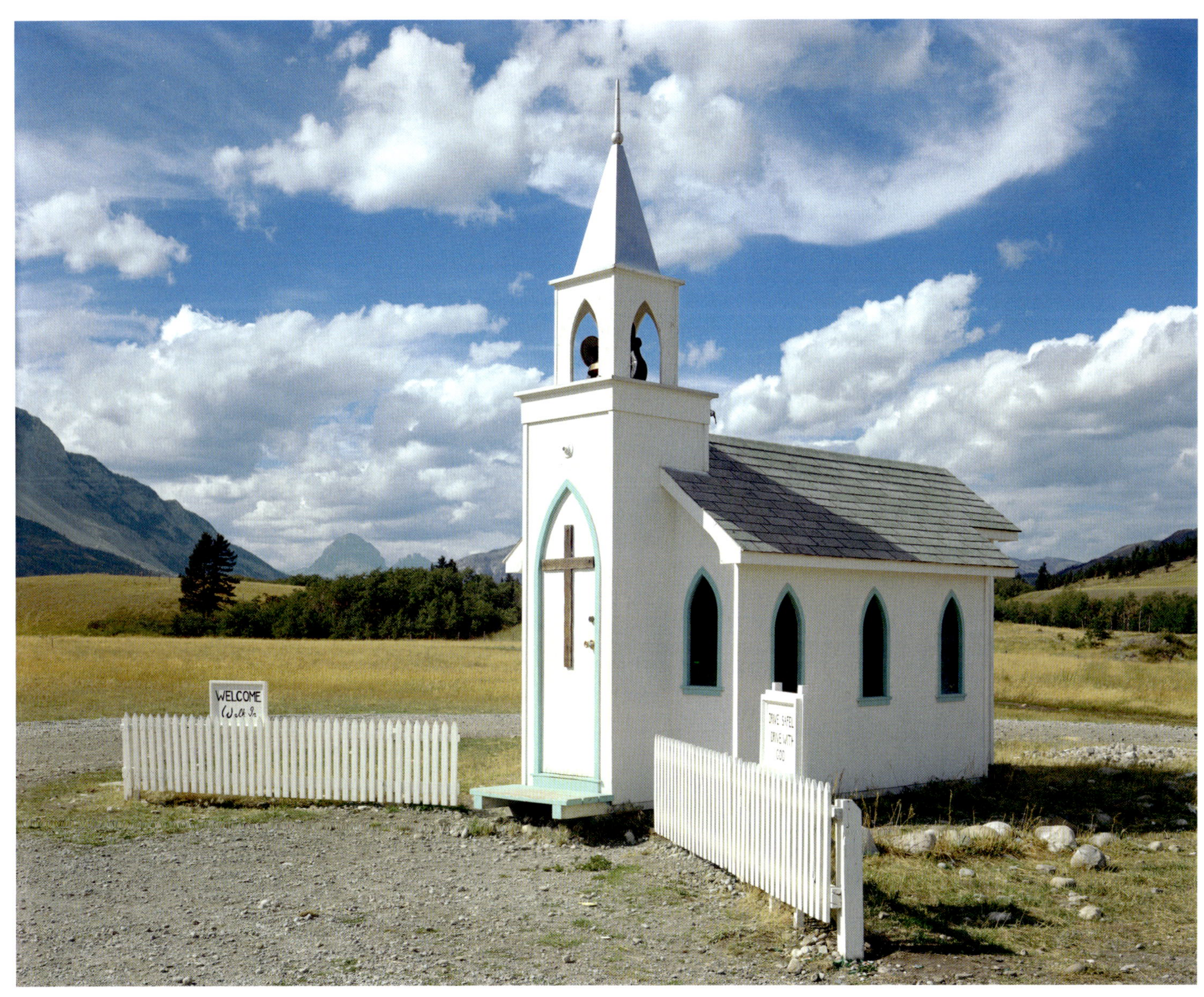

***Bellevue, Alberta, August 21, 1974.* 1974**

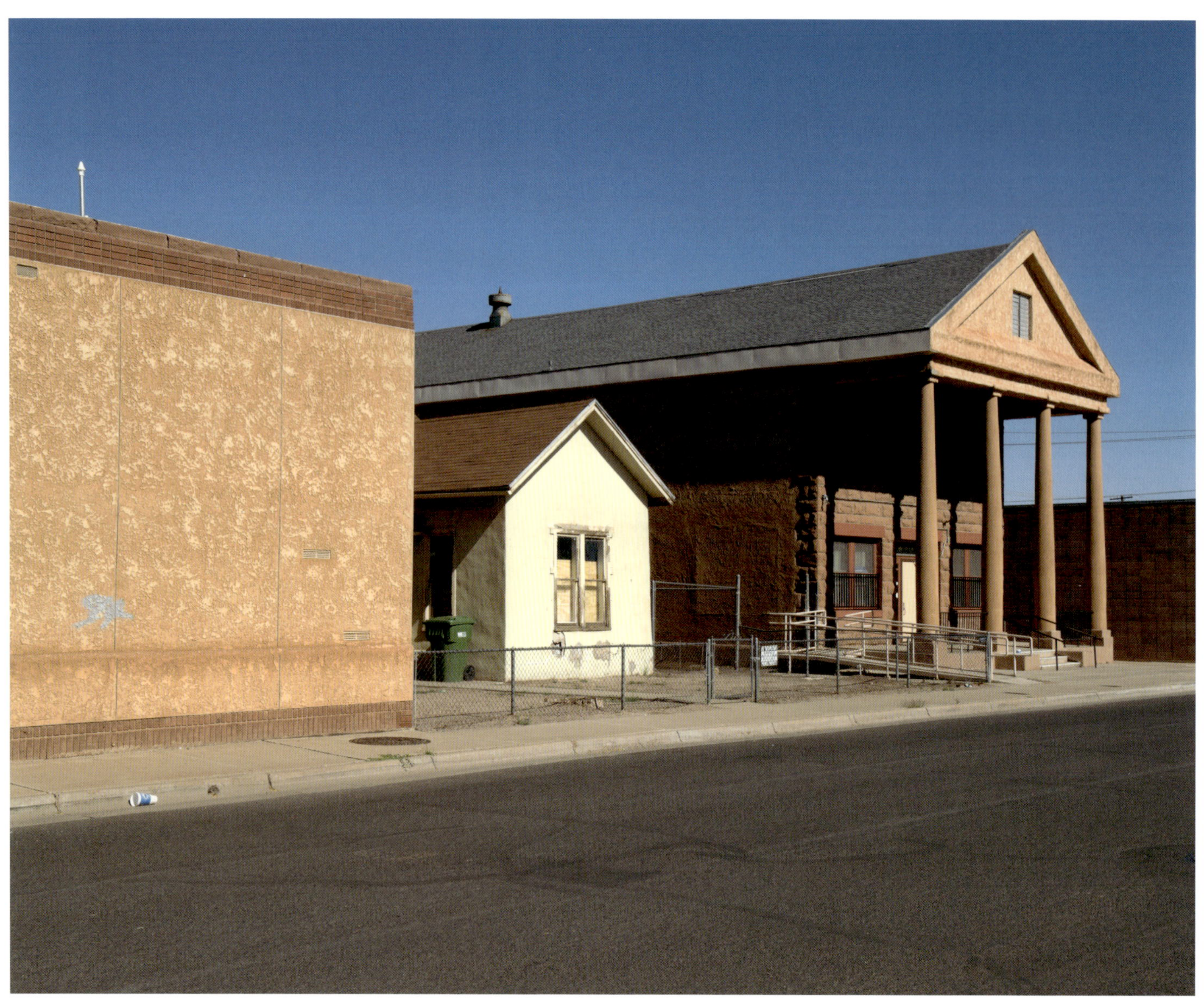

Winslow, Arizona, September 19, 2013. 2013

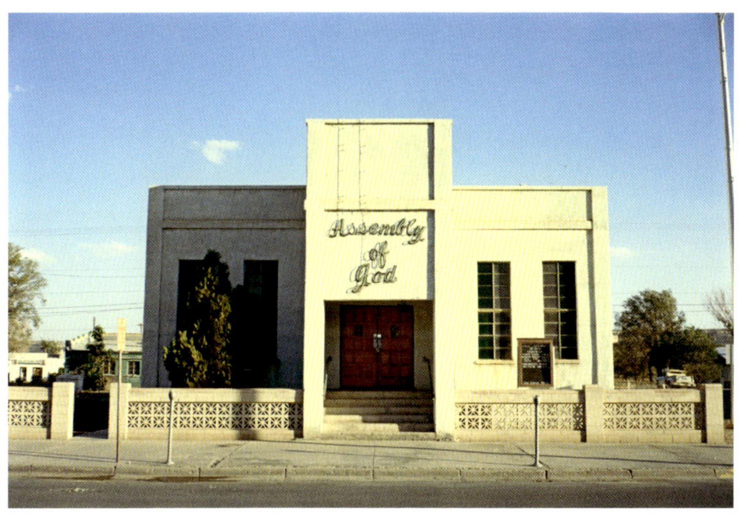

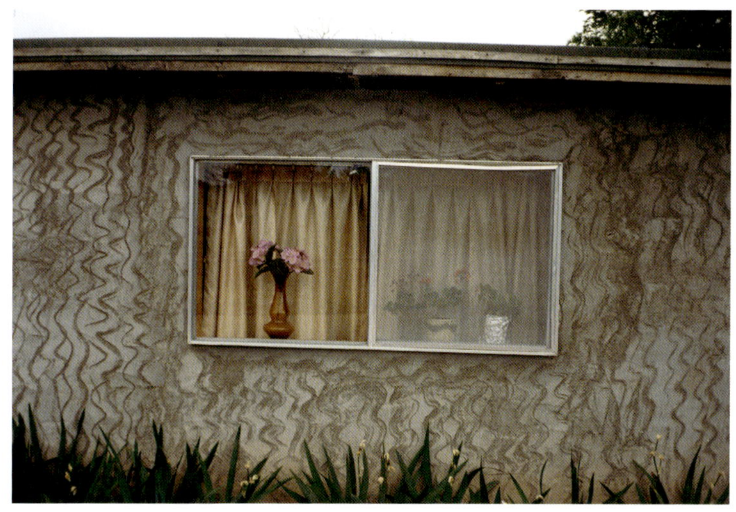

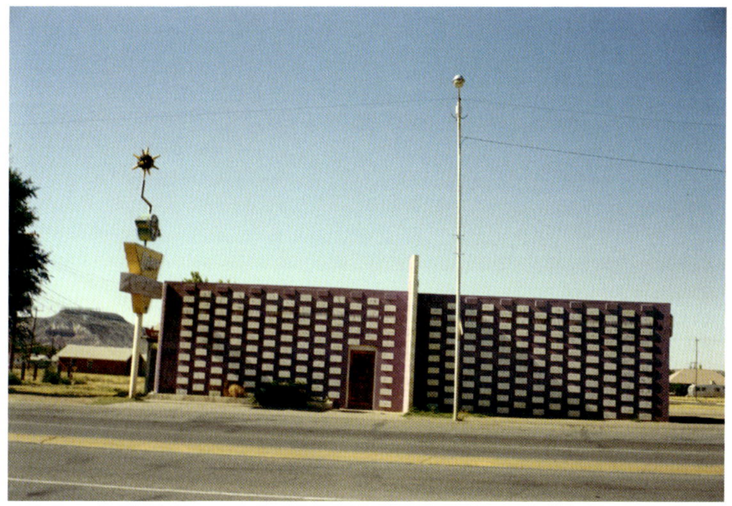

***Farmington, New Mexico, June 1972.* 1972**

***Carrillos, New Mexico, June 1972.* 1972**

***Tucumcari, New Mexico, July 1972.* 1972**

Shore has recounted a telling anecdote regarding the topographic methodology that demonstrates his deep investment in the history of photography. When the influential American photographer Paul Strand in the early 1950s visited the northern Italian village of Luzzara, he reported in a letter to a friend that it was a difficult place to photograph because it lacked buildings of architectural interest.[2] Taking this observation as a cue, when Shore traveled to Luzzara himself in 1993 on a commission, he applied his topographic approach to the town, returning with pictures of inconspicuous buildings, storefronts, and workshops. Unlike his pioneering color photography in *Uncommon Places*, in this work Shore used black and white, evoking, in combination with the worn facades of the featured buildings, a sensation of melancholy or even nostalgia. While the former was present in *Uncommon Places* from the beginning as well, the latter has equally invaded these pictures through the visible passing of time. Photography is invariably charged with temporality, and the shadow of time is involuntarily cast over the instant when the photo was taken.[3]

Shore's interest in the idiosyncrasies of the contemporary American vernacular did not go unnoticed in the architectural discourse of the 1970s. In 1975, as a result of their common interest and affinity, he was commissioned by the architects Robert Venturi, Denise Scott Brown, and Steven Izenour to contribute photographs of roadside iconography and typical streets in American suburbia to the 1976 exhibition *Signs of Life: Symbols in the American City*. The architects had for some time pursued a theoretical and visual investigation of the American suburban landscape and, through research projects such as "Learning from Las Vegas," would fundamentally shift the profession's attention away from the heroic propositions of late modern architecture and toward the aesthetic and spatial "logic" of these seemingly unplanned places. In Shore's topographic approach the architects found a methodology that rendered their project visible.

Shore's take on American architecture and place is not without precedent. Walker Evans's *American Photographs* (1938) comes to mind, and Shore has readily acknowledged the lasting impression this work made on him when he received a copy of the book for his tenth birthday. Evans is considered the inventor of the so-called documentary style, in which the ordinary subject matter of his images is kept at arm's length, almost like a clinical investigation; and it is this deadpan, detached aesthetic that we find in Shore as well,[4] albeit in color, which, until he and photographers such as William Eggleston pursued similar interests in the 1970s, had been reserved almost exclusively for commercial photography. Shore also took inspiration from the paintings and photographic artist's books of Los Angeles–based artist Ed Ruscha, and from the photo series of postindustrial architecture by the Bechers. But apart from his very early Conceptual series from 1969 and 1970 and some later commissioned works, Shore became increasingly uninterested in the notion of seriality as manifest in the work of the Bechers. Instead of taking hundreds and hundreds of images of American main streets, as was their approach, Shore pursued a different path. "I wanted to find that quintessential main street," he explained.[5] It is this search for the essence of things that lends Shore's architectural photographs, beyond the surface, their metaphysical depth. (Martino Stierli)

See also: *Courthouses*; *Evans, Walker*; *Luzzara*; *New Topographics*; *Shopwindows*; *Signage*; *Signs of Life*; *Uncommon Places*

1. See Stephen Shore, "Photography and Architecture," in *Sze Tsung Leong: History Images* (Göttingen: Steidl, 2006), 142.
2. Ibid.
3. See Roland Barthes, *Camera Lucida: Reflections on Photography* (New York: Hill and Wang, 1981).
4. Conversely, Cervin Robinson has argued that Evans's and Shore's photography is not documentary in style, but picturesque. See Cervin Robinson, "Architectural Photography: Complaints about the Standard Product," *Journal of Architectural Education* 24, no. 2 (1975): 14.
5. Jennifer Thatcher, "Artworker of the Week #23: Stephen Shore @ Sprueth Magers Lee," *Kultureflash*, no. 71 (January 7, 2004).

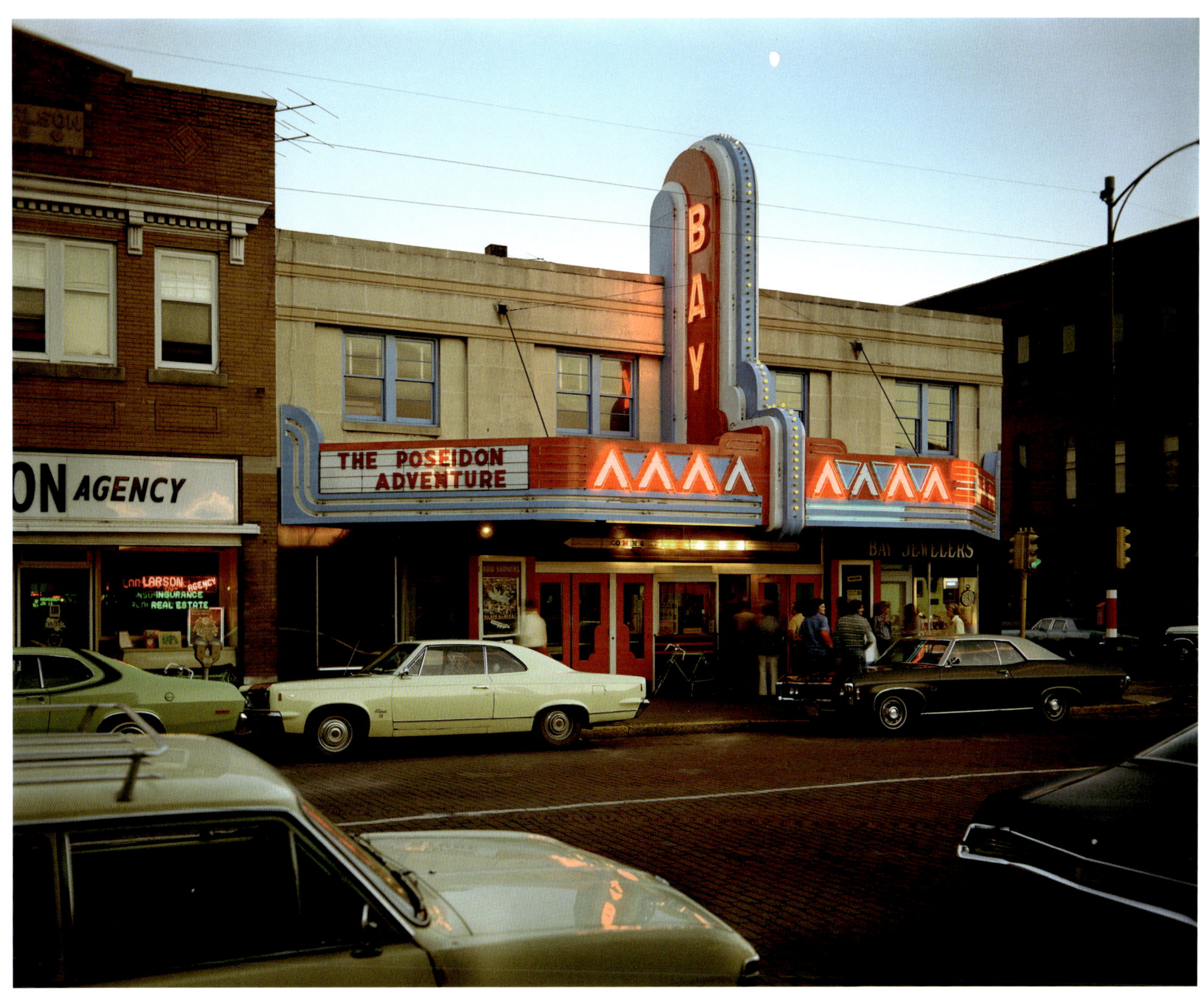

2nd Street, Ashland, Wisconsin, July 9, 1973. 1973

47.

THE REST OF NEW YORK

... Now you don't have to go there

PHOTOGRAPHS BY STEPHEN SHORE

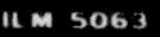

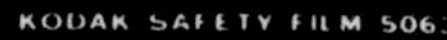

The famous Apollo Theater on 125th St.

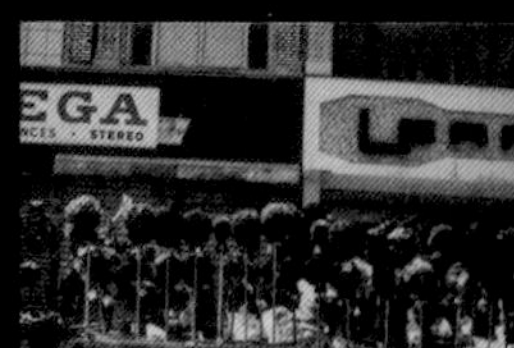

125th St. wig stand

Cathedral Church of St. John the Divine

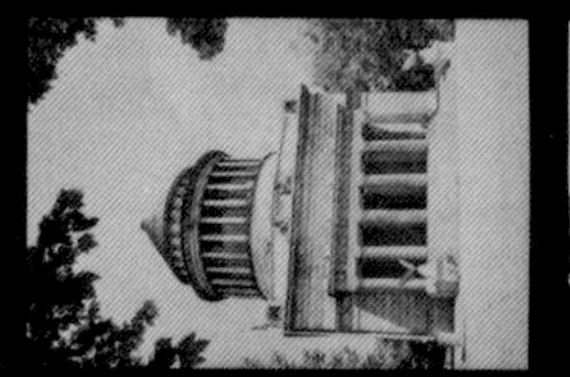

Grant's Tomb

Metropolitan Museum of Art

Lincoln Center

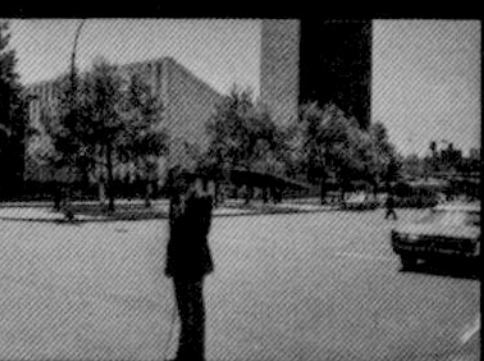

Channel 5 newscaster in front of U.N.

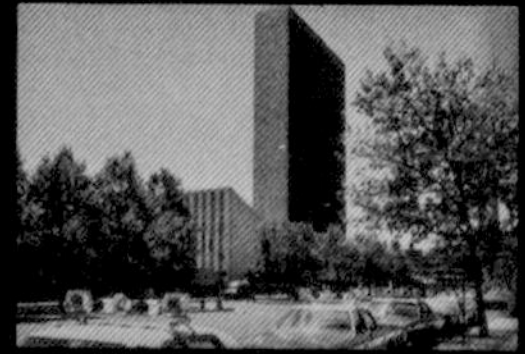

U.N. with police car

Famous view of Trinity Church up Wall St.

Statue of Liberty on a clear day

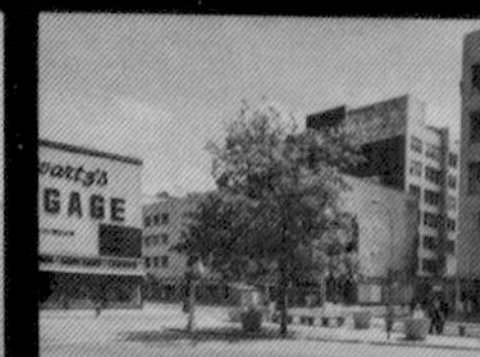

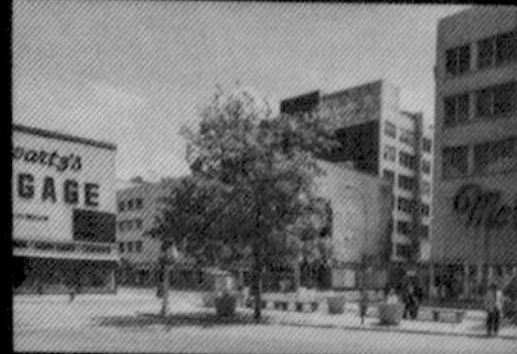

Downtown Brooklyn

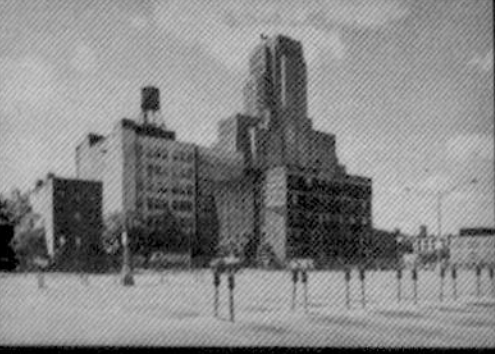

Downtown Brooklyn again

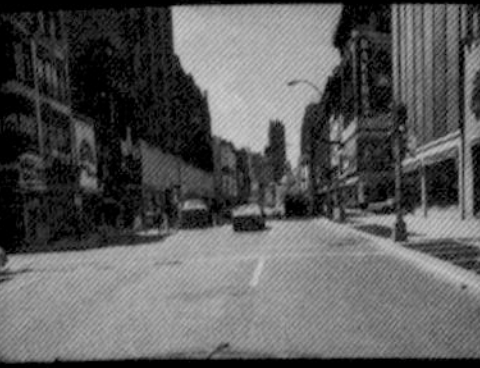

Heart of downtown Brooklyn--Fulton St.

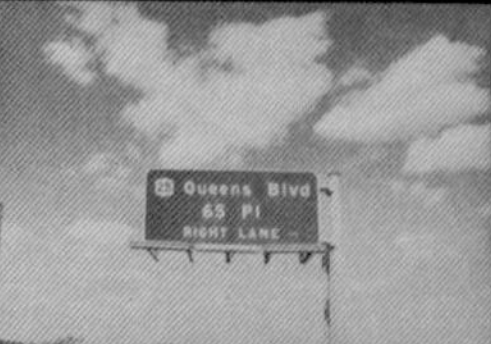

A typical street in Queens

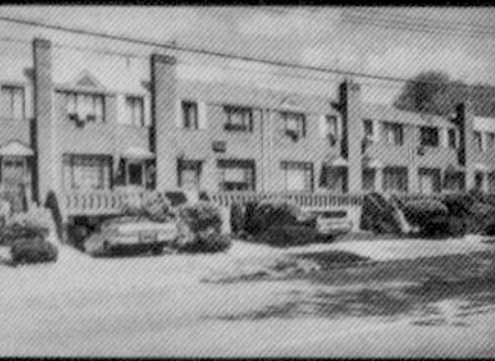

Another typical street in Queens

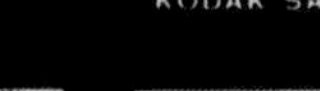

View of Manhattan from Brooklyn Hts. Esplanade

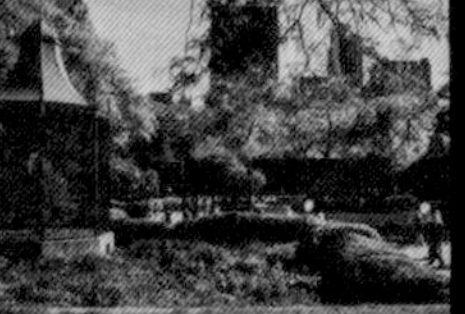

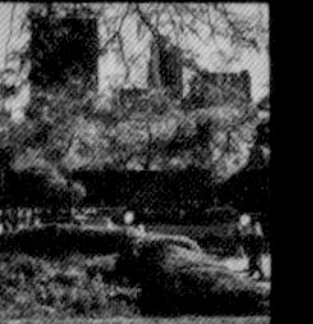

Central Park Zoo

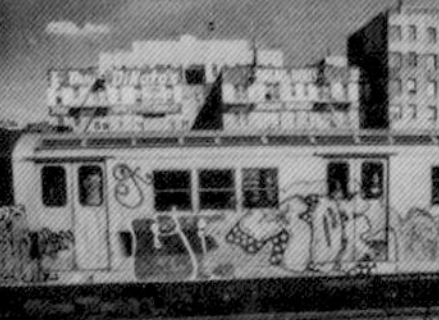

Subway car

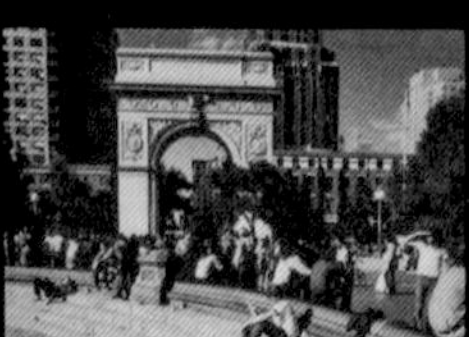

Washington Sq. Park and Arch

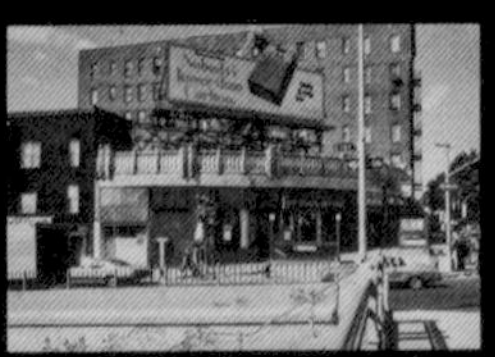

The Bronx outside Yankee Stadium

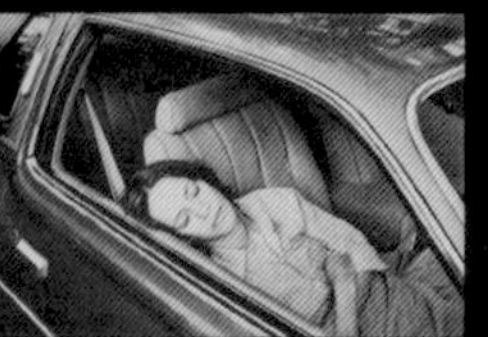

Caption writer on Staten Island

"The Rest of New York," *The Real World*, July/August 1976

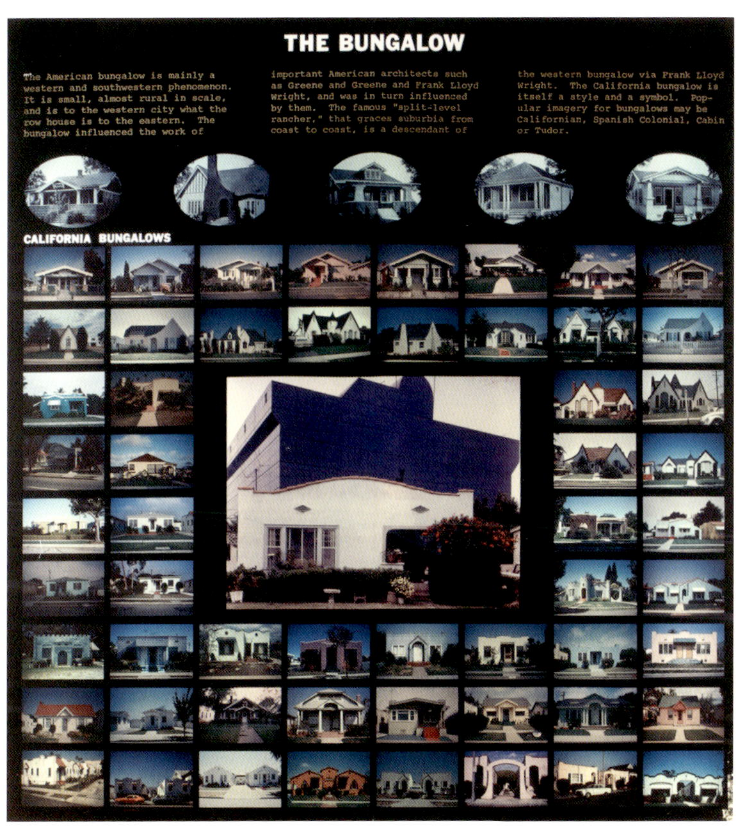

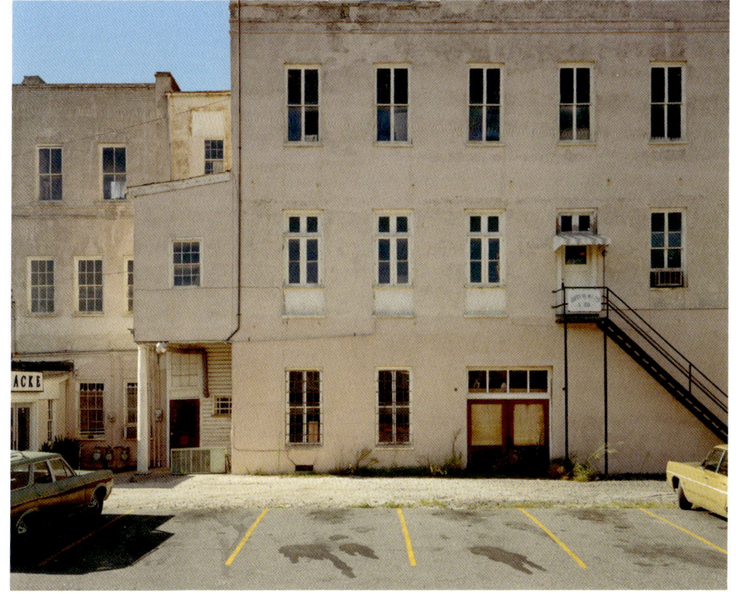

Transparency with photographs by Stephen Shore and others, from *Signs of Life: Symbols in the American City*, organized by Robert Venturi, Steven Izenour, and Denise Scott Brown, 1976

***Meeting Street, Charleston, South Carolina, August 3, 1975*. 1975**

Baseball

Baseball was a childhood passion for Shore that has continued into adulthood. In the late 1970s he and his future wife, Ginger, were avid supporters of the Yankees, attending as many as thirty games a year. This was a glorious time for the Yankees, the era of Ron Guidry and Graig Nettles, which concluded in October 1978 with the team's twenty-second World Series win, beating out the Los Angeles Dodgers.

It was at the start of this victorious season, in February and March of 1978, that Shore photographed the Yankees at spring training in Fort Lauderdale, Florida, for a commission he received from AT&T.[1] The project offered Shore the opportunity to tackle a subject he was passionate about, but also to play with conventional approaches to photographing sports. There is no mythology of the "decisive moment" here, nor of the heroism typical in sports photography. When the players are present, they seem static, as in the image of Graig Nettles standing in a batting cage (right). But often the players are not visible, either because they have been reduced to tiny figures within a sumptuous landscape, or because Shore focuses on close-up details, baseball equipment, or locker rooms devoid of human presence. This approach was very different from the more intimate one he would adopt in 2000 when he photographed a Minor League team in the Hudson Valley for *Details* magazine.[2]

Ultimately, baseball also provides Shore with a valuable metaphor for the practice of photography, as he explained in 1979: "It's like if you were a baseball player and you're playing the outfield. Someone hits a fly ball, you can't think about the trajectory of the ball and how fast you have to run to be able to intersect with it and catch it. At some point your muscles have developed a kind of memory [. . .]. It comes naturally, after years of experimenting."[3] (Quentin Bajac)

See also: *Commissions and Editorial Work*

1. Several images from the project would be published in the *New York Times Magazine* in April of that year (April 9, 1978, 38–39) and shown at Light Gallery a few weeks later.
2. "Farm Hands," *Details*, November 2000, 136–47.
3. Meg Ryan, "The Venerable Stephen Shore Shares Wisdom Through the Lens of His Latest Project," April 4, 2016, http://www.americanphotomag.com/venerable-stephen-shore-shares-wisdom-through-lens-his-latest-project.

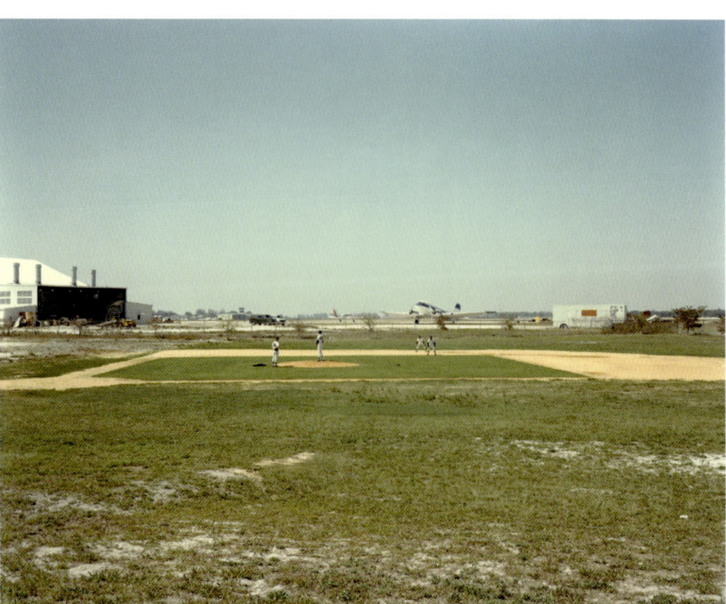

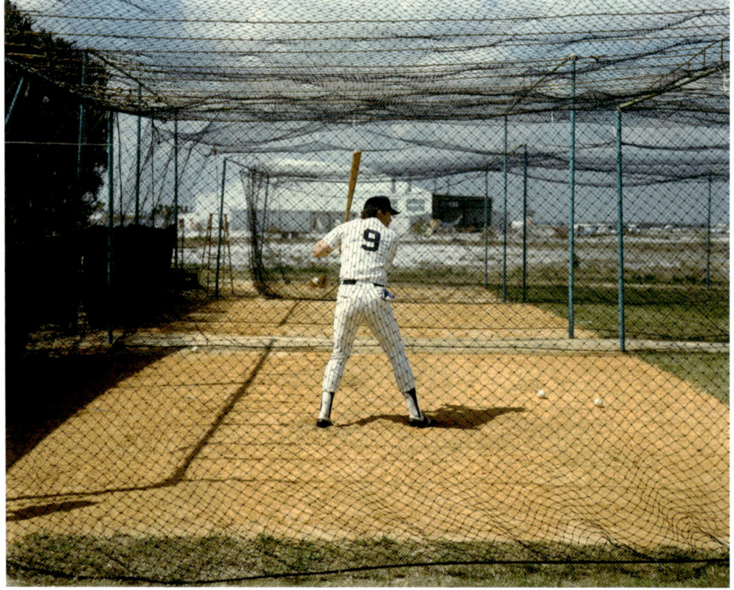

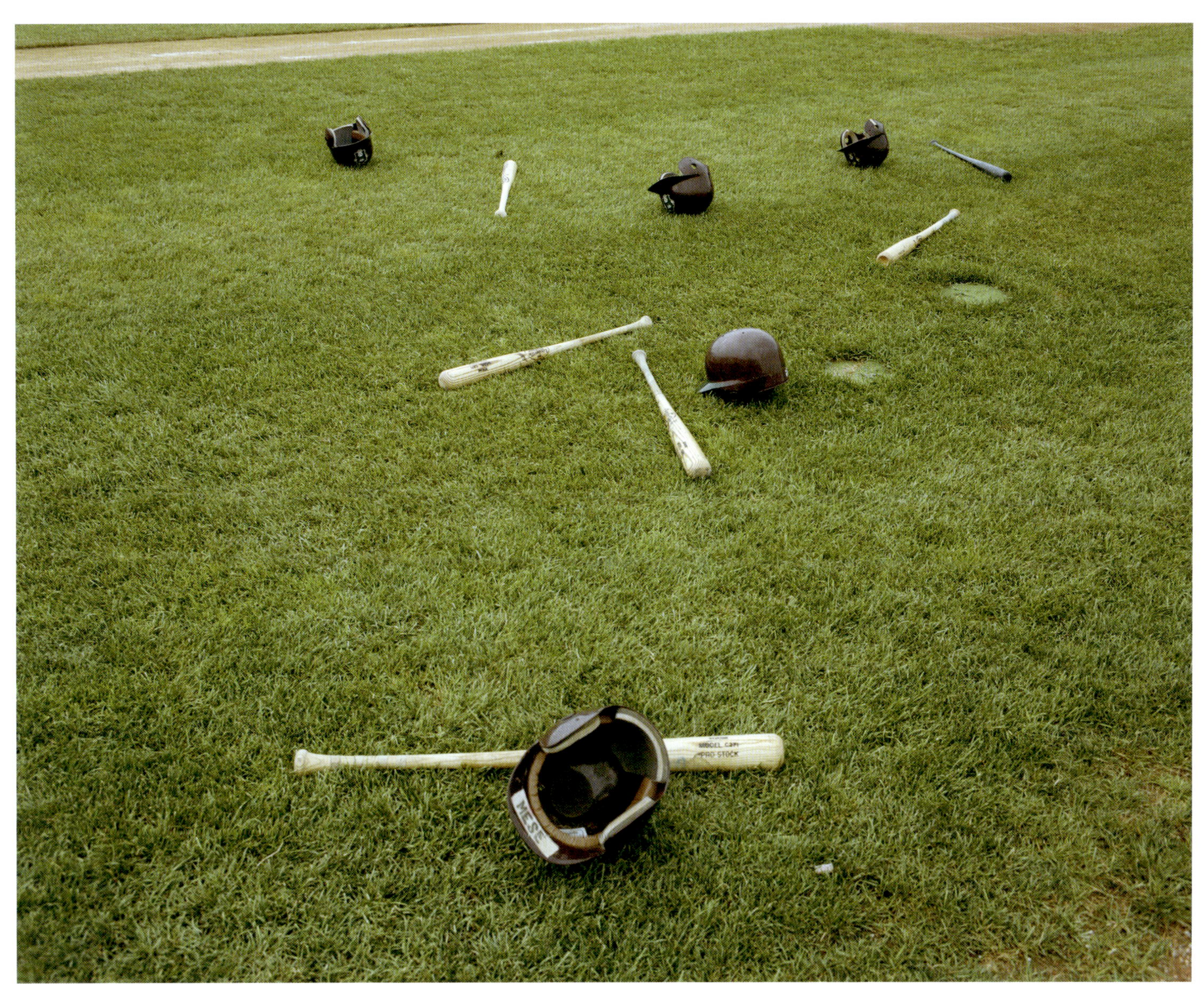

Fort Lauderdale, Florida, March 5, 1978. **1978**

Graig Nettles, Fort Lauderdale, Florida, March 1, 1978. **1978**

Hudson Valley Renegades. **2000**

Beverly Boulevard and La Brea Avenue, Los Angeles, California, June 21, 1975

Beverly Boulevard and La Brea Avenue, Los Angeles, California, June 21, 1975 is one of Shore's most beloved images. Throughout the 1970s, as he made various road trips around the United States, Shore would switch between photographing with disarming pictorial simplicity and making highly complex compositions, such as this. In his 2011 essay "Form and Pressure," Shore noted:

> I was drawn to this scene because it seemed to be such a quintessential Los Angeles experience: the gas stations, the jumble, the signage, the space. I was also, for my own personal reasons, exploring visual structure. [. . .] I was also interested in how the frame of the picture forms a line that all the visual elements of the picture relate to. It is the image's proscenium, as it were. I recognized that when three-dimensional space is collapsed into a flat picture, objects in the foreground are now seen, on the surface of the photograph, in a new and precise relationship to the objects in the background. For example, look at the relationship between the "Standard" sign and the light pole underneath it in the L.A. picture. I was interested in seeing how many of these visual interstices I could juggle on a single image.[1]

Los Angeles is a city of crazed interstices. Nothing human-made in the streetscape we see here was built to last, and none of it has. Today there is still a Chevron gas station on the corner, but its architecture has changed. In a token gesture to the planet, rectangles of grass the size of doormats now edge its forecourt. What does survive is Shore's photograph, a far sturdier structure, and with a far more eminent history. Via a friendship with the photographers Bernd and Hilla Becher, this was one of a group of pictures Shore presented in 1977 at the great art exhibition Documenta 6, in Kassel, Germany. Four years later it was published in Sally Eauclaire's anthology *The New Color Photography*, perhaps the single most influential book in establishing color photography as a serious medium of artistic expression in the United States. In 1982 the image appeared in Shore's first major book, *Uncommon Places*. In recent decades, it has become one of a select band of pictures that symbolize the great flowering of American color photography in the 1970s.

To the extent that this photograph is a document of a time and a place, its value is clear. It is thick with information, all in pin-sharp focus from foreground to distant horizon. When the world finally weans itself off fossil fuels, our descendants will look upon this image with fascination. The artistic value of a photograph may be less predictable, less definable, than its documentary value, but few would doubt the mastery here. Whatever technological and aesthetic changes befall photography, whatever future generations make of the world it depicts, there will always be a place for pictorial structure. (David Campany)

See also: *Uncommon Places*

1. Stephen Shore, "Form and Pressure," *Aperture* 205 (Winter 2011): 44–45.

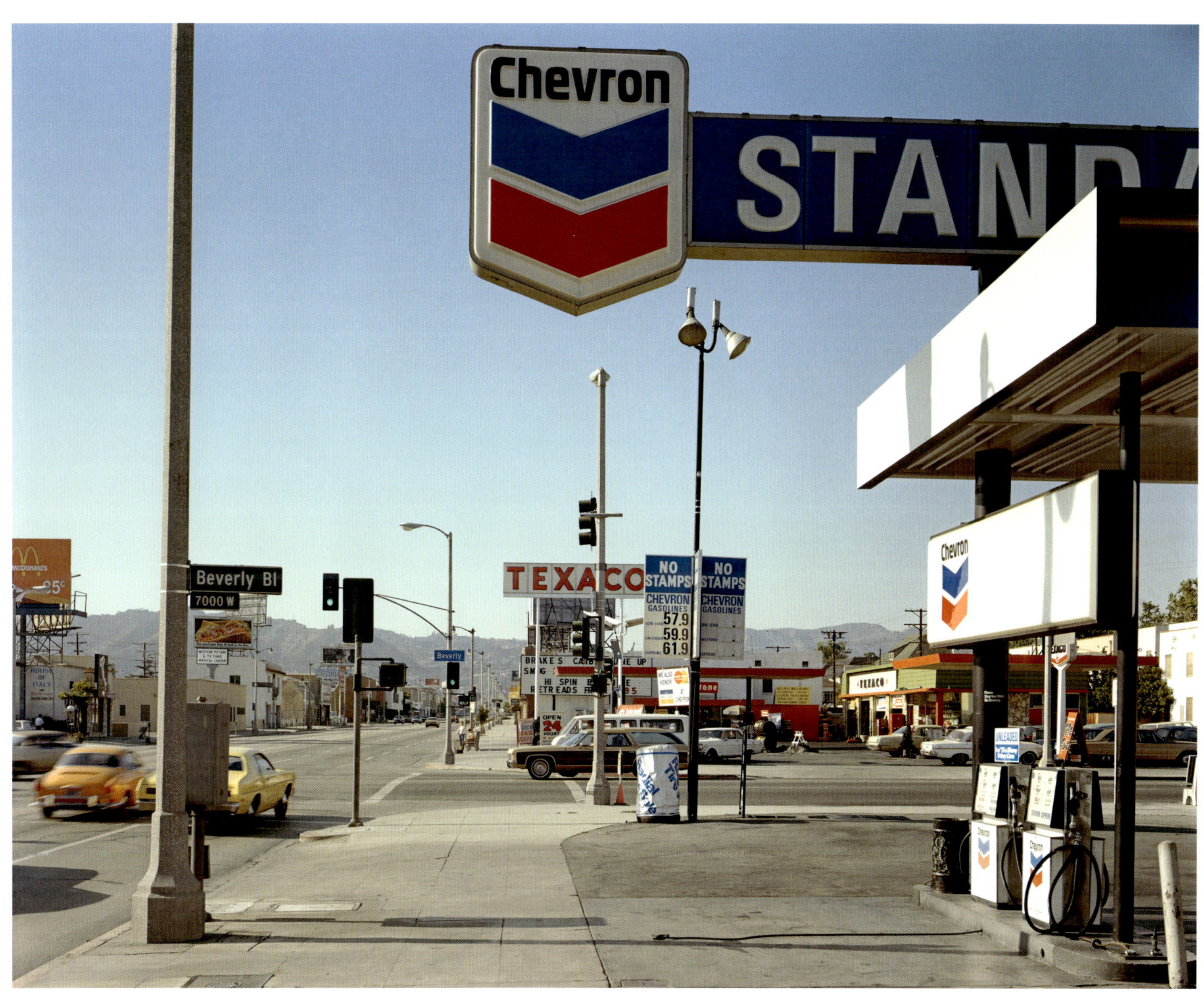

Beverly Boulevard and La Brea Avenue, Los Angeles, California, June 21, 1975**. 1975**

53.

Black and White

Shore entered photography working in black and white. His photographic "family of origin" in the 1950s and early 1960s, from Walker Evans to Lee Friedlander, evinced a lack of interest in and even a distrust of color. As a young amateur photographer in the sixties, shooting in New York in the tradition of his predecessors' street photography and printing his own pictures, black and white was a natural choice for Shore. While he also worked in color during this period, it remained marginal to his production. For noncommercial photographers at the time, using black and white was more than an aesthetic choice; it was a moral imperative. Color was the domain of the commercial photographer and the hobbyist, black and white the domain of the photographer who aspired to become an auteur.

The pictures that Shore took at the Factory in 1965–67, shooting in black and white, have an immediacy and a testimonial quality that verge on reportage. He would later say that "the feel of the place, the sense of action, the rawness, everything about [the images] feels very appropriate in black and white."[1] His serial imagery of 1969–70 came out of a different black-and-white tradition, a more Conceptual and documentary form linked to Ed Ruscha's work, with which Shore became acquainted in 1967–68.[2]

After experimenting with various black-and-white approaches in the sixties, Shore made the transition to color in the early seventies. Two decades later, he would revisit black and white, notably in the series *Essex County* (1992–95), *Luzzara* (1993), *Archaeology* (1996–97), and *New York, New York* (2000–2002). This return to black and white may be explained by several factors. First, as is often the case with Shore, was a desire for reinvention, this time after twenty years of working in color. Second was his penchant for a kind of contrariness, a tendency to take the opposite approach from prevailing trends: at a time when much of the photography world had converted to color, he decided to return to black and white. In addition, black-and-white printing was an essential component of teaching photography, which he had been doing at Bard College since 1982. A final factor was the two commissions Shore received in the early nineties that echoed black-and-white works by nineteenth- and twentieth-century photographers. The first, from the Getty, was a commission to make (color) images based on those by the French photographer Camille Silvy in the late 1850s; the second was in Luzzara, an Italian city photographed in black and white four decades earlier by Paul Strand. During this same period Shore was writing his book *The Nature of Photographs* (1998), which served in many ways as a personal and subjective history of photography. His panoramic images of New York, which brought the decade to a close, were also inscribed in a black-and-white tradition, that of his early street photography (Shore himself has described them as "Winogrand-esque street pictures"[3]), whose sense of instantaneity and movement he revisited using a slow and cumbersome 8-by-10 camera.

Like his color work of the same years, his new black-and-white prints (with the exception of *Luzzara*) tended toward the monumental: those of *Essex County* and *Archaeology* measure 30 by 38 inches, and *New York, New York* 38 by 95. Shore's black-and-white work of the nineties was created in a completely different context, technically and aesthetically, from that of his younger days. Using such large formats, as well as choosing Iris prints—an inkjet print that gives a much more graphic look to images—moved Shore away from a photographic tradition toward something more pictorial, even sculptural. "It's taken me a while to figure out what form I want to see them in," he said in 2000, "but now I've started to use Iris prints, mostly three-by-four feet. [. . .] I think I'm heading more toward making objects, so that's why I'm attracted to the Iris prints. They impress themselves more as physical objects than an 8x10 black-and-white photograph."[4] (Quentin Bajac)

See also: *Archaeology*; *Conceptual Sequences*; *Factory, The*; *Luzzara*; *Prints*; *Street Photography*

1. "Stephen Shore Interview," *Wallpaper*, July 26, 2007, https://wallpaper.com/art/Stephen-Shore-interview.
2. "A Ground Neutral and Replete: Stephen Shore and Gil Blank in Conversation," *Whitewall*, no. 7 (Fall 2007): 59.
3. David Campany, "Ways of Making Pictures," in Marta Dahó, ed., *Stephen Shore* (Madrid: Fundación MAPFRE; New York: Aperture, 2014), 47.
4. "Stephen Shore with Peter Halley," *Index* 23 (April 2000): 36.

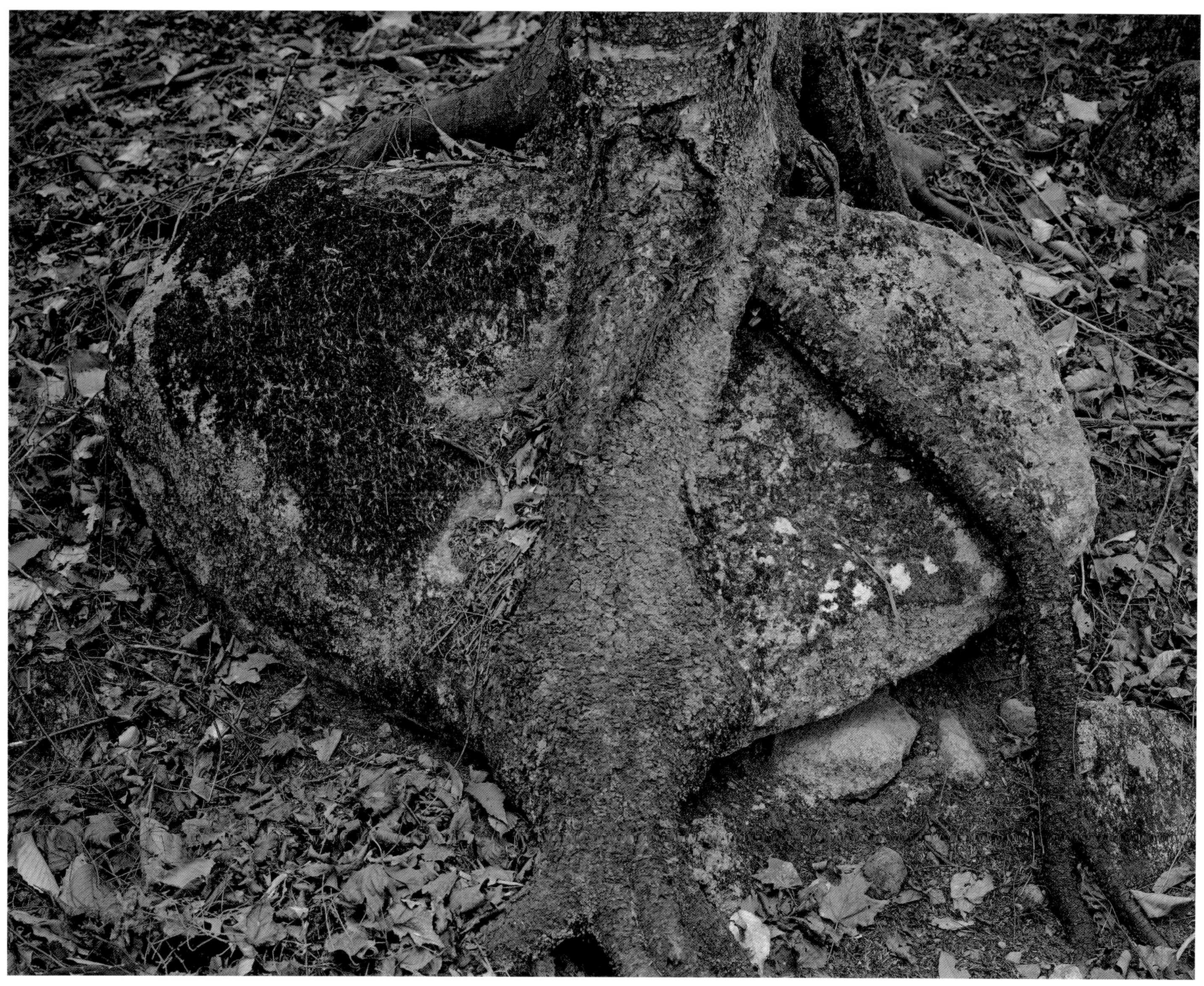

***Essex County*. 1992**

55.

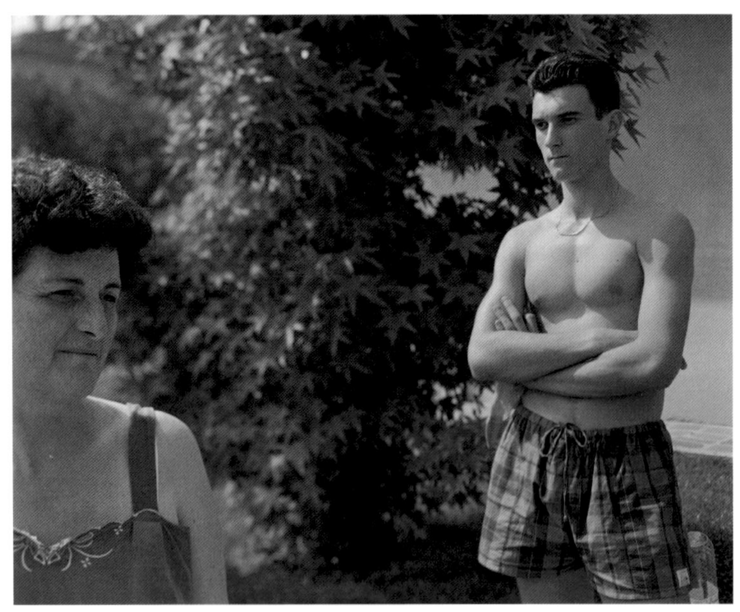

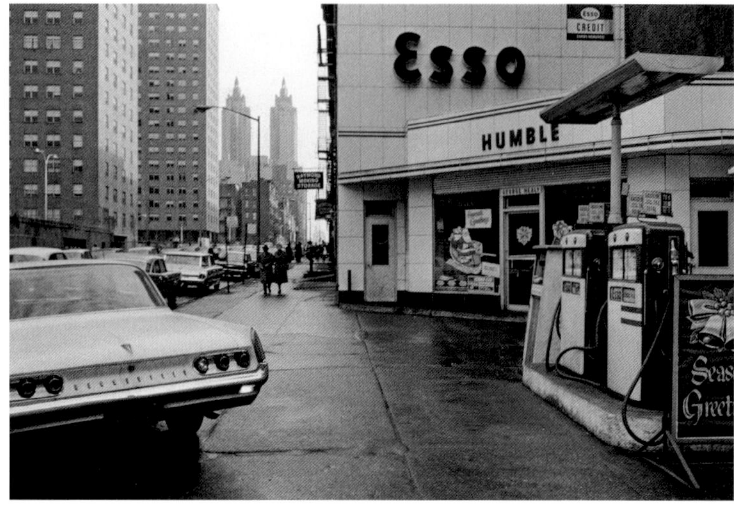

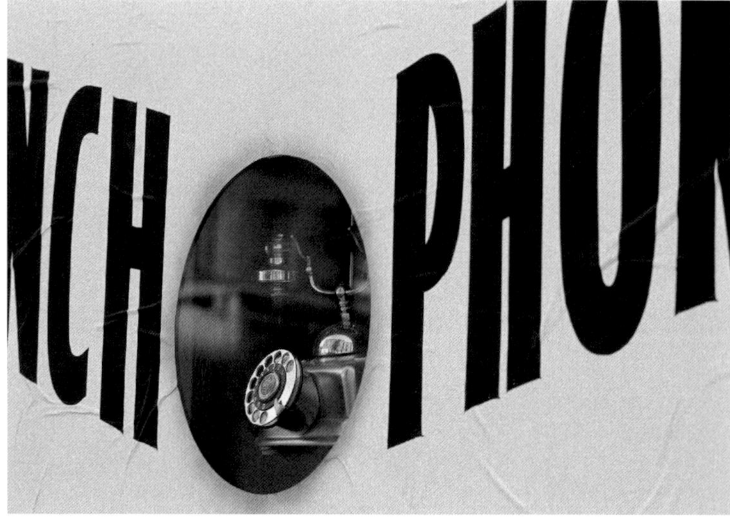

***Luzzara, Italy, 1993*. 1993**

***New York, New York*. 1964**

Untitled. 1964

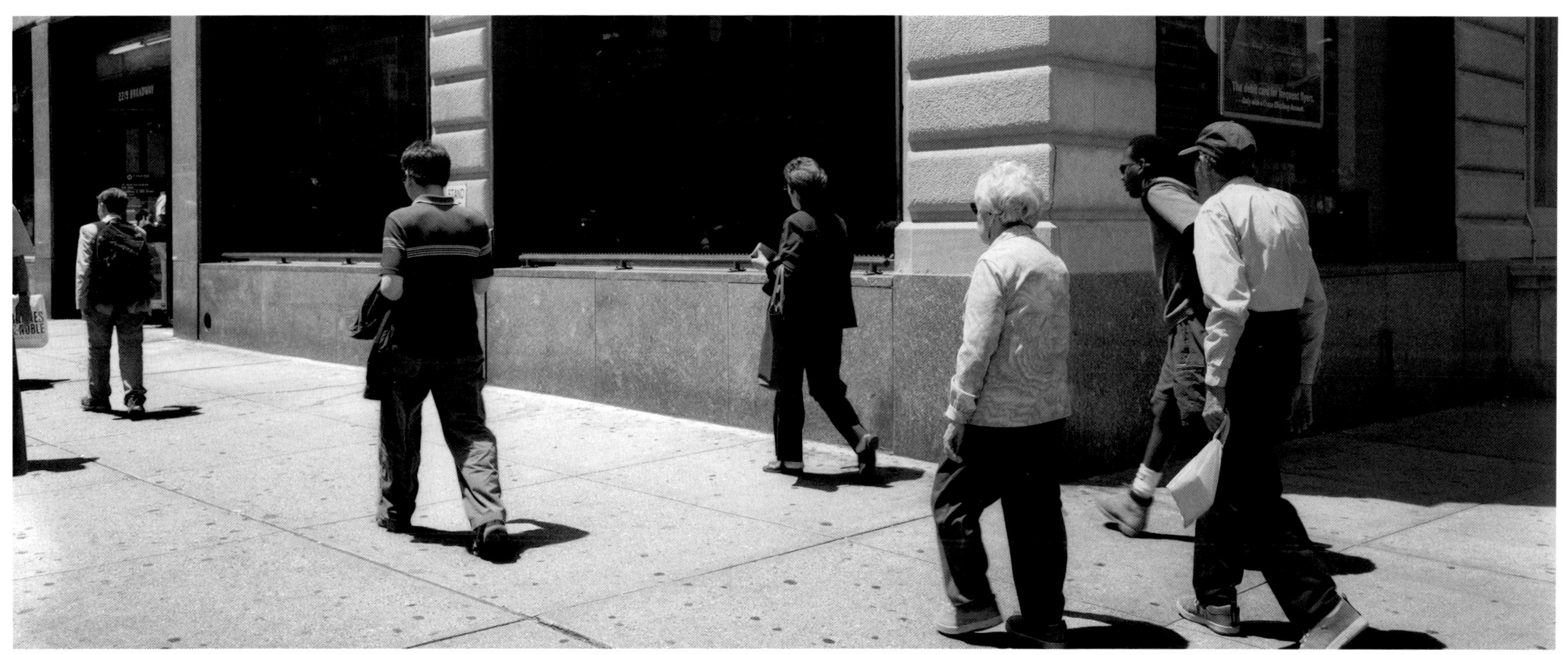

***New York, New York*. 2000–2002**

Cameras

Shore's very first experiments with photography were not with a camera: after being given a darkroom kit when he was six years old, he processed negatives of pictures his parents had taken with their Brownie Hawkeye.[1] Almost three years later he was given his own camera, a Ricoh 35mm rangefinder, which he would use for his black-and-white photographs of the 1960s. But the first camera that clearly influenced both Shore's form and his content was the 1971 Mick-a-Matic camera he used to take informal snapshots and portraits. As he was planning the road trip that would turn into *American Surfaces* the next year, Shore wanted to continue pursuing a similarly "natural" snapshot quality and so began using a Rollei 35, which he chose over other cameras he had acquired by that time (including a Nikon F, a Leica M2, and a Hasselblad 500EL) because it was "innocuous-looking," and he had already noted how different cameras shaped how subjects responded to him.[2] Shot with Kodacolor 35mm film that he would ship back to New York to be processed, the resulting images evidence a looseness and spontaneity that came to define the series.

Shore was interested in making larger prints, but his enlarger experiments with 35mm negatives were untenably grainy, so in late 1973 he started using a Graflex Crown Graphic 4-by-5. He has explained that even though for a time he used the two cameras simultaneously while working on both *American Surfaces* and the series that followed, *Uncommon Places*, the delineation between them was tied to the difference in equipment: photographs for the former were taken with the Rollei and for the latter with the Graflex.[3] Shore quickly found that the large-format camera encouraged deliberation, in part because of the expensive negatives and cumbersome equipment. As a result, he has said, "you begin to learn conscientious decision-making and develop a taste for certainty."[4] He adapted his subject matter to the new format, photographing fewer meals, for instance, after eating a pancake that had cooled during his effort to set the Graflex with its tripod on top of his chair in the middle of a restaurant (page 108), and fewer people unless they were posing.[5] "But I don't want to blame it on my technique," he has said. "If having lots of people in my pictures was that important, I would have chosen a different technique."[6] Shore enjoyed working with the large format, and in 1973 and again in 1974 he borrowed an 8-by-10 Calumet from his friend Weston Naef, a curator at the Metropolitan Museum of Art. He knew he had found the format he wanted to use for years to come, and purchased an Arca Swiss 8-by-10; he almost exclusively used 8-by-10 cameras through the 1990s.

In the last decade Shore has mainly used digital cameras and has explored their limitations and strengths as thoroughly as he did with previous equipment. "[Digital] allows me to take a picture that is more spontaneous but with the resolution, the detail, and the tonality of a large-format camera," he has explained.[7] For his 2009–11 projects in Israel and the West Bank he worked with both a large-format camera and a Nikon D3X, setting up incredibly dense photographs of the desert and urban landscapes with the former and capturing daily life with the latter. He shot on many different digital cameras for his print-on-demand books of 2003–10 (including an Olympus, a Casio Exilim, and a Contax) and the Nikon D3X and a Nikon D800 for his 2012–13 series in Ukraine. And for a few years now Shore's most-utilized camera has been the one on his iPhone, on which he shoots the images he posts on Instagram. He has continually used cameras as one more way to challenge himself, explaining, "I'm not interested in developing a style and playing it to death. I'll change the medium, or I'll go to a different camera, just to be confronted with new problems or new possibilities."[8] (Kristen Gaylord)

See also: *American Surfaces*; *Instagram*; *Israel and the West Bank*; *Mick-a-Matic*; *Print-on-Demand Books*; *Stereographs*; *Uncommon Places*

1. An example of a print Shore developed when he was six is in the collection of the Center for Creative Photography, Tucson, Arizona, object number 79.109.15.
2. David Campany, "Ways of Making Pictures," in Marta Dahó, ed., *Stephen Shore* (Madrid: Fundación MAPFRE; New York: Aperture, 2014), 30. See also Steve Lafreniere, "Stephen Shore," *Vice*: The Photo Issue, 2009, 168–73.
3. "A Ground Neutral and Replete: Stephen Shore and Gil Blank in Conversation," *Whitewall*, no. 7 (Fall 2007): 54.
4. Aaron Schuman, "*Uncommon Places*: An Interview with Stephen Shore," *Seesaw* 3 (Summer 2005): http://seesawmagazine.com/shore_pages/shore_interview.html.
5. "A Ground Neutral and Replete," 64.
6. Glenn O'Brien, "American Landscape," *Tokion*, 2006, 47.
7. Alexis Dahan, "Stephen Shore on Photography vs Instagram," *Purple Magazine* 24 (Fall/Winter 2015–16): http://purple.fr/magazine/fw-2015-issue-24/stephen-shore/.
8. O'Brien, "American Landscape," 48.

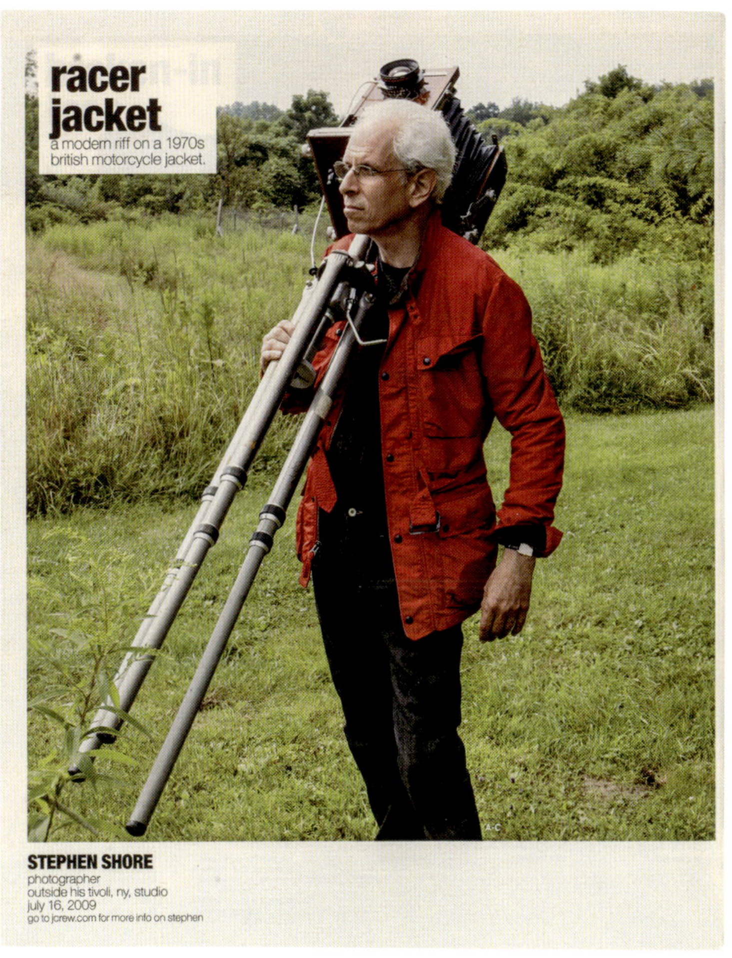

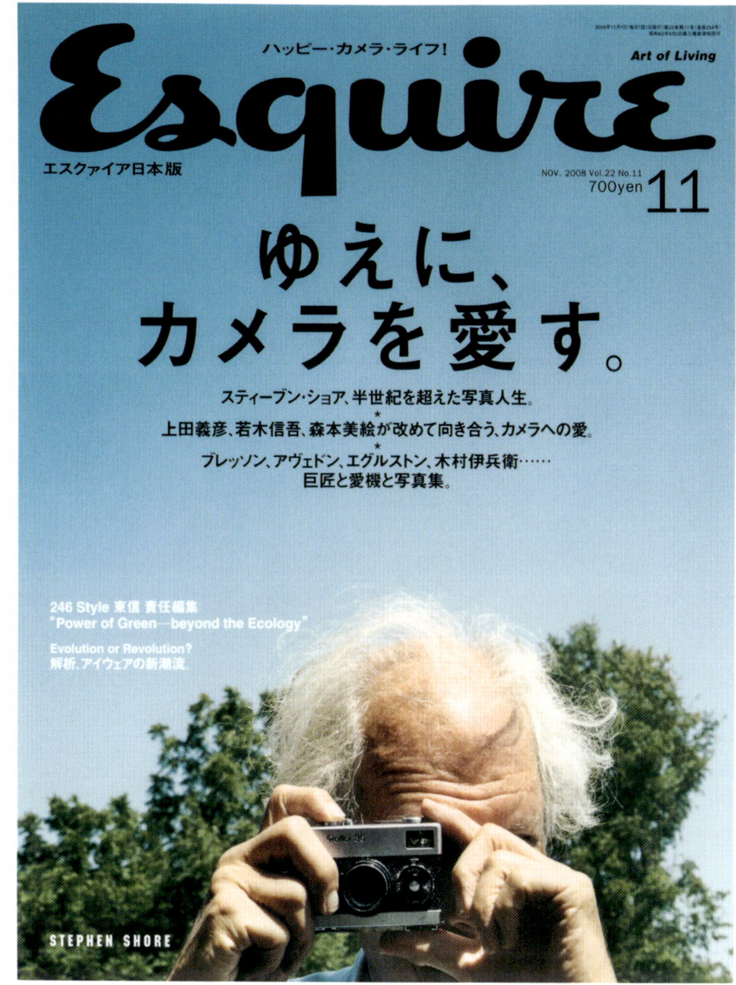

Page from J. Crew catalogue, October 2009

Cover of *Esquire* (Japan), November 2008

Color

Kodachrome / They give us those nice bright colors / They give us the greens of summers / Makes you think all the world's a sunny day.

The lyrics of Paul Simon's 1973 song seem to echo Shore's early *Uncommon Places* photographs of the same period, which convey the photographer's enthusiasm for various shades of green and his fascination with the blue skies and bright light of the American West. In the seventies and early eighties, Shore was one of the primary representatives of what was known as the New Color Photography in America, along with William Eggleston, Jan Groover, Joel Meyerowitz, and Joel Sternfeld. Images from *Uncommon Places* were included in the 1981 exhibition *The New Color: A Decade of Color Photography*, at the International Center of Photography in New York, and in the exhibition catalogue, which was published retrospectively and served as a sort of consecration of the movement. The publication, written by Sally Eauclaire, who curated the exhibition, was followed by two other books by her on the subject: *New Color/New Work: Eighteen Photographic Essays* (1984) and *American Independents: Eighteen Color Photographers* (1987), in which Shore was represented by his landscapes of Montana and the Hudson Valley, respectively.

As Max Kozloff pointed out in the pages of *Artforum* in 1975, color photography was then "coming of age."[1] For Shore's generation color photography was a given, not a secondary subgenre as it had been for the previous generation. It was no longer about using color film only to highlight the properties of color photography but rather about using the most contemporary and natural technology available to capture the world without nostalgia. This generation finally left behind the disdain with which their predecessors—not only photographers but also critics and journalists—had viewed color, an attitude perfectly illustrated by Walker Evans's often-quoted remark about rising up against the "bebop of electric blues, furious reds, and poison greens."[2] In a 2010 interview, Shore recollected a conversation he had with Paul Strand in 1974 during which the older photographer confided that the "higher emotions could not be communicated in color."[3] The same observation was sometimes made of Shore's early work. A 1975 review of an exhibition of photographs by Shore, Duane Michals, and Harry Callahan in Boston was critical of Shore's color images in comparison to the black-and-white work of the other two photographers: "Colors themselves prevent Shore's photographs from obtaining the extremes which black and white can reach. Color lays hold of the viewer more impetuously and thus leaves less wonderment."[4] This impression was reinforced by the fact that his use of color was deliberately antiheroic, eschewing the spectacular aspects of color found in commercial, advertising, and even news photography of the time. In response to this unconventional approach to color, the printer of Shore's 1971 postcards of Amarillo, his first color series, returned them with the chromatic values heavily corrected to conform to the outrageously blue skies and unnaturally green grass typical of commercial postcards.

Although some of the early images from the series *Uncommon Places*, like *2nd Street, Ashland, Wisconsin, July 9, 1973* (page 47) or *West 3rd Street, Parkersburg, West Virginia, May 16, 1974* (page 207), succumbed to a more seductive use of color, over the years Shore's color would become increasingly natural and unspectacular. In the manner of Walker Evans's postwar photo-essays in color, published primarily in *Fortune* magazine,[5] the chromatic values in Shore's pictures were deliberately muted. In a review of the 1975 group exhibition *New Topographics: Photographs of a Man-Altered Landscape*, in which Shore was the only photographer working in color, the critic from *Artweek* did not distinguish his images from those of the other photographers in the show: "[Shore's] works are as transparent as the rest, for the colors are neutral and not overwhelming."[6] The following year, during his first exhibition at MoMA, the *New York Times* described his color as "equally bland and unemphatic," and explained: "Unlike the expressive and distorted color of so many magazine photographs, it is, one suspects, as close as possible to the real color of the objects photographed."[7]

The model of color photography that Shore emulated early on was that of amateur snapshots and other vernacular pictures, a vision he shared with a number of Conceptual artists, foremost among them John Baldessari and Robert Smithson. For a young professional photographer who had been working in black and white, Shore's transition to color implied that he had distanced himself from technique and

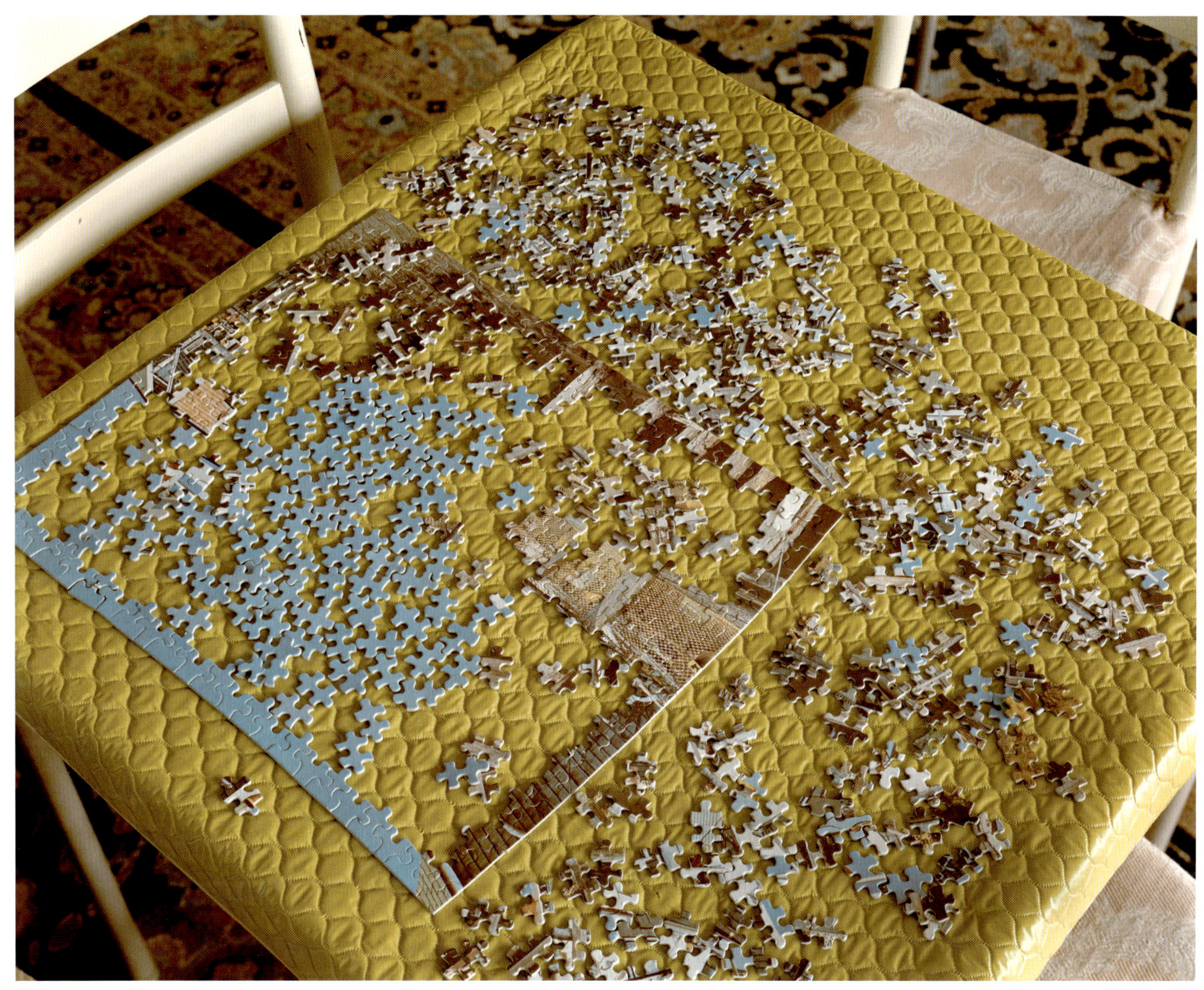

Lookout Hotel, Ogunquit, Maine, July 16, 1974. 1974

61.

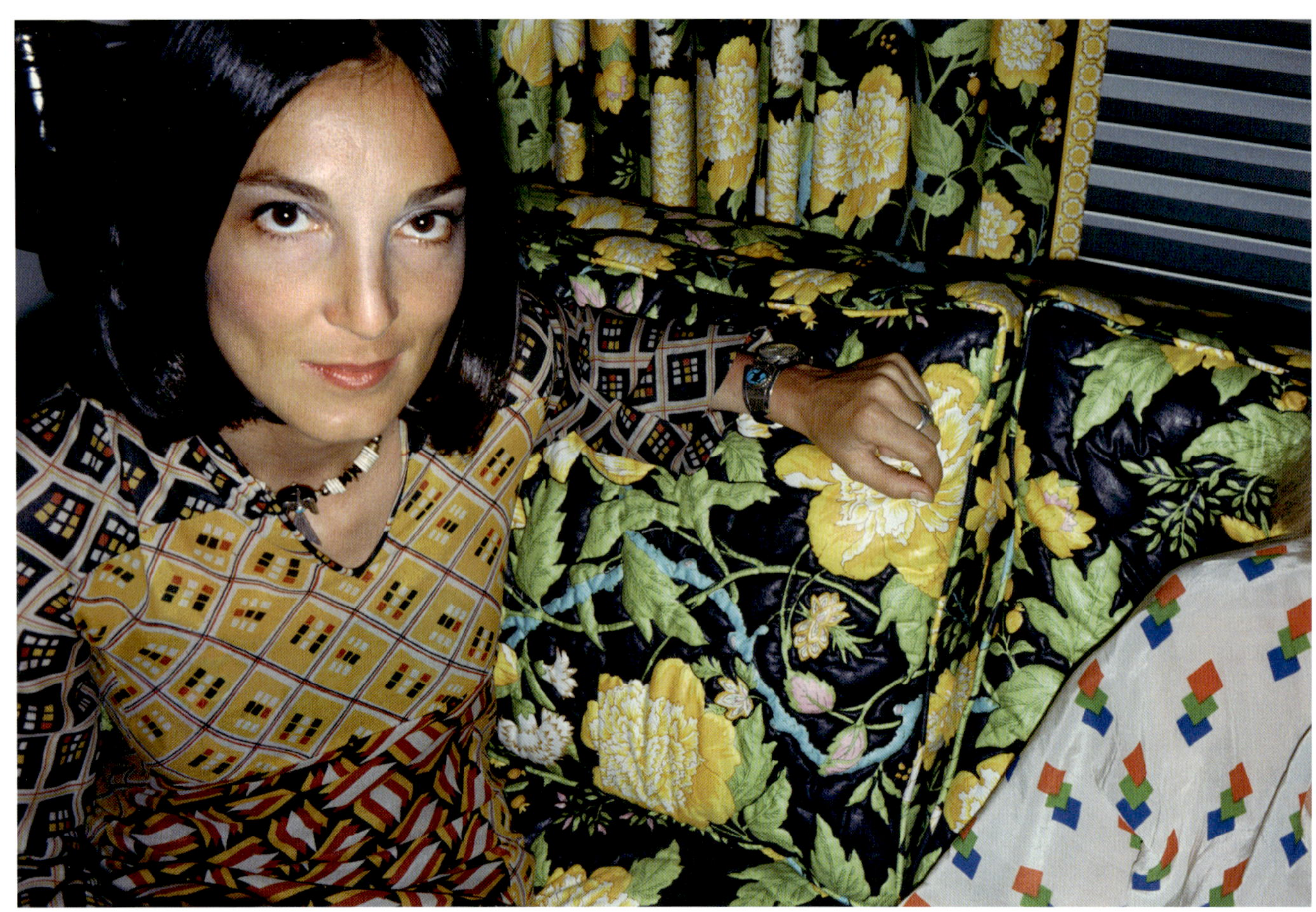

***Palm Beach, Florida, April–May 1973.* 1973**

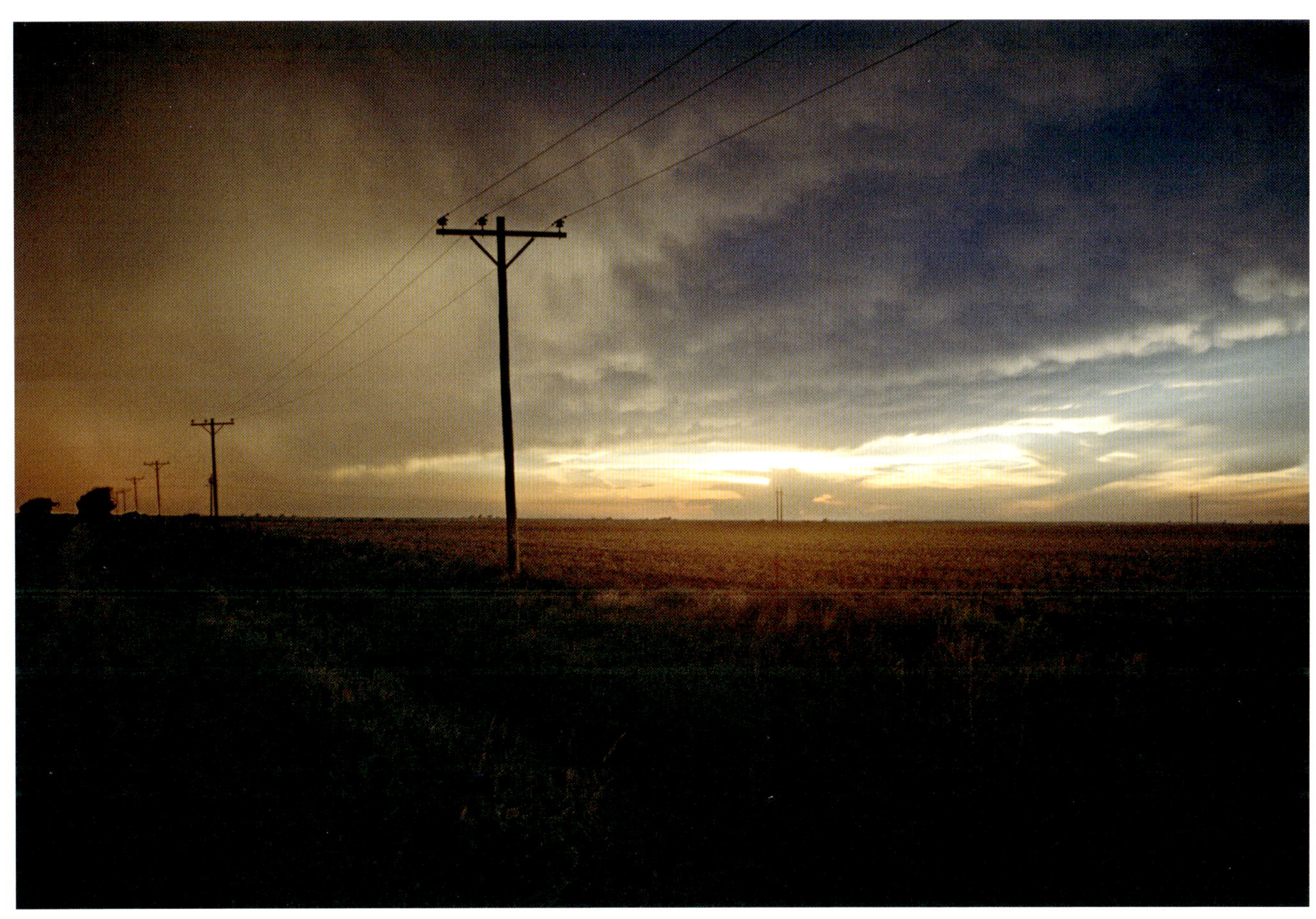

Granite, Oklahoma, July 1972. 1972

accepted his loss of control over the production of the image—in other words, that he had relinquished his status as an auteur. For his series *American Surfaces,* Shore made this loss of control systematic by mailing rolls of Kodacolor film to Kodak for developing, so that the end result, in terms of both aesthetics and mode of production, was a kind of mass-produced image.

With *Uncommon Places*, Shore's choice of large-format negatives reintroduced a measure of photographic skill, professionalism, and compositional control into his practice, first with Ektacolor (1973–75) and then Vericolor (from 1976) Type L film. His use of color then took on a different significance, representing above all a desire to capture the small and endless variations of luminous tonalities up close. "Color film is wonderful because it shows not only the intensity but the color of light," he said in 1982. "There is so much variation in light between noon one day and the next, between ten in the morning and two in the afternoon."[8] In keeping with his ideal of simplicity, Shore intentionally chose a commonplace and unremarkable printing process: the chromogenic print. As John Szarkowski pointed out regarding Shore in 1979: "Type C prints are so *immaterial*—you don't have the sense of a body of dye, of any physical deposit. It's just colored light—like a transparency."[9] Unlike William Eggleston's dye transfer prints of the mid-1970s, which have a strong physical presence, Shore's prints are infused with a luminosity that makes us forget their presence. This creates the impression that, rather than *seeing* his images, we are *seeing through* them. (Quentin Bajac)

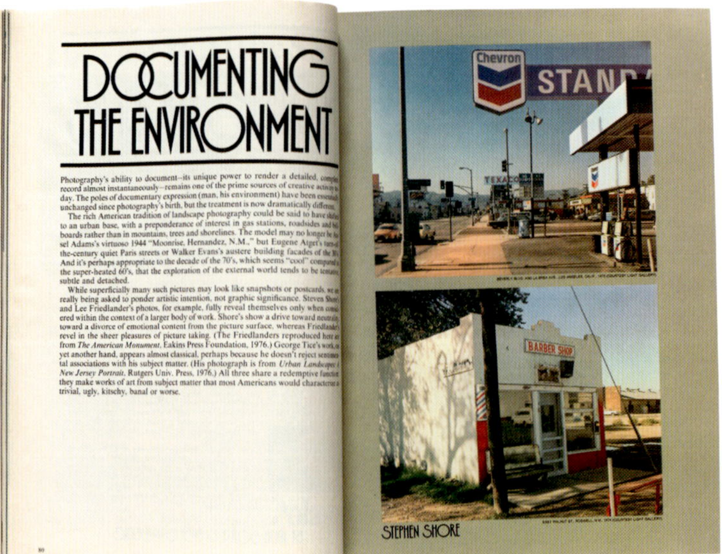

DOCUMENTING THE ENVIRONMENT

Photography's ability to document—its unique power to render a detailed, comple[illegible] record almost instantaneously—remains one of the prime sources of creative activity to- day. The poles of documentary expression (man, his environment) have been essentially unchanged since photography's birth, but the treatment is now dramatically different.

The rich American tradition of landscape photography could be said to have shifted to an urban base, with a preponderance of interest in gas stations, roadsides and billboards rather than in mountains, trees and shorelines. The model may no longer be Ansel Adams's virtuoso 1944 "Moonrise, Hernandez, N.M.," but Eugene Atget's turn-of-the-century quiet Paris streets or Walker Evans's austere building facades of the 30's. And it's perhaps appropriate to the decade of the 70's, which seems "cool" compared to the super-heated 60's, that the exploration of the external world tends to be tentative, subtle and detached.

While superficially many such pictures may look like snapshots or postcards, we are really being asked to ponder artistic intention, not graphic significance. Steven Shore's and Lee Friedlander's photos, for example, fully reveal themselves only when considered within the context of a larger body of work. Shore's show a drive toward neutrality, toward a divorce of emotional content from the picture surface, whereas Friedlander's revel in the sheer pleasures of picture taking. (The Friedlanders reproduced here are from *The American Monument*, Eakins Press Foundation, 1976.) George Tice's work, on yet another hand, appears almost classical, perhaps because he doesn't reject sentimental associations with his subject matter. (His photograph is from *Urban Landscapes: A New Jersey Portrait*, Rutgers Univ. Press, 1976.) All three share a redemptive function: they make works of art from subject matter that most Americans would characterize as trivial, ugly, kitschy, banal or worse.

See also: *American Surfaces*; *Evans, Walker*; *New Topographics*; *Uncommon Places*

1. Max Kozloff, "Photography: The Coming of Age of Color," *Artforum* 13, no. 5 (January 1975): 30–35.
2. Quoted in David Campany, *Walker Evans: The Magazine Work* (Göttingen: Steidl, 2014), 59.
3. David Land, "Unmediated Moments," *Royal Photographic Society Journal*, October 2010, 458.
4. Ann Parson, "Harry Callahan, Duane Michals, Steven Shore," *New Boston Review*, Fall 1975, 22.
5. See, especially, the photo essays "Before They Disappear," *Fortune*, March 1957, 141–45; "Color Accidents," *Architectural Forum*, January 1958, 110–15; "The Pitch Direct," *Fortune*, October 1958, 139–43; and "The Auto Junkyard," *Fortune*, April 1962, 132–37. Shore was not familiar with this aspect of Evans's oeuvre when he began working in color.
6. Robert W. Woolard, "Man-Shaped Landscapes," *Artweek*, March 27, 1976, 12.
7. Gene Thornton, "Formalists Who Flirt with Banality," *New York Times*, November 1976, D34.
8. Stephen Shore, *Uncommon Places* (New York: Aperture, 1982), 63.
9. Tony Hiss, "The Framing of Stephen Shore," *American Photographer*, February 1979, 36.

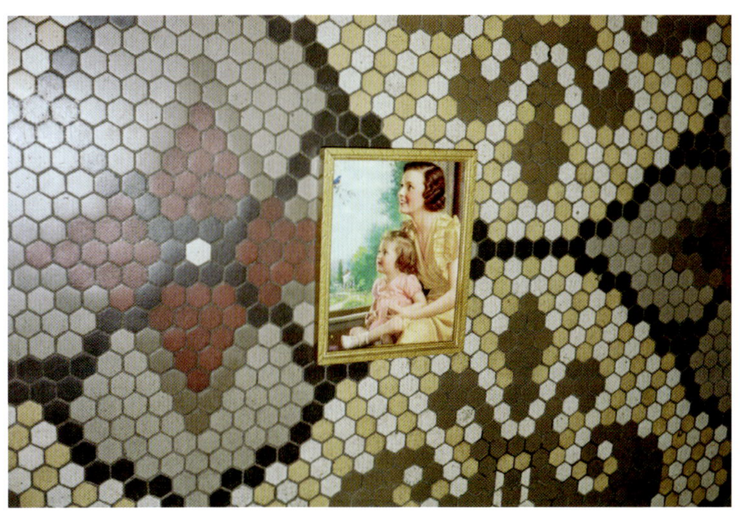

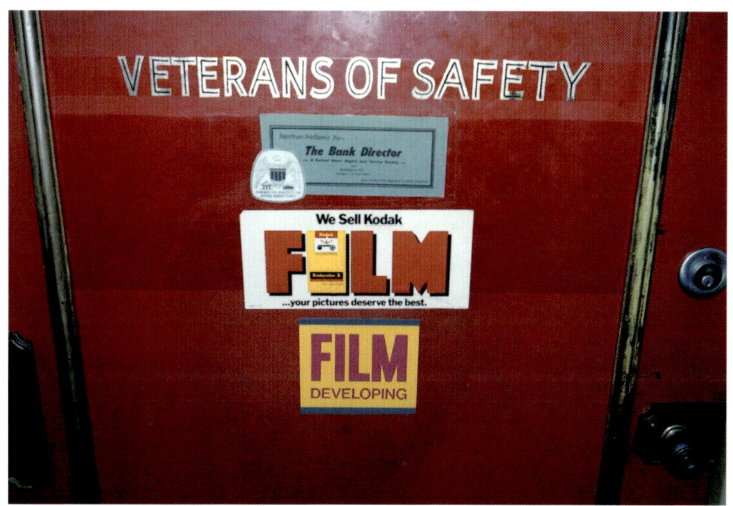

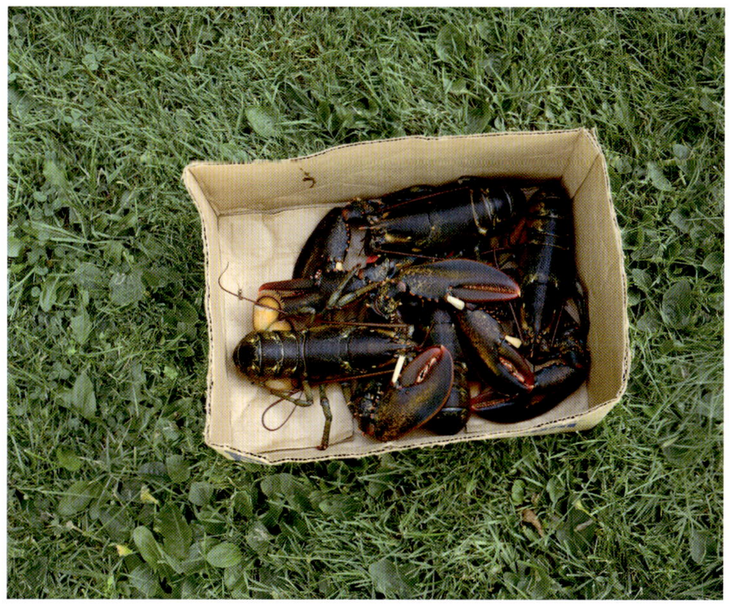

Spread from Julia Scully and Andy Grundberg, "U.S.A.: Pushing the Limits," *Modern Photography*, July 1976

***Joplin, Missouri, July 1972*. 1972**

***New York, New York, August 1972*. 1972**

***Castine, Maine, July 18, 1974*. 1974**

65.

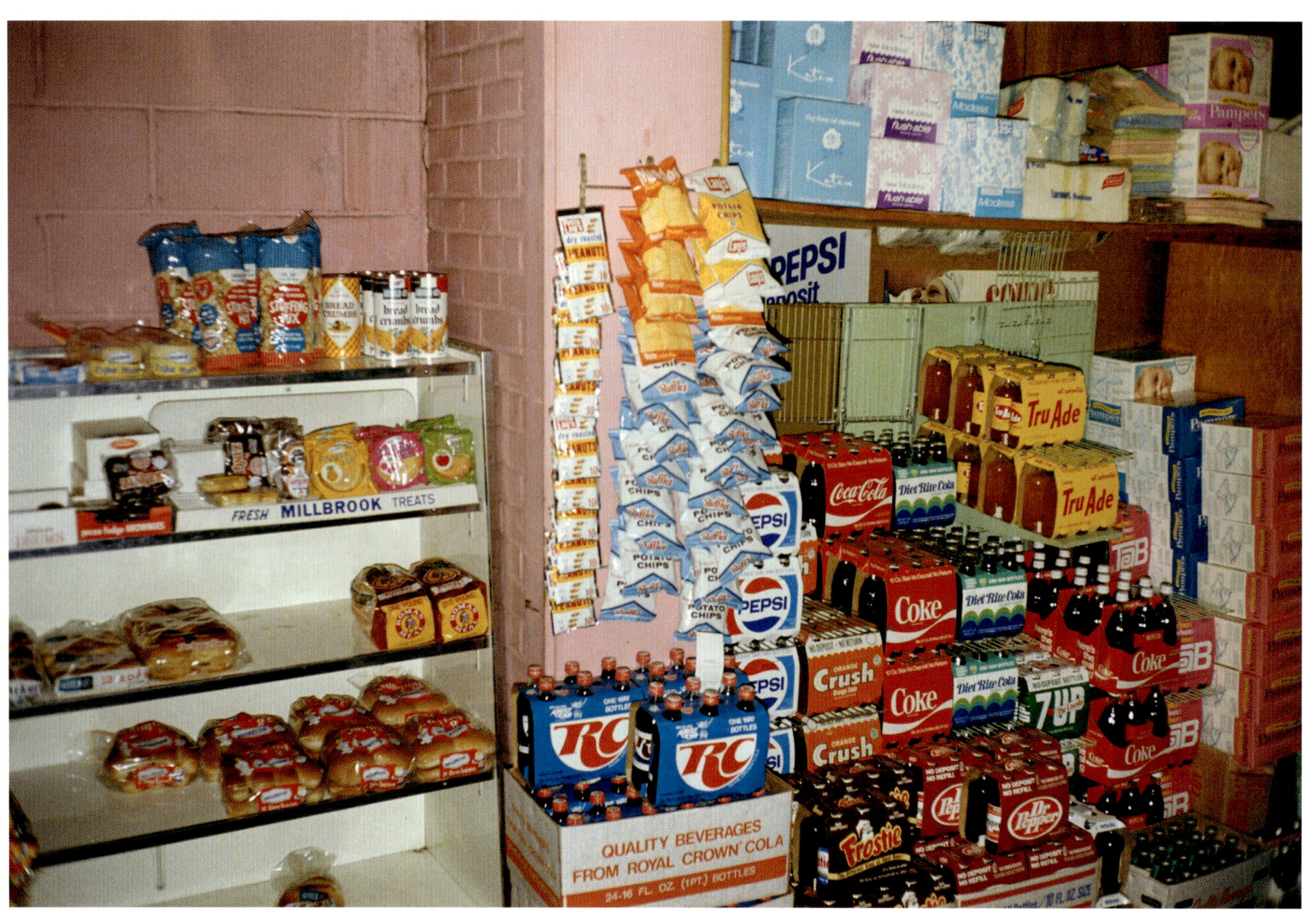

Petersburg, New York, September 1972. 1972

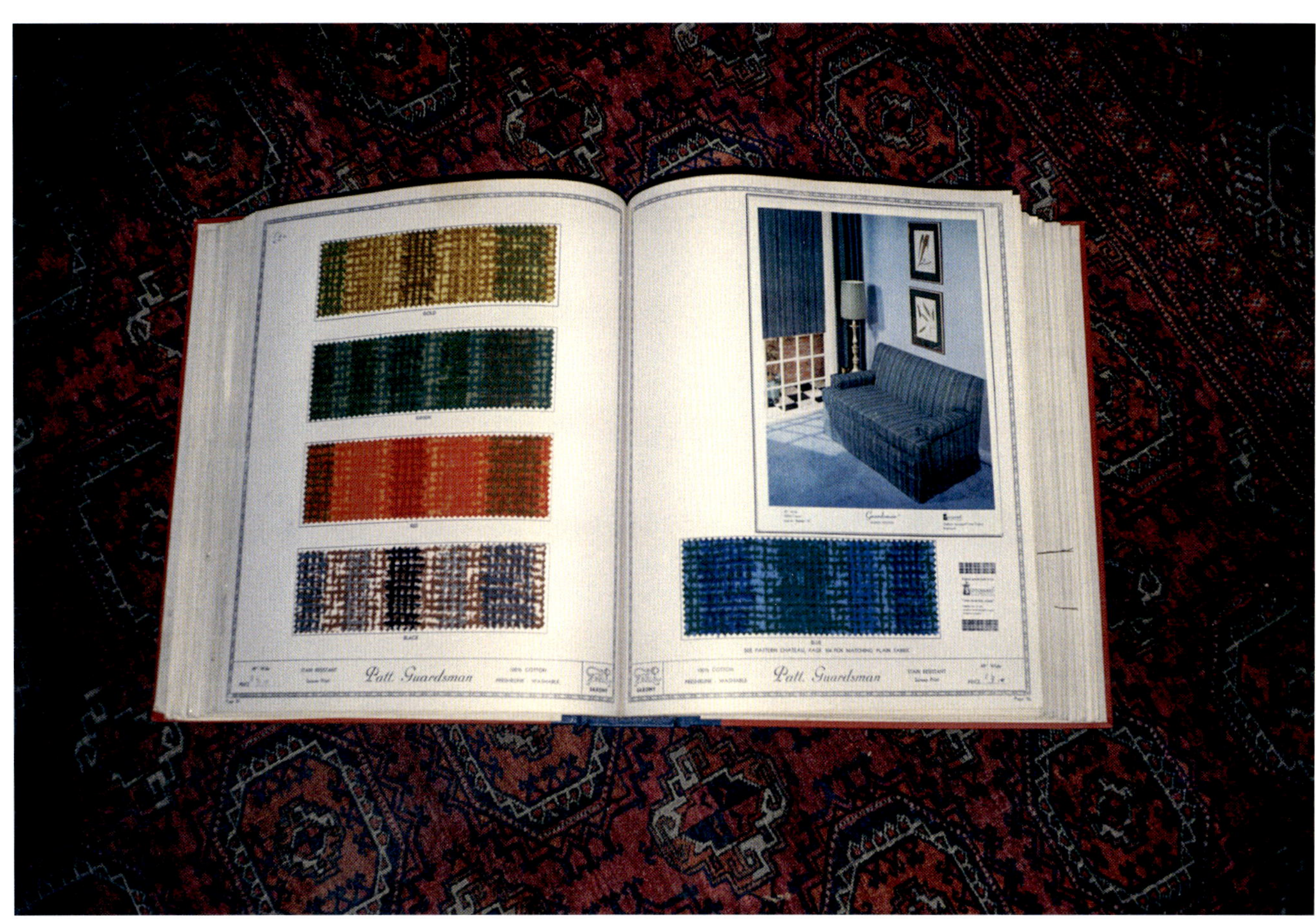

***New York, New York, September–October 1972*. 1972**

67.

Commercial Work

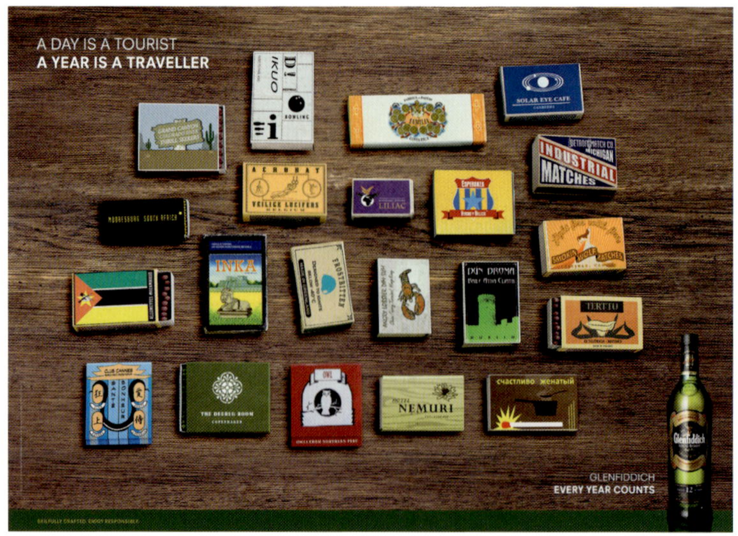

Although known primarily as an art photographer, Shore has worked on advertising campaigns since 2000—for Titleist, Glenfiddich, Bottega Veneta, Nike, Trussardi, Cadbury, Esso, Orange S.A., and Acorda Therapeutics, among other companies. Compared to the interpretive work that is sometimes possible with an editorial commission, commercial commissions often involve an entire creative team, of which the photographer is only one member, concretizing a preexisting sketch.[1] A shoot can involve dozens of people, including an art director, account executive, company representative, prop director, location scout, tech staff, and various assistants. Shore has used both digital and film cameras for these projects, although digital is far more common. Either format can involve extensive postproduction editing, whether stitching together a few negatives because of difficult light conditions or combining dozens of digital fragments to create a fictional location or scene.[2]

Although some of the creativity is taken out of his hands in commercial work, Shore finds it challenging in other ways. He has said, for instance, that he enjoys the problem of "clarifying" a specific object or product in a photograph after decades of learning how to clarify space and distance.[3] Clients hiring him know what sort of photographs he takes, but Shore has said that he always advises them, "'Don't feel embarrassed about telling me what you want.' I know that I have a reputation as an artist, and sometimes [clients] are hesitant about saying what their needs are. But what interests me as an artist is satisfying their needs. They're giving me the aesthetic problem, and that's fun for me to solve."[4] (Kristen Gaylord)

See also: *Cameras*; *Commissions and Editorial Work*; *Fashion Work*

1. Stephen Shore, phone conversation with the author, July 6, 2017.
2. In an interview in *Vice* magazine, Shore described how much easier his Nike advertisements were to create with digital tools than they would have been before digital cameras were widely used. See Steve Lafreniere, "Stephen Shore," *Vice*: The Photo Issue, 2009, 168.
3. Alexis Dahan, "Stephen Shore on Photography vs Instagram," *Purple Magazine* 24 (Fall/Winter 2015–16): http://purple.fr/magazine/fw-2015-issue-24/stephen-shore/.
4. Ibid.

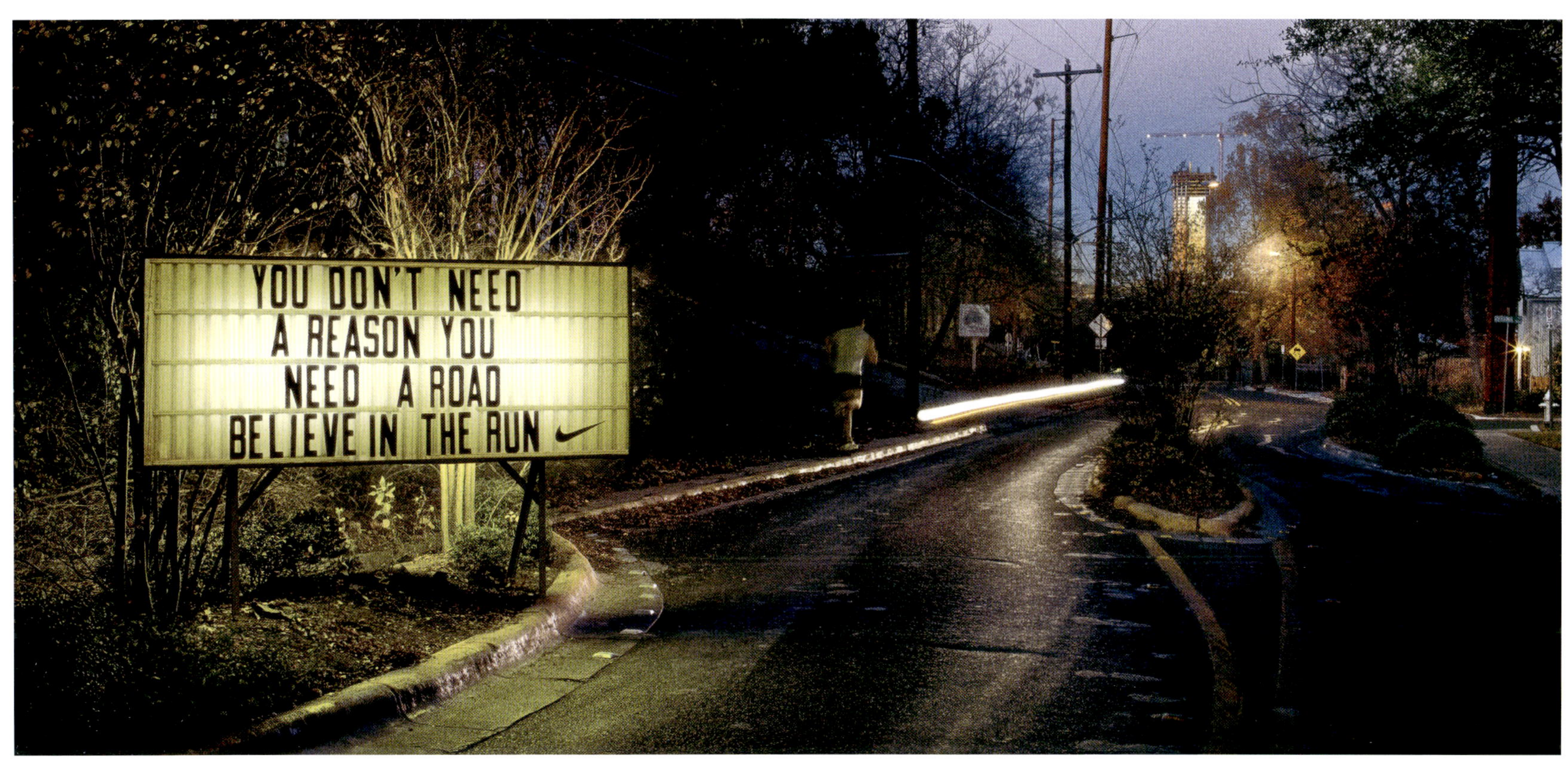

Glenfiddich advertisement, 2006

Nike advertisement, 2009

Commissions and Editorial Work

"At least one of the photographers in this show [. . .] has actually done commercial assignments," wrote the critic Gene Thornton in his 1981 review of the exhibition *The New Color: A Decade of Color Photography* at the International Center of Photography.[1] That photographer was Shore, for whom the second half of the 1970s and the early 1980s represented one of his most active periods of commissions and editorial work. During this time, the photography market was still in its infancy and emerging photographers could not live on the sale of their prints. In 1975, having gradually spent the small inheritance at his disposal and still several years away from securing the teaching position that would ensure a steady income, Shore began to accept photographic commissions, not only for editorial work but also for various institutions and companies.

A number of these commissions, completed while Shore was working on *Uncommon Places*, show some affinity with that series in their attention to both architecture and to what might be seen as a certain American-ness. In 1975 and 1976 Shore was given the opportunity to create two very different bodies of work on American architecture: the first, for the 1976 exhibition *Signs of Life: Symbols in the American City*, organized by Robert Venturi, Steven Izenour, and Denise Scott Brown, focused on contemporary vernacular architecture; the second, commissioned by Joseph E. Seagram & Sons, documented courthouses in small towns across the country and gave rise to an exhibition and a book.[2] Shortly thereafter, Shore had the opportunity to photograph steel towns in the Rust Belt for a 1977 story in *Fortune* magazine and Fairfield County, Connecticut, in the summer of 1979 for *Geo* Magazine, but to do so in a style that followed in a direct line from *Uncommon Places*, alternating between urban landscapes, portraits, and storefronts.[3] These two commissions show radically different aspects of white America in the late 1970s, illustrating the scope of places, subjects, and social classes that Shore was focusing on at the time, from upper-middle-class Connecticut during the summer months to steel towns in western New York, western Pennsylvania, and eastern Ohio. Speaking about the *Fortune* commission, Shore recalled that this was "for the last of the old-format issues. It was the last chance to run a large photographic portfolio. [. . .] The people in these pictures were being thrown out of work as their plants were closing. While some today blame trade agreements for the loss of manufacturing jobs, these pictures were fifteen years before the North American Free Trade Agreement was ratified."[4]

An invitation in 1981 to document (along with several other photographers) the filming of John Huston's *Annie* in Burbank, California, led to a series of images whose common element is the architectural decor itself.[5] The film's reconstruction of the Lower East Side in the 1930s inspired a few of Shore's images that are most indebted to the history of photography (Walker Evans, of course, but also Paul Strand, Jacob Riis, and Berenice Abbott) as well as some of the most detached and ironic pictures—postmodern, one might even say. The film's stage sets are to the original architecture of the Lower East Side what Shore's photographs are to those of his predecessors: reconstructions under the influence. The *Annie* photographs, in turn, shed new light on many of the images in *Uncommon Places* that, in their strange emptiness, appear to be so many stage sets.

These commissions from 1975 to 1981 were a welcome and even beneficial exercise for Shore. The photographer often said during this period that, by requiring him to focus on a specific theme and capture a place or subject in a few images, some of the commissioned work served as an antidote to his innate formalism.

In 1977 the Metropolitan Museum of Art commissioned Shore to photograph Claude Monet's home and garden at Giverny for an exhibition on the subject at a time when the garden was emerging from a long restoration. Five years later Shore returned to Giverny, for a related commission, to produce new work. Presented at the Met and reproduced in the *New York Times Magazine* and subsequently in a number of other magazines, Shore's photographs of Giverny were published in a 1983 book and included in three different portfolios, produced in 1978, 1984, and 2002.

The borders between Shore's commissioned photographs of Giverny and his personal body of work were very porous. This was also true of his images of the Yankees, shot during spring training in 1978 for a commission from AT&T, which gave him carte blanche to photograph

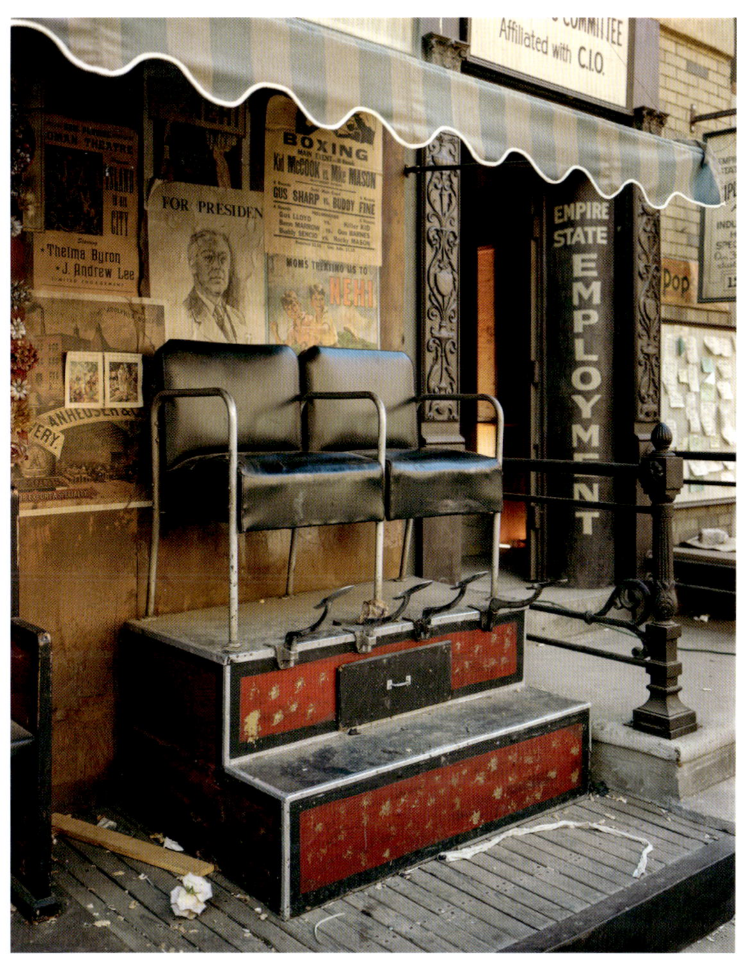

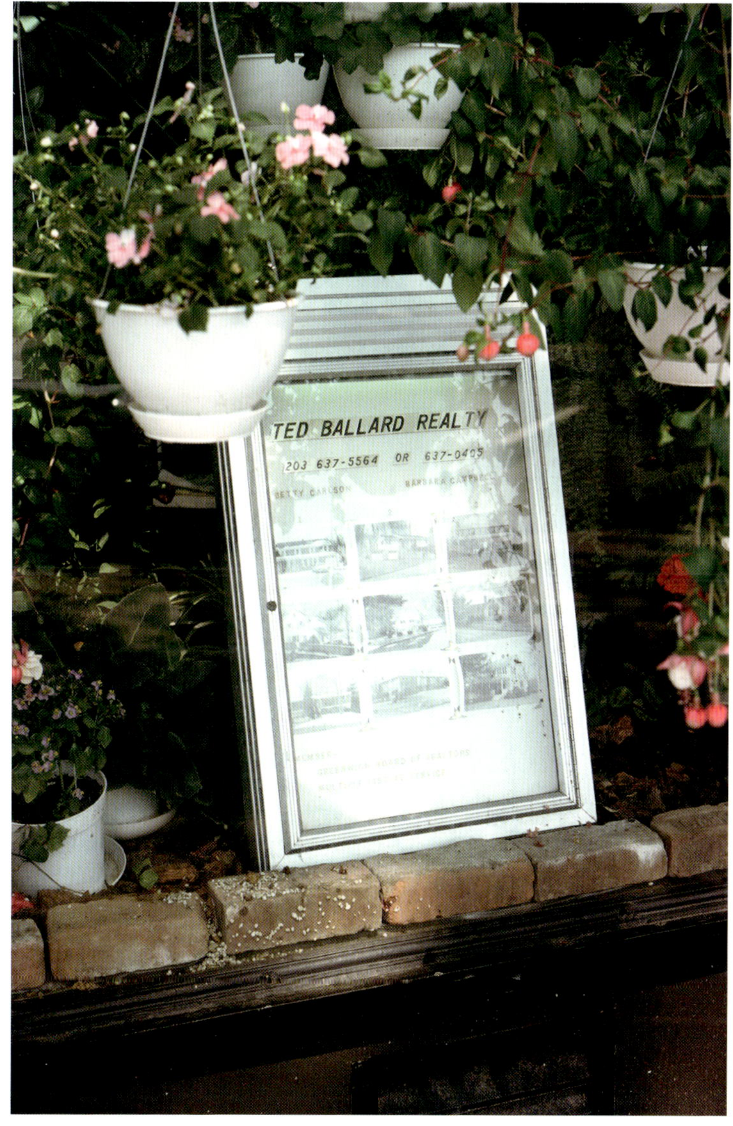

***Burbank, California, August 11, 1981.* 1981**

***Fairfield County, Connecticut, June 1979.* 1979**

whatever he liked.[6] Some of these pictures were published by the *New York Times Magazine* in April of that year,[7] others were presented in a solo exhibition at Light Gallery shortly thereafter, and one (a photograph of Graig Nettles, page 50) was included in his first book, *Uncommon Places*, in 1982. *Merced River, Yosemite National Park, California, August 13, 1979* (page 153), also published in *Uncommon Places* and one of Shore's most reproduced images today, was the result of a commission from the photographic film company Fuji. By the early 2000s, however, when Shore once again took on commissions and editorial work and opened himself up to other arenas—particularly advertising and fashion work—the fluidity between commissioned and personal work no longer existed. (Quentin Bajac)

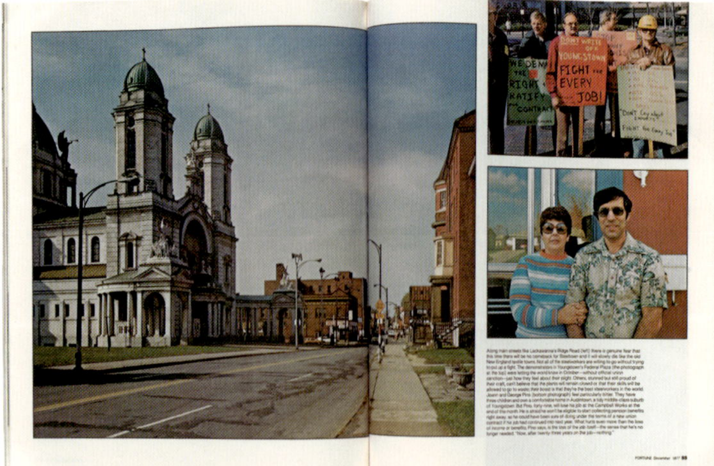

See also: *Baseball*; *Commercial Work*; *Courthouses*; *Gardens*; *Fashion Work*; *Merchandise*; *Uncommon Places*

1. Gene Thornton, "Is the New Color Work So Different from the Old?," *New York Times*, November 8, 1981, D27.
2. Richard Pare, ed., *Court House: A Photographic Document* (New York: Horizon Press, 1978).
3. Lee Smith, "Hard Times Come to Steeltown," *Fortune*, December 1977, 86–93.
4. Personal communication with the author, March 18, 2017.
5. *Annie on Camera: Nine Photographers*, text by Anne H. Hoy (New York: Abbeville Press, 1982).
6. Renato Danese, ed., *American Images: New Work by Twenty Contemporary Photographers* (New York: McGraw-Hill, 1979).
7. "Steinbrenner's Yanks," *New York Times Magazine*, April 9, 1978, 38–39.

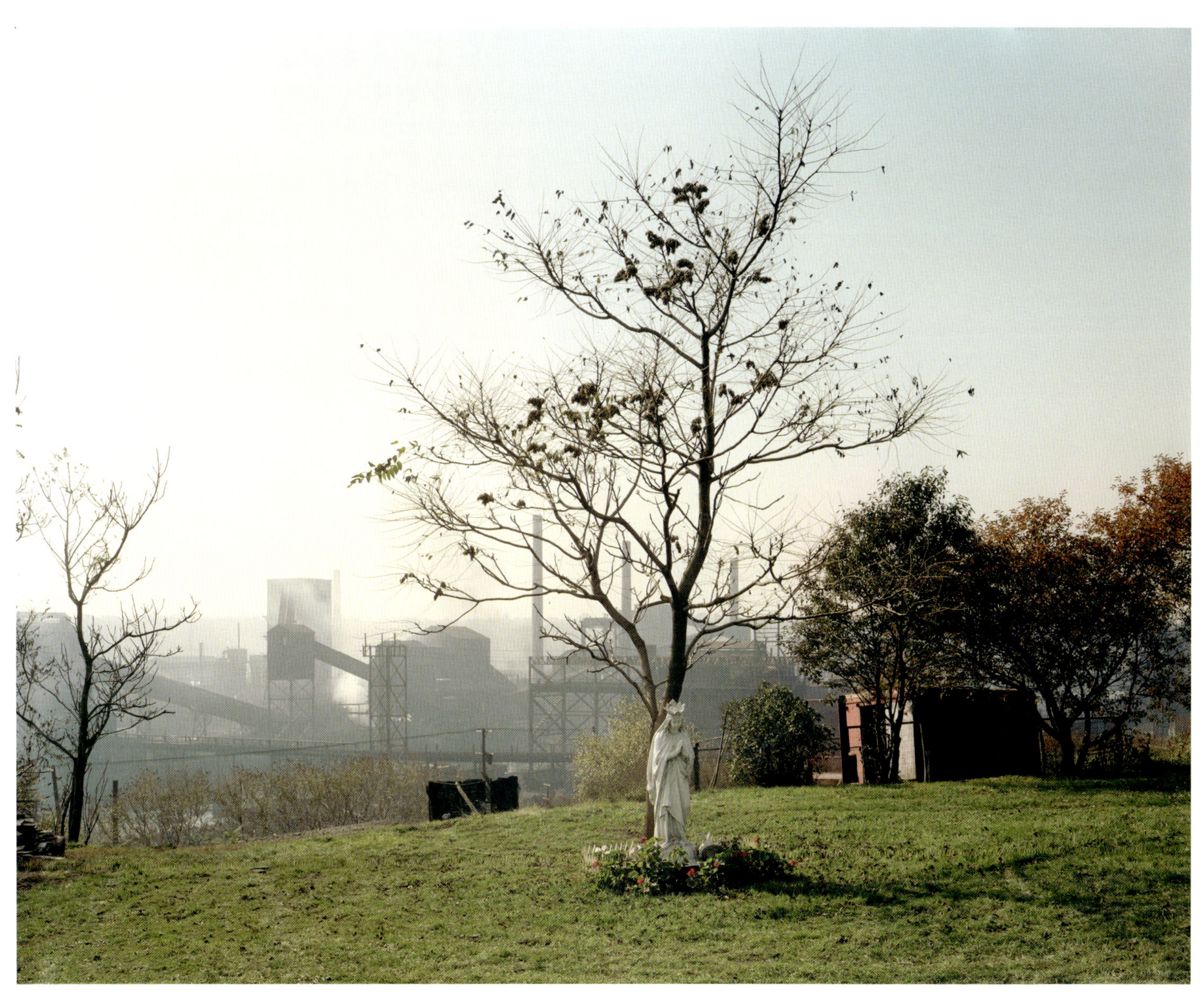

Spread from Lee Smith, "Hard Times Come to Steeltown," *Fortune*, December 1977

***Washington Street, Struthers, Ohio, October 27, 1977*. 1977**

73.

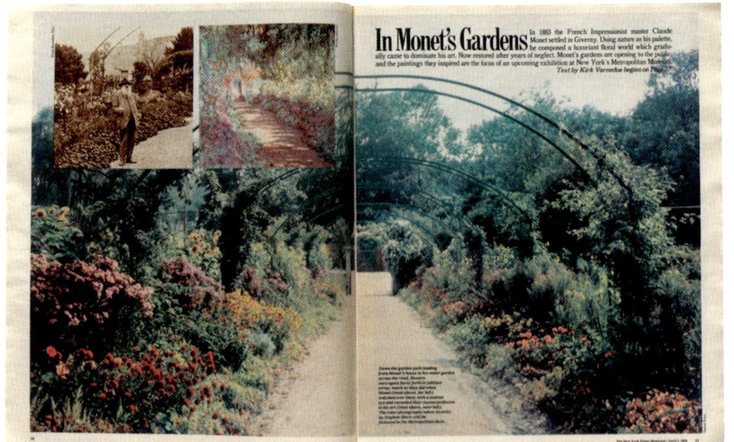

In Monet's Gardens

In 1883 the French Impressionist master Claude Monet settled in Giverny. Using nature as his palette, he composed a luxuriant floral world which gradually came to dominate his art. Now restored after years of neglect, Monet's gardens are opening to the public and the paintings they inspired are the focus of an upcoming exhibition at New York's Metropolitan Museum.

Text by Kirk Varnedoe begins on Page 37.

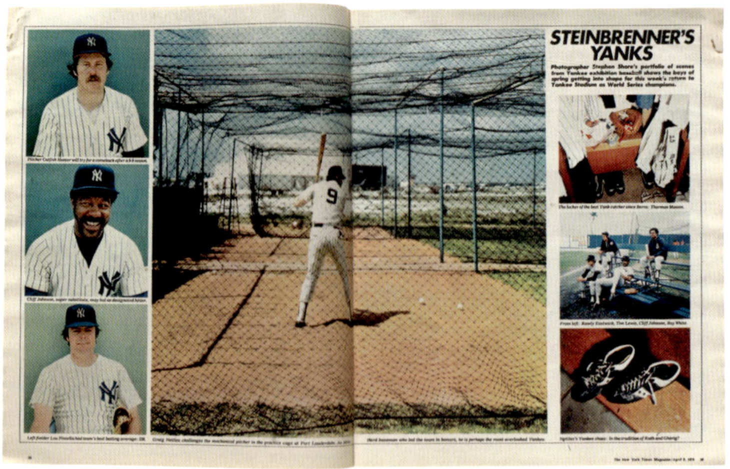

STEINBRENNER'S YANKS

Photographer Stephen Shore's portfolio of scenes from Yankee exhibition baseball shows the boys of spring getting into shape for this week's return to Yankee Stadium as World Series champions.

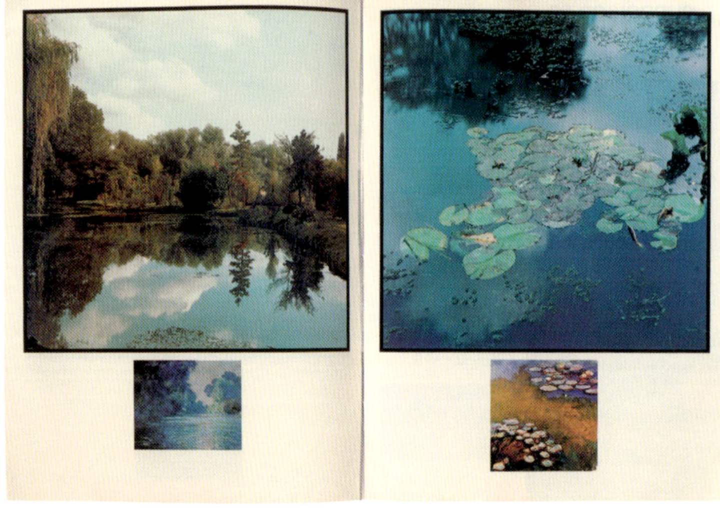

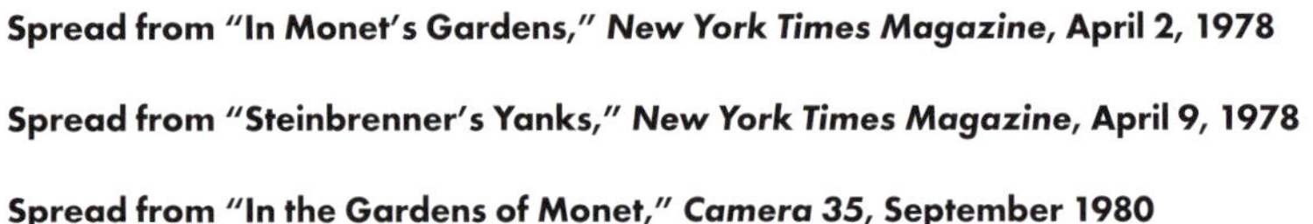

Spread from "In Monet's Gardens," ***New York Times Magazine*****, April 2, 1978**

Spread from "Steinbrenner's Yanks," ***New York Times Magazine*****, April 9, 1978**

Spread from "In the Gardens of Monet," ***Camera 35*****, September 1980**

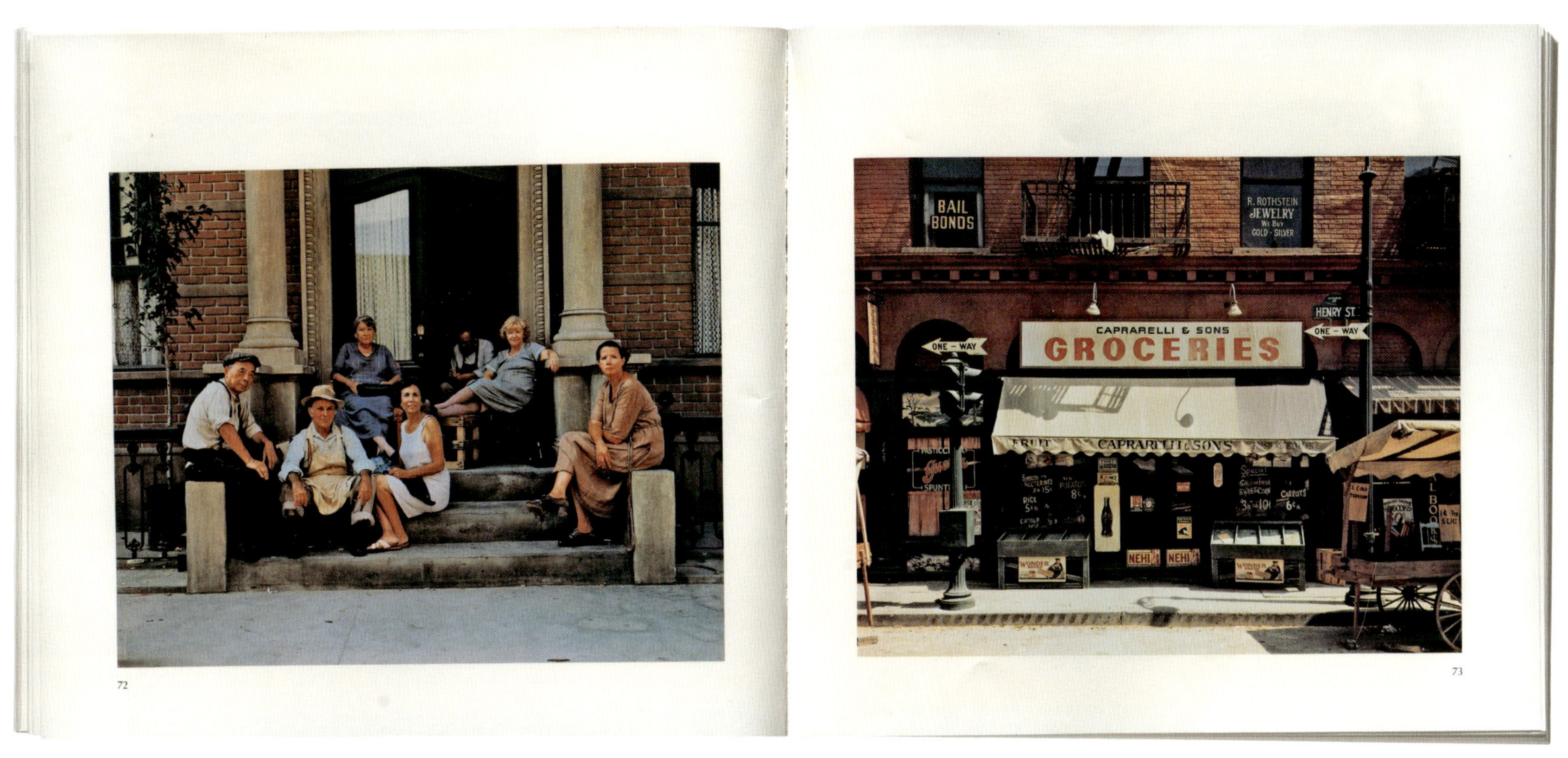

Spread from *Annie on Camera: Nine Photographers* (New York: Abbeville Press, 1982)

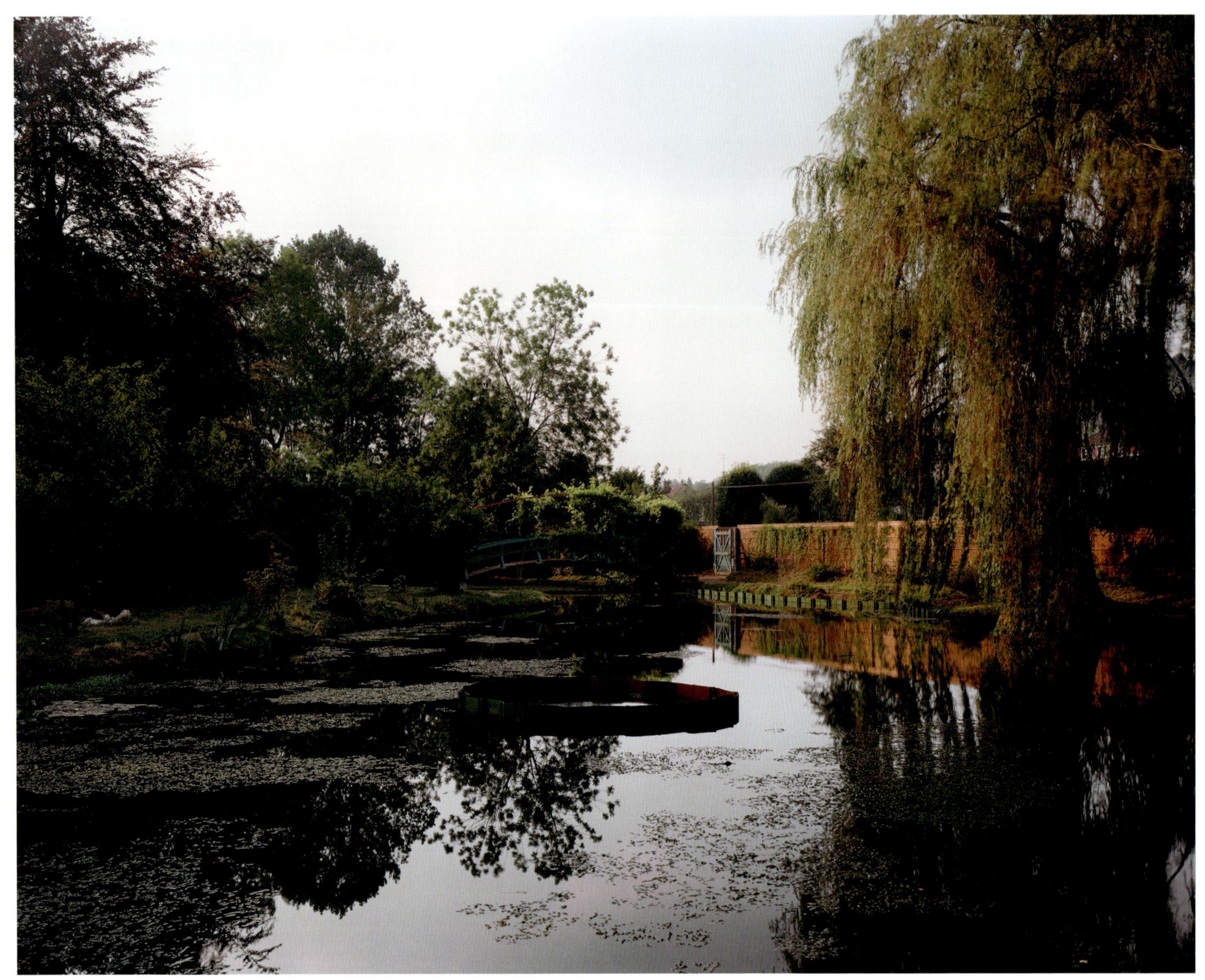

***Giverny, France, 1977*. 1977**

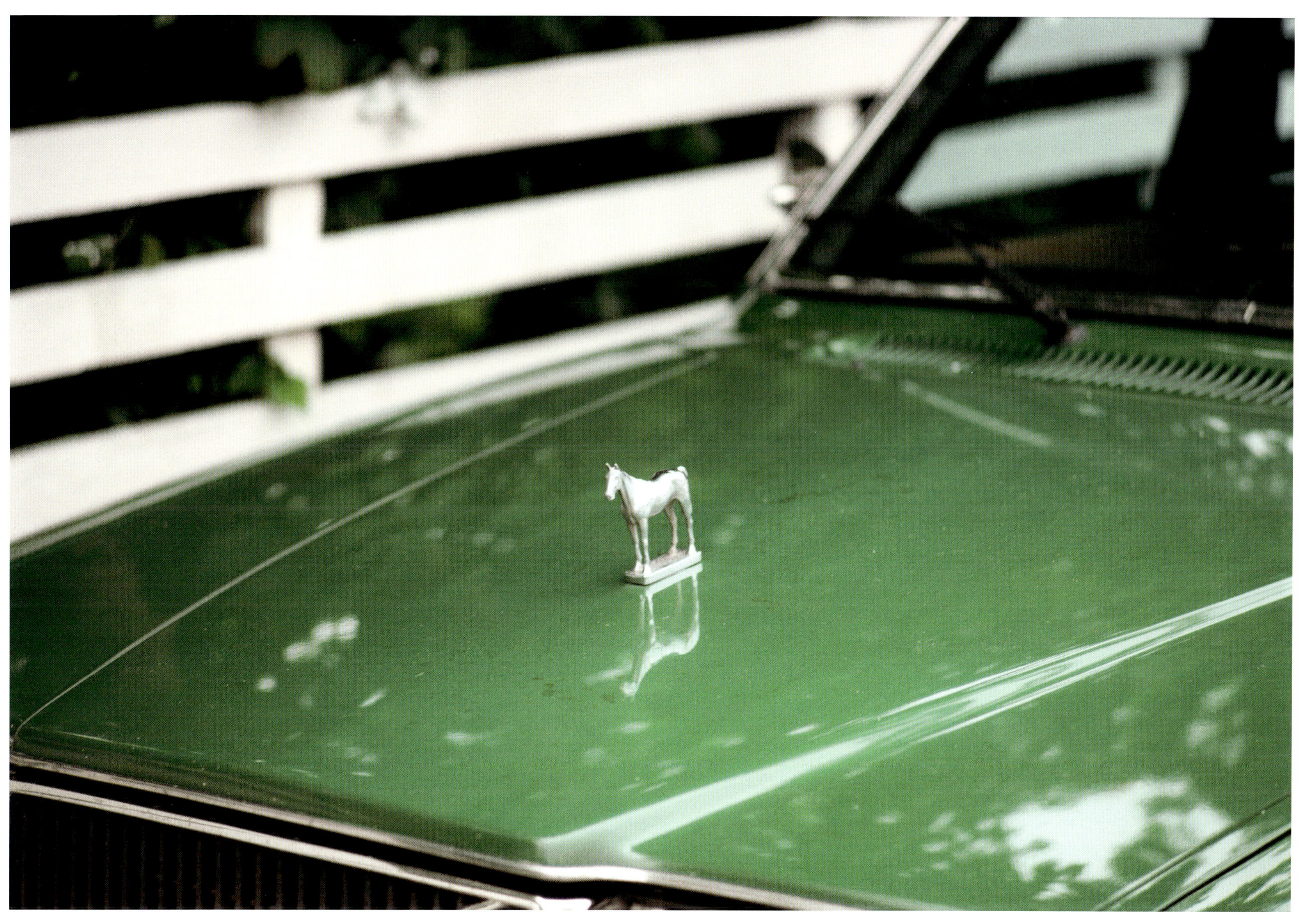

Fairfield County, Connecticut, June 1979. 1979

77.

Conceptual Sequences

Though in the late 1960s and early 1970s Shore never exhibited with Conceptual artists, when several of his serial black-and-white images were included in his solo exhibition at the Metropolitan Museum of Art in 1971, a few reviews explicitly associated his work with the Conceptual movement and used that term.[1] The time Shore spent at the Factory in the mid-1960s and the Pop example of Andy Warhol introduced him to the serial and detached approach that would characterize a good deal of Conceptual art. Shore's work of this period also owes much to his reading of the catalogue for *Serial Imagery*, in which the curator of the 1968 exhibition, John Coplans, analyzes various forms of seriality in modern, contemporary, and especially Minimalist art.[2] In addition, Shore was becoming familiar with certain photographic works that were directly linked to Conceptual art and a systematic or serial approach. One was Ed Ruscha's *Every Building on the Sunset Strip* (1966), a book that Shore discovered in 1968 through the critic and curator Kasper König and led him to acquire most of the artist's earlier publications. Another was *Anonyme Skulpturen*, the first major work of Bernd and Hilla Becher, which he encountered around 1970. In the late 1960s Shore also was friendly with several artists connected with Conceptual art, some of whom spent time with the Marsh brothers in Amarillo, Texas (as Shore did), and others who were associated with the John Gibson Gallery, such as Christo, Peter Hutchinson, Dennis Oppenheim, Richard Long, and Dan Graham.

At a time when there was virtually no critical literature on photography and the medium had yet to secure its status as art, these artists provided Shore with a way to envision a new form of photography. After essentially taking a break from photography in 1968, while he worked with his father in investment banking, Shore returned to it in 1969, using his serial black-and-white projects to deconstruct photography and rebuild it on a more detached and intellectual foundation. In these works, which he started in Amarillo in the summer of that year, with his friend Michael Marsh as his main model (pages 81–82), Shore was striving to free himself from certain photographic conventions: the concept of photography as the art of creating isolated and "significant" images, and the related cult of the "decisive moment," perfect framing, and the expressive subjectivity of the photographer.

From this point on, the principle of multiplicity would prevail in Shore's work—series, suites, and sequences that resisted all narrative temptation. No single image dominated the others; the whole was more important than each component part; and installation on the wall in the form of a grid or line reinforced the works' repetitive nature. Executed according to rules that Shore established for himself ahead of time, these works systematically investigated the two main parameters of the photographic process, time and space. In their attempt to eliminate subjectivity, these series, in both intention and form, are related to a number of Conceptual photographic works of the same period, including most notably Douglas Huebler's *Variable Pieces* and *Duration Pieces*.

Beyond the serial work in black and white, Shore's clear interest in nonartistic forms of photography during the same period can also be seen within the broad context of Conceptual art. His postcard series *Greetings from Amarillo, "Tall in Texas"* (1971, pages 19–21), for instance, echoes the mail art of On Kawara, both of them communicating the mundane consumerist aesthetic that was a central investigation for many artists of the period—the idea of the artist as tourist. As for the exhibition *All the Meat You Can Eat*, which Shore organized in 1971, it reminds us that at the same time a number of Conceptual artists, in the United States in particular, saw vernacular or nonartistic photography (amateur, journalistic, documentary, and even commercial) as a means of critiquing the traditional languages of art; here the artist plays the role of sociologist. Concluding this phase of his work, Shore's adoption in 1971 of popular and amateur forms of image production—Kodacolor film, Mick-a-Matic and Rollei cameras—was clearly a part of this desire to embrace artistic practices on the margins, echoing the work of artists like Robert Smithson (a fan of the Instamatic) and Allen Ruppersberg. Thus Shore's exhibition *American Surfaces*, shown at Light Gallery in the fall of 1972, can be seen in relation to Ruppersberg's *Where's Al?* (which Shore did not know about), presented for the first time in Claremont, California, at exactly the same time. The two "installations" evinced a similar adoption of serial forms arranged in grids, the most ordinary Kodacolor commercial printing, a grammar inspired by snapshots, and a certain level of detachment from

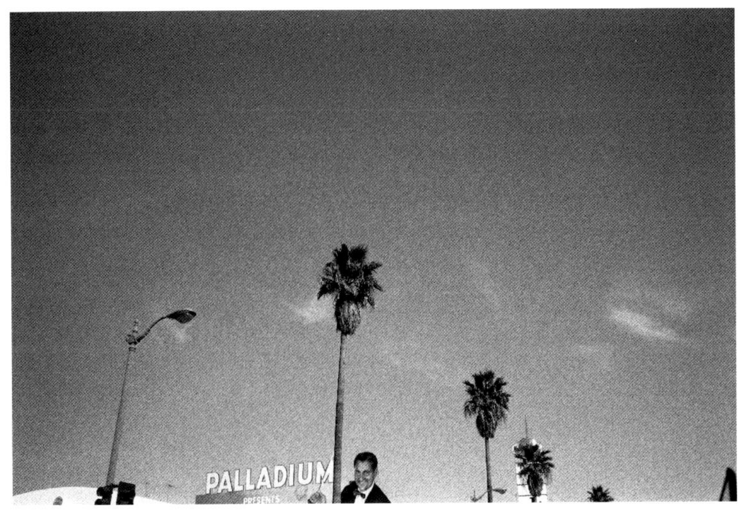

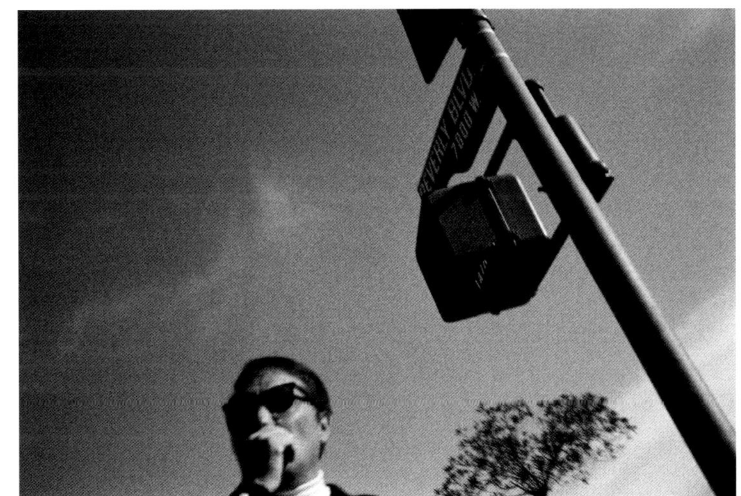

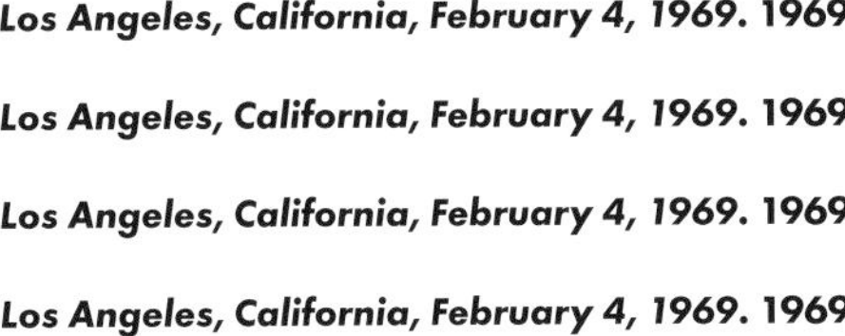

Los Angeles, California, February 4, 1969. **1969**

Los Angeles, California, February 4, 1969. **1969**

Los Angeles, California, February 4, 1969. **1969**

Los Angeles, California, February 4, 1969. **1969**

their subject. For Shore, the choice of very manageable cameras, even one made for children (the Mick-a-Matic), also represented a deliberate attempt to embrace the concept of the artist as amateur, and to rid himself of a number of "professional" ideas and practices inherited from history and from the photographic tradition of which he was a part. It is worth remembering that during this same period, even Shore's touchstone in the field of photography, Walker Evans, succumbed to the charms of the color Polaroid, a popular mode of photography requiring no skill and reducing "everything to your brains and taste," to a pure idea, like a ready-made.[3]

At the time of Shore's first exhibition at the Met, the critic A. D. Coleman noted disparagingly that the photographer was attempting to dematerialize art, in the tradition of Marcel Duchamp.[4] In its often systematic and repetitive nature, enthusiasm for unsophisticated forms, rejection of bravado and expressiveness, and deliberate search for the commonplace, Shore's work from 1969 until the beginning of *American Surfaces* in 1972 represents a deconstruction of artistic practices, a disavowal of the artist/auteur figure, and a form of dematerialization with obvious ties to Conceptual art. Far from disappearing in his later work, these ideas and preoccupations are expressed again in various forms and to varying degrees, particularly in his print-on-demand books of the 2000s and the series *Winslow, Arizona* of 2013. (Quentin Bajac)

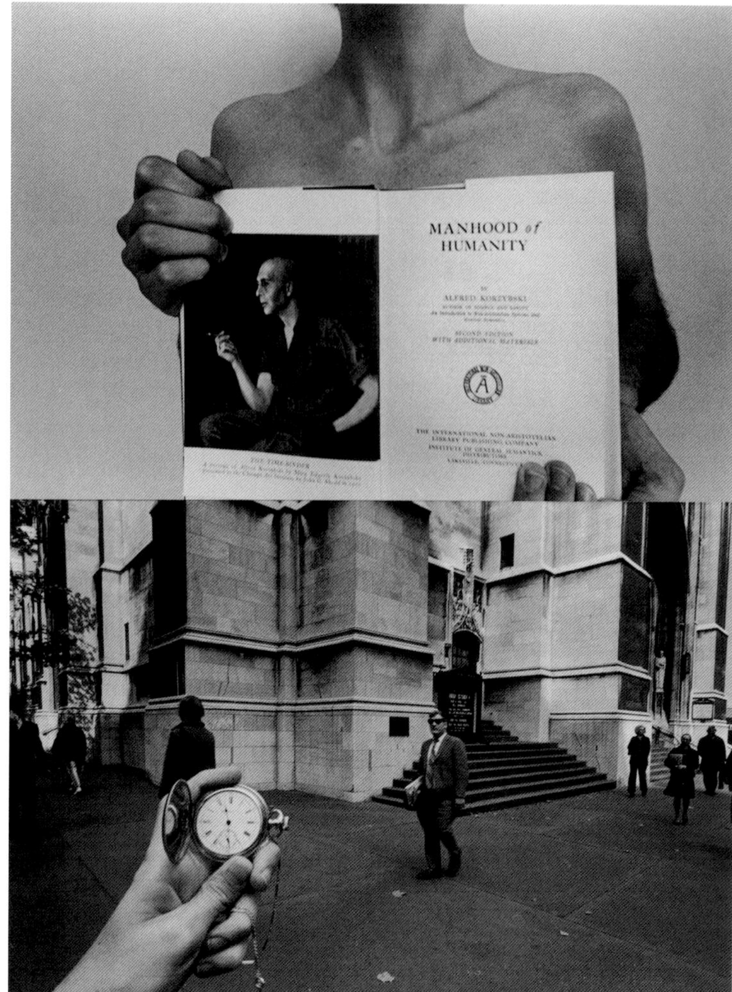

See also: *All the Meat You Can Eat*; *Amarillo, Texas*; *American Surfaces*; *Deadpan*; *The Institute of General Semantics*

1. A. D. Coleman, "Latent Image: Little Seen, Less Said," *Village Voice*, April 1, 1971, 24, 26; David. L. Shirey, "Prints and Photographs On View at Metropolitan," *New York Times*, February 24, 1971, 34; and Gene Thornton, "Is It Necessary To Ask What They Mean?," *New York Times*, March 7, 1971, D30.
2. John Coplans, *Serial Imagery* (Pasadena, Calif.: Pasadena Art Museum, 1968).
3. Quoted by Mia Fineman, '"The Eye Is an Inveterate Collector': The Late Work," in *Walker Evans* (New York: The Metropolitan Museum of Art; Princeton, N.J.: Princeton University Press, 2000), 137.
4. Coleman, "Latent Image: Little Seen, Less Said," 24.

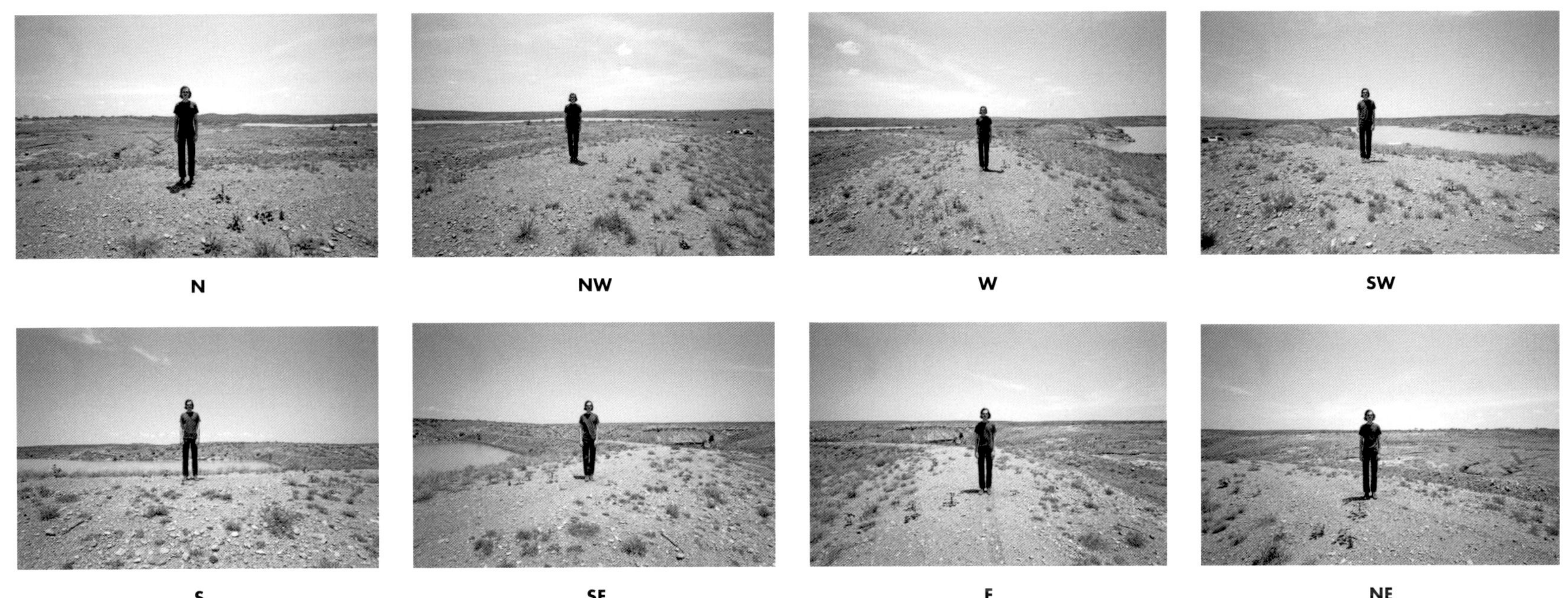

Manhood of Humanity. 1970

Circle No. 1, July 1969. 1969

81.

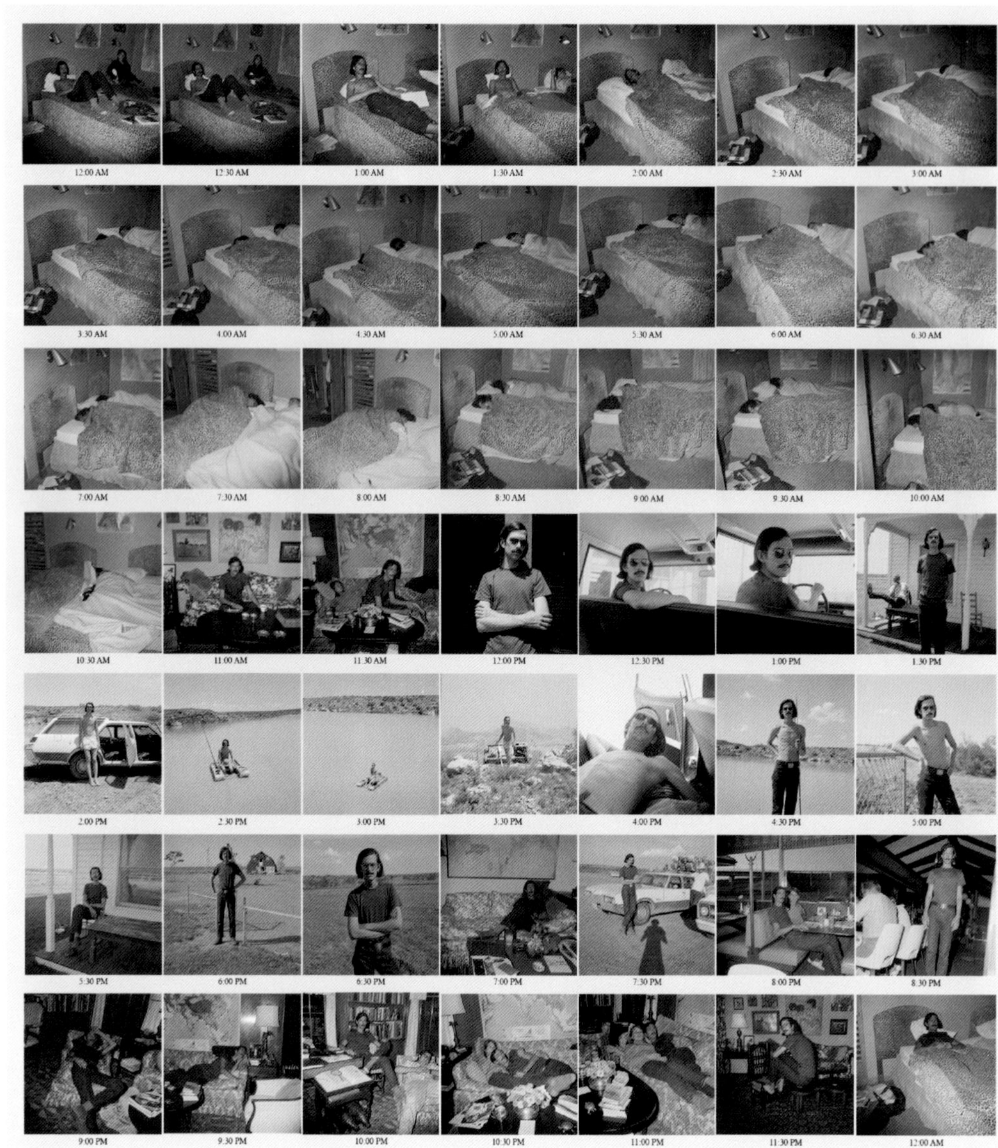

***July 22–23, 1969*. 1969**

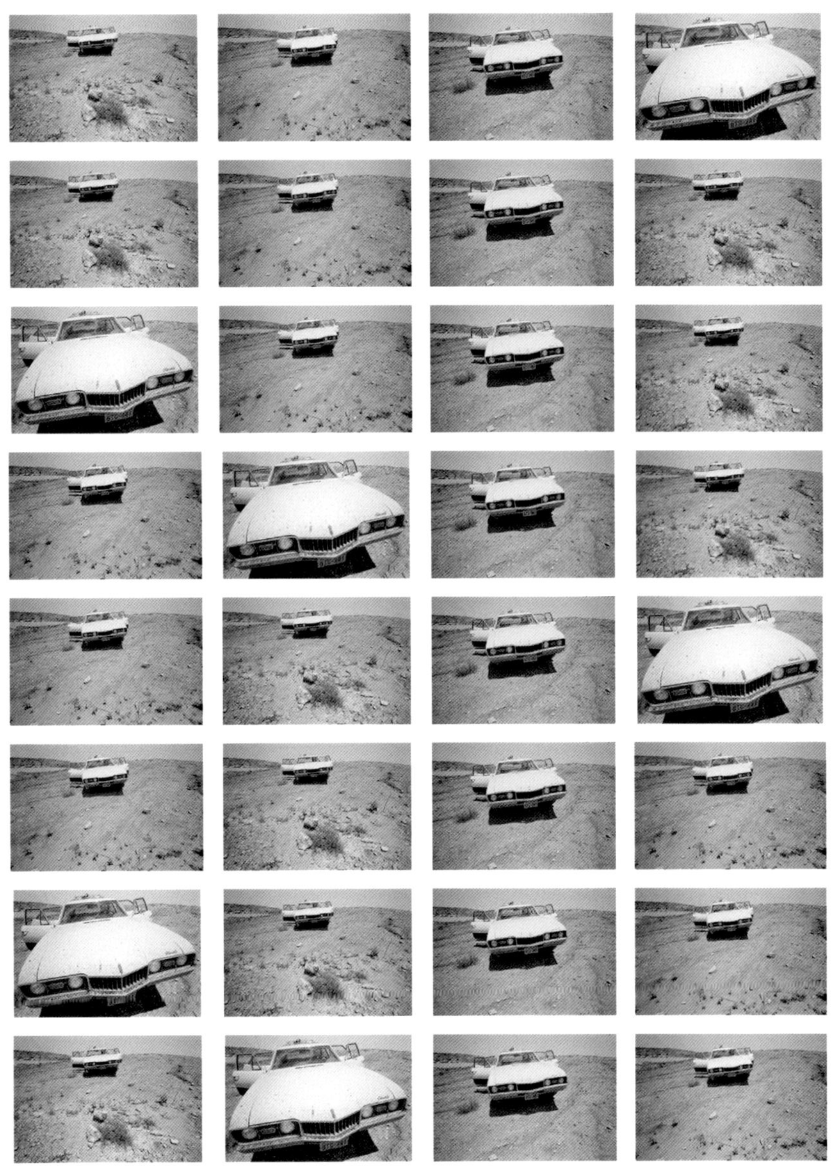

4-Part Variation, July 1969. 1969

Courthouses

In advance of the bicentennial of the United States on July 4, 1976, institutions and companies across the country prepared patriotic books, festivals, and exhibitions.[1] The contribution of Joseph E. Seagram & Sons was a large project that commissioned Shore and twenty-three other photographers—including Lewis Baltz, Frank Gohlke, and Nicholas Nixon, who, like Shore, were featured in the 1975 exhibition *New Topographics: Photographs of a Man-Altered Landscape*—to document county courthouses throughout the country.[2] As a group they took more than eight thousand view-camera photographs intended to "encourage respect for the important buildings that survive and stimulate further research into their architectural history."[3]

Reviewing an exhibition of twenty-six of the prints at Seagram House, Gene Thornton wrote in the *New York Times* about the grand vision of the project, noting, "Nothing quite like this has been undertaken since the government-sponsored Farm Security Administration program of the 1930's."[4] But he expressed disappointment with what the photographs betrayed about American official architecture: he complained that although courthouses were often the most important buildings in a small county, the nineteenth-century examples in the survey were smaller and less impressive than even the average eighteenth-century European palace or church. And in Thornton's eyes, the structures were getting worse every day, with "recent additions—wall clocks, vending machines, fluorescent lighting fixtures—that show a callous indifference to or ignorance of the intentions of the original builders."[5] He did detect, though, a political resonance between the modest buildings and American ideals: "There is no need for big buildings when there is small government," he wrote.

Several exhibitions came out of the project, including one that opened at MoMA in 1977 and toured the Midwest; six photographs by Shore were included. The next year many of the images were compiled in the large publication *Court House: A Photographic Document*, edited with an introduction by architectural photographer Richard Pare. The other texts in the book included a preface about architectural documentation by Phyllis Lambert, the director of the project and the daughter of the founder of Seagram; an essay about the American county court system by Paul C. Reardon, associate justice of the Supreme Judicial Court of Massachusetts; a reflection on personal experience with courthouses by journalist and memoirist Calvin Trillin; and architectural notes by historians Henry-Russell Hitchcock and William Seale. Twenty-four images by Shore are featured, including rare examples of black-and-white large-format work from the 1970s, which he made when lighting conditions weren't ideal for color. In 1980 Seagram gave 11,000 negatives and 2,500 prints from the project to the Library of Congress, and three years later gave all sixty-three prints from the MoMA exhibition to the Museum. (Kristen Gaylord)

See also: *Architecture*; *Commissions and Editorial Work*; *Museum of Modern Art, The*; *Signs of Life*

1. Shore was involved with two other bicentennial projects: *Signs of Life: Symbols in the American City*, at the Renwick Gallery in Washington, D.C., and *200 Years of American Sculpture*, at the Whitney Museum of American Art in New York.
2. The full list comprised Harold Allen, Lewis Baltz, Richard Bartlett, Douglas Baz, Caldecot Chubb, William Clift, Jim Dow, Frank Gohlke, Allen Hess, Pirkle Jones, Lewis Kostiner, Ellen Land-Weber, Patrick Linehan, Nicholas Nixon, Ira Nowinski, Tod Papageorge, Richard Pare, Stephen Shore, Bob Thrall, Jerry Thompson, Charles H. Traub, Paul Vanderbilt, Laura Volkerding, and Geoff Winningham.
3. Richard Pare, "Court Houses: County Symbols," *Historic Preservation*, October–December 1977, 36.
4. Gene Thornton, "A Strong Sense of Grass-Roots America," *New York Times*, July 18, 1976, D22.
5. Ibid.

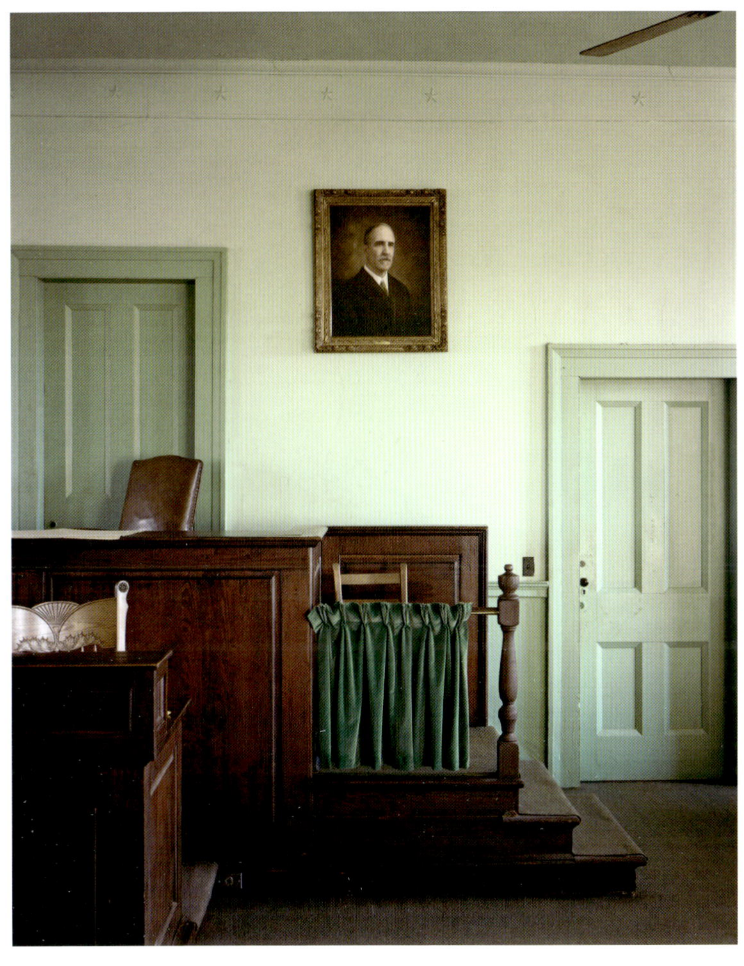

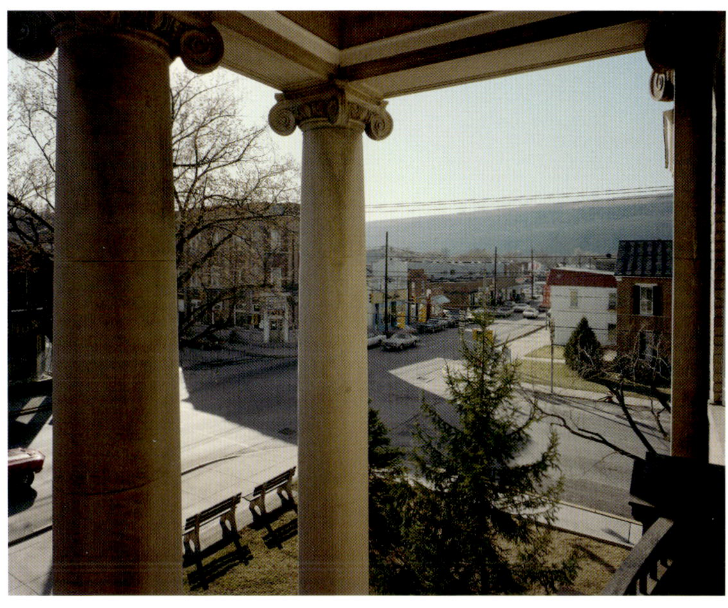

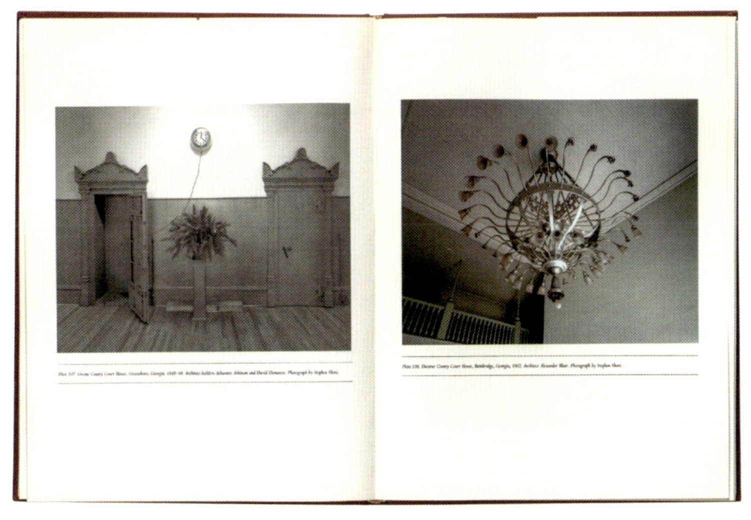

Greene County, Greensboro, Georgia, January 28, 1976. **1976**

Hampshire County, Romney, West Virginia, February 27, 1976. **1976**

Spread from Richard Pare, ed., *Court House: A Photographic Document* (New York: Horizon Press, 1978)

85.

Deadpan

The adjective *deadpan*, used in the 1960s and early 1970s to describe works by several artists Shore was interested in—Ed Ruscha and Andy Warhol, in particular—would be applied to his own work, beginning with the first exhibition of the series *Uncommon Places* at Light Gallery in 1973. A review of the exhibition published in *Artforum* ascribed to the photographs "a deadpan quality," which the writer attributed to Warhol's influence, "accentuated here by the 8 x 10 scale, and also the sheer amount of high focus detail."[1] Three years later, an exhibition of *Uncommon Places* at The Museum of Modern Art elicited similar commentary in the same magazine: the critic noted "the deadpan vernacular of most of Shore's shots," linked this time not to Warhol but to Conceptual art.[2] *Deadpan* refers not only to Shore's fascination with transparency and surfaces, but also to his attitude of neutrality. Like the architects Robert Venturi and Denise Scott Brown, who, while working on *Learning from Las Vegas*, developed a method of "looking nonjudgmentally at the environment" in the hope of "learning from everything," Shore approached all of his subjects with equal attention and lack of criticism.[3]

Even when the word *deadpan* was not explicitly used, reviews of *Uncommon Places* emphasized qualities generally associated with the concept—an absence of expression and judgment, with a soupçon of indifference or even ennui. In discussing his images in the 1975 exhibition *New Topographics: Photographs of a Man-Altered Landscape*, the *Los Angeles Times* spoke of their "bored detachment," although it acknowledged that they had an air of "peace" and "serenity."[4] And while his exhibition at MoMA in 1976 received fewer negative reviews than William Eggleston's, which preceded his by a few months, many observers remained puzzled by the detached nature of Shore's work and its lack of clear meaning. Reviewing the exhibition, Gene Thornton in the *New York Times* compared his photographs to postcards, characterizing them as "bland and uncritical" images in which all subjects "have equal value," while a 1978 review in the *Village Voice* commented on the "perplexing dullness [of his work] despite its often flawless execution."[5] During these years, Max Kozloff was one of the few critics to assign meaning to Shore's detachment, seeing it as an exploration of solitude: "If his art *illustrates* anything, it is the theme of being *alone* in color."[6]

Faced with the photographs' evident lack of expression, critics in the 1970s moved from *deadpan* to *formalist* to describe Shore's style, Thornton being the first to unleash the word in his 1976 article. "The new photographic formalists imitate the purely photographic effects of the snapshot, the picture postcard and the old fashioned 8x10 stand camera," he wrote.[7] Tired of looking for meaning in the work, reviewers chose to speak of its rigorous formalism; according to some critics, the banality of the subject matter forced viewers to focus only on the formal qualities of the image. In 1982, for instance, a writer for *Artweek* expressed admiration for several of Shore's images, including *Merced River, Yosemite National Park, California, August 13, 1979* (page 153), but mentioned that some observers saw his pictures as "boring formalist exercises"; he went on to say that Shore "avoids social questions and retreats to a individualistic sense of harmony," rendering his photographs "precious objects suited primarily for connoisseurs of the medium."[8] Shore's formalism was not always viewed in a negative light, however: a *Washington Post* review in 1979 celebrated him as "the classic example of a 'tough,' formalist photographer who manages to use both his head and his heart," concluding that "one can feel both the passion and restraint in his work."[9] (Quentin Bajac)

See also: *Conceptual Sequences*; *New Topographics*; *Signs of Life*; *Uncommon Places*; *Warhol, Andy*

1. James Collins, "Stephen Shore, Light Gallery," *Artforum* 12, no. 6 (March 1974): 76.
2. Ross Skoggard, "Stephen Shore, Museum of Modern Art," *Artforum* 15, no. 5 (January 1977): 65.
3. Robert Venturi, Denise Scott Brown, and Steven Izenour, *Learning from Las Vegas* (Cambridge, Mass.: MIT Press, 1972), 3.
4. William Wilson, "Camera Artists: Truth in Focus," *Los Angeles Times*, March 15, 1976, E10.
5. Gene Thornton, "Formalists Who Flirt with Banality," *New York Times*, November 14, 1976, D34; Ben Lifson, "Taking All the Way," *Village Voice*, June 19, 1978, 76.
6. Max Kozloff, "Photography: The Coming of Age of Color," *Artforum* 13, no.5 (January 1975): 31.
7. Thornton, "Formalists Who Flirt with Banality."
8. Ted Hedgpeth, "Saturated With Actuality," *Artweek*, January 9, 1982, 11.
9. Jo Ann Lewis, "Galleries," *Washington Post*, July 14, 1979, D8.

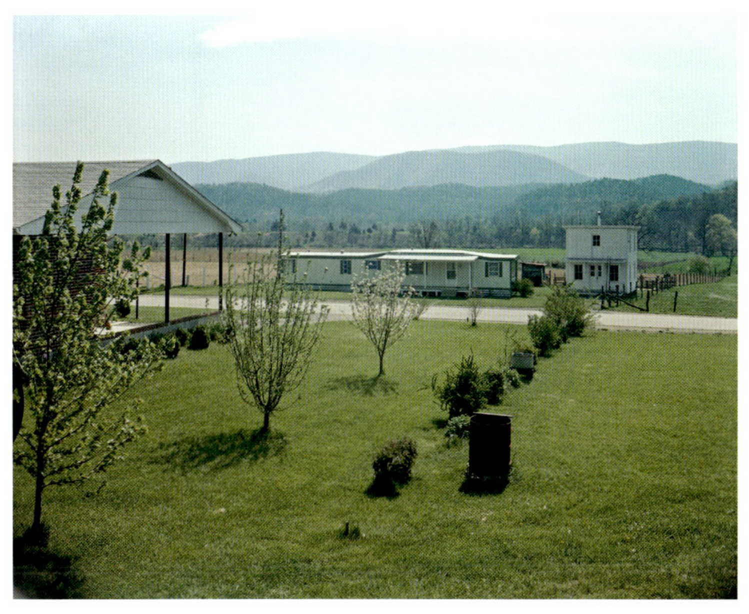

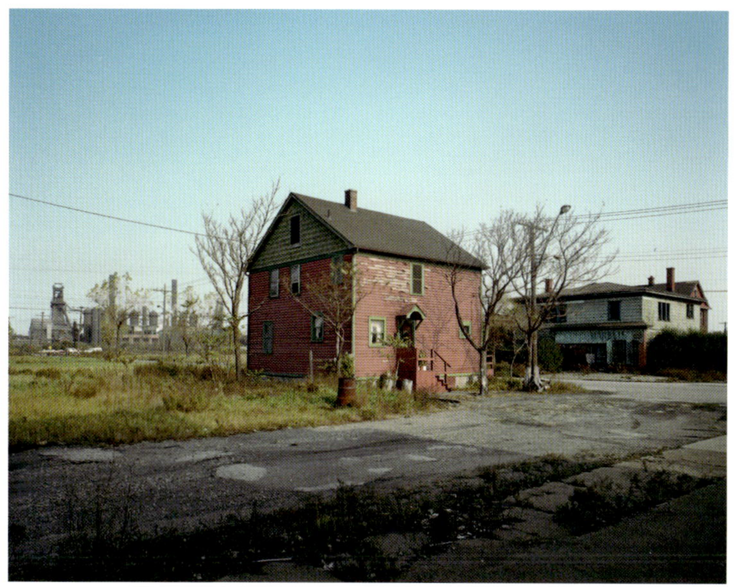

Fort Seybert, West Virginia, April 29, 1974. **1974**

Gilbride Street and Sixth Street, Lackawanna, New York, October 24, 1977. **1977**

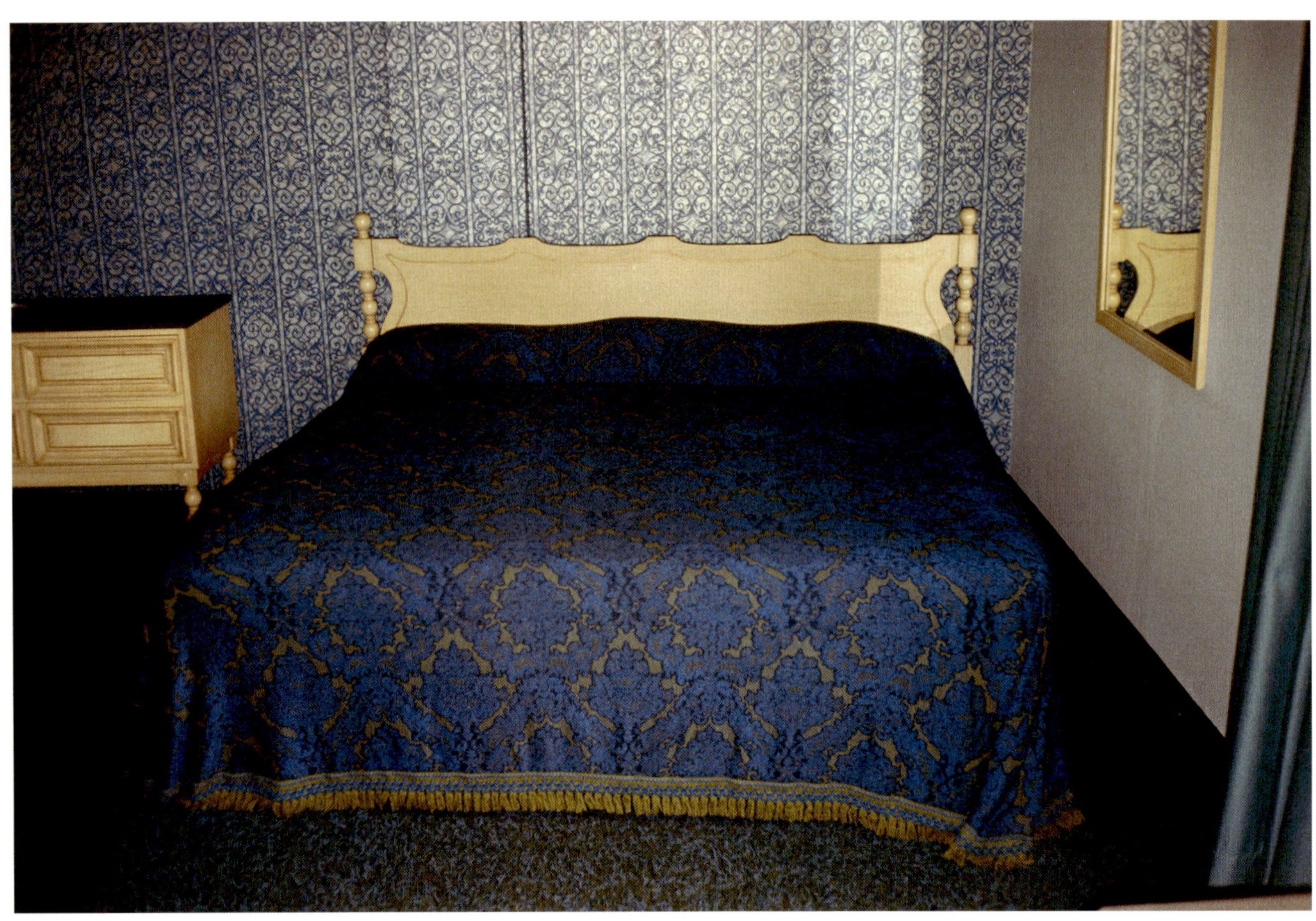

***Dayton, Ohio, August 1972.* 1972**

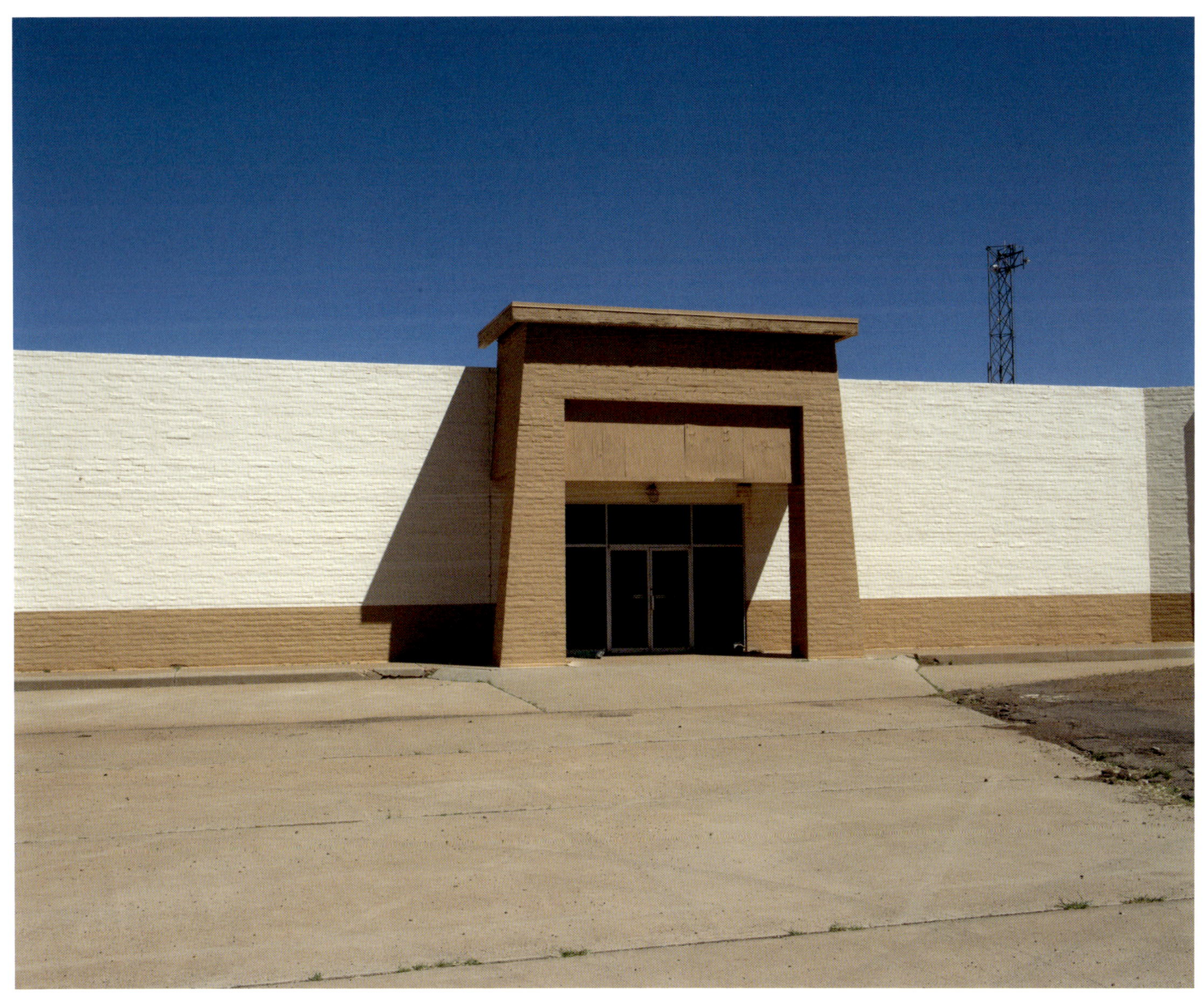

Winslow, Arizona, September 19, 2013. 2013

El Paso Street, El Paso, Texas, July 5, 1975

Several of the best-known photographs from Shore's project *Uncommon Places* were made at the intersections of urban streets. The visual complexity of these spaces is a great pictorial challenge. How are static elements (buildings, curbs, lampposts, trees) to be balanced with changing ones (shadows) and fleeting ones (people and moving cars)? Solving this with a cumbersome view camera requires great concentration, switching attention from the multitude of small details to the more abstract schema of the composition as a whole, and back again.

El Paso Street, El Paso, Texas, July 5, 1975 is one of Shore's most intricate photographs and at the same time one of his most harmonious. The balance is very fine. Any small difference in framing or timing would have likely resulted in a substantially different picture. For example, cutting off the bottom of the tree on the left or of the pole on the right would have undermined the illusion of three-dimensional space. Waiting for the figure on the edge of the curb to pass would have altered the picture's impression of both space *and* time.

In 1998, twenty-three years after it was taken, Shore included this image in *The Nature of Photographs*, his book of thoughts on the medium. He wrote: "For some pictures the frame is active. The structure of the picture begins with the frame and works inward. While we know that the buildings, sidewalks, and sky continue beyond the edges of this urban landscape, the world of the photograph is contained within the frame. It is not a fragment of a larger world."[1]

Strictly speaking, every photograph *is* a cut in space and time from the larger world. It is always a fragment, never a whole. Even if this scene were a set on a Hollywood back lot and the streets didn't continue beyond the frame, *something* continued. So, a photograph that has been structured to feel like a world unto itself is, in a way, a negation of the cutting that is a fundamental aspect of the medium. Or, more accurately, it is a *disavowal* of it: we know very well that all photographs are fragments, but nevertheless this particular one appears not to be. And in appearing not to be, this photograph allows all the elements within its frame to stand as representatives for the countless other similar elements that are beyond it.

When a photographer does this exceptionally well, the result exceeds the picture's documentary value but also undermines it a little. The image is almost too perfect. The world begins to resemble a distilled illustration of itself. We cannot imagine the scene any other way, while knowing it could be many other ways. (David Campany)

See also: *Uncommon Places*

1. Stephen Shore, *The Nature of Photographs* (Baltimore: Johns Hopkins University Press, 1998), 62.

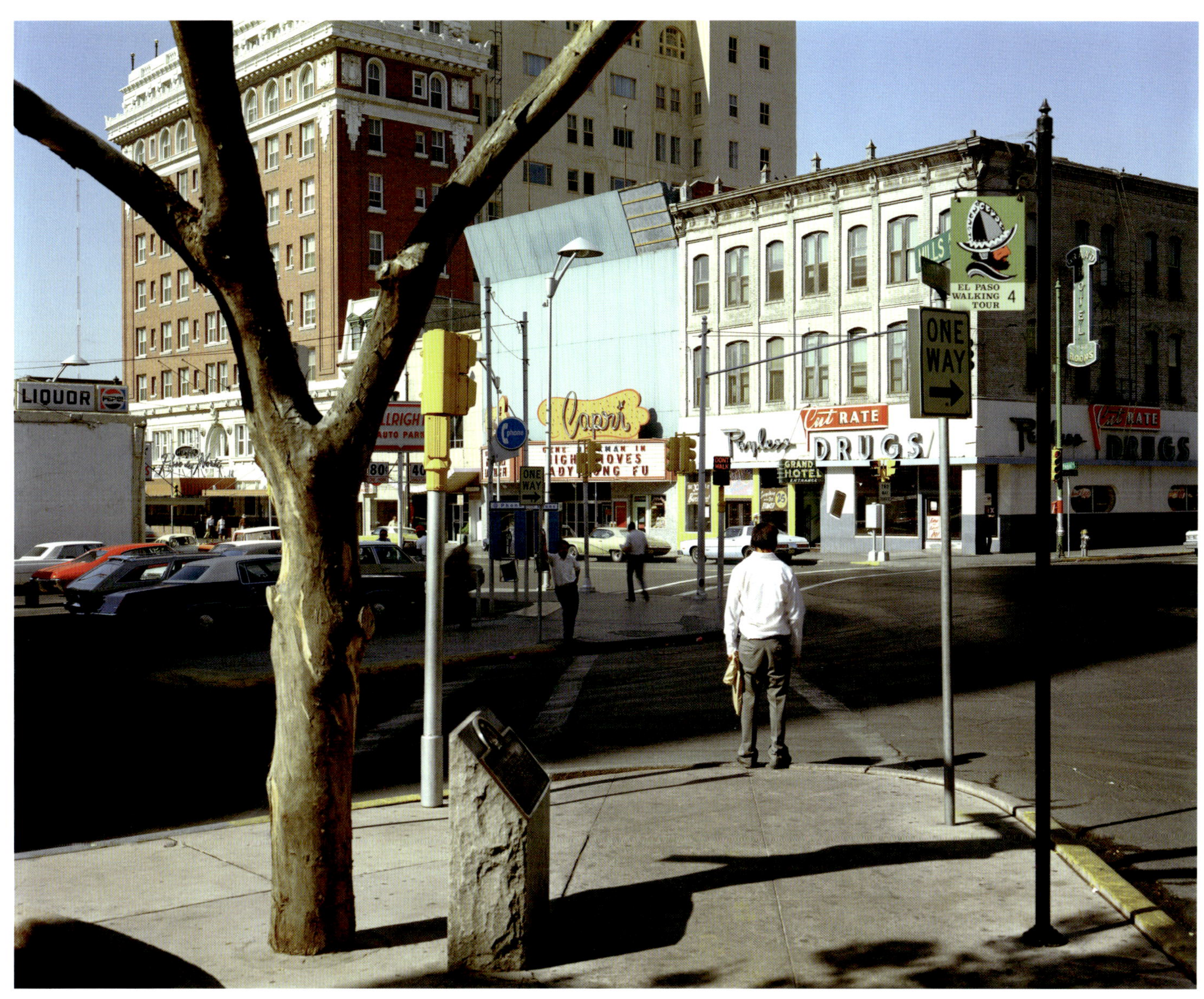

***El Paso Street, El Paso, Texas, July 5, 1975.* 1975**

91.

Evans, Walker

"If I were to say in the photographic world the one person whom I used as a springboard for ideas and a resource to learn from, it was Walker Evans," Shore asserted in 2004.[1] Among the photographers that Shore refers to, Evans holds a special place. This is evident not only in the frequency of Shore's references to him—since the 1980s, he has been the photographer whose name invariably comes up in interviews—but also in Evans's wide-ranging influence on the younger photographer, sometimes to the point of apparent pastiche, as in Shore's 1981 series *Annie*.

More than an "influence," a difficult word to define, Shore prefers to characterize his relationship with Evans in another vein, something on the order of sentiment ("a kinship") or a way of being ("the same constitutional type").[2] Evans was among Shore's earliest photographic references, by way of his book *American Photographs* (first published in 1938), which was given to Shore for his tenth birthday. Moreover, Shore came of age as a photographer in the early seventies, a time when Evans was undergoing a major rediscovery. Two exhibitions of his work were mounted in 1971: a large retrospective organized by John Szarkowski at MoMA and a smaller show, more focused on recent work, at the Yale University Art Gallery. Evans would achieve a new status during this period, embodying a photographic approach characterized as "lyric documentary," an alliance of poetic and documentary modes that Shore would go on to fine-tune in his own work. Indeed, Shore's choice of the title *American Surfaces* for his first photographic series on America was a nod to Evans's *American Photographs*.

The focus on America, particularly strong in Shore's images of the seventies, is clearly one of the main common denominators in the two photographers' work. In one of Shore's first interviews, he discussed the ways in which his work aligned with Evans's, "in terms of both of us photographing the same country at different times, both using the same type of camera, both having an interest in architecture, etc."[3] Elaborating on his relationship to architecture, Shore later added, "I see architecture as an external representation of the forces political, social, aesthetic, at play in our culture. This I got from Evans."[4] The ties between their work are numerous, going beyond those cited by Shore: both are fascinated by endangered forms of popular culture, such as the postcard, and by the centrality of the automobile in American culture. (Shore has always been interested in the cars in Evans's photographs, and especially the role they play as markers of time.)[5]

Yet in one aspect the two photographers are very different: their attitude toward color. Evans's distaste for color is well known, a position he declared in 1969, two years before Shore began making color photographs: "Color photography is vulgar. When the *point* of a picture subject is precisely its vulgarity or its color-accident through man's hand, not God's, then only can color film be used validly."[6] Paradoxically, it is this same photographer who is most often cited in articles from the mid- to late seventies as the spiritual father of the new American color photography.[7] In both the favored subject matter of Shore's generation—a resolutely American contemporary landscape marked by human presence—and the kind of detachment linked to the widespread use of the view camera, the influence of Evans seemed ever-present, despite his antipathy toward color. In a sense, Shore took to heart Evans's remark about the validity of applying color to "vulgar" subjects. Unremarkable architecture (motels, gas stations), fast-food joints, and other non-places: Shore chose to devote himself to these subjects in "bad taste," one might be tempted to say, when he began using color and as he worked throughout the seventies on *American Surfaces* and *Uncommon Places*. (Quentin Bajac)

See also: *Architecture*; *Color*; *Nature of Photographs, The*; *Uncommon Places*

1. Philip Gefter, "Travels with Walker, Robert and Andy," *New York Times*, July 4, 2004, D28.
2. "Heroes & Mentors: Stephen Shore and Gregory Crewdson," *Photo District News*, July 20, 2011, https://www.pdnonline.com/features/heroes-mentors-stephen-shore-and-gregory-crewdson/; David Campany, "Ways of Making Pictures," in Marta Dahó, ed., *Stephen Shore* (Madrid: Fundación MAPFRE; New York: Aperture, 2014), 24.
3. Michael Auping, "An Interview with Stephen Shore," in *Stephen Shore: Photographs* (Sarasota, Fla.: John and Mable Ringling Museum of Art Foundation, 1981), 15.
4. Suzie Mackenzie, "The Beauty of the Disregarded," *The Guardian*, May 16, 2003, https://www.theguardian.com/artanddesign/2003/may/17/photography.artsfeatures.
5. Aaron Schuman, "*Uncommon Places*: An Interview with Stephen Shore," *Seesaw*, Summer 2004, http://seesawmagazine.com/shore_pages_/shore_interview.html.
6. Walker Evans, "Photography," in Louis Kronenberger, ed., *Quality: Its Image in the Arts* (New York: Atheneum, 1969), 208.
7. See, for example, Carol Squiers, "Color Photography: The Walker Evans Legacy and the Commercial Tradition," *Artforum* 17, no. 3 (November 1978): 64–67, and Douglas Davis and Mary Rourke, "New Frontiers in Color," *Newsweek*, April 19, 1976, 56–61.

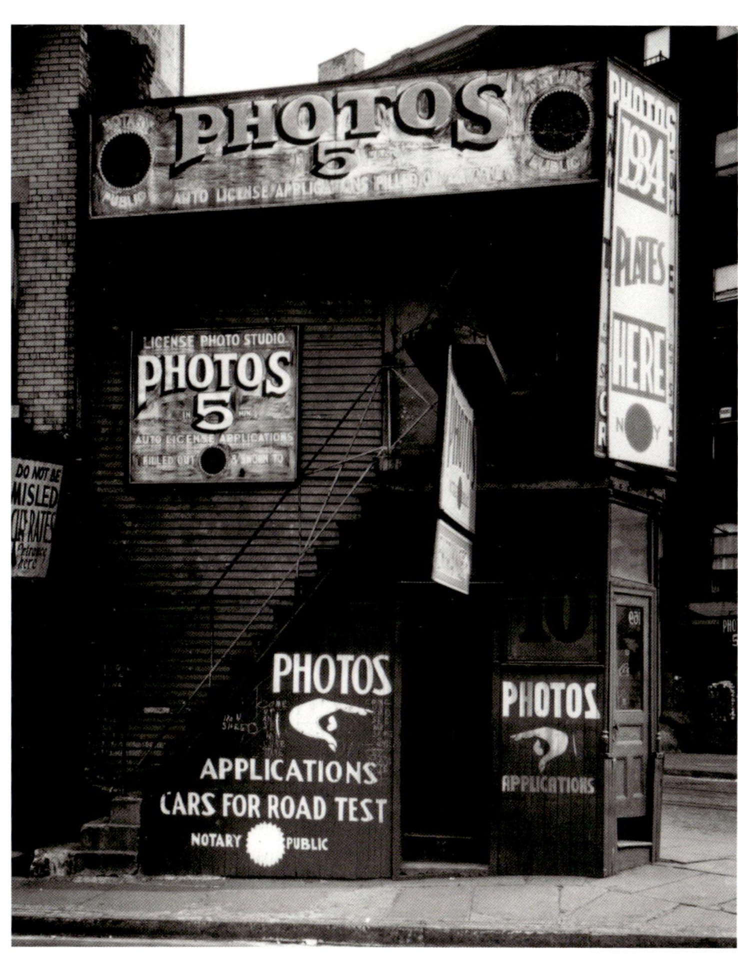

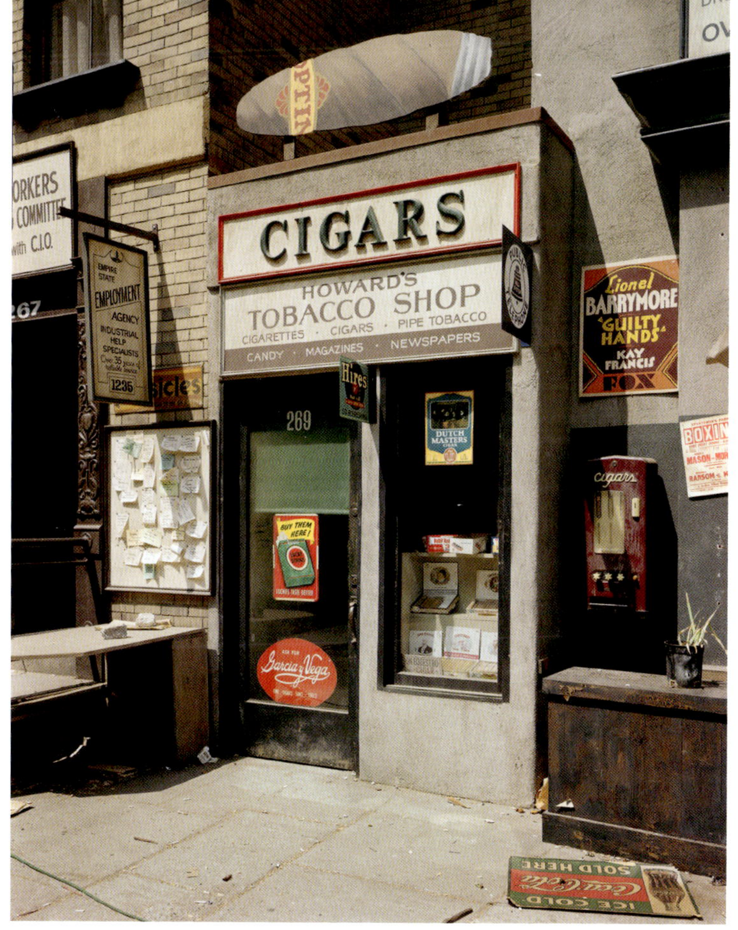

Walker Evans. *License Photo Studio, New York*. 1934

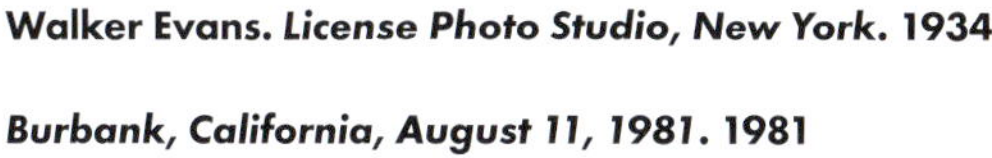

***Burbank, California, August 11, 1981*. 1981**

93.

Factory, The

"I rejected my Factory period for a long time," Shore has said. "For so many of the others involved, it was the pinnacle of their lives. For me it just wasn't. It was the beginning."[1] Shore began spending time at Andy Warhol's Factory in May of 1965, and would be a presence there for about two years—first, on a regular basis after deciding to drop out of high school, and then more sporadically. Located at the time on the fifth floor of 231 East Forty-seventh Street, between Second and Third Avenues, Warhol's studio—its walls entirely covered in sheets of tinfoil and aluminum paint like the interior of a spaceship—was a mecca of the New York art scene, even though Warhol had not yet acquired the aura and renown he would enjoy by the end of the sixties. During the period when Shore frequented the Factory, Warhol was devoting himself primarily to film, putting his other work aside to some extent. He was also serving as manager for the Velvet Underground, who regularly played there as part of the Exploding Plastic Inevitable, a series of multimedia events organized by Warhol. When not taking photographs, Shore helped with tasks such as lighting for the various performances that took place in New York.

Shore joined in with the regulars on the scene and got along especially well with Billy Name, the unofficial Factory photographer, whom Warhol had entrusted with keeping a photographic record of life in the studio, and who had installed a darkroom there. But Shore was also friendly with John Cale and Sterling Morrison, who were members of the Velvet Underground, and other habitués of the Factory—notably Sandy Kirkland, who would later marry his friend Michael Marsh. Shore's photographs were taken with an insider's perspective, by a photographer who was sharing the everyday life of his subjects. "Most of the time we were completely unaware that [Shore] was taking pictures, so casually did he go about his work," one of the protagonists would assert in the nineties.[2] There is no search for the spectacular, the event, or even the anecdote, and no declared or conscious intention to record things for posterity either. We see Warhol at work; portraits, sometimes posed, sometimes candid; a few party scenes; and a lot of people lounging on couches and in armchairs. Shore's photographs are snapshots of friends—intimate images, we might be tempted to say, if they didn't in most cases take a detached or neutral stance, for which he was already becoming known. In comparison with Shore's photographs, Name's pictures—the other main photographic body of work on the Factory at this time—appear to be more explicitly expressive but also more concerned with conveying an image, with valorizing their subjects and constructing a story or even a mythology.

This contrast is evident in the catalogue of the 1968 Warhol exhibition at the Moderna Museet in Stockholm, based on images by Name and Shore, who oversaw the selection and layout of his photographs in collaboration with Kasper König, one of the curators of the show. Some 170 of Shore's images were included in the book, the first to reproduce these photographs in such quantity. The structure of the book, two thirds of which consists of photographic documentation, affirms the central place of the Factory in Warhol's body of work. Printed in extremely high contrast, in which the grain of the images boldly stands out, and on inexpensive paper like that of a tabloid, the catalogue would have a lasting influence on a large segment of the photography world in the late sixties and seventies, especially in Japan. Later, however, aside from a few reproductions here and there in the press and the inclusion of a portrait of Warhol in a group exhibition in the Hague in 1970, Shore's Factory photographs would remain invisible for more than twenty years. In 1990 an exhibition at the Fondation Cartier in Paris would be the first in a long series of shows and publications on Warhol, including the 1995 book *The Velvet Years: Warhol's Factory, 1965–67*. During the nineties, when his color work was still awaiting rediscovery, Shore seemed to be celebrated above all as the photographer of the Factory and the Velvet Underground. (Quentin Bajac)

See also: *Black and White*; *Warhol, Andy*; *Youth*

1. "Stephen Shore Interview," *Wallpaper*, July 26, 2007, https://www.wallpaper.com/art/Stephen-Shore-interview.
2. Edmund Hennessy quoted in *The Velvet Years: Warhol's Factory 1965–67*, photographs by Stephen Shore; text by Lynne Tillman (New York: Thunder's Mouth Press, 1995), 126.

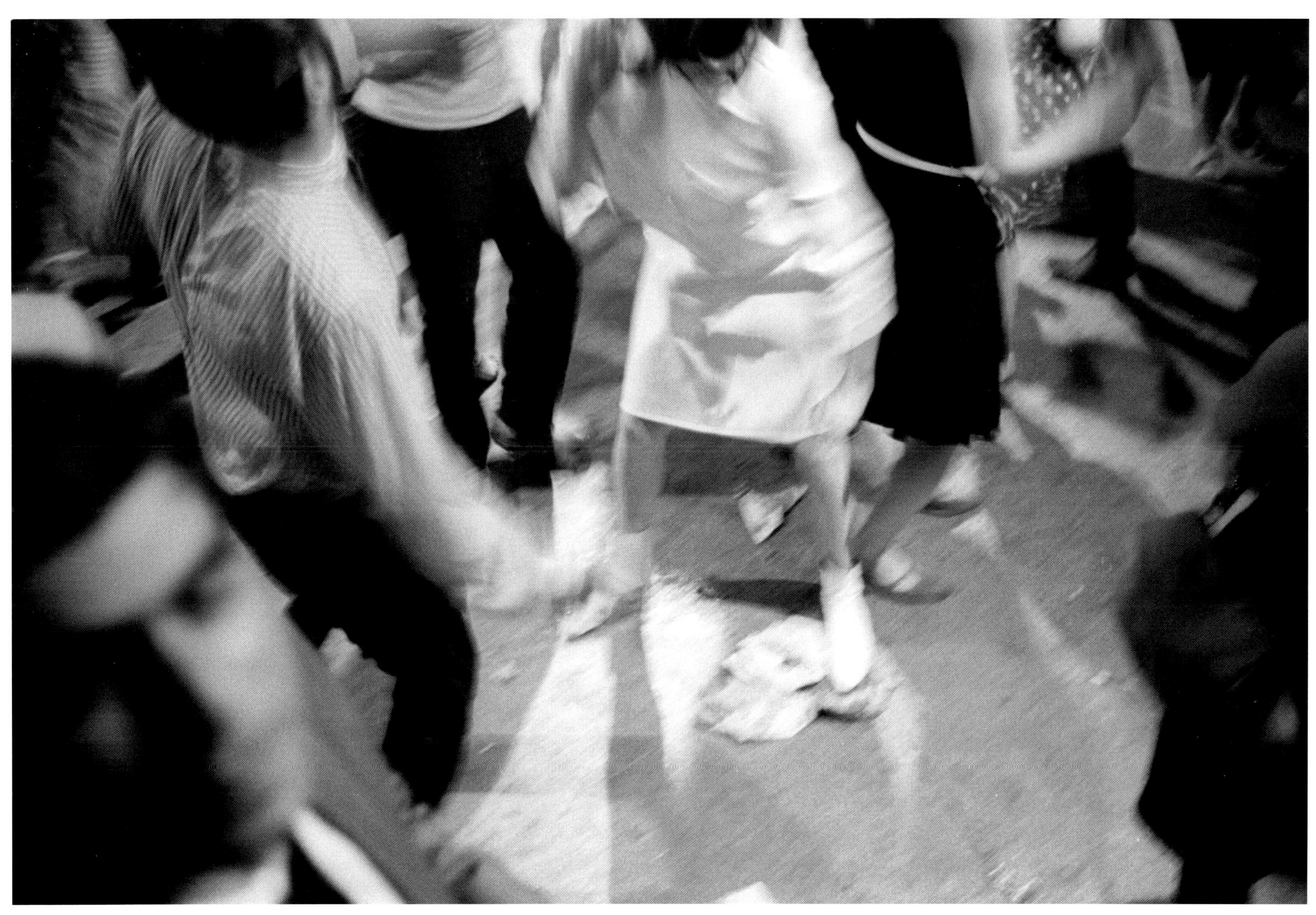

***Ivy Nicholson, Factory Party, New York, New York.* 1965–67**

95.

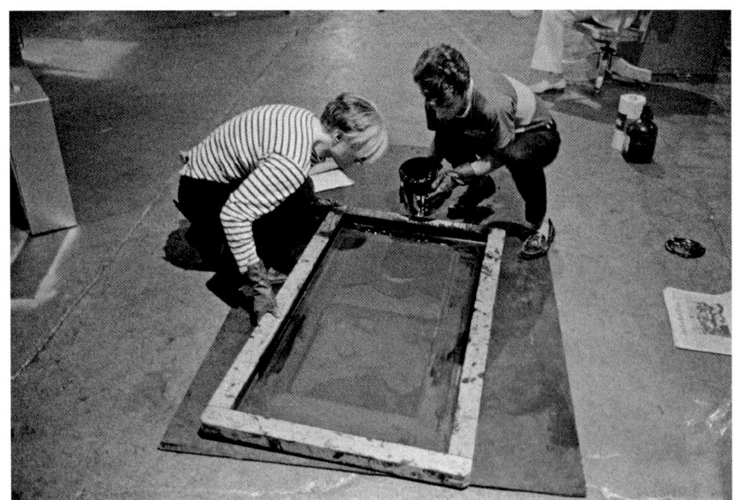

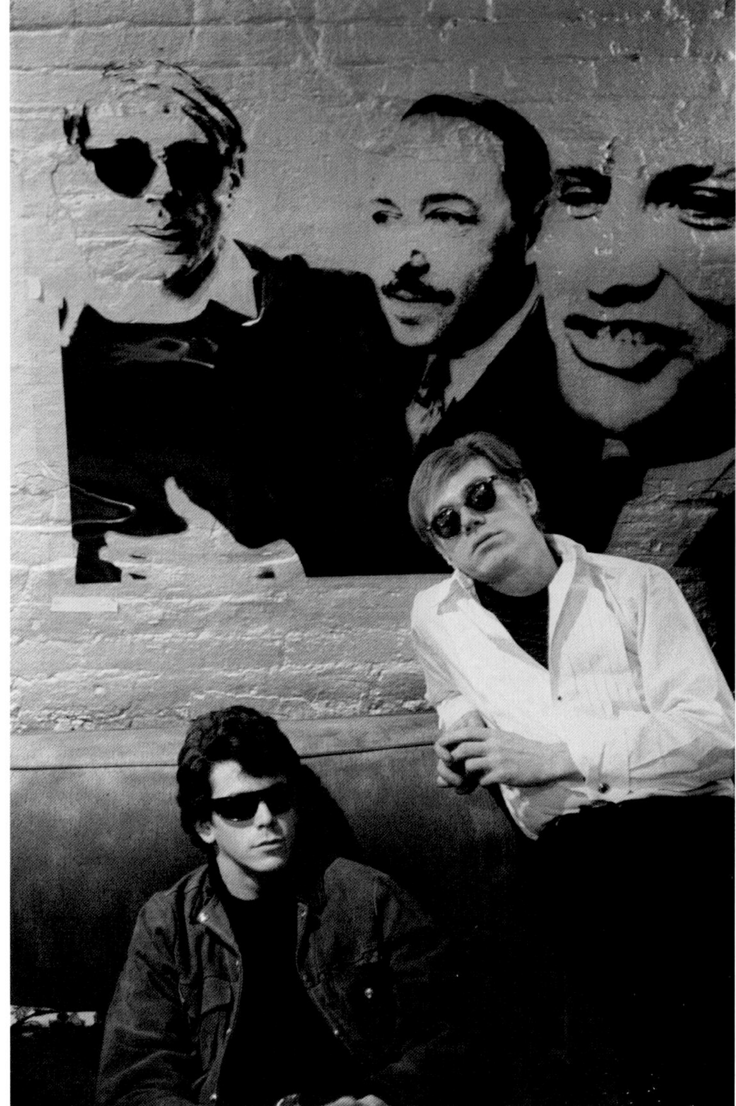

Andy Warhol and Gerard Malanga, the Factory, New York, New York. **1965–67**

Lou Reed and Andy Warhol, the Factory, New York, New York. **1966–67**

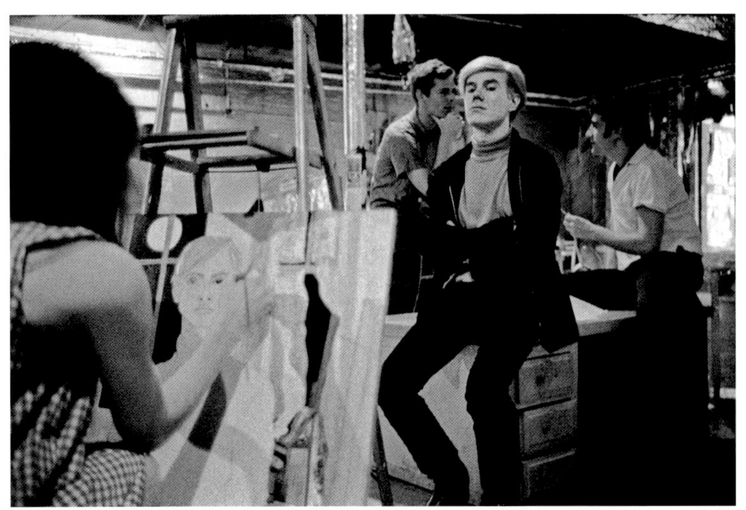

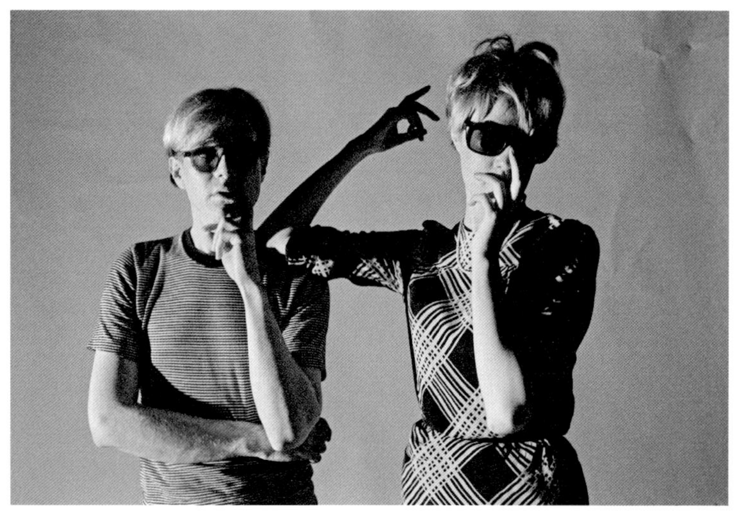

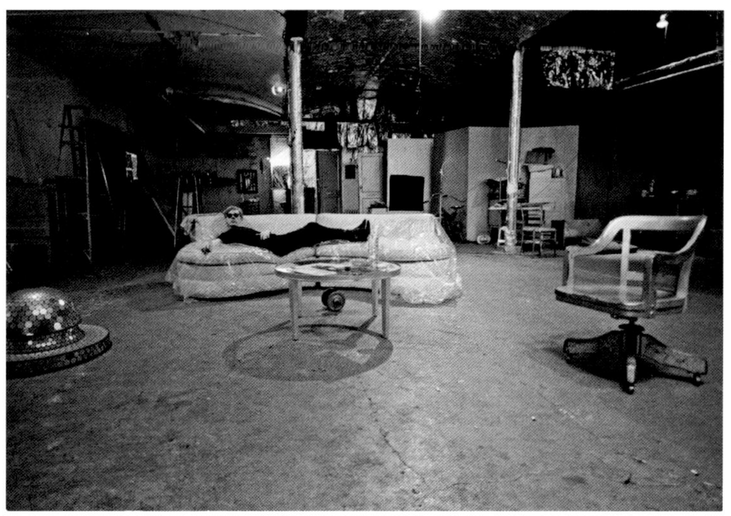

Ivy Nicholson and Andy Warhol, the Factory, New York, New York. 1965–67

Andy Warhol and Ingrid Superstar, the Factory, New York, New York. 1965–67

Andy Warhol, the Factory, New York, New York. 1965

97.

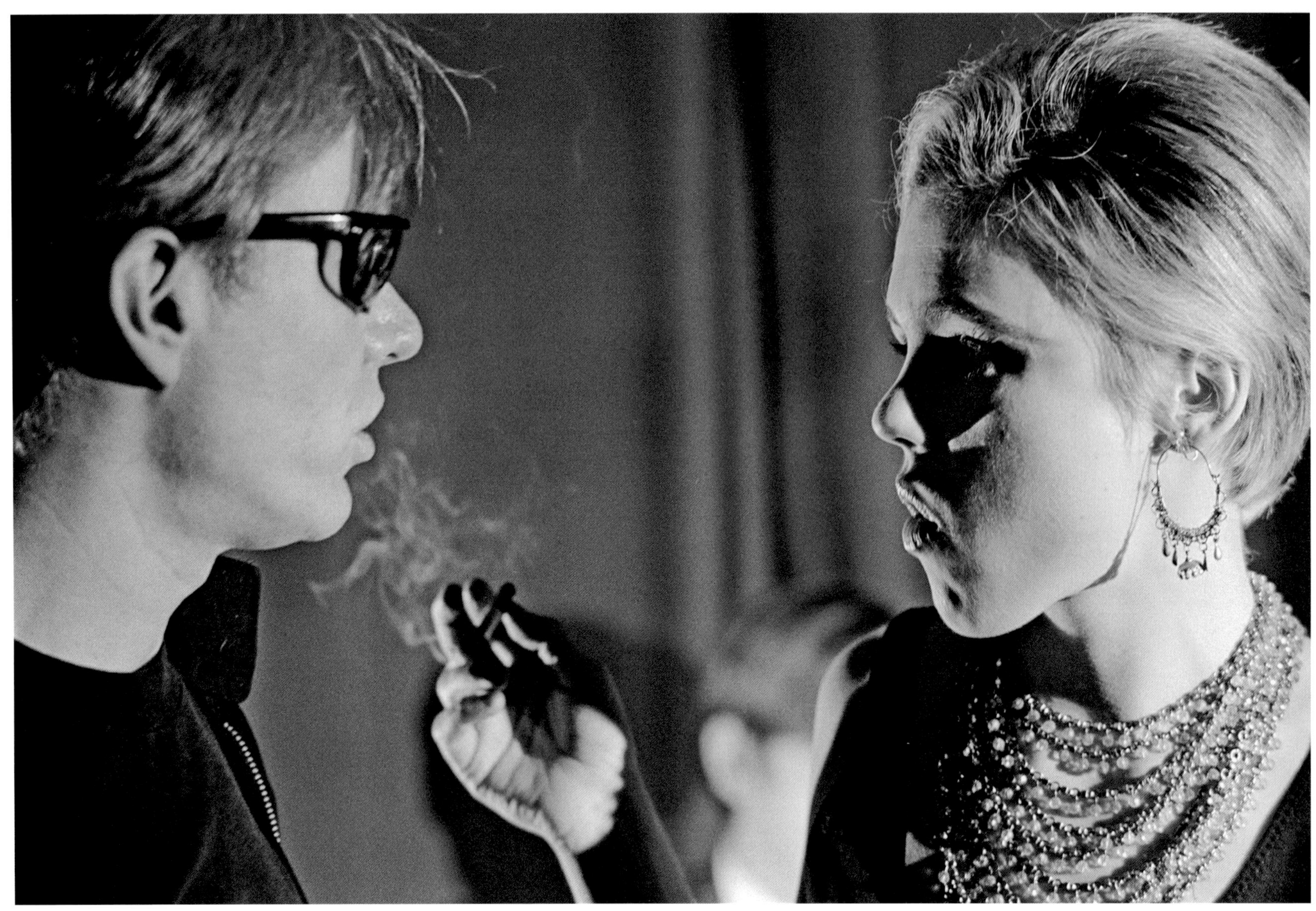

Andy Warhol and Edie Sedgwick, New York, New York. 1965

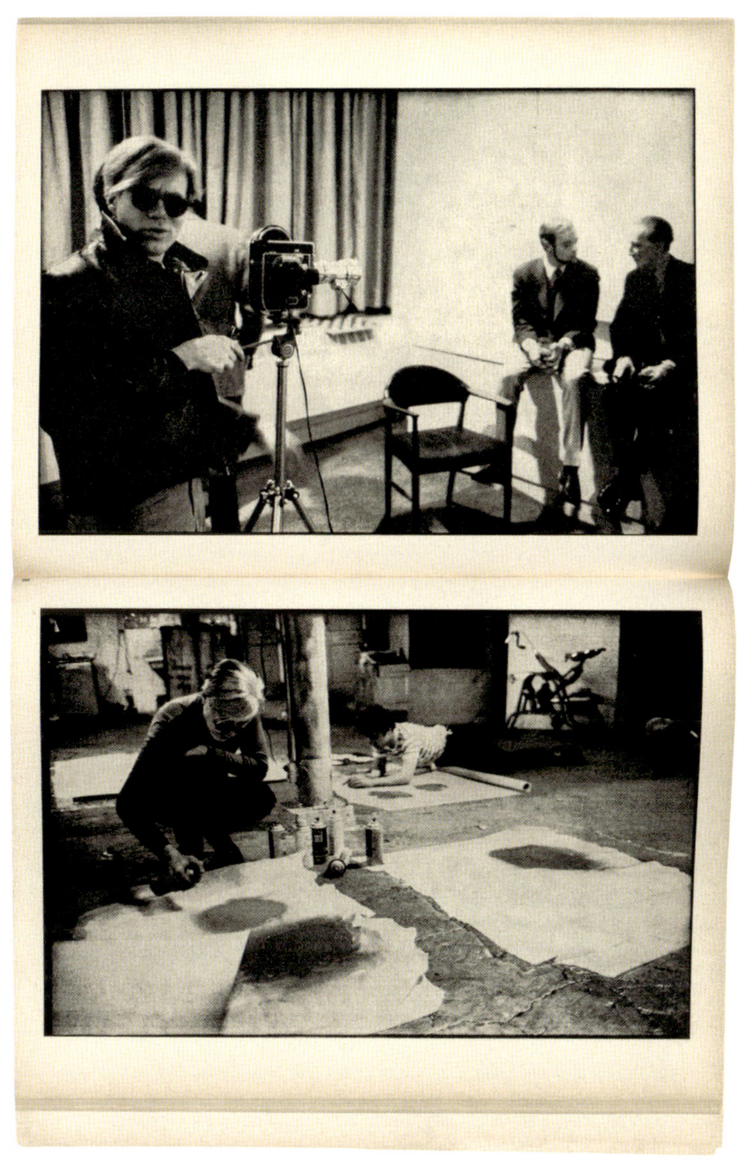

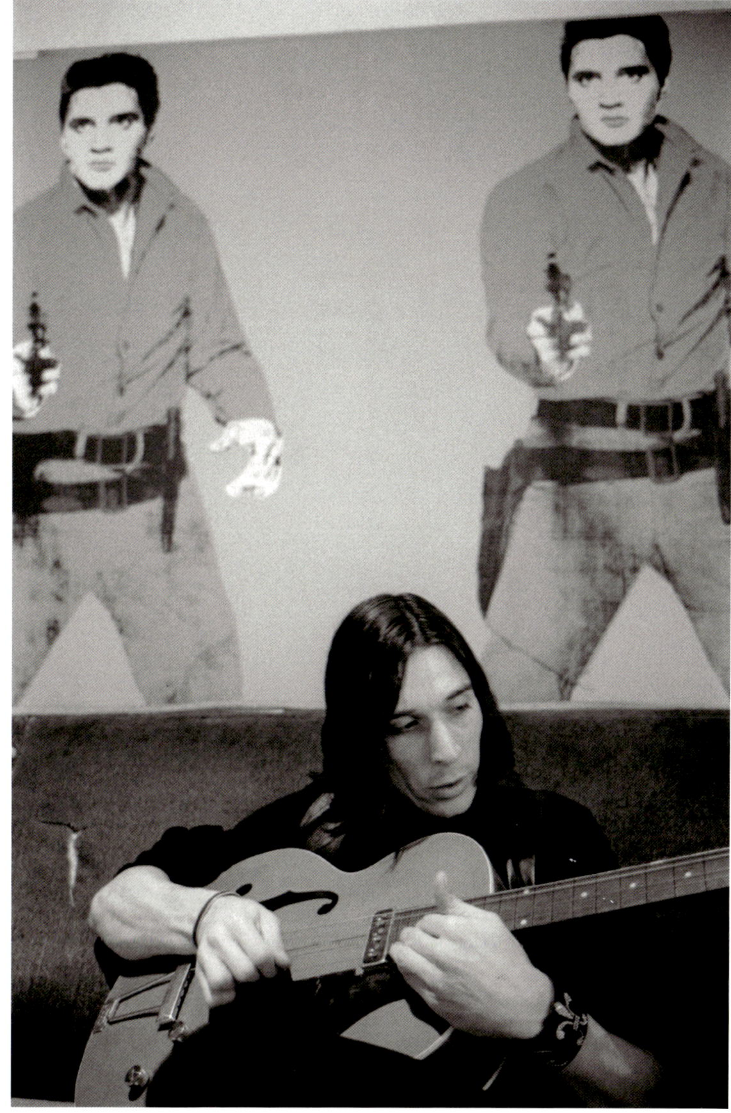

Spread from Kasper König, ed., *Andy Warhol* (Stockholm: Moderna Museet, 1968)

***John Cale, the Factory, New York, New York.* 1966–67**

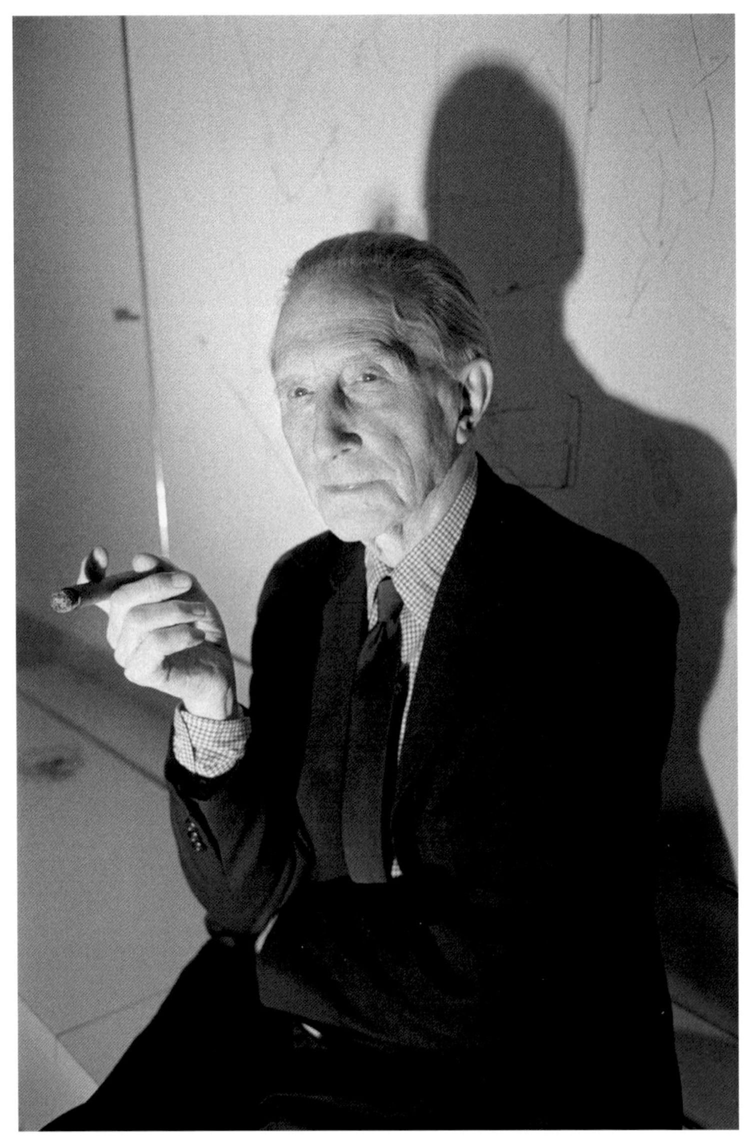

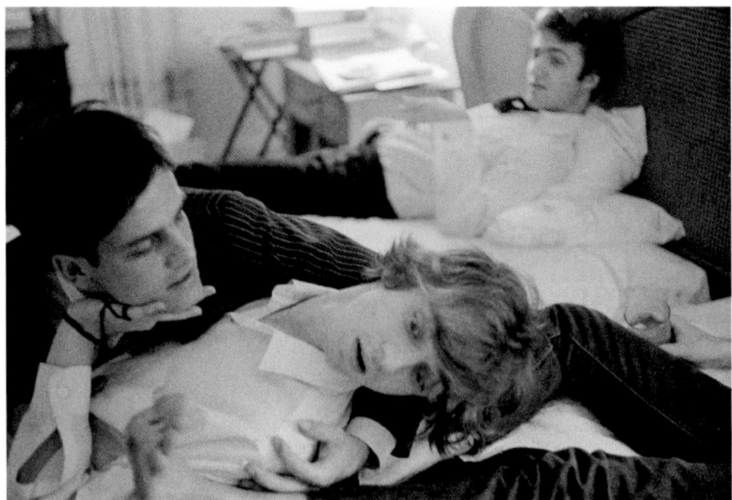

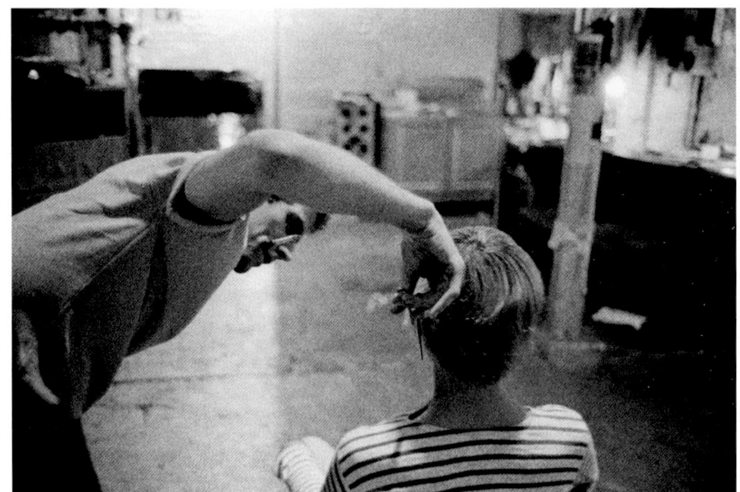

Marcel Duchamp, New York, New York. 1966

Rene Ricard, New York, New York. 1965–67

Billy Name and Chuck Wein, the Factory, New York, New York. 1965–67

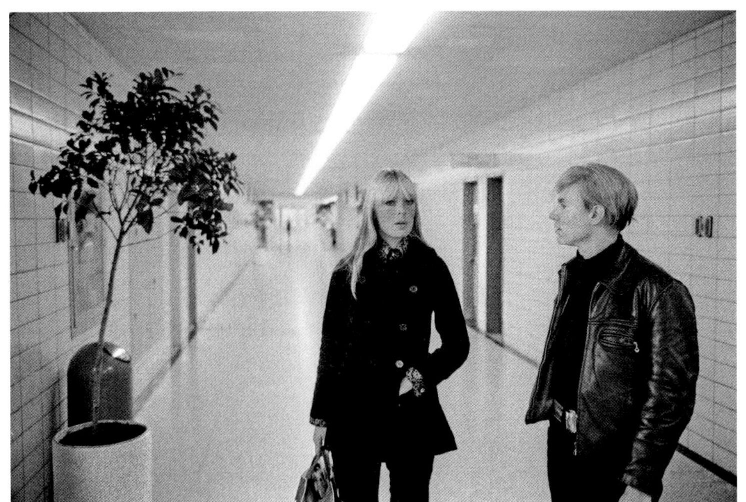

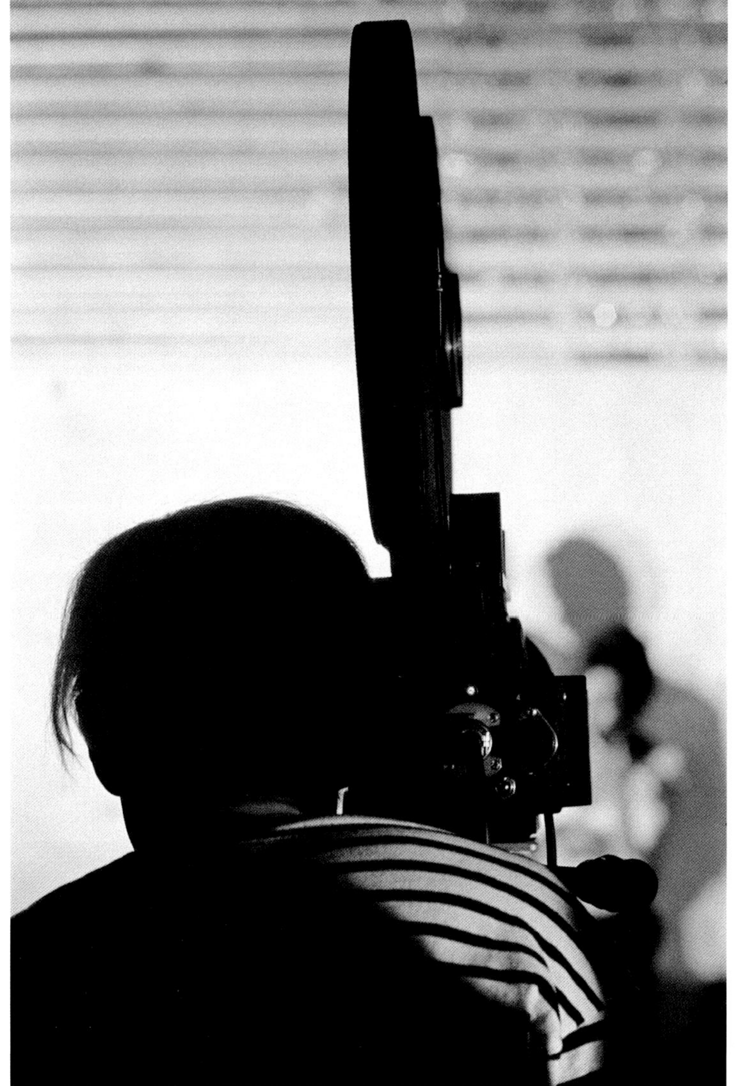

Nico and Andy Warhol, Rutgers University, New Jersey. 1966

Andy Warhol, the Factory, New York, New York. 1965

Fashion Work

Although he had taken on photographic commissions since the 1970s, Shore did not shoot a fashion commission until 2005, when Bottega Veneta's creative director, Thomas Maier, approached him for an advertisement that would be published in *W* magazine in March 2006. His next shoot, for *Another Magazine*, features settings that are consistent with his best-known 1970s subjects—suburban lawns and driveways, greasy-spoon diners, motels, and even a baseball diamond—but much of Shore's fashion work is not immediately recognizable as his. Since then he has photographed models in the U.S.—including Tivoli, New York, where he lives—and abroad, in India, Italy, and Dubai. His shoots have been most often featured in *Elle*, but have also appeared in *Telegraph, Amica, Lucky,* the *Wall Street Journal Magazine,* and an Urban Outfitters catalogue, and he has collaborated with fashion houses including Giorgio Armani, Roberto Cavalli, and Rodarte.

After decades of photographing alone, Shore enjoys the collaborative aspect of working with other people, often including art directors, stylists, and models. Like using new and different equipment, he sees commissions as both challenging and freeing: "If I only try to solve the problems I set for myself, then I'm limited by what I can conceive of. I can't solve a problem I can't conceive. But if someone else gives me a visual problem, it can be out of the whole realm of my normal practice."[1]

Fashion and modeling have appeared in his work in other ways, too. In 2007 Shore visited the Chanel factory in Paris, where he photographed the machinery and workstations used to make handbags. The images became part of the Mobile Art Pavilion, designed by Zaha Hadid, which housed artworks created in response to Chanel's iconic quilted purse. And he has even done some modeling himself, wearing the Racer Jacket (page 59) and the Workwear Corduroy Sportcoat with the Crewneck Merino Sweater in the October 2009 J. Crew catalogue. (Kristen Gaylord)

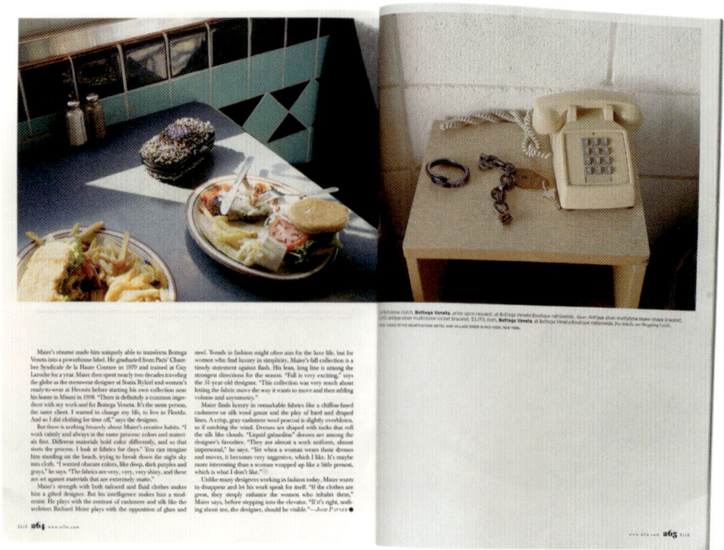

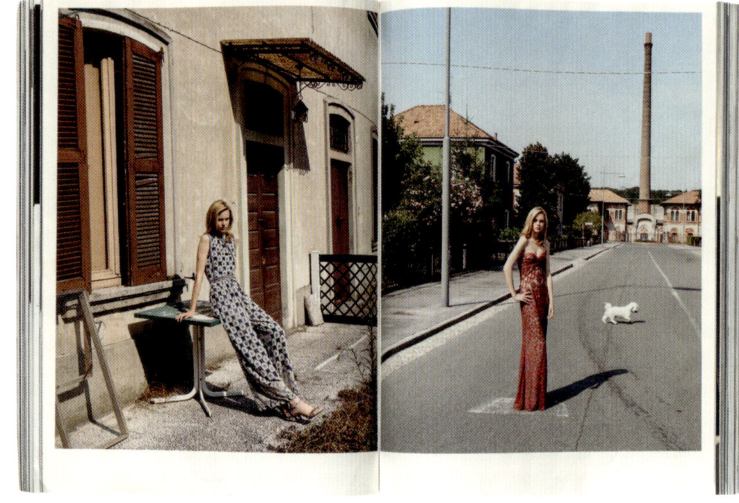

See also: *Commercial Work*; *Commissions and Editorial Work*

1. Alex Gartenfeld, "A Shore Thing," *Interview,* June 11, 2009, http://www.interviewmagazine.com/art/stephen-shore.

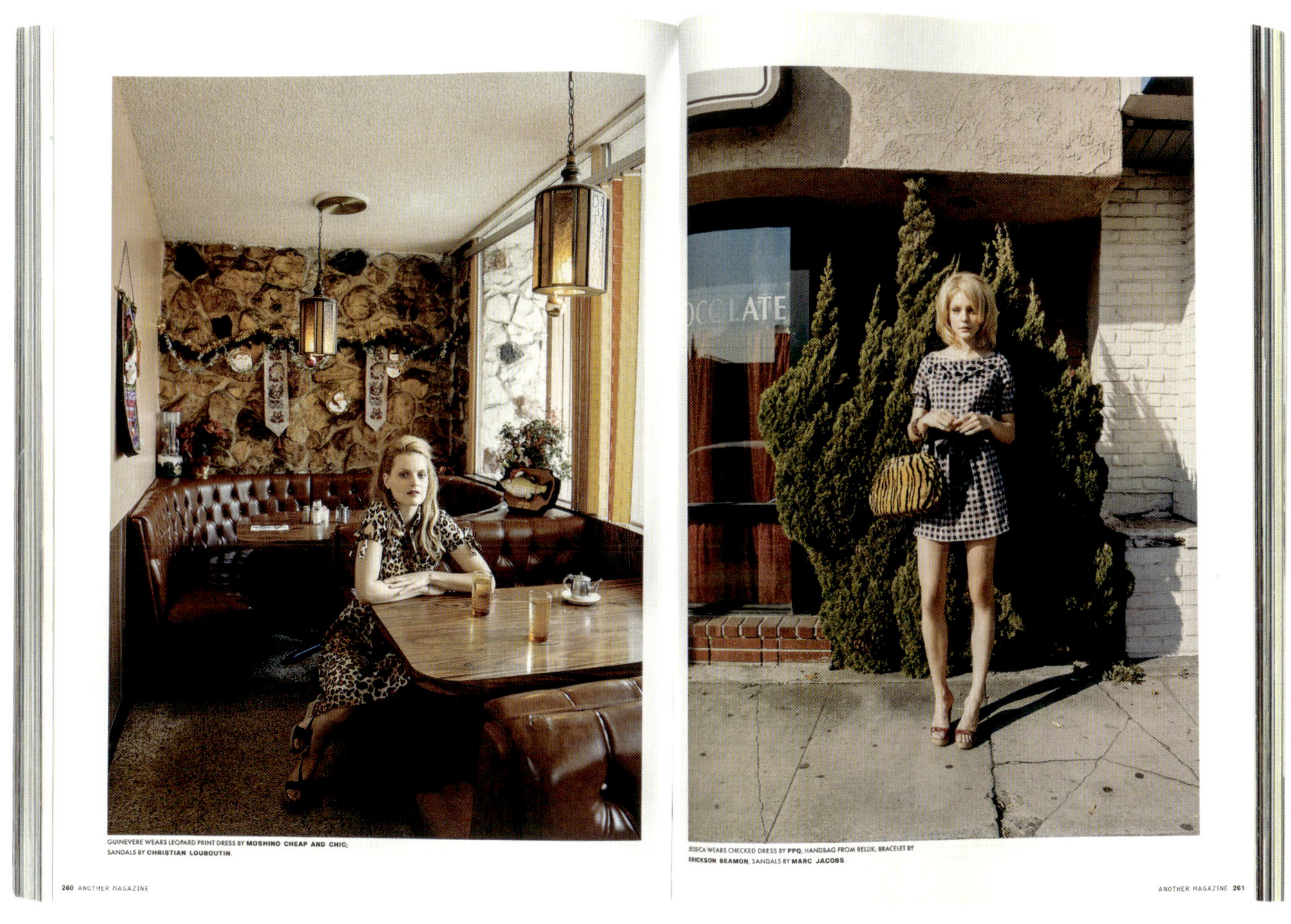

Spread from "Brief Encounter," *Elle*, August 2008

Spread from "Un Racconto," *Amica*, October 2010

Spread from "In Back of the Real," *Another Magazine*, Spring/Summer 2006

Food

"Nutrition determines, more largely than any other physiological function, the nature of social groupings, and the form their activities take," wrote Audrey Richards, the founder of nutritional anthropology, in her 1932 study of Bantu tribes.[1] Shore's America, that of *American Surfaces* and, to a lesser extent, *Uncommon Places*, is an America of consumption, in which food plays a central role as exemplified in a few recurring motifs: stored food (the interiors of open refrigerators), food being prepared (pots and pans on the stove), and, above all, food being consumed. Like the television programs he watched or the hotel rooms he stayed in, the meals Shore ate are among his favorite subjects. Invariably framed from above, using the simplest and most natural angle for a photographer who sometimes stands but more often sits—alternating between a "top-down" view and a "three-quarter" view—Shore's images of meals are among the most graphic in the series *American Surfaces*. Objects and plates of food, shown at the beginning or end of the meal, are photographed with no depth of field against a surface that is generally uniform, where the reflection of the flash is particularly visible, reinforcing the amateur and improvised look of the image.

In their banality and lack of artifice, Shore's pictures seem to fly in the face of typical food photography, which always seeks to beautify the meal being photographed. In contrast, the food on display here—that of travelers and people in a hurry, in cafeterias, motels, drive-ins, diners, planes—is repetitive, unsophisticated, and rarely appetizing. It epitomizes generic American food during a time when "fast food," a term that entered the dictionary in 1951, was rapidly expanding throughout the United States. We should also note that in *American Surfaces*, Shore generally eats alone; a meal is not a convivial ritual or an occasion for socializing but a solitary practice, an experience of isolation further reinforced by the harsh lighting in most of the locations. In *Uncommon Places*, he began by photographing similar subject matter, but as the images became more posed—a result of the different cameras he used for the two series—he took on different subjects. Shore has explained how the snapshot quality of *American Surfaces* became too difficult to achieve when he switched from his Rollei 35 to an 8-by-10 view camera.

Curiously, although the appearance of food in Shore's images seems inseparable from his use of color, when he took on professional food photography—to illustrate a 1978 book on Chinese cooking—he shot in black and white.[2] Shore's almost anthropological attention to food as representative of a society's material culture in his work of the 1970s reemerges sporadically in later photographs taken in the Yucatán (1990), Israel (2009–11), and especially Ukraine (2012–13). In the Ukraine images, food-related themes are omnipresent, suggesting the tradition of an almost anachronistic model of domestic subsistence agriculture in a number of his pictures. Finally, we might note that while the photographer of *American Surfaces* may rightly be considered a precursor to today's foodie and an early pioneer of the food photography that abounds on the Internet, Shore has also practiced the genre himself from time to time since he began posting pictures on Instagram in 2014. (Quentin Bajac)

See also: *American Surfaces*; *Cameras*; *Print-on-Demand Books*; *Ukraine*

1. Audrey I. Richards, *Hunger and Work in a Savage Tribe: A Functional Study of Nutrition among the Southern Bantu* (London: Routledge & Kegan Paul, 1932), 1.
2. The book was *Henry Chung's Hunan Style Chinese Cookbook* (New York: Harmony Books, 1978). Around the same time, Shore also participated in a project called "The Photographers' Cookbook," to which he contributed his recipe for Key Lime Pie Supreme along with a photograph. Conceived in 1977 by Deborah Barsel, the book did not come to fruition until 2016, when it was published by Aperture with an essay by Lisa Hostetler.

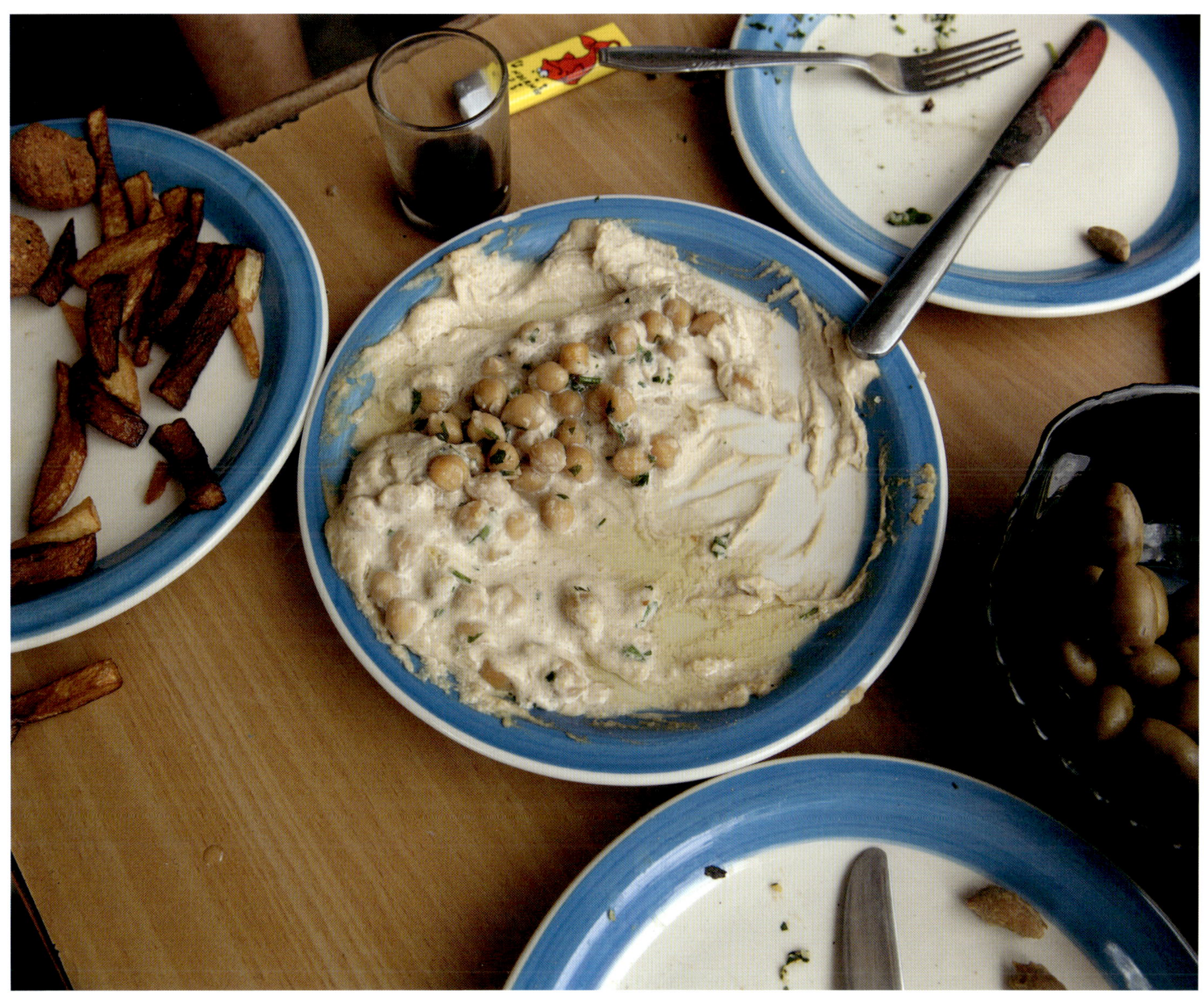

Peqi'in, Israel, September 22, 2009. 2009

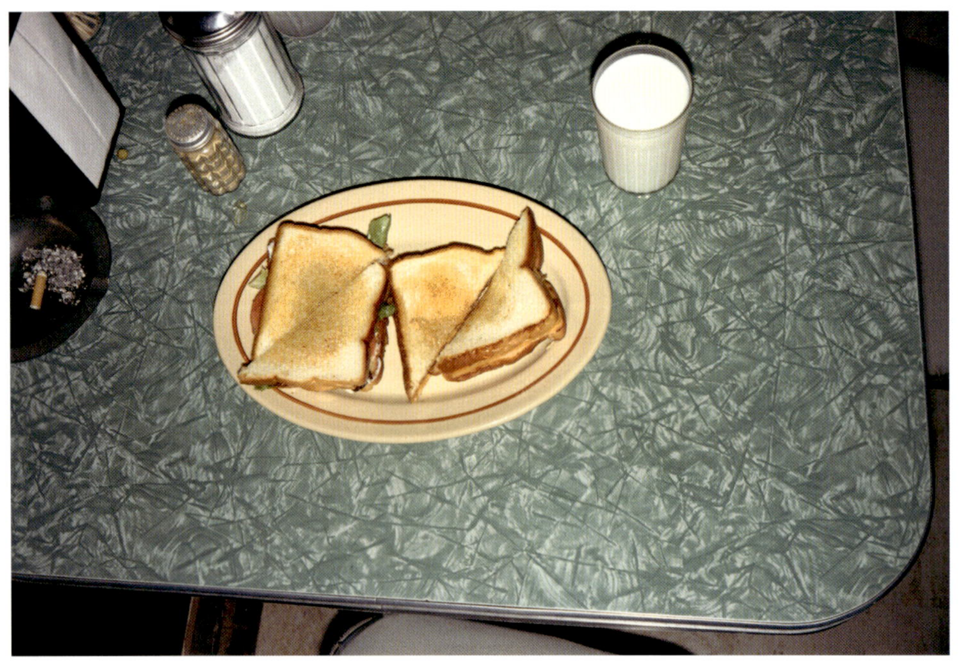

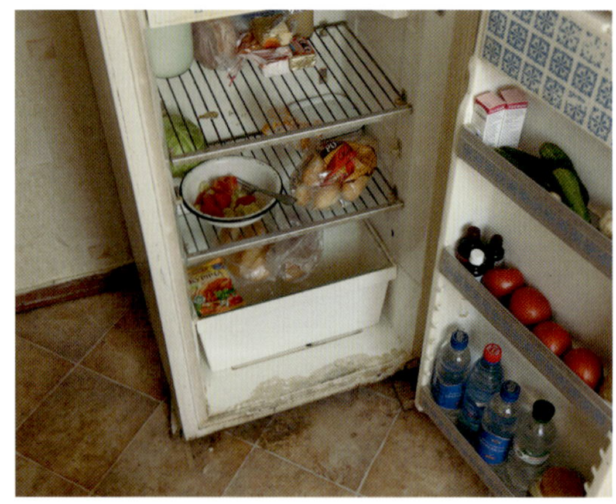

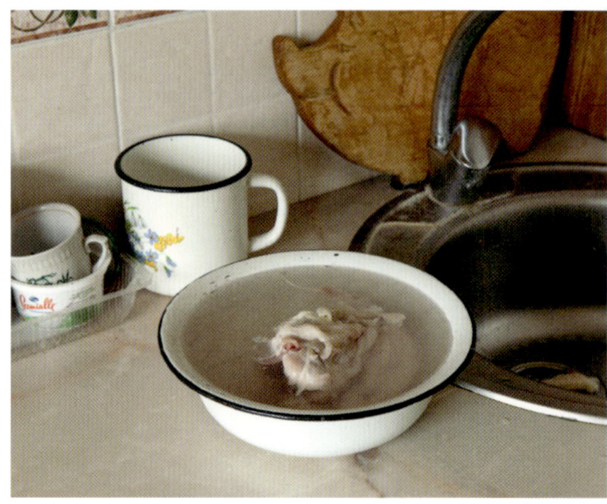

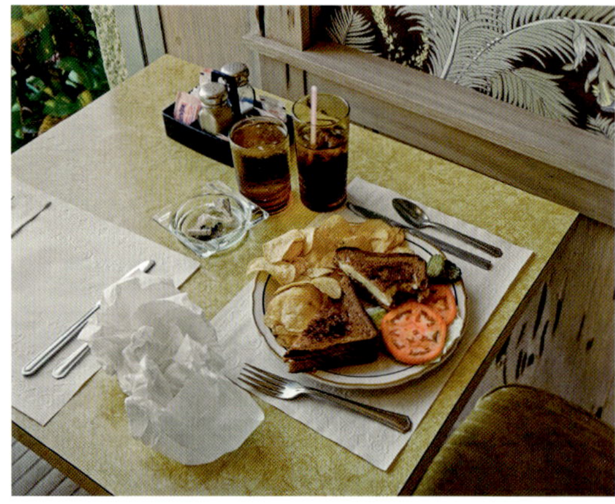

***Granite, Oklahoma, July 1972*. 1972**

***Home of Tzylia Bederman, Bucha, Ukraine, July 18, 2012*. 2012**

***Home of Tzylia Bederman, Bucha, Ukraine, July 18, 2012*. 2012**

***Palm Beach, Florida, November 8, 1977*. 1977**

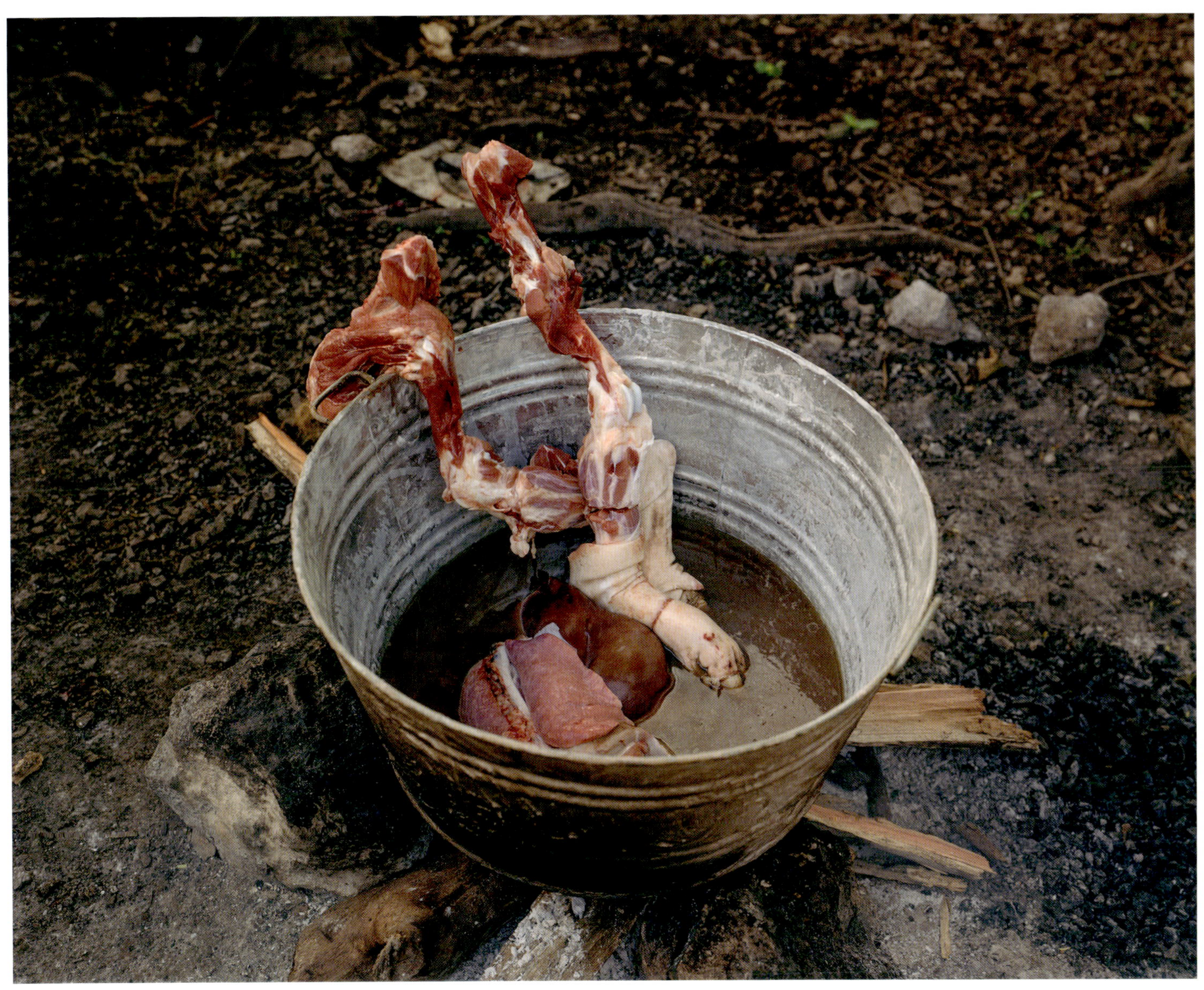

Yucatán, Mexico, 1990. 1990

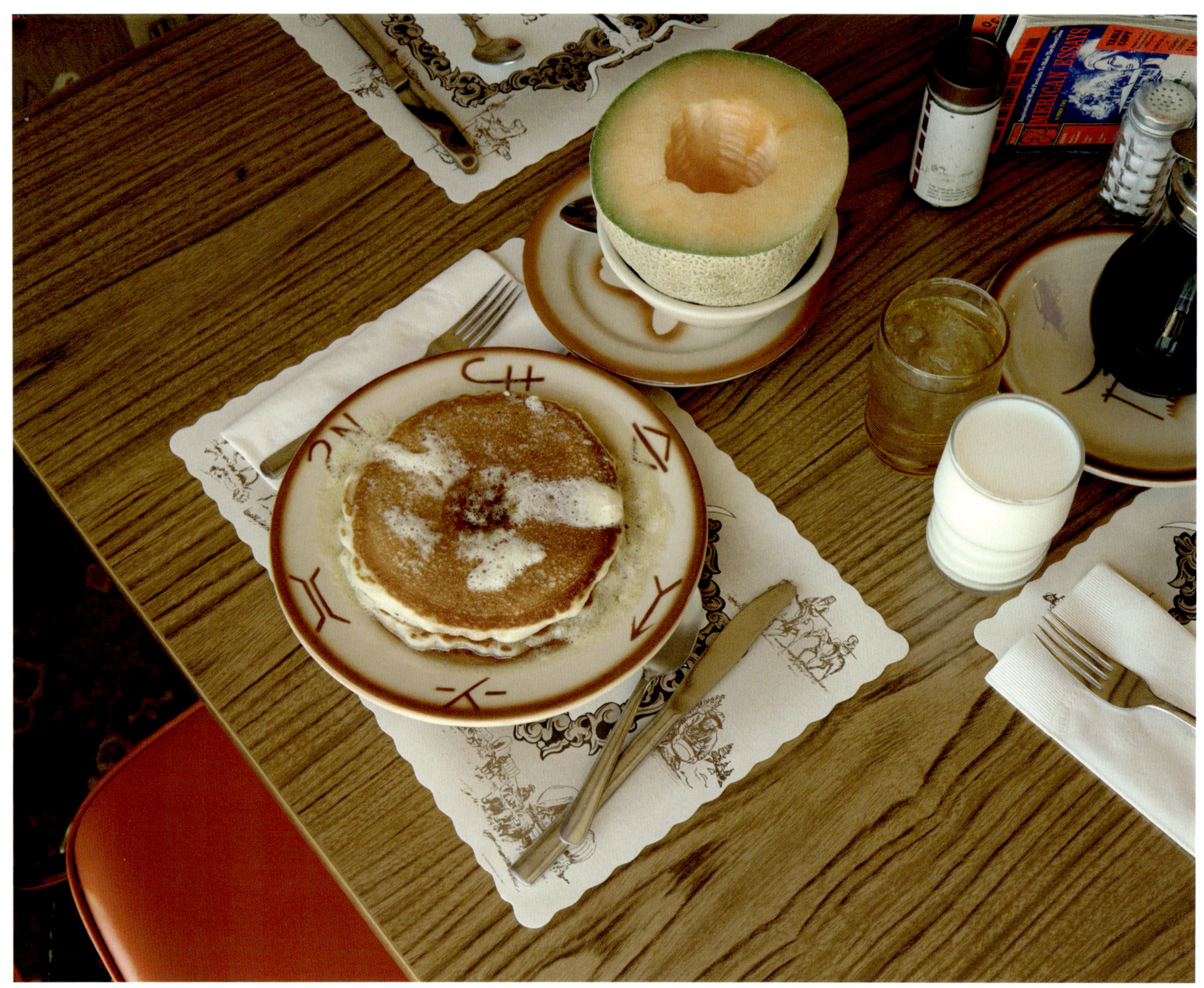

***Breakfast, Trail's End Restaurant, Kanab, Utah, August 10, 1973*. 1973**

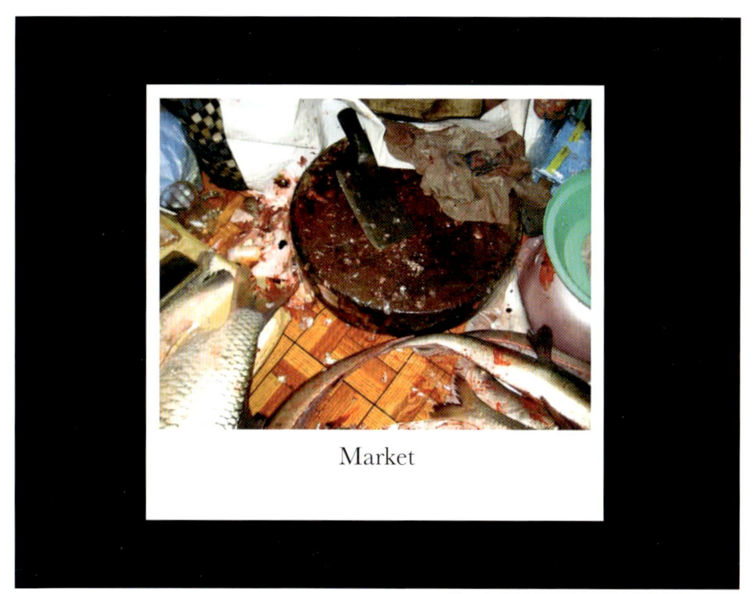
Market

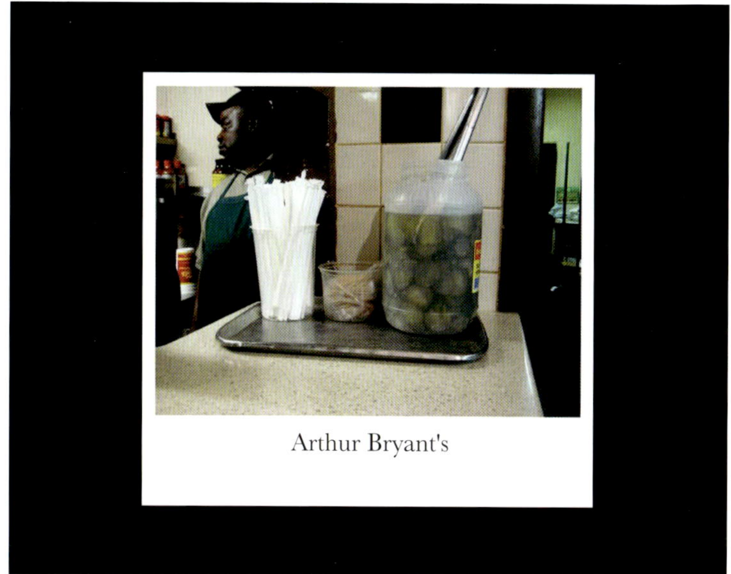
Arthur Bryant's

***Market*. 2008**

***Arthur Bryant's*. 2008**

Gallatin County, Montana, July 10, 1982

By 1981 the epic series of photographic road trips Shore had been making over the previous eight years had come to a natural end. A selection of the pictures from his travels was showcased in the book *Uncommon Places*, published the following year. Some of the very last photographs from that project were taken in Bozeman, Montana. With his wife, Ginger, Shore had spent two summers in Montana; feeling he was at an artistic watershed, they decided to relocate there. Recently, he recalled:

> I had got to a point where I could walk into any town in America and have an understanding of the forces at play and come to a sense of what to photograph. But when I walked out into the land in Montana, I was just a New Yorker in paradise: "Oh gosh, isn't this beautiful!" I knew if I took a picture of that, it wouldn't have a deeper perception of the land. So, what I did was just live there without taking pictures of it for two years—just walking on the land, cross-country skiing on it, seeing it in different light, until I felt I was at a point where I had something to communicate about it other than its beauty. [. . .] An open landscape is not differentiated like an intersection. That became a real challenge: how to articulate three-dimensionality in a photograph of that kind of landscape.[1]

Shore's Montana work includes some of the most minimal pictures he has ever made, although the term *minimal* ought to be approached with care. In terms of pictorial space, he was working with very few elements—in this example, a grassy hill punctuated by rocks, and a sky punctuated by clouds. One can feel the picture, and by extension the landscape, as something schematic, like a simple diagram of three-dimensional space converted into a two-dimensional picture.

Even so, whether a camera is pointing at a plain white wall, a green pasture, or a stadium full of individual human faces, every square inch of a sheet of film is transformed equally in the single act of exposure. Where a painter begins with a blank canvas and may be done after adding just a few marks, photographic film goes from unexposed to entirely exposed in one step. Open the shutter and the world-as-light will flood in, unbidden—from empty to full, with no intermediate stages. In this sense, a minimal photograph is an unexposed one, and a maximal photograph is an exposed one.

The photographer Harry Callahan once remarked: "Every artist continually wants to reach the edge of nothingness—the point where you can't go any farther."[2] In the rolling hills of Montana, Shore was exploring his own kind of pictorial limit. (David Campany)

See also: *Landscape*

1. David Campany, "Ways of Making Pictures," in Marta Dahó, ed., *Stephen Shore* (Madrid: Fundación MAPFRE; New York: Aperture, 2014), 40-41.
2. Harry M. Callahan, *Water's Edge* (Lyme, Conn.: Callaway Editions, 1980), 47.

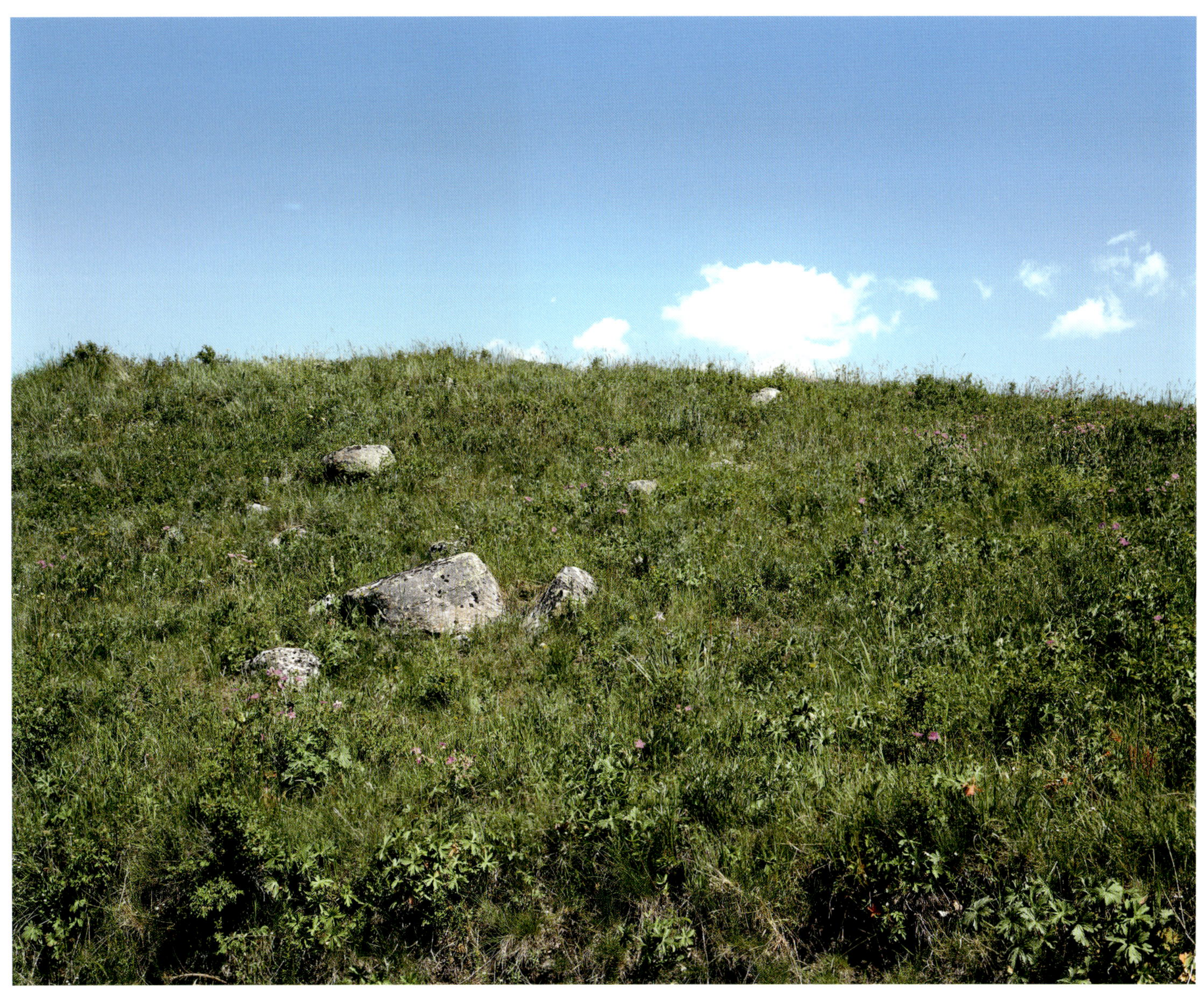

Gallatin County, Montana, July 10, 1982. 1982

111.

Gardens

Although Shore's most sustained engagement with landscape was in the 1980s, his first project dealing with nature was in 1977, when he photographed the restoration of Claude Monet's gardens at Giverny. While he had shot suburban lawns for *American Surfaces* and *Uncommon Places*, Giverny provided a fresh challenge: to organize an overwhelmingly green and lush space in a way that would provide Shore's usual clarity and structure without succumbing to picturesqueness, or what he described as the "pitfalls in photographing flowers in a garden."[1] His photographs of gardens are beautiful, but they also deal with the realities of gardening: growth and dormancy, arrangement and wildness, harmony and contrast, simplicity and abundance.

Shore became increasingly interested in gardens over the next decades, evidenced in his 1980s photographs but also in more recent work. In 2003 his son used white spray paint to cover several plants in their garden in Tivoli, New York; Shore photographed these, as well as a naturally white Queen Anne's Lace, and compiled a print-on-demand book of the images called *White Garden* (right). Many of his Instagram photographs are of this garden, ranging from overviews of the organized landscape to isolated, technical studies of soil, water, leaves, and bark (often these latter images provoke arguments among commenters about their value as photographs). He frequently photographs the New York Botanical Garden, and in 2016 he traveled throughout southern England, posting images of important gardens; he has described the English garden style as "an exaggeration of nature but with an understanding of a natural order."[2] And although in the past decade he has mainly worked with digital cameras, in 2014 and 2015 Shore took black-and-white large-format photographs of his garden that, without the visual shorthand of color, emphasize texture, depth, and light. (Kristen Gaylord)

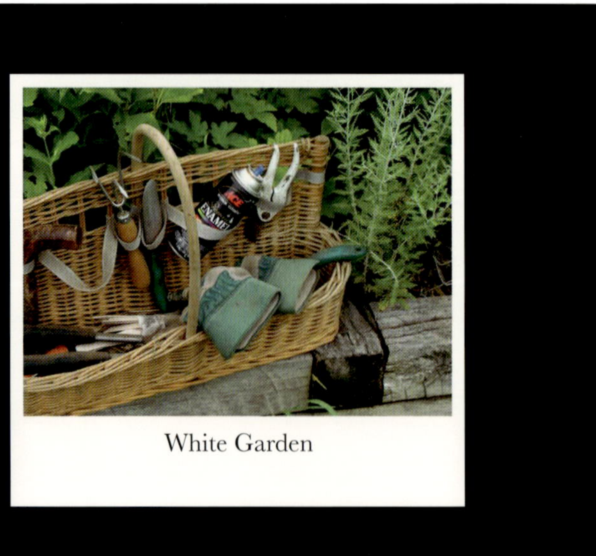

See also: *Color*; *Commissions and Editorial Work*; *Instagram*; *Landscape*

1. "Stephen Shore with Peter Halley," *Index* 23 (April 2000): 36.
2. Ibid.

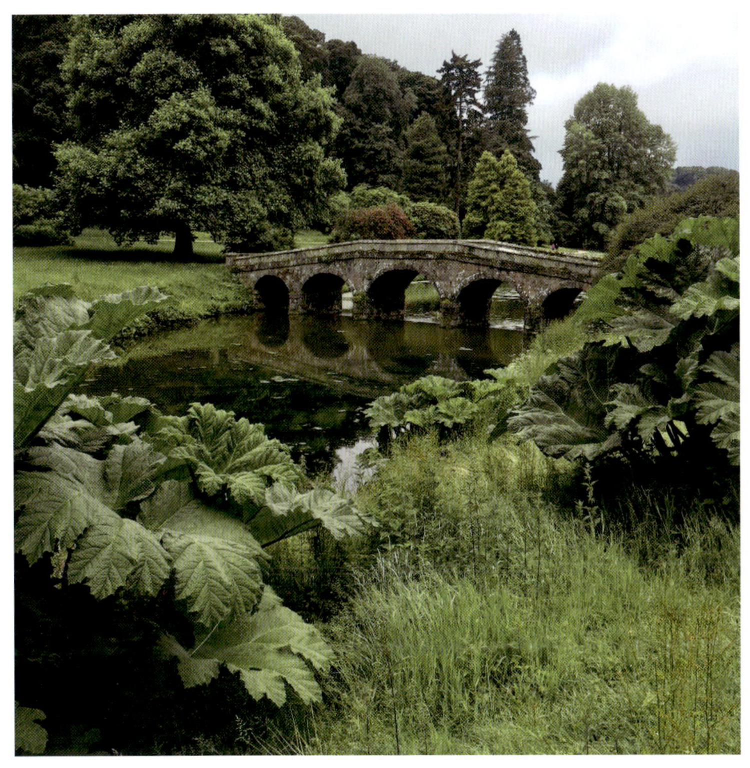

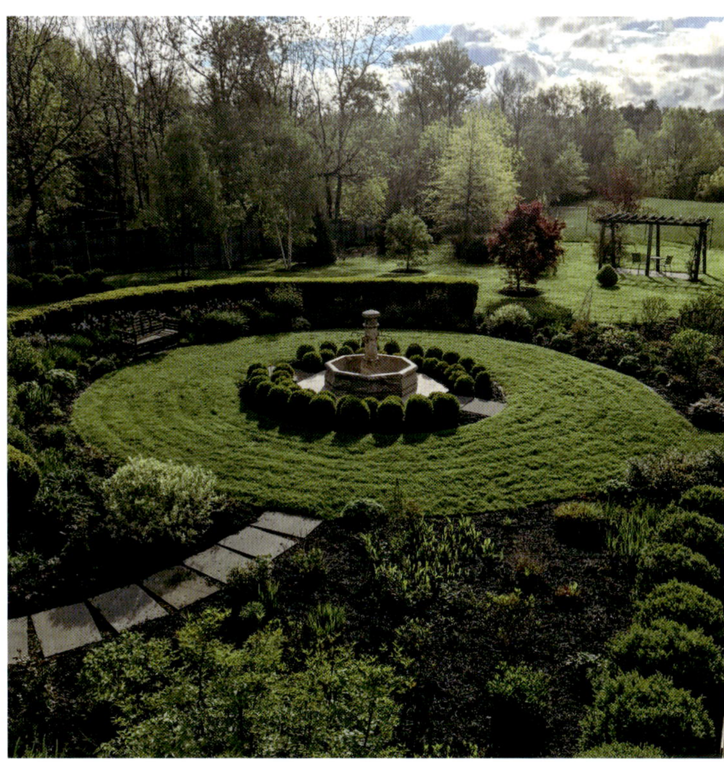

***White Garden*. 2003**

***Stourhead Gardens, Stourton, Warminster, U.K., June 19, 2016*. 2016**

***Tivoli, New York, May 8, 2017*. 2017**

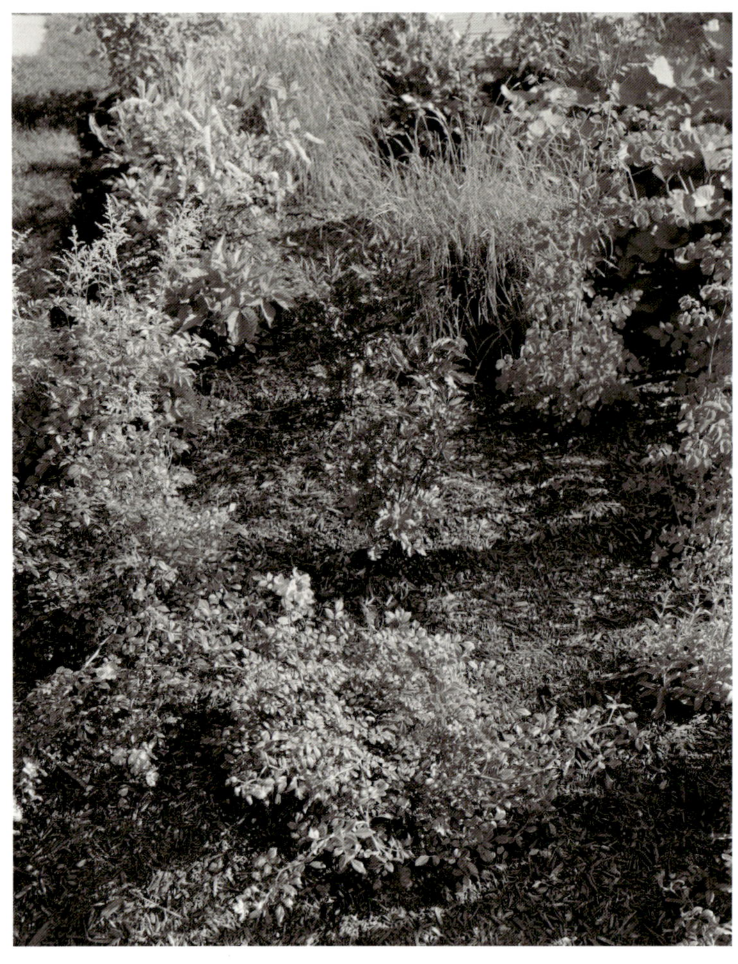

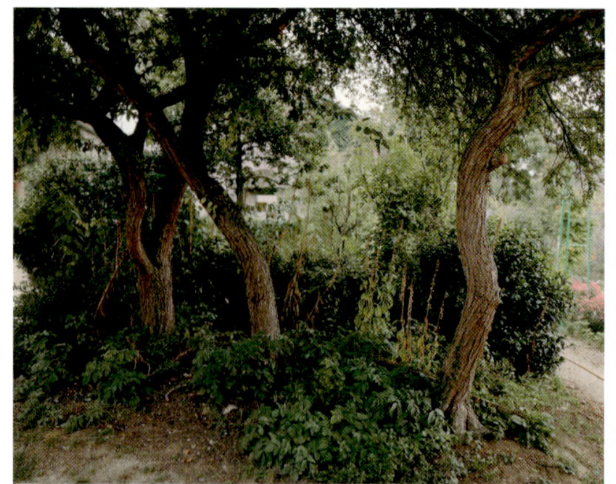

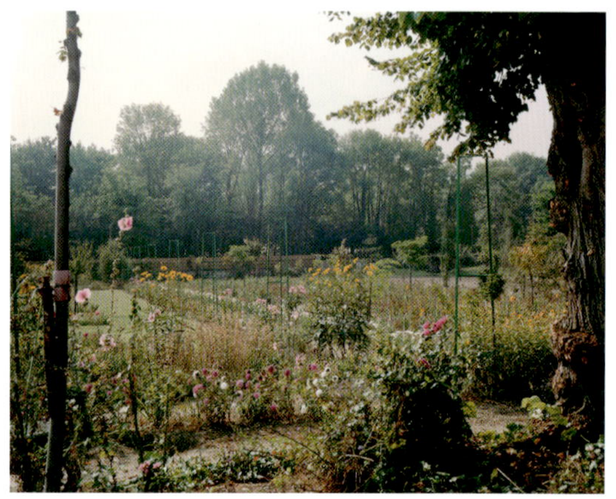

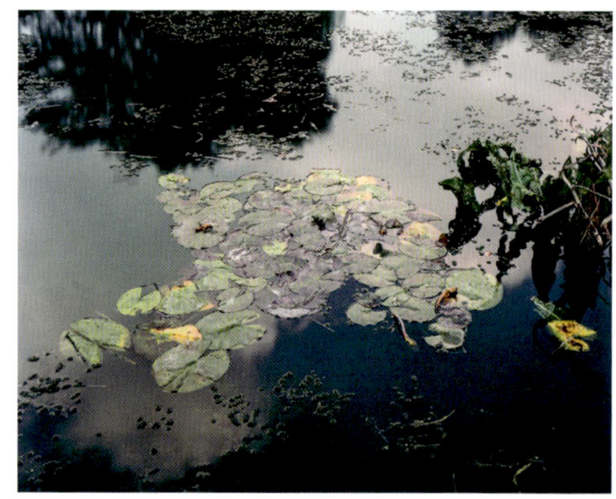

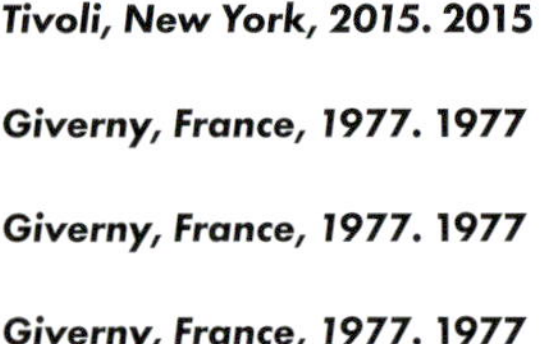

***Tivoli, New York, 2015*. 2015**

***Giverny, France, 1977*. 1977**

***Giverny, France, 1977*. 1977**

***Giverny, France, 1977*. 1977**

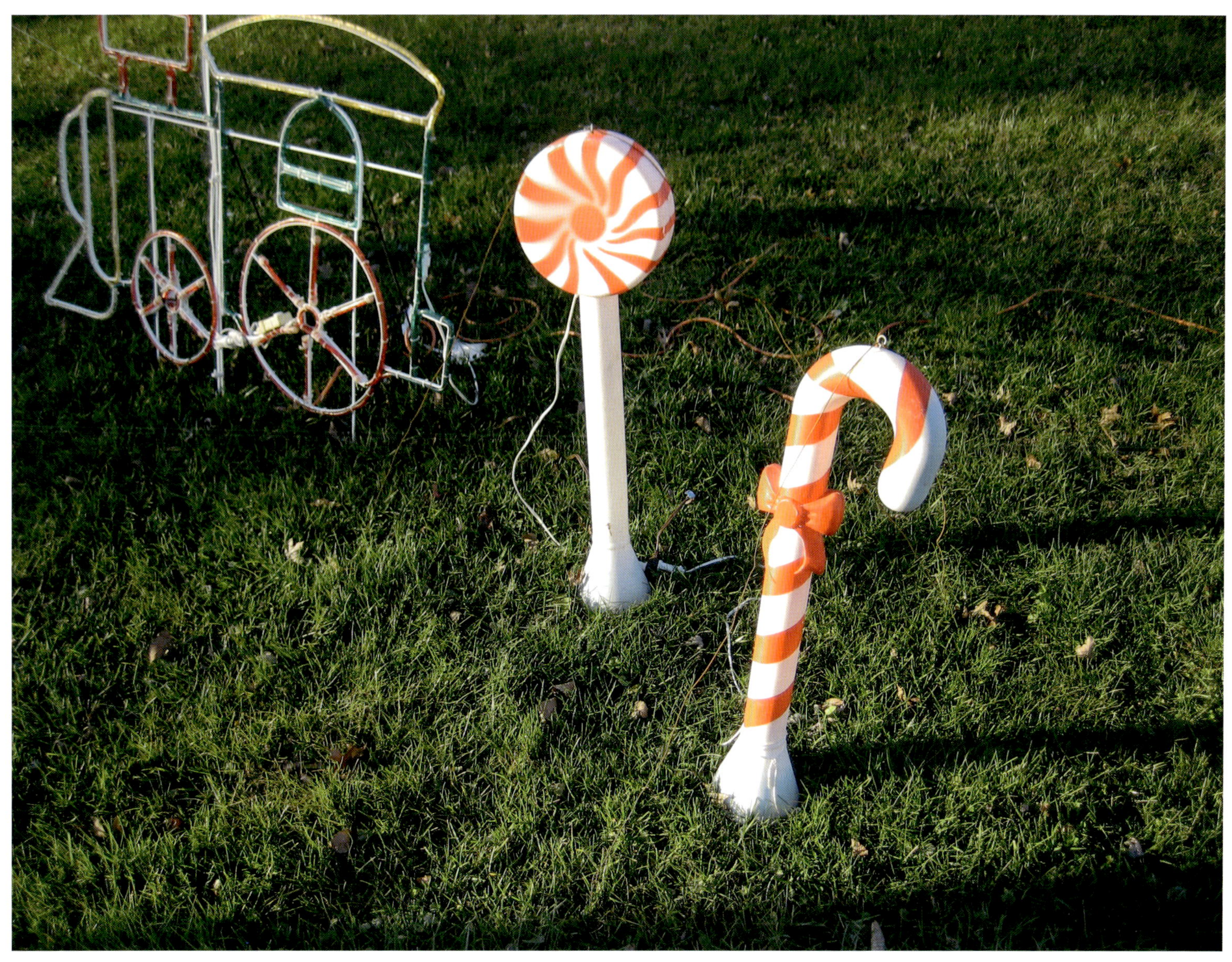

Image from *Merry Christmas*, 2006

Germany

After receiving little attention for almost fifteen years, Shore's work was rediscovered in the 1990s, largely as a result of exhibitions in Germany. In 1995 Heinz Liesbrock organized the first retrospective of Shore's work, at the Westfälischer Kunstverein in Münster, which included twenty years of photographs, from *Uncommon Places* to his works of the early nineties; this was also the photographer's first international traveling exhibition, touring to three cities in Germany and elsewhere. Four years later, in 1999, his series *American Surfaces* was shown for the first time since 1972 in an exhibition in Cologne and then Frankfurt that was accompanied by a book published by Munich-based Schirmer/Mosel. These two exhibitions would contribute significantly to the revival of interest in Shore's work on both sides of the Atlantic.

His rediscovery occurred in the context of the international success of a number of German photographers who had studied with Bernd Becher at the Kunstakademie in Düsseldorf in the seventies and eighties, including Andreas Gursky, Candida Höfer, Thomas Ruff, and Thomas Struth, and allowed a reexamination of the role played by American color photography—and Shore's in particular—for this generation of practitioners.[1] Early on, Shore had garnered interest in German photographic and artistic circles, thanks primarily to Bernd and Hilla Becher's enthusiasm for his work. In an interview published in the 1995 exhibition catalogue, the Bechers discussed for the first time the importance they accorded Shore's work and the attitudes they shared with him in the seventies: a similar interest in the documentary-style approach of photographers like Walker Evans, and a similar embrace of an architecture "without qualities"—for the Bechers, buildings that had emerged from the industrial revolution, and for Shore, the postwar remnants of a disappearing American culture.[2] Not only were the Bechers and Shore bound by friendship and mutual respect, but the proximity of their interests was also reflected in the fact that they were all included in the 1975 exhibition *New Topographics: Photographs of a Man-Altered Landscape* at George Eastman House in Rochester.

In the seventies, the Bechers began collecting prints from the *Uncommon Places* series, and they introduced German gallerists to Shore's work.[3] One of these was Rudolf Kicken, who exhibited Shore's photographs in his Aachen gallery in 1975. This was the first in a series of exhibitions in Germany in which Shore was held up as the exemplar of the new American color photography. Bernd Becher showed Shore's images in his classes in the late seventies and early eighties, a time when art photography in Germany (including the Bechers') was still being shot almost exclusively in black and white. It is a testament to Shore's influence that almost all of the first generation of Becher's students would end up adopting color photography. Gursky acknowledged the extent to which the 1981 publication *The New Color Photography*, the first major book on this new wave of American color photographers, had been a touchstone for him (he called it his bible), while in 1987 Struth named his first work about architecture *Unconscious Places*, in a tribute to Shore's *Uncommon Places*, published five years earlier.

Shore's influence on German photography was not, however, restricted to the Düsseldorf scene. The Werkstatt für Photographie in Berlin, for example, founded by Michael Schmidt in 1975, introduced artists and viewers to a number of American photographers of the period, notably those in the *New Topographics* exhibition.[4] In 1978 Shore showed at the Werkstatt in the company of other photographers from that show, including Frank Gohlke, Joe Deal, and Lewis Baltz.

The German interest in Shore's work is still evident: in 2010 a portfolio of six German photographers (Jens Liebchen, Max Regenberg, Oliver Sieber, Olaf Unverzart, Robert Voit, and Janko Woltersmann) working with Shore's well-known image *Beverly Boulevard and La Brea Avenue, Los Angeles, California, June 21, 1975* (page 53) was published under the title *The La Brea Matrix*.[5] (Quentin Bajac)

See also: *American Surfaces*; *Beverly Boulevard and La Brea Avenue*; *Uncommon Places*

1. Werner Lippert and Christoph Schaden, eds., *Der Rote Bulli: Stephen Shore und die Neue Düsseldorfer Fotografie* (Düsseldorf: NRW–Forum Düsseldorf, 2010).
2. "His pictures have the quality of a first encounter," Bernd and Hilla Becher in conversation with Heinz Liesbrock, in Heinz Liesbrock, ed., *Stephen Shore: Photographs 1973–1993* (Munich: Schirmer/Mosel, 1995).
3. The Becher archives, conserved at the SK Stiftung Kultur, Cologne, contain nine prints from the early years of Shore's *Uncommon Places*.
4. Florian Ebner et al., eds., *Werkstatt für Photographie 1976–1986* (London: Koenig Books, 2017).
5. *The La Brea Matrix: Six German Photographers and a New Color Icon by Stephen Shore* (Culver City, Calif.: Lapis Press, 2010).

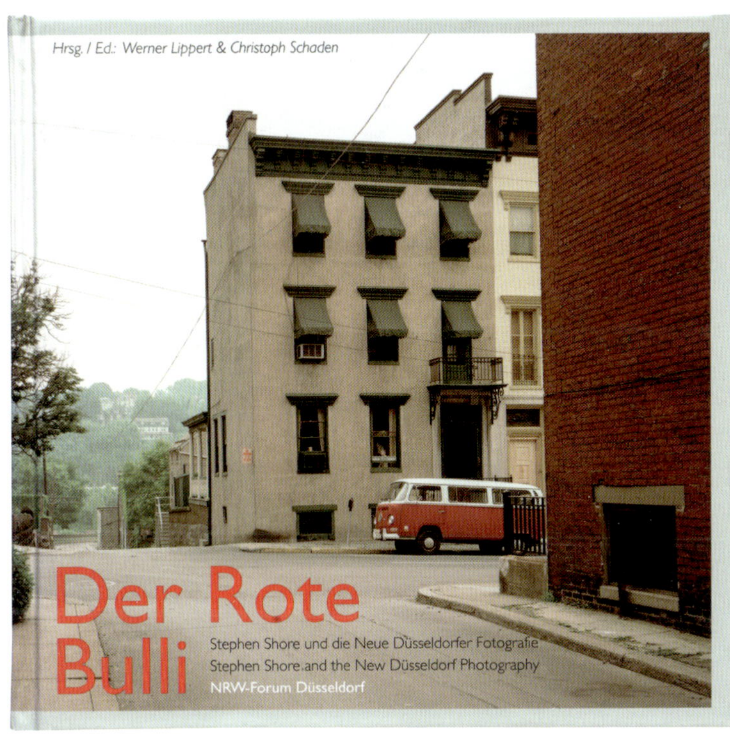

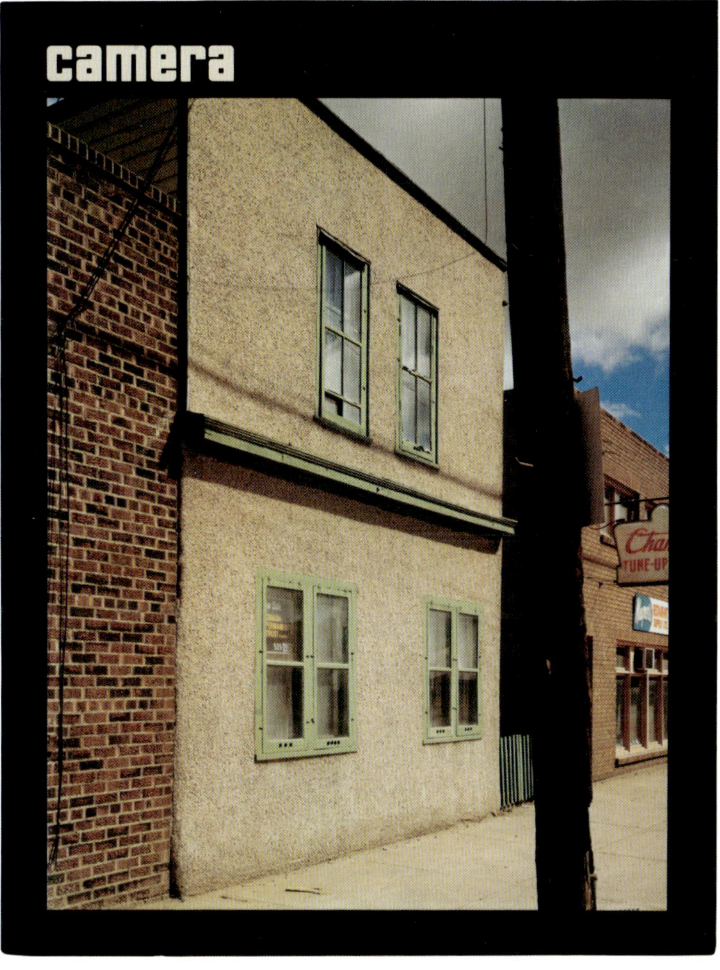

Cover of Werner Lippert and Christoph Schaden, eds., *Der Rote Bulli: Stephen Shore und die Neue Düsseldorfer Fotografie* (Düsseldorf: NRW-Forum Düsseldorf, 2010)

Cover of *Camera*, January 1977

Ginger

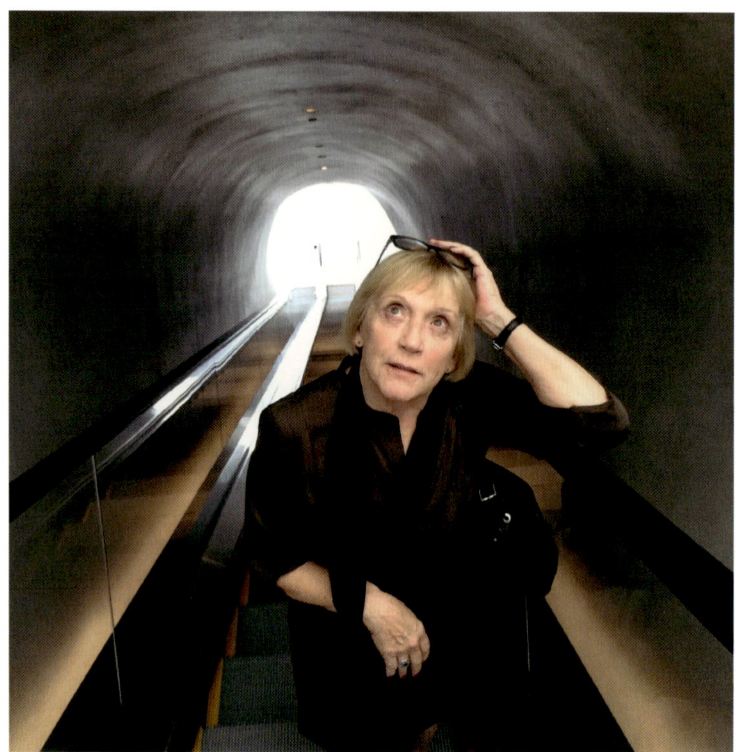

Ginger met Stephen in 1976 while she was working at Time-Life Books, which had been founded in 1961 and was known for its subscription book series including The Good Cook, The Enchanted World, and the Life Library of Photography.[1] She was working on the annual publication *Photography Year 1977*, and interviewed Shore for a section on trends called "Return to Landscapes." In 1977 she started to work at *Fortune* (where she took over what had been Walker Evans's office when he had been an editor), and they met again when she asked Shore to do a portfolio for the magazine. They dated until 1980, when they married in Berkeley, California; Tod Papageorge photographed the wedding. They spent their honeymoon in Montana, indulging in their mutual love of fly-fishing (which Ginger had introduced Stephen to) and beginning a relationship with the state that continues to this day.

Although Shore almost always photographs alone, when Ginger's work schedule allowed she would go with him on his shoots, sometimes carrying his gear, as she does in what he has called his "favorite portrait": his image of her in front of a tiled wall (opposite).[2] She shows up often in images from the 1970s, and also went with Shore on many of his shoots in the 1980s, sometimes taking notes about his shots.

Ginger has continued to be a subject of Shore's photographs through his print-on-demand books of the early 2000s and, currently, his Instagram feed, where she appears eating, playing with the couple's pets, photographing, traveling with him, and napping. Perhaps the simplest explanation for his dozens of images of her is the one Shore gave in a 2005 questionnaire from *Frieze*. In response to the question "What do you like the look of?" he answered, "My wife, Ginger."[3] (Kristen Gaylord)

See also: *Commissions and Editorial Work*; *Portraiture*; *Road Trips*; *Uncommon Places*

1. The Life Library of Photography series published volumes on different aspects of photography; Shore was featured in *Color* and the second edition of *Great Photographers*.
2. *Stephen Shore: New American Photography*, directed by Ralph Goertz (Düsseldorf: Institut für Kunstdokumentation und Szenografie, in cooperation with NRW-Forum Düsseldorf, 2010), DVD.
3. "Questionnaire: Stephen Shore," *Frieze* 95 (November–December 2005): 148.

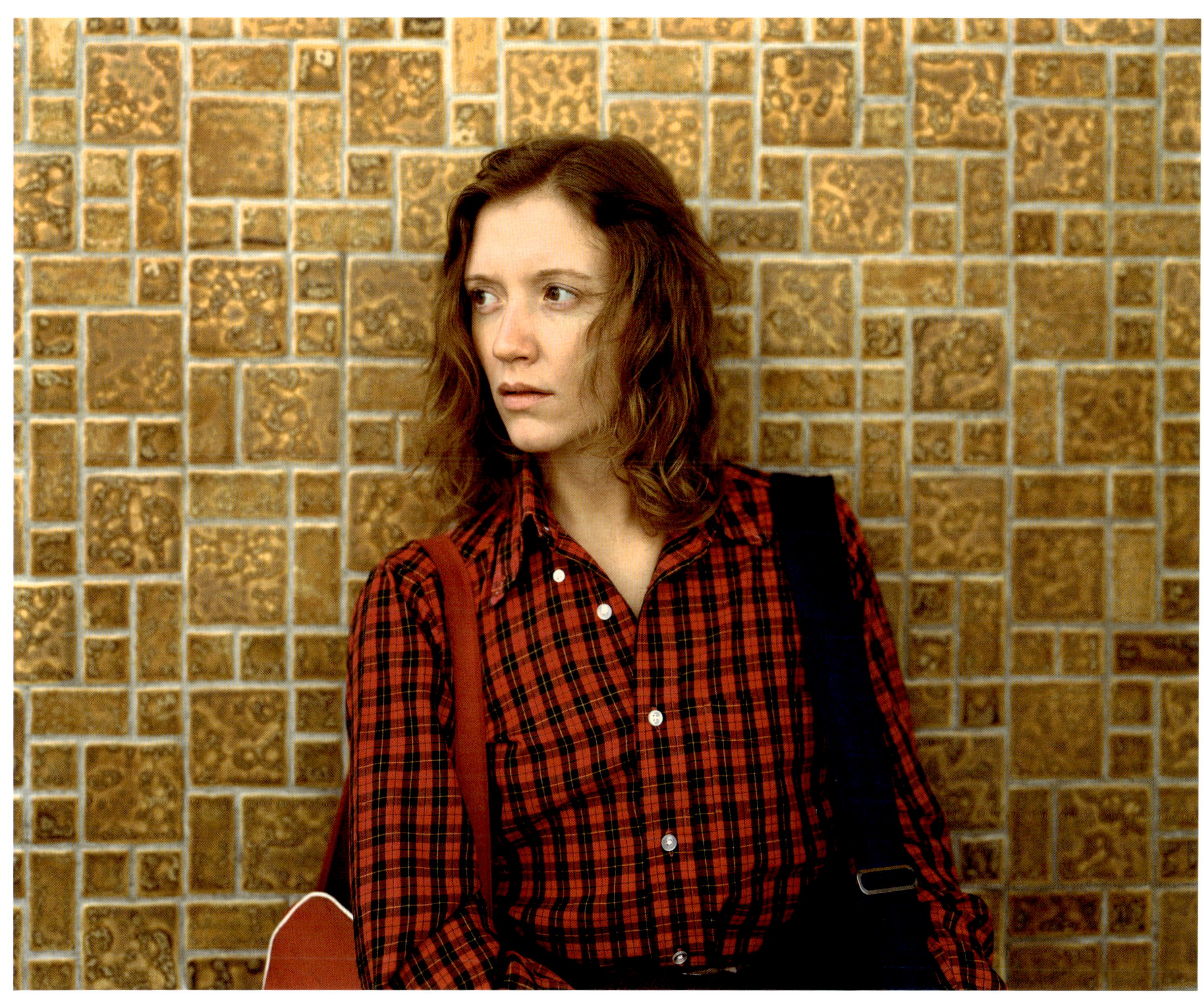

***Ginger Shore, The Broad, 221 South Grand Avenue, Los Angeles, California, September 24, 2015.* 2015**

***Ginger Shore, Flagler Street, Miami, Florida, November 12, 1977.* 1977**

Instagram

"Taking fun seriously" was how Shore described his relationship with Instagram in 2015, before adding, "Andy Warhol would have loved it."[1] In the summer of 2014, Shore decided to devote most of his photographic activity to Instagram, where he posts images almost every day. While he continues to take on commissions, the bulk of his personal production of the past three years has been through the social networking app; he considers this output his current "work," although to date it has not been translated into any form with commercial ends.[2]

Shore's interest in Instagram follows directly from his longtime enthusiasm for popular forms of photography, whether related to the manufacture of images (the Mick-a-Matic and Rollei cameras of the 1970s) or their dissemination (postcards, print-on-demand books). Like some of the iBooks he created beginning in 2003, shooting and printing each in a single day, or the print book *Winslow Arizona*, which presented photographs taken during one day in 2013, with Instagram Shore has reestablished a rapid, instantaneous practice, one that requires him to be on constant alert. "Paying attention all the time is a very interesting way to go through a day," he has said, a different way of being in the world.[3]

Instagram also presents a new, dual aesthetic challenge for Shore in the square format, which he was not used to, and the small size of the image (although he prefers to look at Instagram on a tablet rather than a mobile phone). These constraints encourage a simplification of the picture, making it more a "notation," in the diaristic sense of the term, than a constructed image. Shore recognizes that many of these photos are not meant to be transformed into framed prints to be hung, individually, on a wall.

For Shore, who has worked with a number of different photographic processes and formats since the early 1960s, Instagram seems to offer a kind of a hybrid. The immediacy, playful character, and small, square format of Instagram pictures are reminiscent of the photographs he took with a Polaroid SX-70 in the 1970s; their brightness on the screen recalls the transparency of slide projections; and the absence of a viewfinder and the distance between the eye and the image on the phone screen is similar to the experience of shooting with a view camera. The real novelty of Instagram resides, though, in the app's instantaneous and universal diffusion of images (the "posts") and especially its worldwide scope. If photography is a language, then the visual messages of Instagram serve what linguists call a phatic function—as communication and contact, as a catalyst of exchange, debate, and conversation. "Instagram is just more like language, like we're talking now," Shore said in a 2015 interview. "We're using language and not in a way a poet or a novelist would use it. We're just using it to communicate. [. . .] There are a lot of people who are using Instagram just as a visual communication. And I find that fascinating and refreshing."[4]

In its often stereotypical and repetitive iconography and its dominant style (colorful, graphic, expressive), Instagram seems to echo certain aspects of Shore's early work, *American Surfaces* in particular. In addition, the luminosity of the screen gives the images a transparency that calls to mind the look of his photographic prints from the 1970s. On his Instagram feed, however, Shore rarely plays to social network clichés, avoiding, for instance, the more self-centered and narcissistic uses of the app. He favors images that for the most part continue in the non-spectacular vein of his work to date, and at times he blurs temporal references by posting some of his older photographs. The images he chooses to post, sometimes after a few days of reflection, usually steer clear of the autobiographical nature of so many Instagram posts, even in his most apparently personal pictures. (Quentin Bajac)

See also: *Cameras*; *Food*; *Gardens*; *Print-on-Demand Books*; *Winslow, Arizona*; *Ziggy, Zelda and Zaza*

1. Aimee Farrell, "Stephen Shore Loves Instagram (and Thinks Warhol Would Have, Too)," *T Magazine*, May 20, 2015, http://tmagazine.blogs.nytimes.com/2015/05/20/stephen-shore-instagram-photo-london-somerset-house/.
2. Stephen Shore, *Instagram*, selected by Hans Ulrich Obrist (London: Mörel, 2015). Published in an edition of 200, this book reproduced all of Shore's Instagram posts since he opened his account.
3. Barry Tanenbaum, "Communication Breakthrough: Legendary Photographer Stephen Shore Makes an Instagram Connection," *Shutterbug*, October 2015, 30.
4. Alexis Dahan, "Stephen Shore on Photography vs Instagram," *Purple Magazine* 24 (Fall/Winter 2015–16): http://purple.fr/magazine/fw-2015-issue-24/stephen-shore/.

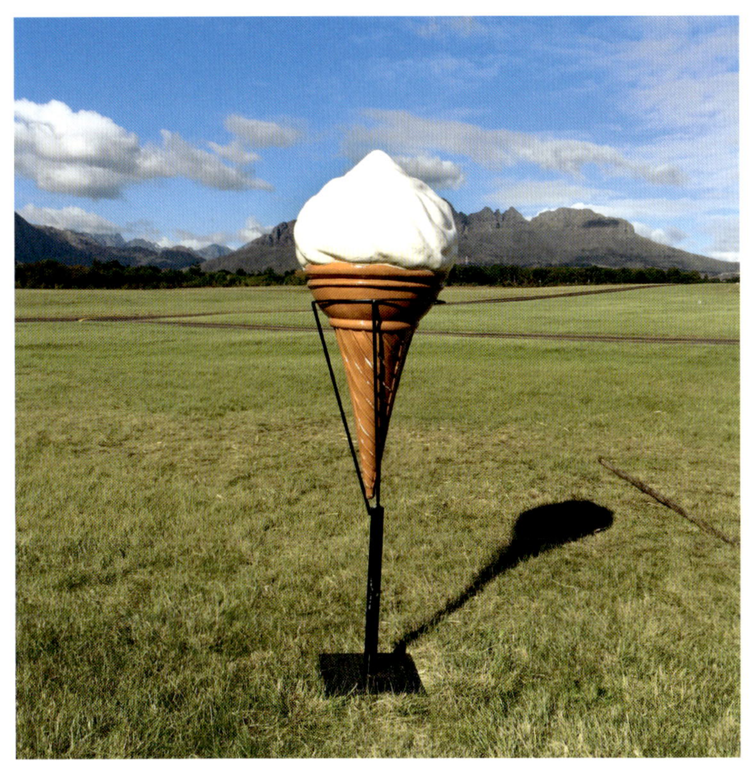

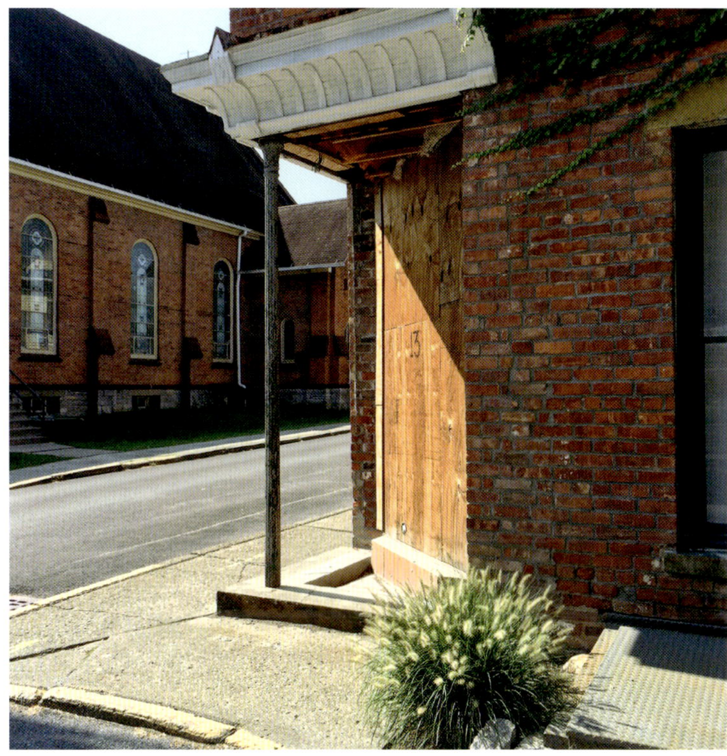

***Stellenbosch Aerodrome, Stellenbosch, South Africa, June 10, 2014.* 2014**

***Hudson, New York, September 7, 2015.* 2015**

121.

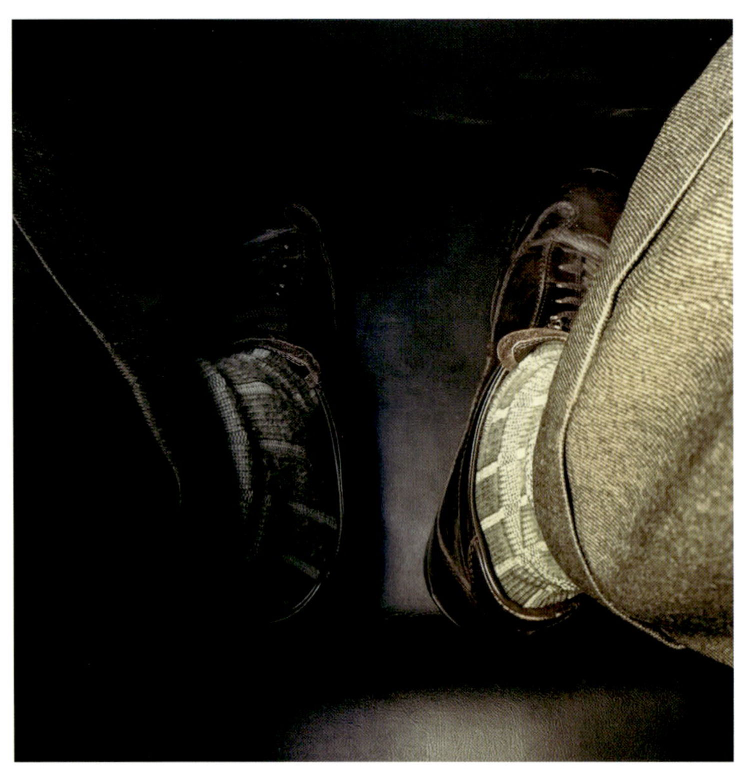

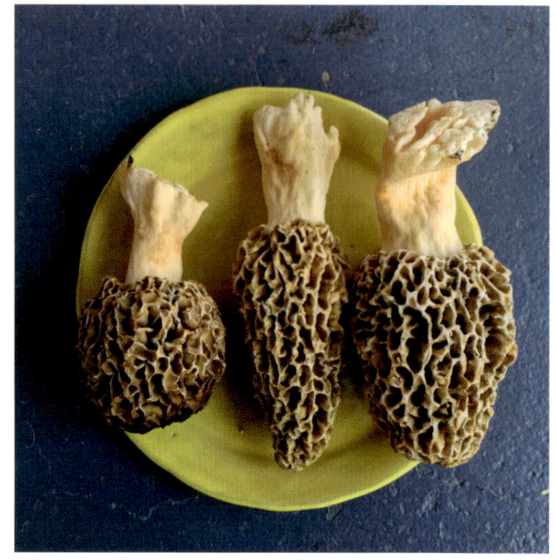

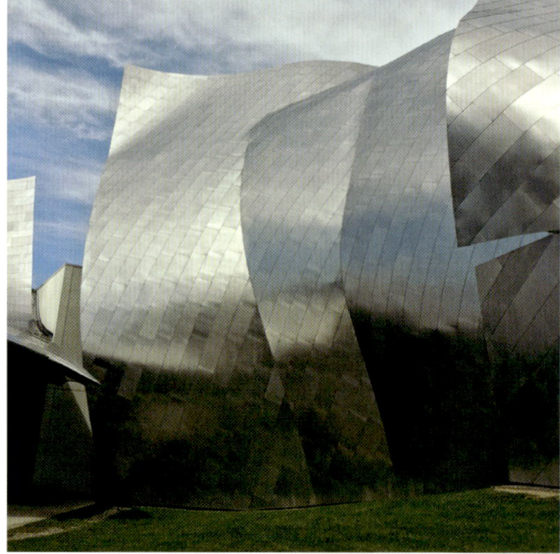

Madison Avenue, New York, New York, December 16, 2015. 2015

Hotel Tivoli, 53 Broadway, Tivoli, New York, May 16, 2016. 2016

Richard B. Fisher Center for the Performing Arts, Bard College, Annandale-on-Hudson, New York, September 3, 2016. 2016

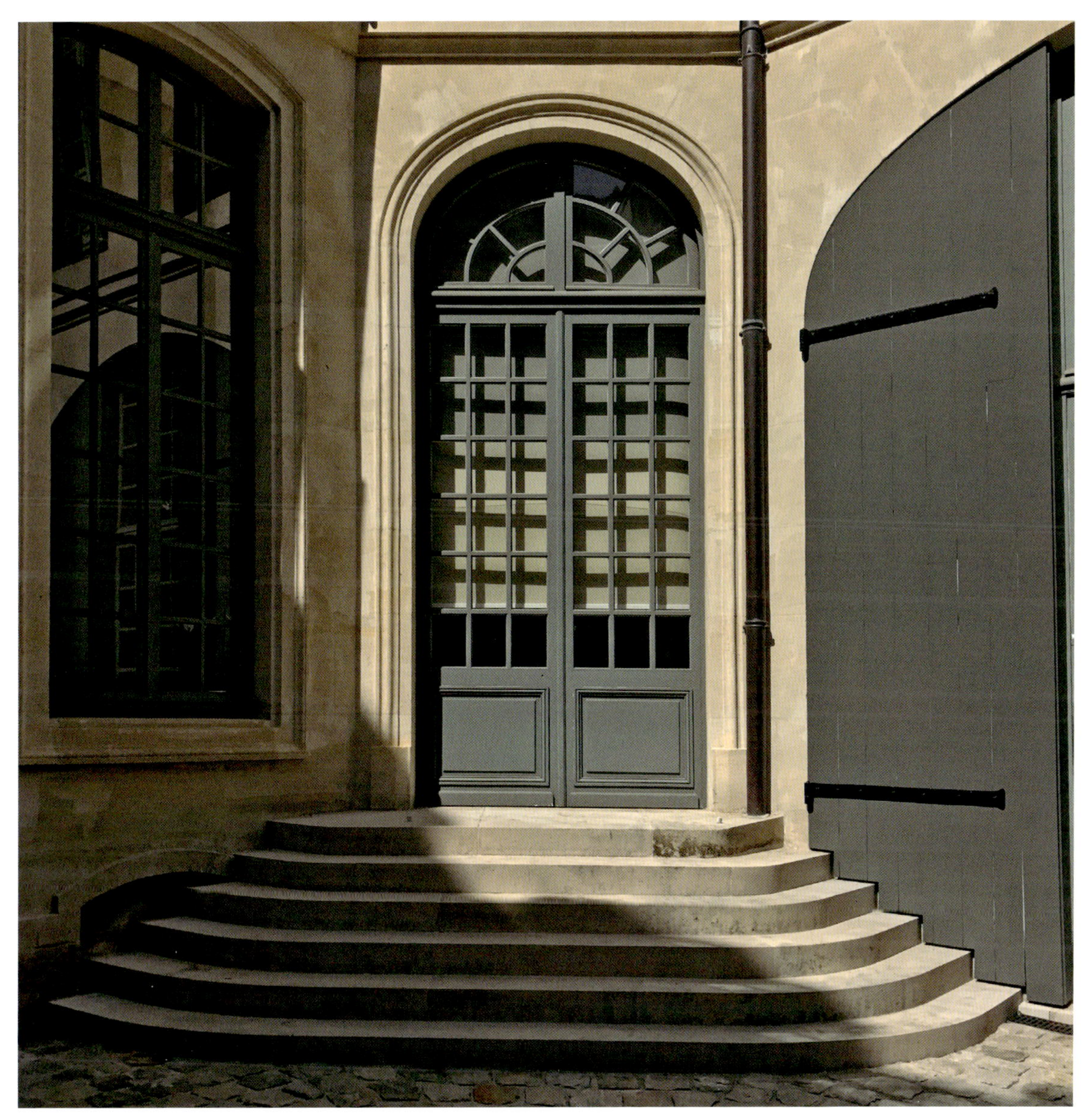

Rue des Capucines, Paris, France, May 31, 2017. 2017

123.

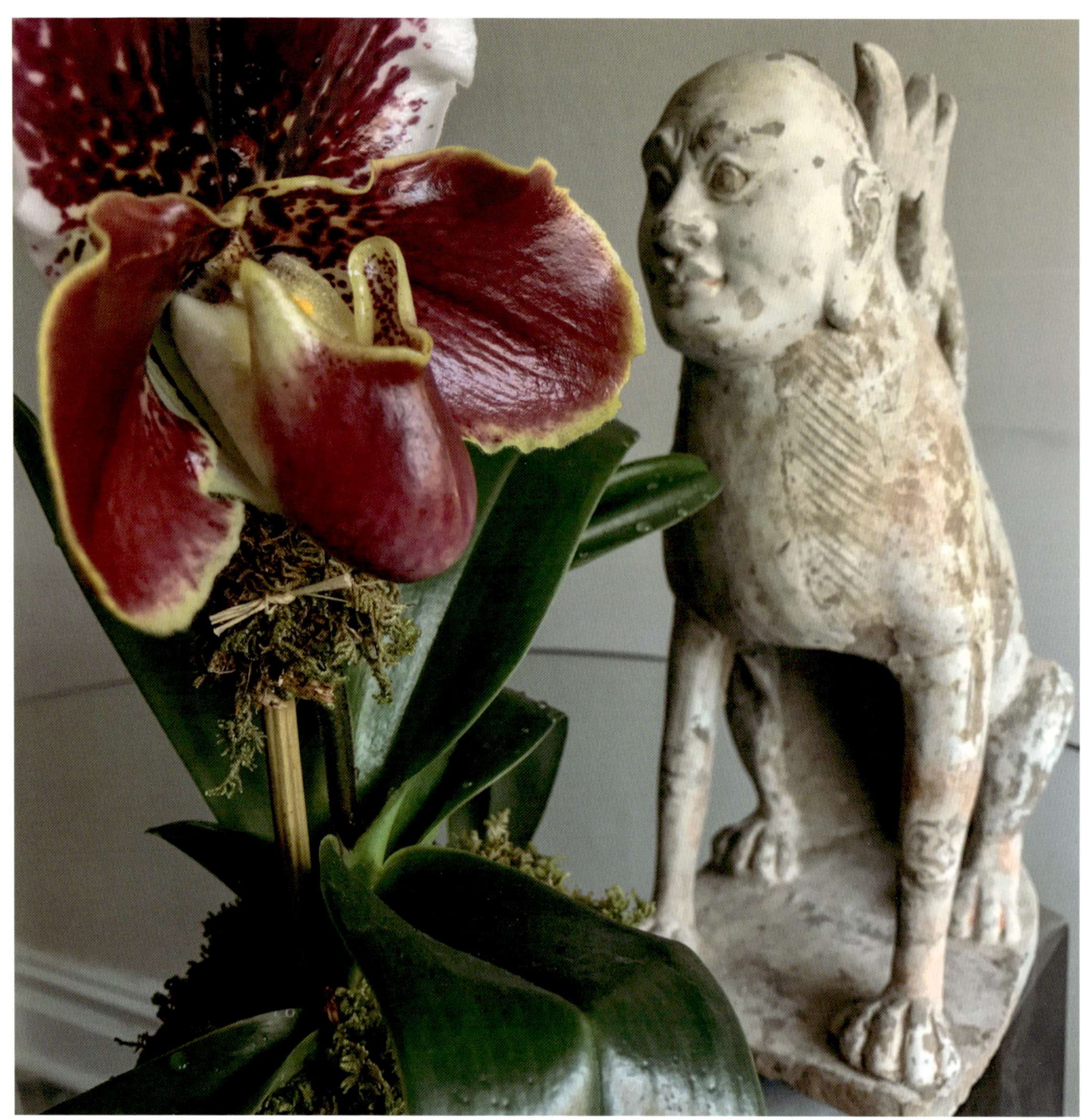

East 94th Street, New York, New York, March 24, 2017. 2017

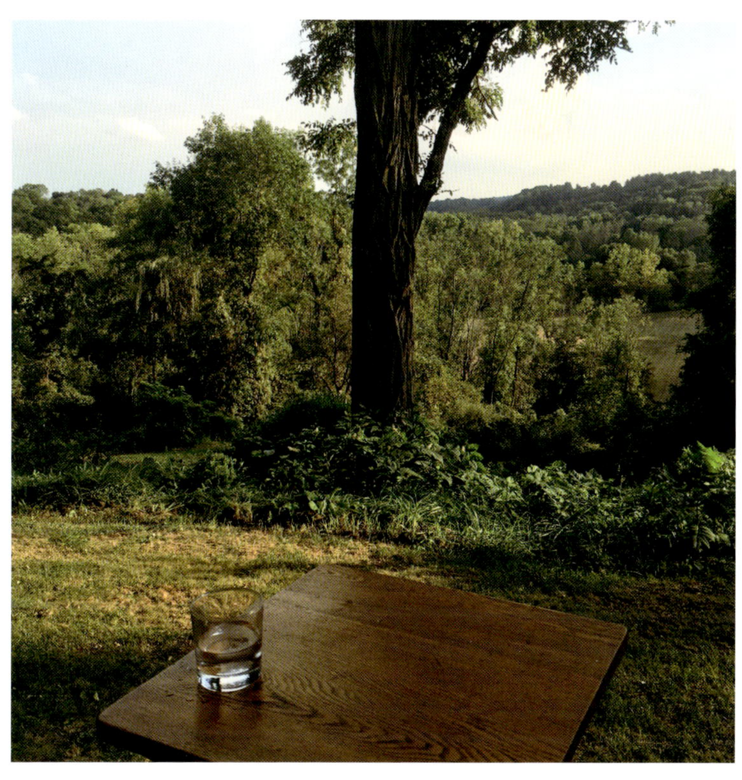

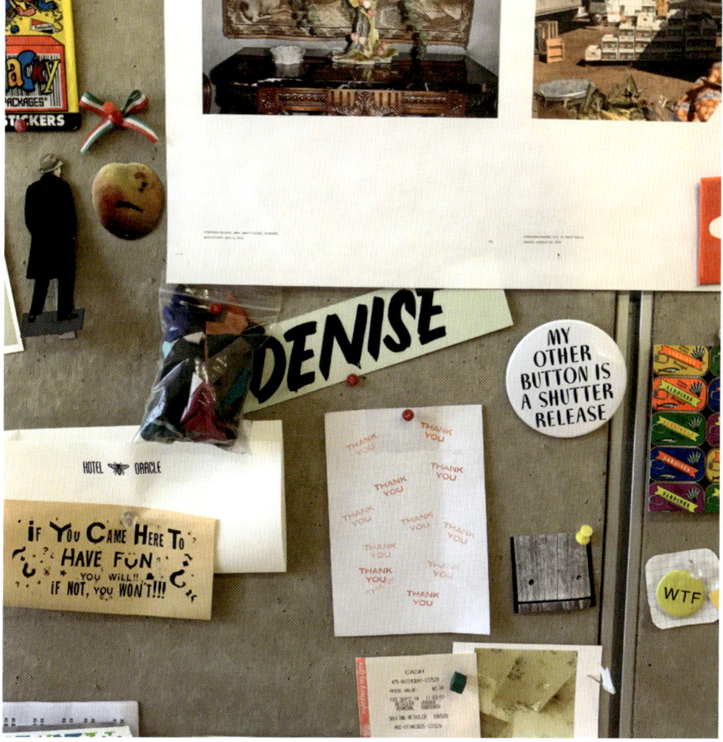

***Wire Road, Germantown, New York, September 10, 2016.* 2016**

***Aperture Foundation, 547 West 27th Street, New York, New York, January 27, 2017.* 2017**

The Institute for General Semantics, Lakeville, Connecticut, June 25, 1970

In keeping with the anti-pictorial urge that informed the avant-gardes of the last century, the "conceptual turn" that placed photography at the heart of contemporary art practice in the late 1960s and 1970s adopted strategies that reduced the image to information, demoted authorship in favor of anonymity, and subsumed individual images into greater protocols and programs. Shore's work *The Institute for General Semantics, Lakeville, Connecticut, June 25, 1970* comprises two sequences of four images each, one above the other. In the upper sequence, the camera moves forward from a view of a large country house and its grounds toward a tree in the center of the image. The closer the camera gets to the tree, the less we are able to see of the house behind; the tree becomes both an obstacle to vision and an object of vision at the same time. The lower sequence comprises four views taken on the same property at ninety degrees to each other. Combined, the camera coverage of the location suggests something systematic, robotic even. Is the couple seated on the lawn the subject of this piece or merely incidental, recorded by the camera's blank indifference? And why is this coldly logical exercise set in the very different aesthetic order of a landscaped estate?

The title of this work may sound like the kind of reflexive intellectual gag typical of the names that Photo-Conceptualists were giving to their work at the time. In fact, the Institute for General Semantics is a real place, set up in Chicago in 1938 by the Polish-American scholar Alfred Korzybski and relocated to Lakeville, Connecticut, in 1946. It is not coincidental for Shore's piece that Korzybski believed that since human knowledge is limited by the structure of our nervous systems and our languages, it can never be fully objective. By extension, neither people nor things nor representations can be reduced to the names we give them.

If Conceptual art often feels like a dry lesson—albeit humorous at times—then artists are their own first pupils, the first to learn and laugh. Looking back chronologically at Shore's career, we can discern what he may have learned from his early Conceptual works such as this one. While he has never returned to quite such rigid systems, there is an underlying recognition in all of his work that photography is an analytical medium as much as an aesthetic one. There is always a tension between the photograph as artwork and as document; between choice and automatism; between intention and chance; between system and intuition; between the individual image and its place in a body of work; and between what can be known consciously and what can only be felt unconsciously. (David Campany)

See also: *Conceptual Sequences*

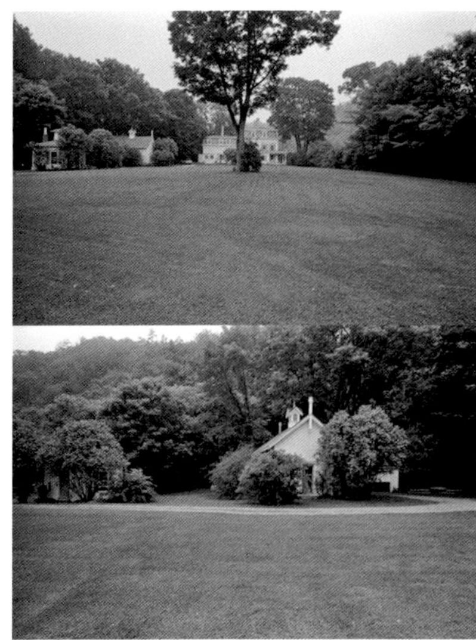
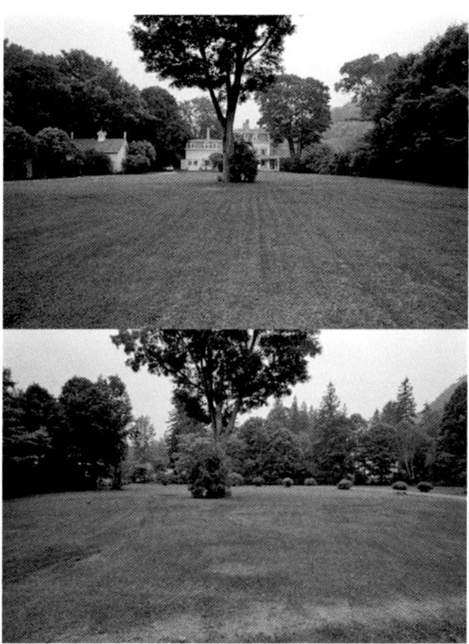
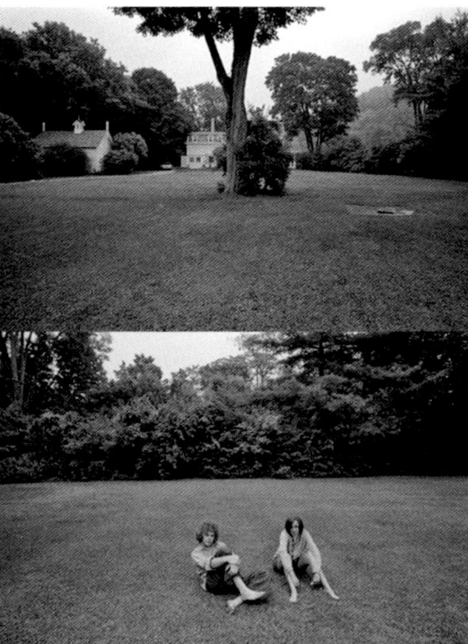
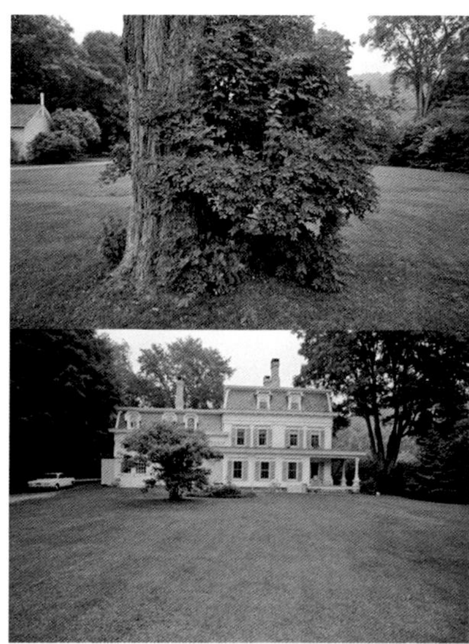

The Institute for General Semantics, Lakeville, Connecticut, June 25, 1970. **1970**

Israel and the West Bank

In 2009 Shore was invited by the French-Israeli photographer Frédéric Brenner to work in Israel and the West Bank, in the company of ten other photographers.[1] The documentary project, entitled *This Place*, was intended to show, through the lenses of foreign photographers, the area in all its diversity and contradictions.[2] Between September of 2009 and the spring of 2011, Shore went to Israel and the West Bank five times, photographing throughout the entire territory, from north to south, or *From Galilee to the Negev*, as he titled the book he published in 2014.[3]

While Shore is not only accustomed to but also very fond of his position as an outsider, a status he deliberately seeks out, *This Place* represented a particular challenge because of its complexity. For the first time, Shore was confronted with an especially complicated political situation in a country with which he was not entirely familiar, even though he had photographed it in the past: on the excavation sites of Ashkelon and Hatzor in 1996, and at various locations in 2008, producing three print-on-demand books on the subject, one in Hebron and two in the Negev Desert. Many of the images for *This Place* would also be used in the 2014 publication, which was presented as an overview of the various phases of Shore's work in Israel and the West Bank over a period of twenty years, eschewing the visual coherence of most of his earlier projects.

Aiming for completeness, Shore took the commission almost literally, attempting—without preconceived notions and within the limits inherent in photography—to create a description of "this place," a land subject to a variety of claims and passions. As indicated by the title and structure of *From Galilee to the Negev*, with its chapters organized geographically, it was a topographical exploration that guided the project; symbolically, the first color image in the book is of a finger pointing to a map of the region (page 133). We see here the desert of Negev; the progressive and modern city of Tel Aviv; the border with Gaza as seen from the Israeli side; Jerusalem, where religion is omnipresent; and the West Bank, including Ramallah and Hebron, where conflict is physically inscribed in the city. In uncharacteristic fashion for a project of this importance, Shore alternated between images taken on the spot and more contemplative landscapes. The former are made with a digital camera, a tool with which Shore could finally combine the precision of a view camera (which allows large prints) and the mobility of a handheld camera (which allows more vertical formats). With the 8-by-10, both inhabited territories and wild lands are captured with gravity and even lyricism.

From Galilee to the Negev, whose large format displays the landscapes to their best advantage, was also a reflection on history, a new dimension for Shore that he would subsequently pursue in his Ukrainian project. By opening and closing on black-and-white images with archaeological content that evoke the history of the country as well as its religious background, the project mixes various temporalities—which are echoed by the diversity of the images—and brings together the short term of humans and events, and the long term of the earth and landscapes. (Quentin Bajac)

See also: *Archaeology*; *Landscape*; *Nabī Musa*; *Travel*; *Ukraine*

1. In addition to Shore and Brenner, the commission involved Wendy Ewald, Martin Kollar, Josef Koudelka, Jungjin Lee, Gilles Peress, Fazal Sheikh, Rosalind Fox Solomon, Thomas Struth, Jeff Wall, and Nick Waplington.
2. See the project's website, www.this-place.org.
3. Stephen Shore, *From Galilee to the Negev* (London and New York: Phaidon Press, 2014).

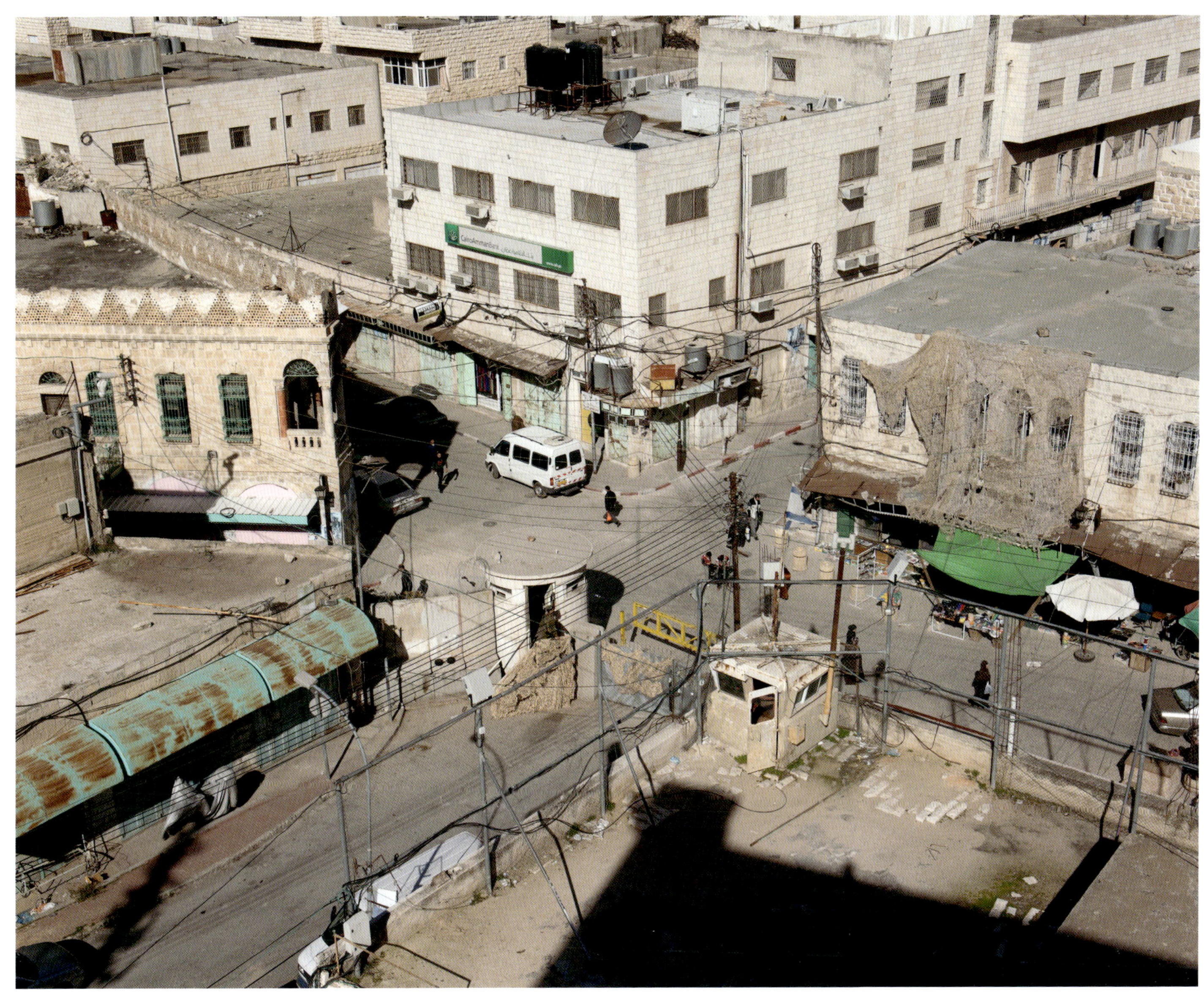

Hebron, West Bank, January 11, 2010. **2010**

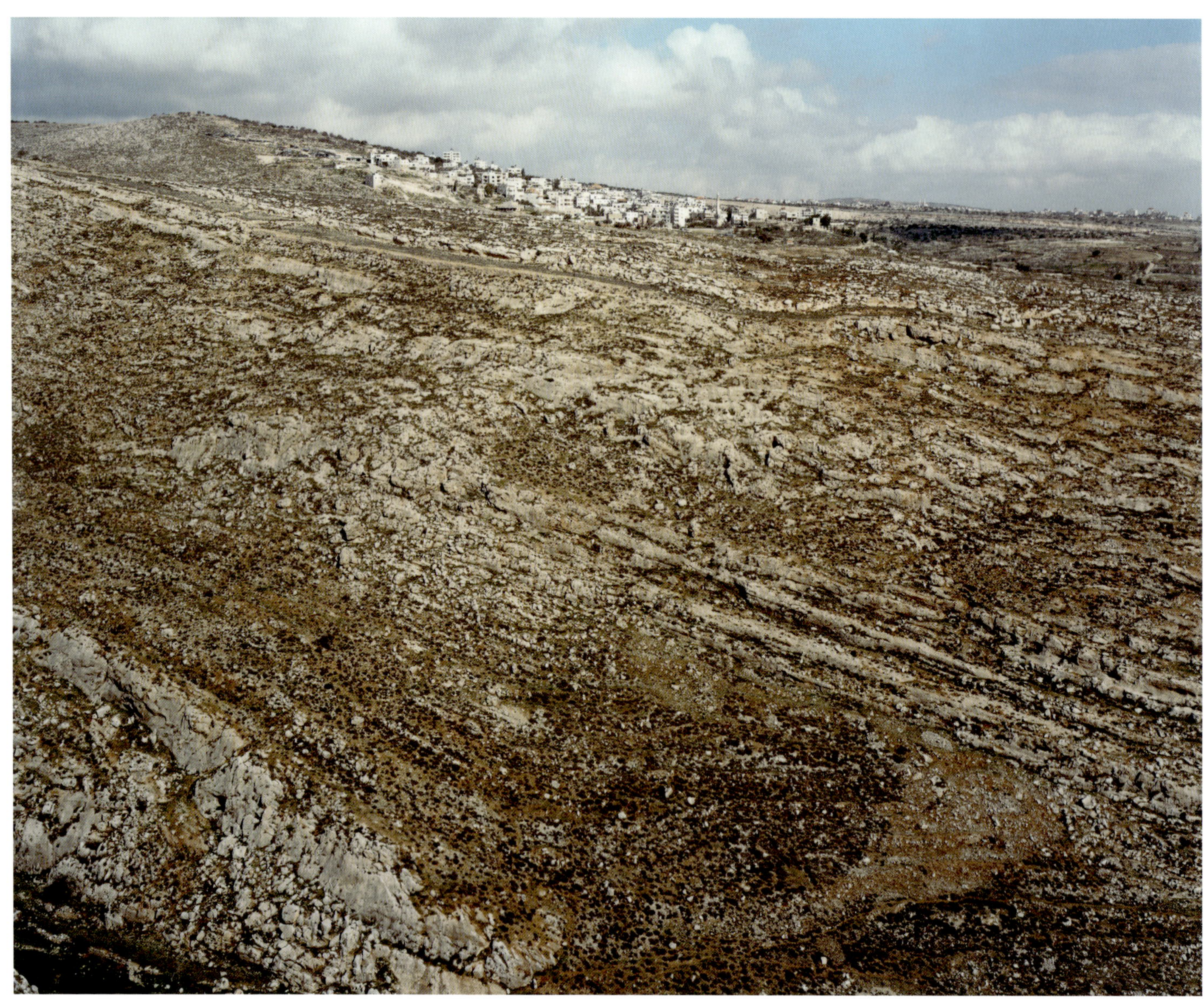

Beitin, West Bank, January 13, 2010. 2010

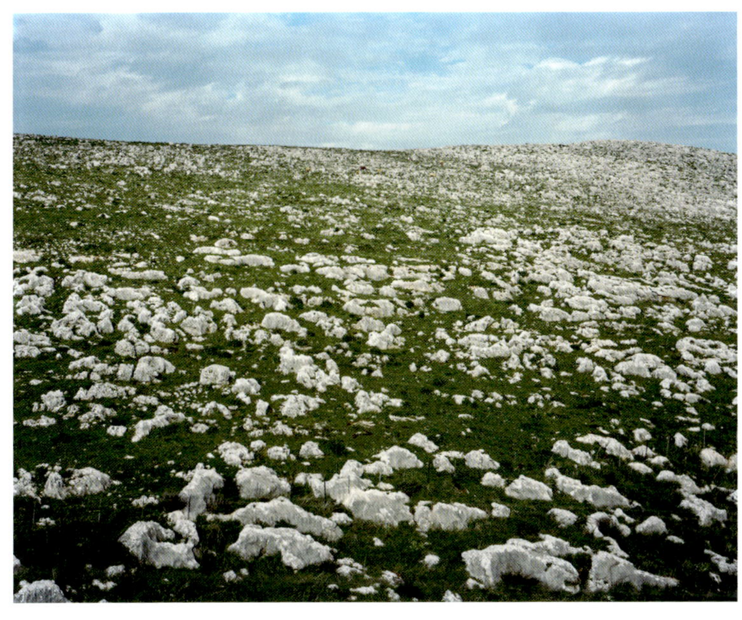

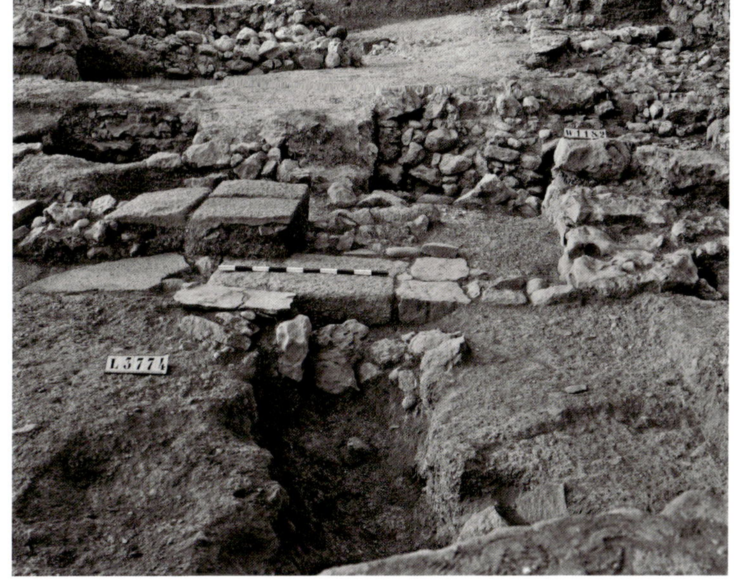

South of Zefat, Israel, January 14, 2010. 2010

Hatzor, Israel, 1996. 1996

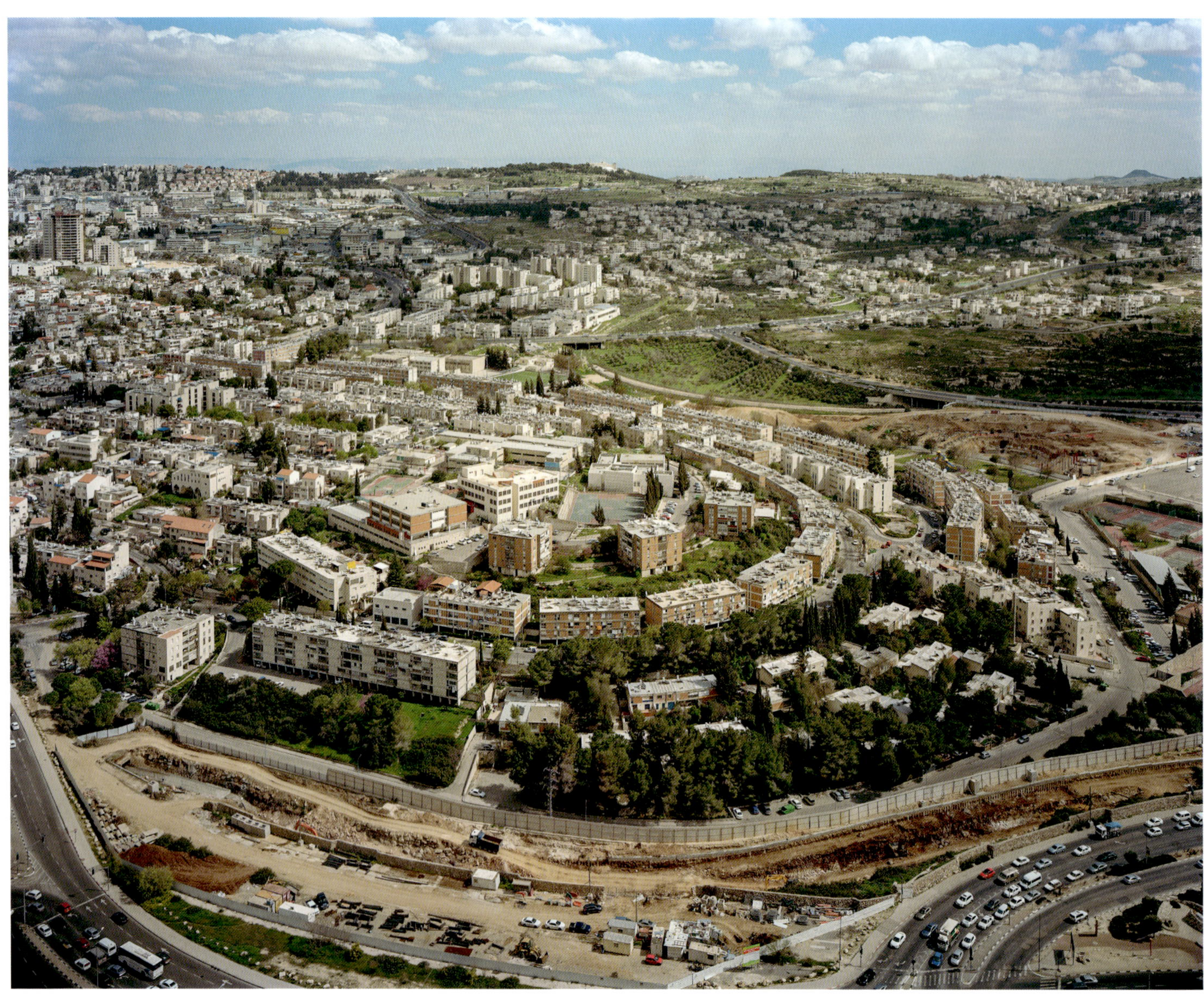

Beit Safāfā, Jerusalem, Israel, March 22, 2011. 2011

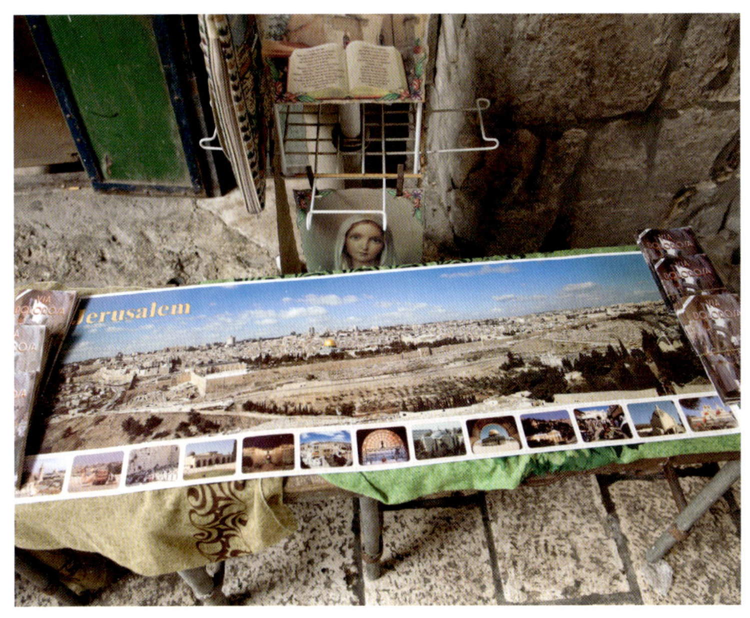

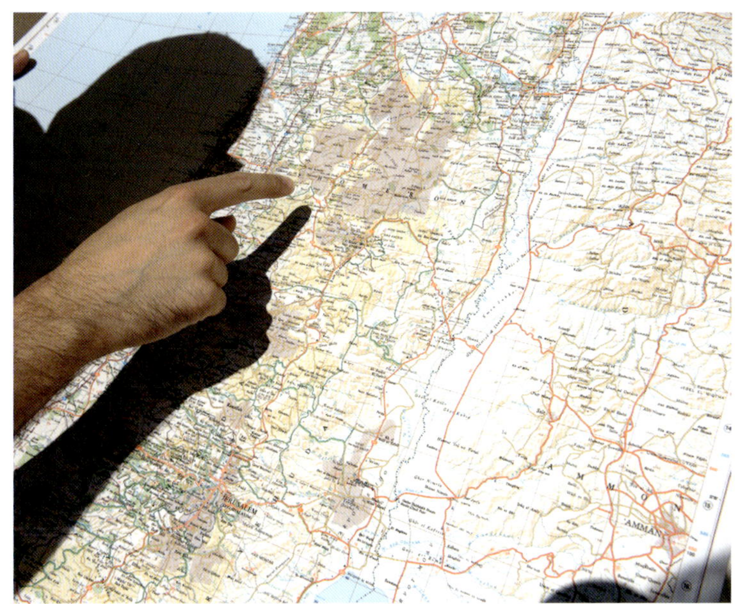

***Jerusalem, Israel, January 1, 2010*. 2010**

***Sderot, Israel, September 14, 2009*. 2009**

Jigsaw Puzzle: Lookout Hotel, Ogunquit, Maine, 7/16/74

Throughout the medium's history, photographs have been produced that function as metaphors for what it is to make an image with a camera. Sometimes the gesture is conscious and explicit, such as pointing the camera at a mirror to take a self-portrait; at other times, it is less so.

Faced with the experience of looking at a picture that appears to be about picturing, it can be instructive (and fun) to try to put the looking into words. In July 1974 Shore tilted his 8-by-10 camera downward at a partially completed jigsaw puzzle on a marigold table cover laid over a small, square table surrounded by chairs in a carpeted interior (page 61). A frame within a frame within a frame. The edge of Shore's picture clips all four corners of the table to different degrees. It also clips one corner of the outer edge of the puzzle. We can make out that the puzzle bears a photographic image of buildings below a blue sky. Whoever has been working on the jigsaw has placed most of the sky pieces within the border. Did Shore build his picture from the edges inward, the way the jigsaw is being approached?

While the photograph is crystal clear, the viewer's eyes are liable to dance across its complex surface, looking for points to hold on to. However, the camera's fixed and monocular lens has rendered the details confusing. The haphazard pattern of the puzzle pieces is scrambled by the interlocking pattern of the table cover. The swirling designs on the chairs and carpet offer no stability either. So, the eyes detach from the minutiae to contemplate the unity of the composition as a whole. But not for long: they will soon be drawn back into a puzzle that will remain bewildering and unfinished forever.

Shore's large-format color negatives contain more detail than you could ever desire, and as a rule he keeps his prints to a scale that hides the fine grains that are the foundation of the photographic illusion. It is the seamlessness of the illusion that allows us to feel we are confronting the jigsaw puzzle as Shore encountered it with his camera, there and then.

Nearly three decades later, Shore made this picture the subject of one of his print-on-demand books. Working from a digital scan of the original negative, he reduced the resolution of the image to 300 dpi (dots per inch). The book begins with an enlarged detail of this file. We cannot see grain, but we can see digital pixels, which are small enough for us to make out a few pieces of the puzzle, but not so small as to reveal the images they bear. Over subsequent pages, the whole of the composition comes into view, the pixels shrinking each time until the illusion is restored.

When the original photograph was made, digital photography and print-on-demand books were the stuff of science fiction. Shore has embraced these new image technologies in his own way, knowing that they do not replace older ones but rather reimagine them.

If the original is a photograph about photography, the book becomes a photograph about the changing technological base of the medium and how it is affecting our viewing habits. But no photograph can be about photography only. This particular one still manages to transport us back to that quiet afternoon in Ogunquit, Maine, in 1974, and to that perfectly named hotel: The Lookout. (David Campany)

See also: *Print-on-Demand Books*; *Uncommon Places*

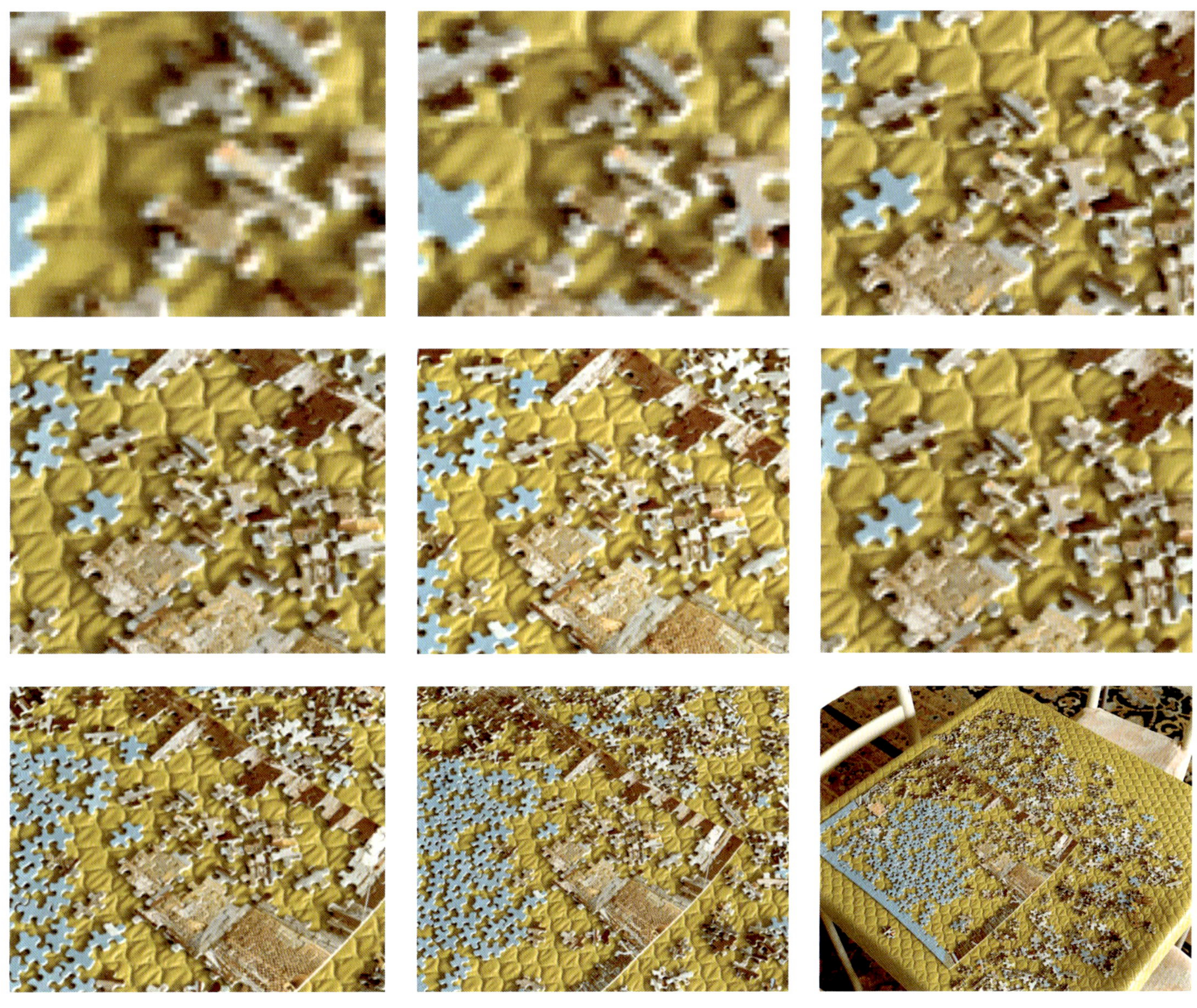

***Jigsaw Puzzle: Lookout Hotel, Ogunquit, Maine, 7/16/74.* 2003**

Landscape

Shore's first American landscapes appeared during a period of accelerated change in the national landscape, especially in areas of suburban sprawl, and a corresponding debate on the adverse effects—both ecological and aesthetic—of this growth on the environment. In 1971, for instance, an editorial in *Life* magazine lamented that "too much of the American landscape has been 'vandalized' with sprawling suburbs, billboard alleys, overhead wires, [and] porcelain gasoline stations hogging all four corners of an intersection."[1] This list seems to point out, several years in advance, some of the recurring motifs of the landscapes in Shore's *Uncommon Places*. It is no surprise, then, that the series was often interpreted at the time in light of this debate, a perception that would be encouraged by the exhibition *New Topographics: Photographs of a Man-Altered Landscape* (1975), which elicited commentary on the new generation of photographers who were focusing on the banal, human-made American landscape.[2] In a review of the exhibition, a critic in *Artweek* called for the creation of a neologism to replace *landscape* when referring to these photographs: "it is perhaps better to describe these as land-shapes or, better still, shaped-land photographs. These photographs differ from what we have come to think of as the traditional twentieth-century approach to landscape photography as represented by Vroman, Adams or Weston."[3]

In Shore's images, as in the work of most of the photographers in *New Topographics*, the landscape has been altered by humans, but they are usually absent, existing only through the traces they have left behind. The absence can also be read in symbolic terms: this landscape transformed by humans could at the same time be rendered inhospitable to them. Shore, however, was less critical of the human effect on the landscape than some of his contemporaries were. Instead, as a journalist at the time asserted, "the transformations he brings about by his affectionate vision seem related to Venturi and Scott Brown's acceptance of 'what is' as the proper starting-point for the redemption of the American scene."[4] Shore's nonjudgmental approach to the ordinary landscape of deep America seems to imply his acceptance of the changes affecting the natural environment. Yet a close look at the hundreds of pictures Shore took during the period of *Uncommon Places* shows that his view of the American landscape is extremely varied and at times contradictory. We find here vestiges of prewar America but also representations of modernity's shining places, small provincial towns as well as metropolises, and buildings both remarkable and banal.

Starting in the late 1970s, Shore gradually abandoned urban and suburban areas and turned to the natural landscape, a subject he would concentrate on almost exclusively during the next decade. The landscapes of Montana (1981–83), where he settled with his wife in 1980, Texas (1983–88), and finally Scotland (1988) seem, in their vastness and the almost complete absence of human traces, to correspond to a classic, somewhat outdated vision of landscape. But far from expressing a simple search for the local picturesque, these are among the most complex of Shore's images. At the heart of his landscape production are pictures that correspond closely to his definition of the photographic shot as a "problem to solve" rather than an image to "compose."[5] Without all the components that allowed him to construct a scene in the urban landscapes of the 1970s—especially the vertical elements, from street lamps to telephone poles—how could a space be structured with perspective to create scale and depth? To make the exercise even more challenging, Shore "chose open, almost uninflected scenes in which to experiment with space."[6] They are landscapes, certainly, but more precisely they are studies of space, guided not by a quest for the picturesque but by an experimental spirit.

In 1990 Shore explained, regarding his images of the Yucatán: "In my recent work, I've been going from completely natural—and by that I mean no sign of the hand of man—landscapes to more man-influenced landscapes."[7] In fact, by the mid-1980s, under the auspices of a commission from the Wallace Foundation, Shore had started a series on the Hudson Valley (where he had moved in 1982), which for him was a chance to revisit the human presence in the landscape. Shore's Hudson Valley is obviously no longer the wild promised land of the Luminist painters but a tamed one, worked and cultivated by humans for habitat, agriculture, and eventually tourism. Here the land is neither excessively domesticated nor excessively brutalized, but exists in an in-between state. Shore's approach to territory is reflected in his 1993 landscapes of the Luzzara region in Italy, some of which, despite being shot in black

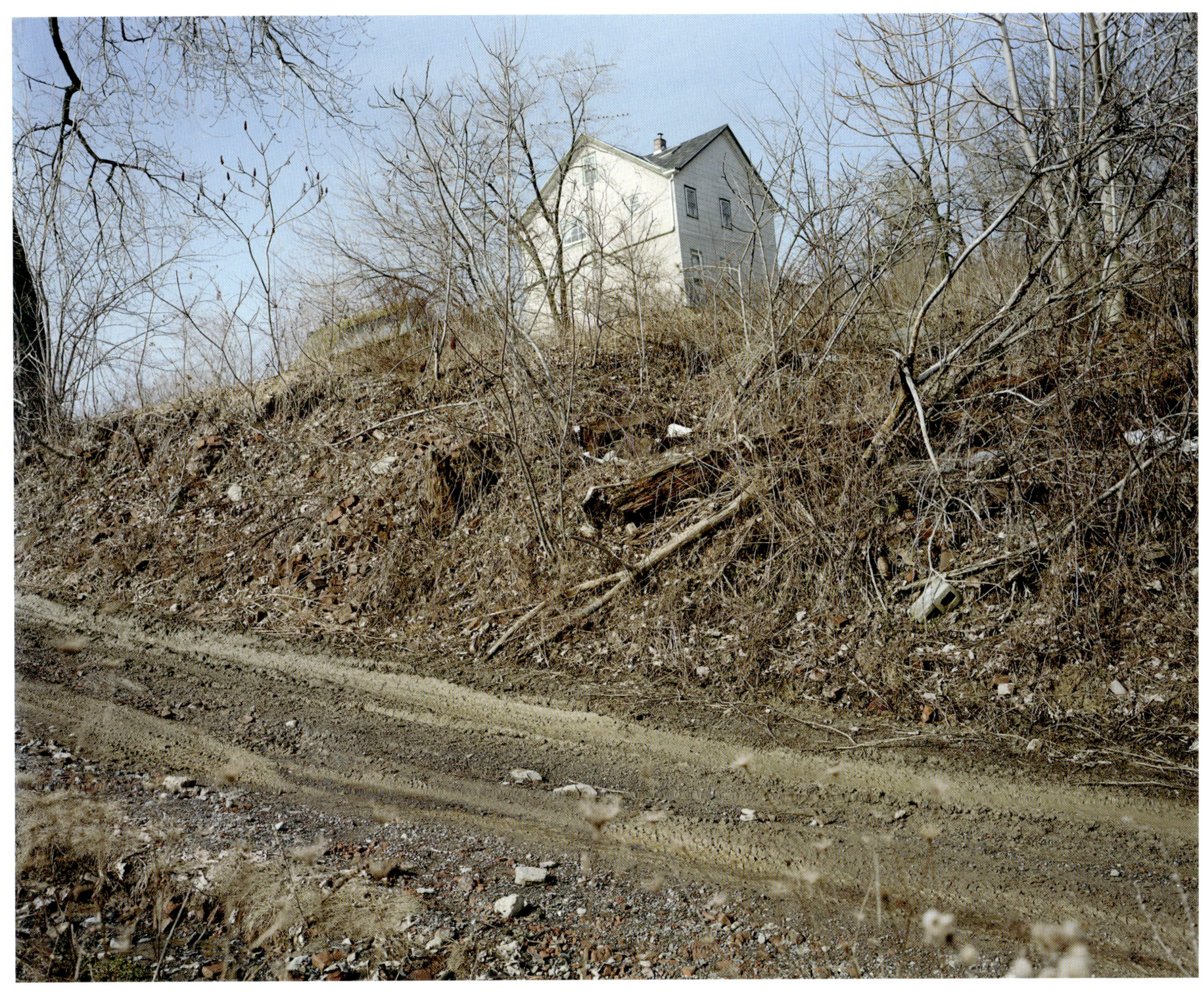

Ulster County, New York, 1984. 1984

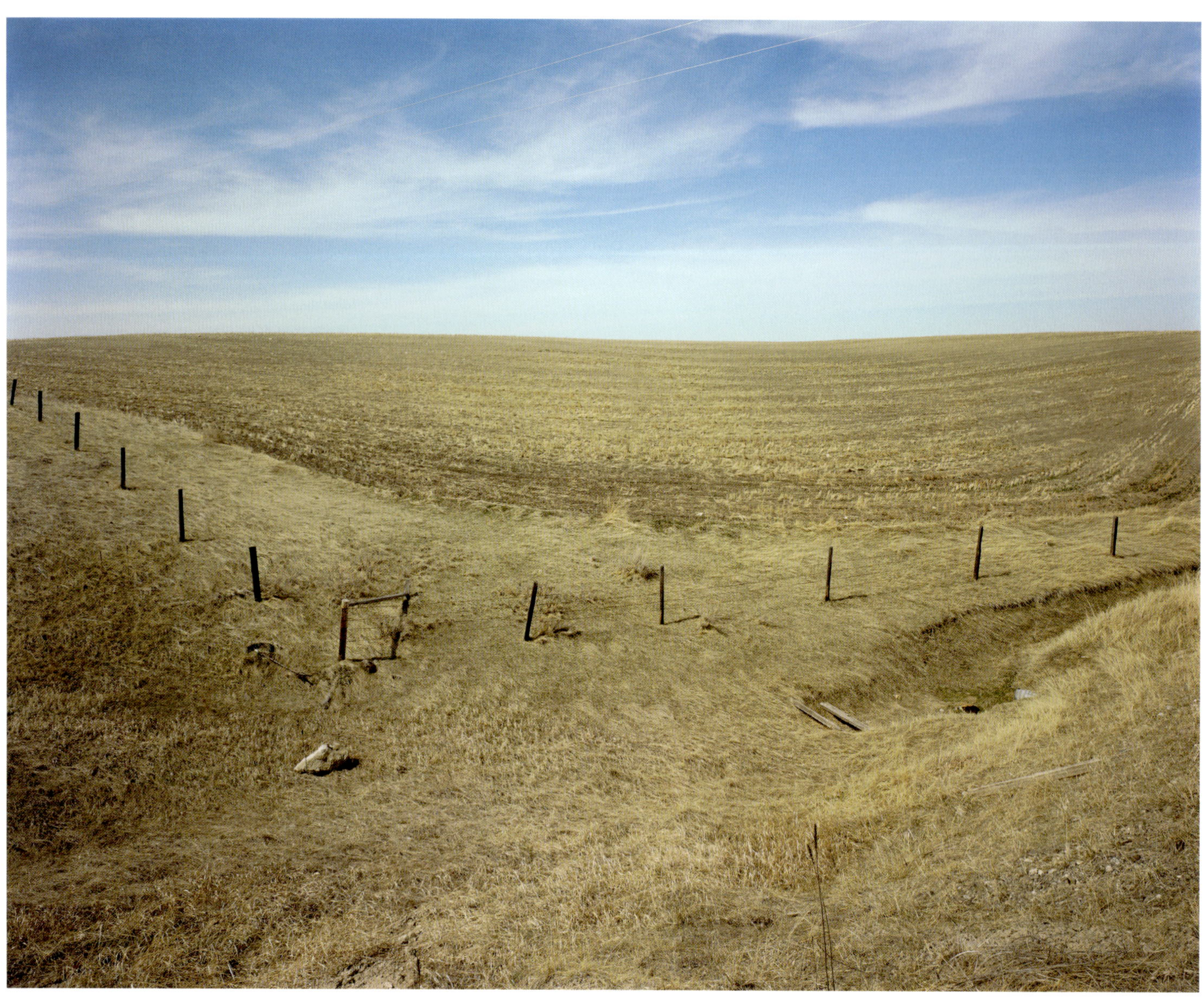

Gallatin County, Montana, April 18, 1981. 1981

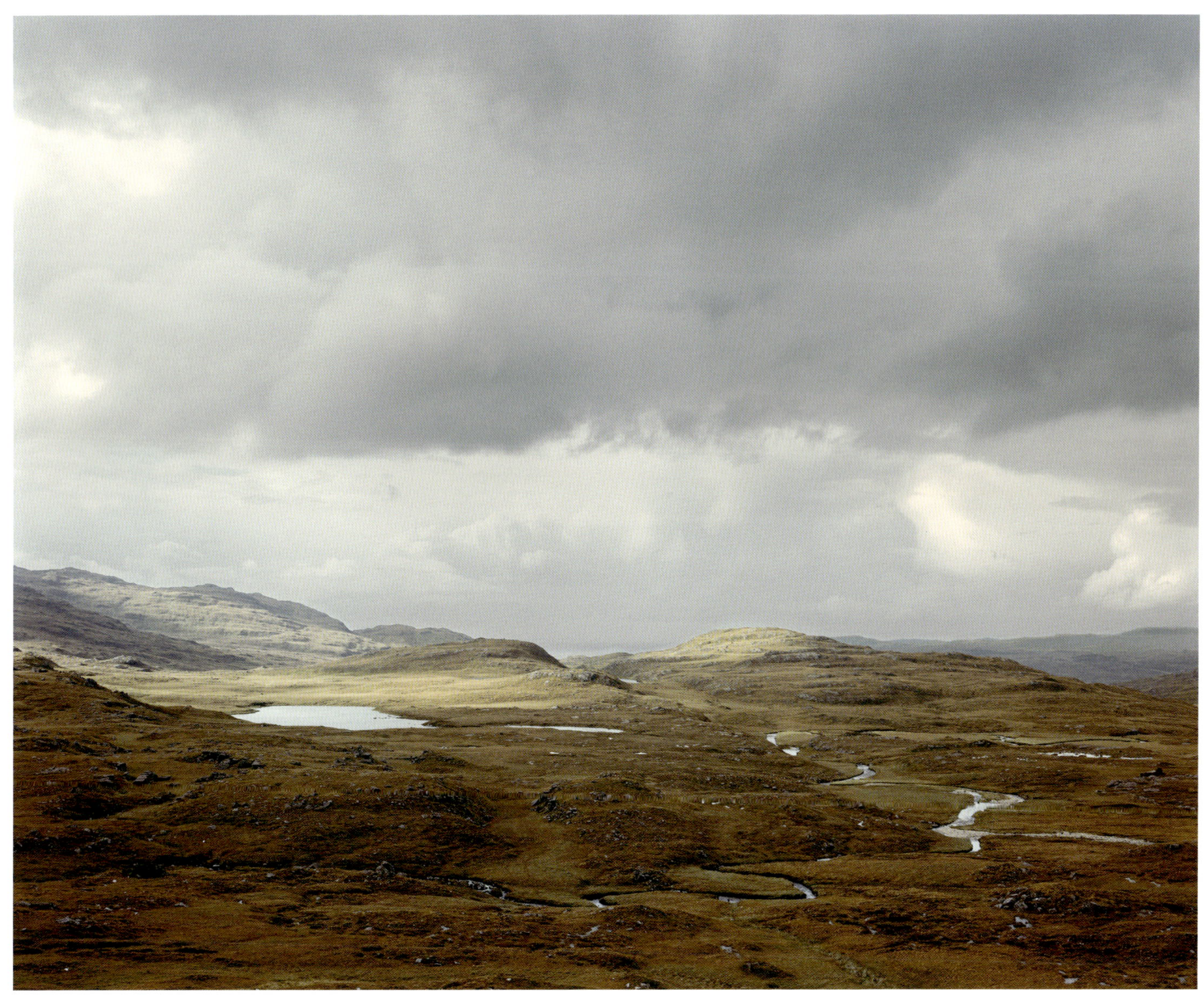

County of Sutherland, Scotland, 1988. **1988**

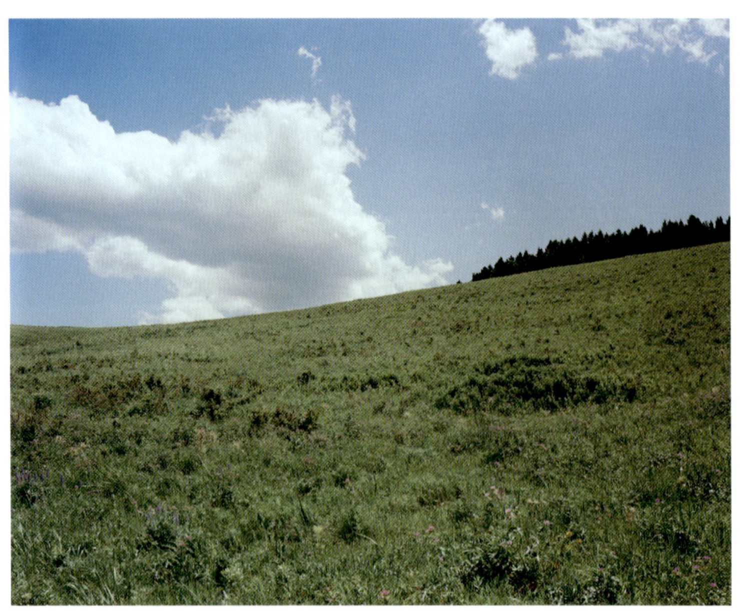

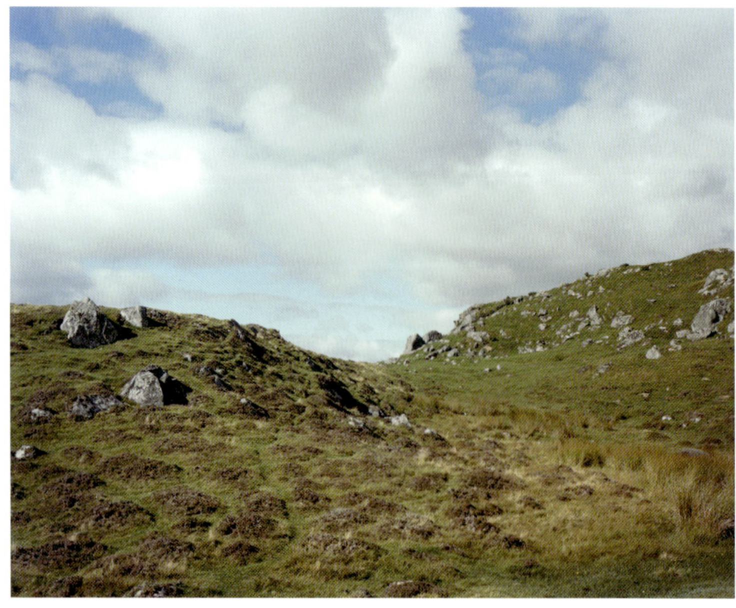

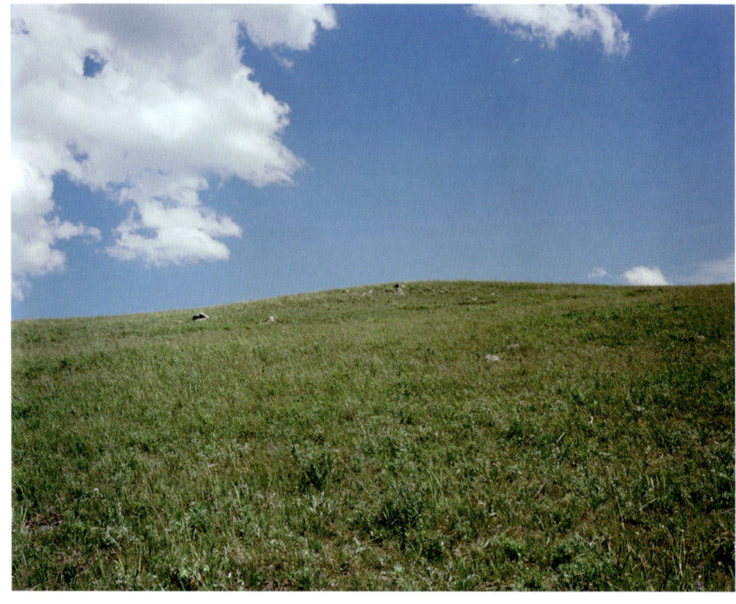

***Gallatin County, Montana, August 2, 1983.* 1983**

***County of Sutherland, Scotland, 1988.* 1988**

***Gallatin County, Montana, August 2, 1983.* 1983**

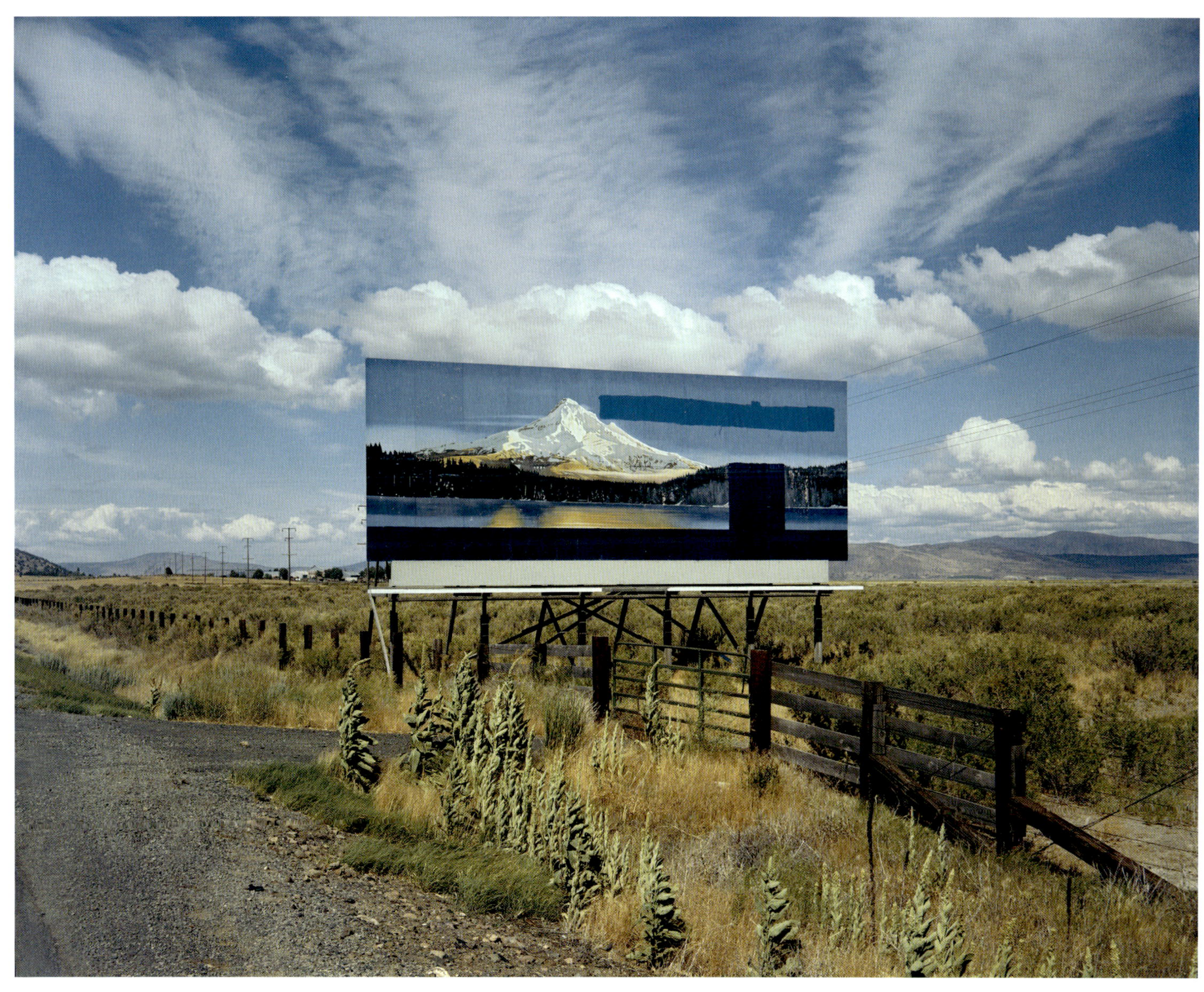

U.S. 97, South of Klamath Falls, Oregon, July 21, 1973. **1973**

141.

and white, echo the color photographs of the Hudson Valley, showing agricultural plains, cultivated forests, and signs of a relatively harmonious relationship of people to their natural surroundings, especially the river.

Since the 1990s, natural and human-altered landscapes have coexisted in Shore's work, as evidenced by his photographs of Israel and the West Bank and of Ukraine. In these major recent series, Shore's approach is almost lyrical, both in his Ukrainian landscapes, marked by vibrant greens, and those in Israel, which communicate a sense of immensity. Both projects express an almost mystical relationship with place, a quality that was already present in Shore's natural landscapes of the 1980s, where he was seeking not just representation, he said, but "physical sensations and shifts in physical, psychological or emotional states."[8] This quality shines through even more clearly in the landscapes he made with an 8-by-10 camera in Israel and the West Bank: "Without sounding too mystical about it," he said, "when I'm photographing the landscape in the American West, I position myself where I feel lines of energy emerge in the land. What I found in Israel and the West Bank is that there was a crazy web of energies."[9] (Quentin Bajac)

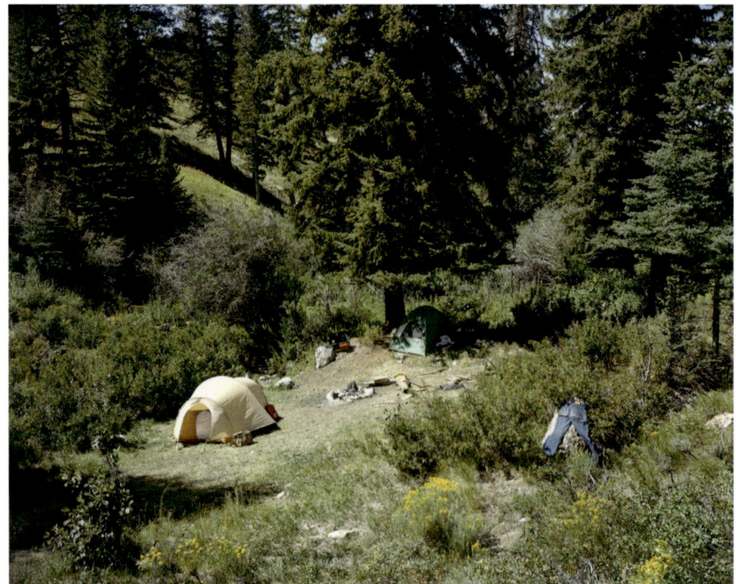

See also: *Gallatin County*; *Gardens*; *Israel and the West Bank*; *Merced River*; *Nabī Musa*; *Ukraine*; *Uncommon Places*

1. "Erasing Grown-Up Vandalism," *Life*, April 9, 1971, 34.
2. Brett Salvesen and Alison Nordström, eds., *New Topographics: Robert Adams, Lewis Baltz, Bernd and Hilla Becher, Joe Deal, Frank Gohlke, Nicholas Nixon, John Schott, Stephen Shore, Henry Wessel, Jr.* (Tucson: Center for Creative Photography, University of Arizona; Rochester, N.Y.: George Eastman House; Göttingen: Steidl, 2009).
3. Robert W. Woolard, "Man-Shaped Landscapes," *Artweek*, March 27, 1976, 12.
4. Carter Ratcliff, "Route 66 Revisited: The New Landscape Photography," *Art in America* 64, no. 1 (January/February 1976): 90.
5. "One thing is that I take pictures to solve problems, visual problems, and the picture is the byproduct of that." Quoted in Steve Lafreniere, "Stephen Shore," *Vice*: The Photo Issue, 2009, 173.
6. Christopher Brayshaw, "An Interview with Stephen Shore," *Doppelganger*, no. 5 (March 2006): http://www.doppelgangermagazine.com/march/chris_brayshaw_march.html.
7. Ellen Handy, "The Curvature of the Earth and the Smell of the Air: Photographs from the Yucatán by Stephen Shore," *Annandale* (Bard College), Spring 1990, 40.
8. Ibid., 49.
9. "Stephen Shore in Conversation with Charlotte Cotton," *This Place*, Summer 2014, http://www.this-place.org/photographers/stephen-shore/.

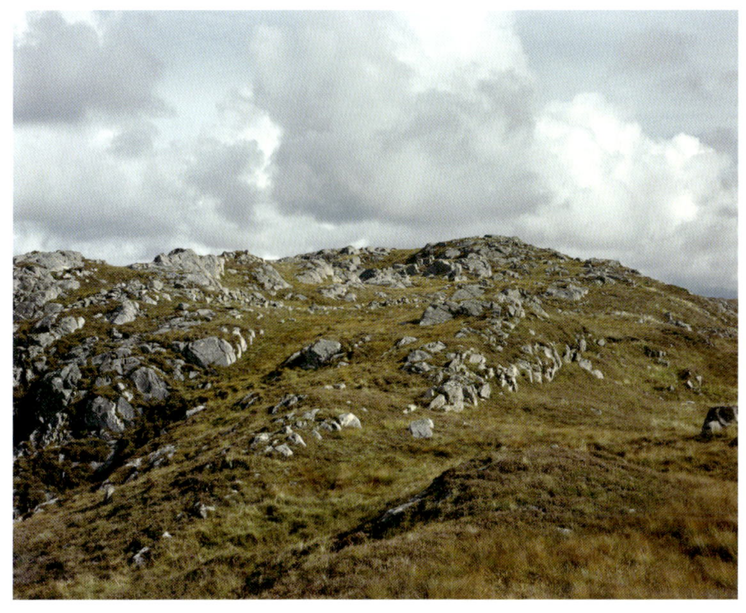

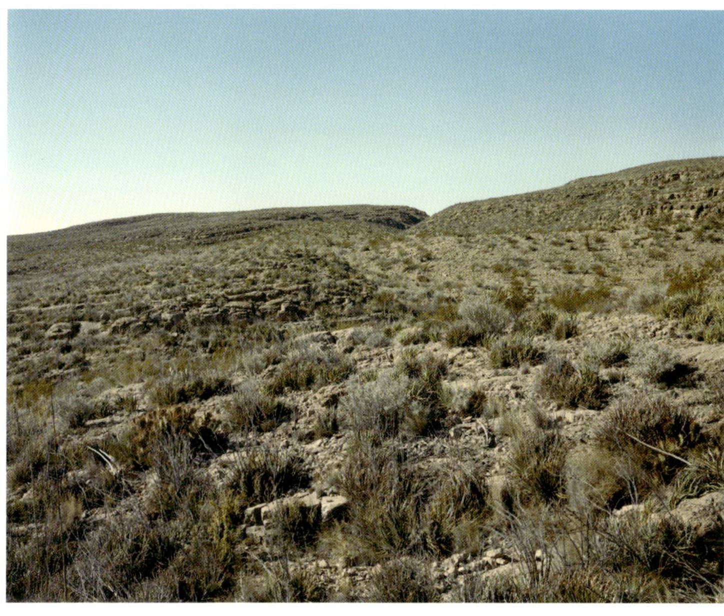

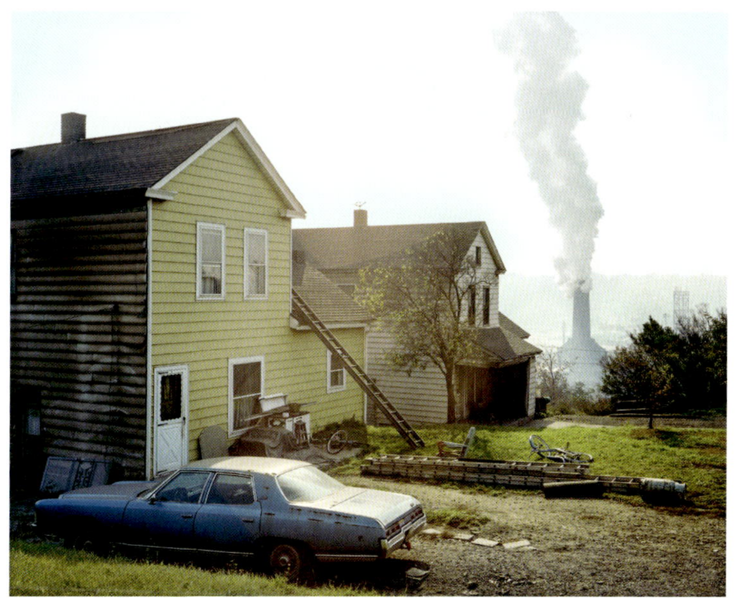

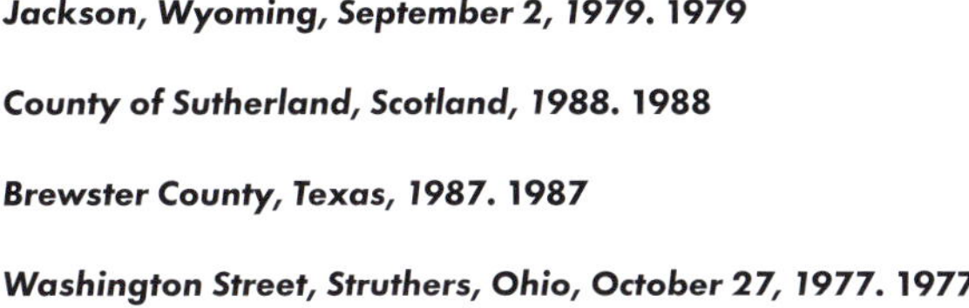

Jackson, Wyoming, September 2, 1979. 1979

County of Sutherland, Scotland, 1988. 1988

Brewster County, Texas, 1987. 1987

Washington Street, Struthers, Ohio, October 27, 1977. 1977

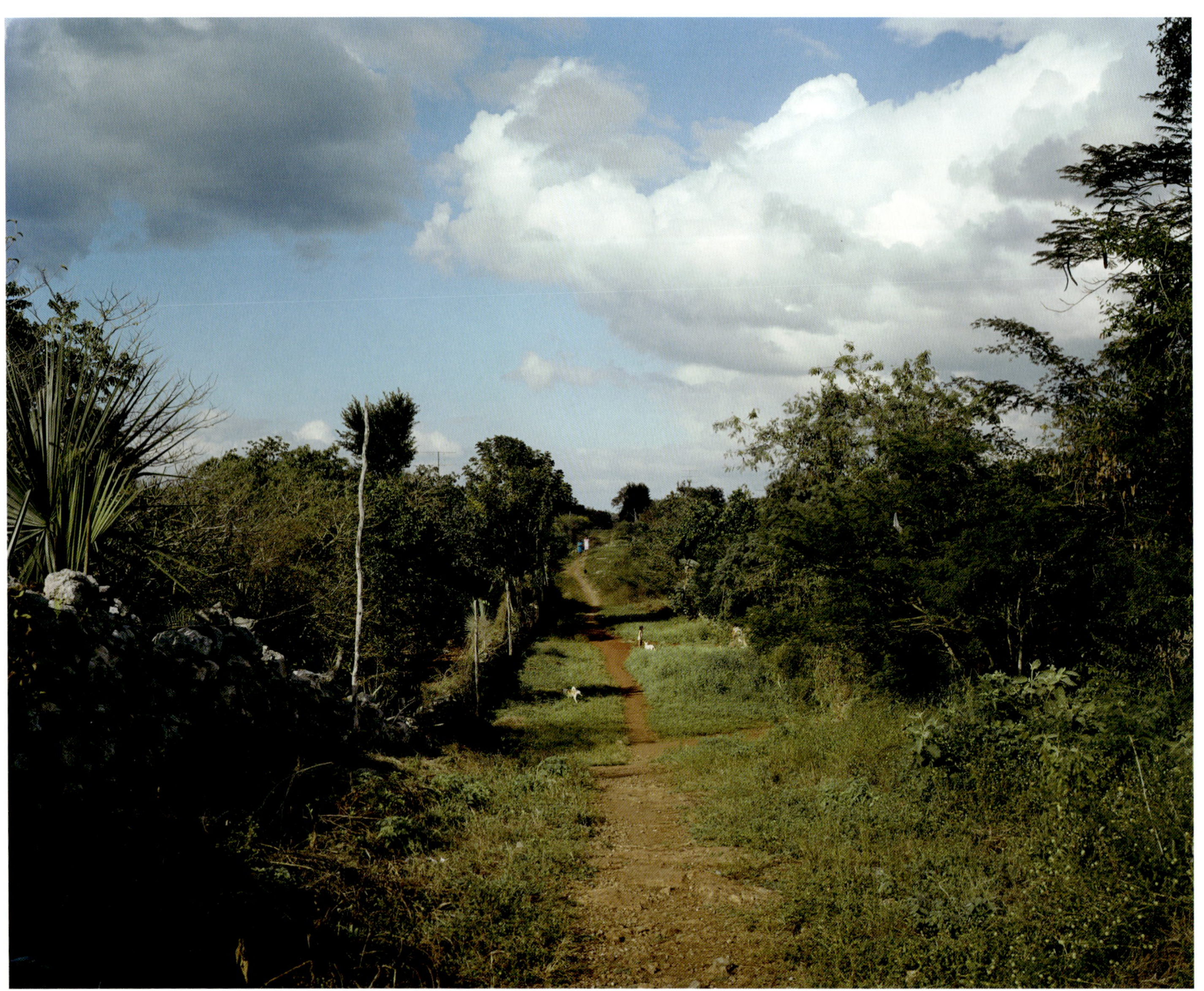

***Yucatán, Mexico, 1990*. 1990**

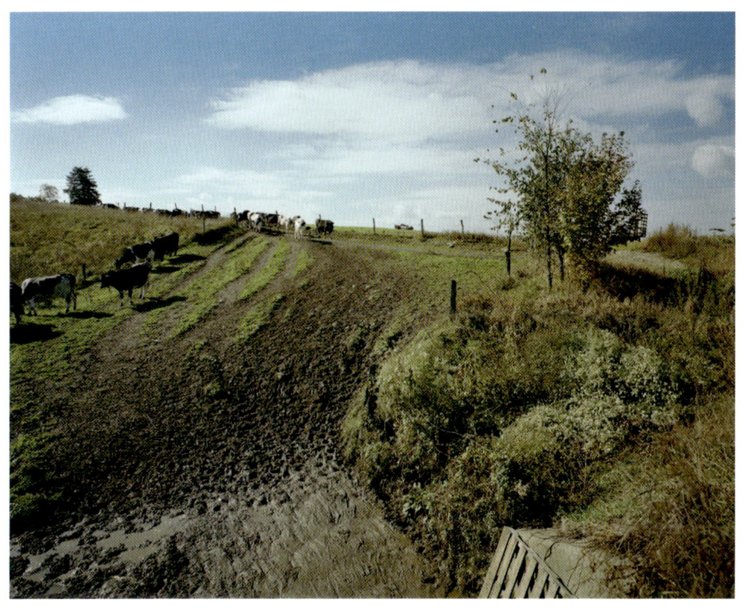

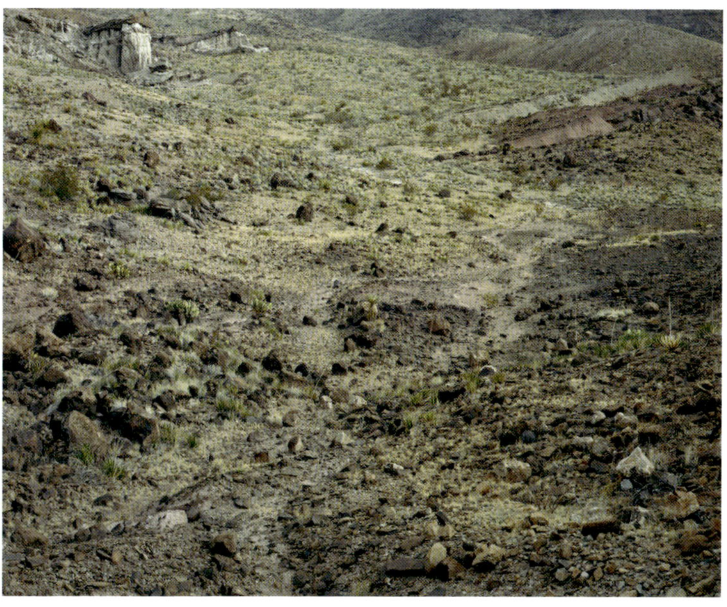

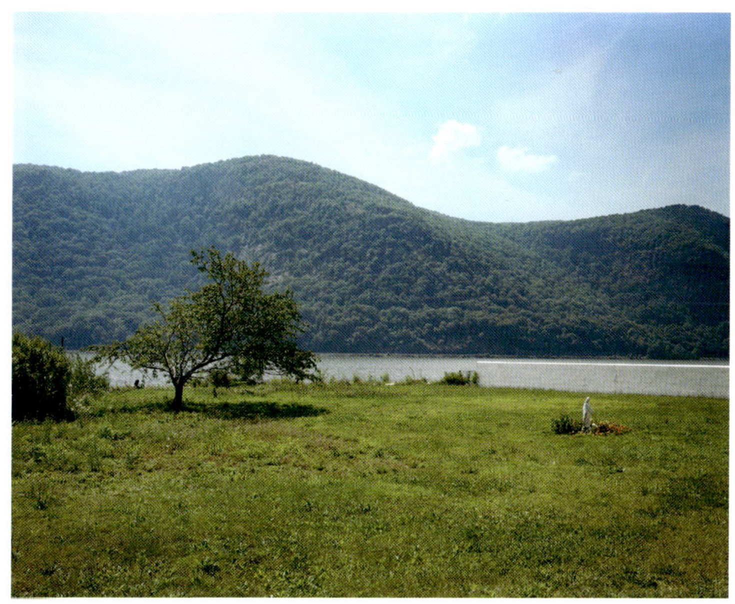

Ulster County, New York, 1986. 1986

Brewster County, Texas, 1988. 1988

Putnam County, New York, 1985. 1985

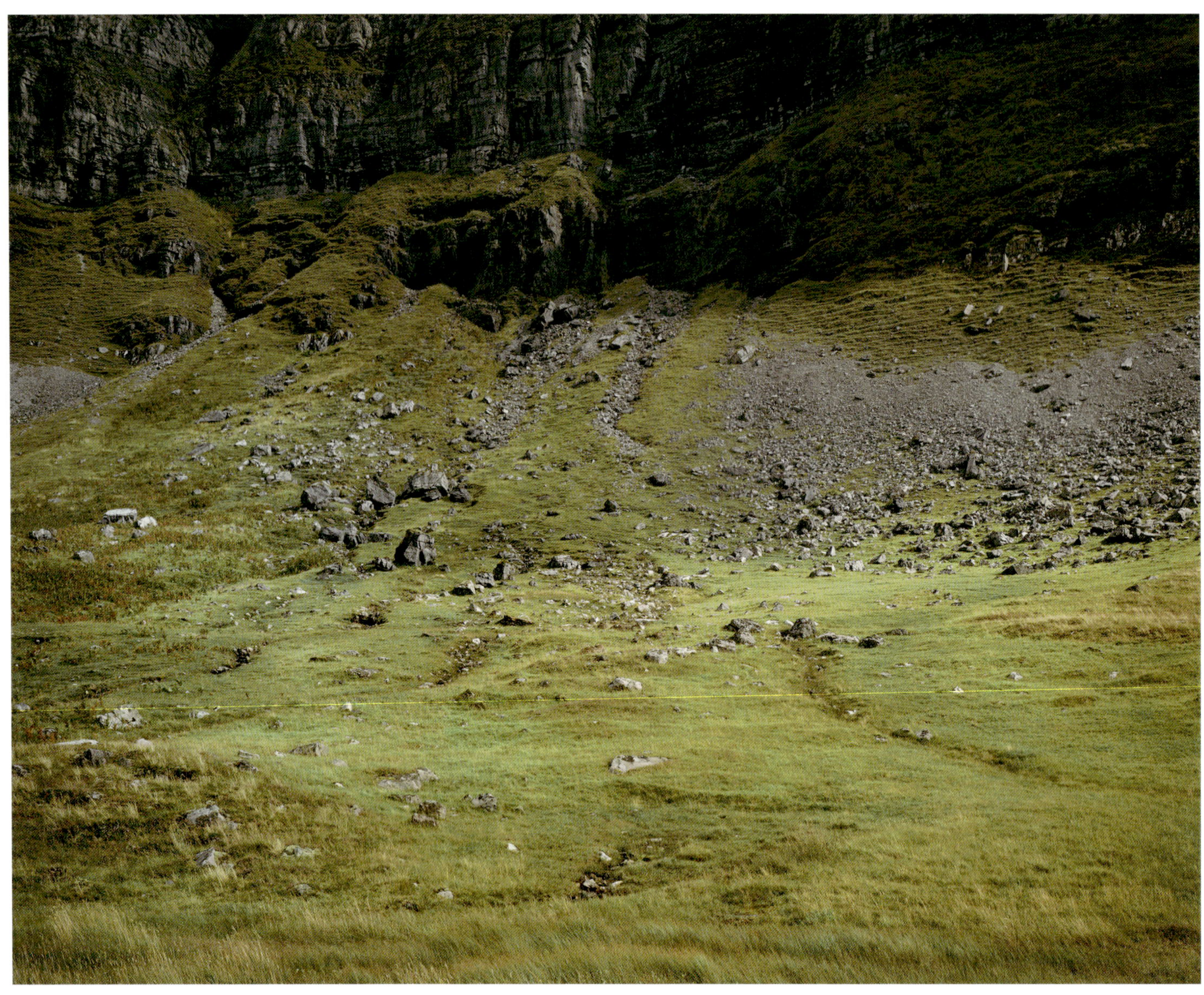

County of Sutherland, Scotland, 1988. **1988**

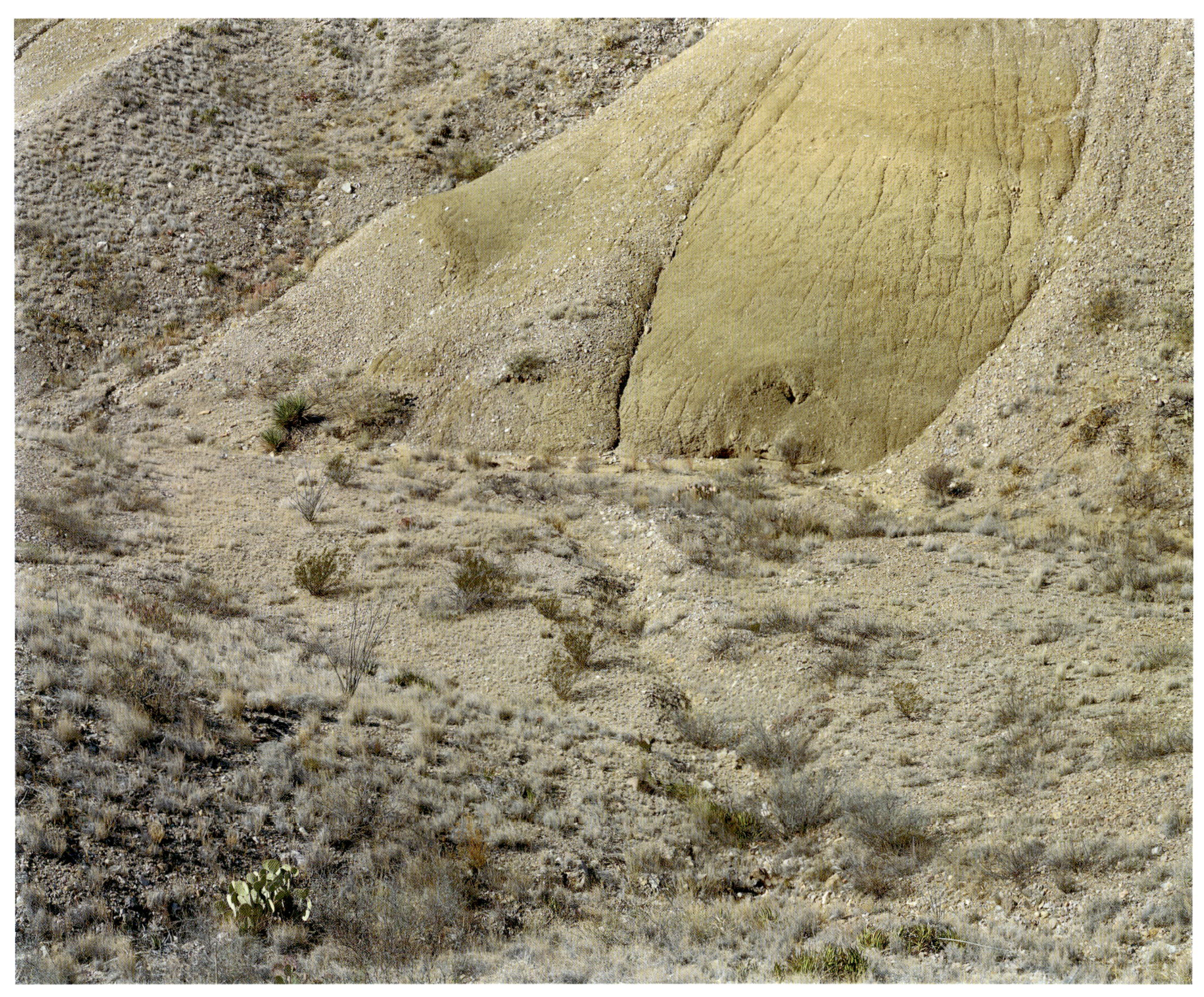

***Brewster County, Texas, 1988.* 1988**

Light Gallery

In November 1971 lawyer Tennyson Schad and curator Harold Jones opened Light Gallery at 1018 Madison Avenue. The 1,500-square-foot space was the first gallery devoted to contemporary photography, and attempted to do for photographers what gallerists had long been doing for painters: arrange exclusive contracts with the artists, and then support them through framing, loaning, exhibiting, advertising, and selling work; they also planned to publish portfolios and books and represent the artists when commissioned.[1] Schad brought the business acumen and the financial backing; Jones, who had been an assistant curator under Nathan Lyons at George Eastman House, brought his curatorial knowledge and experience.

Shore's first inclusion at Light was in the 1972 summer show. Critic Gene Thornton, who had disapproved of Shore's Conceptual turn in his exhibition at the Metropolitan Museum of Art, wrote that his Amarillo postcards at Light demonstrated an "academic preoccupation" with "photography as kitsch."[2] The month after that show closed, his first solo exhibition with Light was *American Surfaces*, and A. D. Coleman, who in August had unfavorably reviewed Shore's contribution to *Summer Light*, reiterated his feelings, classifying Shore as a "conceptual" photographer "intent on proving that anyone can photograph as well as he can." He concluded, "I must admit he's building an airtight case."[3] Even with Coleman and Thornton's criticism, Shore immediately began to sell work through Light (starting with the entirety of *American Surfaces* being bought by Met curator Weston Naef) and appeared in another group exhibition and solo exhibition the next year.

In 1974 Light started exclusively representing Shore.[4] His solo exhibitions that year and the next were of recent large-format work that would eventually become *Uncommon Places*. Visitors who signed the guest book in 1975 disagreed—sometimes quarreling directly with each other—about the quality of the photographs, often related to the use of color. Photographer Elliott Erwitt wrote that it was "One of the few (very few) instances, that color seems appropriate—also some very good pictures."[5] The gallery continued to sell his work to institutions and individuals, as well as loaning it to galleries throughout the country. Light was well positioned to promote its artists as the prices of photographs rose through the 1970s.[6] As Shore has said, "It was an extraordinary place. Until then, photography galleries had [. . .] I would call it a camera club mentality of prints. Pins and burlap on the walls. Light was the first gallery that showed photographs the way they were presented at the Modern. Freshly painted white walls, an uptown space."[7]

In 1976 Light moved to 724 Fifth Avenue, and Shore had two solo exhibitions there.[8] Charles Traub took over as director in July 1978, and the next year Shore renewed his contract with the gallery, which at that point was representing thirty-six artists, with a staff of ten.[9] In 1980 a 3,400-square-foot Los Angeles outpost was founded, under the direction of curator Renato Danese, meant to both extend the reach of Light's current artists and to broaden its stable with California artists.[10] It opened in October with a large exhibition of Harry Callahan's work and a smaller show of Shore's Giverny photographs. At the same time, the New York gallery expanded its space, and Shore also had an exhibition there. The Light / Los Angeles opening garnered much publicity, especially in California, but with the extra rent and the cost of renovations the gallery had financially overextended itself. Light / Los Angeles closed, and the New York space gradually scaled back its operations, eventually closing in 1987. (Kristen Gaylord)

See also: *American Surfaces*; *Color*; *Uncommon Places*

1. Natalie Rosenheck, "Light Gallery Opens: Room at the Top?" *Popular Photography* 70, no. 3 (March 1972): 106.
2. Gene Thornton, "Time-Travel, Other Trips," *New York Times*, August 6, 1972, sec. 2, D14.
3. A. D. Coleman, "Latent Image: American Yawn, Irish Wail," *Village Voice*, October 5, 1972, 31.
4. Contract between Stephen Shore and Light, 1974, Light Gallery Archive, AG 194, Center for Creative Photography, University of Arizona, Tucson (hereafter CCP).
5. Guest book, 1975, Stephen Shore Collection, 1973–1978, AG 50, CCP.
6. See Manuela Hoelterhoff, "Why the Photography Market is Booming," *Wall Street Journal*, October 8, 1974, 28, and Gene Thornton, "Prices of Modern Photographs Zoom," *New York Times*, March 9, 1975, D1, D35.
7. "Stephen Shore with Peter Halley," *Index* 23 (April 2000): 34.
8. His 1977 exhibition was of work from 1974 to 1976, and the 1978 one was of his Yankees photographs (which were not received well by reviewers). See Carol Squiers, "Color Photography: The Walker Evans Legacy and the Commercial Tradition," *Artforum* 17, no. 3 (November 1978): 64–67, and Ben Lifson, "Taking All the Way," *Village Voice*, June 19, 1978, 76, 79.
9. "History of Light Gallery," September 18, 1979, Light Gallery Archive, AG 194, CCP.
10. Press release announcing Light / Los Angeles, September 1980, Light Gallery Archive, AG 194, CCP.

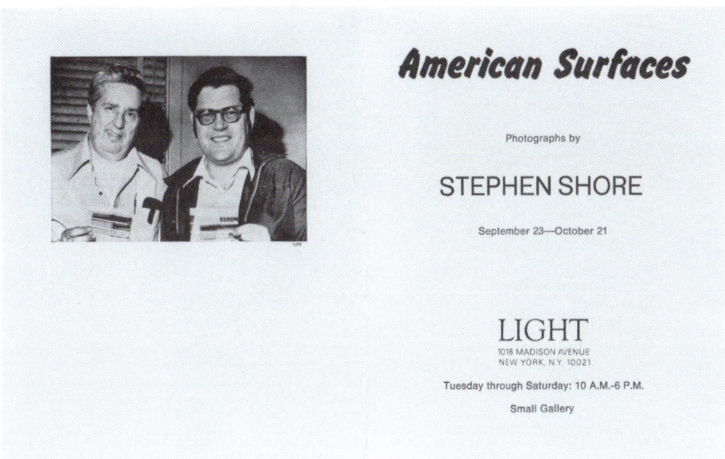

American Surfaces

Photographs by

STEPHEN SHORE

September 23—October 21

LIGHT
1018 MADISON AVENUE
NEW YORK, N.Y. 10021

Tuesday through Saturday: 10 A.M.-6 P.M.

Small Gallery

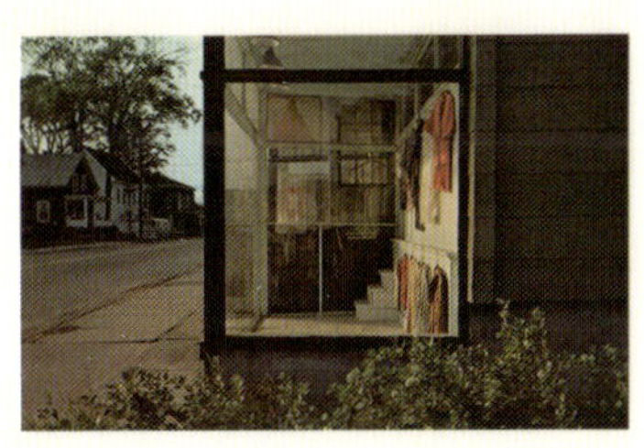

STEPHEN SHORE

FEBRUARY 4 - MARCH 1

Opening reception: February 8, 4-6 pm

St. Francis was respected for his piety and his ability to communicate with animals. Whenever anyone asked him how he had become so holy, he always answered: "I know what is in the Bible."

One day he had just given this reply to an enquirer in the town square, when an imbecile asked: "Well, what IS in the Bible?"

"In the Bible," said Francis, "there are two pressed flowers and a letter from a friend."

Traditional Tale

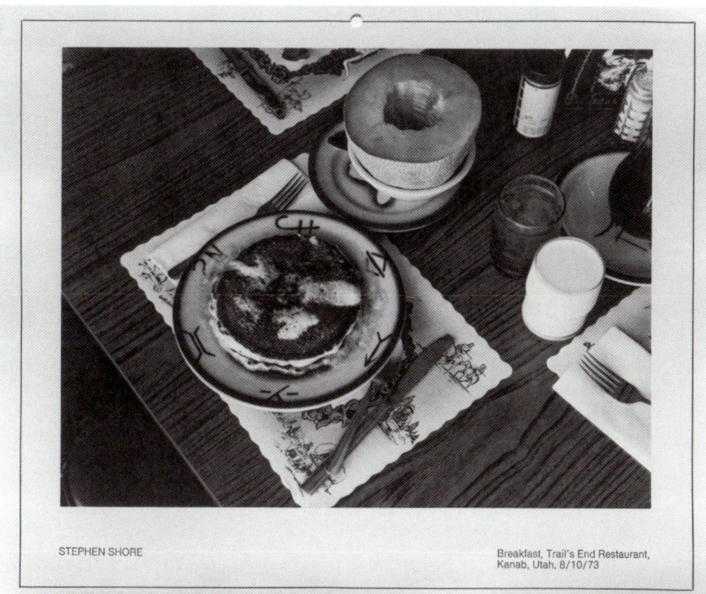

STEPHEN SHORE

Breakfast, Trail's End Restaurant, Kanab, Utah, 8/10/73

FEBRUARY

SUNDAY	MONDAY	TUESDAY	WEDNESDAY	THURSDAY	FRIDAY	SATURDAY
						1 1971: Raoul Hausmann died in Limoges, France 1935: Television Committee of British Government recommends England establish television as a public service
2	3	4 1902: George N. Barnard died in Cedarvale, N.Y. 1902: Manuel Alvarez Bravo born in Mexico City	5 1839: Bayard presents pictures by his process to members of L'Institute de France 1841: Talbot announces his Calotype process	6	7	8 1841: Talbot patents the Calotype process
9 1864: Mathew Brady photographs Lincoln in Washington, D.C.	10 1852: James Wallace Black, first to take a successful aerial photograph, born in Francetown, New Hampshire	11 1847: Thomas Edison born in Milan, Ohio 1800: William Henry Fox Talbot born in Melbury, Dorset, England	12 LINCOLN'S BIRTHDAY 1857: Eugène Atget born in Libourne, France	13	14 ST. VALENTINE'S DAY 1848: Hugo Erfurth died in Germany 1849: James Polk first president to have portrait made by daguerreotype; by Brady, N.Y.C.	15
16 1884: Robert J. Flaherty, documentary film maker, born in Iron Mountain, Michigan	17 WASHINGTON'S BIRTHDAY 1902: Photo-Secession founded by Alfred Stieglitz and friends	18 1947: Dr. Edwin Land announces the Polaroid-Land process	19 1856: Hamilton L. Smith awarded patent for the tintype process	20 1902: Ansel Adams born in San Francisco, California 1962: John Glenn makes first manned orbital flight of earth	21 1901: Henry Peach Robinson died in Turbridge Wells, England	22
23	24 1913: Exhibition of Alfred Stieglitz's photographs at "291" coinciding with Armory Exhibition	25	26	27 1860: Mathew Brady photographed Lincoln at 359 Broadway, New York City	28 1839: Sir John Herschel coins word "photographed"	

Invitation to *American Surfaces*, Light Gallery, New York, September 23–October 21, 1972

Invitation to *Stephen Shore*, Light Gallery, New York, February 4–March 1, 1975

Light Gallery calendar, 1975

Luzzara

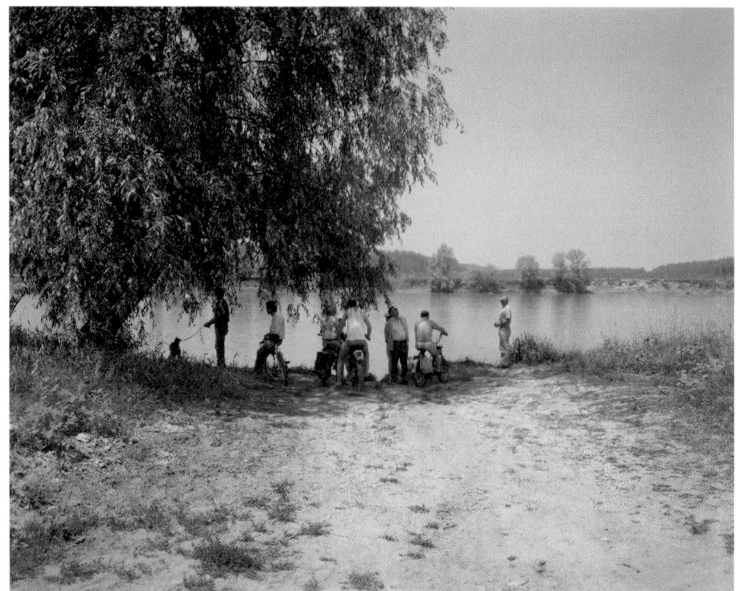

In 1993 Shore was invited to photograph the Italian city of Luzzara under the auspices of the program Linea di Confine per la Fotografia Contemporanea, his first international commission. Shore spent the month of June there, taking photographs in black and white while also conducting a workshop with Italian photographers. A vast program established in 1990 to document the changing landscape of Emilia-Romagna, Linea di Confine was part of a revival of landscape photography in Europe at the time. The project was a matter of exploring not so much the landscape as the territory—that is, going beyond the physical geography to the human activity and history of the region.

In Shore's eyes, Luzzara had the special distinction of having been photographed forty years earlier by the American photographer Paul Strand, who, in collaboration with the writer and screenwriter Cesare Zavattini, published a book of his Luzzara photographs, *Un Paese*, in 1955. As Shore wrote about the commission:

> There was no way I could approach Luzzara as though I was not familiar with Strand's work. At the same time, even though I was going to Luzzara exactly forty years after Strand, I was not interested in producing a re-photographic survey—taking pictures which document the inevitable changes in the scenes and, where possible, people he photographed. In a certain way, Strand's work does not need simple updating. Because the kinds of people and farms and landscapes he photographed still exist in very much the same form today. But, they exist side by side with the modern world. A key feature of Italian life, at least to my New World eyes, is the presence of the traditional within the modern. My aim, then, was to produce a companion volume to *Un Paese*; to produce a group of pictures, which to the limit of the subjectivity of my vision, supplement Strand's work.[1] (Quentin Bajac)

See also: *Black and White*; *Commissions and Editorial Work*; *Landscape*; *Portraiture*

1. Stephen Shore, *Luzzara*, Laboratorio di Fotografia 6 (Rubiera: Arcadia Edizioni, 1993); new rev. ed., London: Stanley/Barker, 2016, n.p.

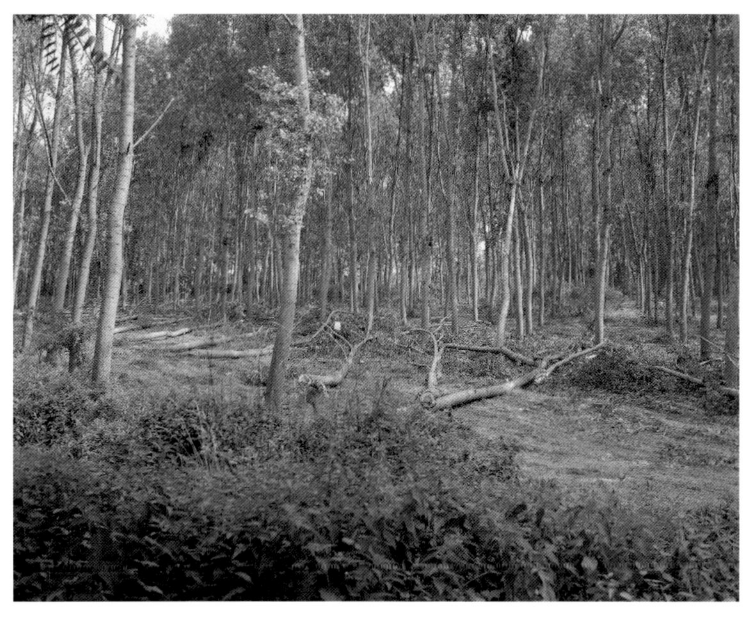

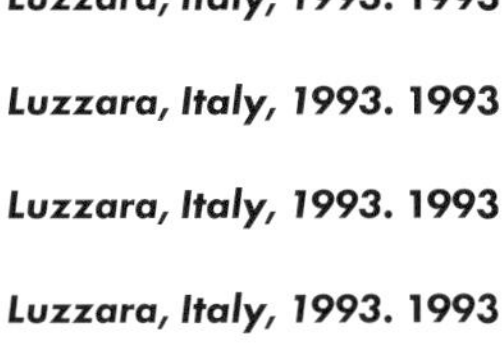

Luzzara, Italy, 1993. **1993**

Luzzara, Italy, 1993. **1993**

Luzzara, Italy, 1993. **1993**

Luzzara, Italy, 1993. **1993**

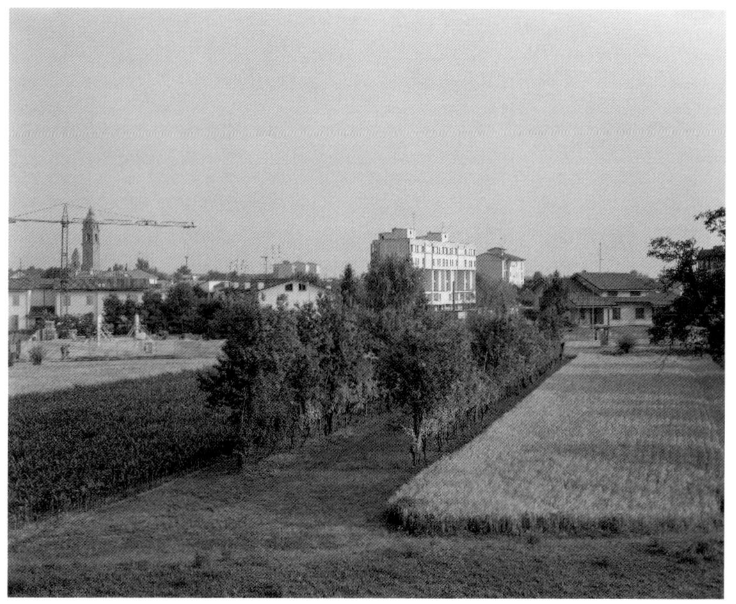

Merced River, Yosemite National Park, California, August 13, 1979

On October 1, 1890, Yosemite became America's third national park, after Yellowstone and Sequoia. It covers around 1,200 square miles of Northern California, but many of today's five million annual visitors spend their time in the seven square miles of Yosemite Valley.

Of all the national parks, Yosemite is the one most closely associated with the history of American photography. Carleton Watkins first photographed Yosemite Valley in 1861, and his images helped to persuade President Lincoln to sign a bill in 1864 to protect the region, paving the way for the national park system. Eadweard Muybridge's 1867 photographs of Yosemite were reproduced in newspapers and as guidebook illustrations, and were also sold in great numbers to a public eager for images that would symbolize a mythic origin for the nation. The wet-plate collodion technique used by these photographers required an intrepid team to travel to the remote region transporting "mammoth plate" cameras that produced 22-by-18-inch negatives.

The promise of the untouched sublime American landscape reached its modern apogee in the photography of Ansel Adams, who first visited Yosemite Valley in 1916 and shot there regularly beginning in the 1920s. One of his best-known images, the monumental *Moon and Half Dome*, was made in 1947, the year Shore was born. By the time Shore came to photograph the location for himself, it was an enormously popular destination, with Californians flocking there from increasingly polluted cities, commercialized road trips bringing busloads of tourists, and international visitors arriving on cheap flights.

On an outcrop overlooking a languorous bend in Yosemite's Merced River, Shore set up his 8-by-10 camera (not as large as the equipment of his early predecessors, but still substantial). He framed the landscape classically, with a defined foreground, middle ground, and background. On the hazy horizon, he included Half Dome, perhaps as a nod to Adams, but to integrate the mountain into his own picture, Shore mirrored its distinctive profile with that of a tree at the extreme right of his frame.

It is the human presence that defines this picture. The rhythms and values of a leisurely day are the counterpoint to the cycle of the seasons and the backdrop of geological time. Casting shadows like sundials, each person in the scene appears suspended in time, but this is not simply the effect of Shore's shutter. The human figures achieve—accidentally and momentarily—an unlikely pictorial ideal, and formal perfection always evokes a suspension of time. As a further accent on this strange effect, one of the figures is photographing another.

Photographs are not narratives, but they do invite us to fill in the blanks, to extrapolate and speculate. So, somewhere in the world, perhaps in a dusty family album, there is a snapshot of a young blond boy standing ankle deep in the Merced River. As he wades into the cool water, he turns, squinting in the sun toward the Instamatic camera of his older sibling. Or perhaps he is looking past that camera to his mother, who holds the hand of the youngest member of the family, who is a little wobbly on delicate feet. What else is in the snapshot we see being taken here? Behind the boy in the water, up on the rocks, is a man. Tall, aged thirty-one, he stands next to a large wooden camera mounted on a tripod. (David Campany)

See also: *Landscape*; *Uncommon Places*

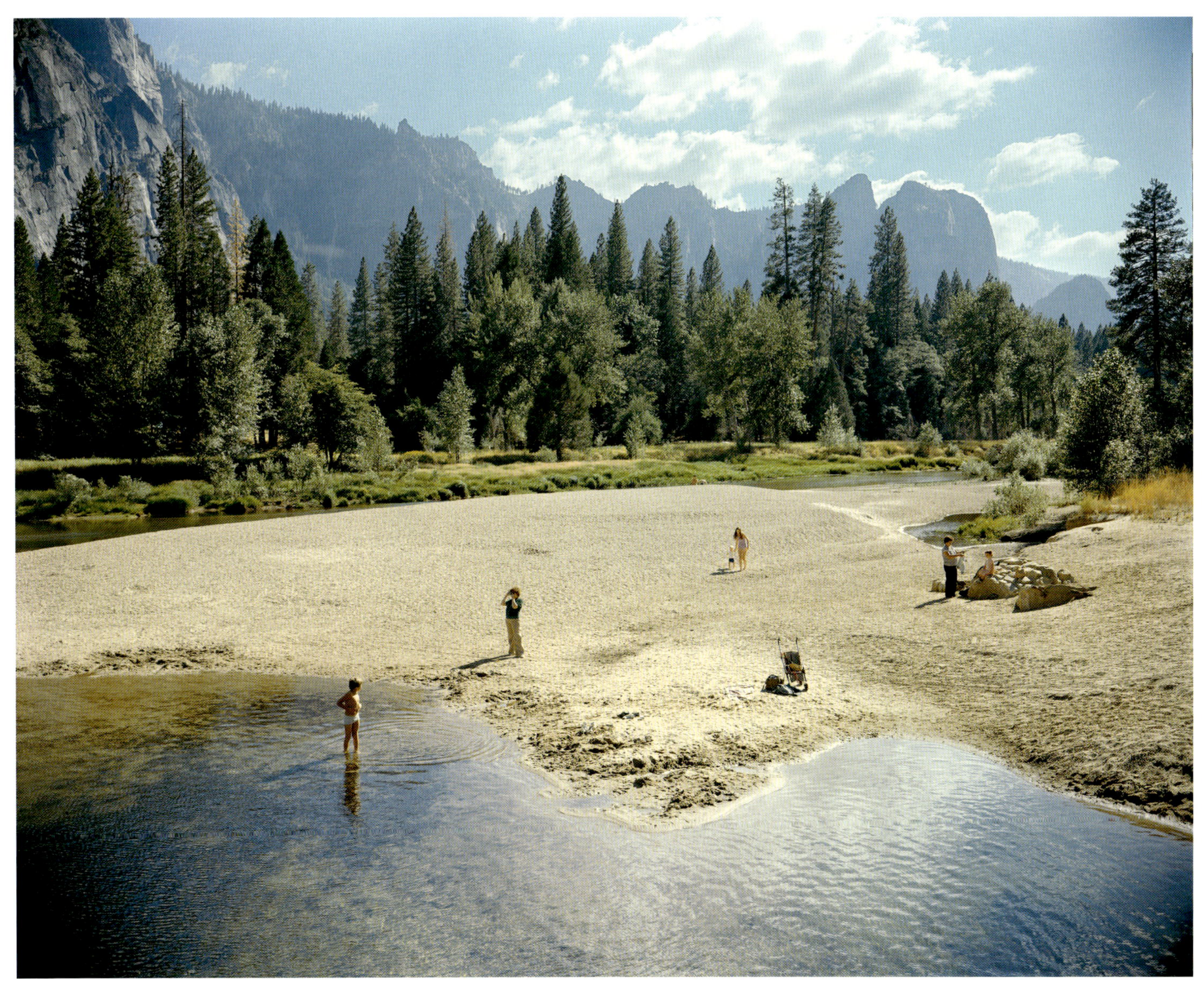

***Merced River, Yosemite National Park, California, August 13, 1979.* 1979**

Merchandise

If we were to classify artists, as Umberto Eco has done with intellectuals, as either "apocalyptic" or "integrated" based on the degree to which they show an explicit critique of mass consumer society and the culture industry, then, like Andy Warhol or Robert Venturi and Denise Scott Brown during the same period, Shore would belong to the latter category.[1] In fact, it was Shore's apparent lack of critical judgment toward the provincial middle America he was photographing—the transparent neutrality of his gaze and his deadpan humor—that some observers in the 1970s, around the time of *Uncommon Places*, reproached him for. In 1977, for instance, the *Village Voice* lamented "the detached eye of a viewer who refuses to comment on the sociological implications of what he sees."[2] Shore has, in fact, always been committed to photographing his subjects without judging them.

The playful attitude he showed toward the signs and symbols of mass culture in his early work can be seen again in the 2000s in his amused and somewhat Warholian interest in the occasional fabrication of ancillary products that recycle his own images and universe, often with a good deal of humor, on cell phone cases, placemats, T-shirts, calendars, and so on. Through this process, his work, which is fed by consumer society, becomes part of it, taking on modest, deliberately banal commercial forms that are far from the traditional distribution channels of both the art market and the luxury industry. (Quentin Bajac)

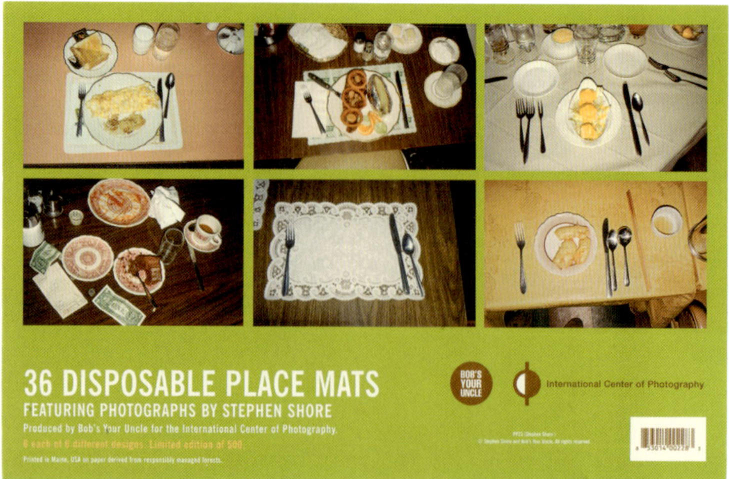

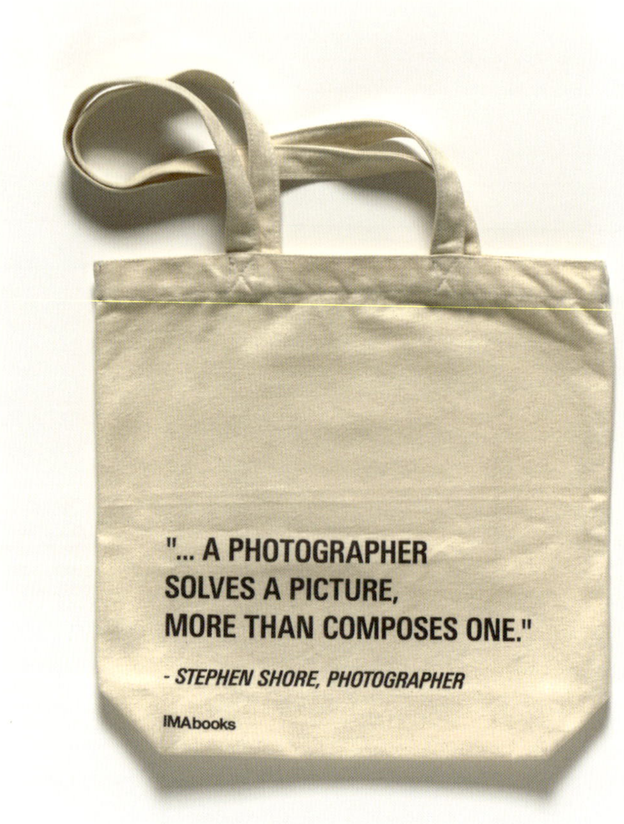

See also: *Commercial Work*; *Commissions and Editorial Work*; *Fashion Work*; *Signage*

1. Umberto Eco, "Apocalyptic and Integrated Intellectuals: Mass Communications and Theories of Mass Culture," in Umberto Eco, *Apocalypse Postponed*, ed. Robert Lumley (London: British Film Institute; Bloomington: Indiana University Press, 1994), 17–34.
2. Shelley Rice, "Stephen Shore: Banal Landscapes Revisioned," *Village Voice*, May 2, 1977, 87.

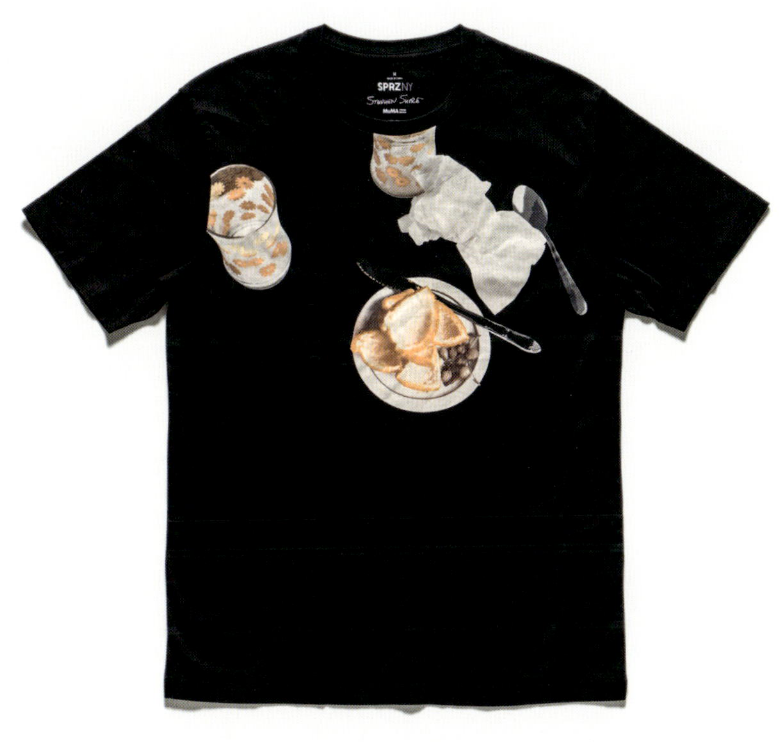

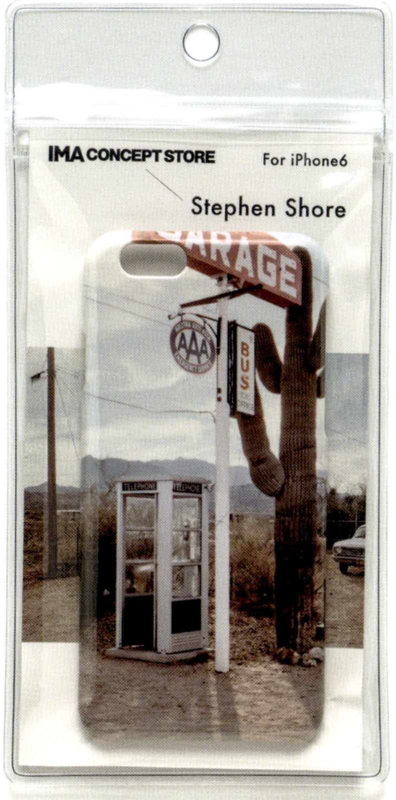

Bob's Your Uncle disposable placemats, 2007

IMA Books tote bag, 2014

UNIQLO SPRZ women's T-shirt, 2014

IMA Concept Store iPhone 6 case, 2015

Metropolitan Museum of Art, The

Raised in New York City, Shore had visited the Metropolitan Museum of Art as a child, but his professional relationship with the institution began in the early 1970s after he left a portfolio of his photographs with John McKendry, curator in the Department of Prints and Photographs at the museum. He thought nothing would come of it, as the Met rarely showed the work of living artists, but in 1971, at the age of twenty-three, Shore found himself only the second living photographer ever to have a solo exhibition there.[1] Organized by curator Weston Naef, the exhibition included photographs of Shore's parents (page 177); of wrecked cars in the woods in upstate New York; of clouds taken from the ground and from airplane windows; *KT Ranch* (opposite); and *The Institute of General Semantics* (page 127). The exhibition was reviewed twice in the *New York Times*: David Shirey called it "extraordinary and beautiful," but Gene Thornton, already familiar with Shore's photographs of Warhol's Factory, disliked his turn toward Conceptual projects, and described the works as inhabiting "those desolate reaches of contemporary art where both subject matter and the artist's feelings are suppressed, where the audience's anticipated responses are systematically nullified, where indeed there may be no work of art at all, but merely an idea."[2] Naef acquired all of the works in the exhibition for the Met's collection; three years later, he gave the museum 230 prints from *American Surfaces*, making the Met the strongest early collector of Shore's work.[3]

The Met remained involved in and supportive of Shore's career. In 1976 it published a portfolio of twelve chromogenic prints from the *Uncommon Places* series (in an edition of fifty, plus six artist's proofs). The following year a commission from the museum sent Shore to photograph the renovation of Claude Monet's gardens in Giverny; the resulting images were included in the 1978 exhibition *Monet's Years at Giverny: Beyond Impressionism*. In 2014 the Met acquired a complete run of Shore's print-on-demand iBooks, making it the only institution to hold all eighty-three, including *Ugolino and His Sons*, a book of twelve images of the eponymous sculpture by nineteenth-century French artist Jean-Baptiste Carpeaux, which Shore photographed in the Met's European Sculpture Court. (Kristen Gaylord)

See also: *American Surfaces*; *Conceptual*; *Youth*

1. Alex Gartenfeld, "A Shore Thing," *Interview*, June 11, 2009, http://www.interviewmagazine.com/art/stephen-shore. He has since said that the show may have happened too early for him: "This is what everyone hopes for, then it happens and you think, 'Oh my God, now what am I going to do?'" Quoted in "Stephen Shore in a Conversation with Lynne Tillman," in *Uncommon Places: The Complete Works* (New York: Aperture, 2004), 173.
2. David L. Shirey, "Prints and Photographs On View at Metropolitan," *New York Times*, February 24, 1971, 34; Gene Thornton, "Is It Necessary To Ask What They Mean?" *New York Times*, March 7, 1971, D30.
3. Naef had purchased the entire 1972 *American Surfaces* exhibition from Light Gallery; he added other prints from the series before he gave the group to the Met in 1974.

Prints and Photographs On View at Metropolitan

By DAVID L. SHIREY

Prejudices that have raised painting and sculpture to a high stature in the arts and relegated prints and photography to a lower level have often been the cause of great esthetic injustices and have frequently been sad deterrents to the discovery of fine works of art in the so-called "secondary media."

Three exhibitions opened yesterday in the Metropolitan Museum of Art's Prints and Drawings Galleries — Prints by Paul Gauguin, Paradise Lost Illustrated and Photographs by Stephen Shore — and at least two are worthy declarations that works in these media can hold their own against the quality paintings and sculptures installed in the Metropolitan's adjoining rooms.

The Gauguin exhibition, from the Met's own collections, stands out as yet another reminder of how rich and unfathomed the museum treasure is and as an eloquent example of how the woodcut and the lithograph were by nature at one—at times more than painting—with the forceful immediacy of spirit and stark simplicity of form in Gauguin's art.

•

There is, on display, a rare first edition of a series of lithographs printed on unusual yellow paper. Mementos of Gauguin's sojourn at Pont-Aven, Martinique and Arles, they are strong in their bold black contrasts of elemental figures moving against an assertive yellow background and offer, as such, remarkable instances of Gauguin's versatility in this medium.

But the woodcut lent itself much more forcefully to the qualities inherent in Gauguin's art. It also afforded him the chance to experiment with various colored ink combinations that could produce, in repetitions of the same cut, a great range of mood and expression. The first artist of a particular eminence since the 16th century to use the woodcut as an art form, Gauguin turned to it as a source of printmaking to illustrate "Noa Noa," his South Seas journal, and later a small newspaper he founded, Le Sourire. Examples from each highlight the show.

The other print exhibition, Paradise Lost Illustrated, a miscellany of isolated prints and prints in books, serves more as a limited display of information on various illustrations of the 17th-century John Milton poem than an esthetic experience of grand scale.

Most of the show is devoted to the prints of the 19th-century English artist John Martin. Highly acclaimed in his day, Martin has been somewhat forgotten. It is understandable. His prints, which found constrained inspiration in theatrical bursts of light, vast spaces, grandiose and disproportionate scale and in classical archeology, rank as only illustration to art but certainly not art in illustration. In fact, the illustrations of Paradise Lost by Fuseli and Blake, some of which are on view, either in the original or in reproduction, make the vision of Martin look regrettably myopic.

The photographs of Stephen Shore give rise to general philosophical concepts such as time and space, permanence and impermanence, relativism and absolutism more readily than they give rise to particular thoughts of certain people, specific events or identifiable places.

•

In this extraordinary and beautiful exhibition of photographs taken with the last two years, Mr. Shore introduces us to a site through a series of photographs taken at various places in the location. By means of a constant, a tree, a cloud or even a recurring format, he forces the viewer to take time to walk around and discover the landscape, piecing together in his own mind's eye what goes on in between pictures. Whether Mr. Shore focuses in on a sidewalk on Avenue of the Americas, a car dump in the woods, a house in the country or a ranch in the Southwest, he seems to be demonstrating a valuable principle of life.

Mr. Shore has considerable respect for the process of making the picture and freely allows observations of his technique and compositional arrangements. Such integrity toward the act of creation heightens, in this case, the creation itself.

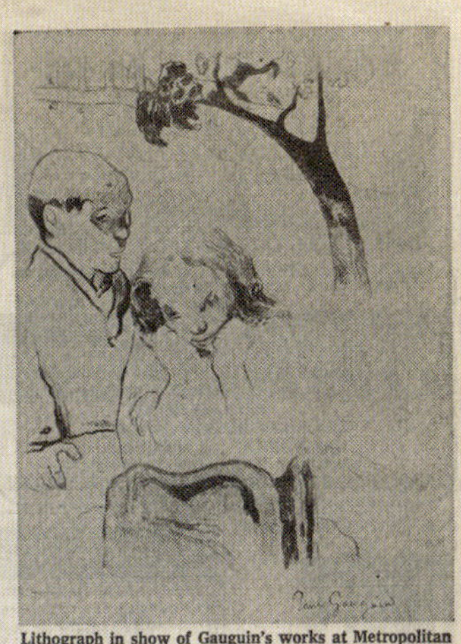

Lithograph in show of Gauguin's works at Metropolitan

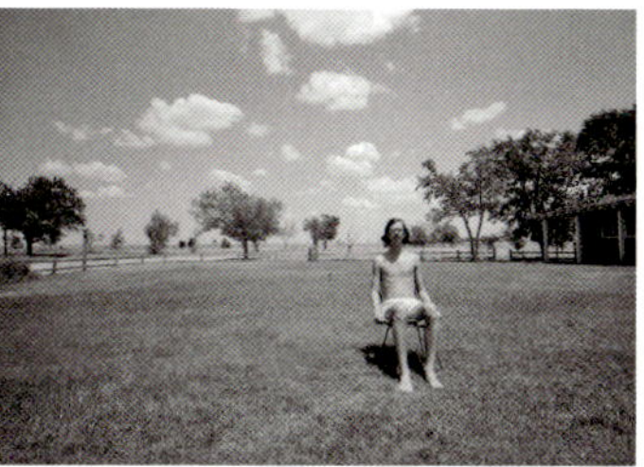
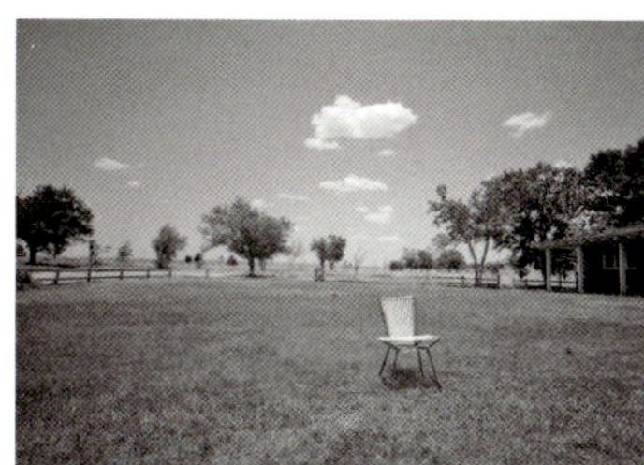
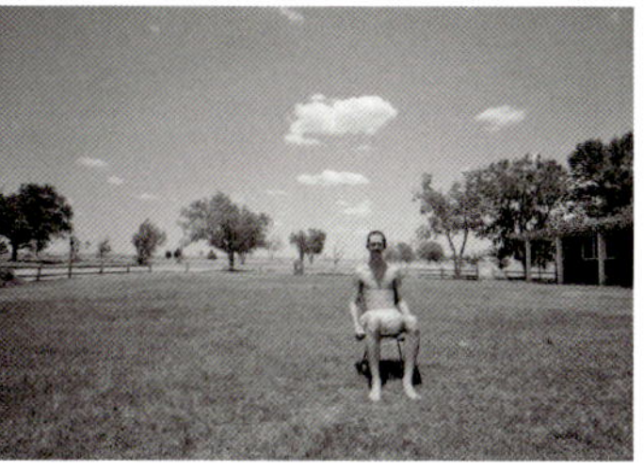
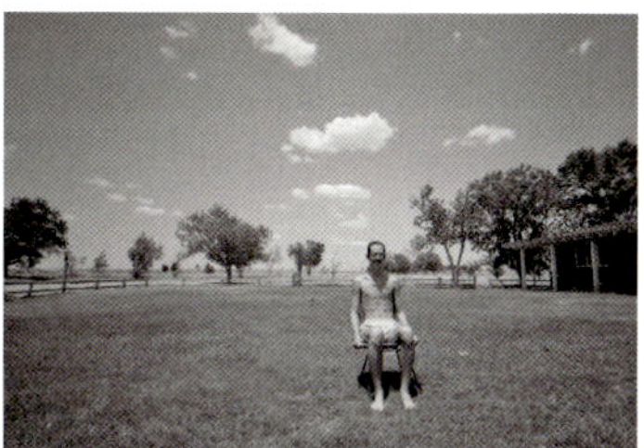
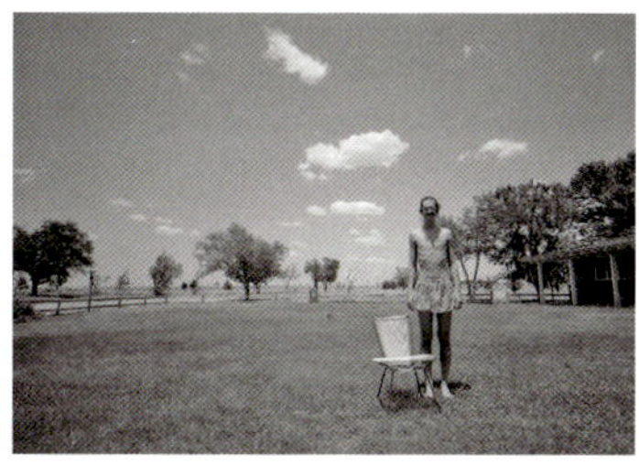
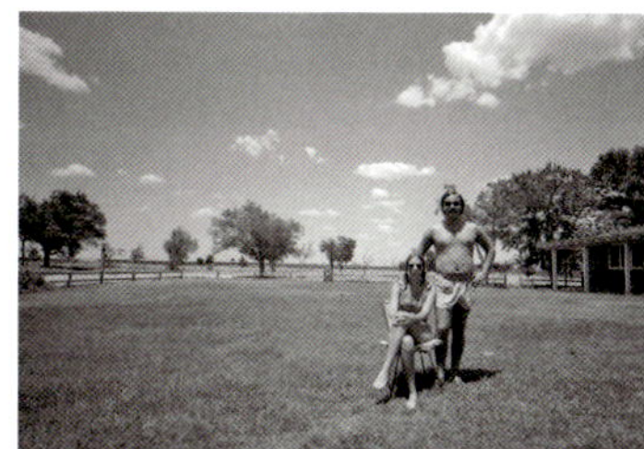
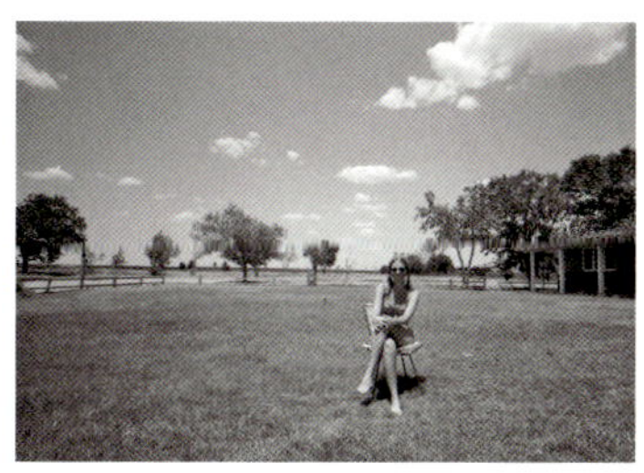
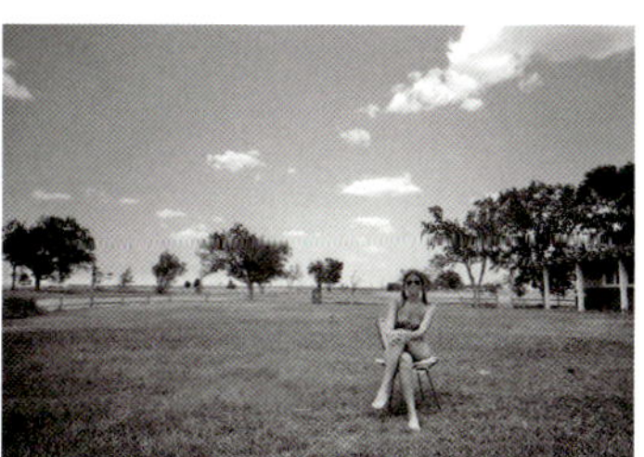
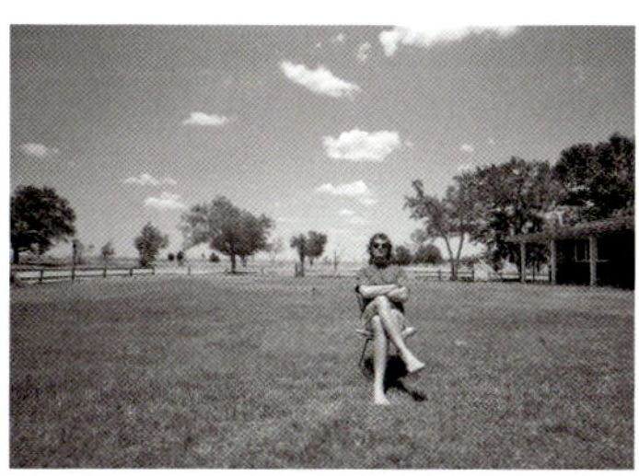
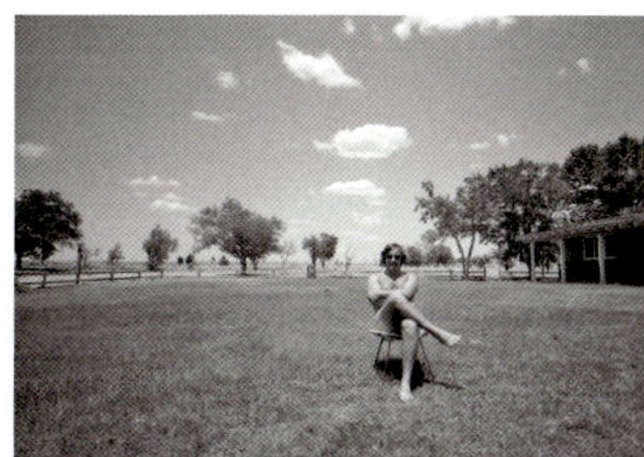

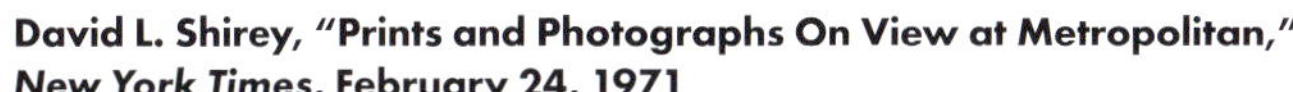

David L. Shirey, "Prints and Photographs On View at Metropolitan," *New York Times*, February 24, 1971

***KT Ranch, July 1969*. 1969**

Mick-a-Matic

In 1971 Child Guidance Products manufactured the Mick-a-Matic camera: a large plastic body shaped like Mickey Mouse's head with a viewfinder in its forehead, a lens in its nose, and a flash between its ears (opposite). Designed for children, the camera had no controls for setting aperture, shutter speed, or focus, and took a 126 cartridge film roll, which didn't require rewinding. Shore used the Mick-a-Matic, which he bought after seeing it in a store, to take dozens of photographs of friends and household objects throughout 1971. These photographs were notable for being Shore's first artistic use of color, which was an outgrowth of his interest in vernacular photography: "All snapshots were in color," he said. "You couldn't take film to your corner drugstore and get black-and-white processing."[1] He included some of the resulting prints, processed by Kodak, alongside material he had collected—such as posters, found photographs, and advertisements—in an exhibition he curated that year, *All the Meat You Can Eat*.

At the time he was especially interested in the "raw, unmediated spontaneity" characteristic of snapshots, which he has described as outside of or unaware of visual conventions, "the result of an accident or chance."[2] The mundane and spontaneous moments in the Mick-a-Matic images foreshadow the aesthetic that Shore would develop in his *American Surfaces* series, shot with a 35mm viewfinder that he bought with a desire for the same "natural quality" of the snapshot, but better optics.[3] Yet despite the fact that these photographs were meant to be as "unmediated" as possible, as Shore explained, the Mick-a-Matic camera itself "played against this because everyone smiles at that camera! You can't avoid smiling."[4] (Kristen Gaylord)

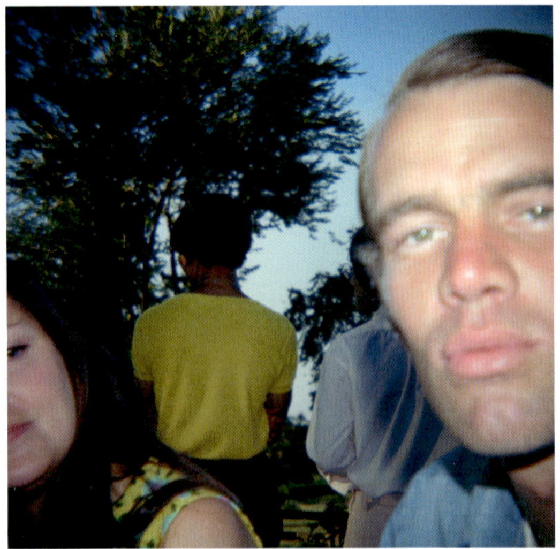

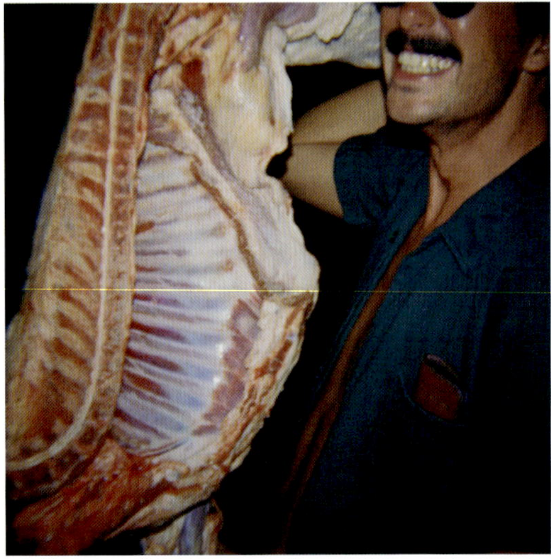

See also: *All the Meat You Can Eat*; *American Surfaces*; *Cameras*; *Color*

1. "Heroes & Mentors: Stephen Shore and Gregory Crewdson," *Photo District News* (August 2011): 26.
2. Ibid., 25; Stephen Shore, "Snapshots," in Ken Miller, *Shoot: Photography of the Moment* (New York: Rizzoli, 2009), 6. He has since noticed that American society has become more visually literate. See "A Ground Neutral and Replete: Stephen Shore and Gil Blank in Conversation," *Whitewall* (Fall 2007): 56.
3. "A Ground Neutral and Replete," 54, 56.
4. David Campany, "Ways of Making Pictures," in Marta Dahó, ed., *Stephen Shore* (Madrid: Fundación MAPFRE; New York: Aperture, 2014), 30.

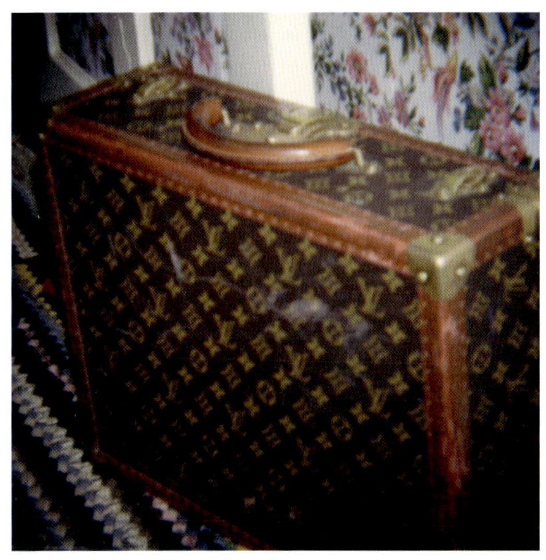

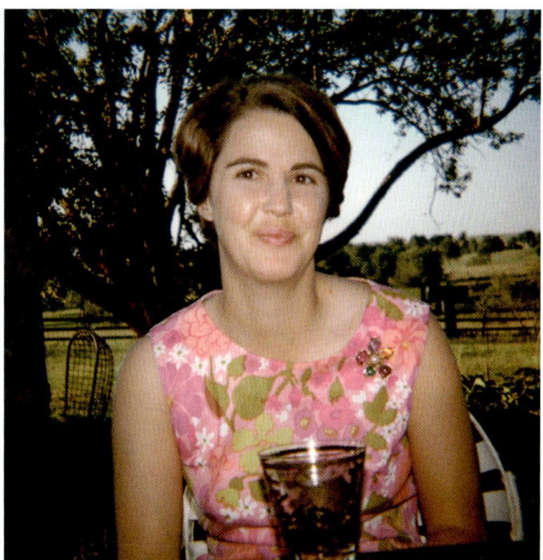

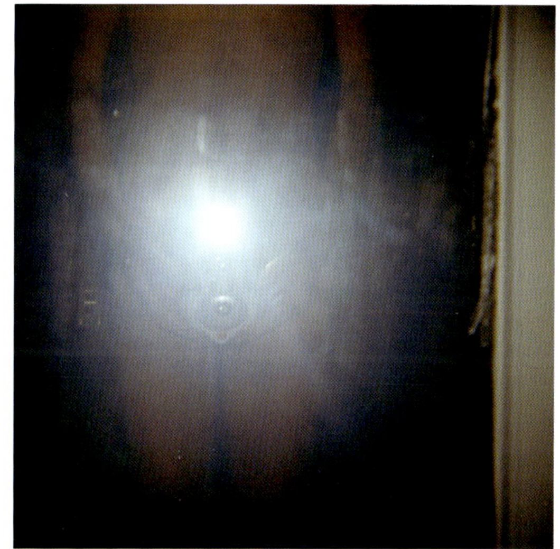

Hugh Russell, Amarillo, Texas (Mick-a-Matic), 1971. 1971

Michael Marsh, Amarillo, Texas (Mick-a-Matic), 1971. 1971

Suitcase (Mick-a-Matic), 1971. 1971

Girl, Amarillo, Texas (Mick-a-Matic), 1971. 1971

Self-Portrait (Mick-a-Matic), 1971. 1971

Stephen Shore's Mick-a-Matic camera, Child Guidance Products, 1971

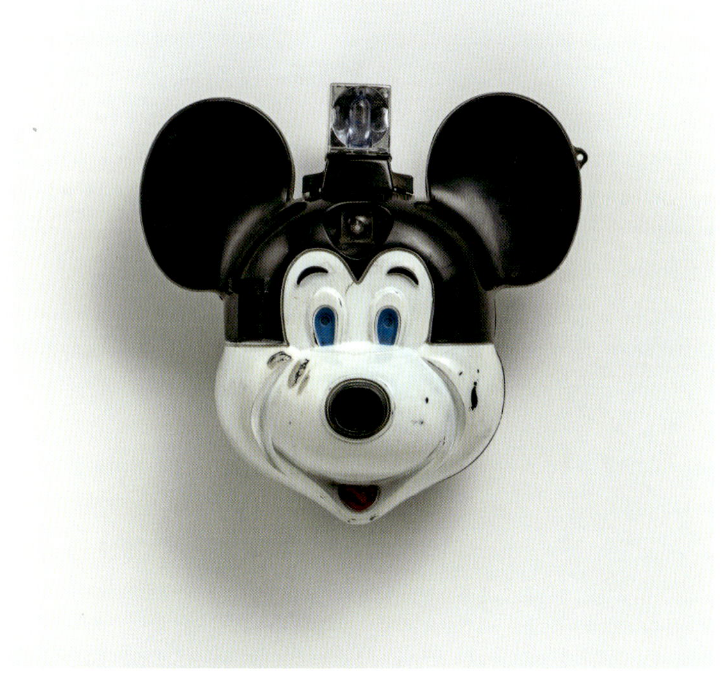

Museum of Modern Art, The

In 1962 Shore, then fourteen years old, dropped by the Department of Photography at MoMA to meet with director Edward Steichen and his personal assistant, Grace Mayer. The young artist, benefiting from the casual atmosphere of the department in those days before the 1970s boom in the value of photographs, had simply called and asked if he could show his work to Steichen. Mayer's notes from that meeting record that Steichen purchased three prints, which joined the department's Study Collection.

The Department of Photography at MoMA has had only five leaders since its founding in 1940, and Shore has had professional relationships with all of them except the first, Beaumont Newhall—an amazing feat that testifies to the length of a career which, in some ways, started at the 1962 meeting. John Szarkowski became the director of the department later that year, and in 1964 Shore came back to MoMA to trade two recent photographs for two that Steichen had purchased. He showed Szarkowski his photographs of Andy Warhol's Factory in the 1960s, and the curator became an important mentor for Shore, who has explained, "I feel that, more than anyone, he was my teacher. Whenever I had a new body of work, I'd bring it to him."[1] In 1974 Szarkowski organized the acquisition of work by Shore for the Museum Collection, consisting of four contact prints from that year.[2]

In 1976 an intern in the department named Maria Morris (who became the founding curator of the Department of Photographs at the Metropolitan Museum of Art in 1992) organized Shore's first solo exhibition at MoMA. Called *Photographs by Stephen Shore*, it included thirty-five prints from 1974–76. Reviews of the exhibition were generally more positive than they had been about his previous Light Gallery shows, with critics especially commenting on his use of color and formal structure.[3] A writer in *Modern Photography* noted that, coming just a couple of months after the exhibition *Photographs by William Eggleston*, Morris's exhibition "proved that the museum is seriously chromatic."[4]

The next year Szarkowski acquired five works that had been in the exhibition, including what would become some of Shore's most iconic images. And he was included in three group exhibitions over the next few years: Szarkowski's *Courthouse* (1977) and *Mirrors and Windows: American Photography Since 1960* (1978) and curatorial fellow Betsy Jablow's reinstallation of the collection in the Edward Steichen Photography Center (1979). The Museum also acquired three of Shore's Yankees photographs, and the courthouse photographs that were part of the gift from Seagram.

Shore did not feature as strongly in the exhibition program of the 1980s, although Szarkowski did acquire a photograph of Scotland the year after it was taken, in a rare contact-print size. Peter Galassi took over leadership of the department in 1991, and the Museum continued to collect Shore's work, especially images from *Uncommon Places* but also a set of the Amarillo postcards and one of the black-and-white panoramas of New York City. Then, in 2013, Galassi organized a large acquisition of Shore's work from throughout his career. Photographs of the Factory were included, along with Conceptual projects and prints from *American Surfaces*, *Uncommon Places*, and much more recent series in Abu Dhabi, Israel and the West Bank, and Ukraine. It was also an opportunity to reflect Shore's contemporary printing practices in the collection, which for many series included larger prints than the Museum had obtained previously and updated color contrast and tonality control, possible with digital technologies and preferred by the artist. With that acquisition, MoMA became one of the most significant repositories of Shore's photographs in the world. (Kristen Gaylord)

See also: *Light Gallery*; *Prints*; *Youth*

1. David Campany, "Ways of Making Pictures," in Marta Dahó, ed., *Stephen Shore* (Madrid: Fundación MAPFRE; New York: Aperture, 2014), 25. When Szarkowski died in 2007, Shore gave the Museum a print of Szarkowski's birthplace—Ashland, Wisconsin—in his memory.
2. One was later published in *Uncommon Places* (1982), and a second in *Uncommon Places: 50 Unpublished Photographs, 1973–1978* (2002).
3. See "New Yorkers Whose Work Invigorates the Avant-Garde," *Village Voice*, December 20, 1976, 73; Gene Thornton, "Formalists Who Flirt with Banality," *New York Times*, November 14, 1976, D34; and George Negroponte, "Stephen Shore," *Art/World*, December 11, 1976, Department of Public Information Records, II.A.722, The Museum of Modern Art Archives, New York.
4. "Miracle on 57th Street," *Modern Photography*, February 1977, PI, II.A.722, MoMA Archives, NY. See also Gene Thornton, "The New Photography: Turning Traditional Standards Upside Down," *Art News*, April 1978, 74–78.

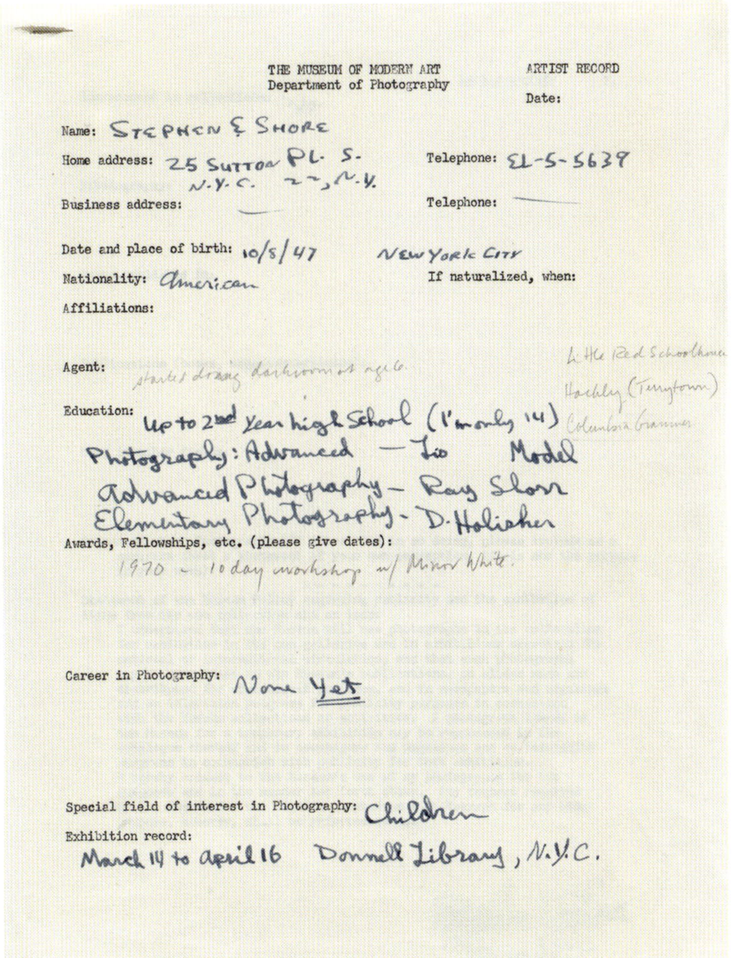

THE MUSEUM OF MODERN ART
Department of Photography

ARTIST RECORD

Date:

Name: STEPHEN E SHORE

Home address: 25 SUTTON PL. S. N.Y.C. 22, N.Y.

Telephone: EL-5-5639

Business address: —

Telephone: —

Date and place of birth: 10/5/47 NEW YORK CITY

Nationality: American

If naturalized, when:

Affiliations:

Agent: started doing darkroom at age 6.

Education: Up to 2nd year high school (I'm only 14)
Photography: Advanced — Lis Model
Advanced Photography — Ray Sloan
Elementary Photography — D. Holisher

Little Red Schoolhouse
Hackley (Tarrytown)
Columbia Grammar

Awards, Fellowships, etc. (please give dates):
1970 — 10 day workshop w/ Minor White.

Career in Photography: None Yet

Special field of interest in Photography: Children

Exhibition record:
March 14 to April 16 Donnell Library, N.Y.C.

Stephen Shore
25 Sutton Place South

14 years old
"very impressive" Mr. Steichen
"You're all right. We're proud of you." Mr. Steichen

Mr. Steichen buys three.

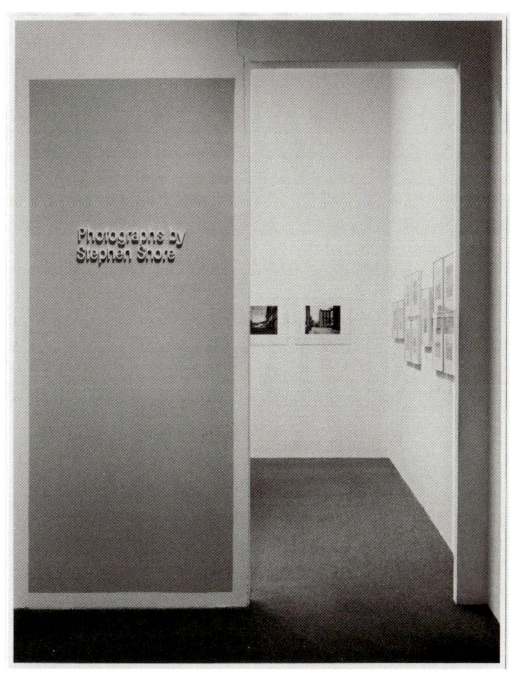

Stephen Shore's artist record, 1962

Grace Mayer's notes from Stephen Shore's meeting with Edward Steichen, 1962

Installation view of *Photographs by Stephen Shore*, The Museum of Modern Art, New York, October 8, 1976–January 2, 1977

Nabī Musa, West Bank, January 19, 2010

In 1853 the photographer Auguste Salzmann traveled from Paris to Jerusalem with very early camera equipment. He hoped to document in great detail holy sites in the city as a way to prove the veracity of the Bible's version of historical events and, by extension, the veracity of biblical claims about the nature of the universe and our place within it. Photography was little more than a decade old and the status of photographs as evidence was untested. That status remains complicated to this day, because photography can show, but it cannot explain. It is a medium of *what*, not of *why* or *how*.

Nevertheless, now we are at least a little clearer in our understanding that the world of proof and the world of religious faith are, to borrow the title of a 1997 essay by Stephen Jay Gould, "Nonoverlapping Magisteria."[1] The validity of faith is not something that can be proved; and provable things are true regardless of our willingness to believe or disbelieve them. To put archaeology and photography at the service of faith is to make a category error. All that Salzmann was able to prove was the limits of proof.

Photography is silent on the matter of whether there are gods, and whether those gods make real estate deals. On January 19, 2010, Shore made a number of photographs of the dry, rolling terrain of Nabī Musa, a site in the West Bank. "Musa" means "Moses" in Arabic, and there is a Palestinian tradition that Moses was buried at the place now called Nabī Musa. However, the Torah claims that Moses died on the east side of the Jordan River, and Nabī Musa is in the Judean Desert, on the river's west side. In this photograph, Shore offers us a view of a cemetery. A few of the headstones are erect and retain their human-made geometry. Others are almost indistinguishable from weathered lumps of rock.

The wealth of visual information recorded here could be of great use to a geologist, archaeologist, or topographer. But our relation to photographs of land is rarely so instrumental. There are always tensions. Although photographs describe according to the particular laws of optics and geometry, our response to them can never be so objective as to avoid the aesthetic dimension—the lure of "landscape" as a pictorial genre. Moreover, land is always subject to ownership, subject to emotional, cultural, political, or religious investment. We cannot look at land with the cold, alien neutrality of an optical machine. Nevertheless, a photograph of land does at least afford us the possibility, however brief, of perceiving land as sheer fact, as sheer existence prior to our projections upon it: land as if it belonged to nobody and no culture, without subject or subjectivity; land as if it were the surface of another planet in some other, equally obscure neighborhood of this enigmatic universe. (David Campany)

See also: *Israel and the West Bank*; *Landscape*

1. Stephen Jay Gould, "Nonoverlapping Magisteria," *Natural History* 106 (March 1997): 16-22.

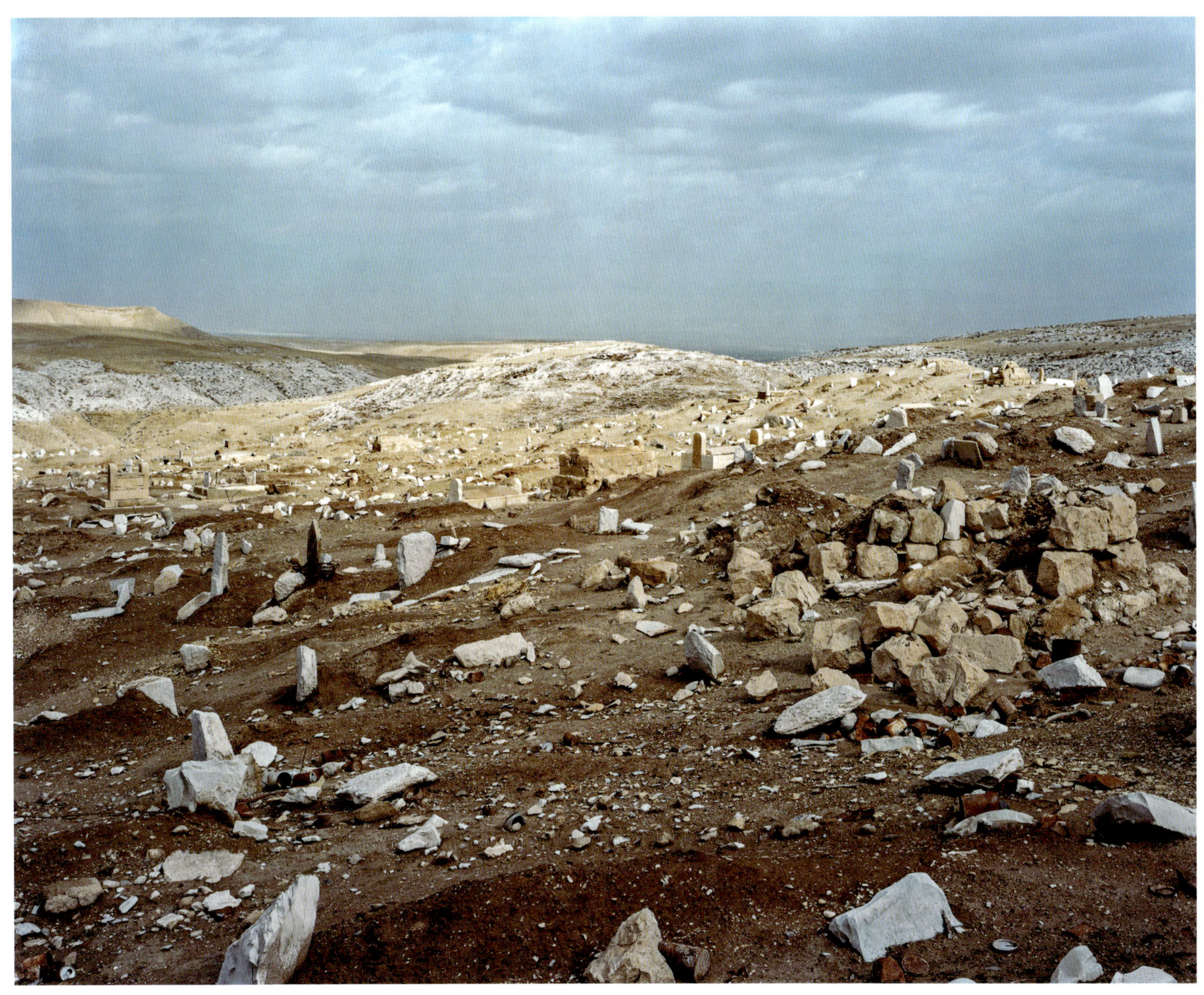

Nabī Musa, West Bank, January 19, 2010. 2010

Nature of Photographs, The

First published in 1998, *The Nature of Photographs* was the result of Shore's experience teaching at Bard College starting in 1982 and, in particular, his reflections on one of his courses, called "Photographic Seeing."[1] The book follows in the tradition of *Looking at Photographs* (1973), by John Szarkowski, who was director of the photography department at MoMA.[2] Szarkowski's book, which Shore began using as a text when he first started teaching, analyzes one hundred photographs in chronological order, from the birth of photography to the 1970s. Not only did Shore partially echo the structure of the book—made up of commentary on images from different periods and by various photographers—but he was also inspired by Szarkowski's very formal, analytical approach. In the same way that Szarkowski deliberately moved away from an essentialist perspective by choosing to write not on photography in general but on specific photographs, Shore was also eager to avoid an ontological approach. It was not "The Nature of Photography" but rather "The Nature of Photographs" that Shore preferred, focusing, like his predecessor, on the images themselves in their physical, descriptive, and symbolic dimensions.

"The aim of this book, then, is not to explore photographic content," he wrote, "but to describe the physical and formal attributes of a photographic print that form the tools a photographer uses to define and interpret that content."[3] To this end, Shore divides his remarks into four parts: "The Physical Level," where he considers the photograph as an object, not an image; "The Depictive Level," the main section, where he analyzes the illusionistic aspect of a medium that is nevertheless also descriptive through a number of processes having to do with framing, the stopping of time, the reduction of three dimensions to two, and focus; and "The Mental Level" and "Mental Modeling," where he discusses the meaning inherent in the reading of the image and its construction.

In his choice of images and the inclusion of five of his own pictures (in the 2007 edition of the book), *The Nature of Photographs* also represents Shore's personal history of photography—though in a detached way, as is often the case with him. Between the lines one can read his trajectory as a photographer, as well as his affinities and tastes, marked by an inclination toward American photography and culture and an interest in the vernacular. The book is also an indirect attempt to evaluate his own place within this same history by focusing on several of his major influences (Eugène Atget, Walker Evans, Carleton Watkins), photographers of his generation with whom he was close and with whom he exhibited (Bernd and Hilla Becher, William Eggleston, Nicholas Nixon), artists from the following generation whose work had a connection with his own (An-My Lê, Paul Graham, Thomas Struth), and even former students (Lisa Kereszi). (Quentin Bajac)

See also: *Museum of Modern Art, The*; *Teaching*

1. Stephen Shore, *The Nature of Photographs* (Baltimore: Johns Hopkins University Press, 1998); a revised, expanded, and redesigned edition was published as *The Nature of Photographs: A Primer* (London and New York: Phaidon Press, 2007).
2. John Szarkowski, *Looking at Photographs* (New York: The Museum of Modern Art, 1973).
3. Shore, *The Nature of Photographs*, 3.

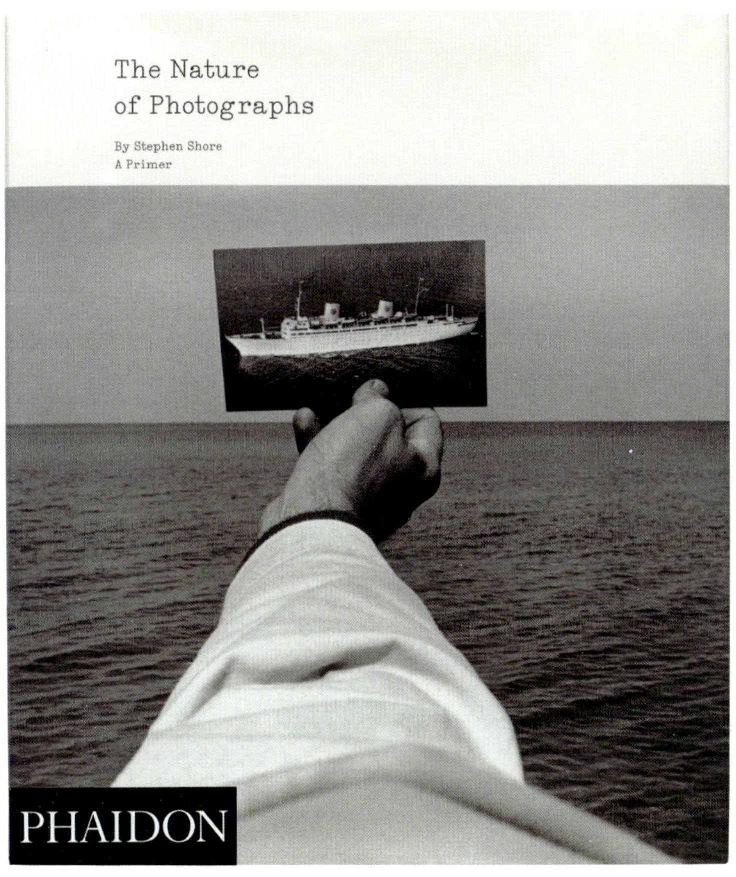

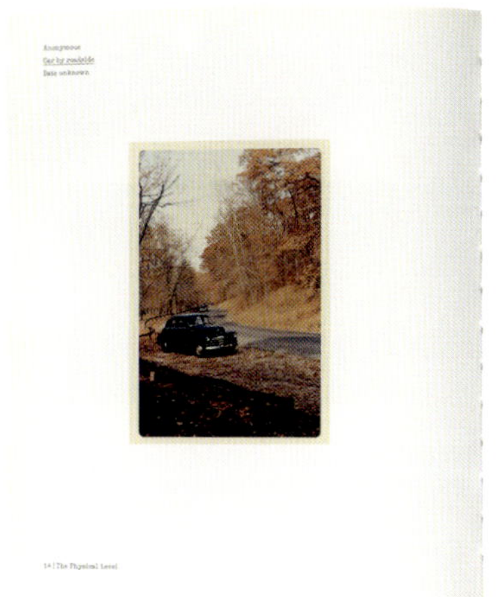

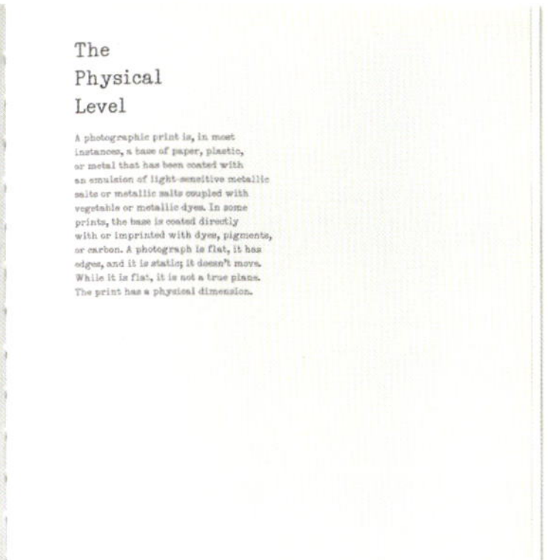
The
Physical
Level

A photographic print is, in most instances, a base of paper, plastic, or metal that has been coated with an emulsion of light-sensitive metallic salts or metallic salts coupled with vegetable or metallic dyes. In some prints, the base is coated directly with or imprinted with dyes, pigments, or carbon. A photograph is flat, it has edges, and it is static; it doesn't move. While it is flat, it is not a true plane. The print has a physical dimension.

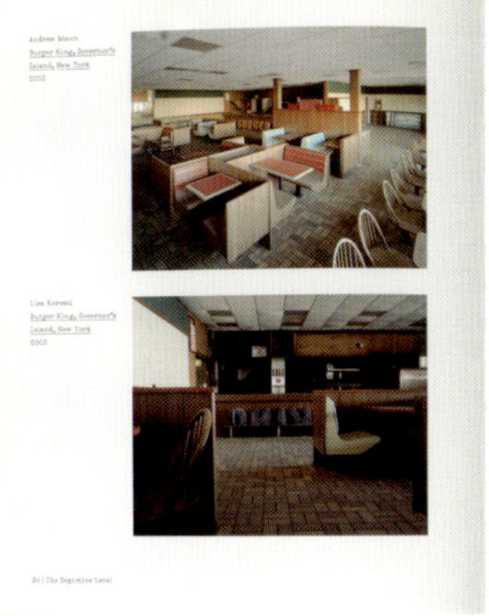

The
Depictive
Level

Photography is inherently an analytic discipline. Where a painter starts with a blank canvas and builds a picture, a photographer starts with the messiness of the world and selects a picture. A photographer standing before houses and streets and people and trees and artifacts of a culture imposes an order on the scene – simplifies the jumble by giving it structure. He or she imposes this order by choosing a vantage point, choosing a frame, choosing a moment of exposure, and by selecting a plane of focus.

***The Nature of Photographs: A Primer*, revised ed. (London and New York: Phaidon Press, 2007)**

New Topographics

The exhibition *New Topographics: Photographs of a Man-Altered Landscape*, organized by then-assistant curator William Jenkins, opened at George Eastman House in Rochester, New York, on October 14, 1975. Shore had already been featured in group exhibitions throughout the United States and Europe, but the artists included in *New Topographics*—Robert Adams, Lewis Baltz, Bernd and Hilla Becher, Joe Deal, Frank Gohlke, Nicholas Nixon, John Schott, Shore, and Henry Wessel, Jr.—would be permanently linked by Jenkins's curatorial vision. His brief introduction to the exhibition catalogue described the artists' affinity as "one of style," or, rather, a "style-less" style. He described a "sense of neutrality," but outlined it with hedged language that conveyed his awareness of the dangers of relying on photography's straightforwardness.[1]

The photographers' refusal to forefront their own subjectivity, to render discernible judgments, and to feature buildings and locations traditionally considered "significant" was compelling. "As good archaeological documents should," one critic wrote, the *New Topographics* photographs "have the transparency of windows through which the man-altered landscape can be viewed."[2] But the differences between the photographers have also been well noted, both at the time and in scholarship since.[3] Shore's photographs in the exhibition were contact prints from 1974 and 1975, including some of the first *Uncommon Places* images shot with an 8-by-10 camera. His work had the most in common with that of Gohlke, Schott, and Wessel, who also photographed everyday buildings from a human vantage point, although Gohlke's comes closest to the precise spatial organization of Shore's.[4]

Shore was the only photographer in the exhibition who worked in color, and the newness of color photography in art museum contexts at the time betrays itself in the sometimes confused responses of reviewers. In the *Los Angeles Times* William Wilson interpreted Shore's images sentimentally, describing their "obvious and gentle affection" (in contrast to the other work, which evinced "detachment" and "critical disdain") and rhapsodizing about the "little gas stations, houses and Ma and Pa stores" that became, in Shore's images, "oases of humanity in a world that can still smile."[5] Carter Ratcliff wrote in a more measured fashion in *Art in America* about Shore's "heavily qualified hope" brought about by "his affectionate vision," which the writer attributed in part to his use of color.[6] This affection was linked by Ratcliff to architects Robert Venturi and Denise Scott Brown, whose 1972 *Learning from Las Vegas*, written with Steven Izenour, made the case for an open and appreciative attitude toward vernacular forms of architecture. In fact, Shore had already traveled across the country fulfilling a commission by the architects to take photographs for *Signs of Life: Symbols in the American City*, a bicentennial project they were organizing at the Renwick Gallery.

During its tenure *New Topographics*, which traveled to the Otis Art Institute in Los Angeles and the Art Museum at Princeton University after its Rochester opening, received relatively little notice. But in the decades to follow it became shorthand for an approach to photography that was borne out—more or less faithfully—by the artists included in it. That approach was described by one visitor in 1976 as "This is it, kid—take it for its beauty and its ugliness."[6] (Kristen Gaylord)

See also: *Color*; *Evans, Walker*; *Uncommon Places*; *Signs of Life*

1. William Jenkins, *New Topographics: Photographs of a Man-Altered Landscape* (Rochester, N.Y.: International Museum of Photography, 1975), 5, 6. Jenkins frames his theses with words and phrases such as "it appears to be," "there is a sense of," and, most tentatively, "it would therefore be possible to conclude," immediately followed by a parenthetical remark calling this not-quite conclusion "questionable."
2. Robert W. Woolard, "Man-Shaped Landscapes," *Artweek*, March 27, 1976, 12.
3. See especially Britt Salvesen and Alison Nordström, eds., *New Topographics: Robert Adams, Lewis Baltz, Bernd and Hilla Becher, Joe Deal, Frank Gohlke, Nicholas Nixon, John Schott, Stephen Shore, Henry Wessel, Jr.* (Tucson: Center for Creative Photography, University of Arizona; Rochester, N.Y:. George Eastman House; Göttingen: Steidl, 2009), and Greg Foster-Rice and John Rohrbach, eds., *Reframing the New Topographics* (Chicago: Center for American Places at Columbia College Chicago, 2013).
4. Much literature about *New Topographics* discusses "the industrial," but these four artists photographed the sorts of structures every American has seen—homes, parking lots, gas stations, motels.
5. William Wilson, "Camera Artists: Truth in Focus," *Los Angeles Times*, March 15, 1976, E10.
6. Carter Ratcliff, "Route 66 Revisited: The New Landscape Photography," *Art in America* 64, no. 1 (January/February 1976): 90.
7. Quoted in Salvesen and Nordström, *New Topographics*, 9.

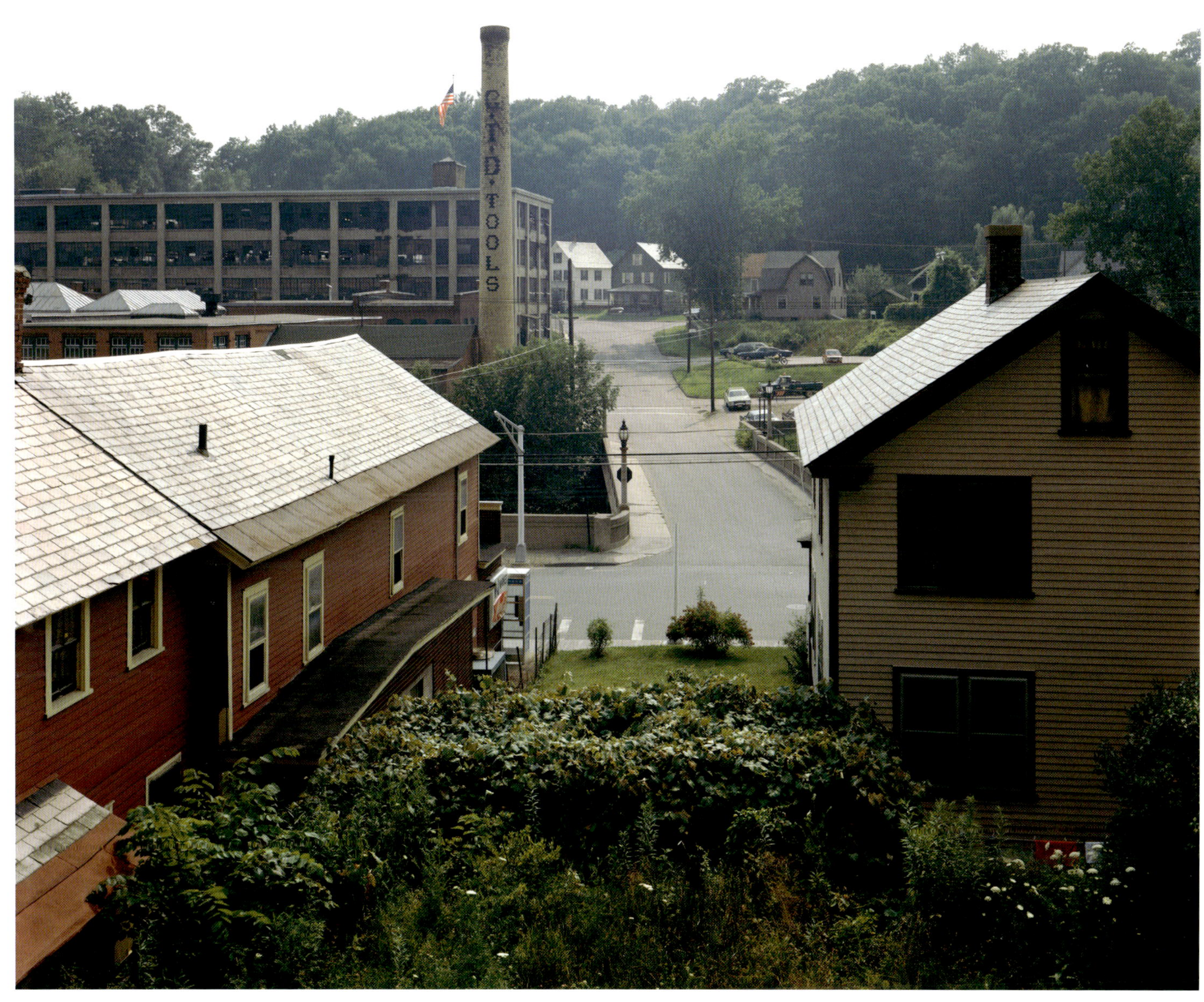

Deerfield Street, Greenfield, Massachusetts, July 15, 1974. 1974

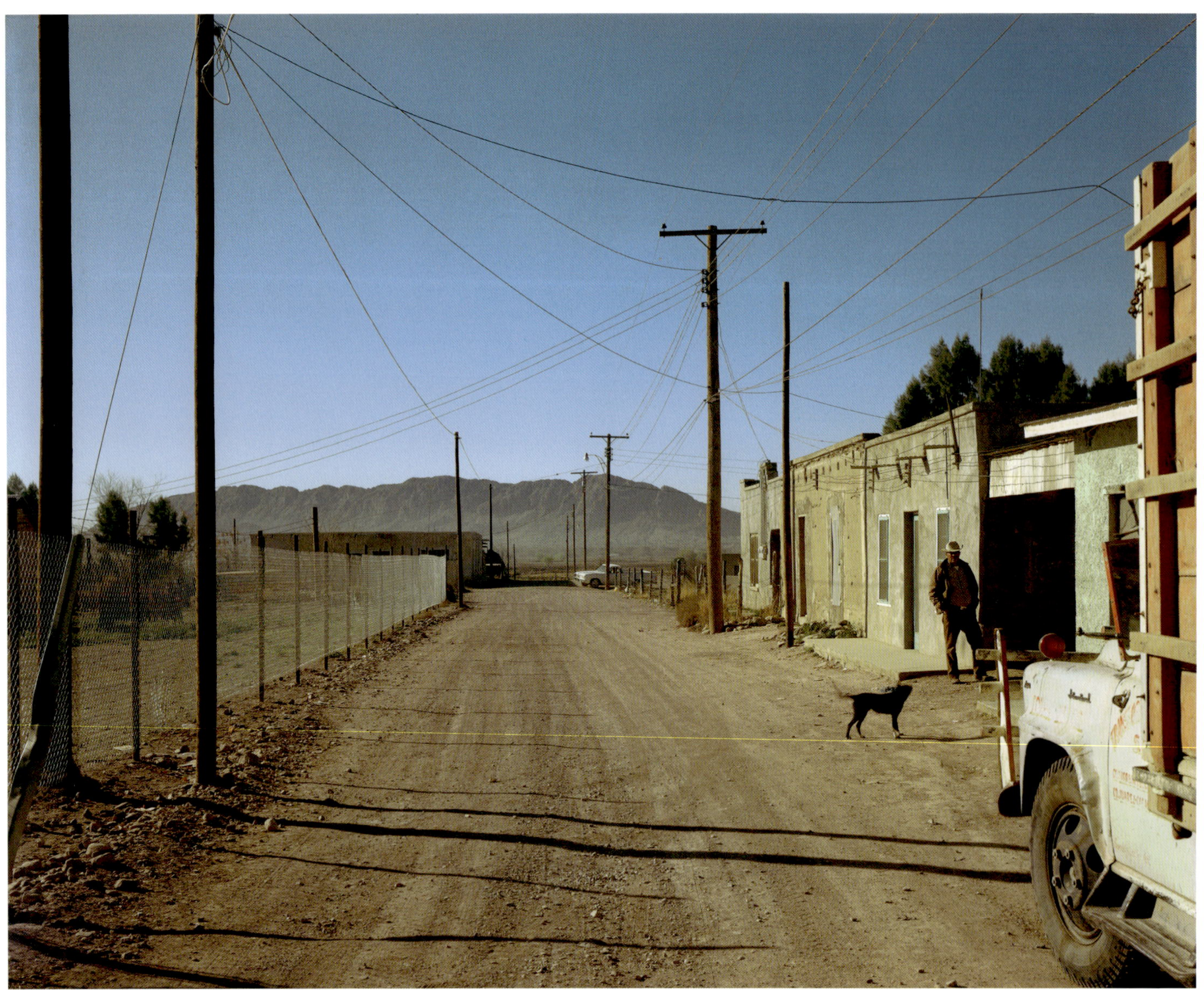

Presidio, Texas, February 21, 1975. 1975

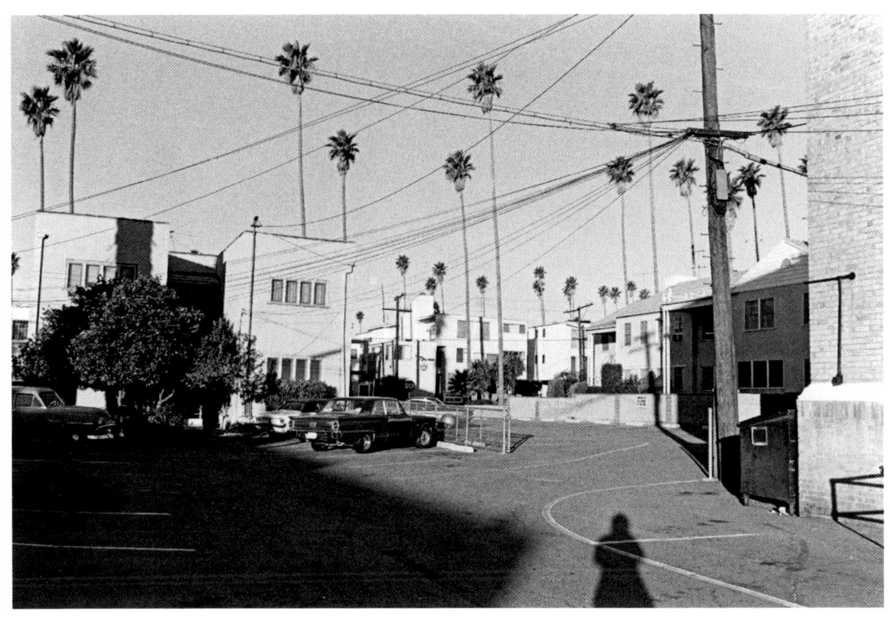

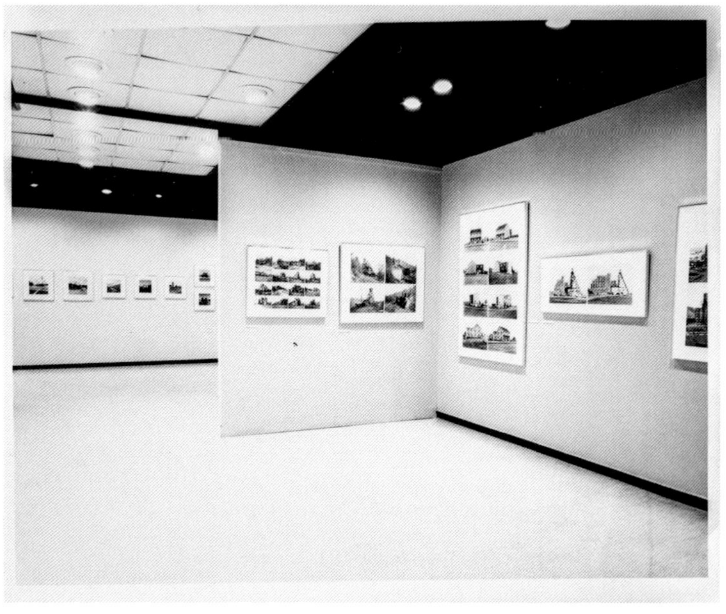

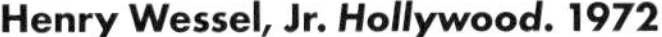

Henry Wessel, Jr. *Hollywood*. 1972

Installation view of *New Topographics: Photographs of a Man-Altered Landscape*, George Eastman House, Rochester, N.Y., October 14, 1975–February 2, 1976, with photographs by Frank Gohlke and Bernd and Hilla Becher

Normal, Illinois, July 1972

Shore's projects generally come to a close when a particular set of pictorial challenges has been met and another is beginning to form. His restlessness leads to renewal:

> I knew by the time I was twenty that [Timothy] O'Sullivan had an active life [in photography] of maybe ten years. I knew all the Walker Evans pictures I loved were made in an eighteen-month period. [. . .] Robert Frank, too. And coming to photography in the late twentieth century, it's impossible to not know all this. And these aren't minor photographers; these are the *best*. These are the people who have changed the medium. Frank and Evans are not lesser because their creative hot streak was a couple of years. [. . .] The people who have had long careers that I respect fall into two categories. There are those who had monomaniacal visions that propelled them, like [Eugène] Atget or the Bechers [Bernd and Hilla]. Then there are people who kept looking at new things, new ways of doing things. They kept changing, like Alfred Stieglitz and Harry Callahan, or in a slightly different way, Lee Friedlander. I know that I'm in this second category. I can't spend my whole career doing one thing.[1]

One aspect of Shore's restlessness derives from a deep fascination with the medium's vernacular practices and popular idioms. The snapshot, the postcard, the print-on-demand book, and the smartphone camera sit in dialogue with his more specialized activities, such as making pictures with a large-format camera. In 1972 he bought a Rollei 35, a very well-made point-and-shoot camera with an exceptional flash. He began to place his ostensible subject matter in the middle of his frame in a way that approximated the most direct kind of human vision and the most "natural" kind of photography. The effect was a disarmingly glassy-eyed stare at the commonplace things Shore was encountering on his early road trips: people and objects, domestic and hotel interiors, plates of food, beds, toilets, telephones, and televisions.

Throughout its history, photography's intersections with other image forms and communication technologies have been very rich. Television in particular has exerted a powerful hold on American photographers. Think of the lonely TV sets buzzing in the corners of Robert Frank's photographs from the mid-1950s, or the little screens Lee Friedlander photographed a few years later. When the 1969 moon landing was beamed into millions of homes, both amateurs and professionals pointed their cameras at their televisions, making souvenirs from an unfolding public event. Even John Logie Baird, the inventor of television, had a camera set up to capture the first images he managed to transmit.

When one medium encounters another in this way, it can have the salutary effect of dramatizing the particulars of each—dramatizing without clarifying or explaining. (David Campany)

See also: *American Surfaces*

1. David Campany, "Ways of Making Pictures," in Marta Dahó, ed., *Stephen Shore* (Madrid: Fundación MAPFRE; New York: Aperture, 2014), 36–37.

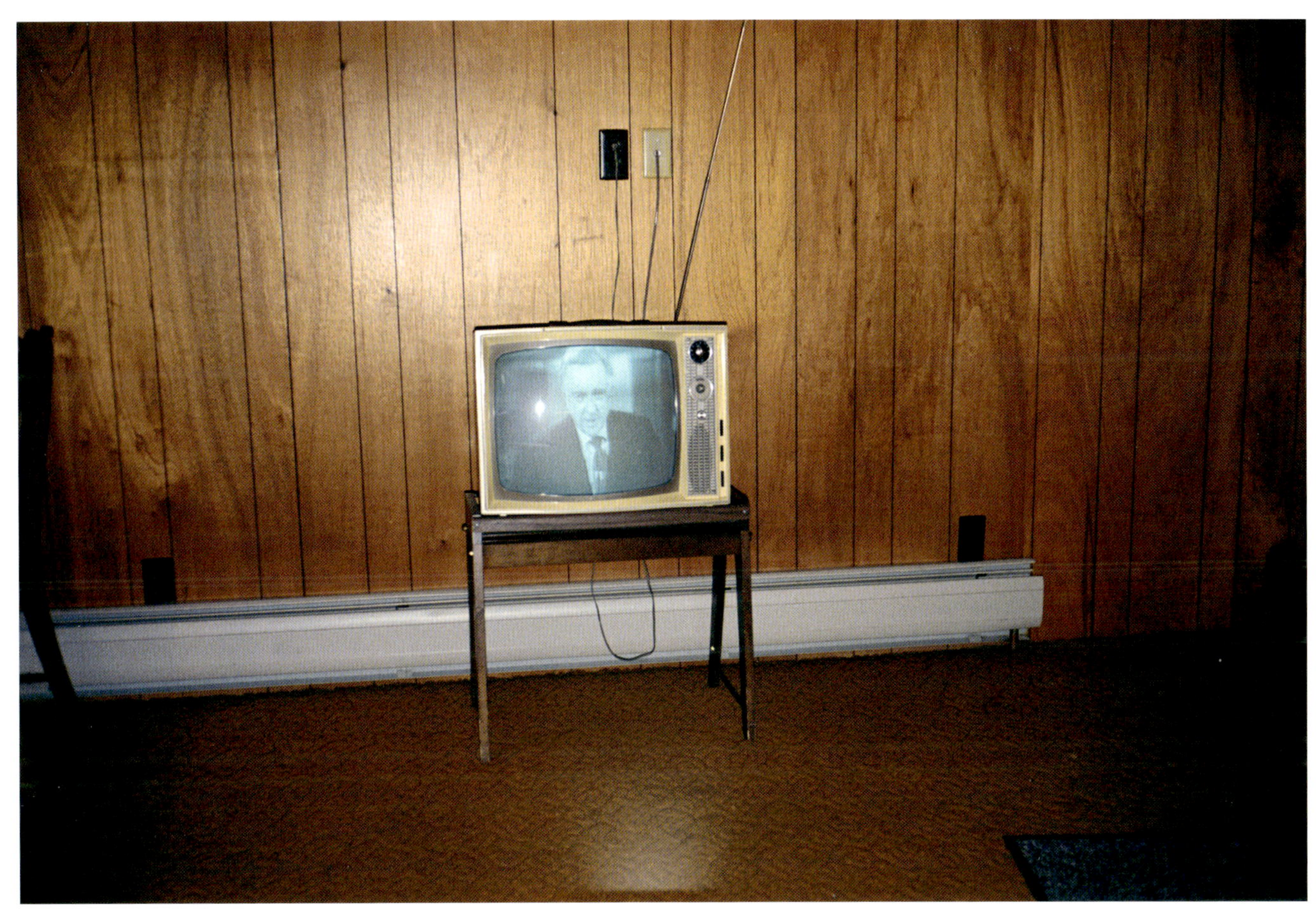

***Normal, Illinois, July 1972*. 1972**

171.

Objective Correlative

When asked what entry he would like to see featured in this book, Shore answered, "objective correlative," a concept that he borrowed from T. S. Eliot and has referred to in several of his interviews. All the images illustrating this entry were chosen by him.

"The only way of expressing emotion in the form of art is by finding an 'objective correlative'; in other words, a set of objects, a situation, a chain of events which shall be the formula of that *particular* emotion; such that when the external facts, which must terminate in sensory experience, are given, the emotion is immediately evoked."[1] —T. S. Eliot

"T. S. Eliot, when he was writing literary criticism, in an essay on Hamlet, used the phrase 'objective correlative.' And what he's saying is that, when he was talking about a piece of literature, that there is a situation which engenders a specific psychological or emotional response in the viewer. That situation is an objective correlative of the emotion or psychological state. So it has some aspect of metaphor, it has some aspect of symbol, it has some aspect of analog, but it's not exactly those things. And this is something photography has dealt with for a long time, where photographers understand that something very ordinary for some reason has some kind of meaning to them that goes beyond cultural or sociological meaning. It does something to them. Walker Evans referred to some of his work as 'transcendent documents,' and I think this is what he was referring to."[2] —Stephen Shore

"[A]fter having made [a photograph] instinctively, unless I feel that the product is a transcendence of the thing, of the moment in reality, then I haven't done anything, and I throw it away. Take [Eugène] Atget, whose work I now know very well. [. . .] In his work you do feel what some people call poetry. I do call it that also, but a better word for it, to me, is, well—when Atget does even a tree root, he transcends that thing."[3] —Walker Evans

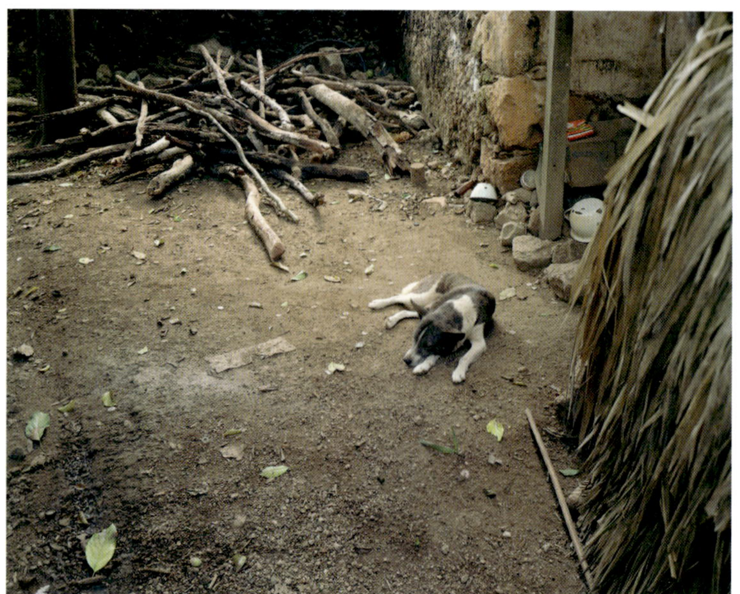

1. T. S. Eliot, "Hamlet and His Problems," in *The Sacred Wood* (New York: Alfred A. Knopf, 1921), 92
2. Kyle Adams, "Stephen Shore's Internal Revolutions," *Register-Star* (Hudson, N.Y.), December 29, 2014.
3. Leslie Katz, "Interview with Walker Evans," *Art in America* 59, no. 2 (March/April 1971): 85.

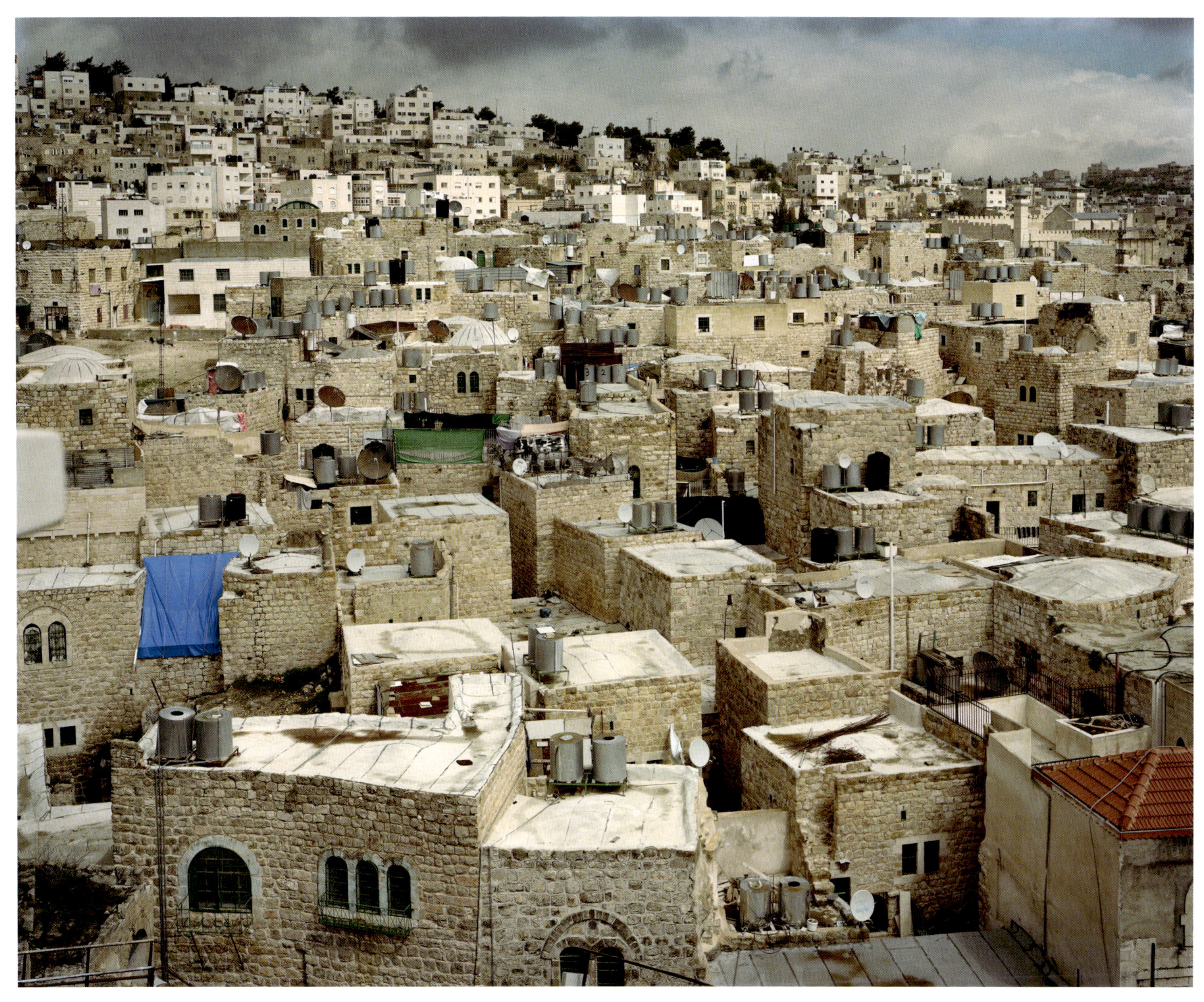

***Yucatán, Mexico, 1990.* 1990**

***Hebron, West Bank, March 25, 2011.* 2011**

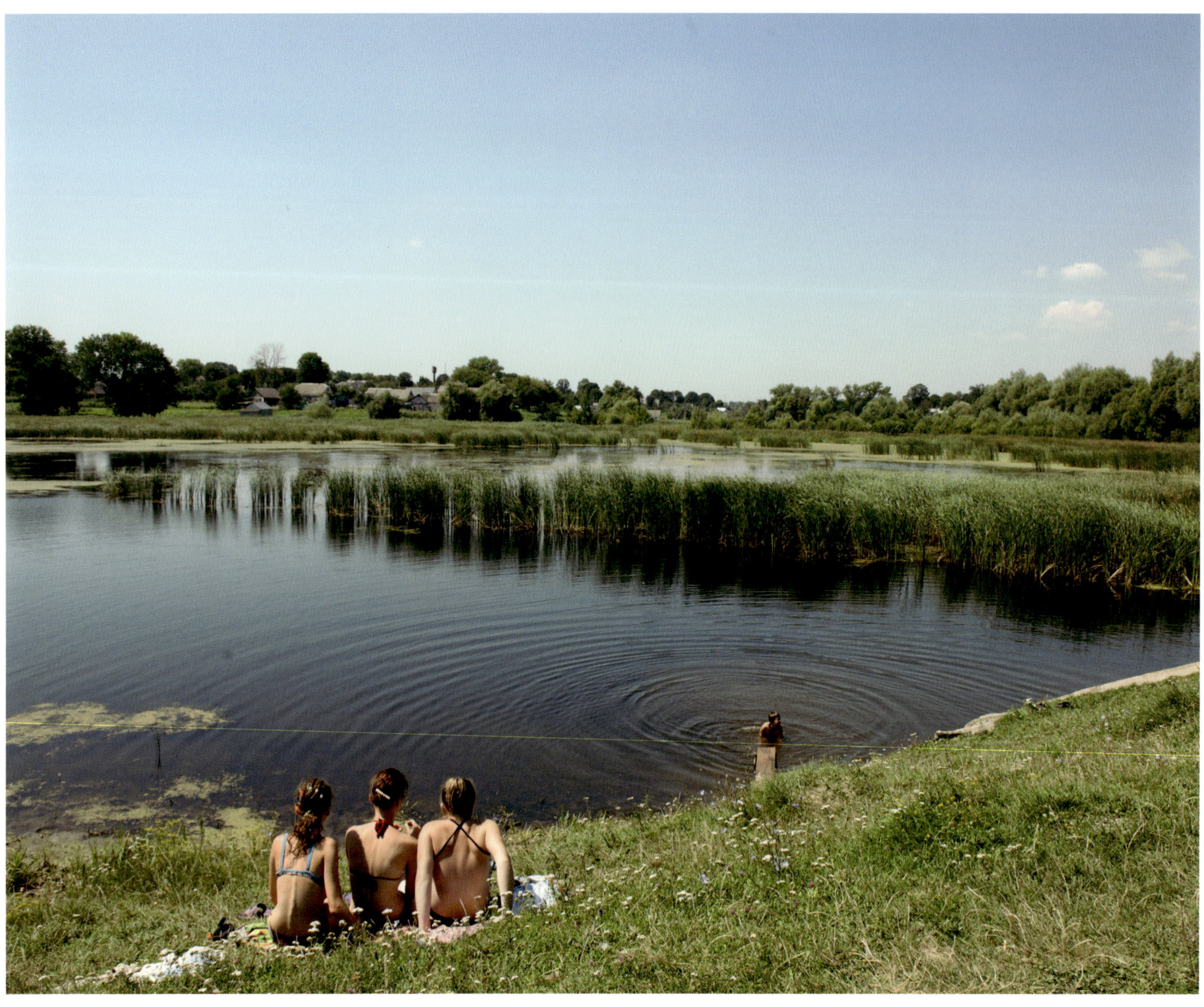

Bazalia, Khmelnitskiy Province, Ukraine, July 27, 2012. 2012

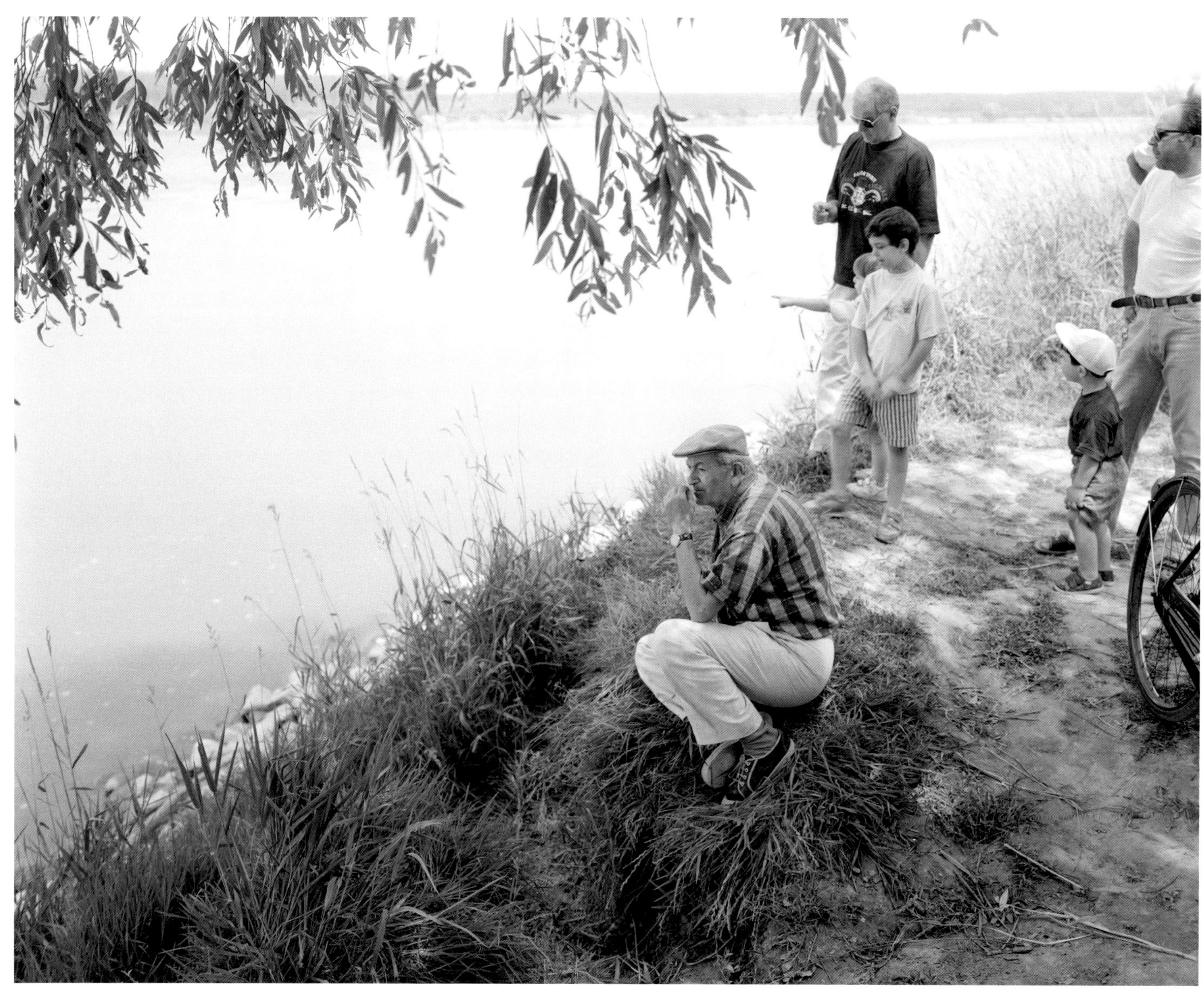

Luzzara, Italy, 1993. 1993

175.

Portraiture

Though often perceived exclusively as a landscape photographer, Shore has always mixed genres and, since his beginnings in the streets of New York in the early 1960s, has also practiced portraiture. In fact, the first article to be published about him, in *U.S. Camera* in 1963 (page 281), features his "straightforward portraits" and discusses his interest in the human figure in the tradition of humanist street photography. It points out that a "strong head-on approach to people typify [*sic*] most of Shore's work when shooting candids," and the young Shore himself explains that he likes to work with "children and older people."[1] His photographs of Andy Warhol's Factory a few years later, in 1965–67, also consist primarily of portraits, intimate shots that were sometimes taken spontaneously and sometimes posed.

While he later distanced himself from portraiture to a certain degree, Shore never totally abandoned the genre, as can be seen especially in *American Surfaces* but also, to a lesser extent, in *Uncommon Places*. Like almost all of Shore's images, regardless of what type of camera he is using, his portraits are typically horizontal and frontal. Though shot on the spur of the moment, they require the complicity or cooperation of the model, who usually looks directly into the camera; "stolen" portraits are rare in *American Surfaces* and almost nonexistent later on. In this sense, they follow the simplest definition of the amateur photographic portrait: a picture taken on the spot of a subject who is aware of being photographed and usually poses for the occasion.

Another consistent quality of Shore's portraits is the lack of distinction (in distance from the subject or in framing) between acquaintances and strangers, close friends and people with whom he had fleeting contact: all are treated as photographic subjects of equal importance. A closer look at *American Surfaces* allows us to isolate individuals who were typical of the liberal, cultured New York milieu to which Shore belonged at the time. In addition to his friends, in these photographs we encounter Michael Marsh and his future wife, Sandy Kirkland (page 27), as well as other people he met at the Factory; Henry Geldzahler, a curator at the Metropolitan Museum of Art (page 30); P. Adams Sitney, a historian of avant-garde film and co-founder with Jonas Mekas of the Anthology Film Archives (page 37); Rogers E. M. Whitaker, an editor at the *New Yorker* and a train specialist; Priscilla Hiss, the widow of Alger Hiss, the government official accused of spying; Harold Jones, the director of Light Gallery (page 28); and so on. There were an equal number of less famous subjects, often from more ordinary walks of life, whom Shore came across during his travels in the summer of 1972—bartenders, sales clerks, waitresses, a Texaco gas station attendant—and who were rarely identified for the viewer. The series mixed the intimate and the public, the known and the unknown, subjects who were chosen not for their identity as 'x' or 'y' but simply for their appearances or surfaces, all captured in the same flash halo. While a similar variety was at work in *Uncommon Places*, the models were generally identified by their names, in keeping with the more explicitly descriptive spirit of that series.

After concentrating solely on landscapes in the eighties, Shore reintroduced the human figure and portraiture into his work in the nineties, somewhat tentatively in his Mexico photographs and more forcefully in his Luzzara images. These portraits no longer display the systematic frontality that characterizes those of the seventies but demonstrate a more varied, more gentle approach, one might say. Portraiture also plays a part in two of Shore's most recent large-scale projects, photographed in Israel and in Ukraine. Of all Shore's series, *Survivors in Ukraine* is undoubtedly the one in which the human figure is most central and the portrait most prominent. Here portraiture becomes the structuring element for the first time, whether in direct, frontal portraits, busts and full-length figures, or indoor and outdoor shots. The series features portraiture in a more abstract sense, too—indirect or fragmented portraits made around the subject, where each part, each detail, both signifies and is equal to the whole, serving as a metonymy for the person. (Quentin Bajac)

See also: *Factory, The*; *Ginger*; *Street Photography*; *Ukraine*

1. "Angry Young Man with a Camera," *U.S. Camera*, June 1963, 52–53.

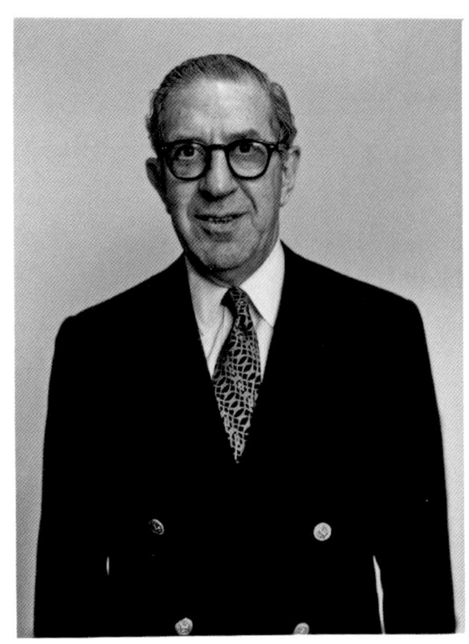
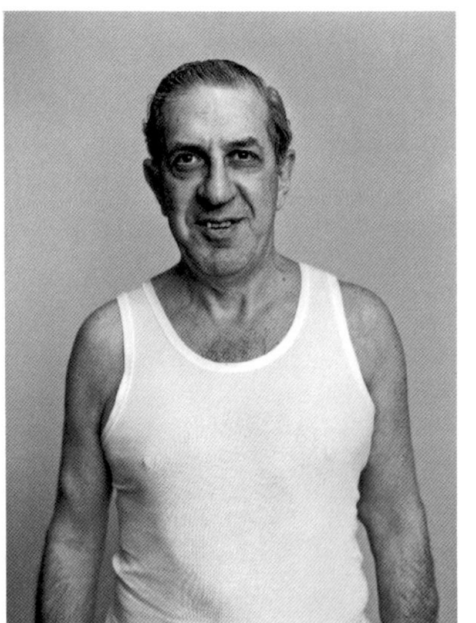
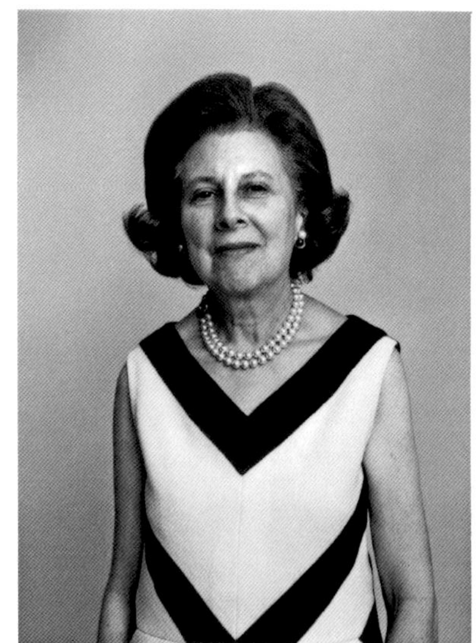
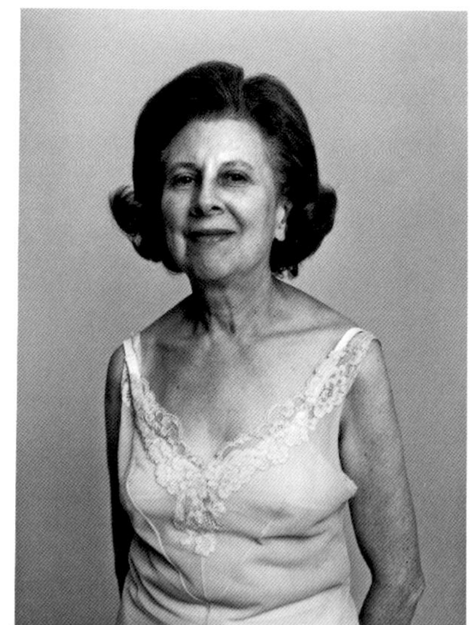

***Fred Shore*. 1970**

***Ruth Shore*. 1970**

177.

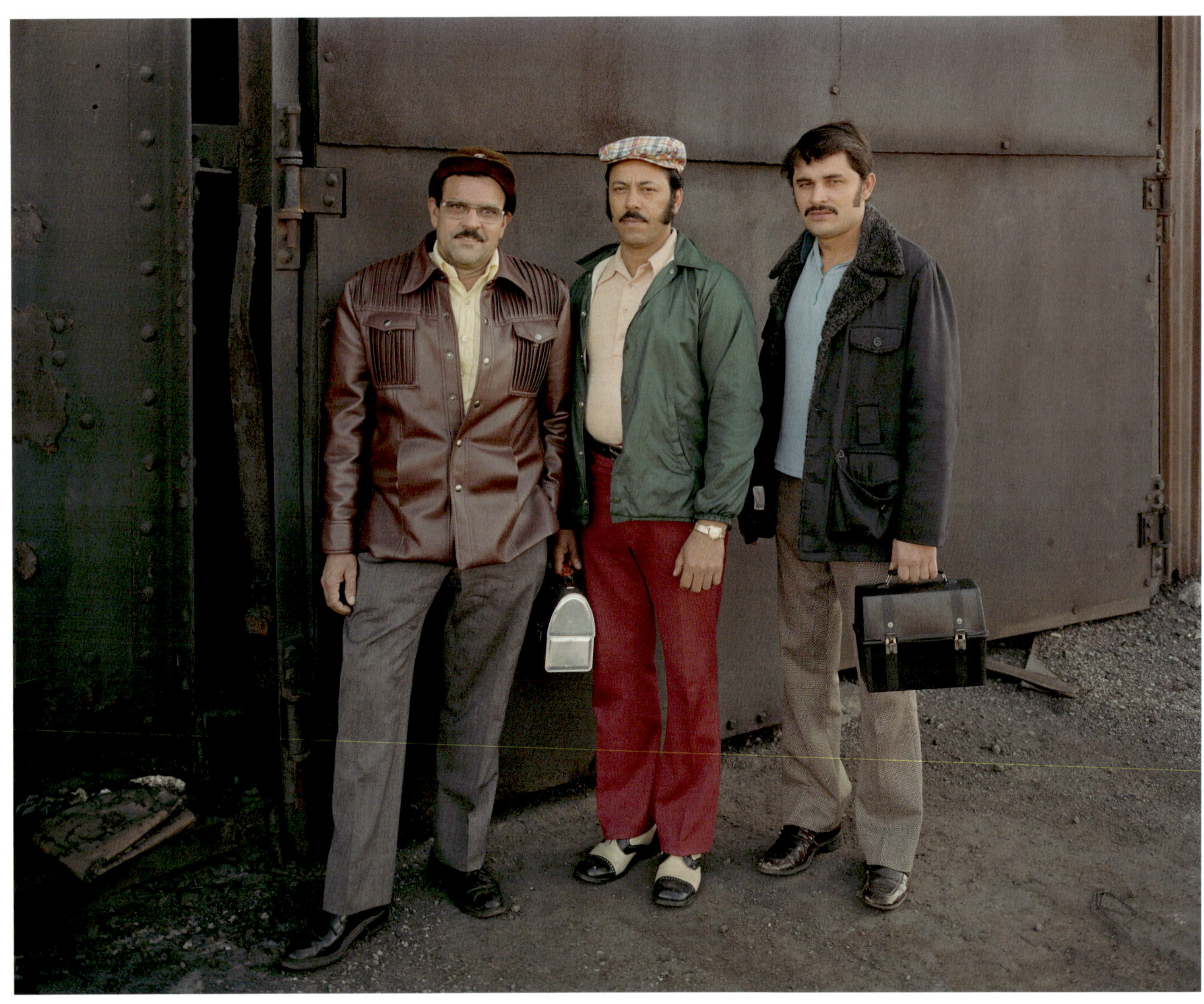

Raphael Rentas, Louis Olivera, and Herminio Cadona, Campbell, Ohio, October 28, 1977. 1977

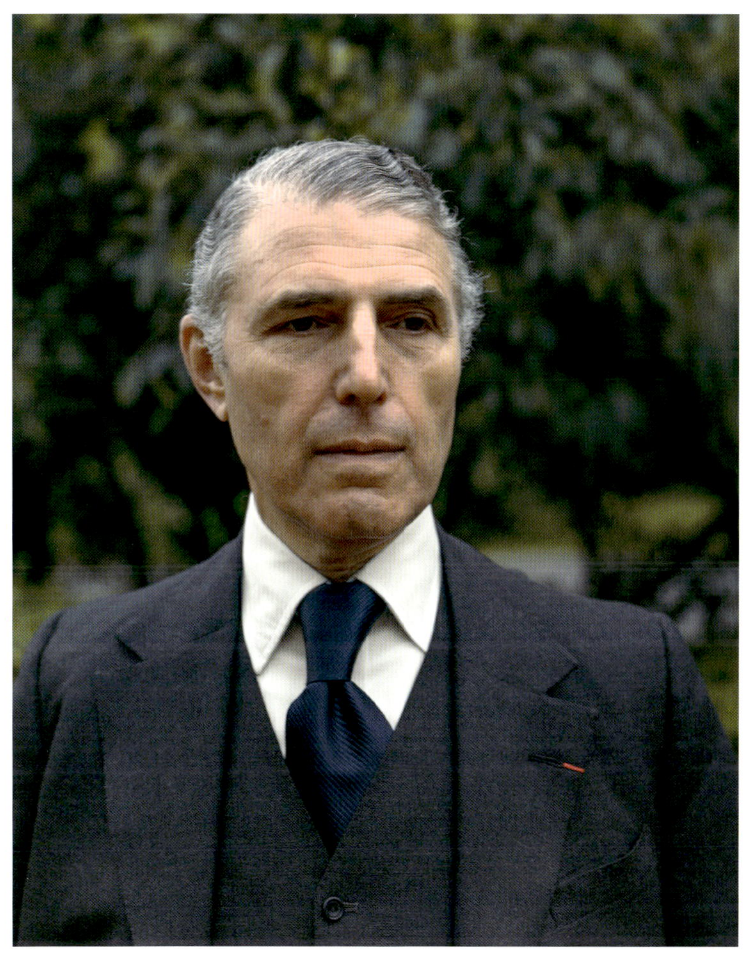

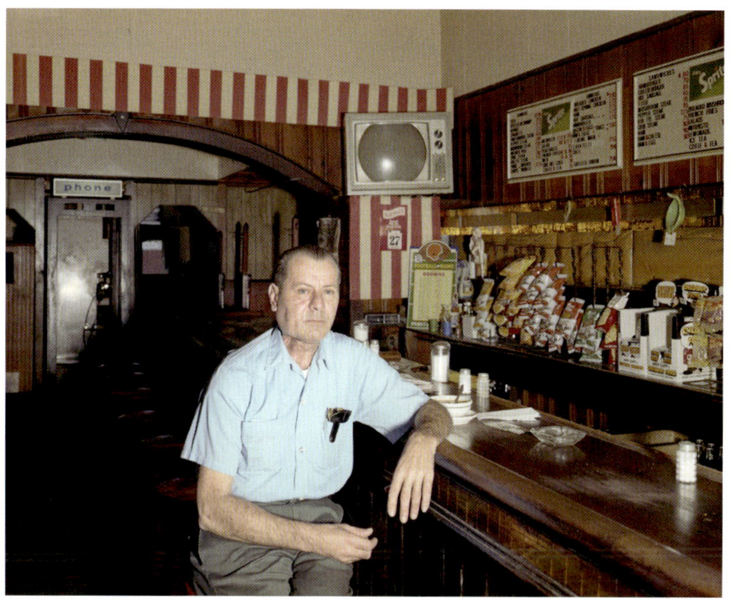

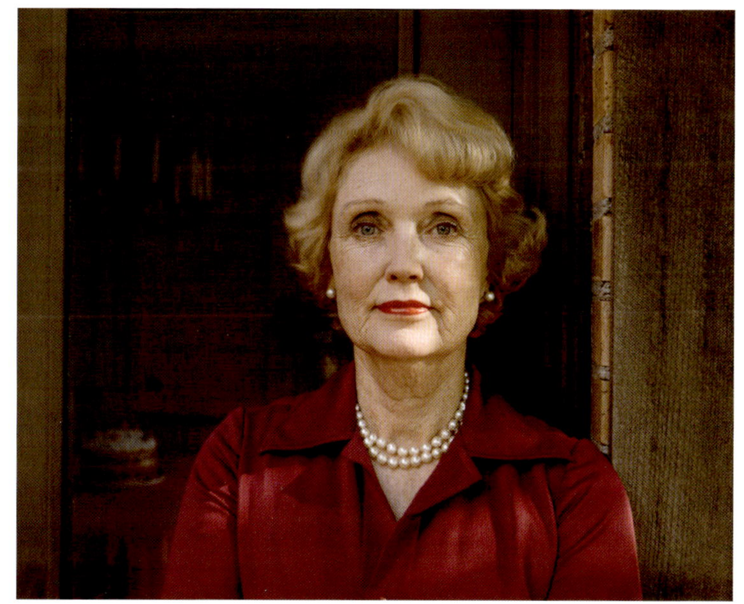

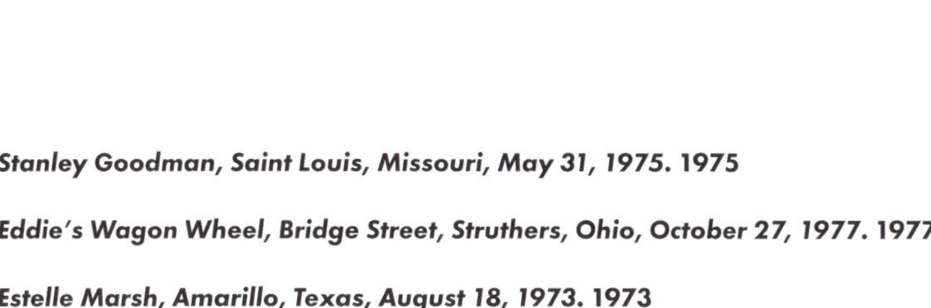

***Stanley Goodman, Saint Louis, Missouri, May 31, 1975.* 1975**

***Eddie's Wagon Wheel, Bridge Street, Struthers, Ohio, October 27, 1977.* 1977**

***Estelle Marsh, Amarillo, Texas, August 18, 1973.* 1973**

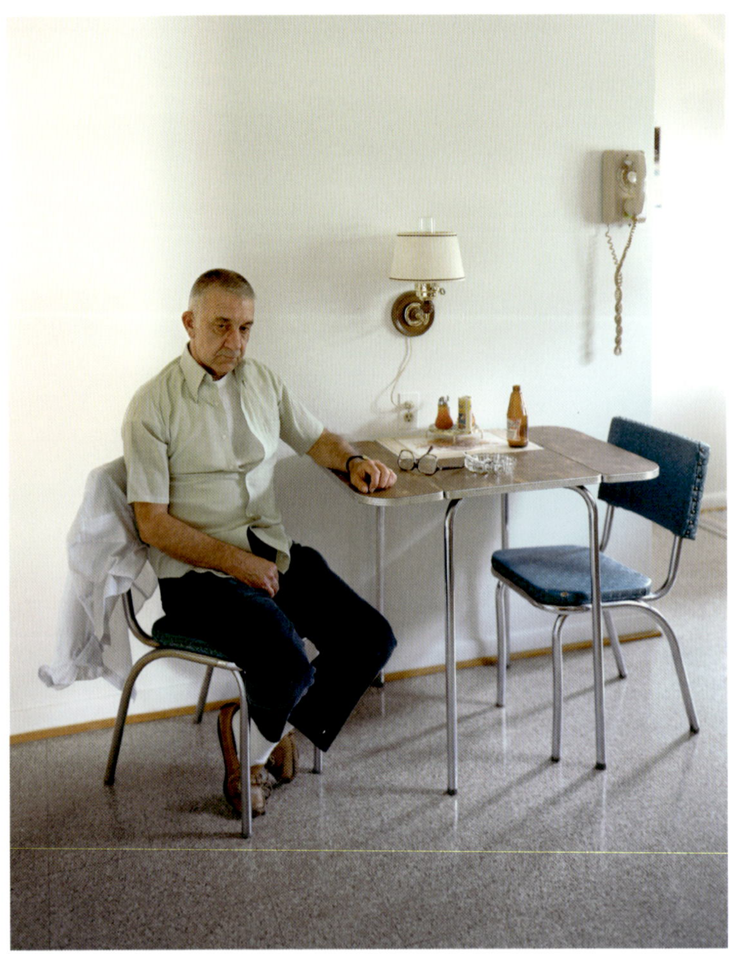

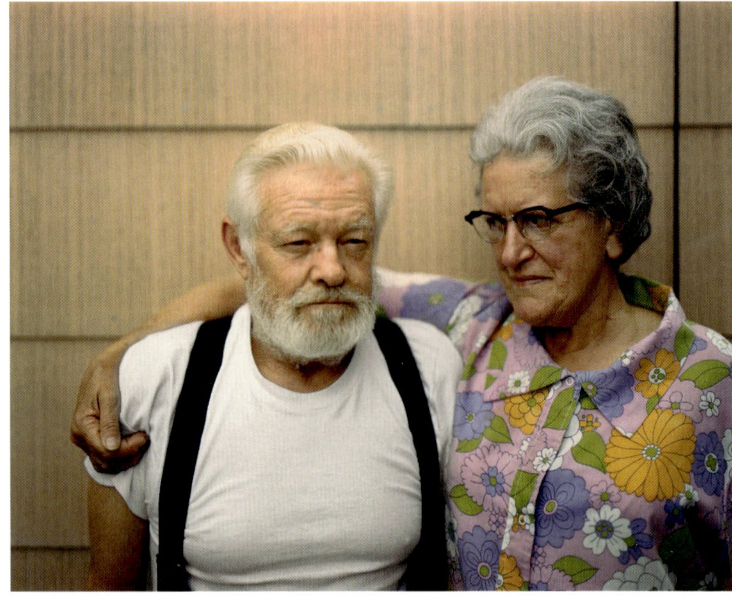

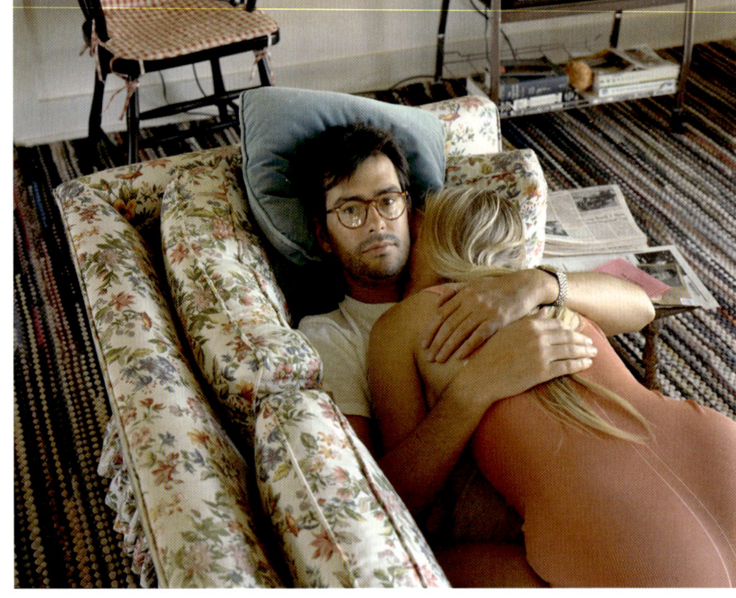

Lee Cramer, Bel Air, Maryland, 1983. 1983

Robert and Lucille Wehrly, Coos Bay, Oregon, August 31, 1974. 1974

Michael and Sandy Marsh, Amarillo, Texas, September 27, 1974. 1974

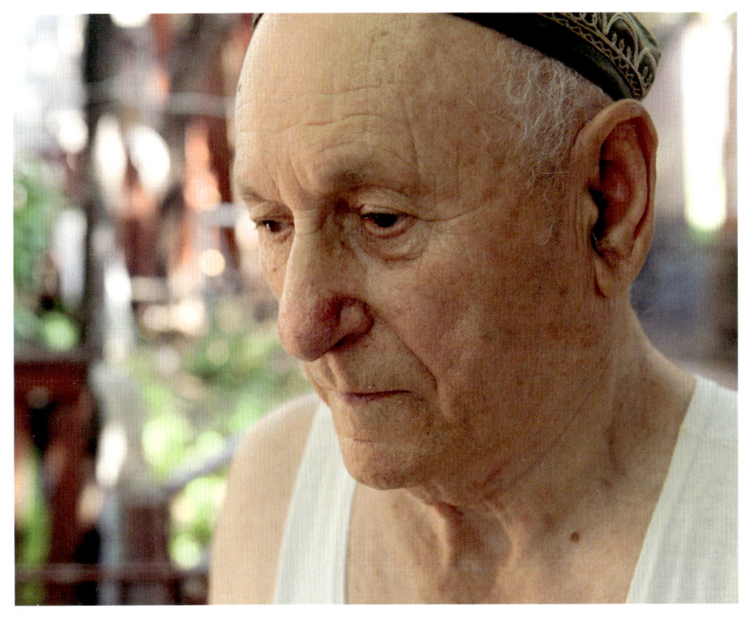

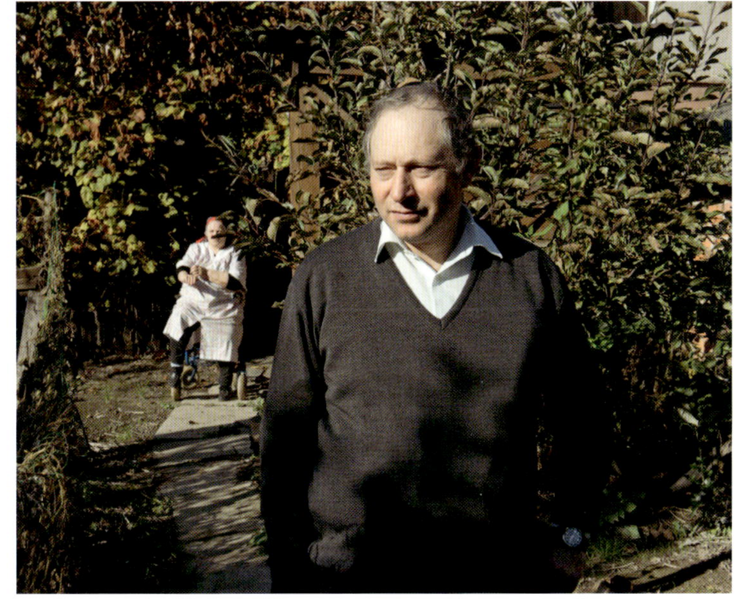

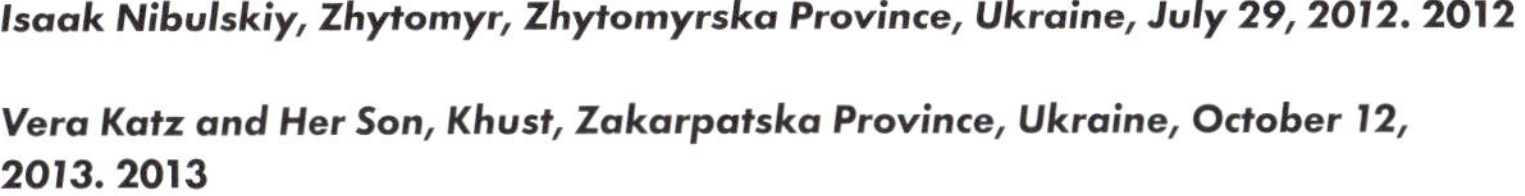

***Isaak Nibulskiy, Zhytomyr, Zhytomyrska Province, Ukraine, July 29, 2012.* 2012**

***Vera Katz and Her Son, Khust, Zakarpatska Province, Ukraine, October 12, 2013.* 2013**

Print-on-Demand Books

"You come back with a disc full of images and you can have a book printed of them—four-color offset lithography," Shore explained in an interview in 2004. "You set up an account with Apple, order the sequence, set up a format, your file is uploaded to a server and three or four days later, FedEx delivers a linen-bound book to your door."[1] With limited layout options and a several-day wait for delivery, the technology of print-on-demand books may appear somewhat archaic in this era of smartphone cameras, widespread immediacy of image transmission via Instagram, and improvements in digital home printing. Nevertheless, when Shore, with his lifelong desire for change and his enthusiasm for mass photographic techniques, adopted it in 2003, the technology constituted a decisive advance and a revolution in books of photography. For more than five years, it formed the core of his photographic work, as Instagram does today.

Between 2003 and 2010, Shore made dozens of print-on-demand books. Each measures 8⅝ by 11 inches and features a photograph on the cover, a page with title and date, and anywhere from one image (*Heavy Metal Alphabet*, 2005, page 191) to fifty (*6-9-06*, 2006, pages 188–89), with no captions whatsoever. All were printed in limited editions of twenty copies, making them similar to artists' books. In the choice of subjects and approaches, the series of books seems both literally and figuratively to be a mini-version of Shore's entire oeuvre, blending and reworking the themes that have always been important to him—an exhaustive exploration of a particular subject or place, a penchant for the vernacular, an interest in sequence, a tendency toward autobiography, a search for a kind of immediacy, and a dry sense of humor—while still retaining its autonomy and specificity.

The monumental work published in 2012 that brings together eighty-three of these books includes an index by subject, allowing us to see the principal motifs of the entire enterprise: an interest in art (especially sculpture), archaeology, and architecture (particularly of the vernacular kind); an anthropological outlook, demonstrated in Shore's fascination with signage, food, and ritual (as in the "Season's Greetings" books); under the rubric "Ways of Seeing," a focus on various modes of perception and visual recording devices (mobile phones, webcams); a frequent use of images within images, and a reuse of his earlier photographs, including the enlargement of details from particular pictures ("Reworkings"); displacement and travel as favorite experiences in his photographic practice ("Journeys"); and, finally, a use of systematic acts of creation in his "New York Times" series.[2] To produce this last group, Shore decided in 2005 to create books on "days that the *New York Times* deems an event so newsworthy that it allocates a six-column, banner headline to it," regardless of his other activities that day.[3] All the books follow the same format, with the front page of the *Times* on the cover, followed by images taken during the day. Shore made eleven books in this series in a three-year period, capturing the ordinary and everyday events of his life, in deliberate contrast to the spectacular news stories. In explaining his mission for the series, he said, "I will make a book, wherever I happen to be that day, that is intended to be a visual time capsule."[4]

With rare exceptions, all of the books-on-demand are time capsules, made in a single day or an even shorter period (the time of a train ride, a plane landing, a visit to the dentist, a rock concert, a walk through Central Park, a trip to a flea market in Vienna). While these images are often arranged chronologically, Shore in some cases displays the sequence out of order. This is a crucial element, as the flow of the individual pictures is essential to understanding the whole, each image serving as a piece of the puzzle that makes up the book. The whole is greater than the sum of its parts, and the images do not lend themselves to being separated or singled out. Moreover, the absence of titles renders the pictures unidentifiable as individual objects, making them the exact opposite of the isolated and precisely captioned images in *Uncommon Places*.

The print-on-demand books were created during a period when Shore was beginning to reexamine his older work more systematically, particularly *Uncommon Places*, and to make digital prints of his photographs in larger dimensions than before; 303 Gallery exhibited the first of the books in 2003 at the same time as these new prints. The reduction in format that the books represent in relation to Shore's previous work goes hand in hand with the simultaneous enlargement of his work. In fact, the series of books entitled "Reworkings" was a

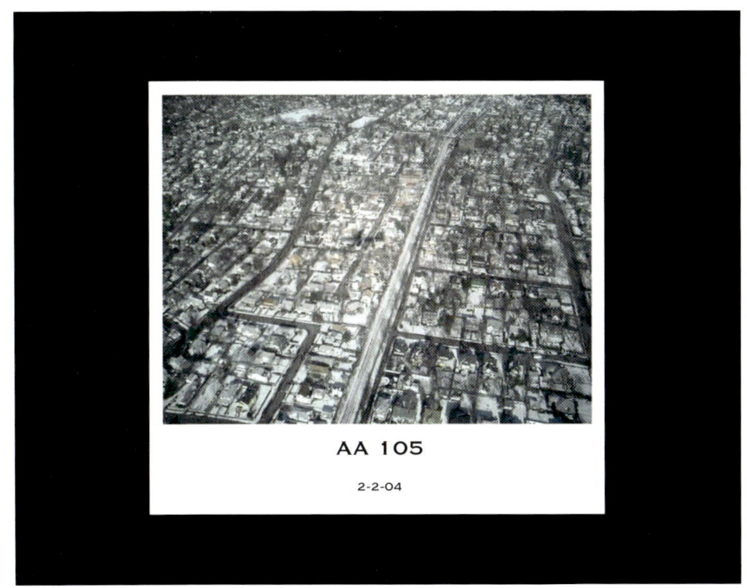

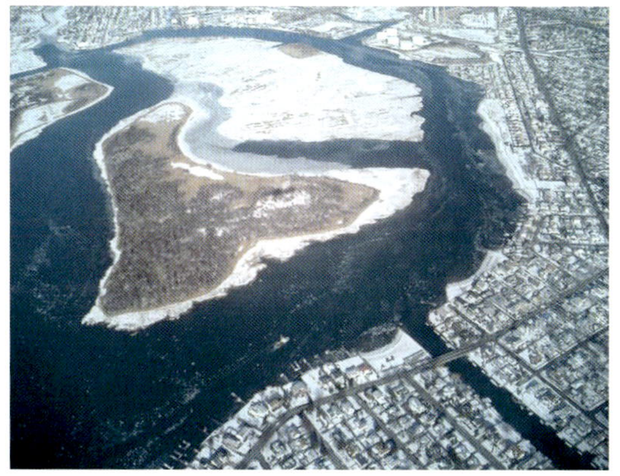

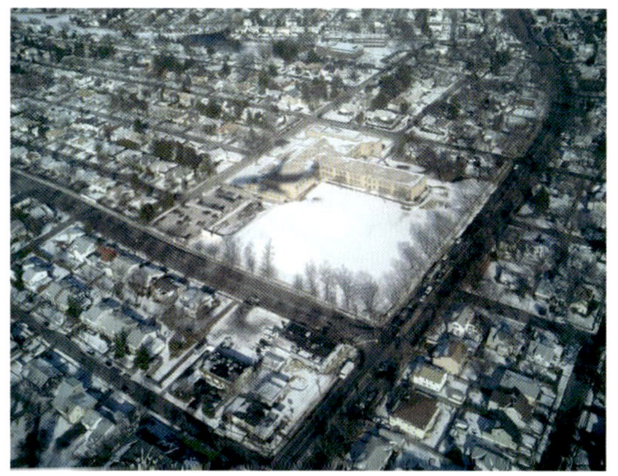

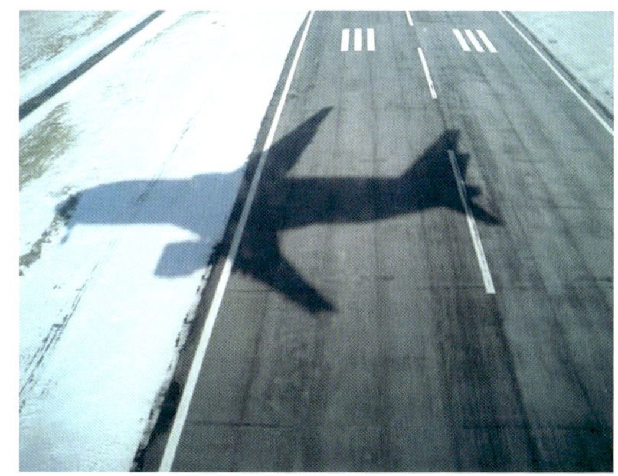

AA 105: **2-2-04. 2004**

183.

product of this practice and of the possibility offered by digital tools to read his older images differently once they were scanned and viewed in greater detail on a computer screen.

In describing the approach taken in these books, Shore speaks of "a light touch," a playful dimension in both their spirit and the simplicity of their layout.[5] The ease of production, speed of execution, democratic nature of the technique used, and modesty of the finished product seem in direct line with the snapshots of *American Surfaces* and the immediacy of Polaroid images. As for the constraints Shore imposed on himself in making these books—from adhering to a random process based on news coverage in the *New York Times* series to working carefully within the rudimentary layouts proposed by the iPhoto program—they bear a similarity to the rules the young photographer established during his Conceptual period to avoid certain idealistic conventions of artistic practice. Shore was reclaiming the position of the amateur, freely exploring a path without worrying about where it would lead, and creating images that were largely outside the art market circuit.

While Shore stopped regularly creating print-on-demand books in 2008, they still resonate in his work.[6] Their influence can be seen in specific projects like *Mose: A Preliminary Report* (2011)—a very original book in its subject matter (the construction of mobile gates to protect the Venetian lagoon), layout, and mix of images—the slide show *Winslow, Arizona*, made in 2013 in a single day, or, starting the following year, his daily use of Instagram. (Quentin Bajac)

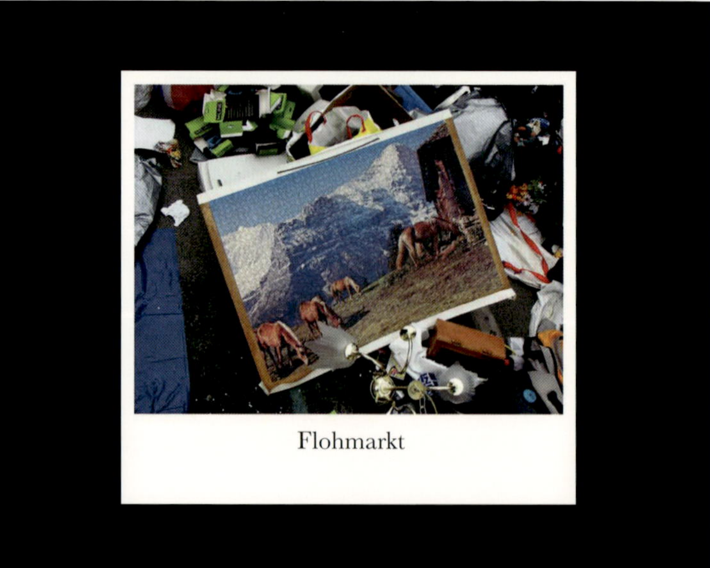

See also: *All the Meat You Can Eat*; *Conceptual Sequences*; *Instagram*; *Jigsaw Puzzle*; *Travel*; *Winslow, Arizona*

1. Kenneth Baker, "Wave of Attention Rushes Back to Stephen Shore's Photography," *San Francisco Chronicle*, May 31, 2004, E5.
2. Stephen Shore, *The Book of Books* (London and New York: Phaidon, 2012).
3. Stephen Shore, "A Book in One Day," *Witness Number One* (New York: Joy of Giving Something, 2006), 13.
4. Ibid.
5. "A Fluttering Knuckleball: Lunch with Stephen Shore and Tim Davis," *Blind Spot*, no. 26 (2004): n.p.
6. Shore created two final print-on-demand books in 2009 and 2010.

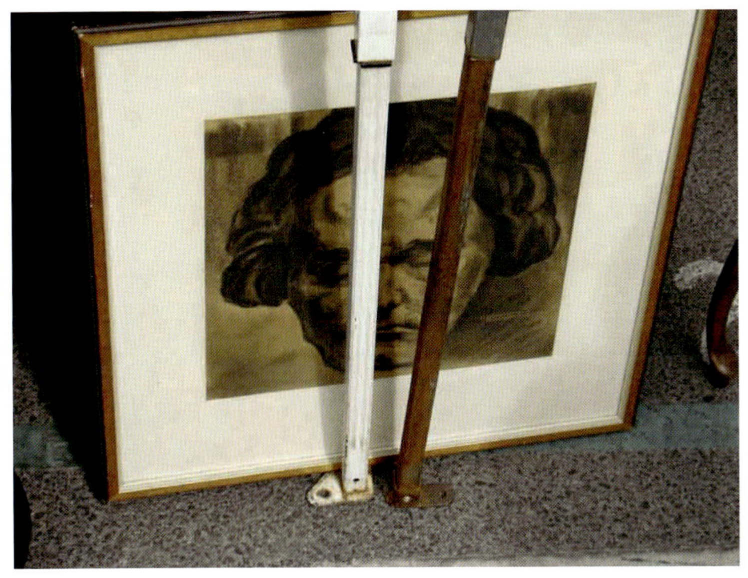

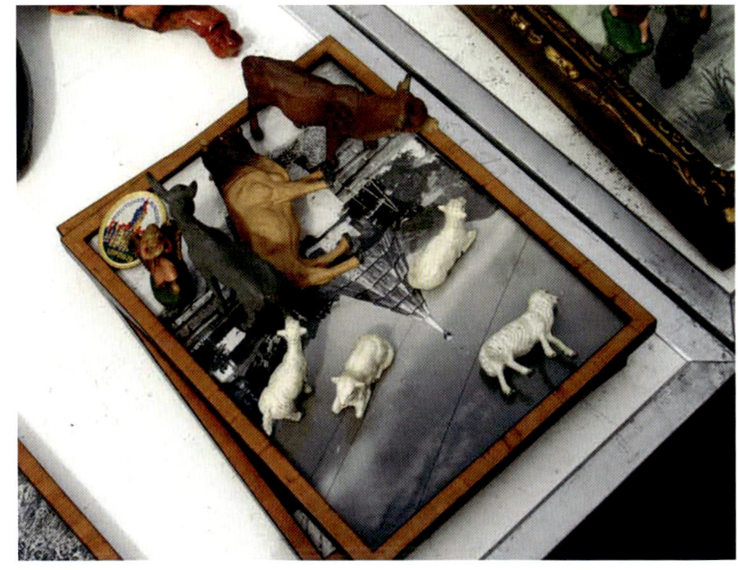

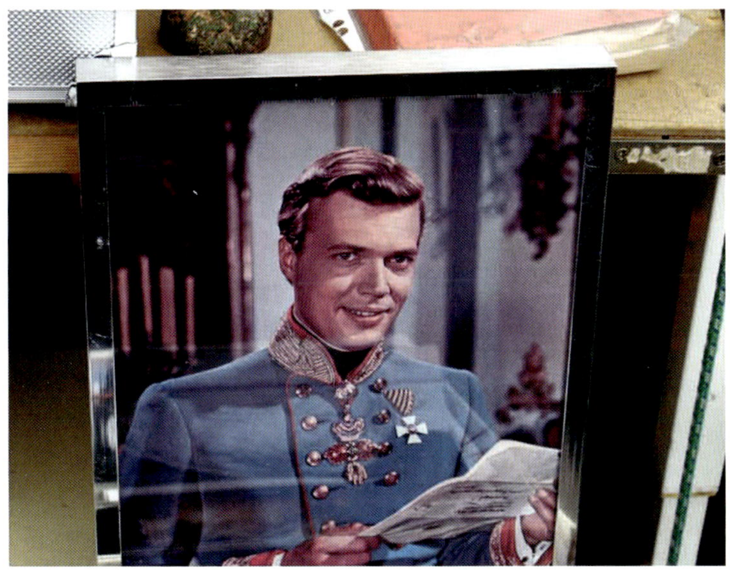

Flohmarkt. 2004

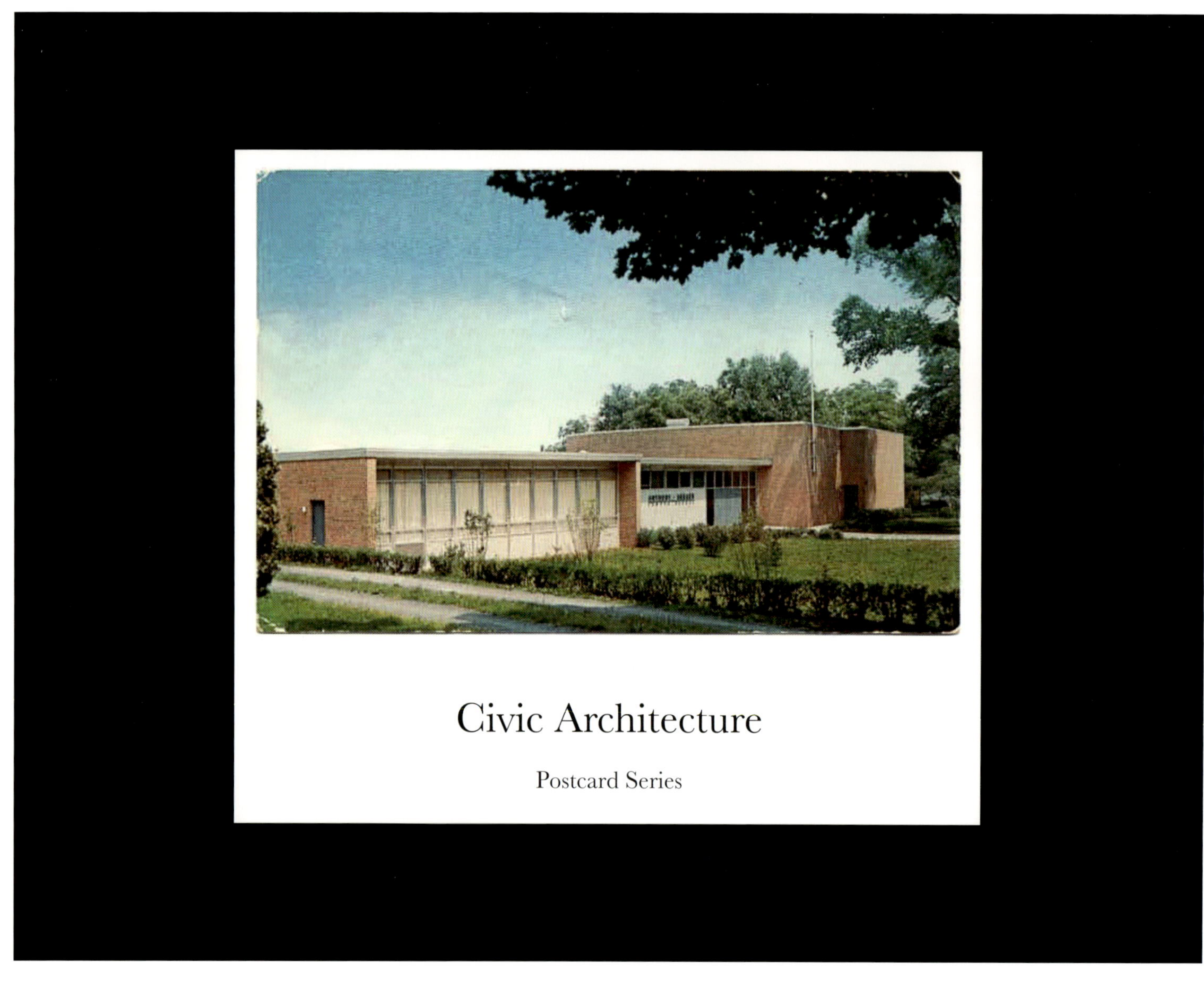

***Civic Architecture: Postcard Series*. 2005**

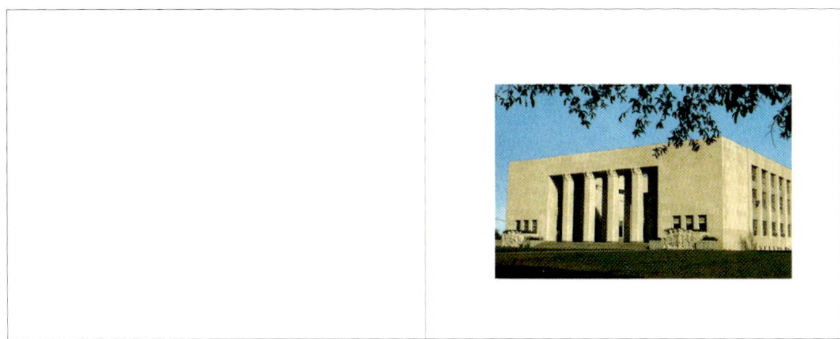

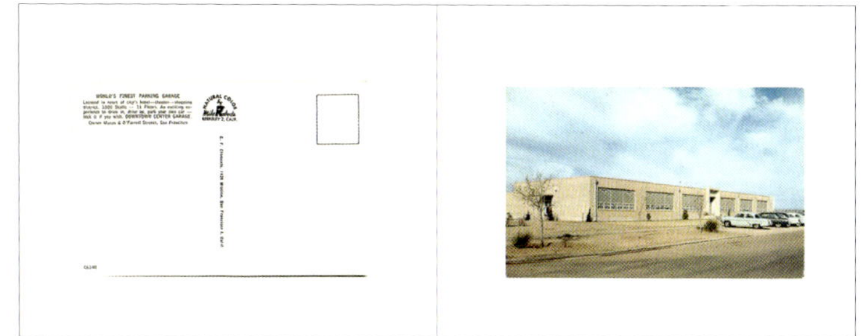

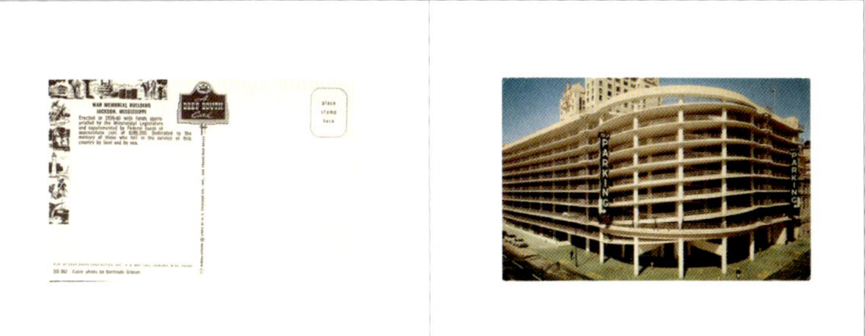

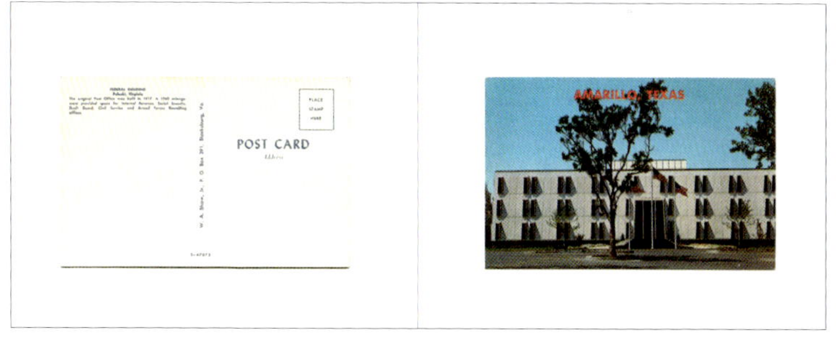
POST CARD
AMARILLO, TEXAS

New York Ti
NEW YORK, FRIDAY, JUNE 9, 2006
.S. Bombs Kill Al Qa
6-9-06

"All the News That's Fit to Print"
The New York Times
Late Edition
NEW YORK, FRIDAY, JUNE 9, 2006
ONE DOLLAR
After Long Hunt, U.S. Bombs Kill Al Qaeda Leader in Iraq
Bush Calls Mission Still Difficult — Cabinet Deadlock Ends
INSIDE
Repeal of Estate Tax Falls Short in Senate
AN INSURGENT'S DEATH
Hatred He Bred Is Sure to Survive Terrorist's Death

SONY
DREAM MACHINE

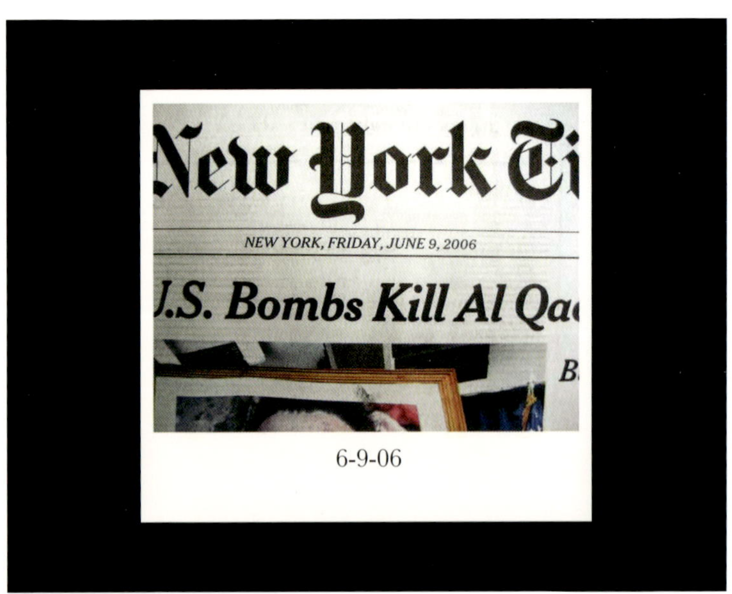

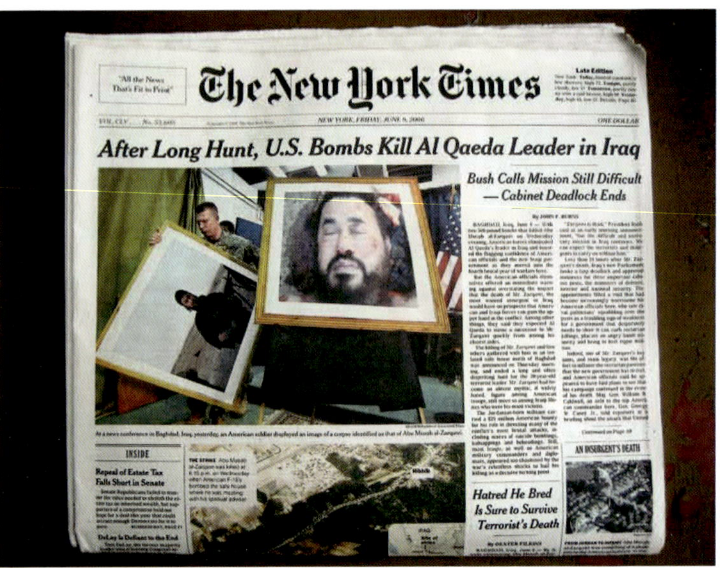

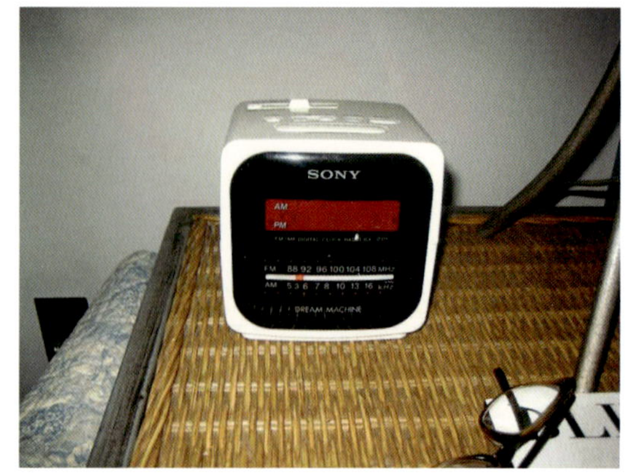

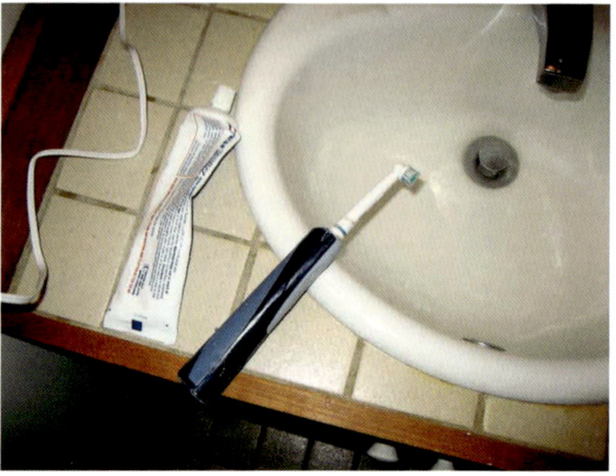

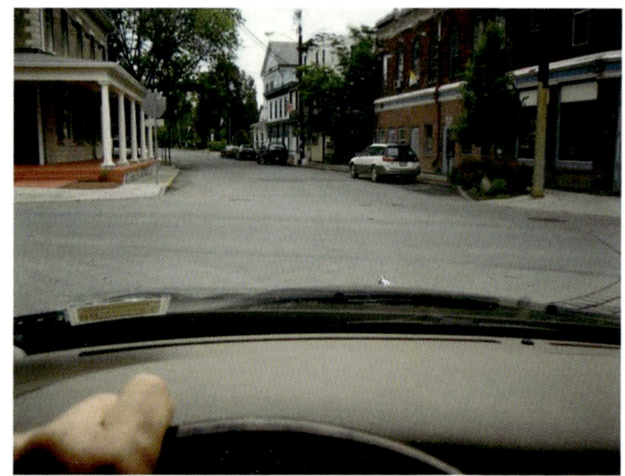

6-9-06. 2006

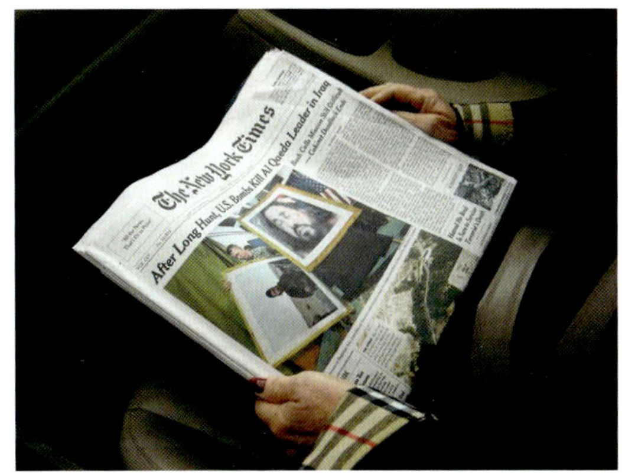
The New York Times
After Long Hunt, U.S. Bombs Kill Al Qaeda Leader in Iraq

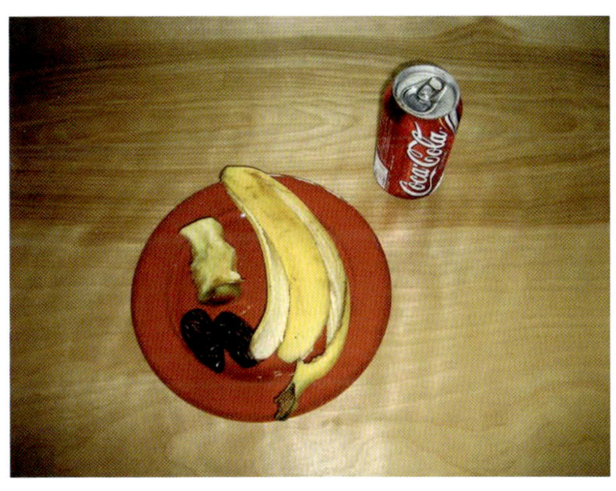
Coca-Cola

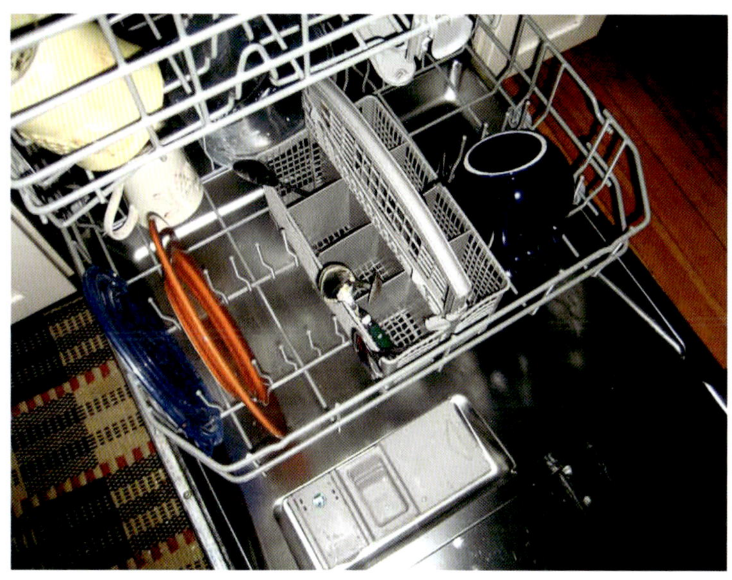

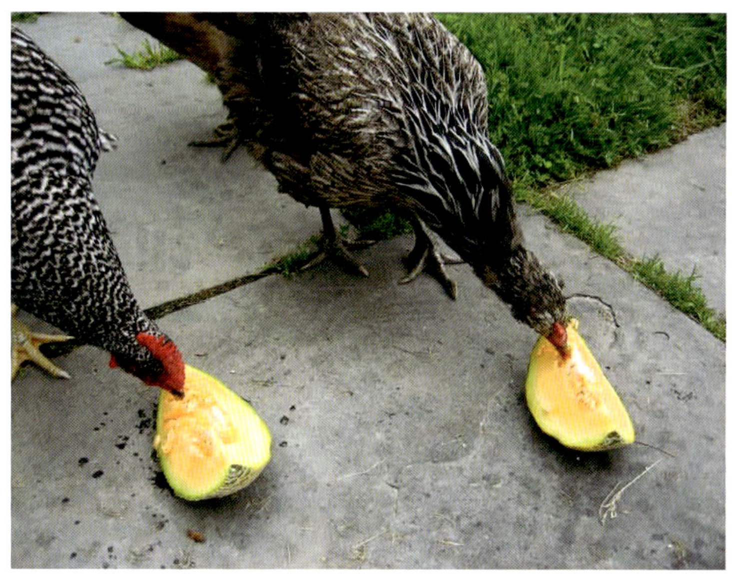

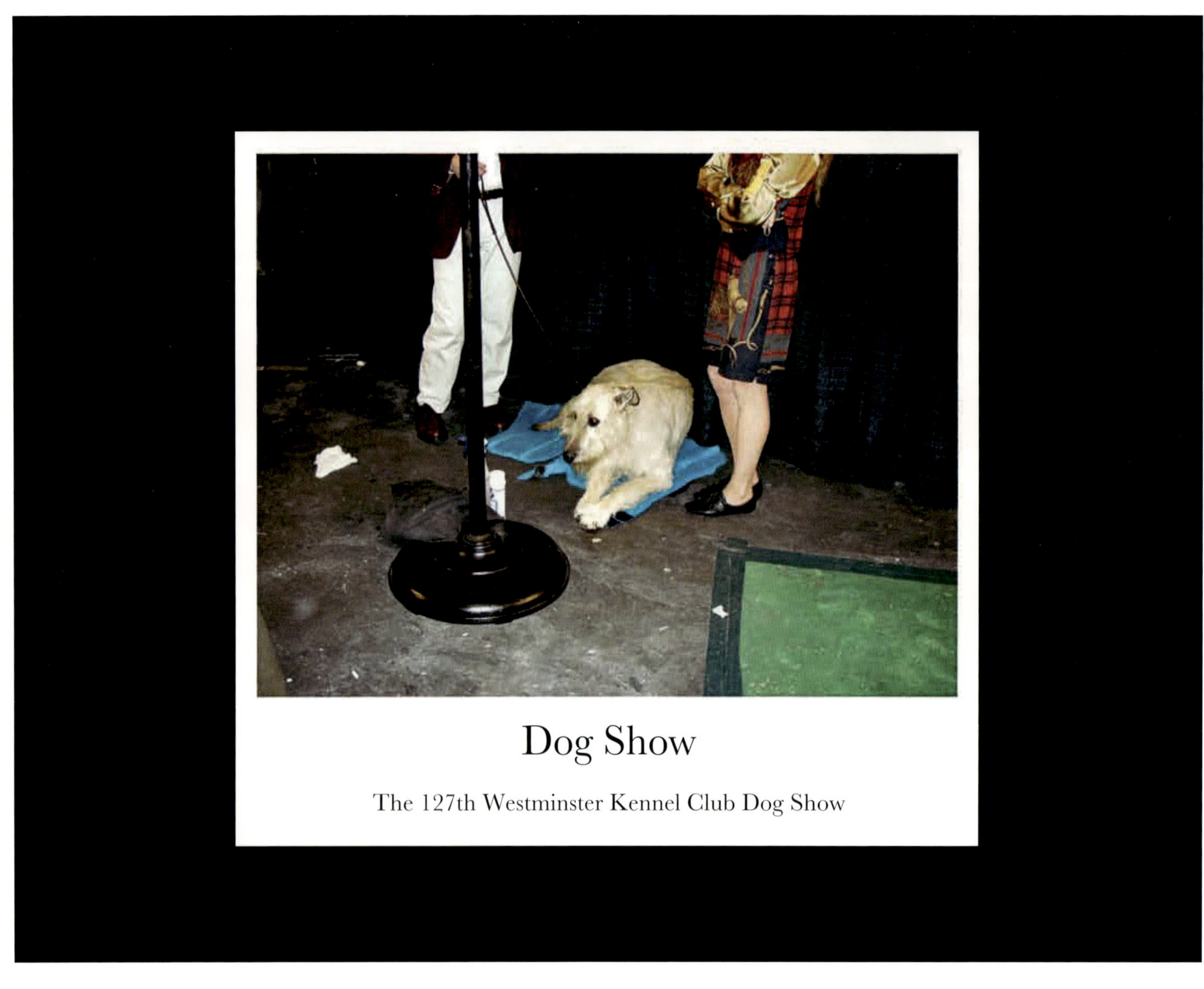

***Dog Show: The 127th Westminster Kennel Club Dog Show*. 2003**

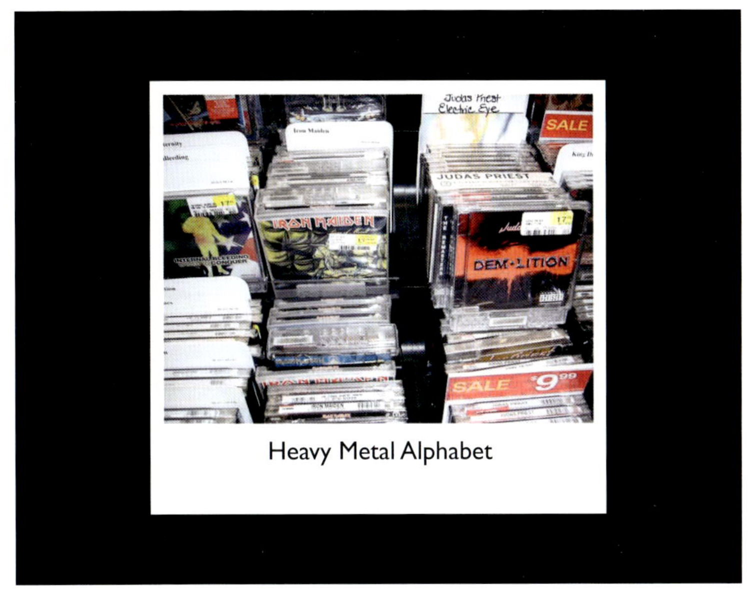

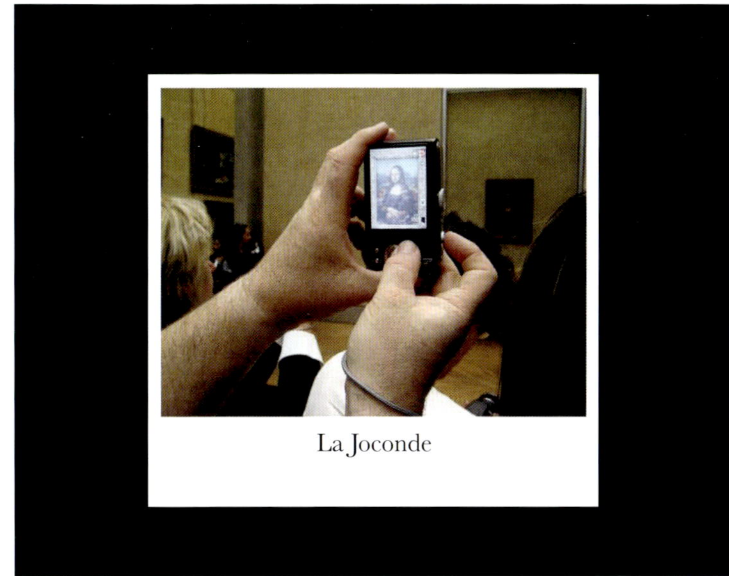

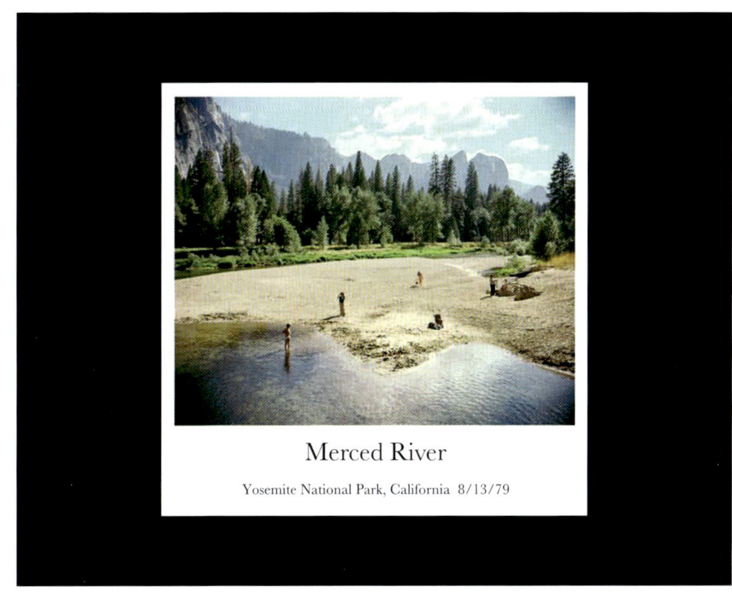

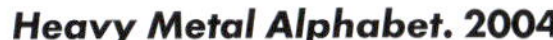

***Heavy Metal Alphabet*. 2004**

***La Joconde*. 2008**

***Merced River: Yosemite National Park, California 8/13/79*. 2003**

Prints

Careful study of Shore's practices from his early work on indicates that far from confining himself to a single format, he has always been interested in varying the dimensions of his prints. In the mid-1970s, Light Gallery offered virtually all of his images in three distinct formats: 8 by 10 (contact prints), 11 by 14, and 16 by 20 inches. The twelve images included in the 8-by-10-format portfolio produced in 1976 by the Metropolitan Museum of Art in a limited edition of fifty copies—pictures that have become among the most iconic of Shore's production—are now available only as 17-by-21 ¾-inch prints. Rather than remaining attached to contact prints, Shore has shown himself to be open to the possibilities offered by enlargement. In 1975, for an exhibition at Phoenix Gallery in San Francisco, he printed one of his images in a 20-by-24 format. Around the same time, his collaboration with the architects Robert Venturi, Denise Scott Brown, and Steven Izenour for the exhibition *Signs of Life: Symbols in the American City* provided the opportunity to see some of his images printed in truly "mural" format, using a technique developed for commercial spaces rather than gallery exhibitions. Also in 1976, in the exhibition *200 Years of American Sculpture*, designed by Venturi and Rauch at the Whitney Museum of American Art, one of Shore's images was enlarged to cover an entire wall, serving as a backdrop for sculptures by David Smith (opposite). As Izenour explained before the exhibition, "a Stephen Shore fifty footer behind some David Smith sculptures [. . .] will be a knockout."[1]

Starting around 2000, Shore began to reinterpret a few of his old images in larger prints—up to 36 by 45 inches for some of his landscapes—an evolution that was made possible by technical advancements but was consistent with his earlier interest in large formats. Like some of Shore's print-on-demand books based on enlargements of details from his past work, these larger prints allow different readings of the image, encouraging close attention to specific details. (Quentin Bajac)

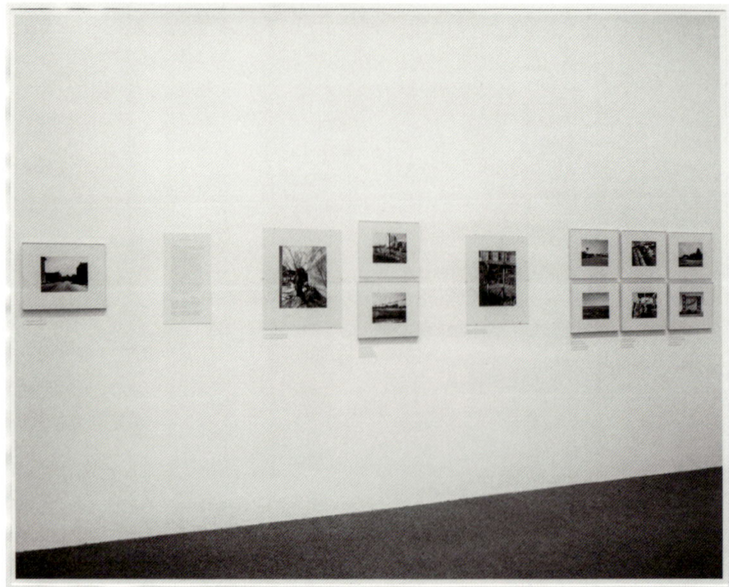

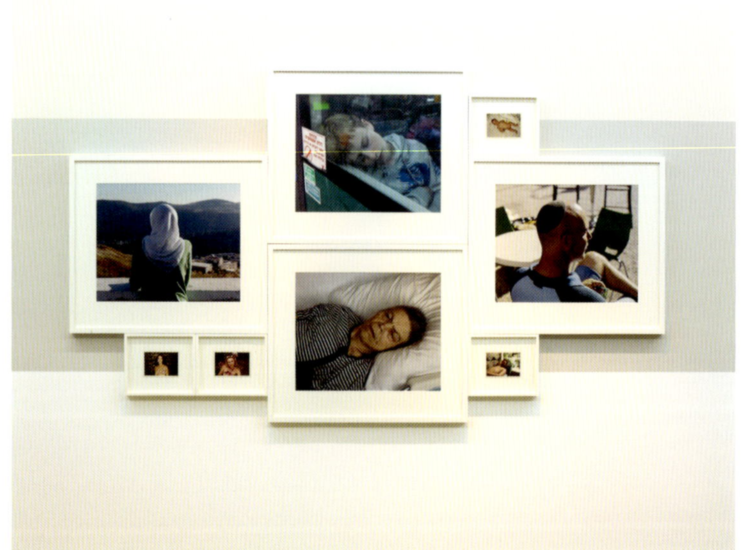

See also: *Black and White*; *Color*; *Signs of Life*

1. "Symbols," Talk of the Town, *New Yorker*, March 15, 1976, 27.

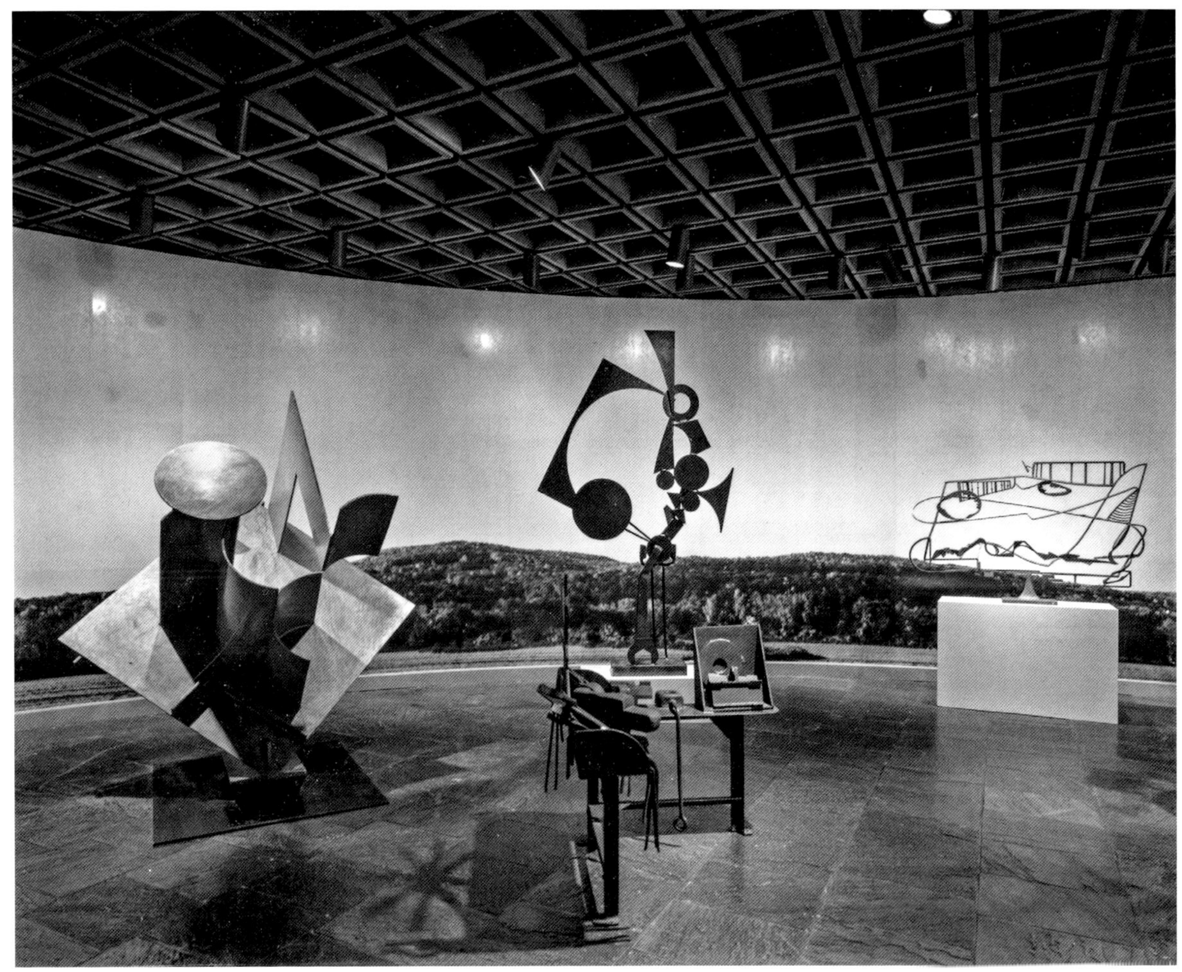

Installation view of *Photographs by Stephen Shore*, The Museum of Modern Art, New York, October 8, 1976–January 2, 1977

Installation view of *Stephen Shore: Something + Nothing*, Sprüth Magers, London, November 26, 2013–January 11, 2014

Installation view of *200 Years of American Sculpture*, Whitney Museum of American Art, New York, March 16–September 26, 1976, with sculptures by David Smith, photographic mural by Stephen Shore, and exhibition design by Venturi and Rauch. Photo: Stephen Shore

Road Trips

Shore grew up a consummate New Yorker, more familiar with Western Europe than with the American West, whose culture was something of a shock to him when he first visited Amarillo, Texas, in 1969.[1] He later wrote that because he didn't drive at the time, "my first view of America was framed by the passenger's window."[2] In some ways, Shore's photography of the next decade took shape in this trip out West, and in similar trips he would make over the next several summers.

In 1972, when Shore was working on *American Surfaces*, he struck out south, swinging west through Georgia all the way to Texas along Interstate 20. He spent about a week in Amarillo, and then continued west through New Mexico, Colorado, Utah, and Arizona, before crossing back and heading north, along Route 66—which was slowly being replaced by interstates—to Chicago, and then straight east back to New York. The entire journey took him about six weeks. He has described the resulting series (which continued through December 1973) as "being a diary, but it's a diary of a life geared to make photographs. It's a diary of a photographic trip—it's things I'm encountering, but it's also things I'm encountering for the sake of encountering them."[3]

The next summer Shore drove west and then up through the Great Lakes states before hitting Big Sky Country, driving down through California, and looping around back east. We know this route, along with the maps of his travels for the next few years, because Shore was an avid, almost obsessive, chronicler of these journeys. *A Road Trip Journal* of his summer 1973 travel is the best-known example (pages 196–97), but Shore kept detailed journals of all these trips, cataloguing how many photographs he took in each of the cities where he stopped.[4] An entry from August 25, 1974, reads:

> Spokane, Wash.
> –Main St. at Howard St.
> –Lincoln St. at Riverside St.
> –Monroe St.
> –Woolworth's, Main St. & Lincoln St.
> –Division St.
>
> Post Falls, Idaho
> –Fruit Stand, U.S. 10
> –As above
> –Cowboy Statue, U.S. 10

Many photographs of the 1970s are the visual evidence of a life on the road: shirts being washed in a sink; motel beds, TVs, and bedside tables; diners and drive-thrus; the homes of friends he stayed with; dirty toilets; gas stations and parking lots; and even a car trunk full of his photographic gear (page 199).

His love of traveling by car (often also manifested in his photographing of cars) continues into the twenty-first century. In 2013 Shore visited Winslow, Arizona, a city he had photographed for *American Surfaces*, and made a series of 183 photographs over one day that begins in the middle of an open road and continues throughout the city. Many images were taken from a vantage point just a few feet away from the previous one, emphasizing the play-by-play nature of the series that makes viewers feel they are on Shore's trail, following him in his travels through the city.[5] (Kristen Gaylord)

See also: *Amarillo, Texas*; *American Surfaces*; *Travel*; *Uncommon Places*; *Winslow, Arizona*

1. David Campany, "Ways of Making Pictures," in *Stephen Shore* (Madrid: Fundación MAPFRE; New York: Aperture, 2014), 29.
2. Stephen Shore, *Uncommon Places* (New York: Aperture, 1982), 63. The photographs he took on an earlier trip to Los Angeles with his parents are an example of "passenger window" vision. See pages 79 and 198 in this volume.
3. Aaron Schuman, "*Uncommon Places*: An Interview with Stephen Shore," *Seesaw* 3 (Summer 2005): http://seesawmagazine.com/shore_pages/shore_interview.html.
4. This self-archiving is what has made the Photographic Chronology in this volume possible. Shore has wondered if his systematic record keeping was a remnant of his 1969–70 Conceptual projects. See "A Ground Neutral and Replete: Stephen Shore and Gil Blank in Conversation," *Whitewall*, no. 7 (Fall 2007): 56.
5. Shore's detailed titling convention has led others to track down the locations of his photographs, for art or personal projects.

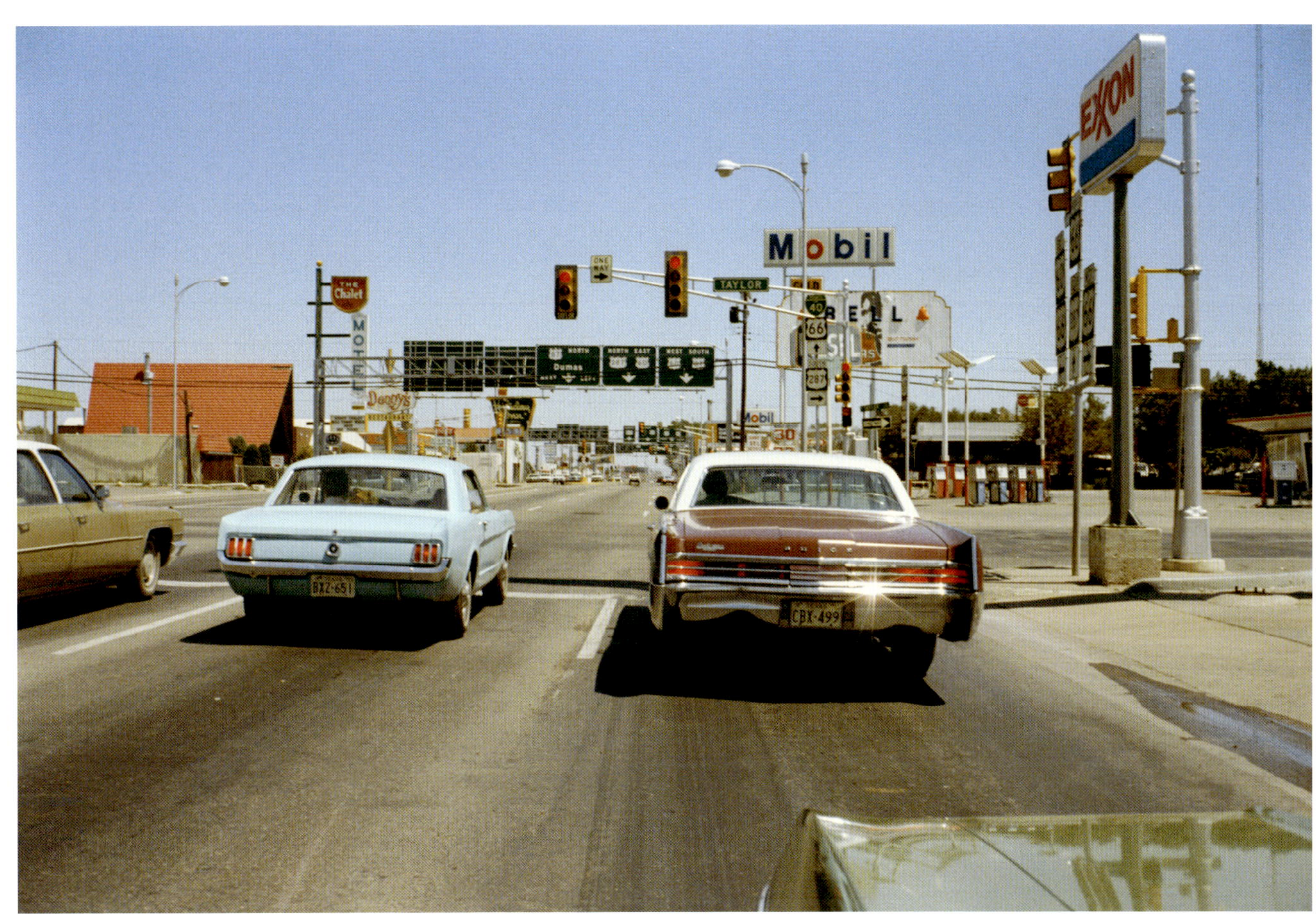

Amarillo, Texas, August 1973. **1973**

195.

JUL 06 1973

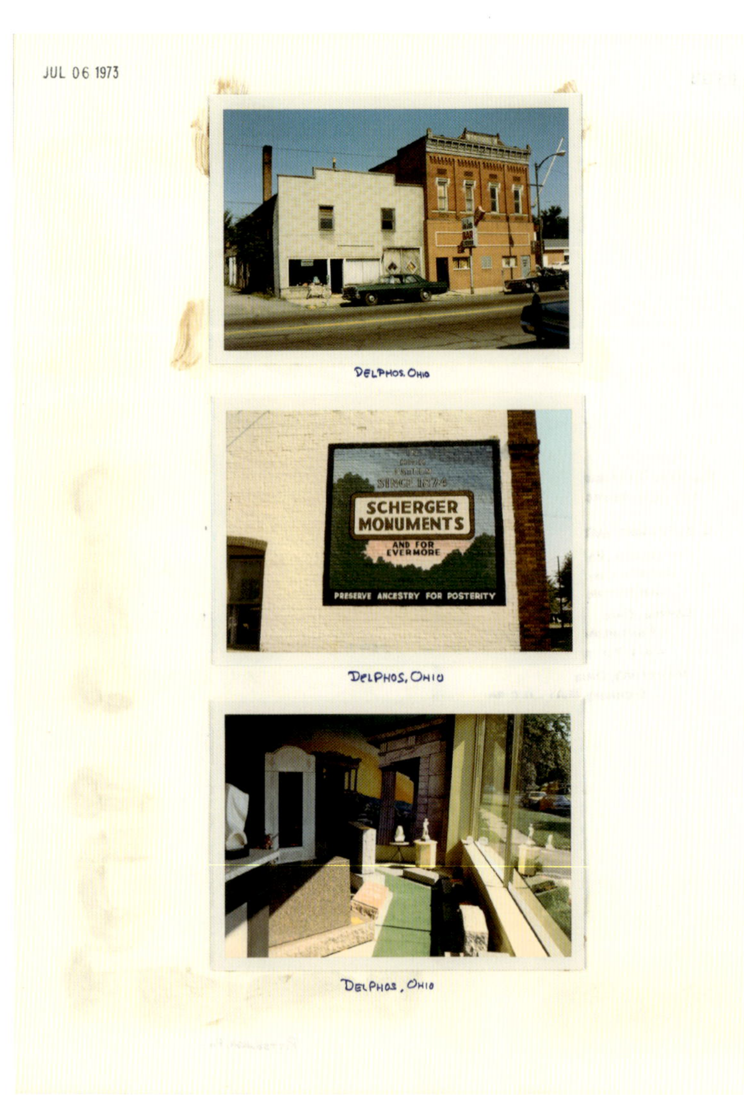

DELPHOS, OHIO

DELPHOS, OHIO

DELPHOS, OHIO

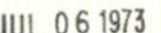

MILAGE: 1424
BREAKFAST: HOWARD JOHNSON'S, LIMA, OHIO (PANCAKES)
LUNCH: PONDEROSA STEAK HOUSE, BATTLE CREEK, MICH. (STEAK)
DINNER: HOWARD JOHNSON'S, BATTLE CREEK, MICH. (TURKEY DINNER)
NIGHT AT: HOWARD JOHNSON'S, BATTLE CREEK, MICH.

TV: CBS EVENING NEWS
60 MINUTES
ROOM 222

POST CARD DIST:
30 – DELPHOS, OHIO

10 EXPOSURES MADE:

LIMA, OHIO
- INTERSEC.: JAMESON & RICHIE
- JAMESON AVE

DELPHOS, OHIO
- INTERSEC.: 4TH & MAIN
- PITSENBARGER SUPPLY CO., 3RD & MAIN
- INTERSEC.: 2ND & MAIN

BATTLE CREEK, MICH.
- MICHIGAN AVE.
- COUPLE, MICHIGAN AVE.
- RM. 316, HOWARD JOHNSON'S
- TOILET, AS ABOVE
- AS ABOVE

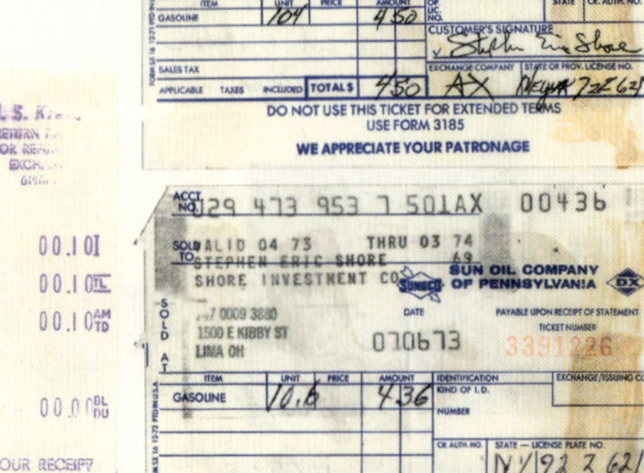

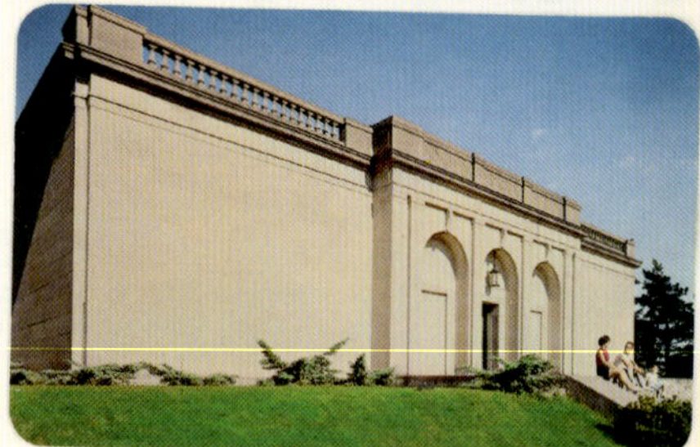

KINGMAN MUSEUM
BATTLE CREEK, MICH.

***A Road Trip Journal*. 1973**

JUL 08 1973

MILAGE: 1838
BREAKFAST: HOLIDAY INN, GAYLORD, MICH. (OMELETTE)
LUNCH: PARADISE RESTAURANT, PARADISE, MICH. (GRILLED CHEESE)
DINNER: SUNNY SHORES FINE FOOD, MANISTIQUE, MICH. (DEEP-FRIED PERCH)
NIGHT AT: STAR MOTEL, MANISTIQUE, MICH.

TV: MCMILLAN AND WIFE

POST CARD DIST.:
80 - GAYLORD, MICH.

8 EXPOSURES MADE:
ALONG MICH. 123
- HIAWATHA NATIONAL FOREST
- ABANDONED CABINS
- AS ABOVE
PARADISE, MICH.
- PARADISE MUSEUM
NEWBERRY, MICH.
- HOUSE, NEWBERRY AVE.
- HOUSES, NEWBERRY AVE.
MANISTIQUE, MICH.
- INTERSEC.: CEDAR & WALNUT
- RM. 11, STAR MOTEL

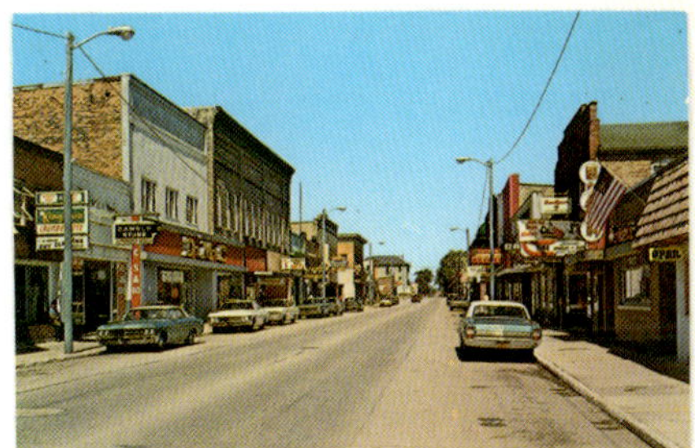

VIEW OF DOWNTOWN BUSINESS DISTRICT, MANISTIQUE, MICH.

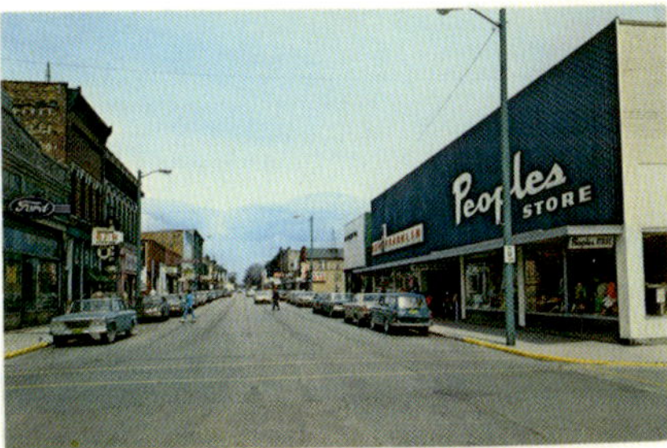

VIEW OF DOWNTOWN BUSINESS DISTRICT, MANISTIQUE, MICH.

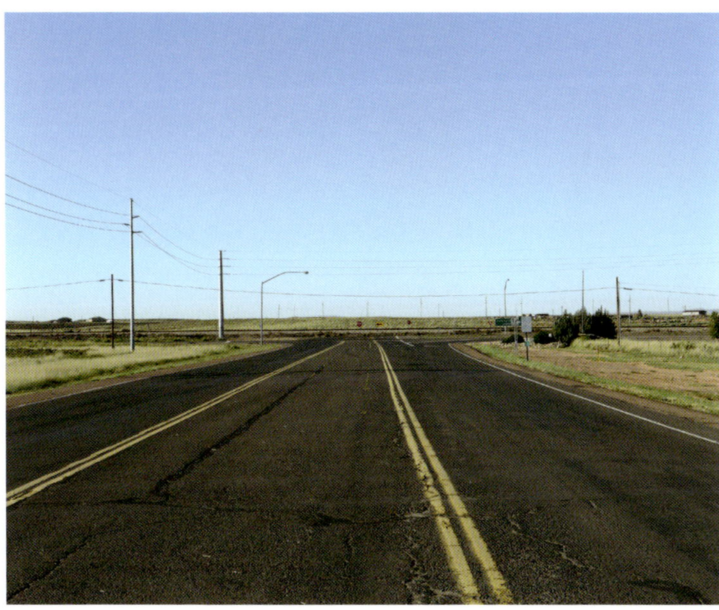

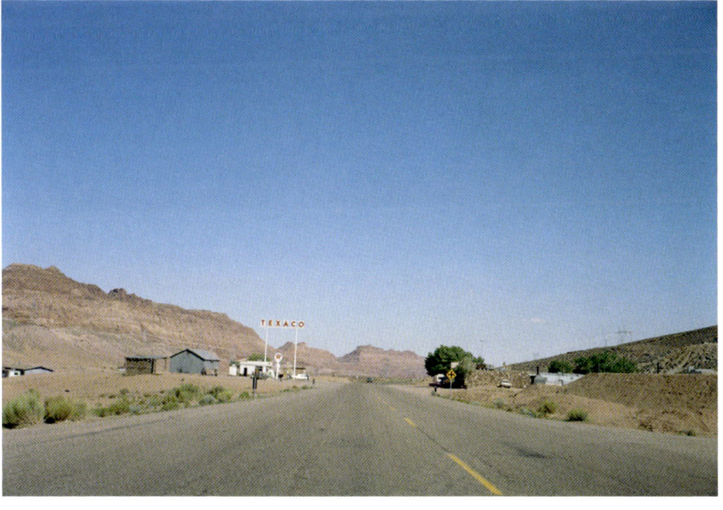

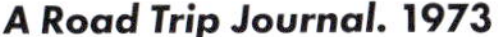

***A Road Trip Journal*. 1973**

***Winslow, Arizona, September 19, 2013*. 2013**

***U.S. 89, Arizona, June 1972*. 1972**

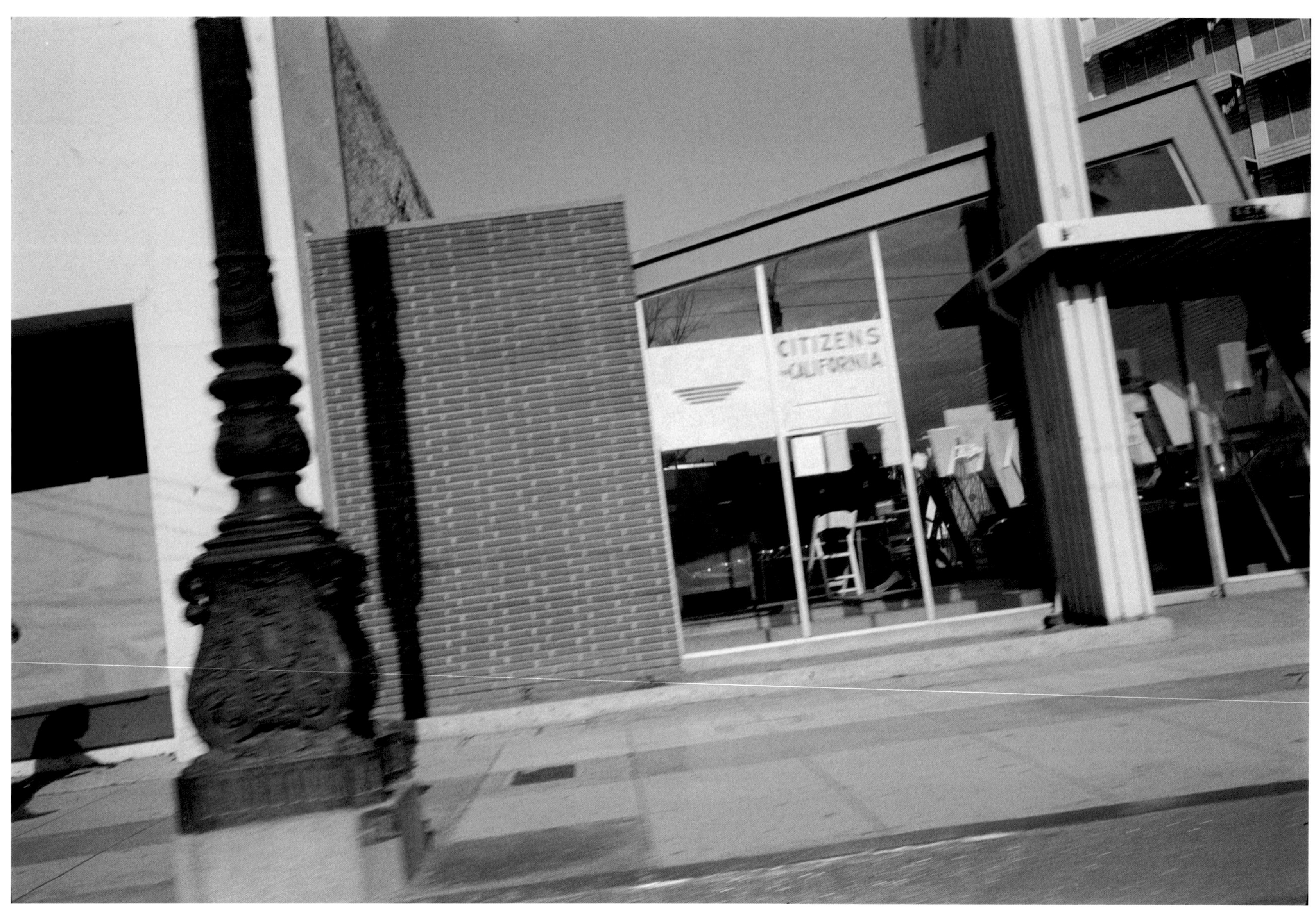

Los Angeles, California, February 4, 1969. **1969**

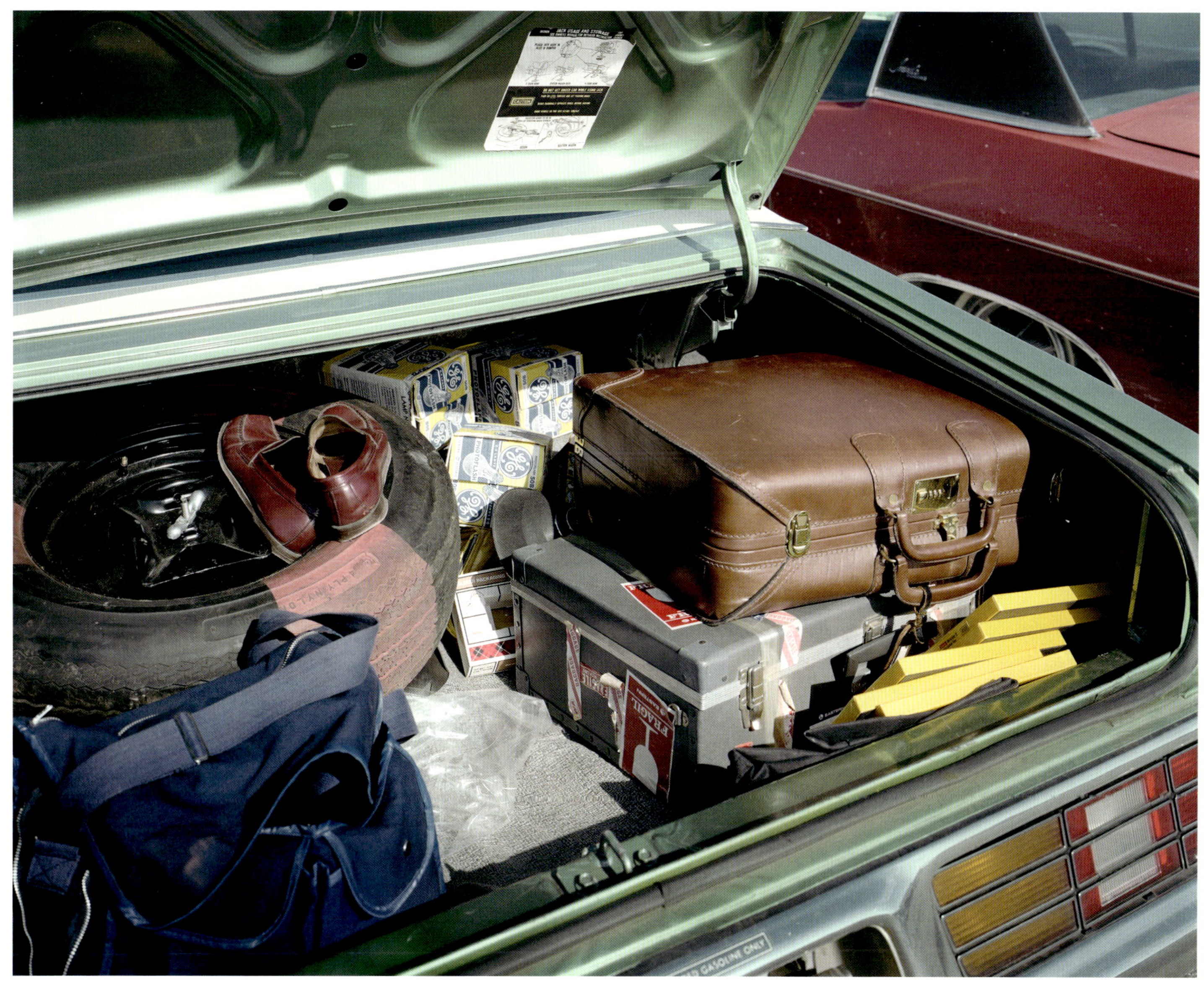

Key Largo, Florida, November 11, 1977. 1977

199.

Shnuriv Lys, Kyivska Province, Ukraine, October 16, 2013

While all photographs are documents to some extent, Shore has not been a documentary photographer in the way the term is generally understood. That is to say, he has not been led primarily by an interest in subject matter and the desire to communicate it. Rather, most of his work has been concerned with solving formal and pictorial problems, for which the typical and the everyday have served as ideal material. His motifs are familiar enough that both the photographer and the viewer can concentrate on the photographic treatment of them. In Ukraine, however, Shore made a break with his usual way of working, although at first glance the images he made there might suggest otherwise.

It was the photographer's wife, Ginger, who came across the Survivor Mitzvah Project, which helps aging Holocaust survivors living in Eastern Europe and the former USSR, and suggested they might make for a rewarding and timely photographic subject. There was also a personal connection to the material, since Shore's paternal grandfather had emigrated to the United States from Ukraine in 1890.

Before the outbreak of World War II, Ukraine had the third-largest Jewish population in Europe. By 1945, around one and a half million Jews had been killed by German SS units in their advance across the country. The great majority of Holocaust survivors moved west, but there were substantial Jewish communities all over Europe. Survivors who moved east—to Moldova, Belarus, and Lithuania, as well as Ukraine—formed small, scattered communities, and today their numbers are dwindling.

Most of the remaining survivors were in their eighties and nineties when Shore first visited in 2012. He photographed the lives of twenty-two people, making portraits, landscapes, interior studies of their homes, and still lifes of personal possessions. This particular photograph was made when Shore came across people setting up a roadside stand to sell preserved mushrooms and dried herbs. Shore recalled:

> I was very aware that I'd never photographed anything that had a really strong emotional resonance. People have feelings about gas stations but not the way they have feelings about the Holocaust. I didn't get drawn into this project for aesthetic or formal reasons, obviously, but if there has been a formal problem on my mind, it is how to take a picture of a subject matter that is so emotionally charged but not have the pictures be illustrations—and not let them rest on that emotion. But not have the pictures avoid that content either. Can I communicate some of the emotional power I feel in that country without it simply being a connection to the label "Holocaust?"[1]

The project was published in 2015 as *Survivors in Ukraine*. As well as being an important record of a nearly forgotten people and representing yet another turn in Shore's restless career, the series also stands as an example of the recent renaissance of the documentary photo book. (David Campany)

See also: *Ukraine*

1. David Campany, "Ways of Making Pictures," in Marta Dahó, ed., *Stephen Shore* (Madrid: Fundación MAPFRE; New York: Aperture, 2014), 54.

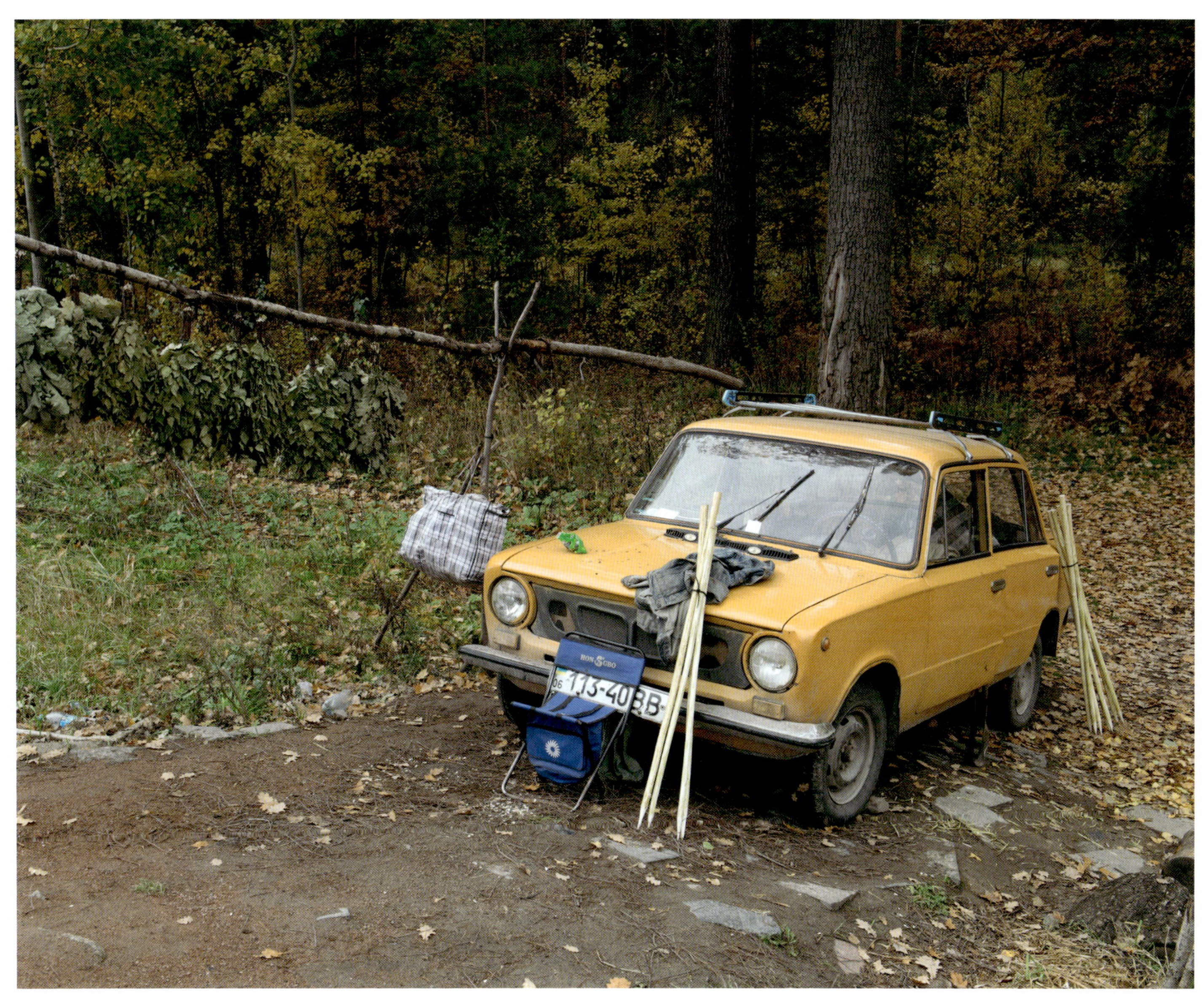

***Shnuriv Lys, Kyivska Province, Ukraine, October 16, 2013.* 2013**

Shopwindows

From *American Surfaces* to the images he made in Israel forty years later, storefronts are plentiful in Shore's work. Regardless of the era of the photograph, the culture being depicted, or the device Shore is using—from the view camera to the stereoscope—shopwindows have consistently been one of the most powerful visual draws for him. "I [find] myself attracted to architecture and artifacts where I can see cultural forces manifest," he says, and storefronts offer particularly rich material for his kind of visual anthropology.[1] Through Shore's lens, shopwindows become cultural artifacts in many different ways. In Jerusalem a hat-maker's window indirectly indicates the strong religious presence of Orthodox Jews in the city (page 207). In Connecticut the photographer smiles at the respectable and slightly outmoded display of what appears to be a thrift shop (page 208), whereas in New York he delights in the Pop confrontation of the male ideal of classical antiquity in a traditional barber shop window (page 206).

With the advent of glass storefronts in the late nineteenth century, shopwindows became one of the great subjects—and one of the great challenges, due to the reflections—of modern photography, appealing to photographers from Eugène Atget to Walker Evans who are sensitive to the poetry of accumulation and the "product." Shore's pictures in this tradition have evolved over the years, going from frontal views where the storefronts are seen as a whole, as in *American Surfaces*, to more fragmented visions, shot at closer range and essentially centered on the window itself and its contents, often photographed at a downward angle, like that of a strolling pedestrian whose gaze might be drawn by an interesting sight.

Some of Shore's shopwindows are the most nostalgic and timeless images of his production. What holds his interest the most are the often slightly outdated storefronts—dusty, sometimes abandoned or without a clear function—that seem to come from another time or to exist outside of time. None of these storefront images celebrate a modern or triumphant consumerism in a Pop way, but instead evoke, often with tenderness and empathy, a world on the verge of disappearing or the vestiges of a world thought to have already disappeared.

If the shopwindow is part of a rich photographic tradition, it is also, paradoxically, the subject where Shore proves closest to painting, especially that of the American Photo-Realists and above all Edward Hopper. This is notably true in *Uncommon Places*, in which Shore takes on the same provincial America that Hopper did. They also share a similar attention to light—even if Shore, unlike Hopper, is interested only in natural light—and a similar enthusiasm for storefronts. For Shore, the lover of natural light, the shopwindow's photogenic aspect resides in the particular quality of light that each one captures, both imprisoning and reflecting light and causing the public space of the street to blend with the private space of the store. (Quentin Bajac)

See also: *American Surfaces*; *Uncommon Places*

1. Madeline Yale, "Stephen Shore and Tarek Al-Ghoussein," *Spot* magazine (Houston Center for Photography), Spring 2012, 27.

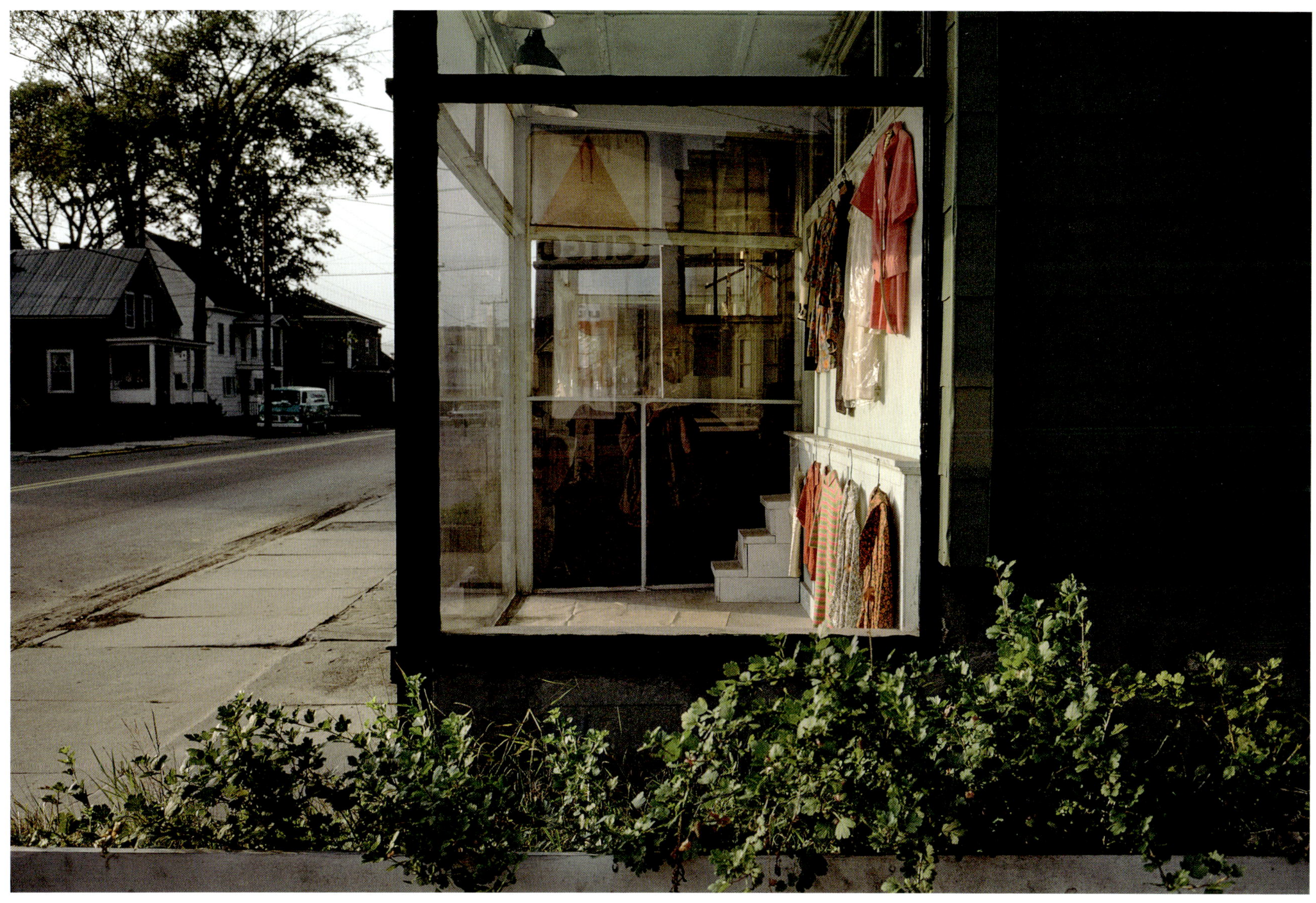

***New Hampshire, July 16, 1974.* 1974**

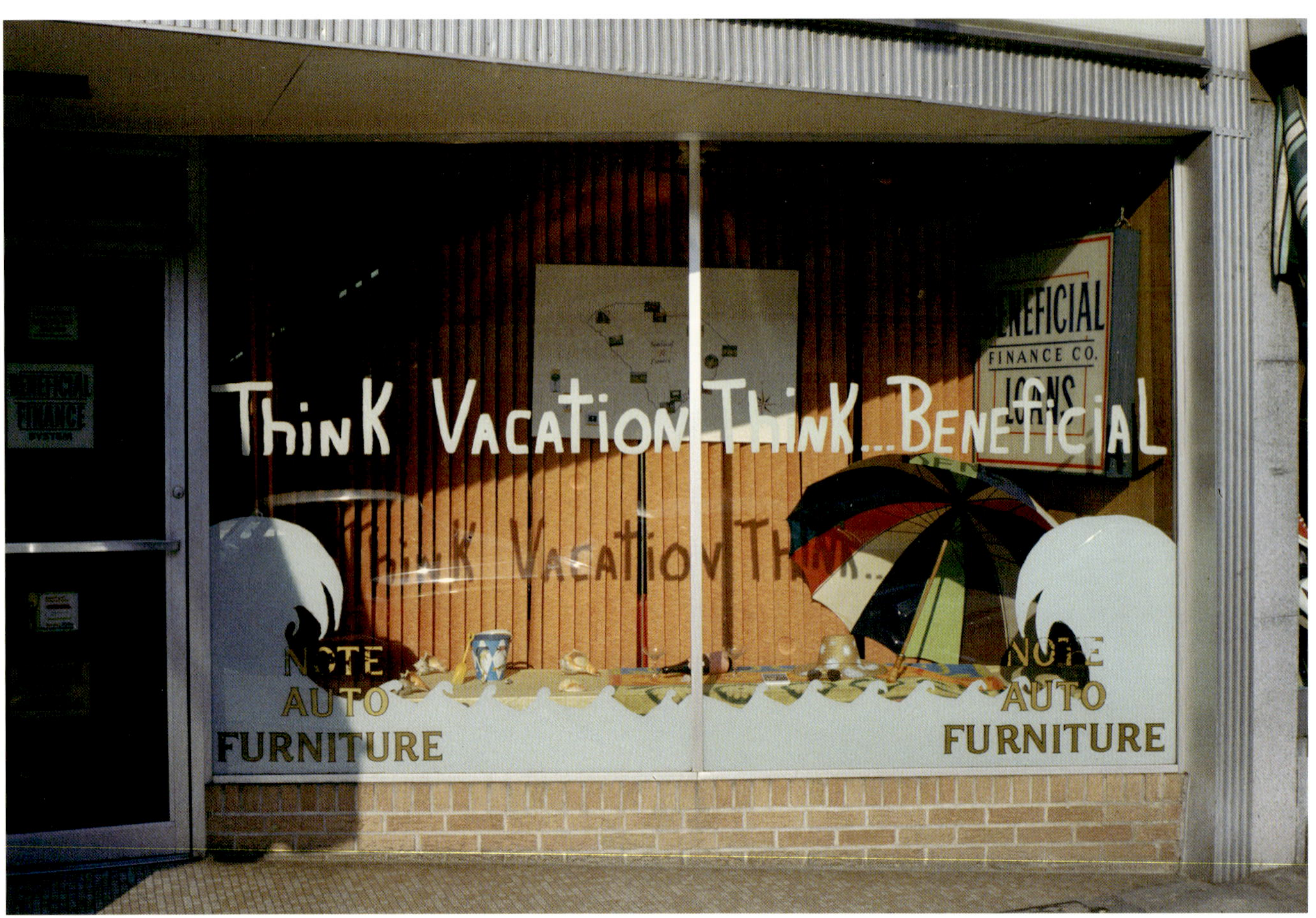

Columbia, South Carolina, June 1972. 1972

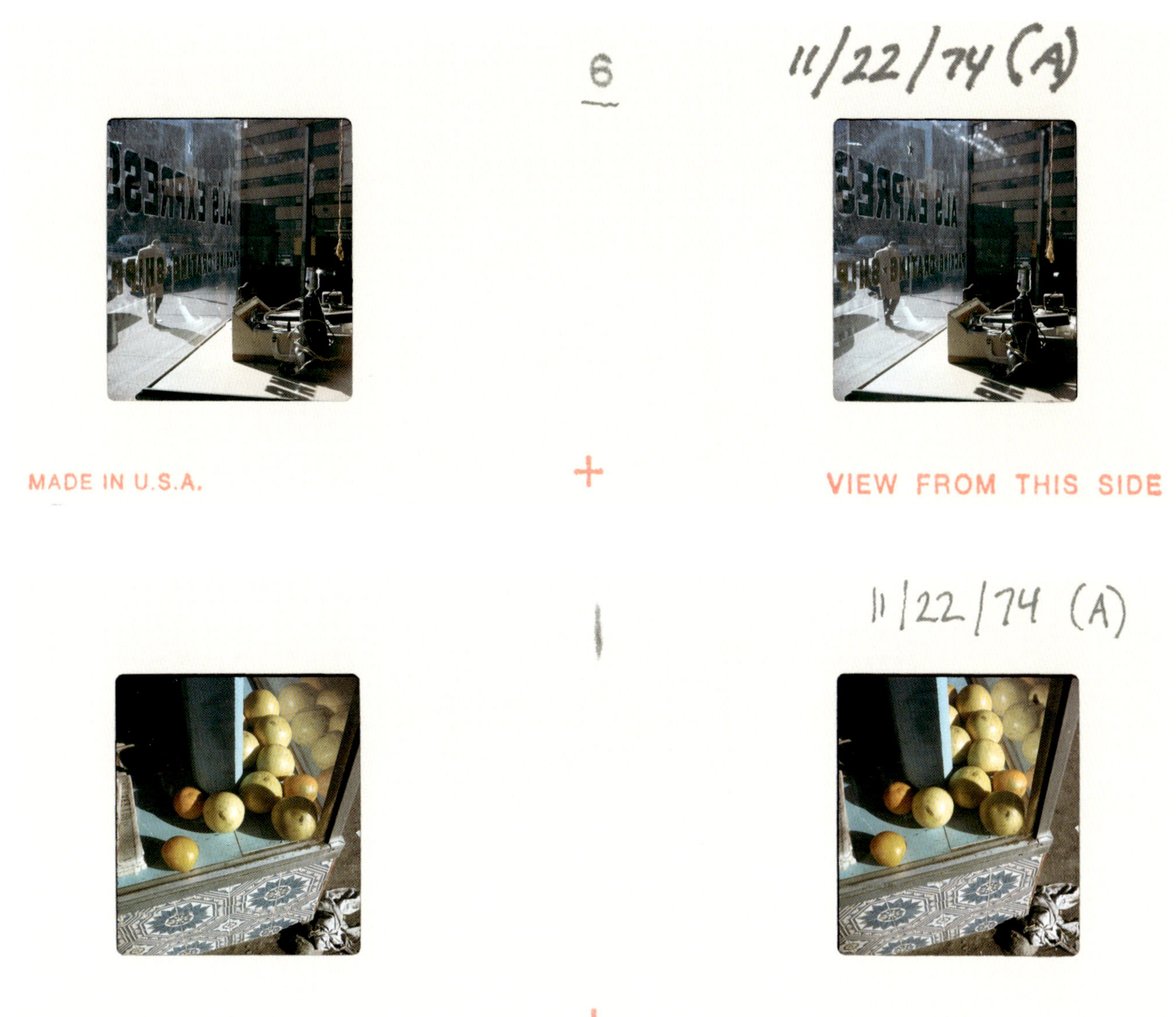

***New York, New York, 1974*. 1974**

***New York, New York, 1974*. 1974**

205.

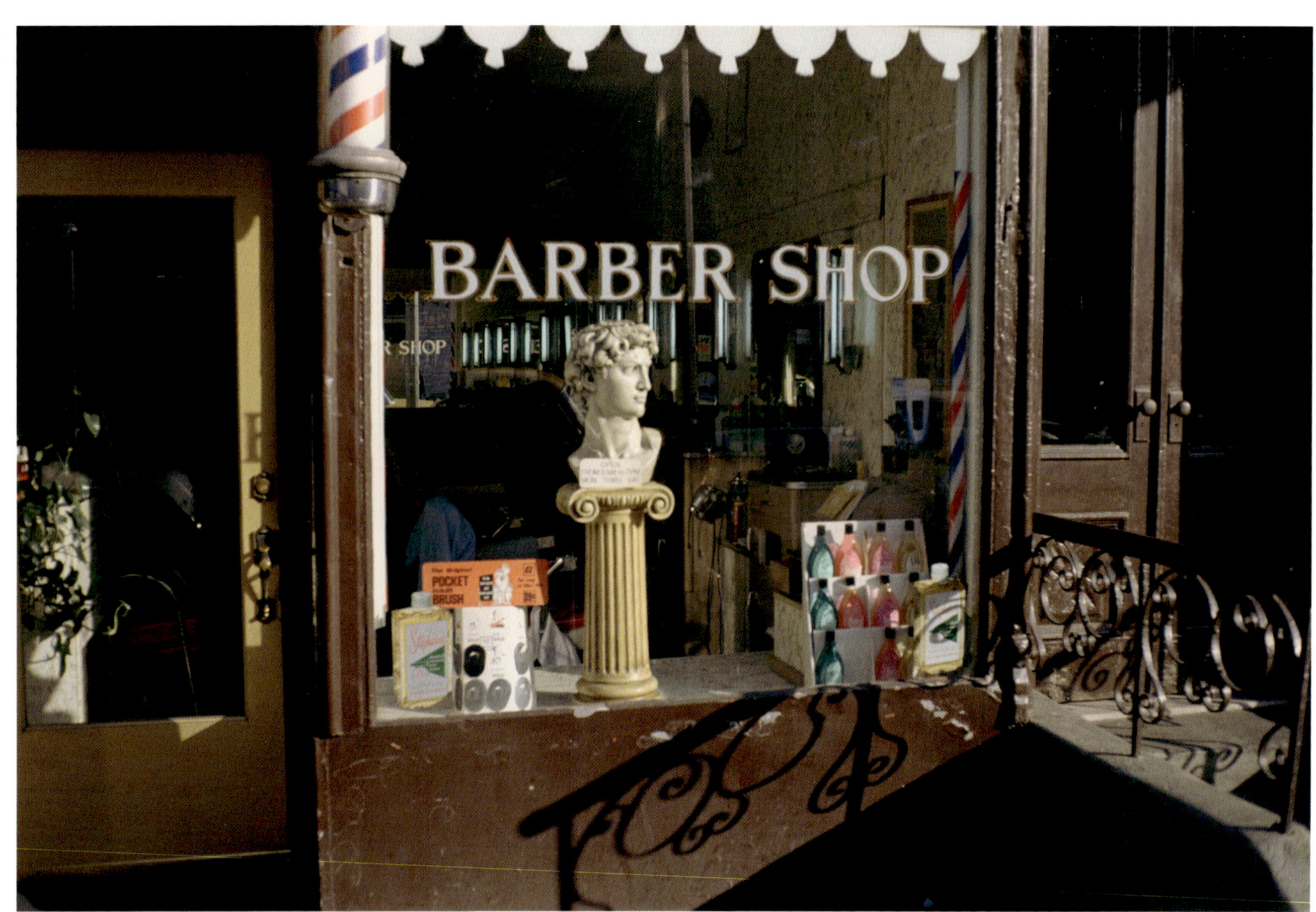

***New York, New York, September–October 1972.* 1972**

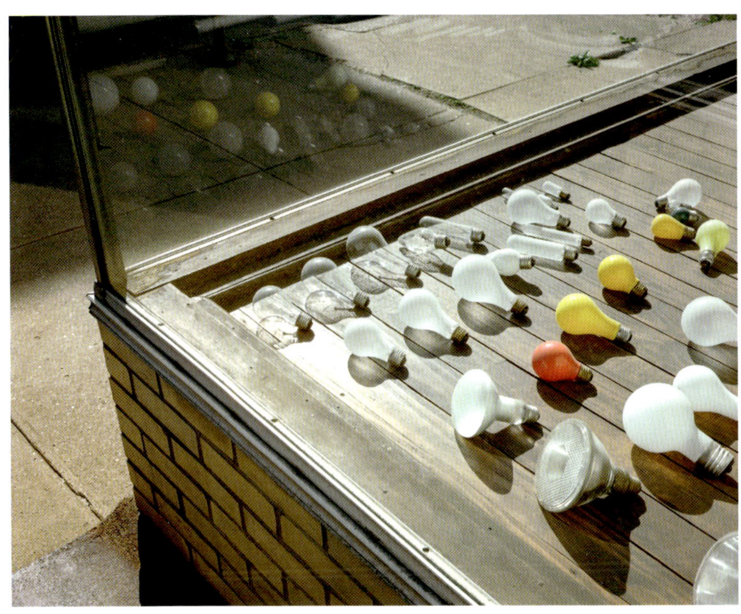

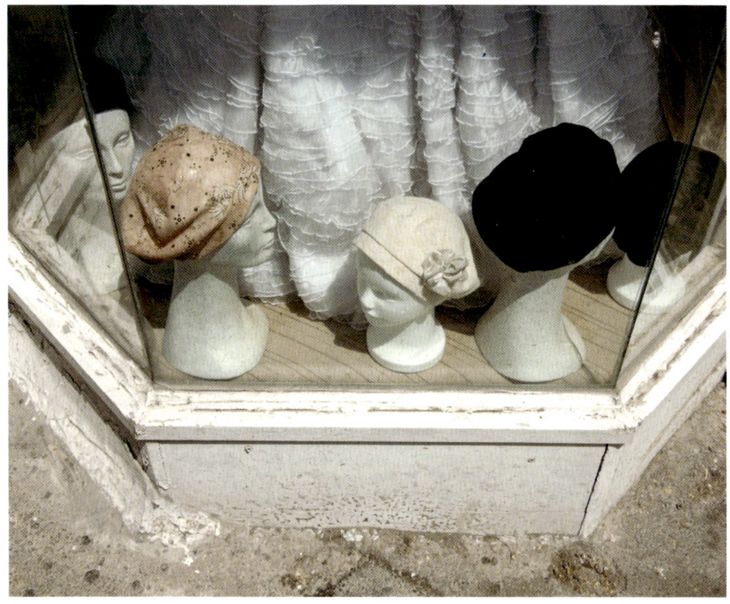

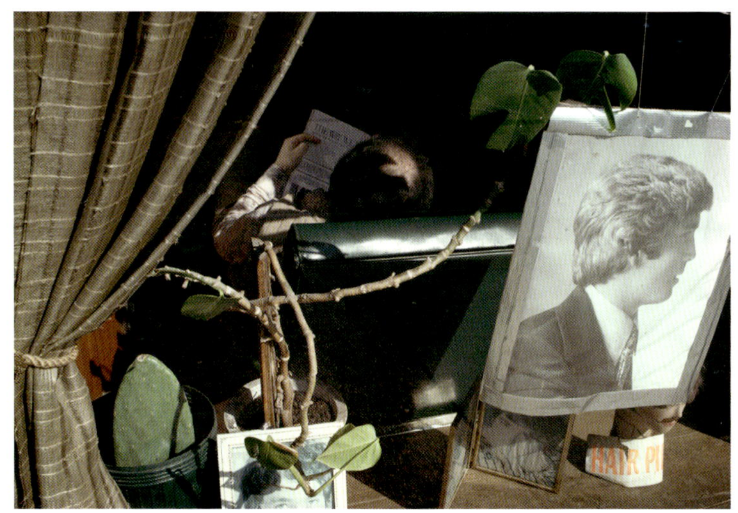

West 3rd Street, Parkersburg, West Virginia, May 16, 1974. 1974

Jerusalem, Israel, September 12, 2009. 2009

Queens, New York, March 1, 1977. 1977

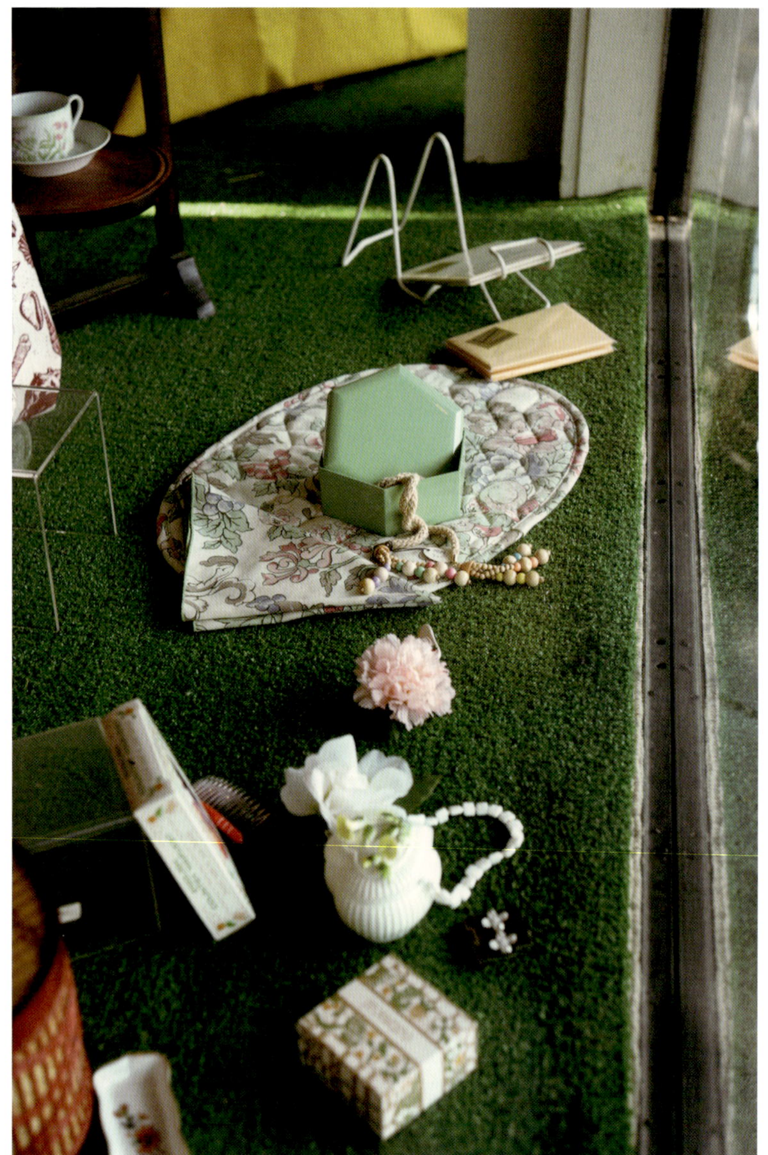

Fairfield County, Connecticut, June 1979. 1979

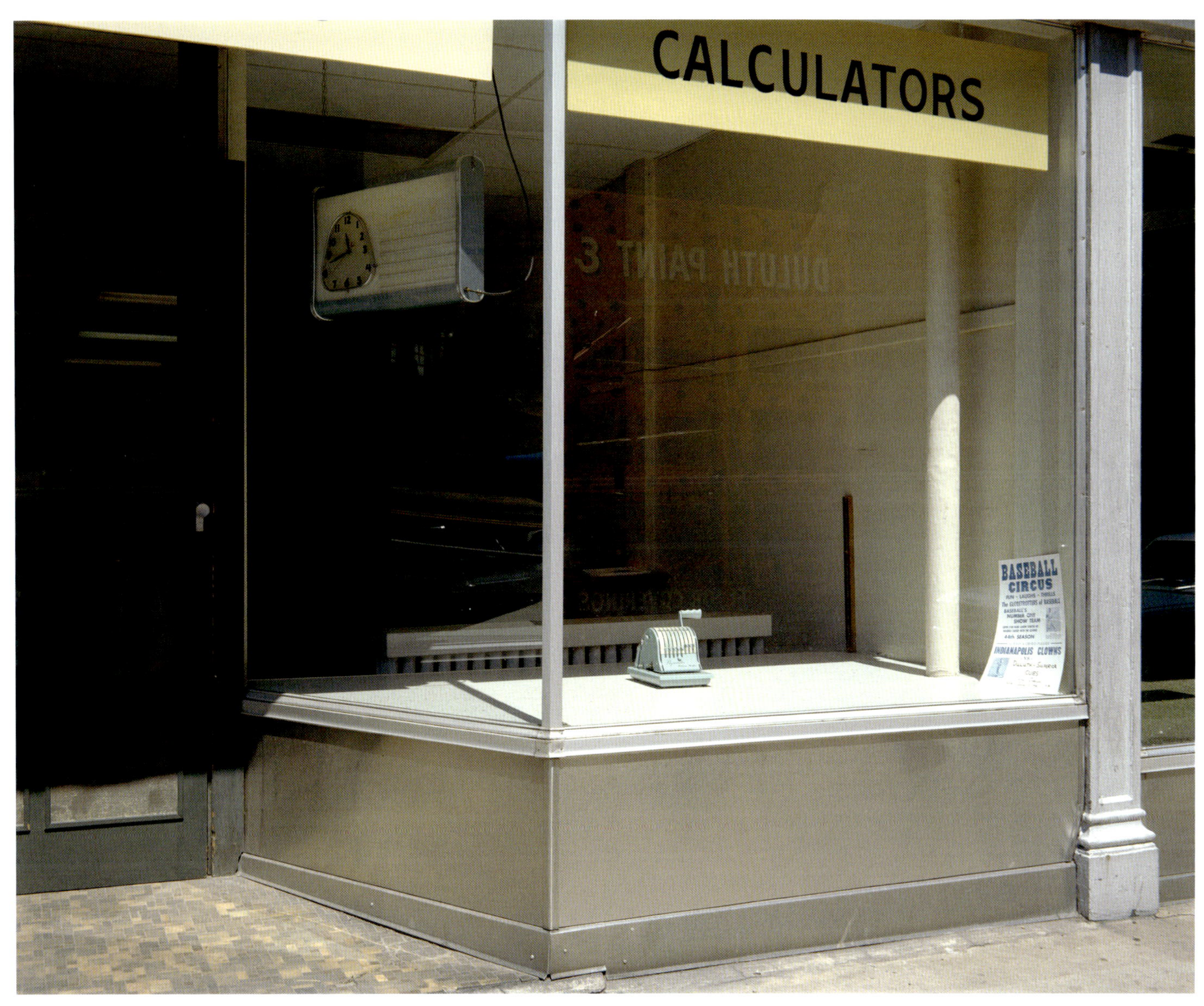

J. J. Summers Agency, 1st Street, Duluth, Minnesota, July 11, 1973. 1973

209.

Signage

"The time has arrived for a scholar to write a doctoral dissertation on signs. He or she would need literary as well as artistic acumen because the same reason that makes signs Pop Art (the need for high-speed communication with maximum meaning) makes them Pop Literature as well."[1] Thus wrote Robert Venturi, Denise Scott Brown, and Steven Izenour in their groundbreaking work *Learning from Las Vegas*, published in 1972, the year before Shore completed his series *American Surfaces* and started working on *Uncommon Places*.

Signs occupy a central place in both series. Ads and billboards, traffic signs, shop signs, writing on walls or storefronts: signs are everywhere in Shore's images from the 1970s, often linked to car culture and intended more for the driver than the pedestrian. In *Learning from Las Vegas* such signs are grouped under the rubric "the architecture of persuasion," a commercial, vernacular architecture—born of the need to inform and seduce the consumer-driver. Signs have continued to appear in Shore's later work, in the series *Winslow, Arizona*, for instance, but also in his print-on-demand books, his photographs of Ukraine and Abu Dhabi, and now his Instagram images.

Just as it did for the authors of *Learning from Las Vegas*, Pop art had a strong influence on Shore's interest in signs generated by popular culture—commercial signs, ads, logos, posters. For Shore, the Pop influence complemented the inspiration he derived from Walker Evans, whose attachment to vernacular American culture could be seen in his collection of road signs and symbols (as well as in his collection of postcards), some of which were on display in a 1971 exhibition at Yale University Art Gallery that Shore saw. The omnipresence of the sign, amplified by the uncompromising precision of the 8-by-10 view camera, explains why a number of Shore's photographs, particularly those from the 1970s, are as much to be read as to be looked at. The sign is envisioned in its plastic form—as a Pop element that contributes to the rhythm and even the construction of the image or landscape—but also in its linguistic form. "Strange Drugs," "Bank Bar," "Mead's Fine Bread": these messages, whether quirky, evocative, or simply informative, are like haiku, forming a minimalist poetics of everyday life. (Quentin Bajac)

See also: *American Surfaces*; *Evans, Walker*; *Signs of Life*; *Uncommon Places*

1. Robert Venturi, Denise Scott Brown, and Steven Izenour, *Learning from Las Vegas*, rev. ed. (Cambridge, Mass.: MIT Press, 1977), 80.

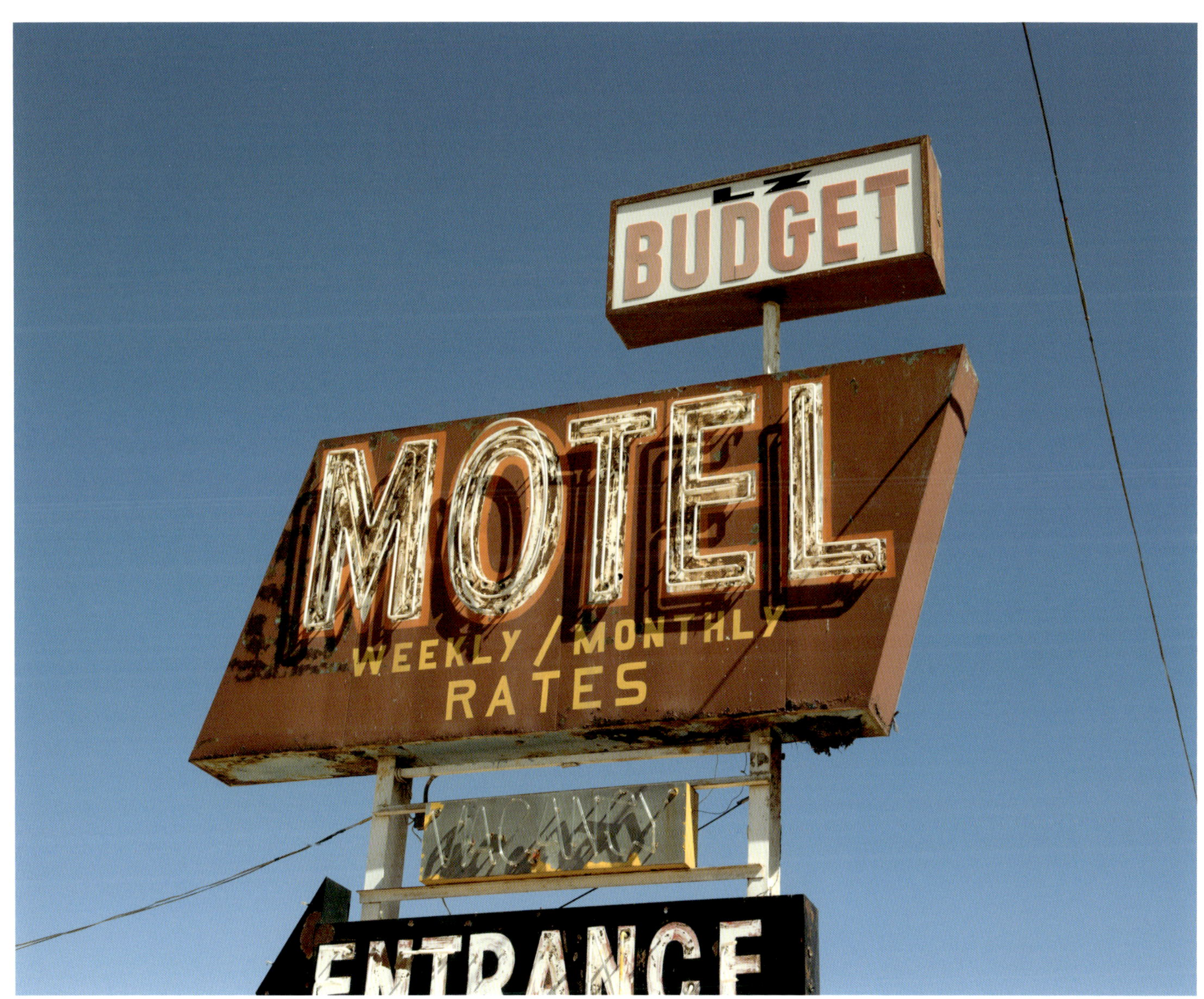

***Winslow, Arizona, September 19, 2013.* 2013**

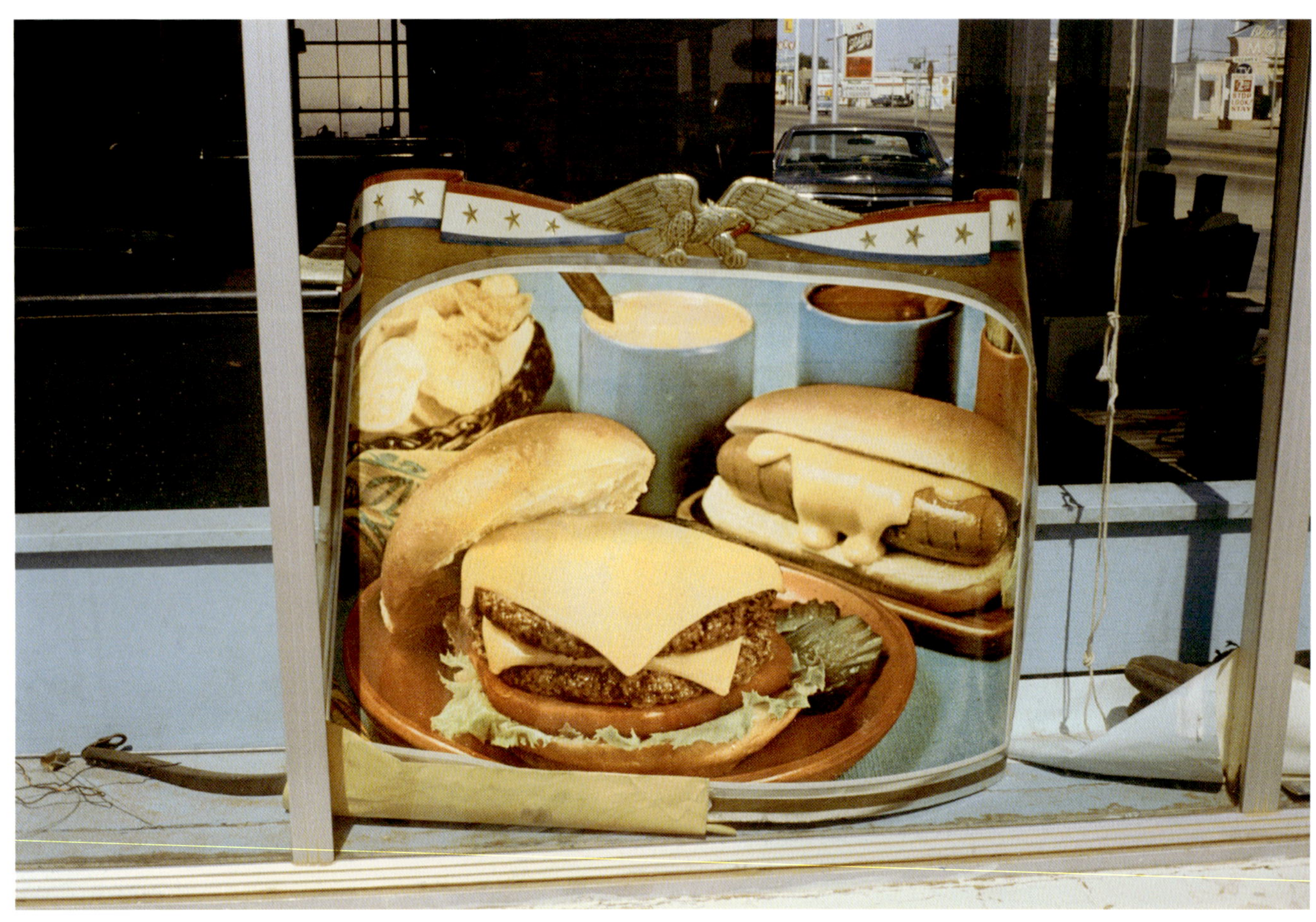

Tucumcari, New Mexico, July 1972. 1972

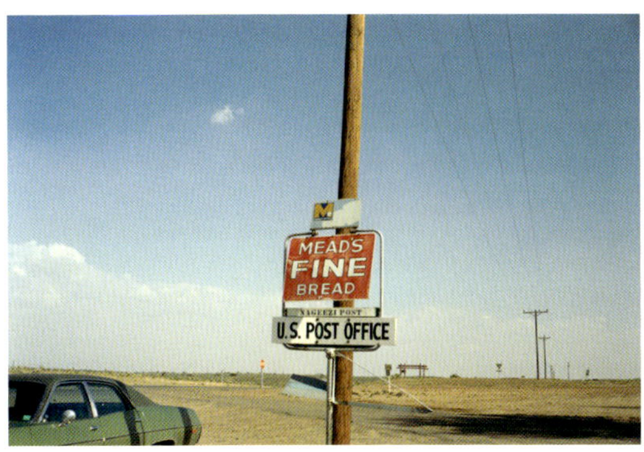

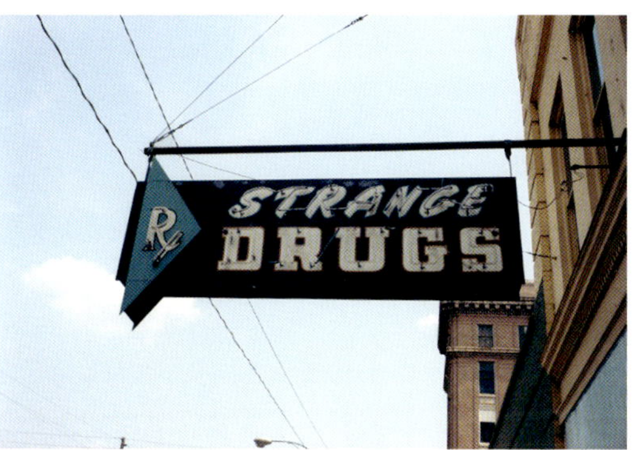

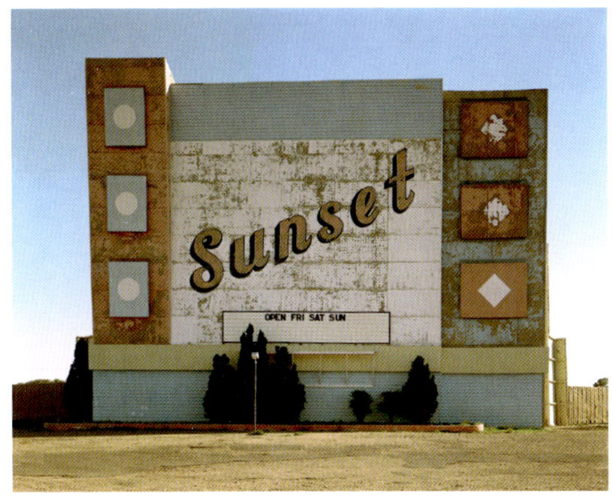

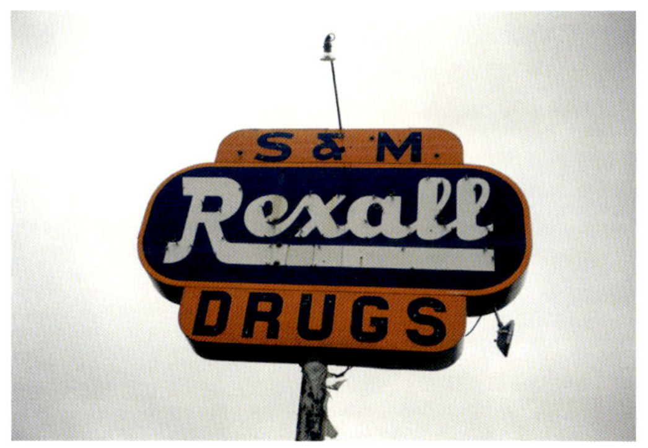

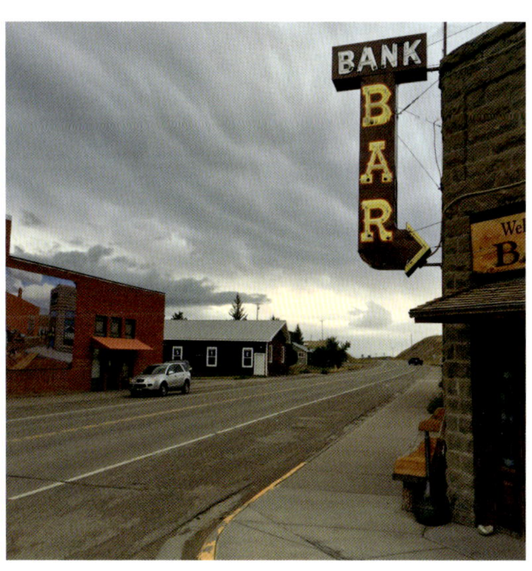

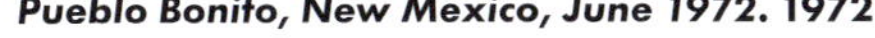

***Pueblo Bonito, New Mexico, June 1972*. 1972**

***West 9th Avenue, Amarillo, Texas, October 2, 1974*. 1974**

***Macon, Georgia, June 1972*. 1972**

***Amarillo, Texas, July 1972*. 1972**

***West Clark Street and South Elliot Street, Wilsall, Montana, September 4, 2015*. 2015**

Signs of Life

Signs of Life: Symbols in the American City was an exhibition organized by the American architects Robert Venturi, Steven Izenour, and Denise Scott Brown (of the firm Venturi and Rauch) at the Smithsonian Institution's Renwick Gallery in Washington, D.C., on the occasion of the American bicentennial celebrations in 1976. The exhibition was conceived, in the words of its creators, as a survey of the "pluralist aesthetic of the American city and its suburbs."[1] Four years earlier, the Philadelphia-based architects had positioned themselves as apologists for American consumer culture and the everyday environment through their groundbreaking book *Learning from Las Vegas*, which not only fundamentally—and controversially—changed the way we think about the contemporary city and its architectural manifestations, but also attracted the attention of the photography world.

While investigating the form and imagery of the ordinary urban and domestic landscapes of mid-century America from an architectural perspective, *Signs of Life* would also prove to be an influential model of how the medium of photography could be used in a contemporary fine art setting, radically challenging the boundaries between "high" and "low" cultures as well as received notions about artistic display. Evidence of the interest this exhibition garnered in the photographic discourse of its time can be seen in the fact that the accompanying catalogue was published by Aperture, a publisher specializing in photography. The visual argument developed in *Signs of Life* relied heavily on photographic images, and was to a large degree predicated on the collaboration between the leading architectural theorists of their time and Shore, though several other photographers were also involved.

Izenour, in charge of organizing the exhibition, had come across the work of the twenty-eight-year-old photographer at Light Gallery in New York, where he immediately recognized their shared affinity for the iconography of the roadside environment as well as their nonjudgmental, "deadpan" attitude toward it. Commissioned by Venturi and Rauch to create a series of photographs for the upcoming exhibition, Shore set out on a cross-continental road trip in the summer of 1975 that led to some of his most iconic works of this period. These color images, many of which were first presented to the public in *Signs of Life*, visually underscored an emerging architectural theory while also redefining the subject matter for the art of photography.

Signs of Life was organized as a sequence of three distinct chapters, each relating to a specific aspect of the urban or suburban landscape under investigation, and privileging a specific form of display. The heavy use of photography in the exhibition was remarkable, central not only for the creators' visual research on the existing landscape but also for its representation; in their view, the photographs constituted a "visual anthropology of American 'settlement forms.'"[2] If the architects were interested in investigating, documenting, and displaying the "reality" of the contemporary American landscape, photography provided the instrument to do so. The gallery space was small, and the display, which included several thousand photographs (by Shore and others) as well as a wide variety of objects, was tightly condensed.

The first section, "The Home," presented interior and exterior views of a working-class row house, a middle-class suburban home, and an upper-class private house in the form of period rooms and painted dioramas. The most conspicuous elements here were photomurals of each home's exterior—both a frontal view of the facade and a perspective of the street—based on monumental enlargements of photographs by Shore. The technological process that made this kind of photomural possible had been developed in Japan and was made commercially available by 3M in the United States. While there was precedent for such an immersive use of photography in avant-garde exhibitions from the late 1920s on (El Lissitzky being one of the pioneers),[3] its presence in a fine arts context proved novel—and controversial—at the time. It is perhaps not surprising that this appropriation of a commercial reproduction technique in a gallery setting was not received favorably by most contemporary critics, but Olivier Lugon has convincingly argued that it served as an important precursor to the rise of the "tableau form" in photography and the ascent of artists such as Jeff Wall or the exponents of the Düsseldorf School in subsequent years.[4]

The second section of *Signs of Life*, titled "The Strip," was a return to the architects' preoccupations in *Learning from Las Vegas*. The gallery was densely filled with neon advertising signs as well as a multitude of backlit photographic images mounted on a translucent wall that

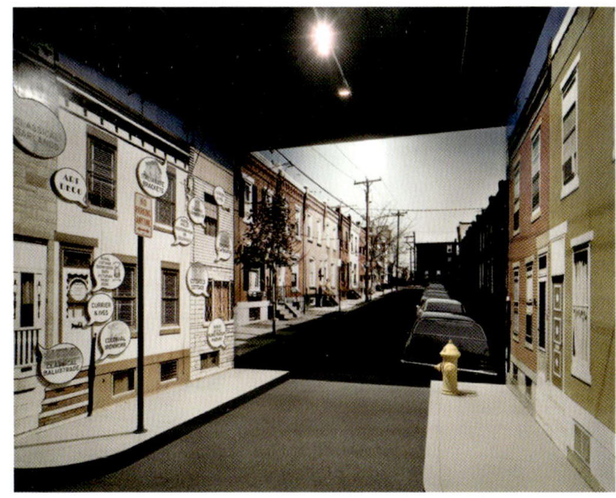

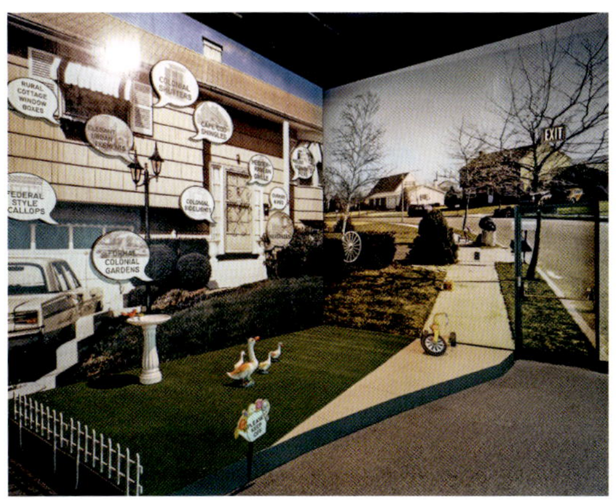

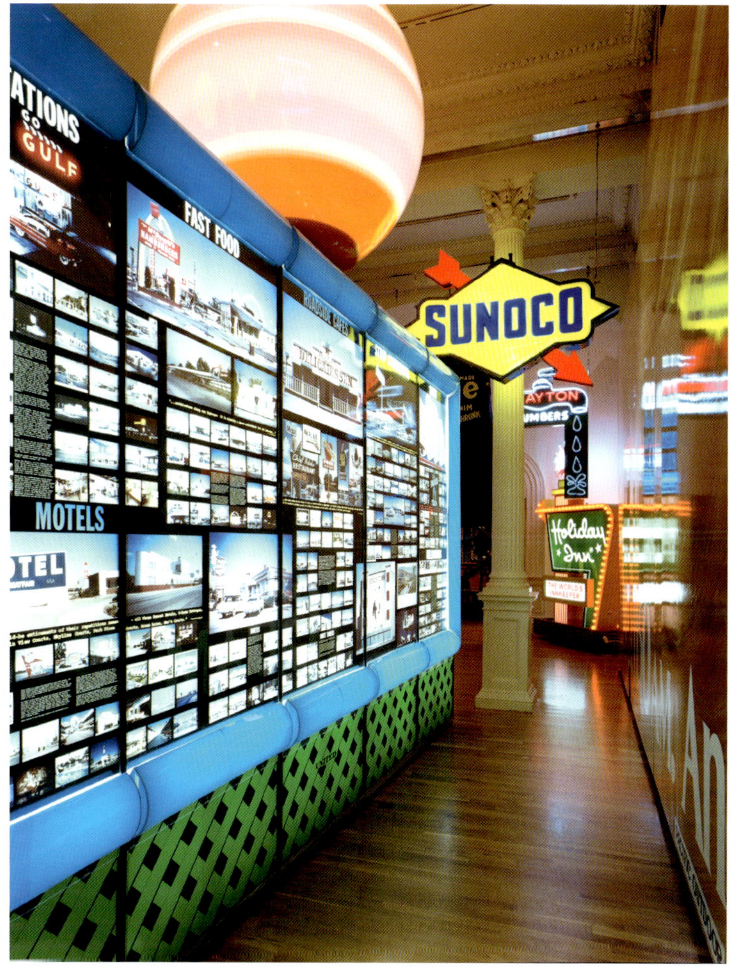

Installation views of *Signs of Life: Symbols in the American City*, organized by Robert Venturi, Steven Izenour, and Denise Scott Brown, Renwick Gallery, Washington, D.C., February 26–October 31, 1976. Photos: Stephen Shore

sketched out a typology of roadside architecture—a device that referenced both large-scale billboards and photographers' light boxes. The final section, "The Street," addressed the traditional Main Street of the American city. Like the others, this gallery made ample use of mid- and large-scale photographs, but here they were displayed in dense rows in the tradition of nineteenth-century salons. In this section, Shore's photographs were presented as discrete objects in the fashion of academic paintings, thereby effecting "the transfiguration of the billboard into a tableau."[5]

Signs of Life proved to be a seminal moment in the history of contemporary photography, appropriating mass cultural techniques of display for the high-art conventions of the museum. (Martino Stierli)

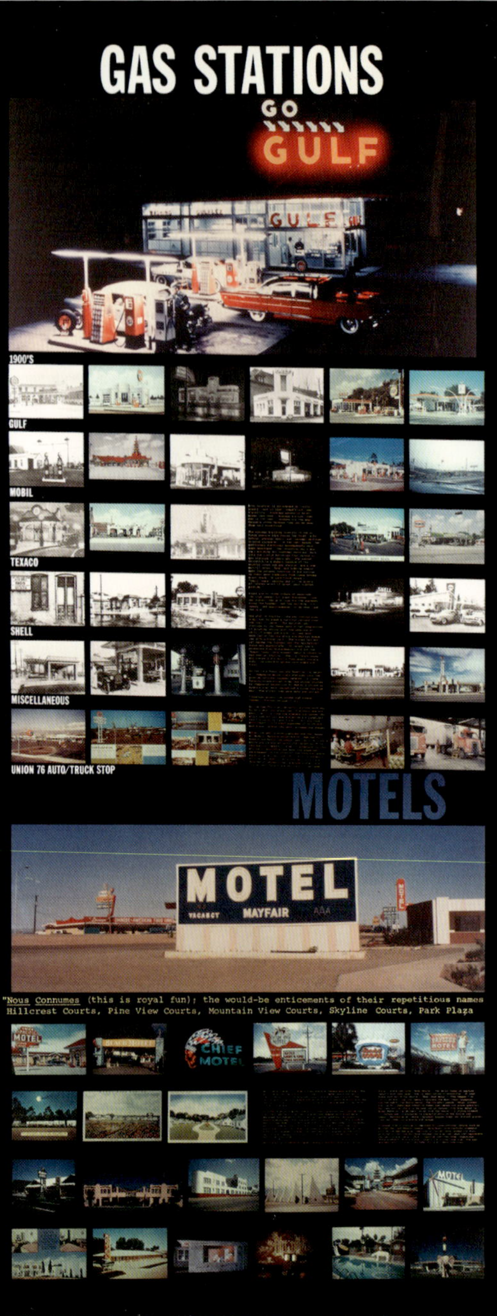

See also: *Architecture*; *Prints*

1. Venturi and Rauch, *Signs of Life: Symbols in the American City* (Washington, D.C.: Aperture, 1976), n.p.
2. Deborah Fausch, "Ugly and Ordinary: The Representation of the Everyday," in Stephen Harris and Deborah Berke, eds., *Architecture of the Everyday* (New York: Princeton Architectural Press, 1997), 81.
3. See Romy Golan, *Muralnomad: The Paradox of Wall Painting, Europe 1927–1957* (New Haven, Conn.: Yale University Press, 2009).
4. See Olivier Lugon, "Before the Tableau Form: Large Photographic Formats in the Exhibition *Signs of Life*, 1976," *Études photographiques* 25 (May 2010): 6–41. The tableau form in photography was first theorized by Jean-François Chevrier in 1989 and later revived by Michael Fried in 2008.
5. Lugon, "Before the Tableau Form," 36.

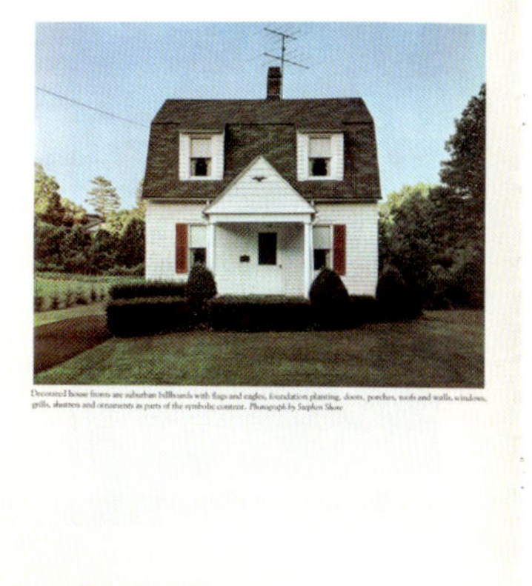

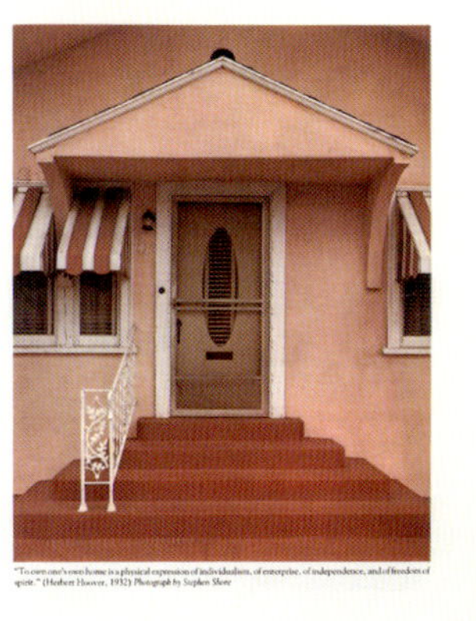

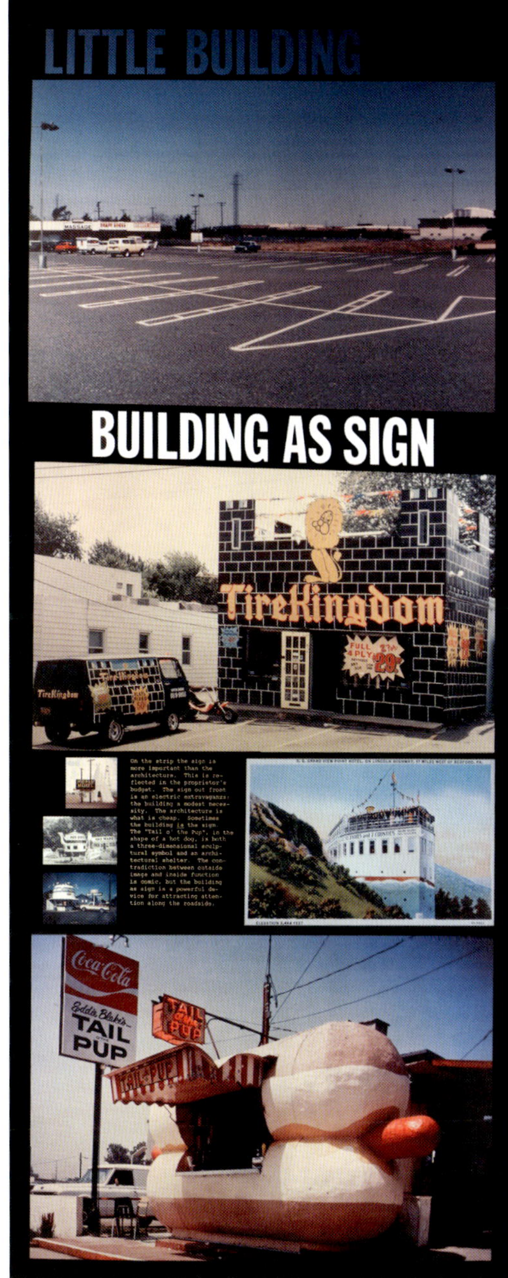

Transparency with photographs by Stephen Shore and others, from *Signs of Life: Symbols in the American City*, organized by Robert Venturi, Steven Izenour, and Denise Scott Brown, Renwick Gallery, Washington, D.C., February 26–October 31, 1976

Venturi and Rauch, *Signs of Life: Symbols in the American City* (New York: Aperture, 1976)

Transparency with photographs by Stephen Shore and others, from *Signs of Life: Symbols in the American City*, organized by Robert Venturi, Steven Izenour, and Denise Scott Brown, Renwick Gallery, Washington, D.C., February 26–October 31, 1976

Stereographs

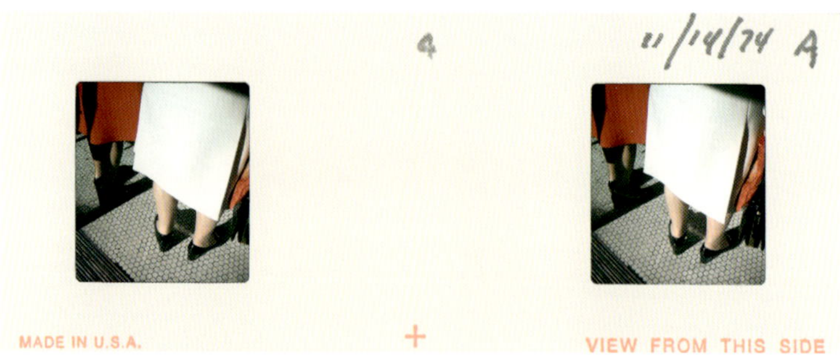

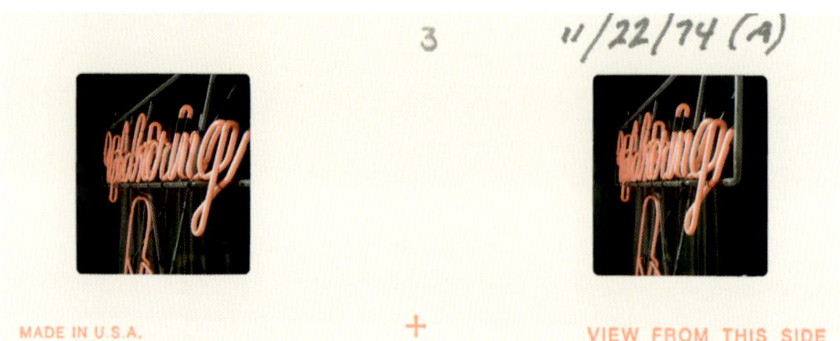

Soon after photography's invention, photographers realized that the vision of the human eye, especially the information it gathers about depth, could be imitated by producing stereo cards, which paired two images of the same scene taken from slightly different places (often the distance between two human eyes). Stereographs had their greatest popularity in the late nineteenth century, bringing three-dimensional views of faraway places into viewers' homes, then faded away in popularity in the second and third decades of the twentieth century. But in the manufacturing boom of the post–World War II years, the David White Company released the Stereo Realist, a stereo camera that fed a smaller, second surge of interest that continues today with digital 3D technology.

For two months in 1974 Shore experimented with a Stereo Realist, taking pictures around New York. Having photographed in the previous four years with a Mick-a-Matic, a Leica 35mm, a Rollei 35, a Crown Graphic 4-by-5, a Calumet 8-by-10, and an Arca Swiss 8-by-10, he was familiar with how different cameras would lead him to changes in composition and subject. His stereographs are beautiful, crystalline images that convey depth through structured and layered forms such as window displays, still lifes, and street scenes. This investigation of photography's ability to convey three-dimensional space would continue through *Uncommon Places* and his landscape images of the 1980s.

Shore's 1975 exhibition at Light Gallery included his stereo views, and visitors rhapsodized about these images in the gallery's guest book (often preferring them to the chromogenic prints). One commenter hoped Shore would start a "stereoscope revolution," and another wrote, "your stereoscopic bathroom sink will haunt me" (opposite). And at least one visitor traced his use of the format to nineteenth-century forebears, writing, "Your stereo realist made my eyes become like way back magic lantern show on Sunday eyes."[1] (Kristen Gaylord)

See also: *Cameras*; *Light Gallery*; *Shopwindows*; *Uncommon Places*

1. Guest book, 1975, Stephen Shore Collection, 1973–1978, AG 50, Center for Creative Photography, University of Arizona, Tucson.

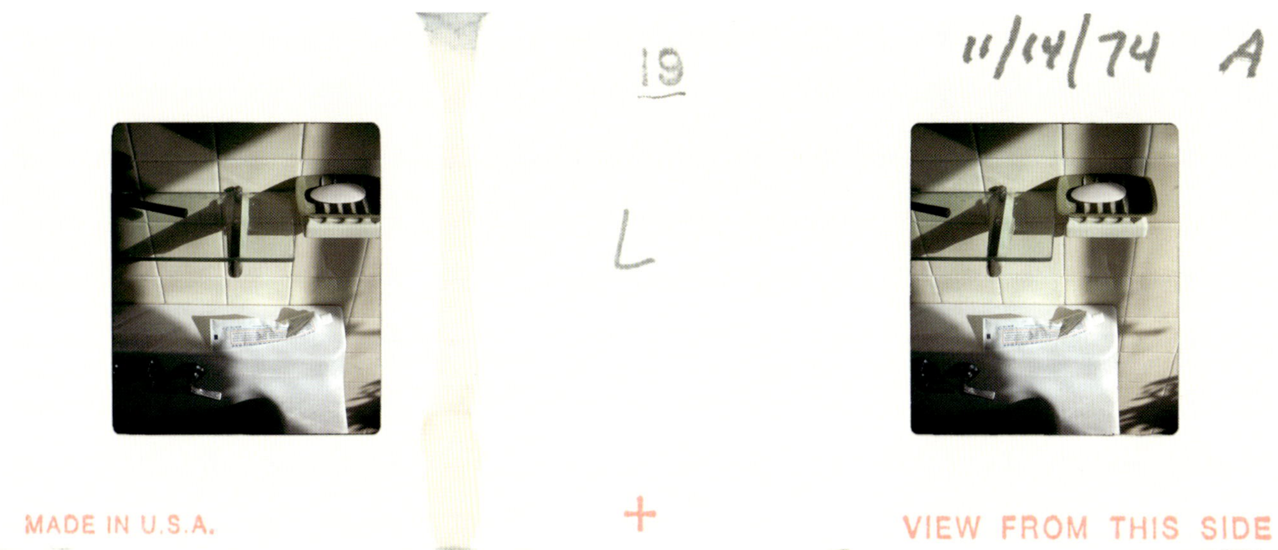

***New York, New York, 1974*. 1974**

***New York, New York, 1974*. 1974**

***New York, New York, 1974*. 1974**

219.

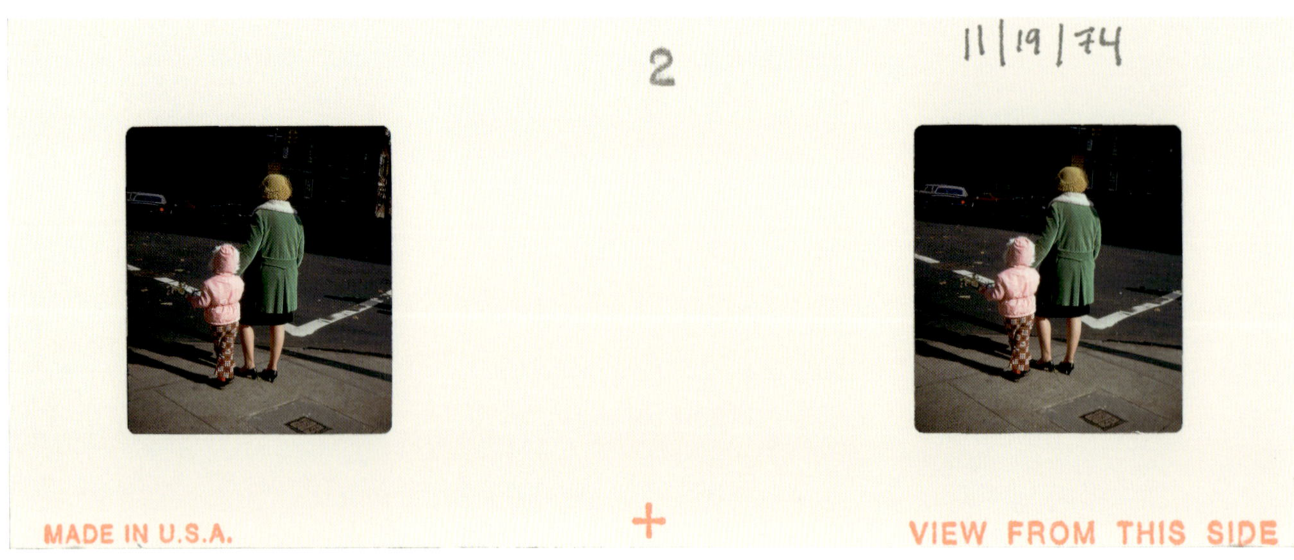

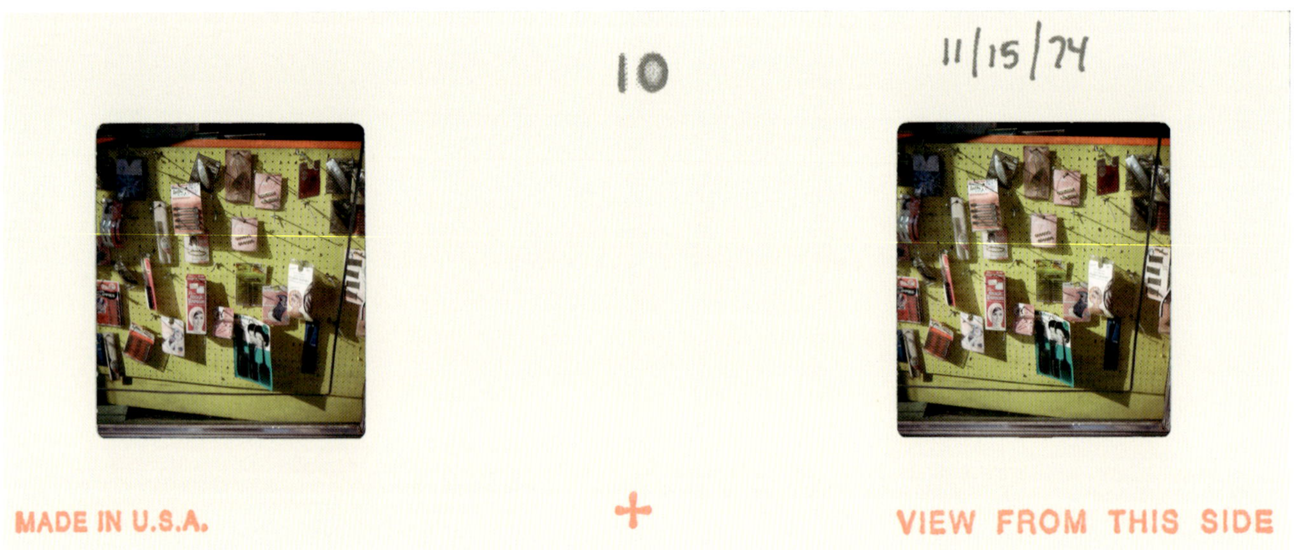

***New York, New York, 1974*. 1974**

***New York, New York, 1974*. 1974**

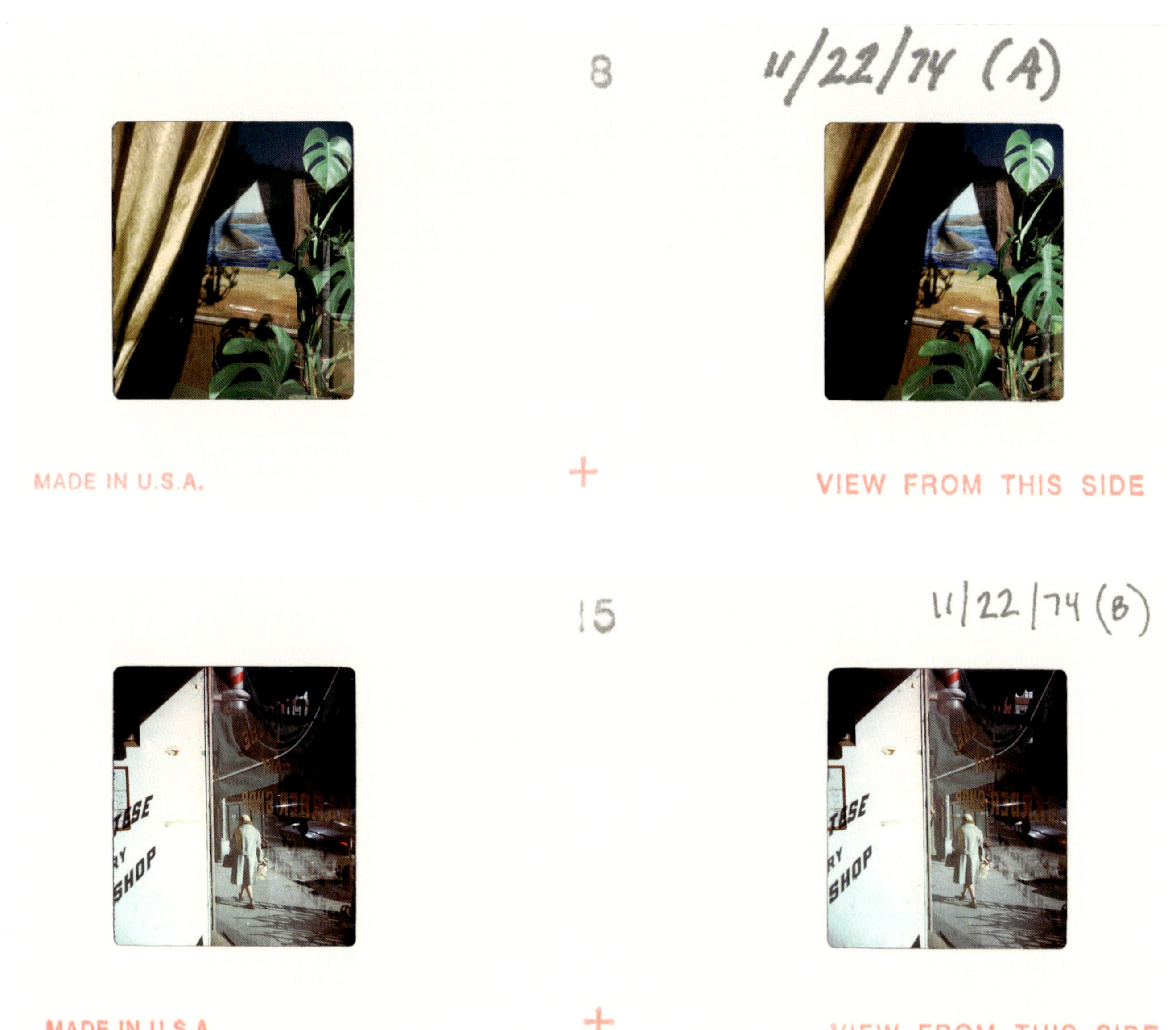

New York, New York, 1974. 1974

New York, New York, 1974. 1974

221.

Street Photography

While Shore remains essentially an urban photographer in the collective imagination, only a few of his series actually have the characteristics of street photography—that is, candid shots, primarily of people, taken in close proximity to the subject. In the 1950s and 1960s, when Shore was teaching himself photography, New York was the epicenter of this genre of photography, and it was amply represented in popular trade magazines that he read, such as *U.S. Camera* and *Popular Photography*.

Shore's images from the early sixties were part of this tradition. Generally taken with a small camera and in black and white, they capture people on the streets of New York, most notably in a series of frontal portraits where the subjects look directly into the camera. These portraits fall somewhere between the ruggedness of William Klein, as seen in his book on New York published in 1956,[1] and the empathy of Dave Heath or Leonard Freed.

Shore demonstrates a photographic vocabulary that is stunningly assertive for an adolescent—fragmented and a little raw, underlining the staccato rhythm of the street, syncopated and almost jazzy—in the creation of these sometimes brutal slices of life. Realized with the use of a hand-held camera pointed at diverse angles and in many directions, the images are generally taken from above and are printed in deliberately high contrast. The shots are rather close, either composed in the camera or reframed in printing. In an article on his street photography published in *U.S. Camera* in 1963, when he was only fifteen years old, Shore mentions the practice of cropping, which he would abandon completely later on, as he would his use of vertical images, a format that appears in his early work but rarely after that.

In the end, Shore's New York—hard-working, gritty Midtown—is not very picturesque, and the young photographer even seems to envision "a book about 42nd Street," a strange subject for someone his age.[2] His world is one of isolated or preoccupied individuals—newspaper vendors, shopkeepers in doorways, preachers, pedestrians—all presented without glorification, in line with the sort of street photography that had been delivering a disenchanted vision of the city since the forties. In addition, the young Shore was drawn to certain signs and symbols that were in the process of becoming commonplaces of street photography, such as the American flag and advertising signs, seeming to follow in the footsteps of older colleagues like Robert Frank and Klein, sometimes consciously and other times in a more distanced and ironic way.

Street photography, then, is intimately linked to Shore's early days. Later, when he returns to the streets of New York, it is from a completely different perspective, in which he shifts the conventions of the genre. In 1970, for instance, in his series *Avenue of the Americas* (page 228), Shore distanced himself from the expressionism and subjectivity inherent in the tradition of street photography in favor of a more Conceptual approach, similar to that of Douglas Huebler. For this series Shore took pictures systematically at every intersection along the avenue, from Forty-second Street to Central Park, using infrared film that produced almost solarized images. Similarly, when he returned to the subject of the New York street in the early 2000s, Shore shot in black and white, as he did in his early work, but he used an 8-by-10 camera in an unusual panoramic format to capture the street and subjects in motion, a choice that ran counter to the mobility typical of street photography. The type of camera used and the panoramic format gave these images a more narrative and monumental character, almost like a frieze. Like Philip-Lorca DiCorcia's series *Streetwork* and *Heads*, which were created around the same time and utilized artificial lighting, Shore's photographs of this period represented a kind of reconstruction of street photography, informed by outside influences, cinema in particular. (Quentin Bajac)

See also: *Black and White*; *Portraiture*; *Youth*

1. See William Klein, *Life Is Good & Good for You in New York: Trance Witness Revels* (Paris: Éditions du Seuil, 1956), although Shore was not aware of this work at the time.
2. "Angry Young Man with a Camera," *U.S. Camera*, June 1963, 52.

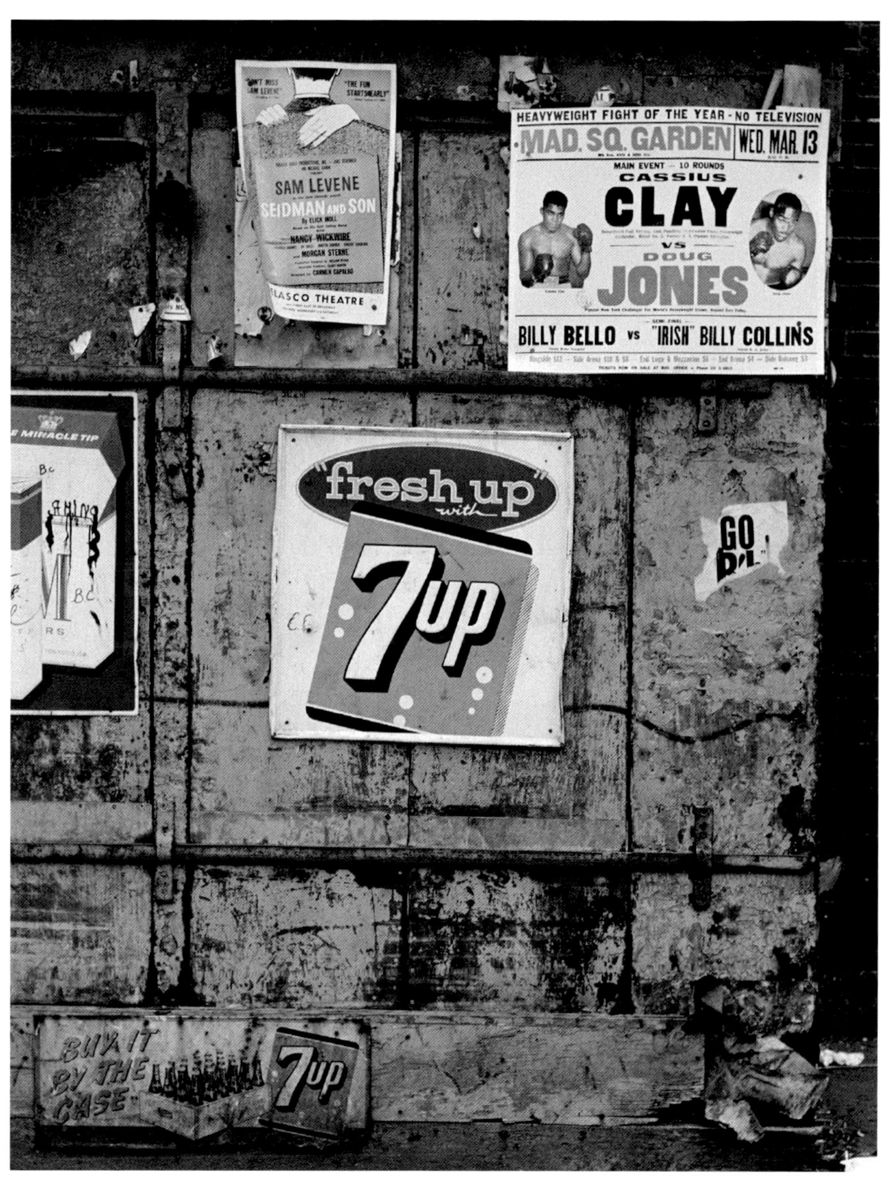

Untitled. 1963

223.

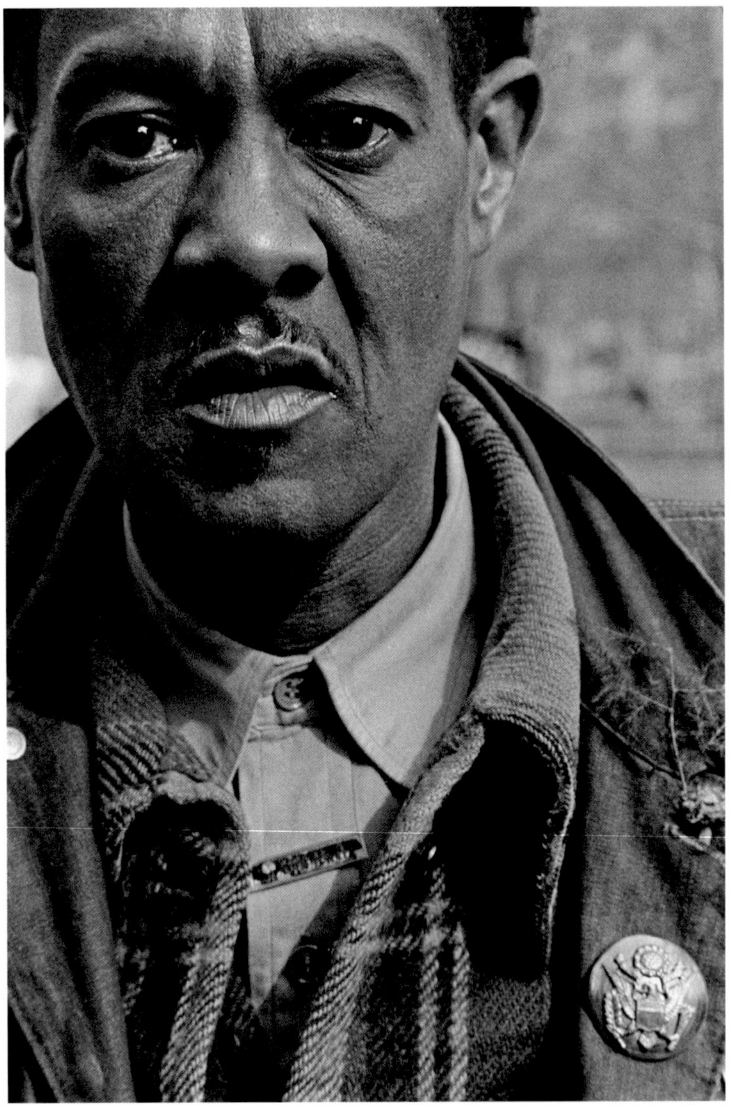

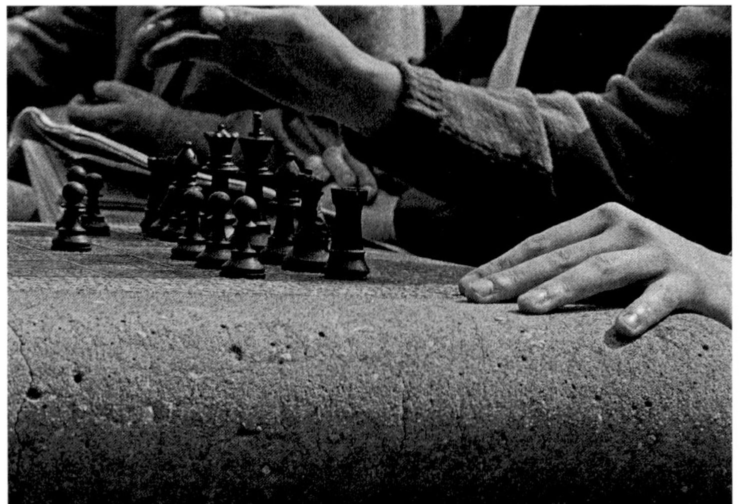

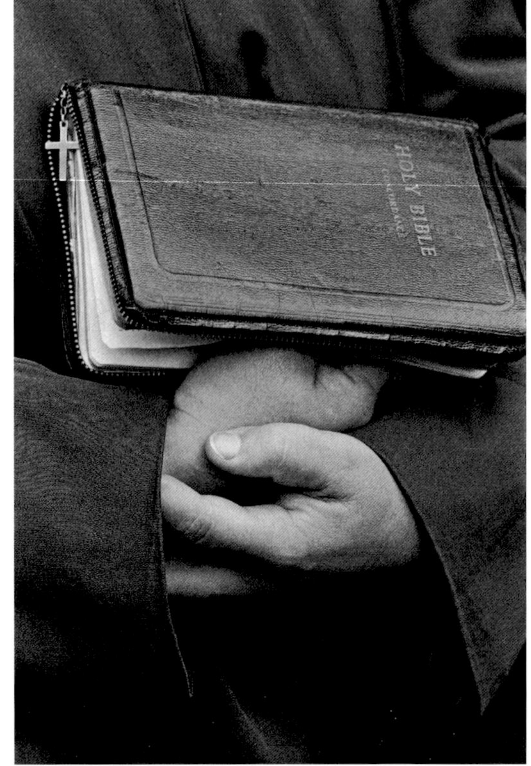

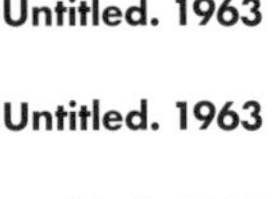

Untitled. 1963

Untitled. 1963

Untitled. 1964

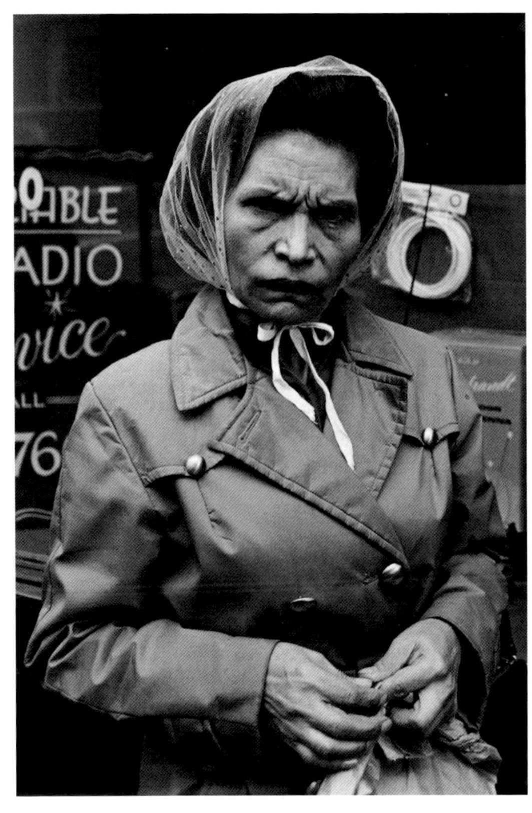

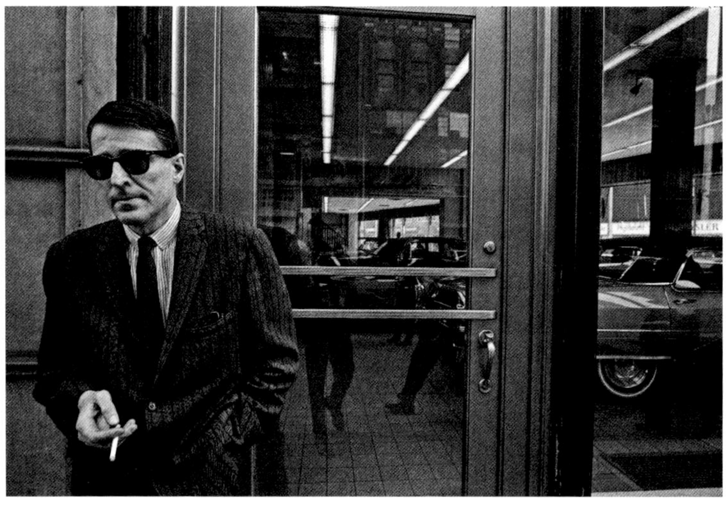

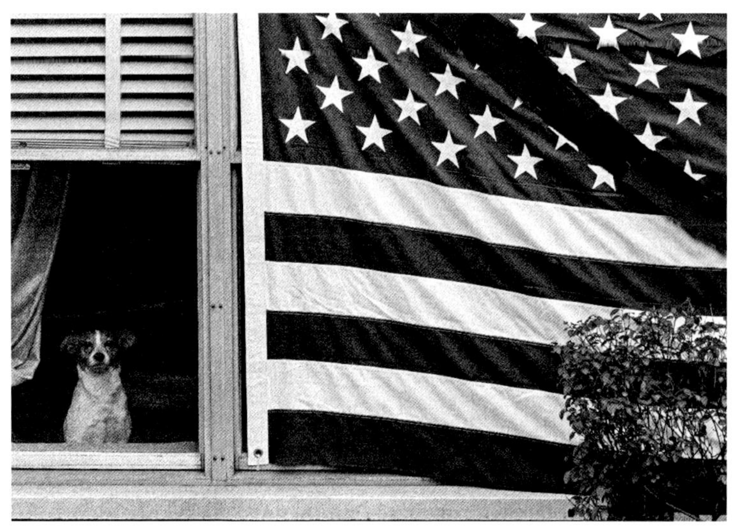

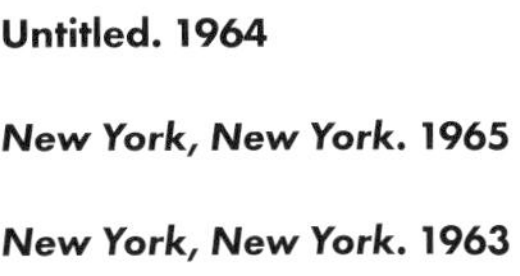

Untitled. 1964

***New York, New York*. 1965**

***New York, New York*. 1963**

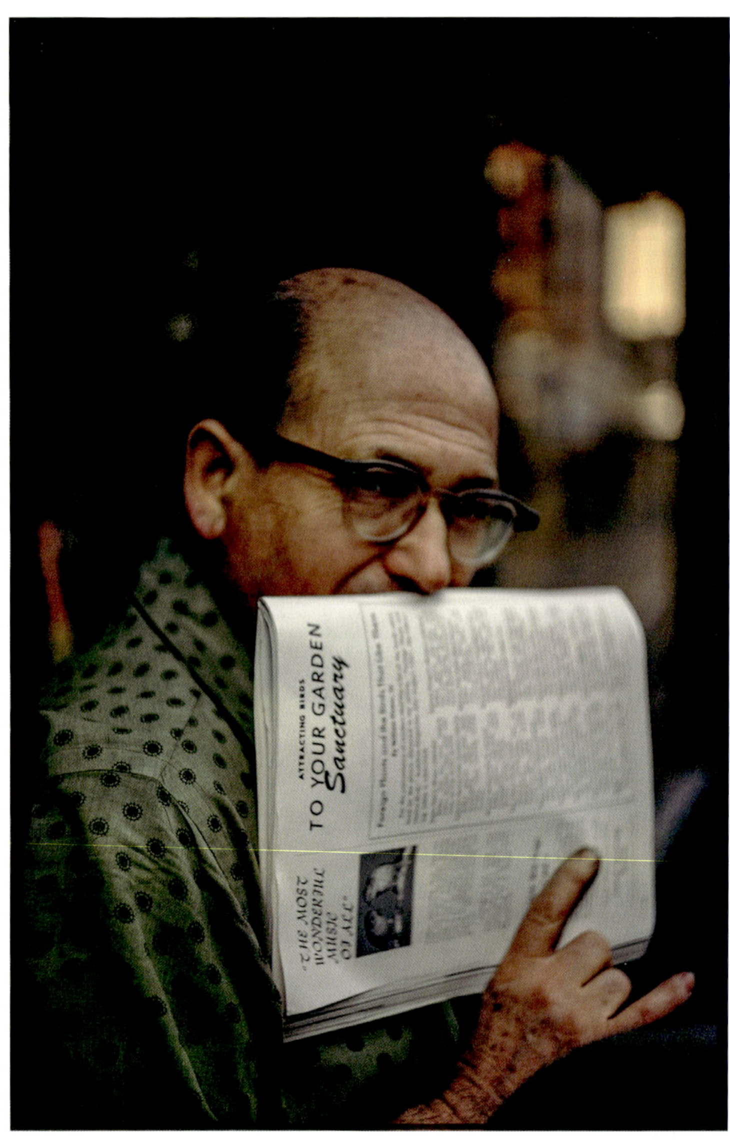

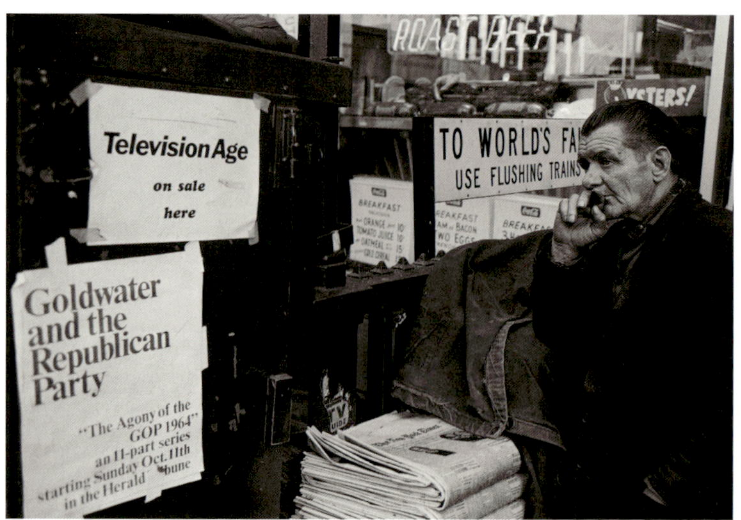

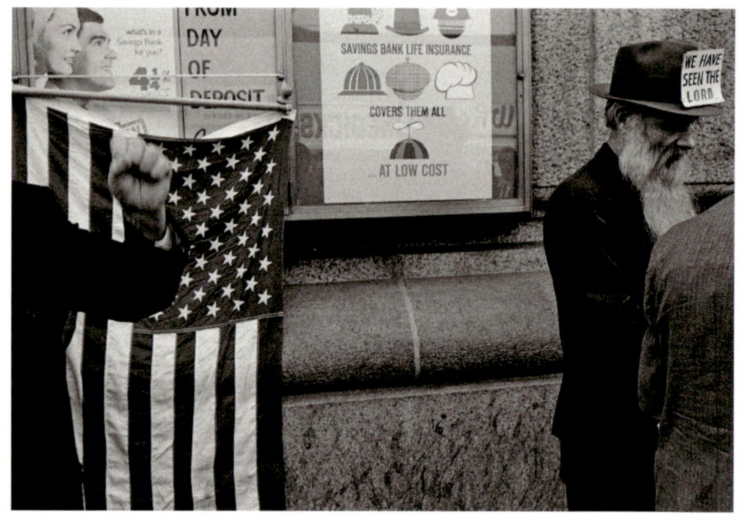

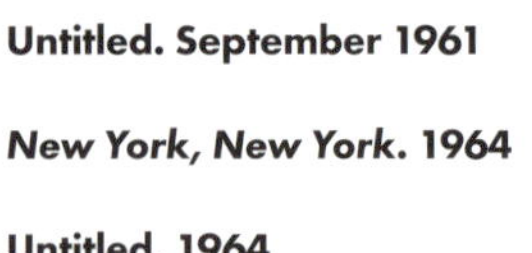

Untitled. September 1961

***New York, New York.* 1964**

Untitled. 1964

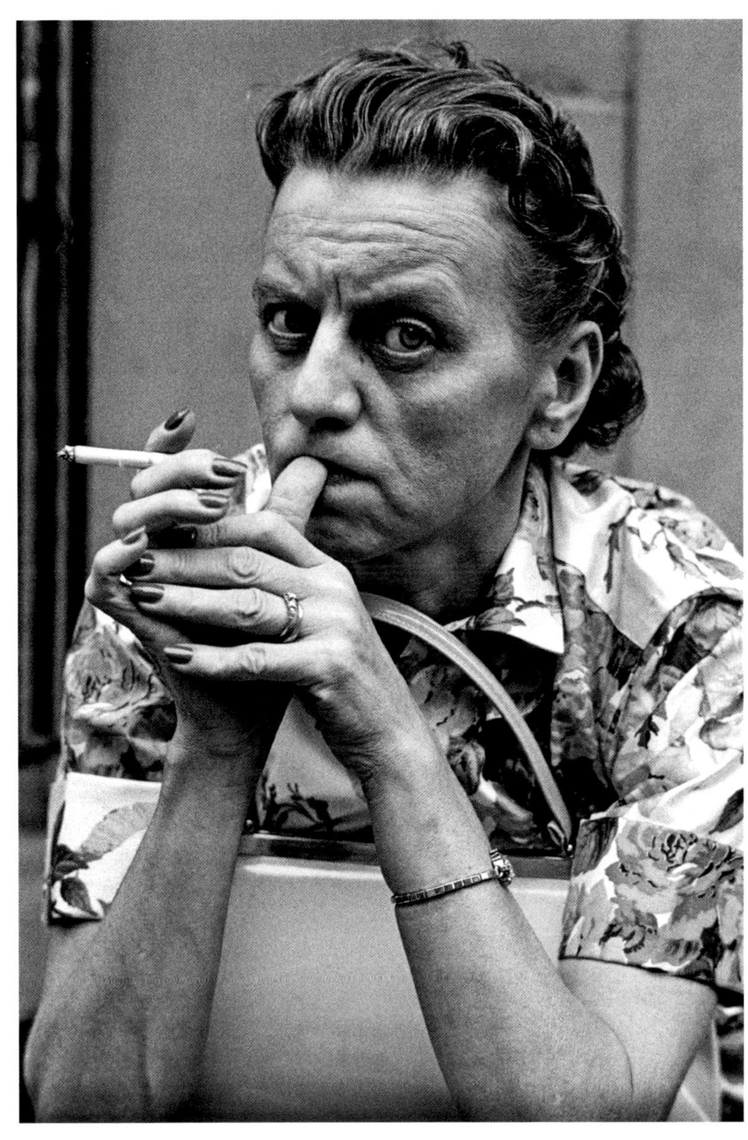

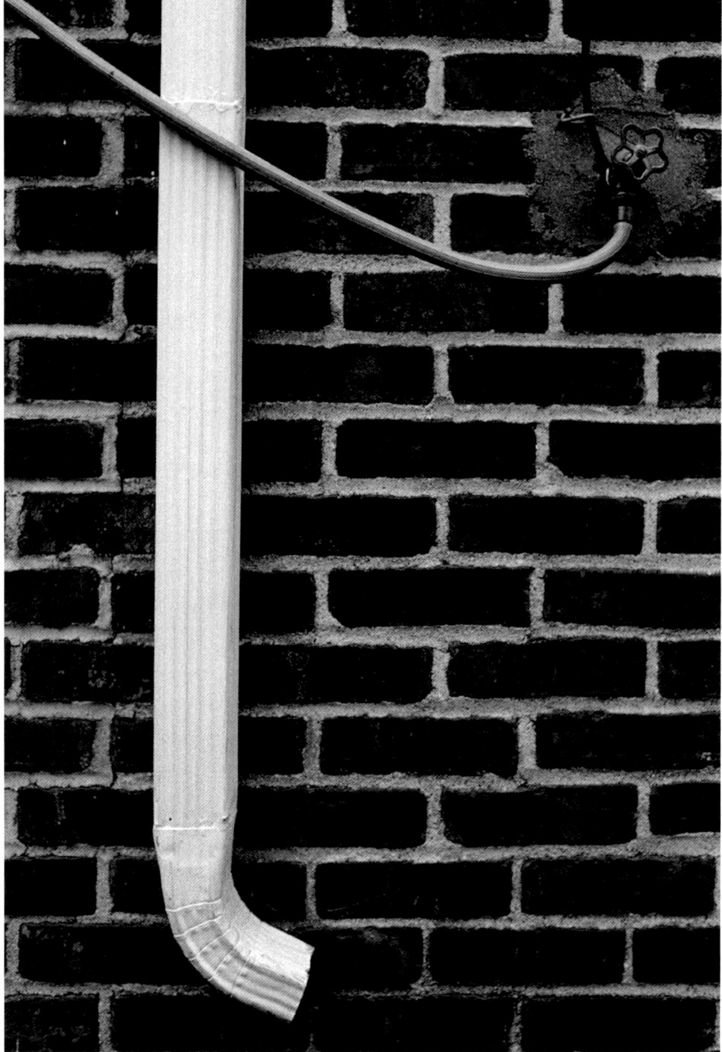

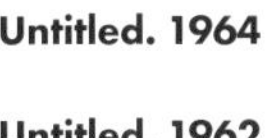

Untitled. 1964

Untitled. 1962

227.

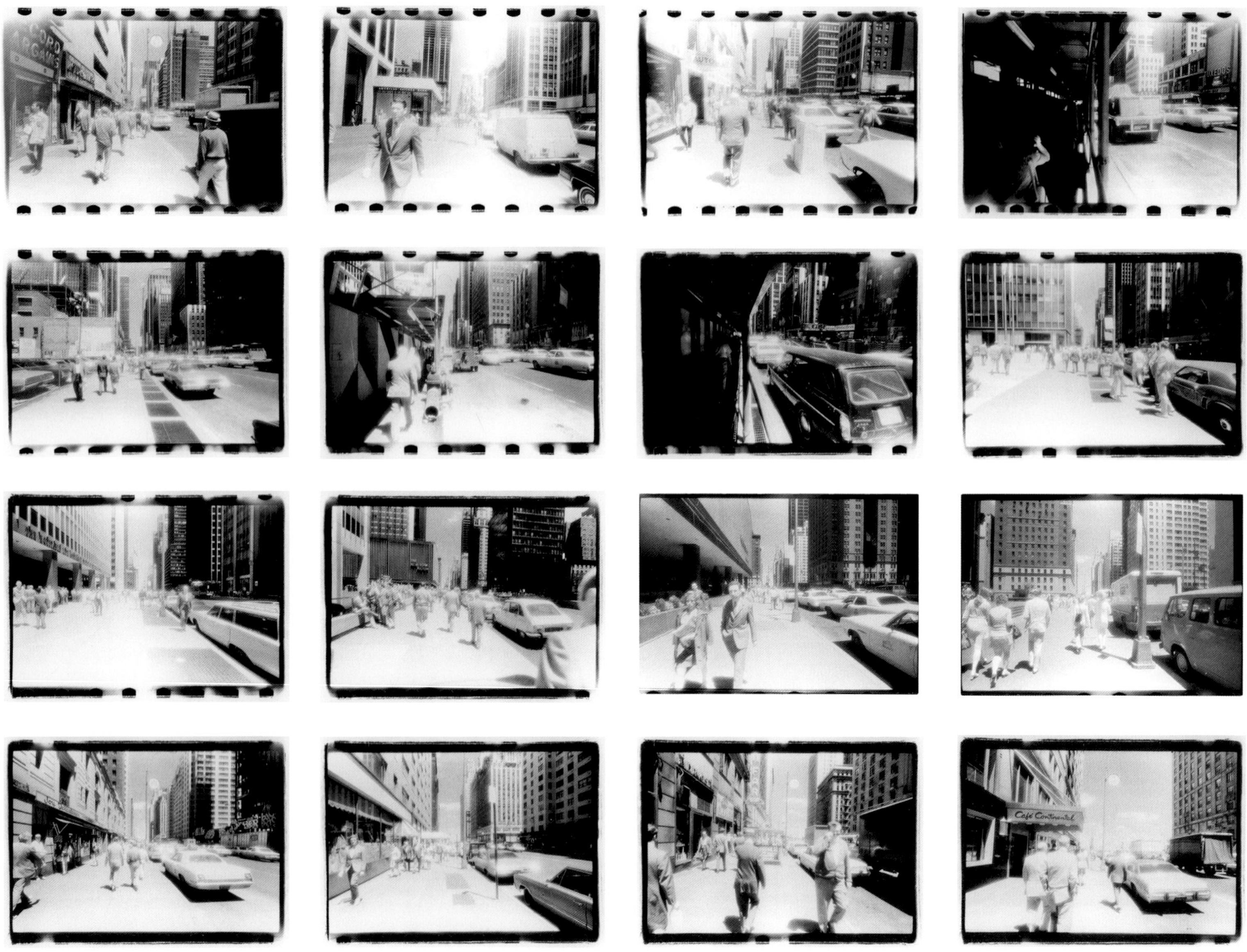

***Avenue of the Americas, June 17, 1970*. 1970**

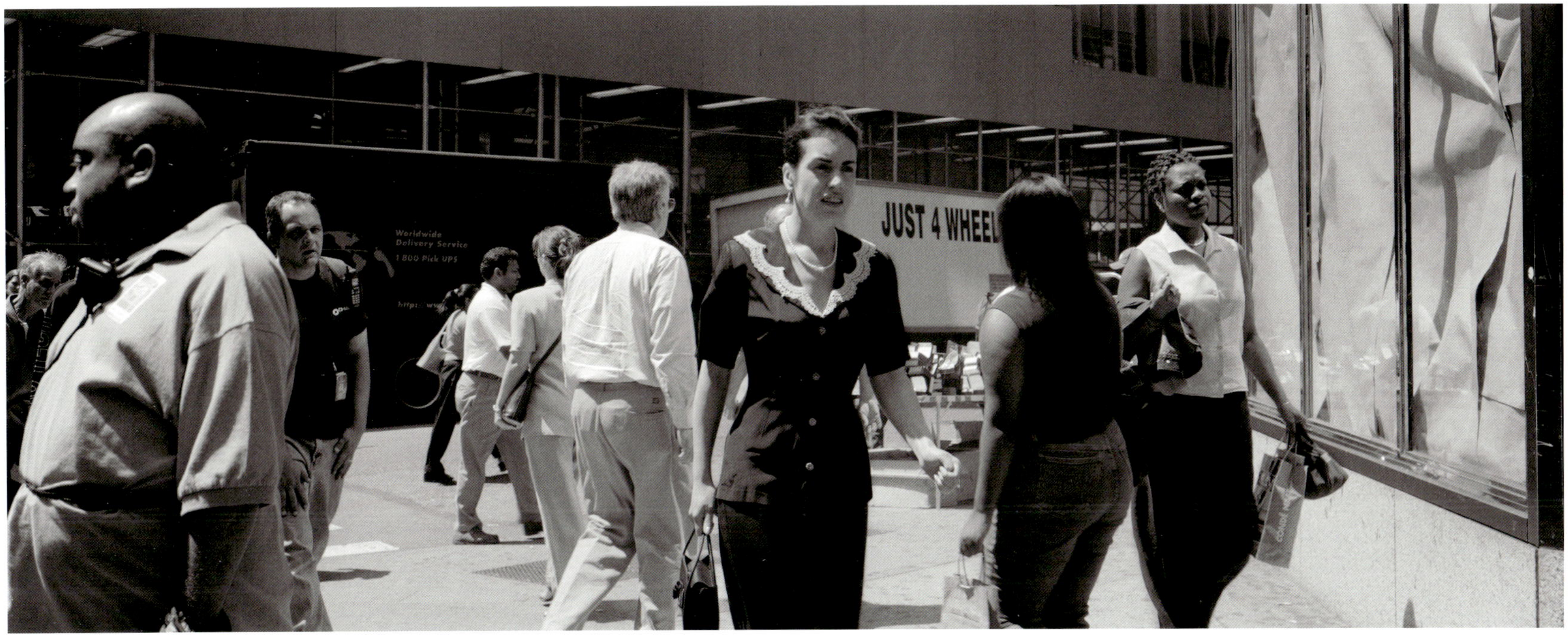

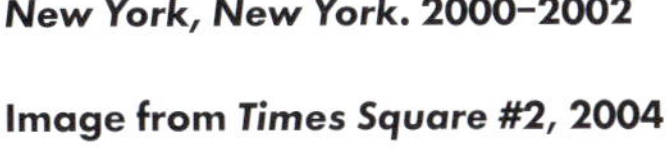

***New York, New York*. 2000–2002**

Image from *Times Square #2*, 2004

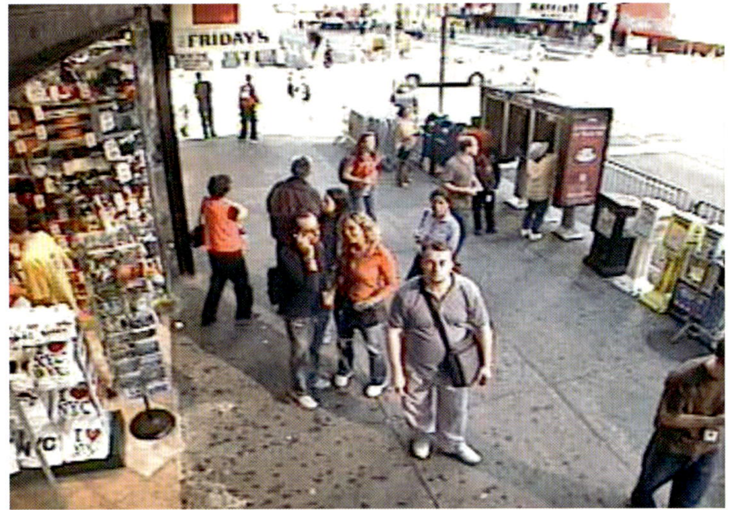

Teaching

Since 1982 Shore has directed the photography program at Bard College in Annandale-on-Hudson, 100 miles north of New York City, a program that he deliberately oriented toward straight photography at a time when most teachers were emphasizing manipulated and constructed photography. For more than thirty years, teaching has been at the core of his activity as a photographer and, notably, was the basis of *The Nature of Photographs*, the book he published in 1998. This may seem an unlikely situation for a photographer who left school at seventeen, was mainly self-taught in his craft (with the exception of some early tutoring and a workshop with Minor White in 1970), and has admitted that before starting to teach he rarely articulated his creative process.

Shore sees his role as a teacher as guiding undergraduate students to their own path, one that may ultimately diverge from the precepts of straight photography they are taught initially. Indeed, some of his best-known former students (such as Walead Beshty, Lucas Blalock, Tim Davis, Shannon Ebner, and Xaviera Simmons) have developed an approach and a photographic universe that are very distant from his own. Nonetheless, Shore's teaching continues to be sustained by ideas closely tied to his own practice, such as the use of film and analog cameras. He sees this type of training as an indispensable prerequisite to understanding certain essential aspects of photography: the discipline of shooting, particularly with a view camera; printing photographs in the darkroom; and using both black and white and color.

Shore considers teaching "a process that is truly altruistic and truly selfish without contradiction."[1] The altruism comes out of a vocation that Shore considers almost a mission: "I see teaching as a separate activity where—this may be too much mystical thinking—for a person to progress in their own evolution it's necessary for them to bring other people to the place they were. I feel that I have a duty to do it."[2] The selfishness resides in the fact that teachers are themselves enriched by the work and thoughts of their students, in a relationship characterized by mutual enrichment rather than a unilateral apprenticeship where the student learns from the master. Shore has at various times explained how his teaching—which forces him to put himself in the shoes of students whose training, tastes, and practices are by definition further and further removed from his own—has kept him vigilant, intellectually and technically, and helped him to envision different solutions that will nurture his own work in turn. (Quentin Bajac)

See also: *Nature of Photographs, The*

1. Michael Grieve, "Master & Servant," *British Journal of Photography*, August 2016, 52.
2. "Heroes & Mentors: Stephen Shore and Gregory Crewdson," *Photo District News*, August 2011, 28.

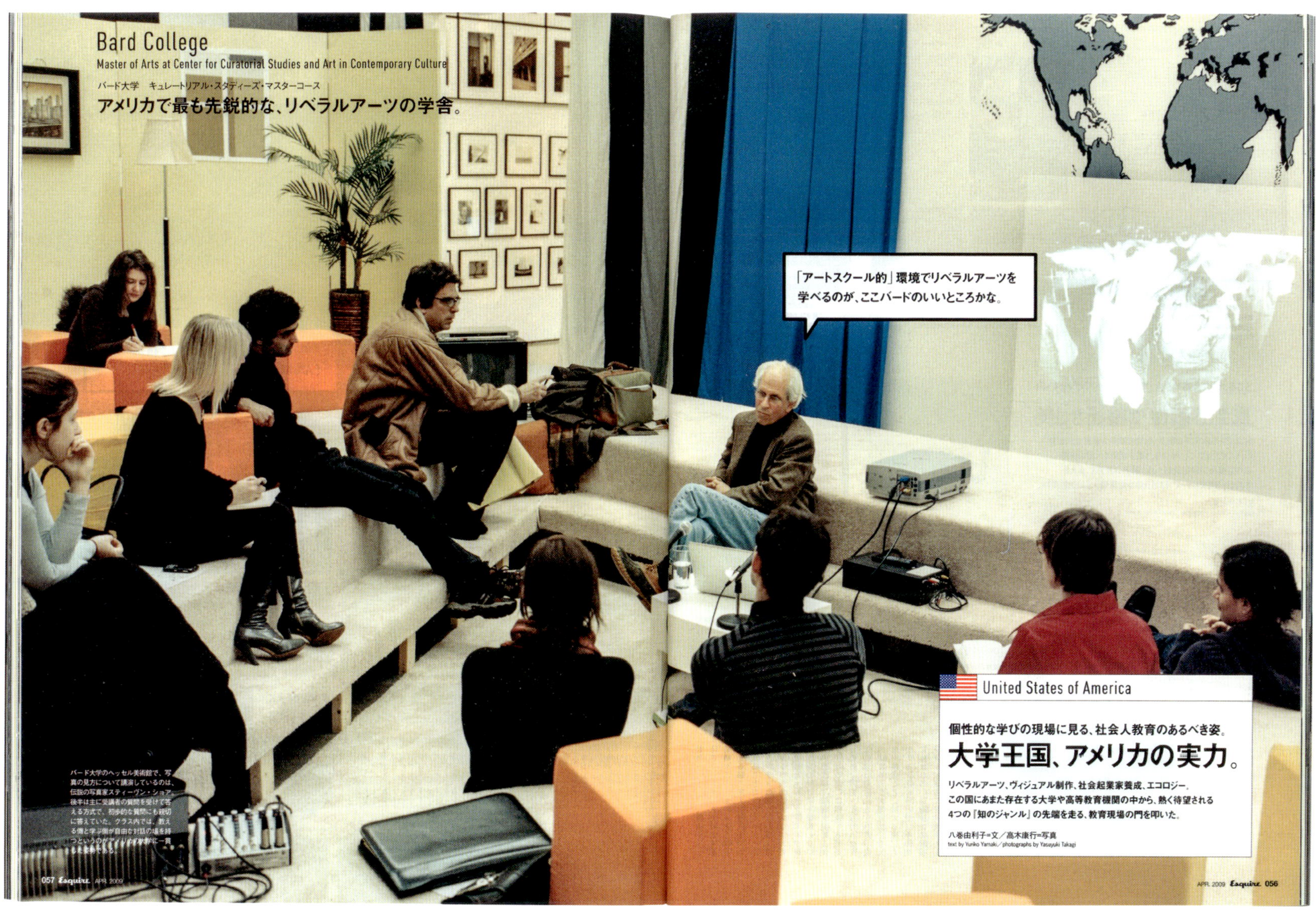

Bard College

Master of Arts at Center for Curatorial Studies and Art in Contemporary Culture

バード大学　キュレートリアル・スタディーズ・マスターコース

アメリカで最も先鋭的な、リベラルアーツの学舎。

「アートスクール的」環境でリベラルアーツを学べるのが、ここバードのいいところかな。

バード大学のヘッセル美術館で、写真の見方について講演しているのは、伝説の写真家スティーヴン・ショア。後半は主に受講者の質問を受けて答える方式で、初歩的な質問にも親切に答えていた。クラス内では、教える側と学ぶ側が自由な対話の場を持つというのがアメリカの大学に一貫した姿勢である。

United States of America

個性的な学びの現場に見る、社会人教育のあるべき姿。

大学王国、アメリカの実力。

リベラルアーツ、ヴィジュアル制作、社会起業家養成、エコロジー。
この国にあまた存在する大学や高等教育機関の中から、熱く待望される
4つの『知のジャンル』の先端を走る、教育現場の門を叩いた。

八巻由利子=文／高木康行=写真
text by Yuriko Yamaki／photographs by Yasuyuki Takagi

057 Esquire APR. 2009

APR. 2009 Esquire 056

Spread from *Esquire* (Japan), April 2009. The speech bubble above Shore's head reads, "The good thing about Bard is that students get to study liberal arts in an art school–like environment."

Travel

During his first trip to Los Angeles in 1969, Shore produced a series of photographs shot exclusively from a car—he was just a passenger and not a driver at the time—and demonstrated how being in a car affects and modifies our perception of the urban landscape (pages 79 and 198). Later, after 2000, he made series aboard planes or trains that would serve as the basis for some of his print-on-demand books, once again closely linking the means of travel with the tools of vision, displacement with new visual experiences, and mobility with a different perspective on his surroundings.

In 1977, in response to an article published in *Artforum* comparing Shore's work to that of Eugène Atget, Shelley Rice in the *Village Voice* drew a distinction between the sedentary working process of Atget and that of Shore, who was constantly in motion.[1] While the former had an intimate knowledge of the place he was photographing (Paris and its environs at the turn of the twentieth century) and strove to capture the local color in all its diversity, the latter was always just passing through, never settling in any of the provincial American cities he visited in the 1970s and chose as his subjects. He was attracted above all to the banal and the quotidian—the repetition of the same, an archetype rather than various types. Shore set himself apart from a typological approach like that of the Bechers. "What I was after," he said, "was not a study of main streets (or gas stations, suburban houses, shopping centers, etc.), but the quintessential main street."[2]

Shore has always been on the move, and since the early 1970s, in addition to his various projects, he has placed traveling in its various forms at the core of his photographic poetics, which has evolved along with the nature of these travels. The early trips in those years were almost all taken by car within the United States (and occasionally on the other side of the Canadian and Mexican borders). Shore feels a kinship with the model of the road trip, linked in American mythology to a sense of freedom and, during the postwar period, a beatnik sensibility or a kind of marginality, but he twists the model and approaches it with his typical detachment. Both in the places he visits (small American towns and their main streets) and his routine on the road (eating in diners, staying at motels), his travels are deliberately more akin to the salesman's humdrum existence than the backpacker's ecstatic discovery of open spaces. The other popular model of the traveler at the time was that of the tourist, who is fully integrated into consumer society but searches for exoticism and the easy picturesque. However, as Max Kozloff pointed out about Shore in a 1975 article in *Artforum*: "It takes, perhaps, some while to adjust to the fact that a traveler to new places has shot these photos in a spirit exactly the opposite of a tourist."[3] Seeking out ordinary, stereotypical subjects (with no particular local color), Shore could be seen as continuing in the tradition of Conceptual artists, from Ed Ruscha, whose book *26 Gasoline Stations* featured a series of very similar gas stations shot on the mythic Route 66, to John Baldessari, who substituted the poetic imaginary of the road trip with its most mundane details in a series of color snapshots called *The Backs of All the Trucks Passed While Driving from Los Angeles to Santa Barbara, California, Sunday 20 January 1963*.[4] Shore is neither a backpacker nor a tourist, then, but an enthusiastic "roving eye," in search of the singular within the ordinary: banal places and moments that the photographer nevertheless sees as "uncommon."

Starting in the late 1980s, international travel would overtake domestic travel for Shore, as he began to photograph abroad more and more frequently, at times on commission. He produced photographic series in Scotland (1988), France (1990), Mexico (1990), Italy (Luzzara, 1993; Aquileia, 1997; Venice, 2008), Israel (Ashkelon and Hatzor, 1996; 2009–11), Abu Dhabi (2009), and Ukraine (2012–13), and created numerous print-on-demand books, between 2003 and 2008, in South Africa, Austria, Cambodia, England, France, Germany, Hong Kong, Israel, Italy, Portugal, and Switzerland. It is therefore no exaggeration to say that the majority of Shore's work after 1990 was made outside the United States, as if he had found a new visual stimulant in his outsider's perspective and his position as a foreigner in these new territories. Initiated in the Yucatán, Mexico, and continued in Luzzara, Italy, this broadening of locales was accompanied by a return to the human element, which had been virtually absent in the 1980s. Reversing Rice's argument of 1977, he was making his status as a traveler the condition of a singular way of looking. He said in 2014, "I want to see

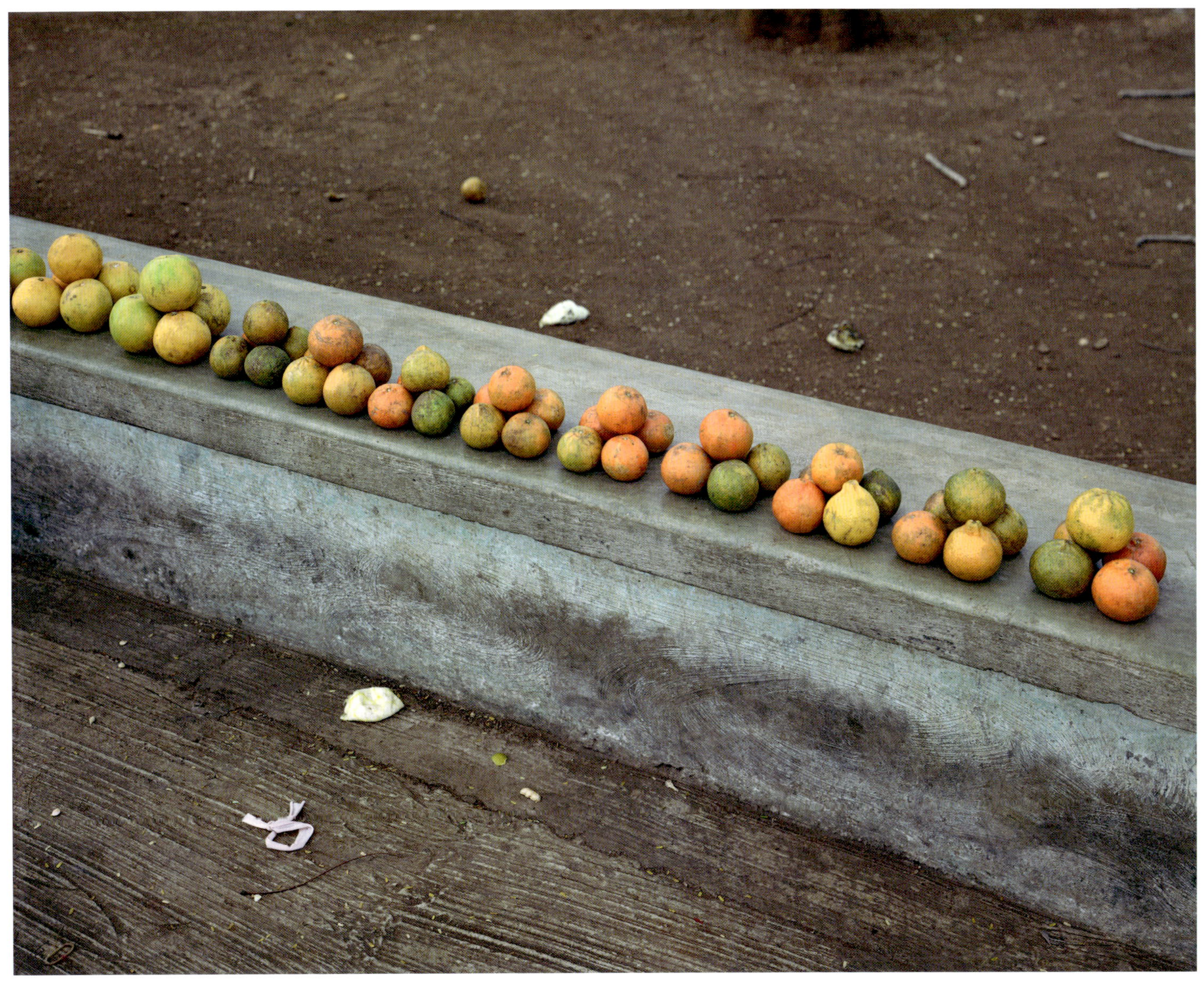

Yucatán, Mexico, 1990. 1990

233.

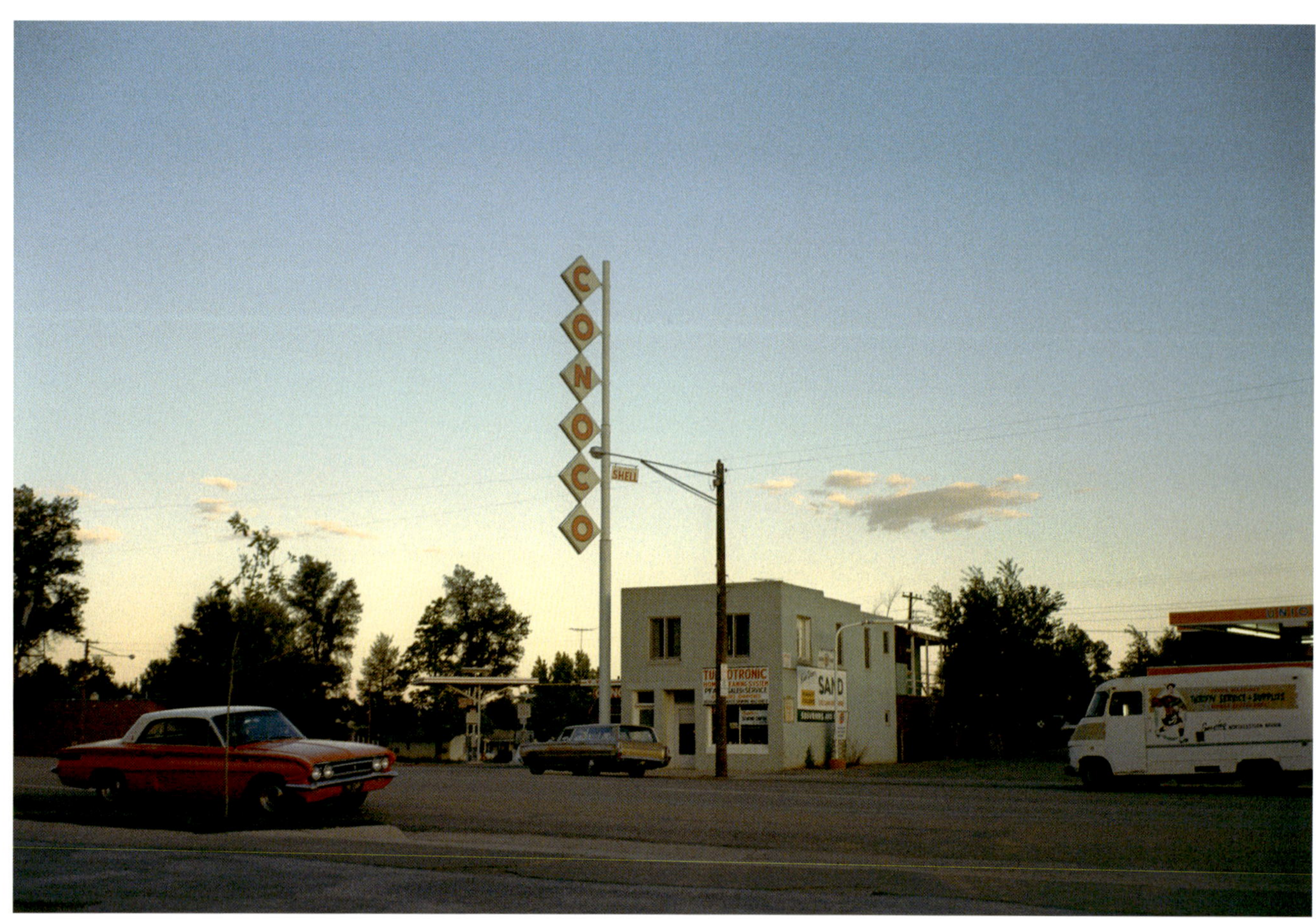

Kanab, Utah, June 1972. 1972

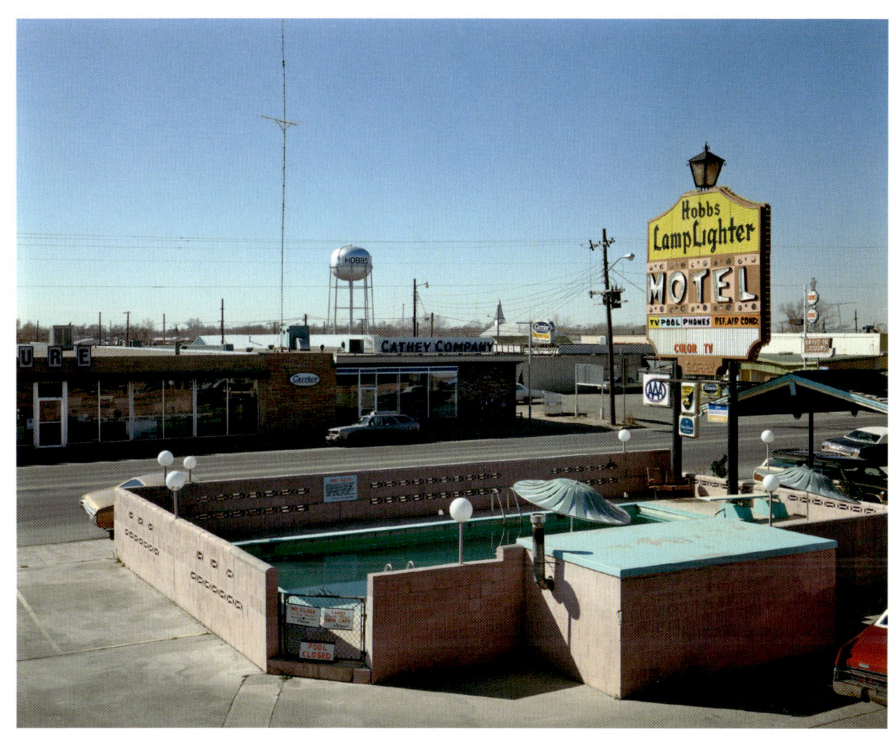

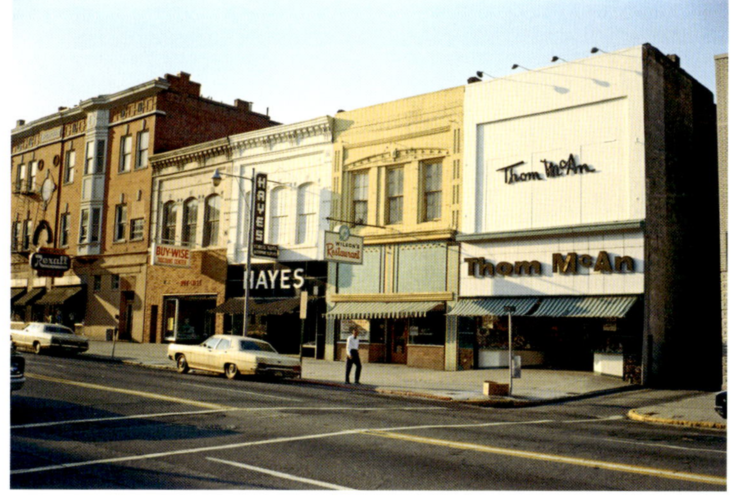

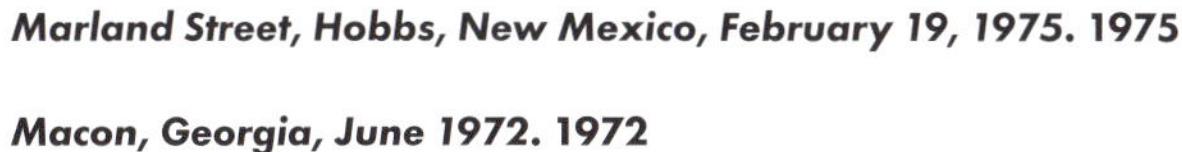

Marland Street, Hobbs, New Mexico, February 19, 1975. 1975

Macon, Georgia, June 1972. 1972

it fresh and see the little bits of everyday life that a native might take for granted, but that are special to the place, while at the same time, not taking a picture that would be a tourist cliché."[5] Although local color is in fact what attracts him, Shore continues to prefer to see himself not as a tourist but as an anthropologist, in search of meaningful signs of the ordinary and the everyday. (Quentin Bajac)

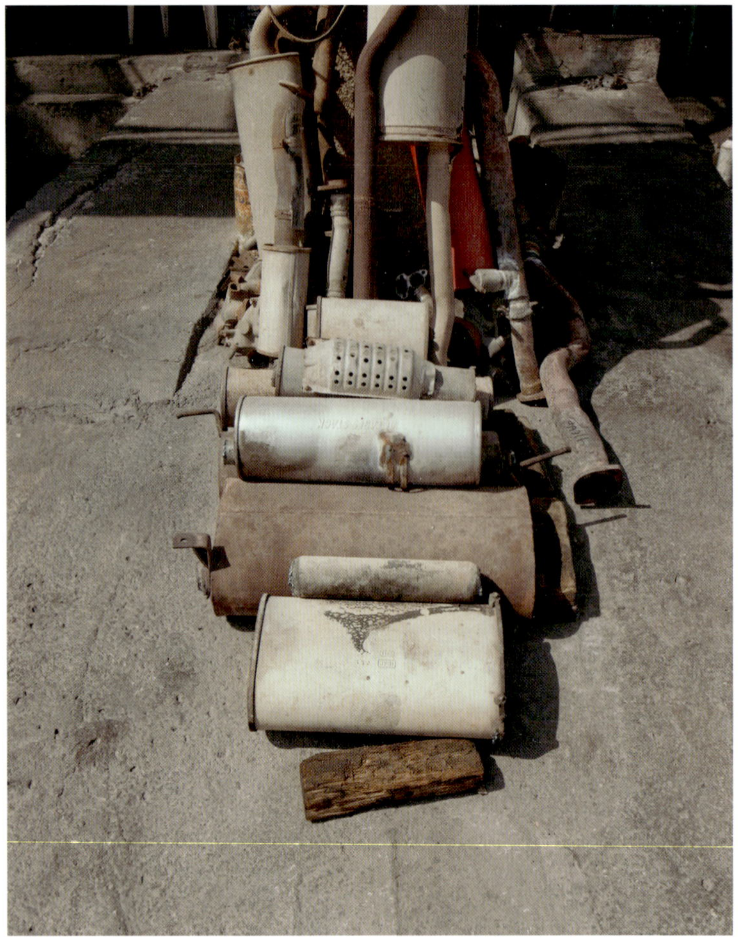

See also: *Israel and the West Bank*; *Luzzara*; *Print-on-Demand Books*; *Road Trips*; *Ukraine*

1. Shelley Rice, "Stephen Shore: Banal Landscapes Revisioned," *Village Voice*, May 2, 1977, 87. The original article was Max Kozloff, "Photography: The Coming of Age of Color," *Artforum* 13, no. 5 (January 1975): 30–35.
2. Susanne Lange, "A Conversation with Stephen Shore," in *Bernd und Hilla Becher Festschrift* (Munich: Schirmer/Mosel, 2002), 50.
3. Kozloff, "Photography: The Coming of Age of Color," 35.
4. See Mark Godfrey, "Across the Universe," in Matthew S. Witkovsky, ed., *Light Years: Conceptual Art and the Photograph, 1964–1977*, 57–65 (Chicago: Art Institute of Chicago; New Haven, Conn.: Yale University Press, 2011).
5. Colleen Kelsey, "Shore to Shore," *Interview*, September 11, 2014, www.interviewmagazine.com/art/shore-to-shore/#_.

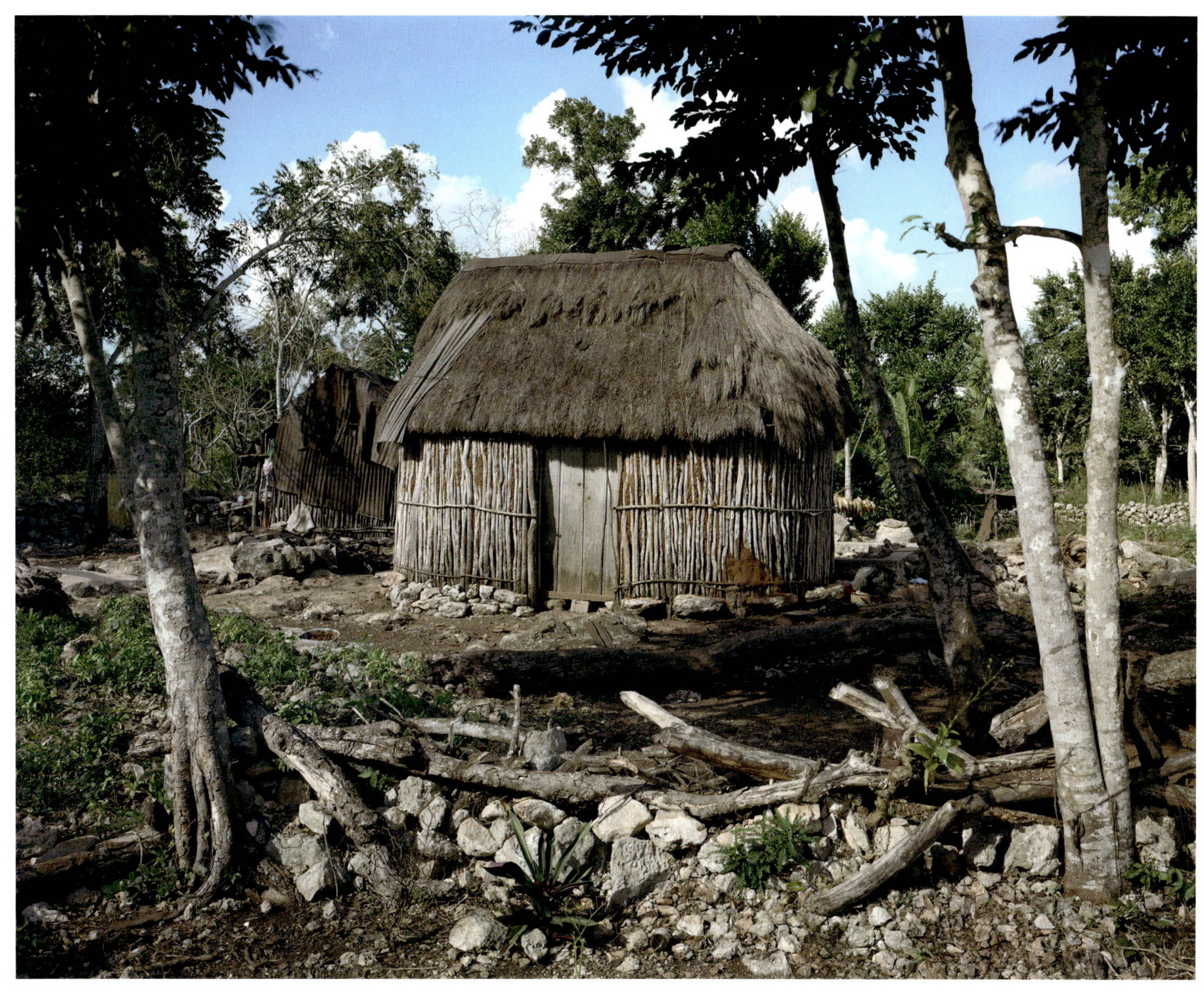

Abu Dhabi, 2009. **2009**

Yucatán, Mexico, 1990. **1990**

Ukraine

The photographs that Shore took in Ukraine in the summer of 2012 and the fall of 2013 have as their subject the country's Jewish community, specifically survivors of the Holocaust who are assisted today by the Survivor Mitzvah Project. This organization, based in Los Angeles, aids the last remaining survivors of the Shoah in Eastern Europe, in which 1.5 million of 2.7 million Ukrainian Jews were killed by the Nazis during World War II. Following three years of photographing primarily in Israel, the series provided Shore with the opportunity to continue working with subjects related to his Jewish roots: his paternal grandfather emigrated from Ukraine to the United States at the end of the nineteenth century. But in Ukraine he pursued a more intense path, both politically and emotionally, than he had in Israel, taking a more personal approach while still retaining, as always, a certain indirectness.

In a break from his norm, Shore structured the Ukraine series around the human figure, and for the first time in a project of this importance he almost always photographed both exteriors and interiors in natural light, a practice made possible by the use of a digital camera. *Survivors in Ukraine*, the book of photographs Shore published in 2015, provides accounts of twenty-two survivors, all more than eighty years old, through a wide range of images: close-ups, busts, and full-length portraits; fragmentary portraits of hands, arms, and legs; views of dwellings and interiors; and still-life details of meals, belongings, and memorials to departed family members. Within the limits inherent in photography's nature as an art of surface, these various images, when seen together like pieces of a puzzle, are an attempt to describe an individual and his or her history, tastes, and way of life.

All of these portraits are marked by fragility, both physical (elderly bodies) and economic (great destitution). The world depicted here is on the brink of disappearing, with each interior evoking a bygone era, as if frozen in time since the war. In this sense, each account is a true time capsule, in which Shore has brought an anthropological and almost archaeological attention not just to things but also, for the first time in such a distinct way, to people. The meandering, often contradictory nature of history is highlighted in the portraits of Isaak Bakmayev and Tsal Groisman, who proudly display their decorations from the "Great Patriotic War" (pages 240–41 and 246).

Like a number of Shore's other projects, *Survivors in Ukraine* is constructed as a journey. The stories of these survivors, told through photographs taken in various places around the country, whether rural or urban, merge with their surroundings, as if they were captured en route, while traveling on country roads or through city streets. The series alternates between close-up, sometimes stifling interior shots and vast, often lyrical landscapes marked by exuberant greens and often bathed in summer light. Giving breathing room to the narrative of the subjects' lives, the outdoor shots place the survivors in the context of Ukraine today, capturing its history and traditions (the presence of religion, vestiges of the Communist past and the Great War) as well as its current social and economic conditions: a country that remains predominantly rural and agricultural but shows a few signs of modernity, especially around Kiev and Lviv. (Quentin Bajac)

See also: *Food*; *Israel and the West Bank*; *Portraiture*; *Shnuriv Lys, Ukraine*; *Travel*

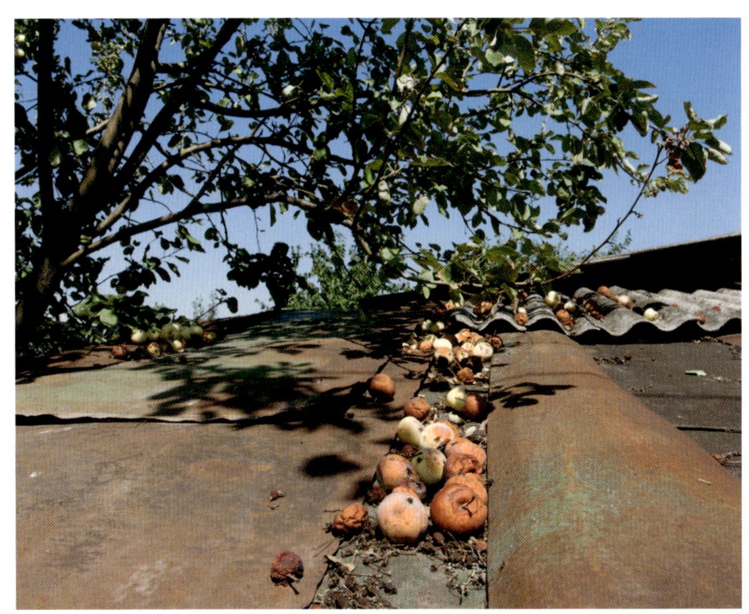

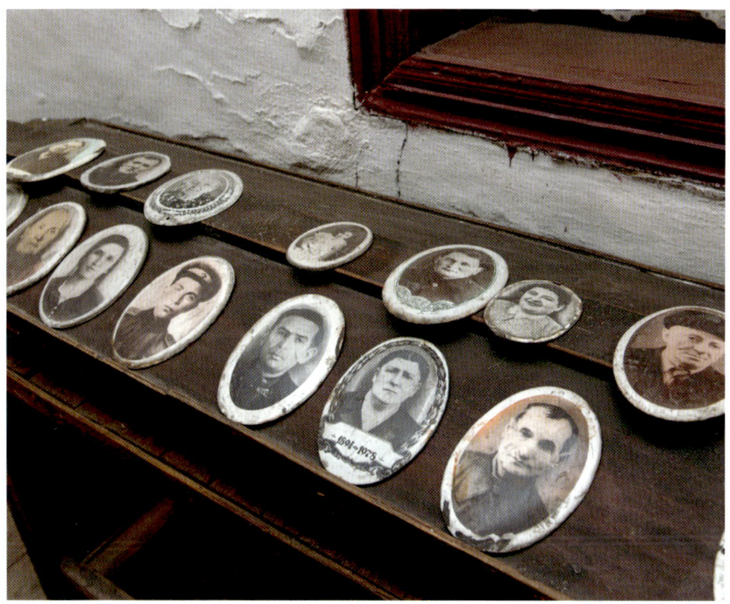

Bershad, Vinnytska Province, Ukraine, July 24, 2012. **2012**

Bershad, Vinnytska Province, Ukraine, July 24, 2012. **2012**

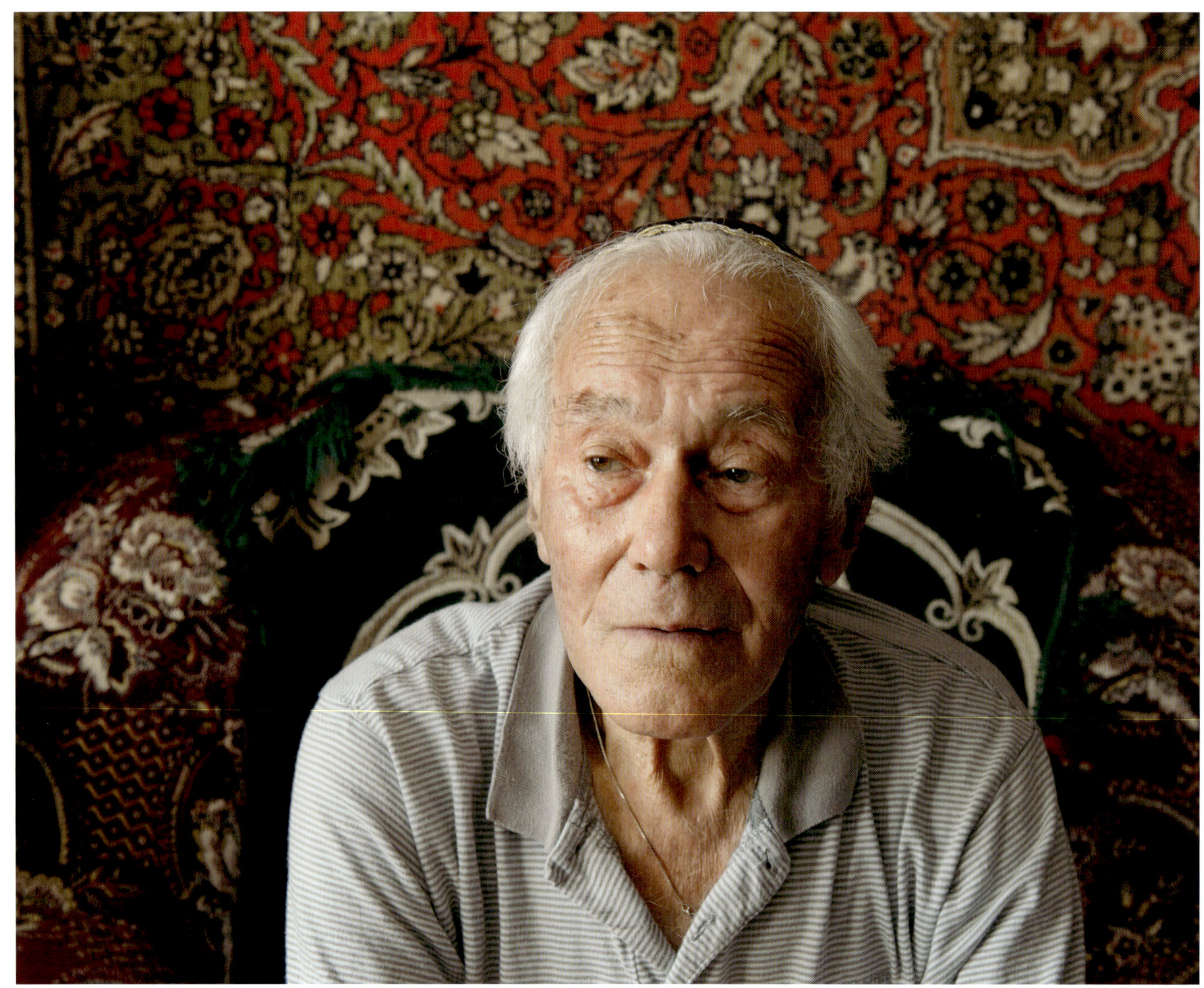

Isaak Bakmayev, Berdychiv, Zhytomyrska Province, Ukraine, July 29, 2012. 2012

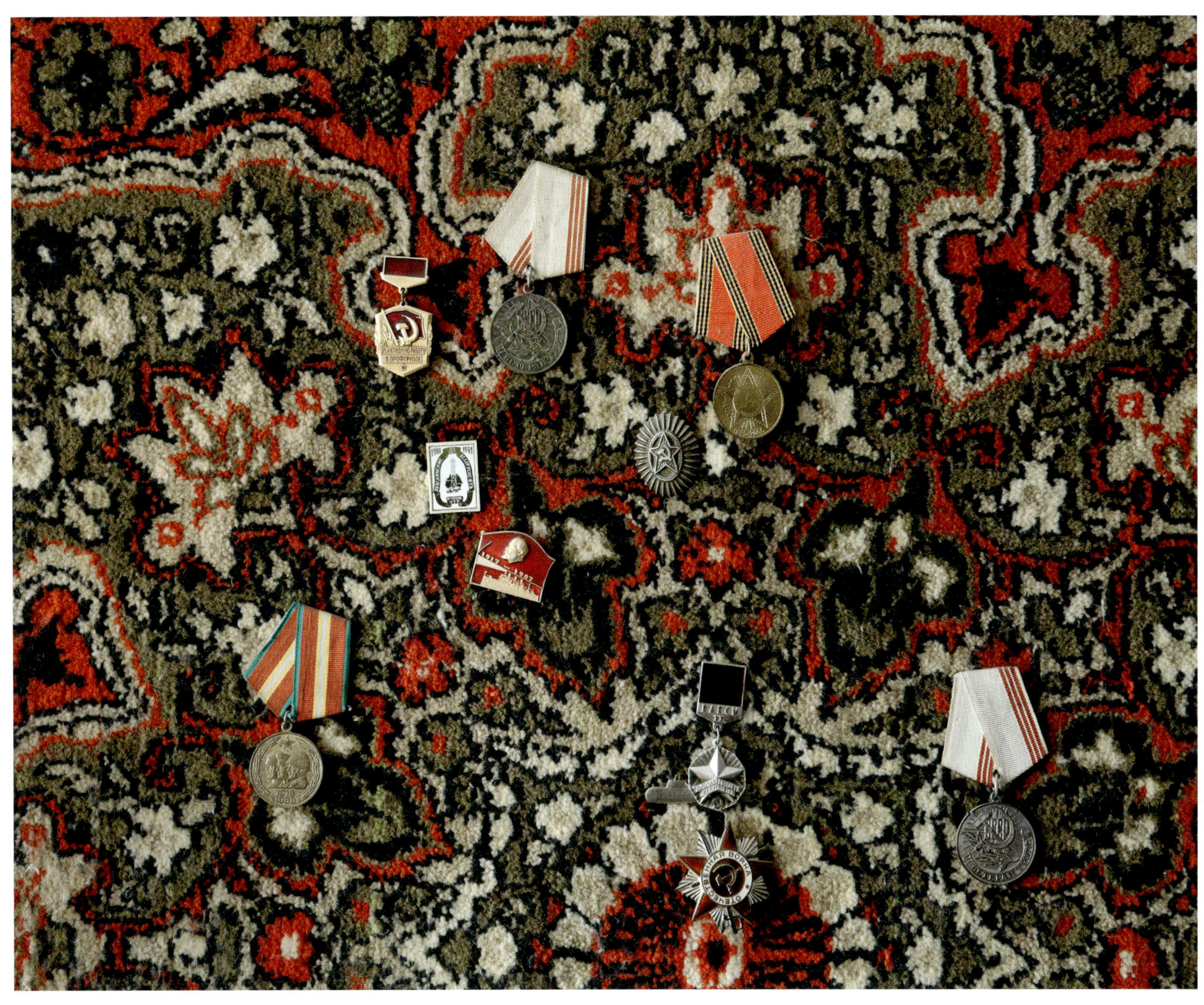

Isaak Bakmayev's Medals, Berdychiv, Zhytomyrska Province, Ukraine, July 29, 2012. 2012

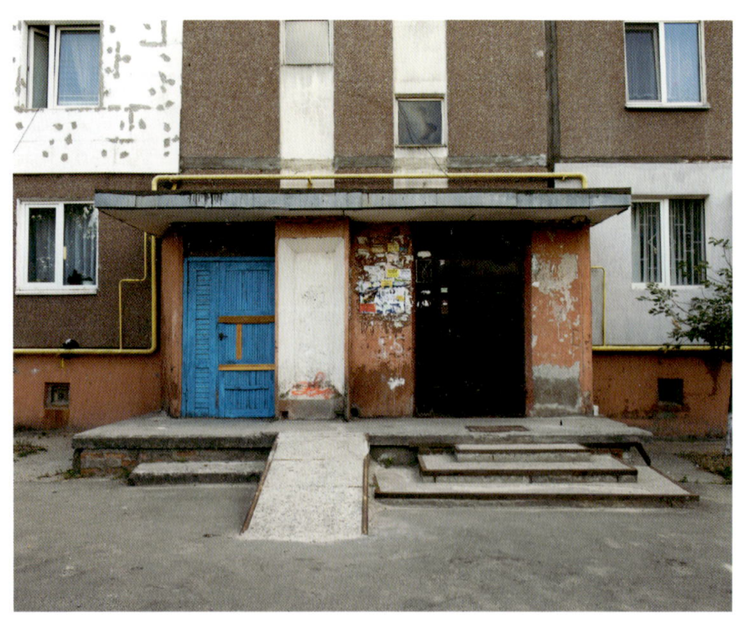

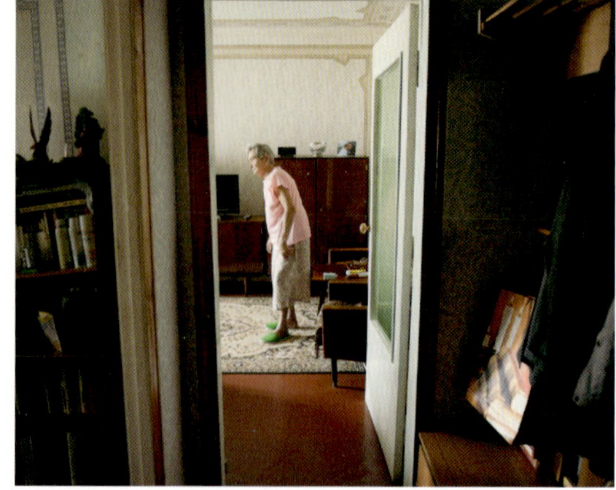

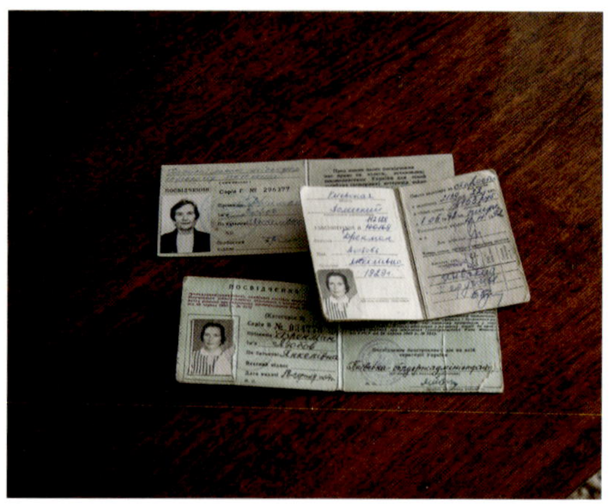

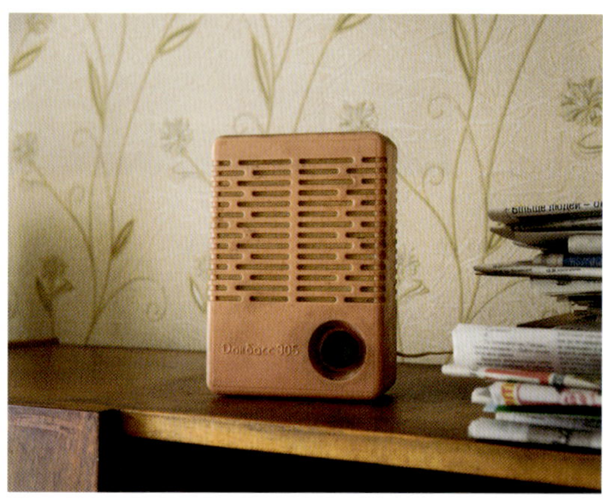

Home of Lyubov Brenman, Boryspil, Kyivska Province, Ukraine, July 19, 2012. 2012

Lyubov Brenman, Boryspil, Kyivska Province, Ukraine, July 19, 2012. 2012

Home of Lyubov Brenman, Boryspil, Kyivska Province, Ukraine, July 19, 2012. 2012

Home of Lyubov Brenman, Boryspil, Kyivska Province, Ukraine, July 19, 2012. 2012

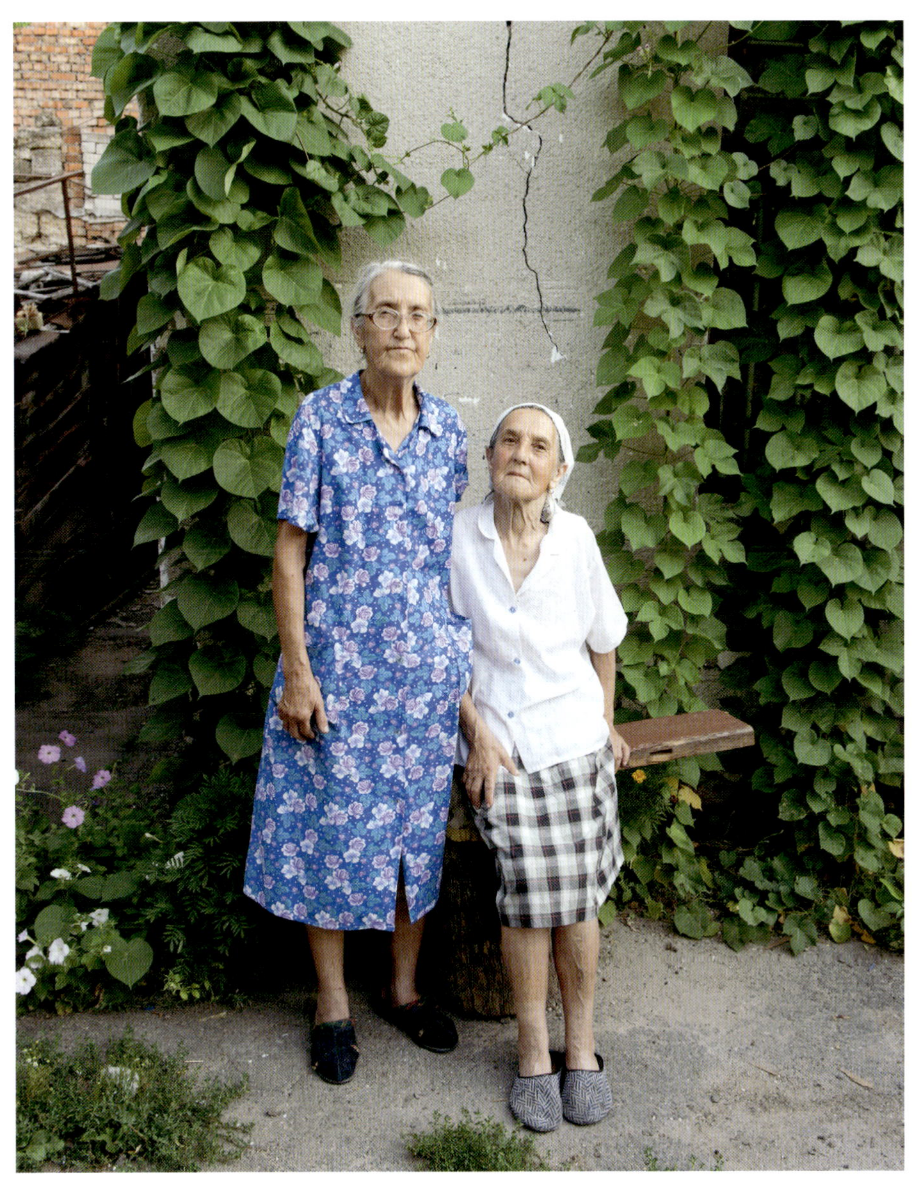

Mira and Beba Pasek, Mykolayiv, Mykolayivska Province, Ukraine, July 23, 2012. 2012

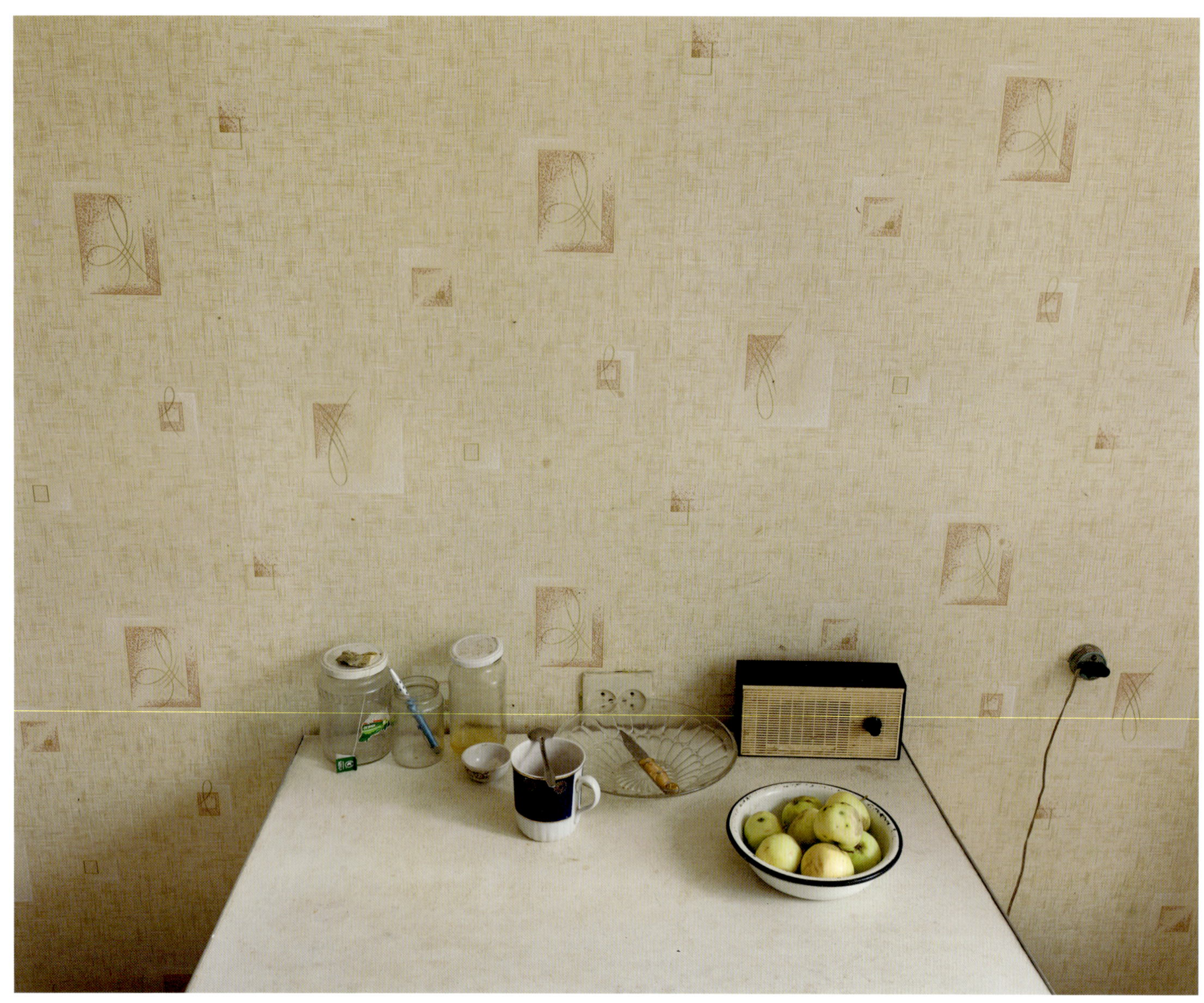

Home of Tzylia Bederman, Bucha, Kyivska Province, Ukraine, July 18, 2012. 2012

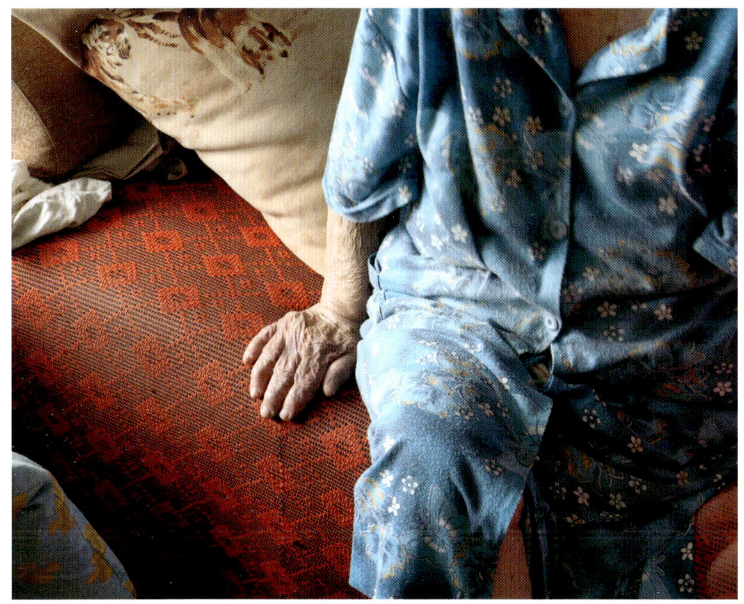

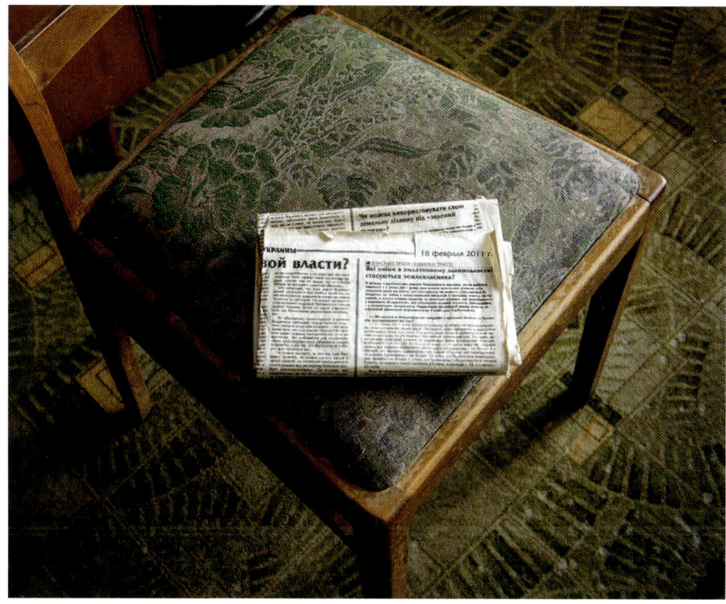

Tzylia Bederman, Bucha, Kyivska Province, Ukraine, July 18, 2012. 2012

Home of Tzylia Bederman, Bucha, Kyivska Province, Ukraine, July 18, 2012. 2012

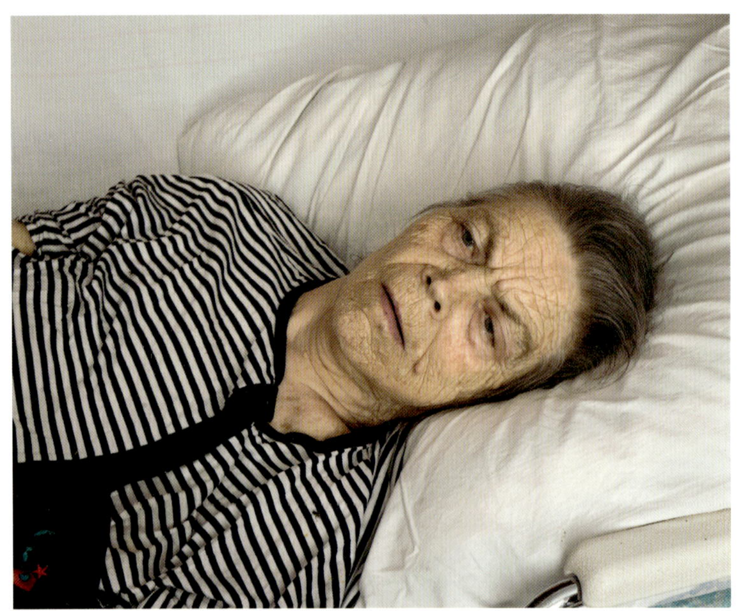

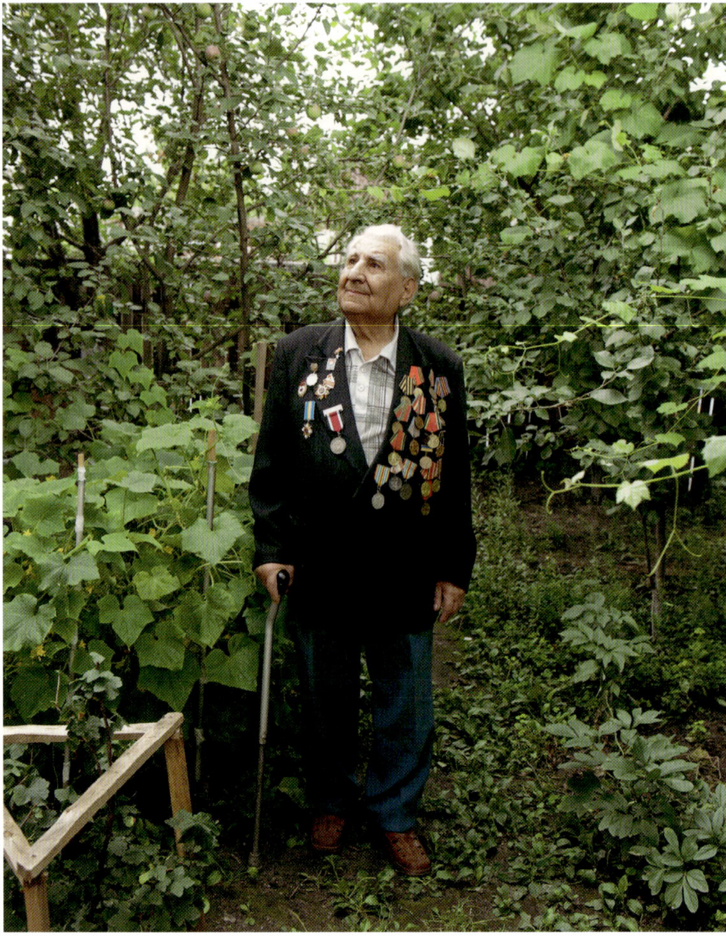

Galina Karpenko, Tomashpil, Vinnytska Province, Ukraine, July 25, 2012. 2012

Tsal Groisman, Korsun, Cherkaska Province, Ukraine, July 20, 2012. 2012

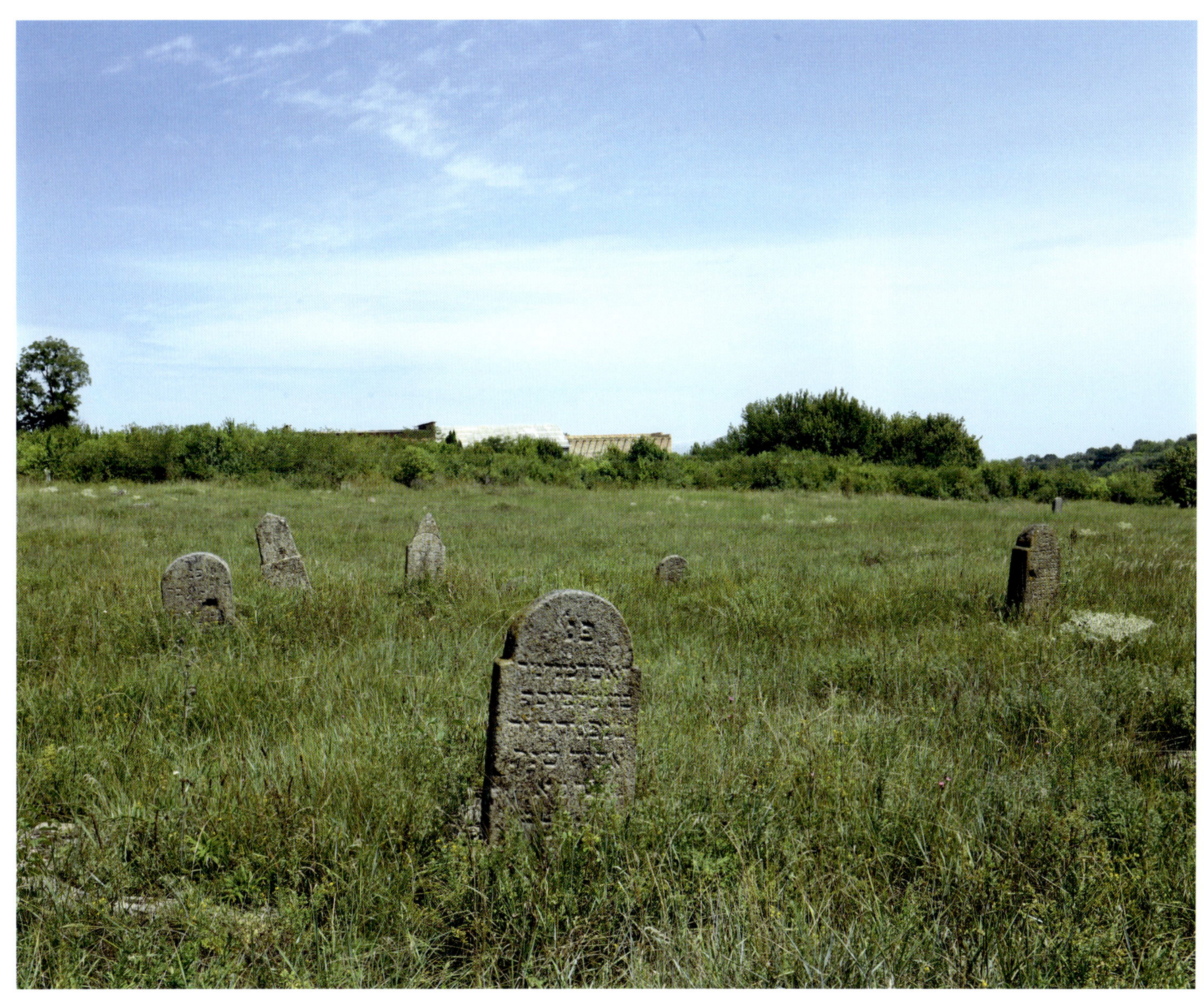

Korsun, Cherkaska Province, Ukraine, July 21, 2012. 2012

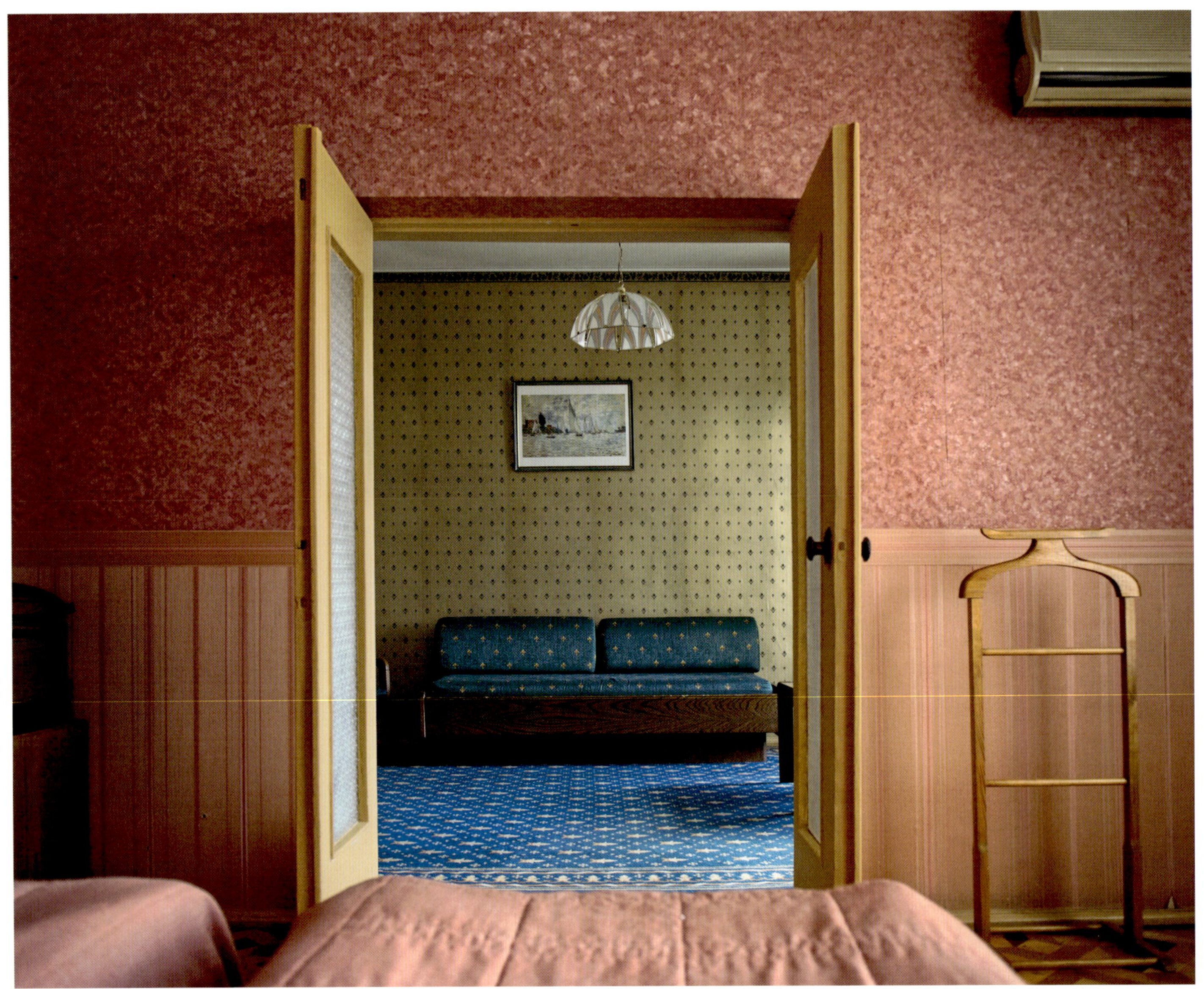

Room 509, Dnipro Hotel, Kiev, Kyivska Province, Ukraine, July 18, 2012. 2012

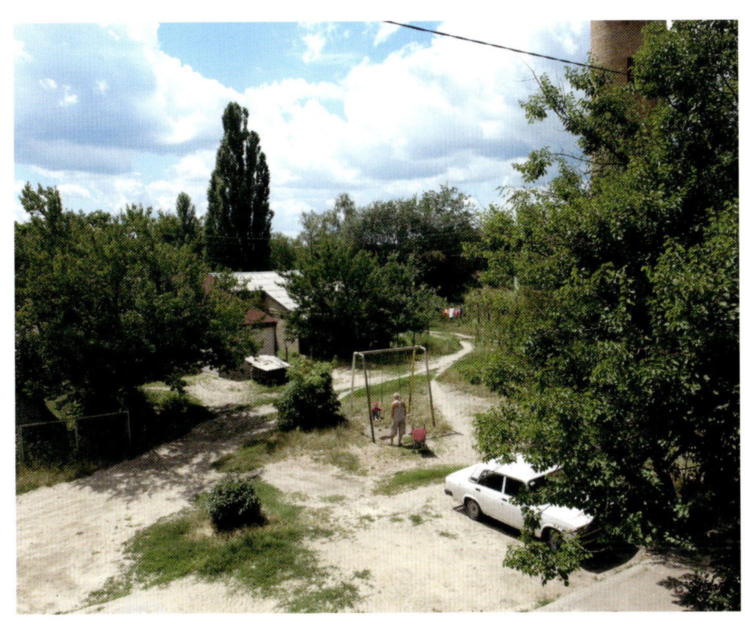

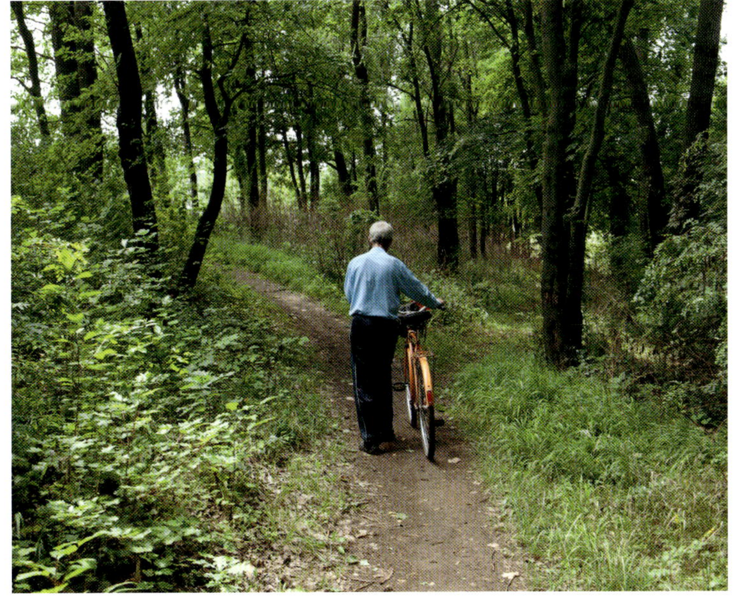

Bucha, Kyivska Province, Ukraine, July 18, 2012. 2012

Uman, Cherkaska Province, Ukraine, July 22, 2012. 2012

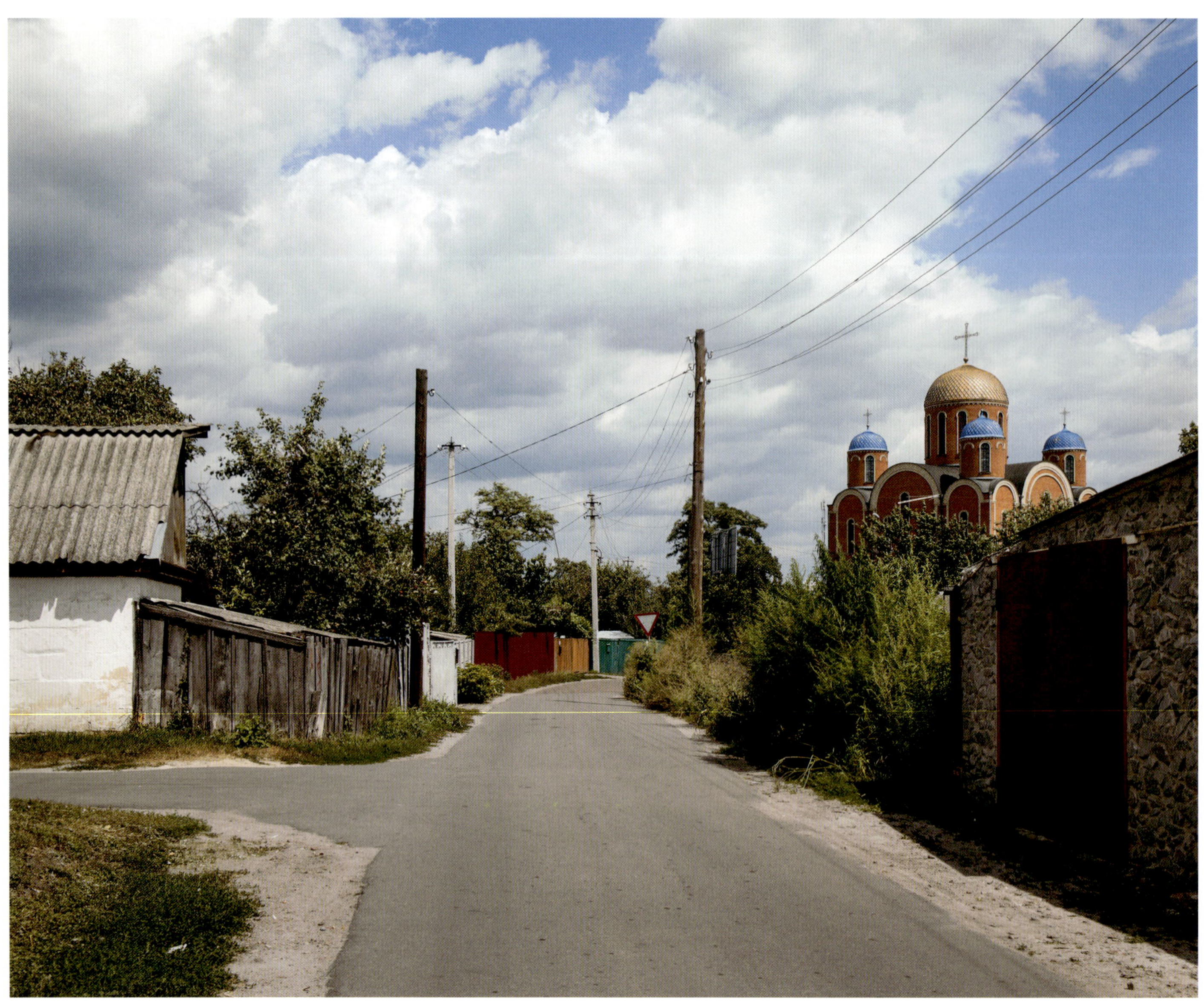

Boryspil, Kyivska Province, Ukraine, July 19, 2012. 2012

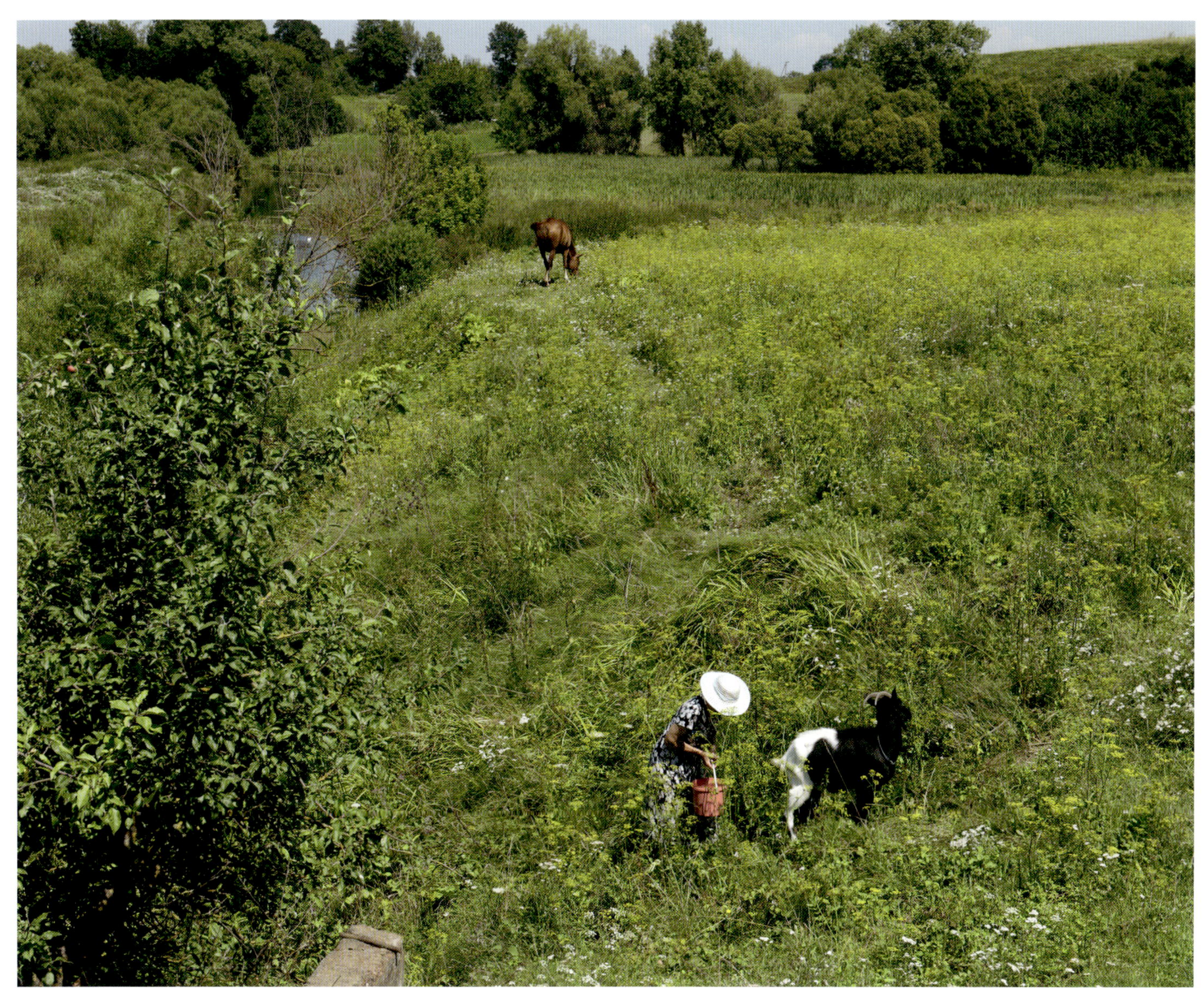

Bazaliya, Khmelnytska Province, Ukraine, July 27, 2012. 2012

Uncommon Places

Begun in 1973 and completed almost ten years later, *Uncommon Places* inhabits the same world, deals with the same themes, and, to a certain extent, uses the same methods as Shore's previous series, *American Surfaces*, in which he photographed the American landscape over many cross-country road trips, from New York to the West, in particular.[1] The continuity between the two series, however, is undercut by a major technical change. With *Uncommon Places* Shore made the transition from a 35mm camera to a view camera, first a 4-by-5 in 1973, and then, starting in 1974, an 8-by-10. As Shore has explained, this change was the result of his desire to make larger prints than he had before: he had found, in trying to enlarge some of his images from *American Surfaces*, that it was impossible without a significant loss of quality due to the small size of 35mm negatives.

A number of Shore's American contemporaries were making a similar choice during the same period. In many respects, the generation that came of age in the 1970s was a cool generation, keeping things at a distance, in contrast to photographers of the 1960s, who favored close proximity to the subject and were still influenced by a snapshot aesthetic, the idea of the "decisive moment," photojournalistic style, and, in some cases, an explicitly engaged perspective. On several occasions Shore has mentioned that *Uncommon Places* has little in common, in either photographic approach or spirit, with *The Americans* by Robert Frank, whose attitude was openly subjective and critical.

The view camera was heavy and bulky, bringing a considerable physicality to shooting photographs and, with it, a less immediate relationship to the world and to the construction of the image. Because the pictures were costly to produce, photographers were forced to limit the number of shots they took, resulting in images that were more thought out, especially in the choice of point of view and framing. Shore quickly got into the habit of taking only one picture of each subject, a discipline he remains attached to today. (This rigor in shooting—the careful framing and construction of an image—was a practice that John Szarkowski, director of MoMA's Department of Photography, indirectly suggested that Shore explore in the early 1970s.) But he also found that the more deliberate method of shooting with an 8-by-10 brought a contradictory loss of control over the tremendous amount of detail the camera can capture. As Shore explained:

> A photographer using an 8x10 camera never sees the whole picture on the ground glass. With a 4x5, you can stretch your arms to hold the dark cloth and stand back far enough to see the whole frame. But you can never be back far enough with an 8x10. Because of this, sometimes the result is disordered and seems almost schizophrenic—decisions, made without reference to each other, bouncing off each other in the same picture space.[2]

Despite the relative consistency of subject matter in the two series, *Uncommon Places* differs significantly from *American Surfaces* in other ways. It features fewer details and close-ups; a more detached, distant approach, which results in a loss in dynamism but a gain in monumentality; and an abandonment of the flash. All the photographs are taken in the daytime, using only natural light, a practice from which Shore would rarely depart in his later work. Beyond these technical features, the quick, diaristic, almost narrative quality of *American Surfaces*, where the flow of the whole takes precedence over the individual image, yields to a slower, more removed quality in *Uncommon Places*. This difference was particularly striking in the way the images were displayed in the 1970s. In the only exhibition of *American Surfaces* at the time, at Light Gallery in 1972, the prints were attached directly to the wall in a grid, creating an allover effect, and were offered for sale as a set, while one year later, in the same gallery, photographs from *Uncommon Places* were presented as individualized, isolated images, mounted and framed.

This change reflected not only the burgeoning market for photographs but, above all, the evolution of Shore's work. The new series called for a more contemplative reading of the separate images, each of which was now given autonomy and endowed with a title. Regardless of the view being represented, the title was neutral and informative, consisting of the place the photograph was taken, followed by the exact date of the picture. For portraits, the name of the model is given if it was known, but for still lifes, the objects are never named. An image of a partially completed jigsaw puzzle, for instance, is titled *Lookout Hotel, Ogunquit, Maine*, not *Jigsaw Puzzle, Lookout Hotel, Ogunquit, Maine*. For Shore, photography is above all about

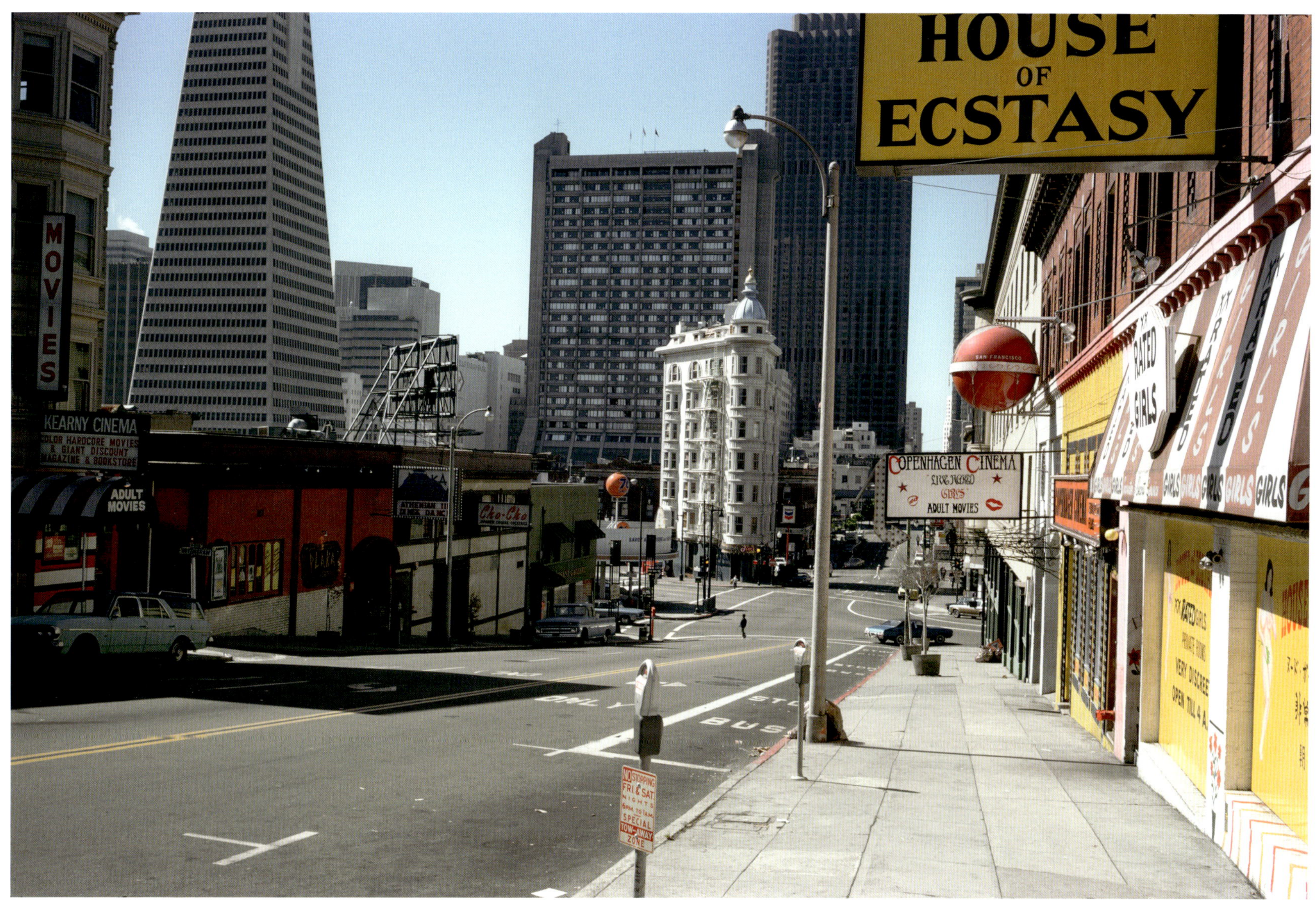

San Francisco, California, September 1974. 1974

253.

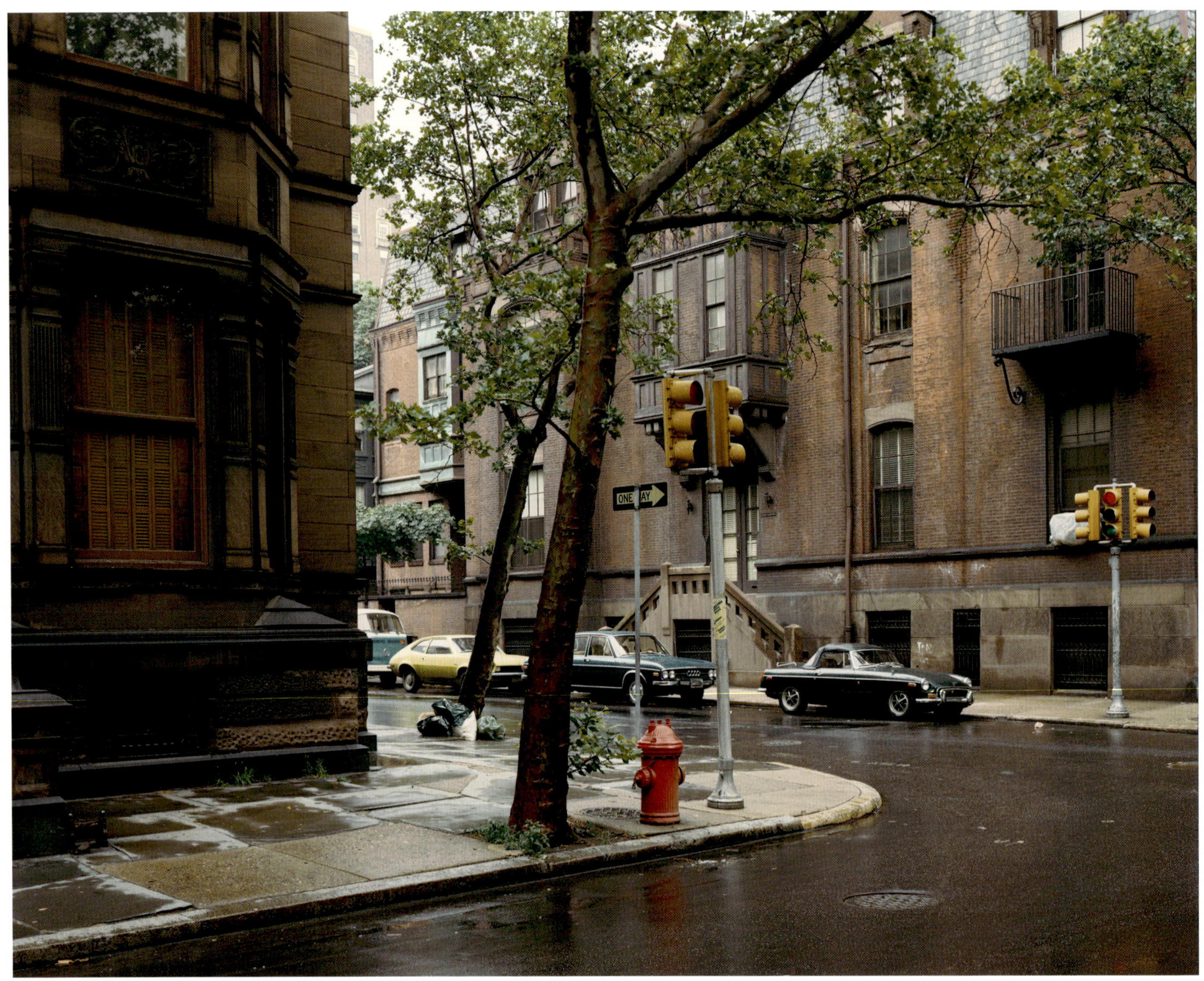

21st and Spruce Streets, Philadelphia, Pennsylvania, June 21, 1974. 1974

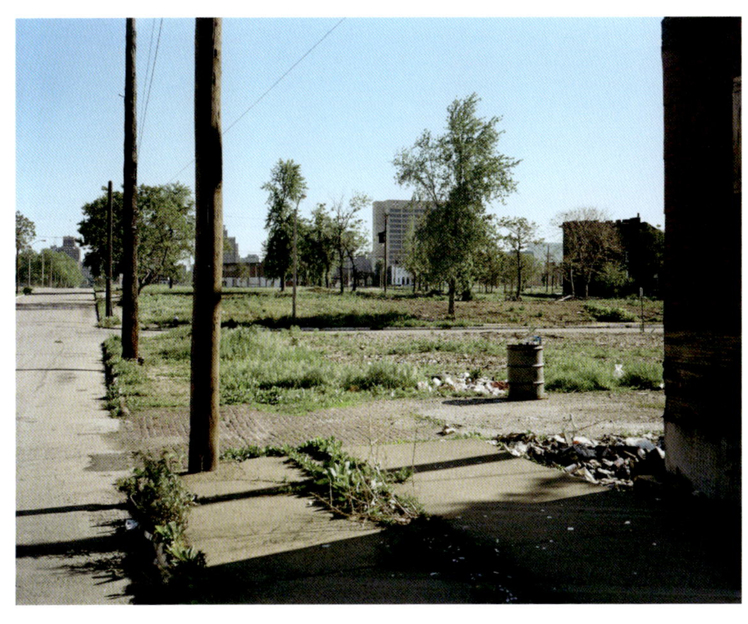

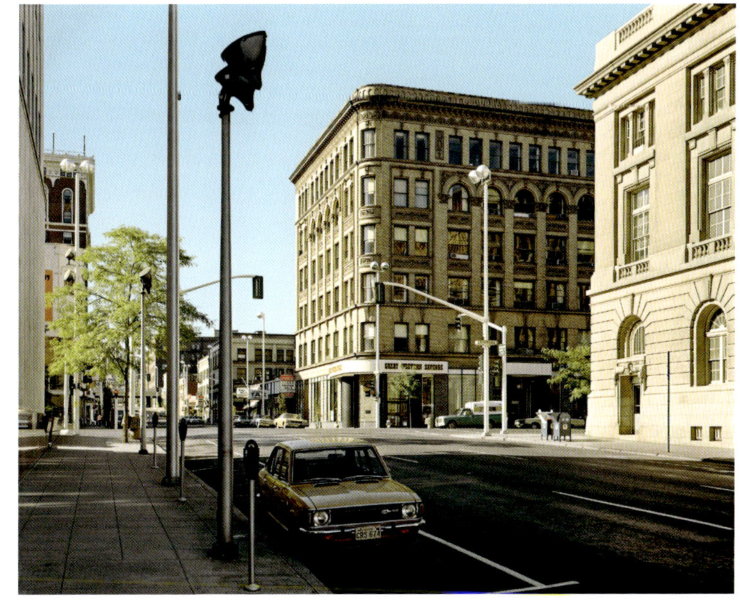

11th Street, St. Louis, Missouri, May 12, 1974. 1974

Lincoln Street and Riverside Street, Spokane, Washington, August 25, 1974. 1974

capturing a place or, more specifically, capturing the conjunction of a place and a moment, when the subject becomes crystallized in time as worthy of consideration. "It is the quality of attention that may make [these subjects] uncommon," Shore said in 2004 when asked about the title of the series.[3]

In their focus on themes of the ordinary and banal in American culture, as well as in their descriptive restraint, the photographs of *Uncommon Places* were, at the time they were first shown, likened to Photo-Realist paintings of the same period. "Your set is conditioned if you've already looked at Photo-Realist painting before seeing Shore's photographs," wrote a critic in *Artforum* in 1974, adding, "Shore and [Photo-Realist] Richard Estes share at least one influence[:] Eugène Atget."[4] Similarly, an essay in *Art in America* two years later said, "Stephen Shore's photographs, Kodacolor images of city intersections and small-town crossroads, have a direct connection to Photo-Realist painting. His disposition of his subject matter is closest, perhaps, to Ralph Goings', but a number of other post-Pop painters are also recalled."[5]

The series gradually ran its course in the late 1970s, when Shore realized his approach had become so natural to him that it might become methodical, offering neither pleasure nor challenge and presenting the ultimate risk of repetition. But seen in its entirety, this body of work is far from a homogeneous whole. Rather than a series that was defined and organized in advance, *Uncommon Places* developed in a very organic way, with porous boundaries, throughout the decade; it even includes photographs Shore made in the context of commissions for Fuji, for AT&T (his baseball pictures), and for Robert Venturi, Steven Izenour, and Denise Scott Brown's 1976 exhibition *Signs of Life: Symbols in the American City*. The title of the series emerged only retrospectively, as Shore was reviewing images for a 1982 book being published by Aperture on his view-camera work of the 1970s. The book includes forty-nine plates, dating from 1973 to 1981, with an epigraph by Louis Sullivan, which reads in part: "Attention is the essence of our powers; it is that which draws other things toward us." At the end of the volume is a short text by Shore, in which he delivers one of his most concise metaphors for photography: "Fishing, like photography, is an art that calls forth intelligence, concentration, and delicacy." (Quentin Bajac)

See also: *American Surfaces*; *Beverly Boulevard and La Brea Avenue*; *Deadpan*; *El Paso Street*; *Landscape*; *Merced River*; *New Topographics*; *Road Trips*; *Shopwindows*; *Travel*

1. See the Photographic Chronology in this volume for a precise description of the trips he took.
2. "A Conversation between Stephen Shore and George Miles," unpublished manuscript, 2017.
3. Kenneth Baker, "Wave of Attention Rushes Back to Stephen Shore's Photography," *San Francisco Chronicle*, May 31, 2004, E5.
4. James Collins, "Stephen Shore, Light Gallery," *Artforum* 12, no. 6 (March 1974): 76.
5. Carter Ratcliff, "Route 66 Revisited: The New Landscape Photography," *Art in America* 64, no. 1 (January/February 1976): 90.

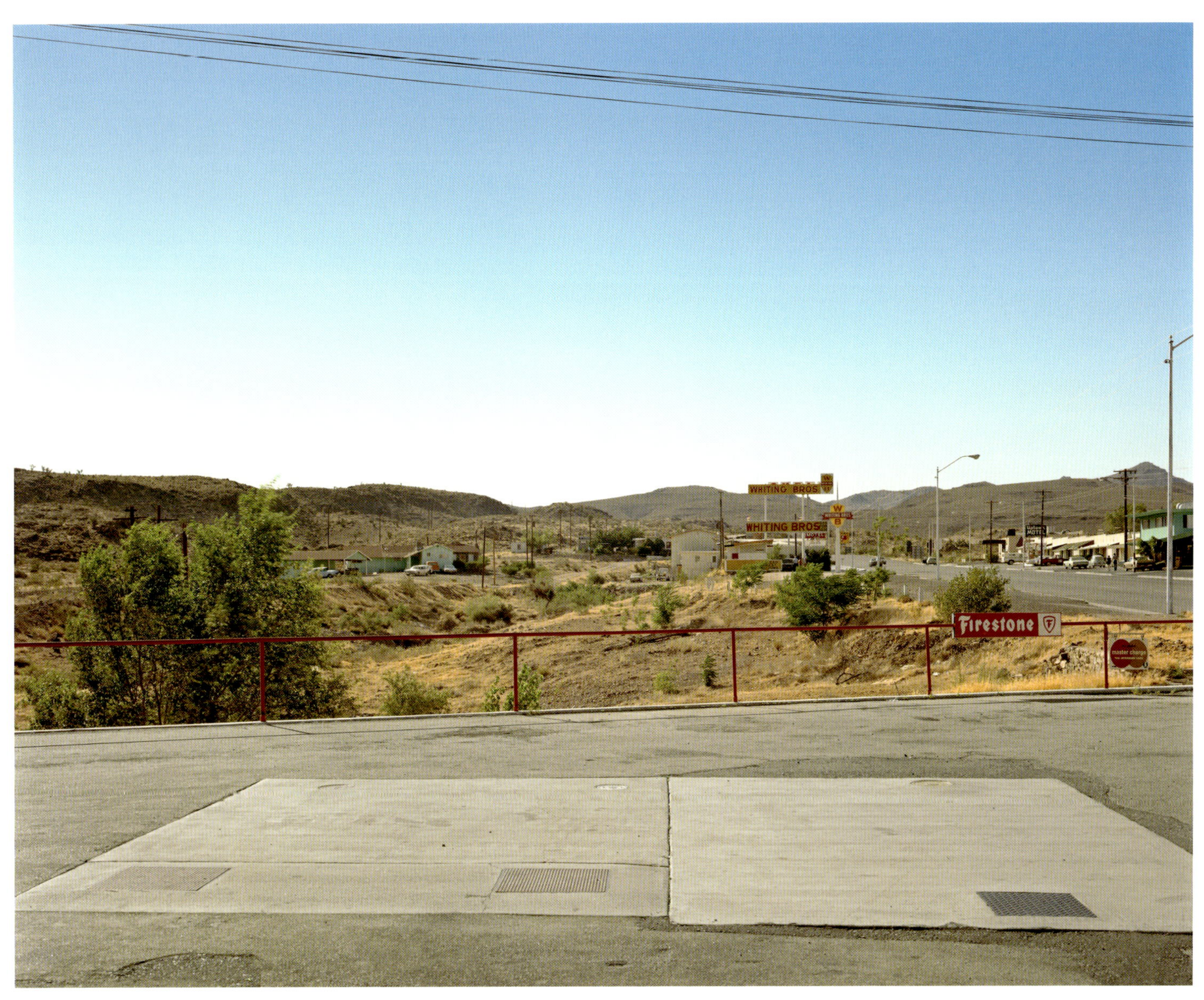

U.S. 93, Kingman, Arizona, July 2, 1975. 1975

257.

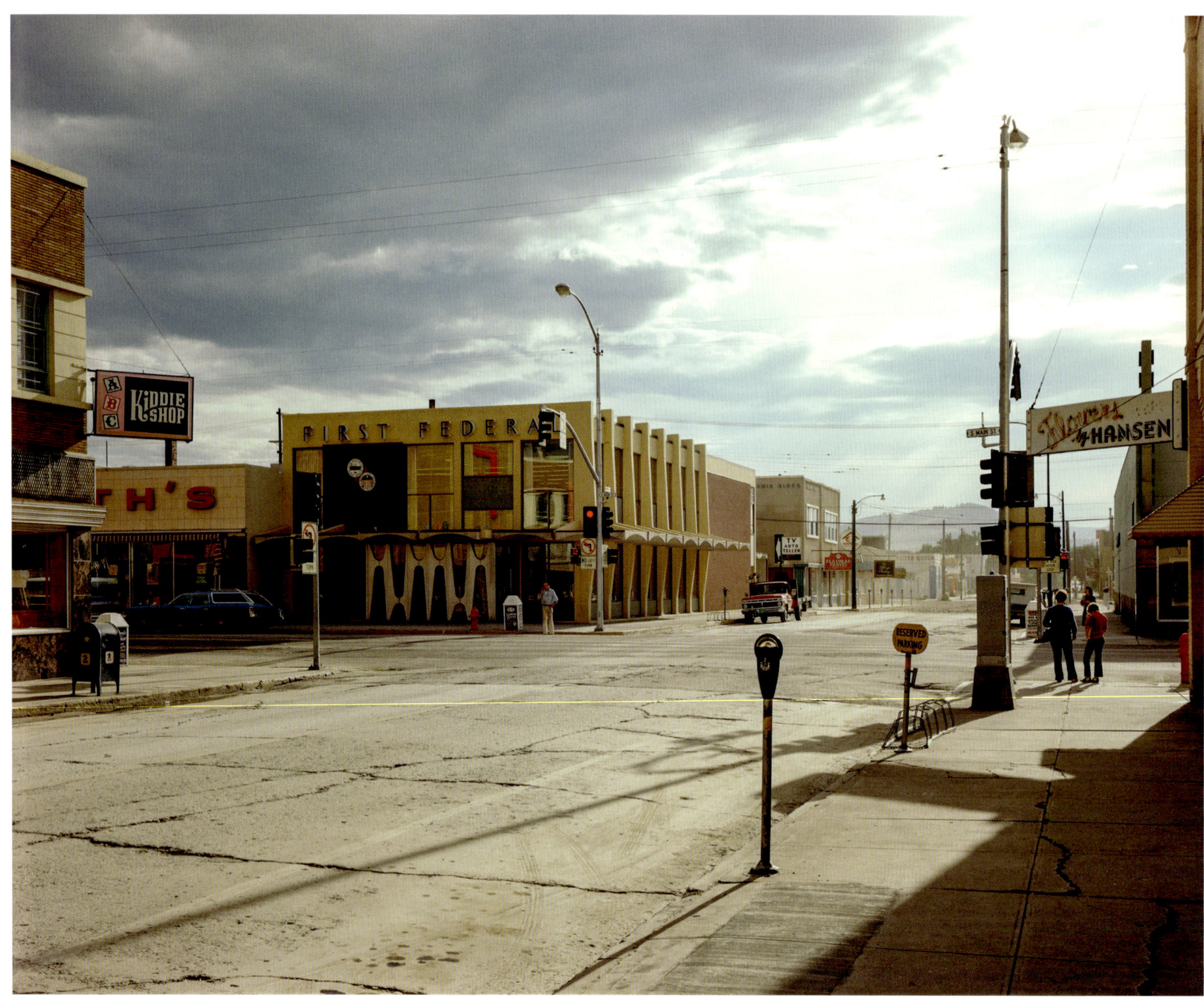

2nd Street East and South Main Street, Kalispell, Montana, August 22, 1974. 1974

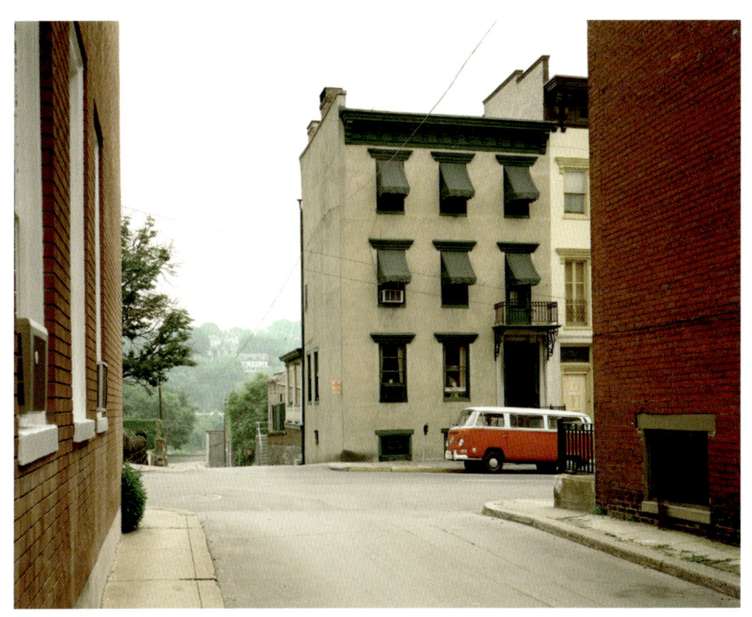

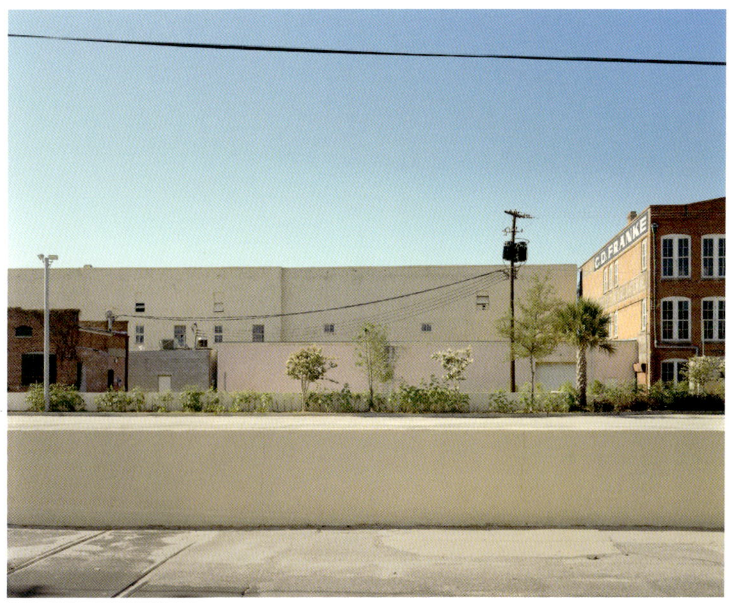

***Church and 2nd Streets, Easton, Pennsylvania, June 20, 1974.* 1974**

***Cumberland Street, Charleston, South Carolina, August 3, 1975.* 1975**

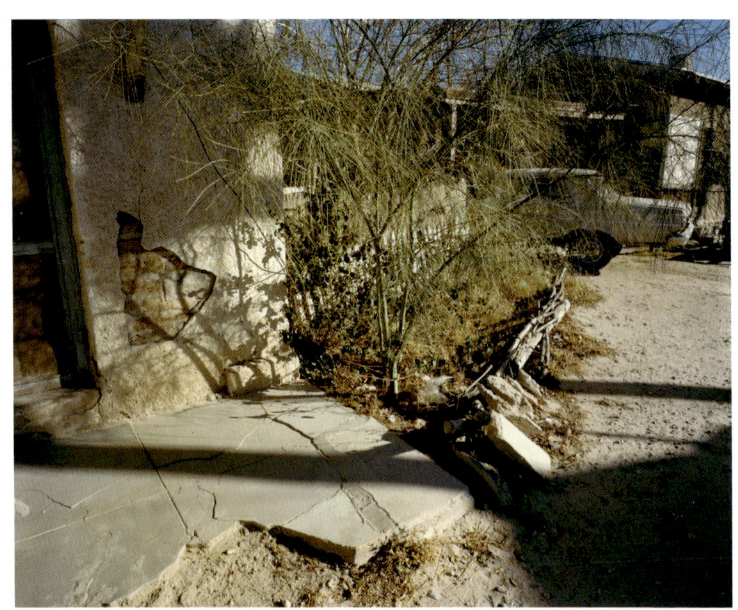

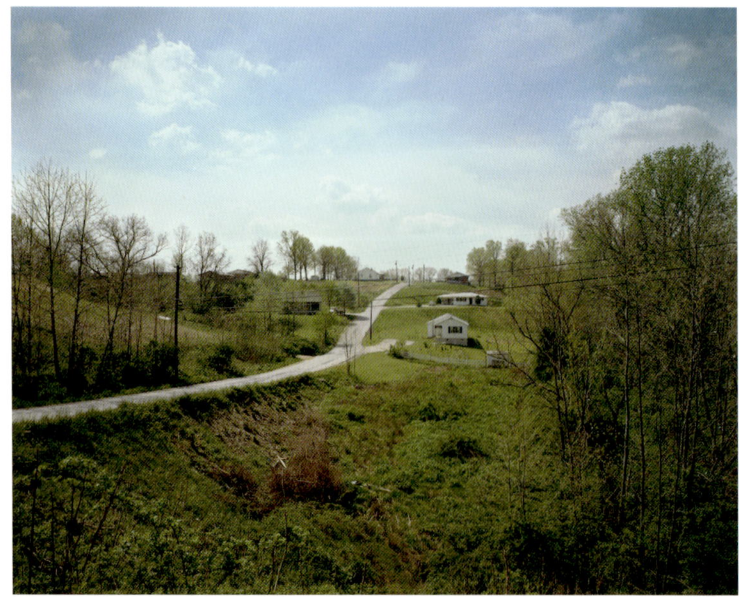

Hoff Avenue, Tucson, Arizona, December 6, 1976. 1976

Grayson, Kentucky, May 1, 1974. 1974

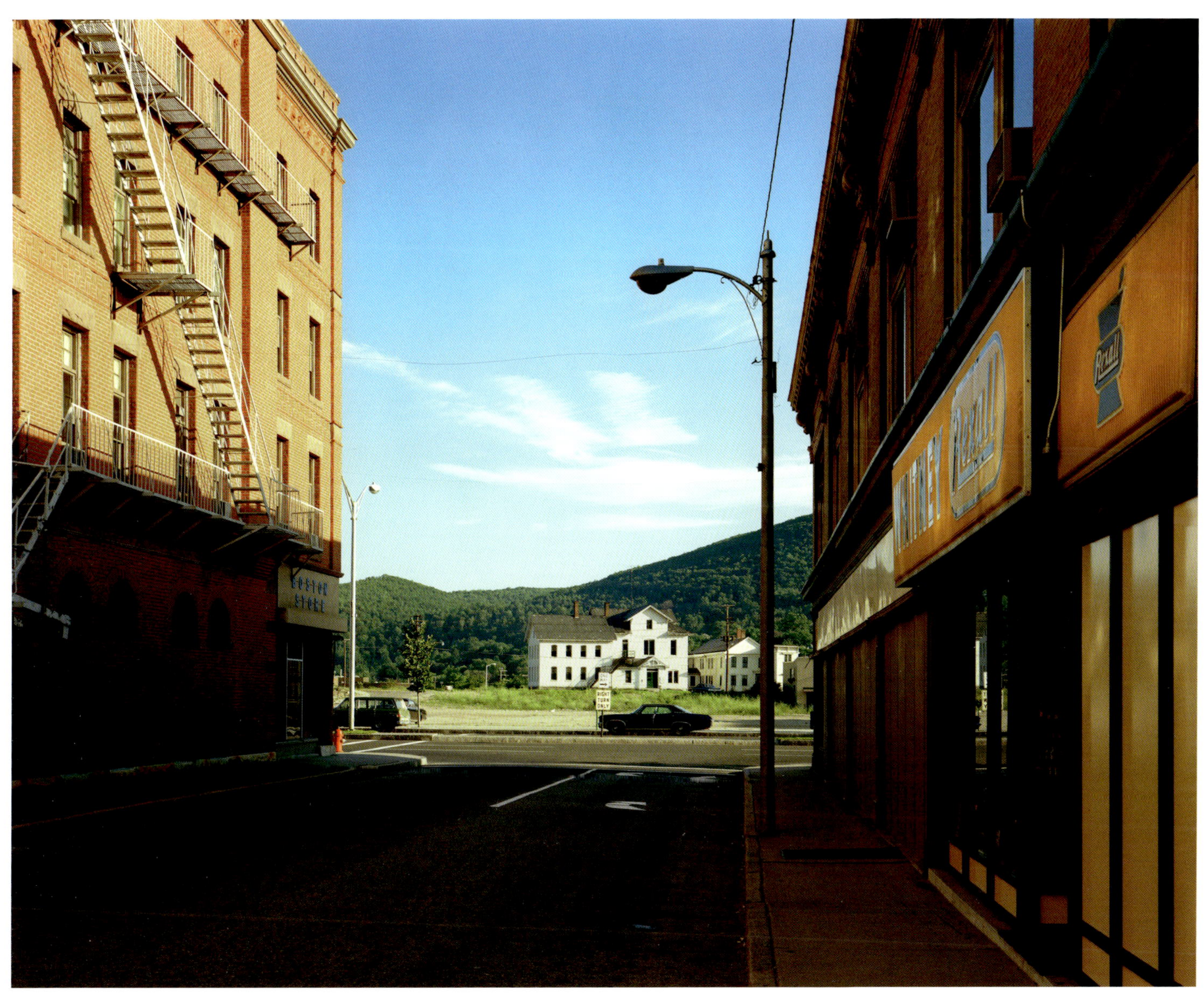

***Holden Street, North Adams, Massachusetts, July 13, 1974.* 1974**

261.

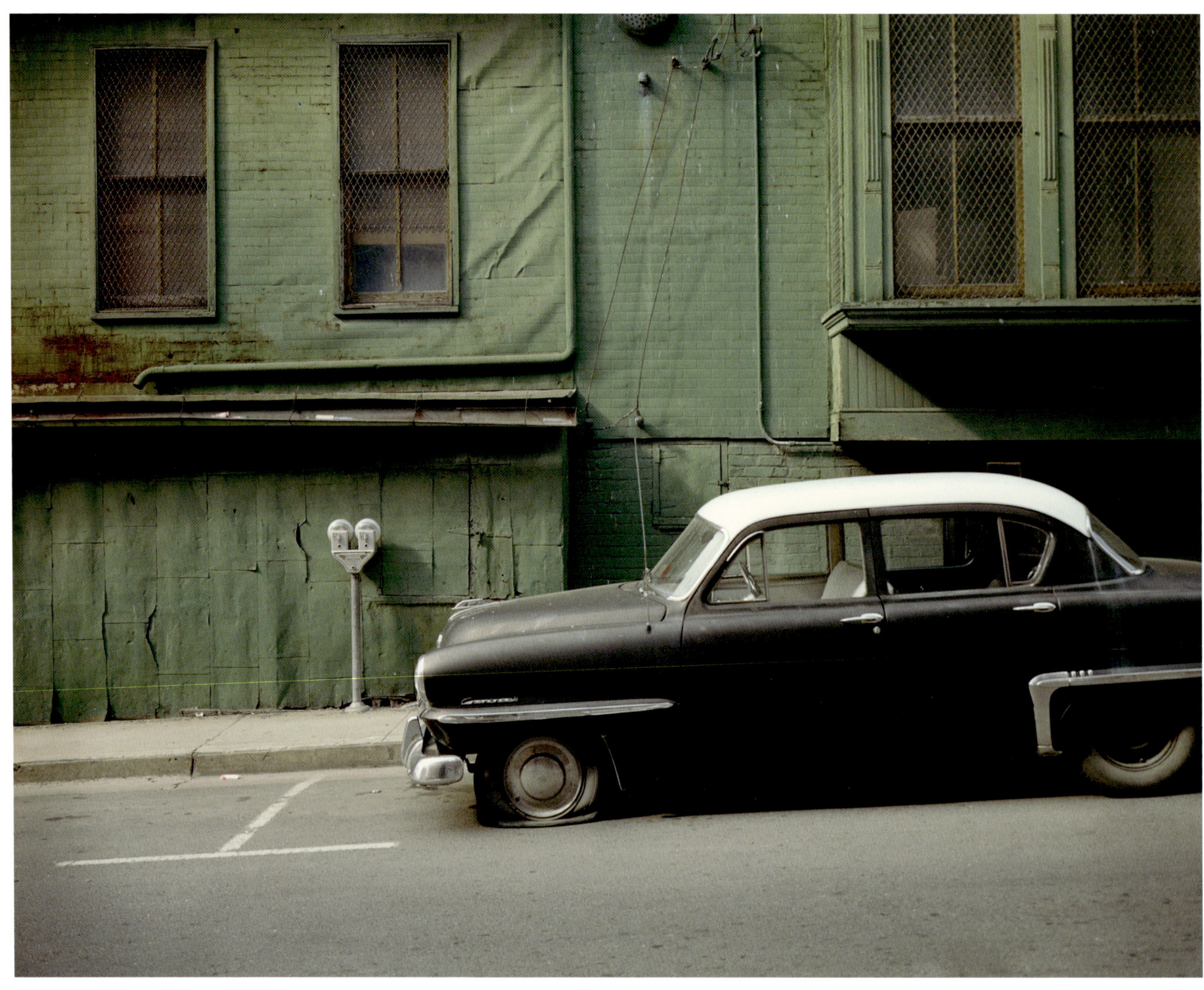

Elizabeth Street, Harrisonburg, Virginia, April 28, 1974. 1974

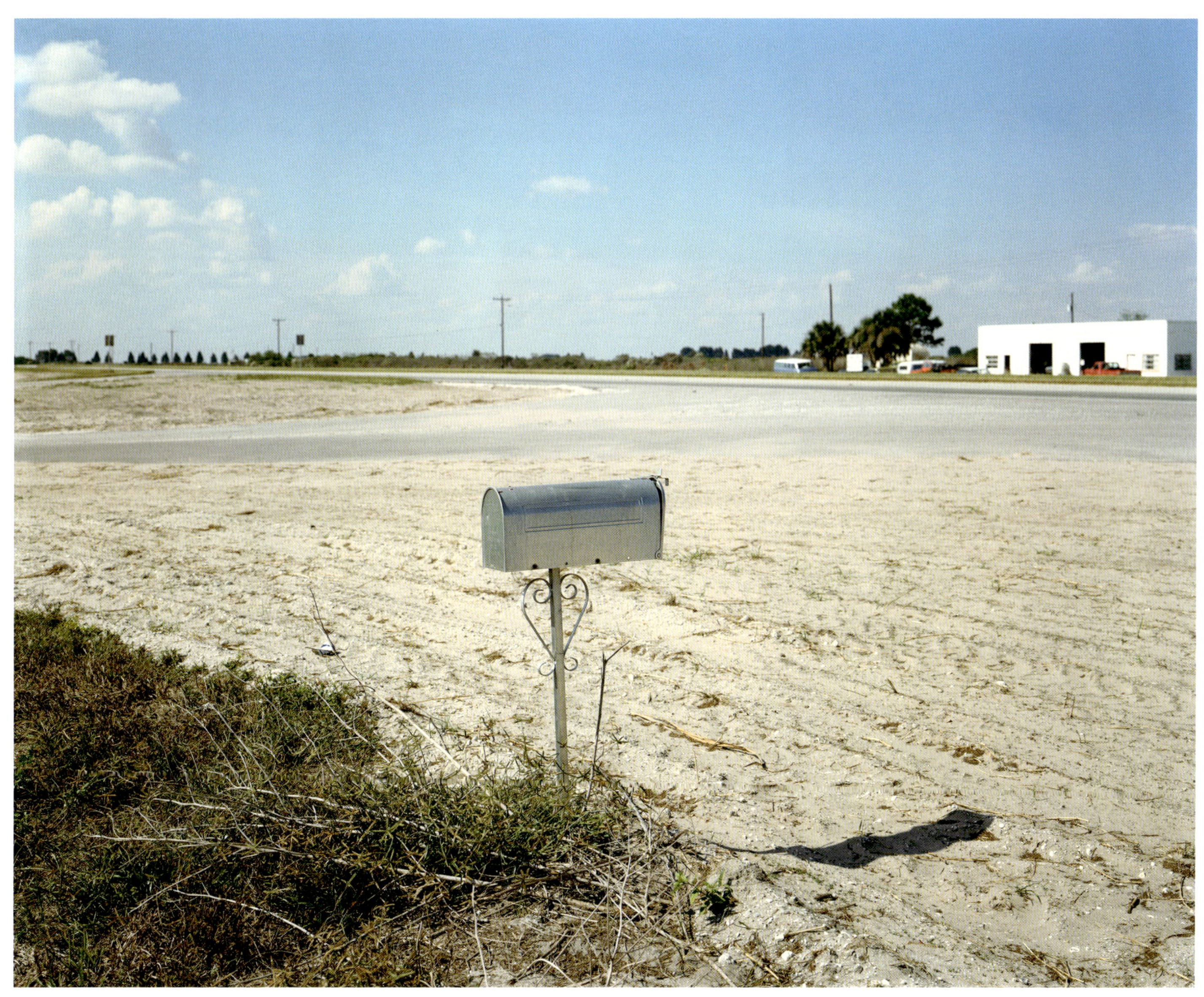

U.S. 27, Moore Haven, Florida, November 15, 1977. 1977

263.

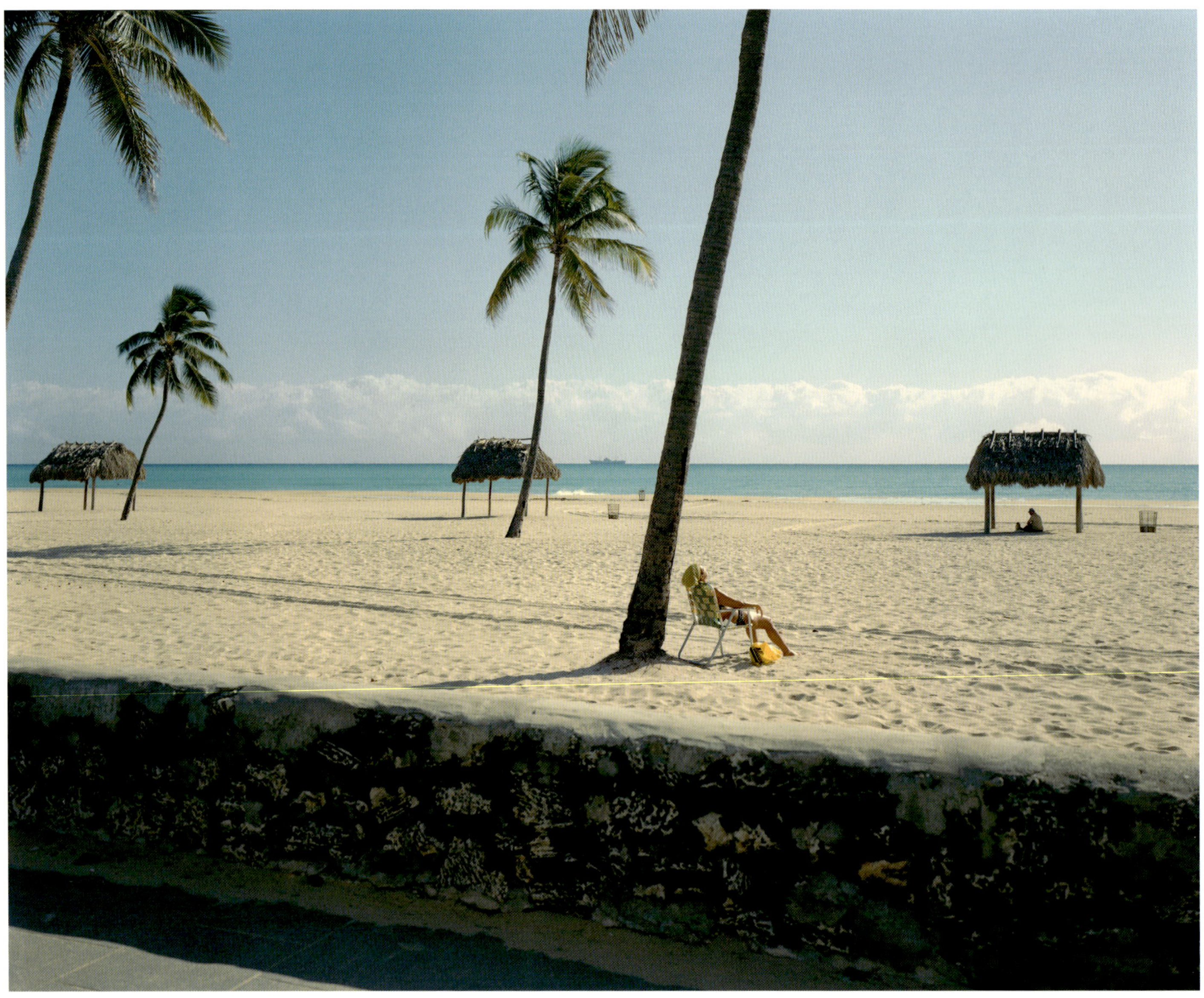

Miami Beach, Florida, November 13, 1977. 1977

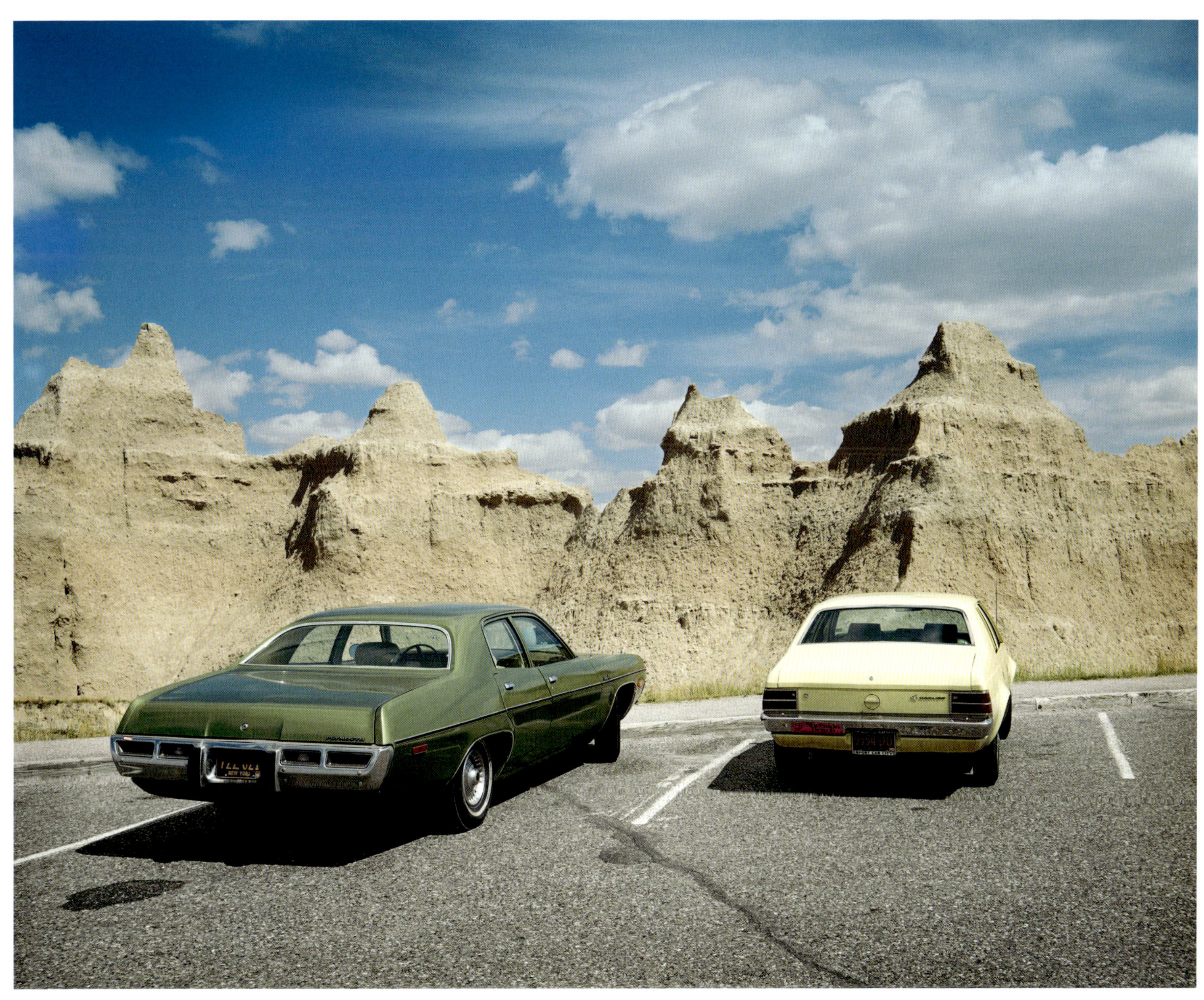

Badlands National Monument, South Dakota, July 14, 1973. **1973**

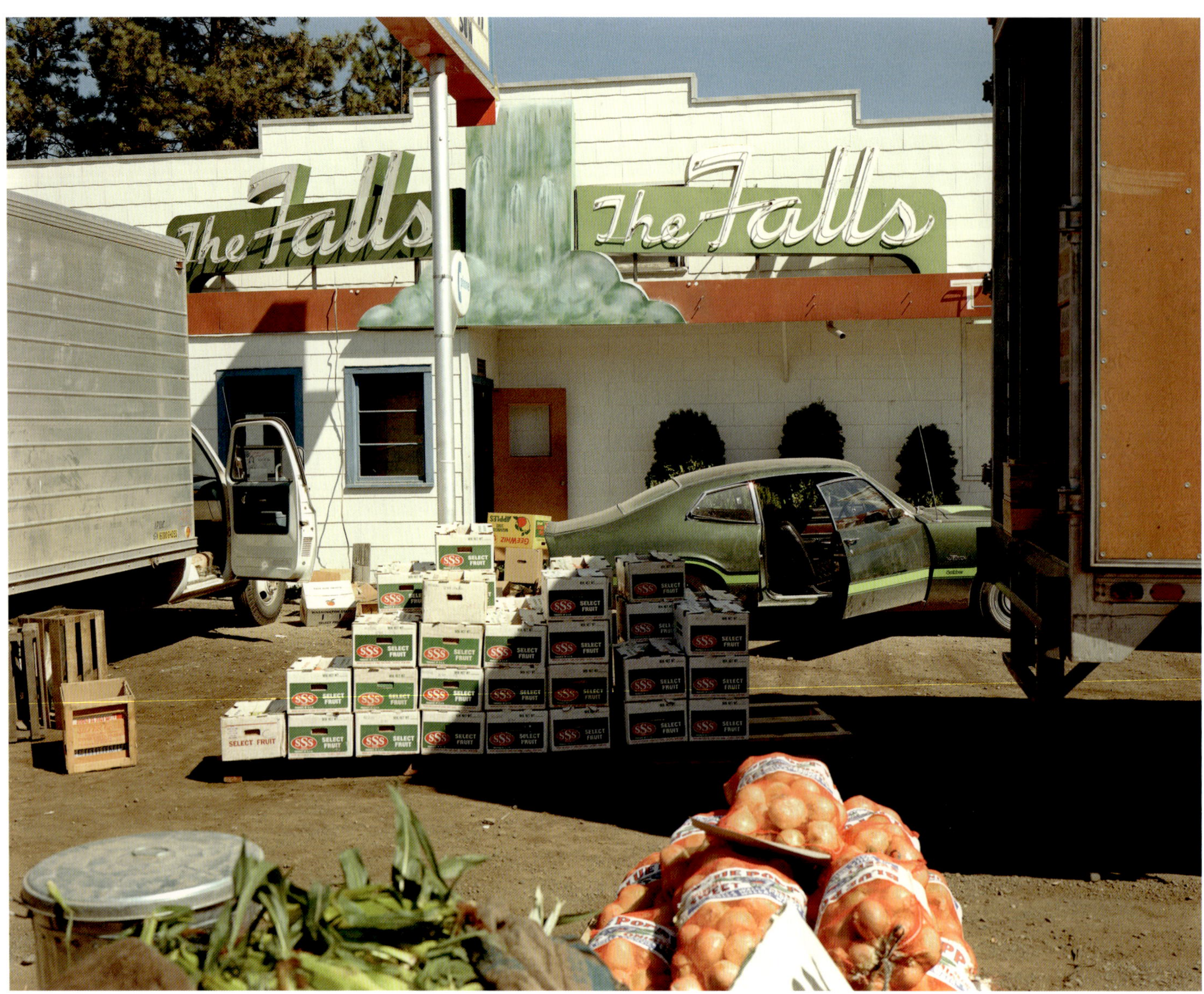

***U.S. 10, Post Falls, Idaho, August 25, 1974.* 1974**

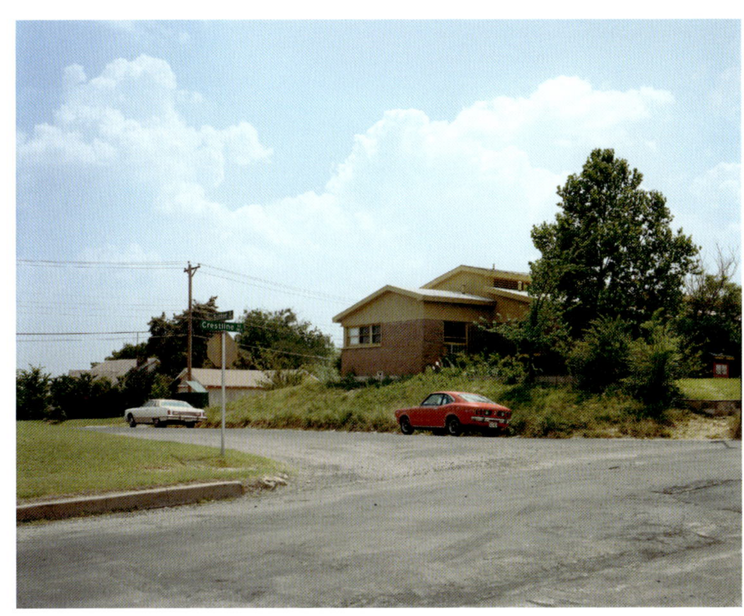

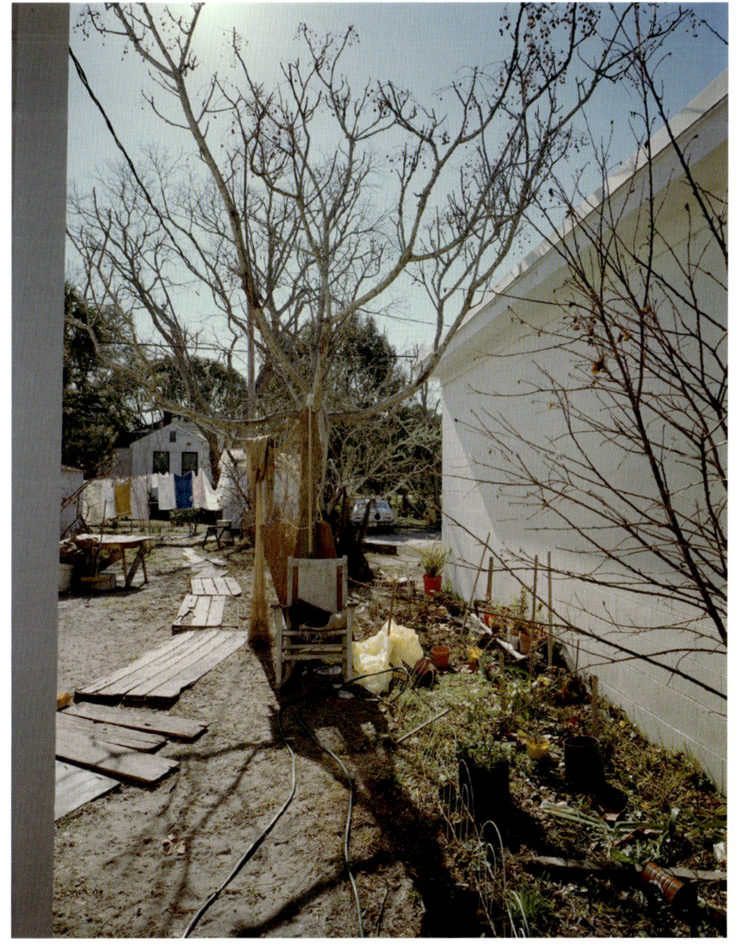

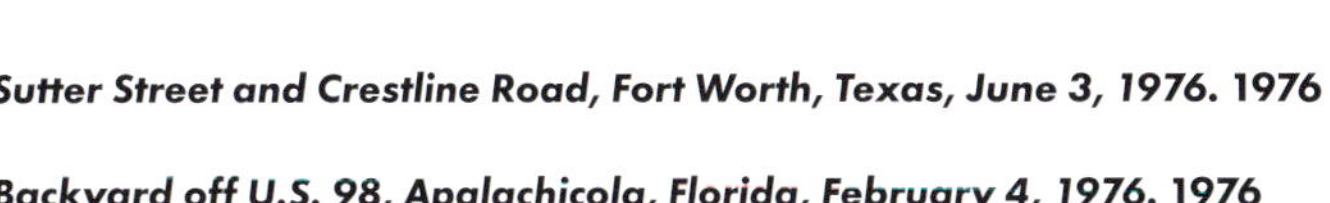

Sutter Street and Crestline Road, Fort Worth, Texas, June 3, 1976. 1976

Backyard off U.S. 98, Apalachicola, Florida, February 4, 1976. 1976

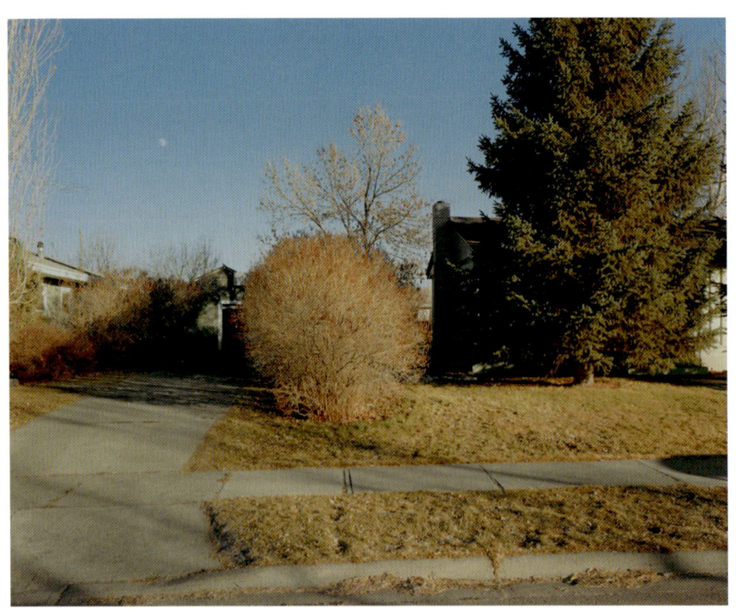

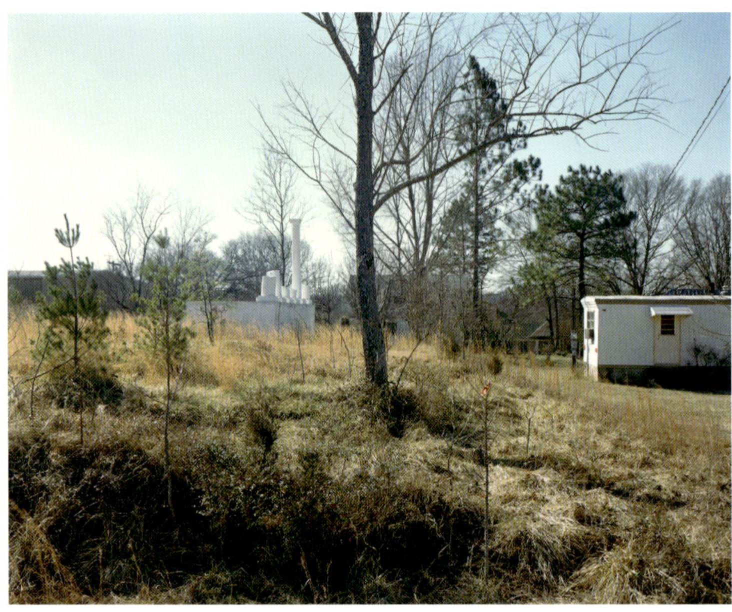

***North Black Avenue, Bozeman, Montana, January 16, 1981*. 1981**

***Carnesville, Georgia, January 29, 1976*. 1976**

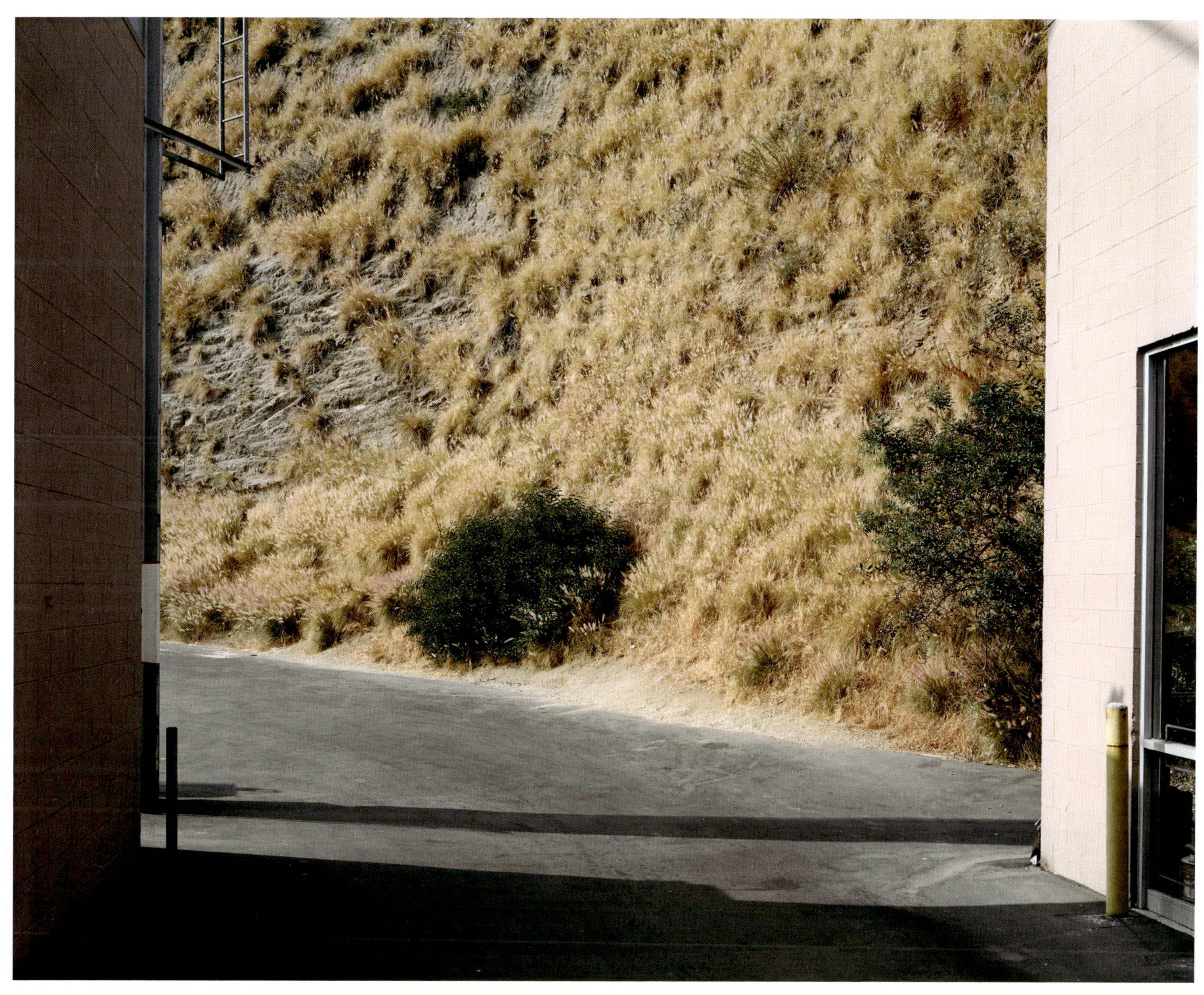

Alley off Sunset Strip, Hollywood, California, June 22, 1975. 1975

269.

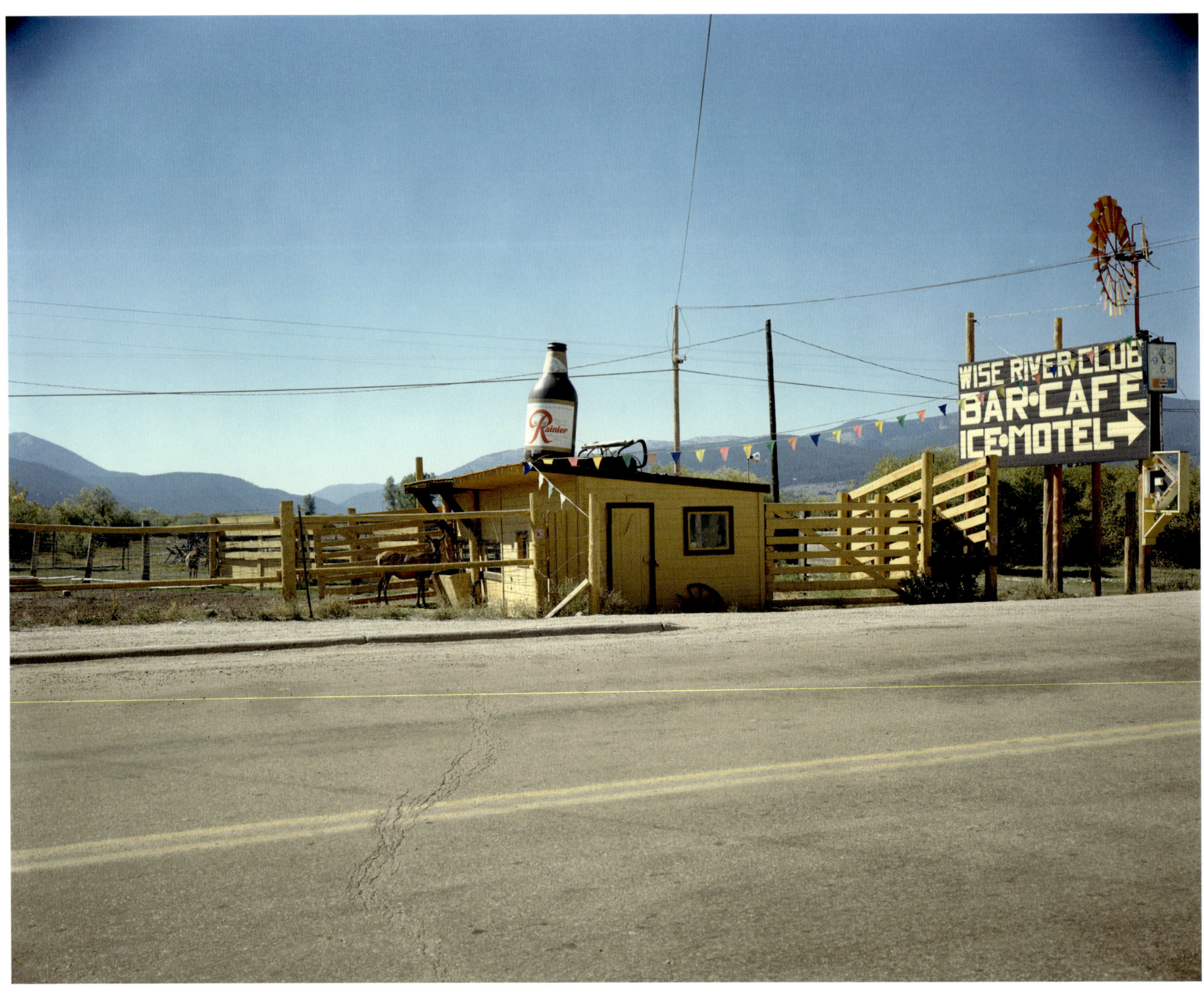

Wise River, Montana, September 18, 1979. 1979

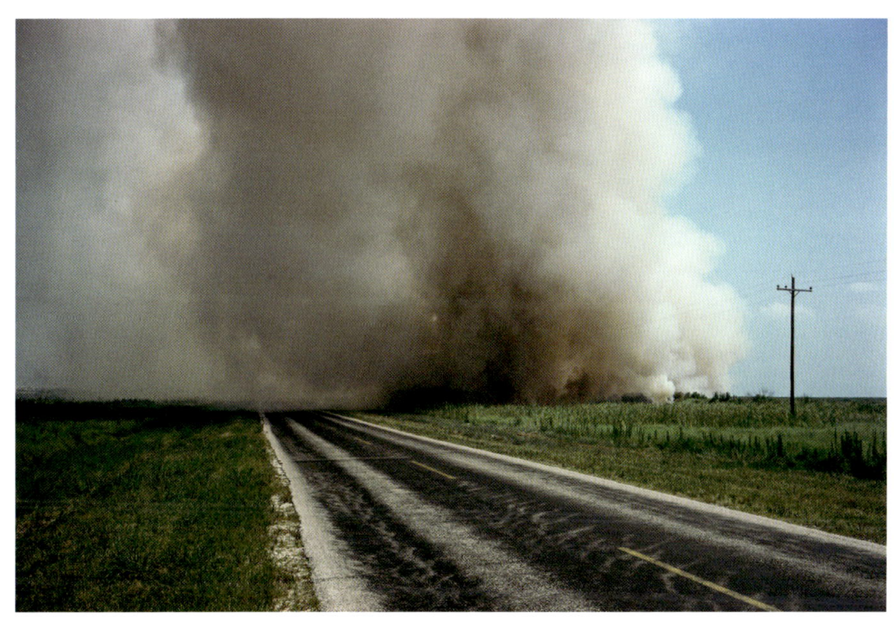

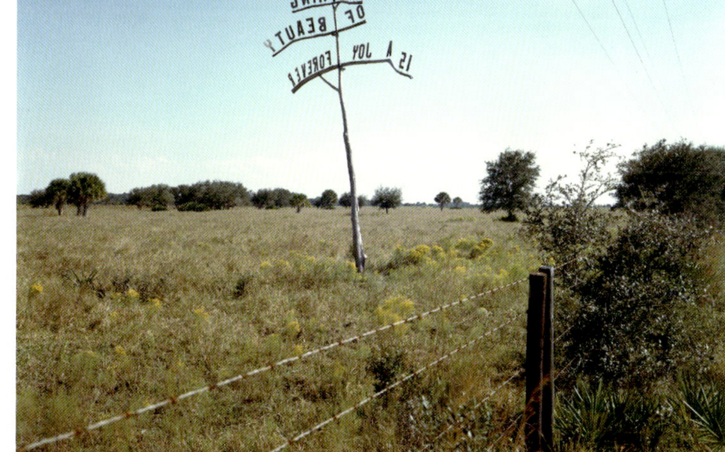

Untitled. 1975

***U.S. 27, Palmdale, Florida, November 15, 1977*. 1977**

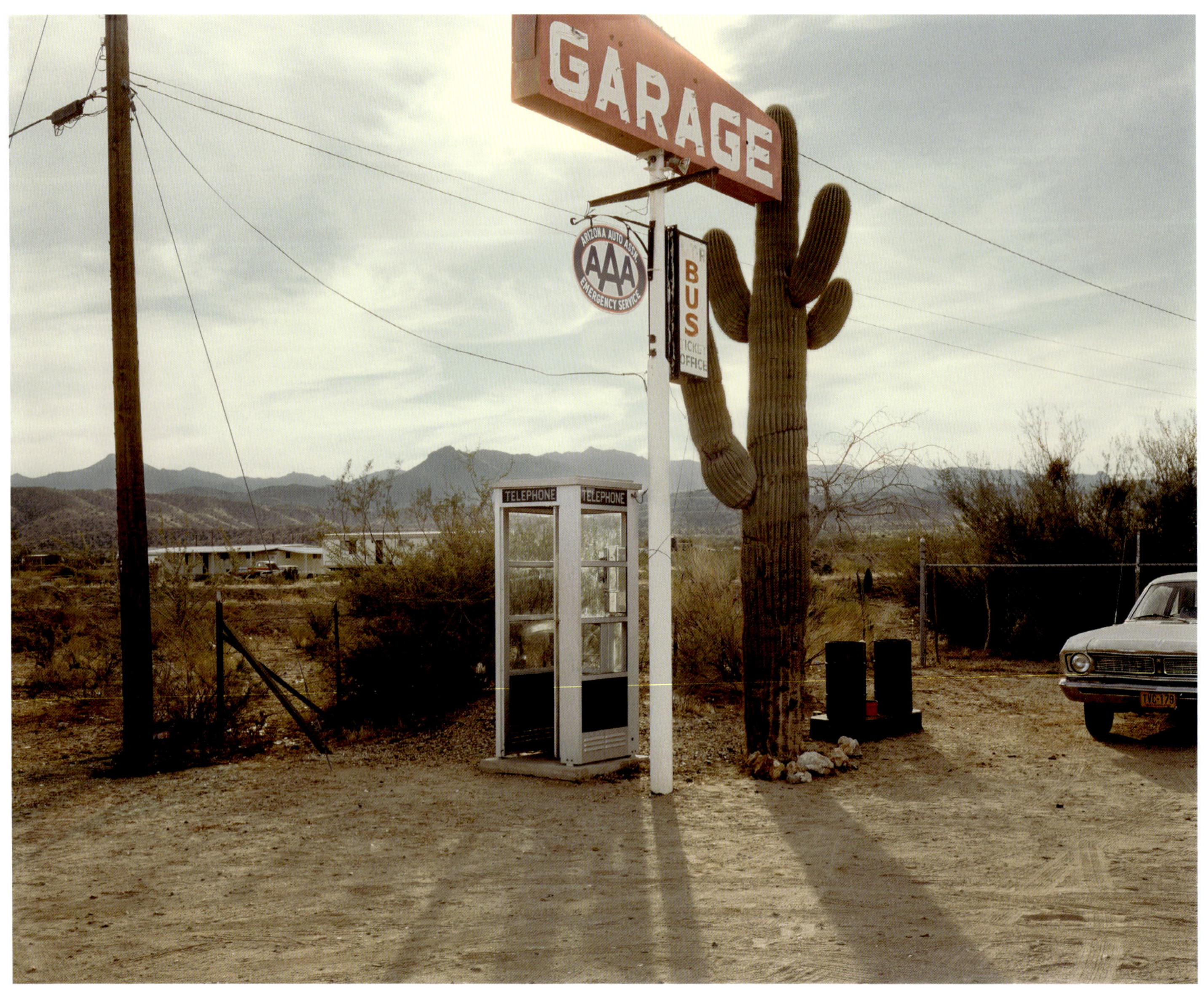

U.S. 93, Wikieup, Arizona, December 14, 1976. 1976

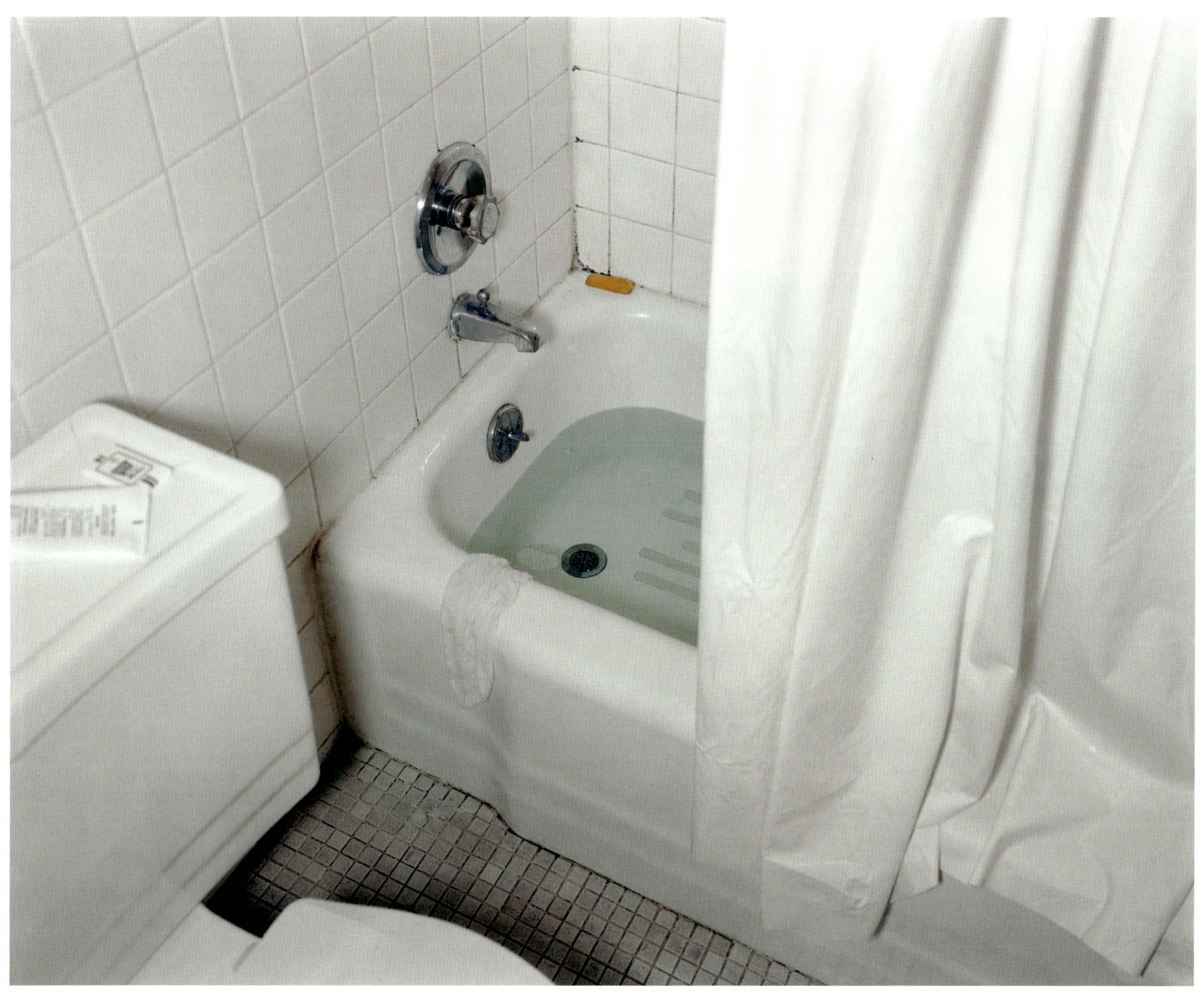

Room 115, Holiday Inn, Belle Glade, Florida, November 14, 1977. 1977

Warhol, Andy

"I think I learned by observing, not observing [Warhol] in order to learn, just by being exposed to the decisions and the actions he was making," Shore wrote in 1995. "More basic was simply a transition to thinking aesthetically. By the end of my stay at the Factory, I found that just my contact with, and observation of, Andy led me to think differently about my function as an artist. I became more aware of what I was doing."[1]

While Walker Evans was Shore's touchstone in the field of photography, it was Andy Warhol who played that role in his apprenticeship as an artist. Shore first met Warhol at the Film-Makers' Cinematheque, headed by the filmmaker and critic Jonas Mekas, in March 1965. The occasion was the screening of *The Life of Juanita Castro*, which Warhol had just completed, and *Elevator*, a short experimental film (possibly inspired by Warhol) that Shore, then seventeen years old, had made. A few weeks after their meeting, Shore began to be a regular at the Factory.

As the pivotal figure at the Factory, Warhol would dominate Shore's photographic production from 1965 to 1967. Whether they capture him at work or in relative privacy, the images of Warhol are often more posed than many of the other Factory portraits, and they convey the artist's acute awareness of the camera's presence and his strong sense of the power of the photographic image. Through Shore's lens, we see Warhol engaging in an assortment of activities, which, when put together like the pieces of a puzzle, create a portrait of the artist in all his diversity. A number of these images show Warhol in action—carrying a camera, moving frames—and give him a physical and material aspect that differs from the prevailing myth of the cerebral artist. The photographs also capture Warhol's social nature, as well as his sense of spectacle and theatricality and his often playful relationship to the camera.

Spending time with Warhol proved to be fundamental for Shore, sensitizing the very young photographer, who had no theoretical grounding, to different methods of working and new ways of looking at the world. The experience introduced Shore to serial imagery, which would have a profound impact on his work in 1969–71 and beyond, and fostered his interest in popular culture as subject matter. Shore learned from Warhol how to approach such subjects with both gentle irony and empathy—a kind of enchanted detachment. "When I photograph a gas station," Shore said, "I take pleasure in it. That is something I learned from Andy. A fascination, an irony and at the same time a delight."[2] (Quentin Bajac)

See also: *Black and White*; *Deadpan*; *Factory, The*; *Youth*

1. *The Velvet Years: Warhol's Factory, 1965–67*, photographs by Stephen Shore; text by Lynne Tillman (New York: Thunder's Mouth Press, 1995), 23.
2. Suzie Mackenzie, "The Beauty of the Disregarded," *The Guardian*, May 16, 2003, https://www.theguardian.com/artanddesign/2003/may/17/photography.artsfeatures.

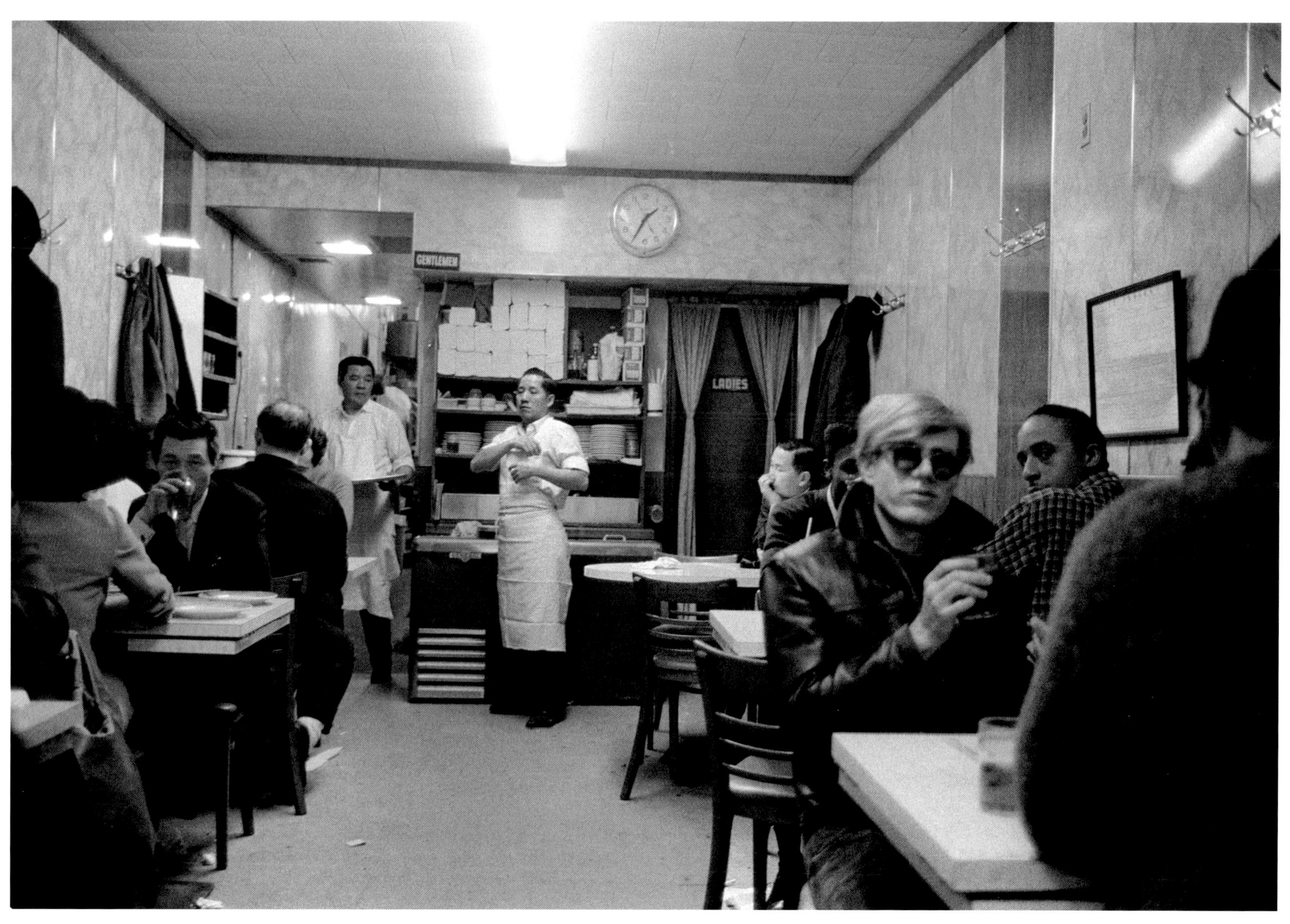

***1:35 a.m., in Chinatown Restaurant, New York, New York.* 1965–67**

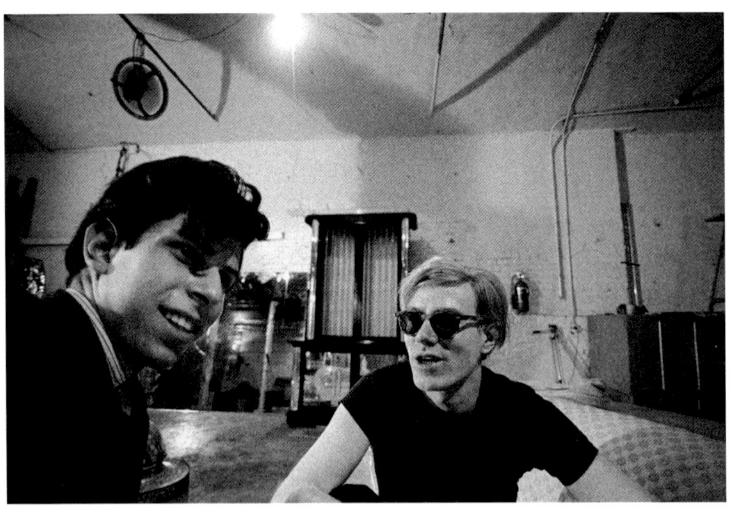

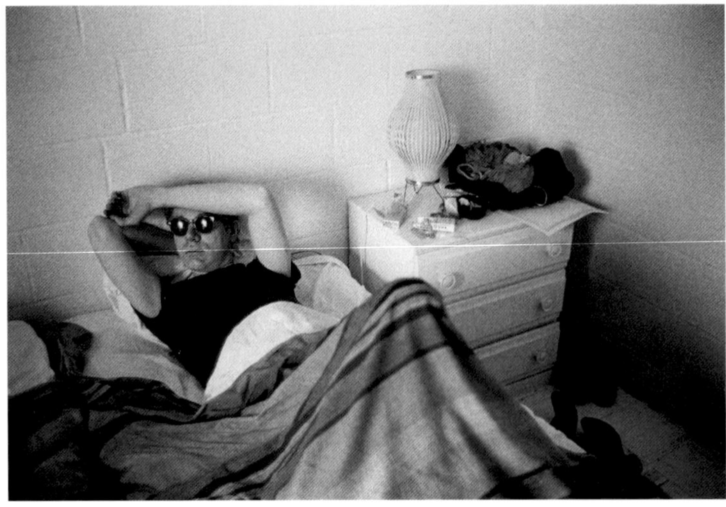

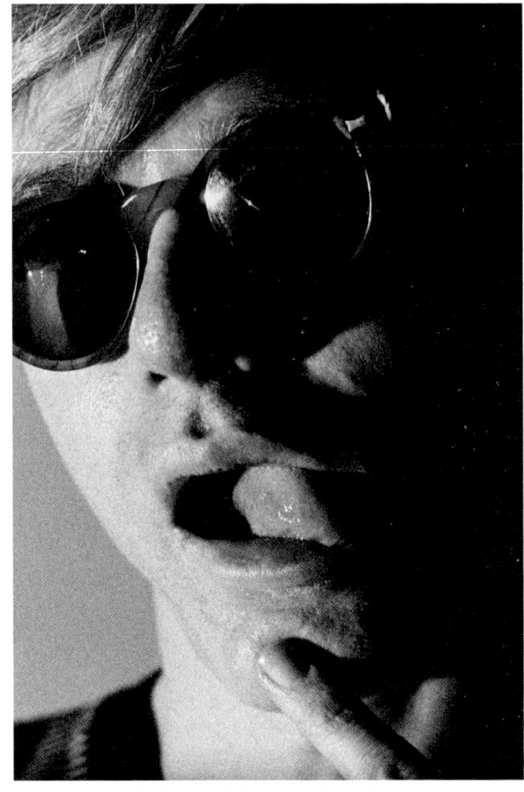

Stephen Shore and Andy Warhol, the Factory, New York, New York. 1965

Andy Warhol, Fire Island, New York. 1965

Andy Warhol, the Factory, New York, New York. 1965

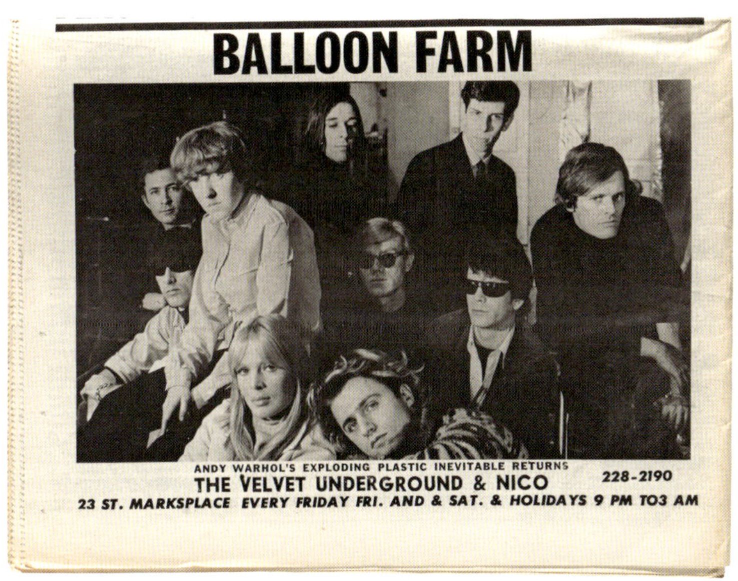

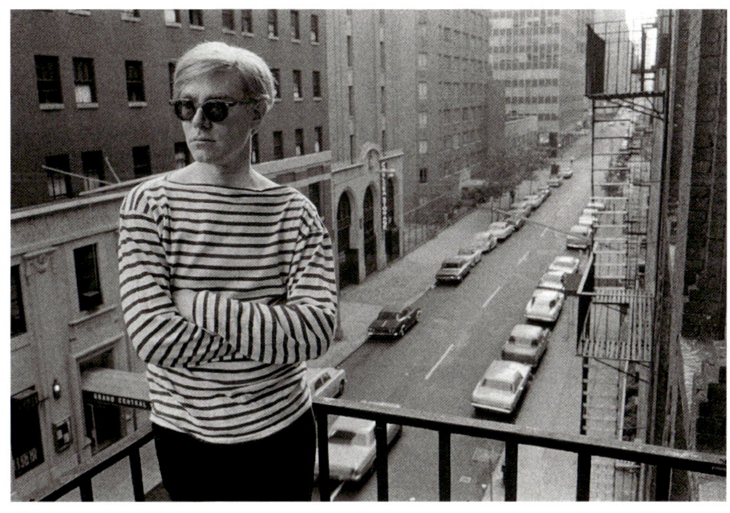

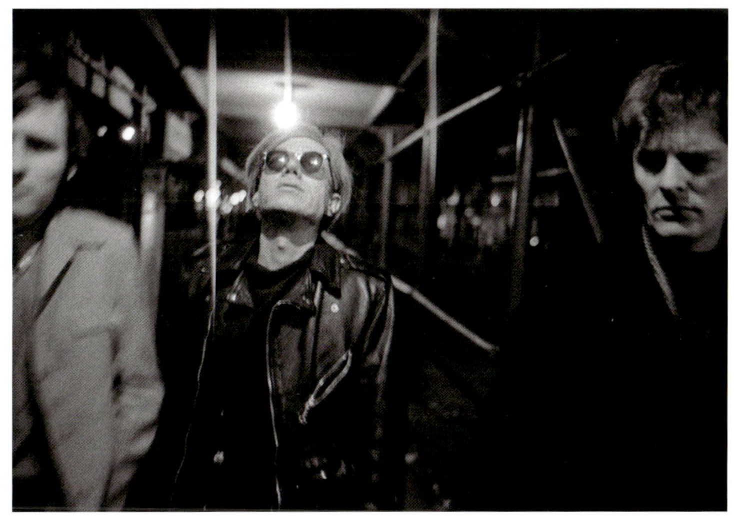

Promotion for the Exploding Plastic Inevitable at the Balloon Farm in the *East Village Other*, October 1–15, 1966

Andy Warhol, the Factory, New York, New York. 1965–66

Rod LaRod, Andy Warhol, and Paul Morrissey, New York, New York. 1966–67

Winslow, Arizona

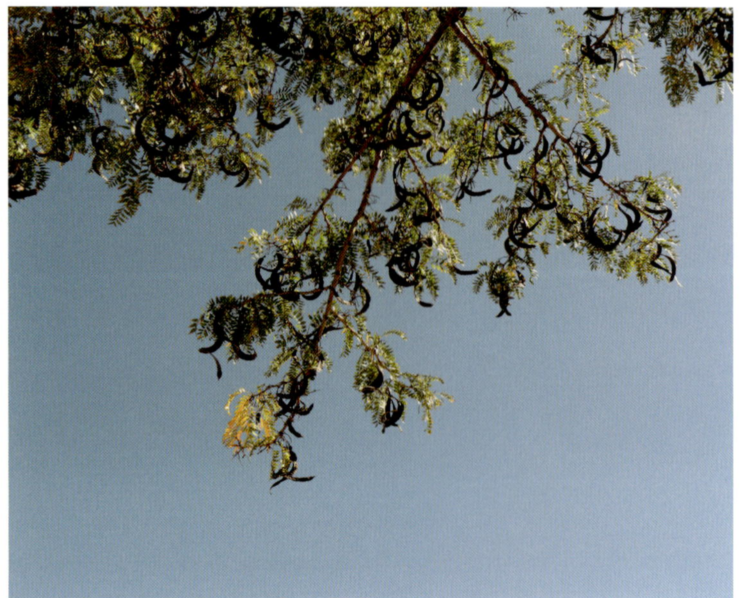

Winslow, Arizona was created in a single day in September of 2013. The precise temporal duration of the series—one day from sunrise to sunset—links it to some of Shore's print-on-demand books from ten years earlier, but it takes on a new performance-based dimension. Shore made the work as part of the project "Station to Station," conceived by the artist Doug Aitken. After chartering a train for three weeks to travel from New York to San Francisco, with numerous stops along the way, Aitken invited about thirty artists to create events or performances at predetermined points en route.

As one of the invited participants, Shore decided to photograph Winslow, a small Arizona town he had shot in 1972 as part of his series *American Surfaces*. He later explained how he created the new work: "I had breakfast at the La Posada hotel, parked my car, and just started walking. I covered the area, then drove, and shot more. I didn't have a plan, [. . .] I wasn't trying to build a narrative. I was just spending the day photographing."[1] All 183 of the pictures Shore took that day were presented, unedited and in the order in which they were shot, in a single slide show, projected on a drive-in screen in Barstow, California, a few days later.[2]

Although the Winslow images are intentionally reminiscent of Shore's photographs of the same town from the early 1970s, his approach was different here. "Because Station to Station is performance-based," Shore explained, "it presented a challenge that I had to figure out how to resolve. If it weren't for that challenge, I wouldn't have gone against my natural inclinations. That's what I like about taking on projects like this: I have to confront new challenges, and it ultimately shakes me out of my own habits in terms of working method and vision."[3] (Quentin Bajac)

See also: *American Surfaces*; *Instagram*; *Print-on-Demand Books*

1. Stephen Shore, "No Filter: How I Captured Winslow, Arizona in 180 Images," *Huffington Post* blogpost, September 25, 2013, http://www.huffingtonpost.com/stephen-shore/no-filter-how-i-captured-_b_3991291.html.
2. A selection of the images would later be published in Shore's book *Winslow Arizona: September 19th, 2013* (Tokyo: Amana, 2014).
3. Shore, "No Filter."

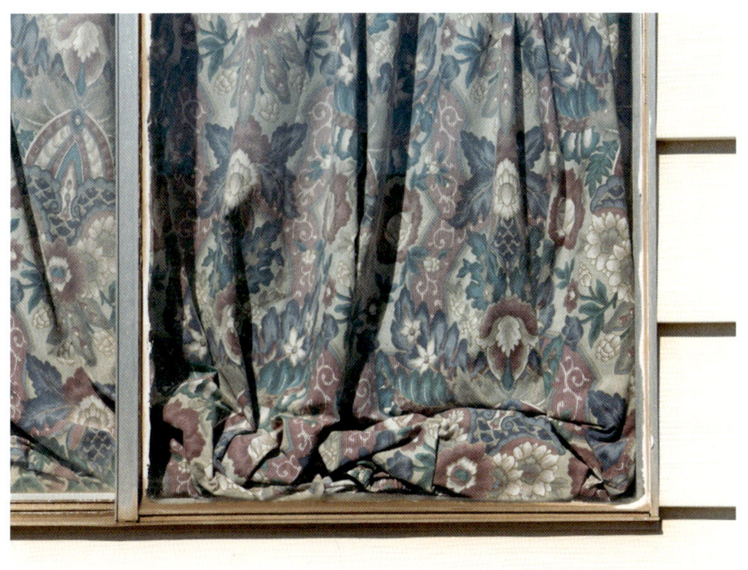

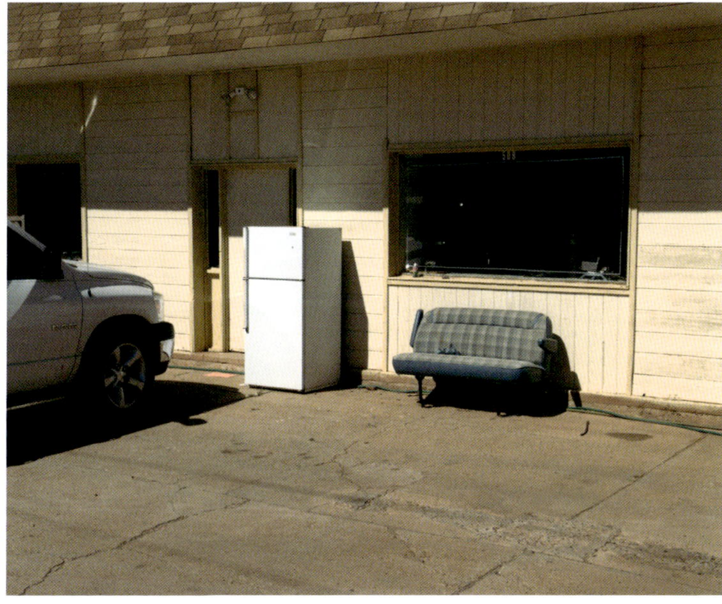

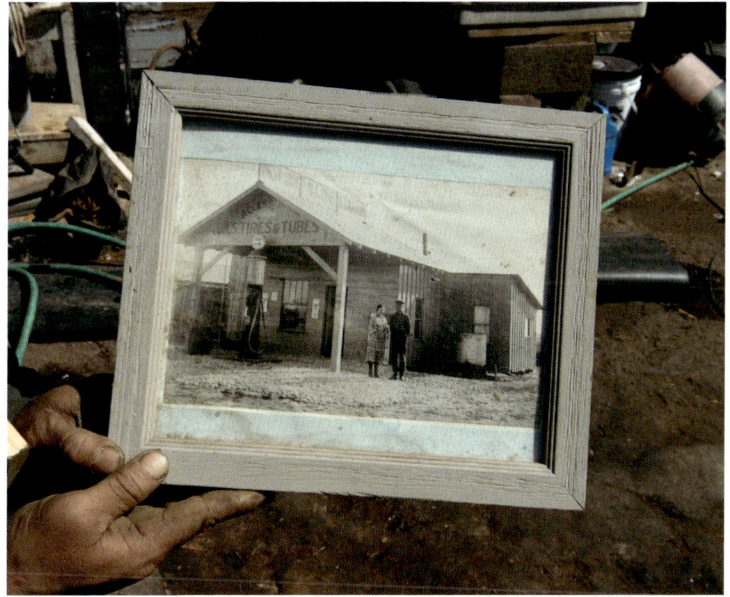

Winslow, Arizona, September 19, 2013. 2013

Winslow, Arizona, September 19, 2013. 2013

Winslow, Arizona, September 19, 2013. 2013

Winslow, Arizona, September 19, 2013. 2013

Youth

Stephen Eric Shore was born on October 8, 1947, in New York, the only child of Ruth and Fred Shore; his mother was a homemaker and his father was the president of a family-owned handbag business. Shore grew up at 25 Sutton Place South, where the family moved from Peter Cooper Village when he was ten years old. He had a cultured, urban childhood. When he was six an uncle gave him darkroom equipment, and Shore started developing the negatives from his parents' Hawkeye Brownie. He got his own camera when he was nine and the next year was given Walker Evans's *American Photographs* for his birthday by a neighbor who was the head of a music-publishing company. He listened to the witty, pun-filled LPs of Broadway soundtracks and Tom Lehrer, the latter given to him by his cousin Jane Kramer (who in 1964 became a staff writer for the *New Yorker*) and watched Robert Cummings play a successful—and dashing—Hollywood photographer on *The Bob Cummings Show*.

In the early 1960s Shore became interested in film, both narrative and experimental. He would skip school to take in features at the Thalia, the New Yorker Theater, the Bleecker Street Cinema, the theater at MoMA, and the Film-Makers' Cinematheque, where he first met Andy Warhol in March of 1965, when Shore screened his early film, *Elevator*. At the same time, he was pursuing his photography career: in 1962 he had his first solo exhibition, at the Donnell Library Center on West Fifty-third Street, and later that year sold three photographs to Edward Steichen across the street at MoMA. In 1963 Shore published his first photograph, a portrait of Kramer on the cover of *The Book Buyer's Guide*, and appeared in his first feature, an article called "Angry Young Man with a Camera" in *U.S. Camera* (opposite). Around this time he became friends with Lee Lockwood—a photojournalist and the editor, in 1963–66, of *Contemporary Photographer*—and through him met photographers such as Dave Heath and saw the work of Lee Friedlander, Jerry Uelsmann, and Duane Michals. Through this group Shore became involved with the Heliography Gallery, a short-lived photography cooperative in Midtown where he would sometimes staff the desk, being paid for his time in prints.[1] And in 1964–65 Shore was the official photographer for the Festival Orchestra of New York, shooting rehearsals and performances weekly and publishing them in several periodicals, including *Newsweek*.

Not surprisingly, Shore was only nominally attending high school at the time. In 1965 he dropped out of Columbia Grammar School and started photographing at Warhol's Factory on an almost daily basis. Although his parents were upset at first, they adjusted to his ambitions, becoming friendly with Warhol and allowing Shore to host people from the Factory at their apartment. After he stopped hanging out with the Factory crowd, Shore continued to spend time with artists, including three months in London with John Chamberlain in 1969. When Shore was twenty-two he moved into his own apartment a block away from his parents', just a year before he was given a solo exhibition at the Metropolitan Museum of Art.

As a professor, Shore has cited ambition as a key indicator of his own students' future success;[2] the youthful drive that led to his own early, flying start in photography is recorded in his *U.S. Camera* article. Although he was only fifteen at the time, his comments about photographic theory and his own career are confident, even brash, perhaps overcompensating for youth with certainty. He was as successful in his youth as many artists aspire to be in their entire careers—in fact, he has described his Met exhibition as "a confusing event," perhaps happening when he was too young.[3] But this precocity was a reflection of Shore's skill, curiosity, and impatience, building an inner momentum that has propelled him for over fifty years. (Kristen Gaylord)

See also: *Evans, Walker*; *Factory, The*; *Metropolitan Museum of Art, The*; *Museum of Modern Art, The*; *Street Photography*; *Warhol, Andy*

1. The gallery existed only from mid-1963 to early 1966 and was most associated with subjective and creative photography, including that of Paul Caponigro, Walter Chappell, Carl Chiarenza, Nicholas Dean, Paul Petricone, and Jerry Uelsmann, but photographers such as Lee Lockwood and Larry Clark were also involved. See Margarett Loke, "From a Vanished Cooperative, Nature in Abstract," *New York Times*, March 6, 1998, E43.
2. David Campany, "Ways of Making Pictures," in Marta Dahó, ed., *Stephen Shore* (Madrid: Fundación MAPFRE; New York: Aperture, 2014), 24.
3. "Stephen Shore in a Conversation with Lynne Tillman," in *Uncommon Places: The Complete Works* (New York: Aperture, 2004), 173.

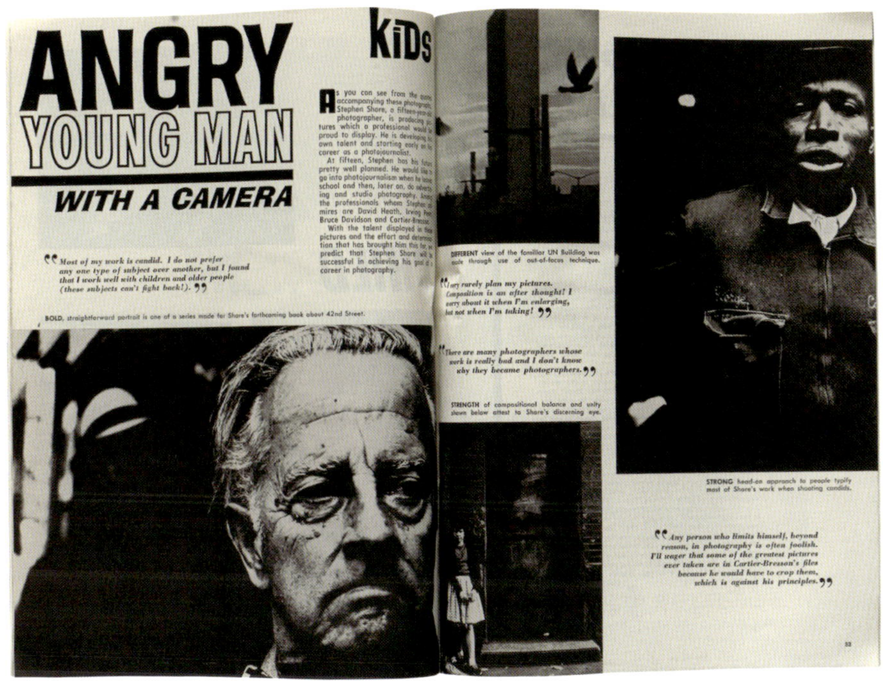

KIDS

ANGRY YOUNG MAN WITH A CAMERA

As you can see from the quote accompanying these photograph Stephen Shore, a fifteen-year-o photographer, is producing pic tures which a professional would be proud to display. He is developing his own talent and starting early on his career as a photojournalist.

At fifteen, Stephen has his future pretty well planned. He would like to go into photojournalism when he leave school and then, later on, do advertis ing and studio photography. Among the professionals whom Stephen ad mires are David Heath, Irving Penn Bruce Davidson and Cartier-Bresson.

With the talent displayed in these pictures and the effort and determina tion that has brought him this far, we predict that Stephen Shore will be successful in achieving his goal of a career in photography.

"Most of my work is candid. I do not prefer any one type of subject over another, but I found that I work well with children and older people (these subjects can't fight back!)."

BOLD, straightforward portrait is one of a series made for Shore's forthcoming book about 42nd Street.

DIFFERENT view of the familiar UN Building was made through use of out-of-focus technique.

"I very rarely plan my pictures. Composition is an after thought! I worry about it when I'm enlarging, but not when I'm taking!"

"There are many photographers whose work is really bad and I don't know why they became photographers."

STRENGTH of compositional balance and unity shown below attest to Share's discerning eye.

STRONG head-on approach to people typify most of Share's work when shooting candids.

"Any person who limits himself, beyond reason, in photography is often foolish. I'll wager that some of the greatest pictures ever taken are in Cartier-Bresson's files because he would have to crop them, which is against his principles."

53

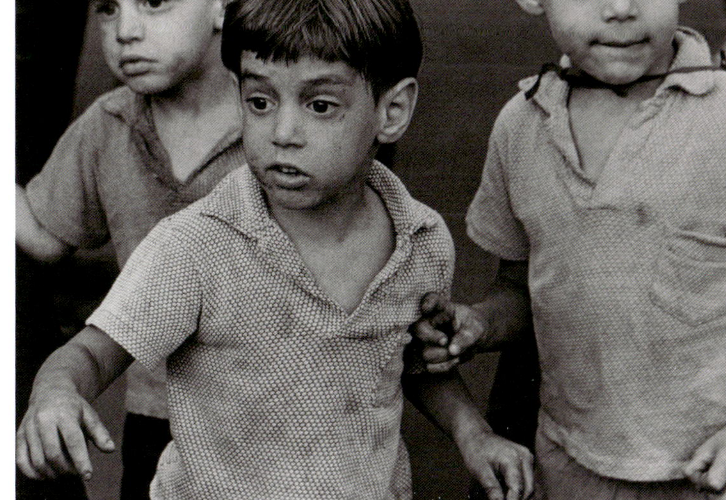

"Angry Young Man with a Camera," *U.S. Camera*, June 1963

Untitled. 1962

Ziggy, Zelda, and Zaza

As a New Yorker, Shore grew up with only a short-lived (and not particularly lamented) goldfish as a pet. But from the 1970s on he steadily accumulated more and more animal companions: cats in his New York apartment with Ginger, dogs in the 1980s when they moved to Montana, and, eventually, goats and chickens in the 1990s while living in the Hudson Valley. Siblings Emma and Chargie were the Shores' first goats, after friends' goats had a litter, and their second group comprised siblings Ziggy, Zelda, and Zaza. The adventurous Ziggy—who climbed trees and jumped on anything he could, including trampolines—died abruptly and tragically as Shore was finishing his *American Surfaces* publication in 2005, and was immortalized with a dedication and image in the back.

All of these animals have been first and foremost pets, not working animals. Shore included many of them in *Pet Pictures*, his 2012 book of 35mm and digital images from the previous three decades. The pictures were taken mostly around Shore's home in Tivoli, New York, and each animal is named—fifteen in all, ending with a signed original photograph of Black Lab and Gordon Setter mix Pete. Animals appear in his print-on-demand books as well: his first was of the Westminster Kennel Club Dog Show (*Dog Show*, 2003, page 190), and others feature a chicken contest at the Dutchess County Fair (*Fowl*, 2003), animals he saw in Africa (*African Idyll* and *The Big Five*, 2004), and images of his daily life with the pets (*6-9-06*, 2006, pages 188–89, and *Season's Greetings*, 2008). Shore remains an animal-lover. When he joined Instagram in 2014 his fourth and eighth posts were of his cat, Oscar, and the first of his images to gain over two hundred "likes." And when reviewing this catalogue and noticing that it began with an A but didn't end with a Z, Shore, ever the completist, suggested an entry featuring Ziggy, Zelda, and Zaza. (Kristen Gaylord)

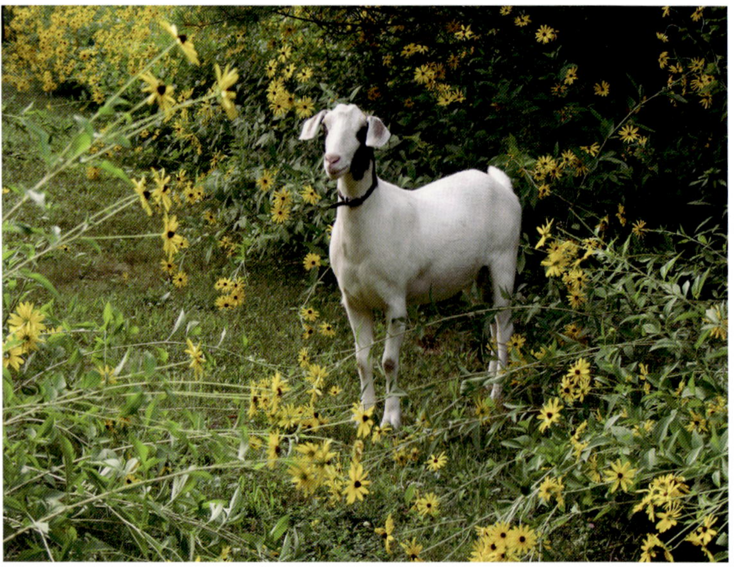

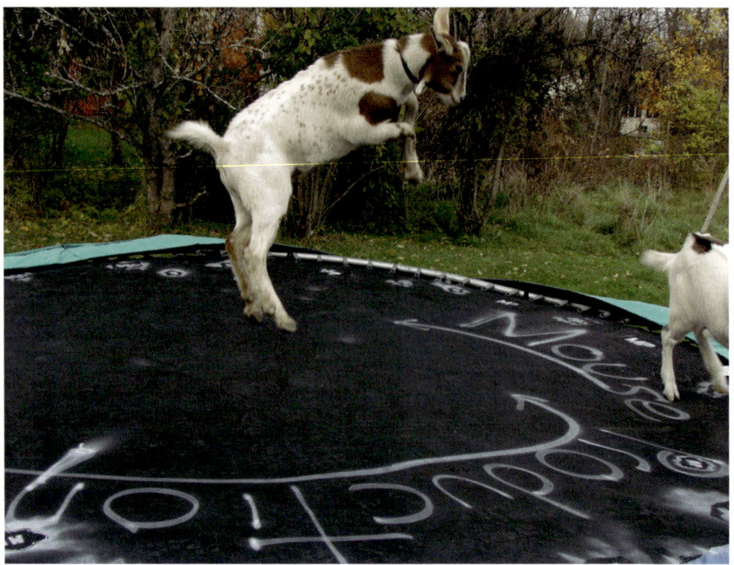

See also: *Instagram*; *Ginger*; *Print-on-Demand Books*

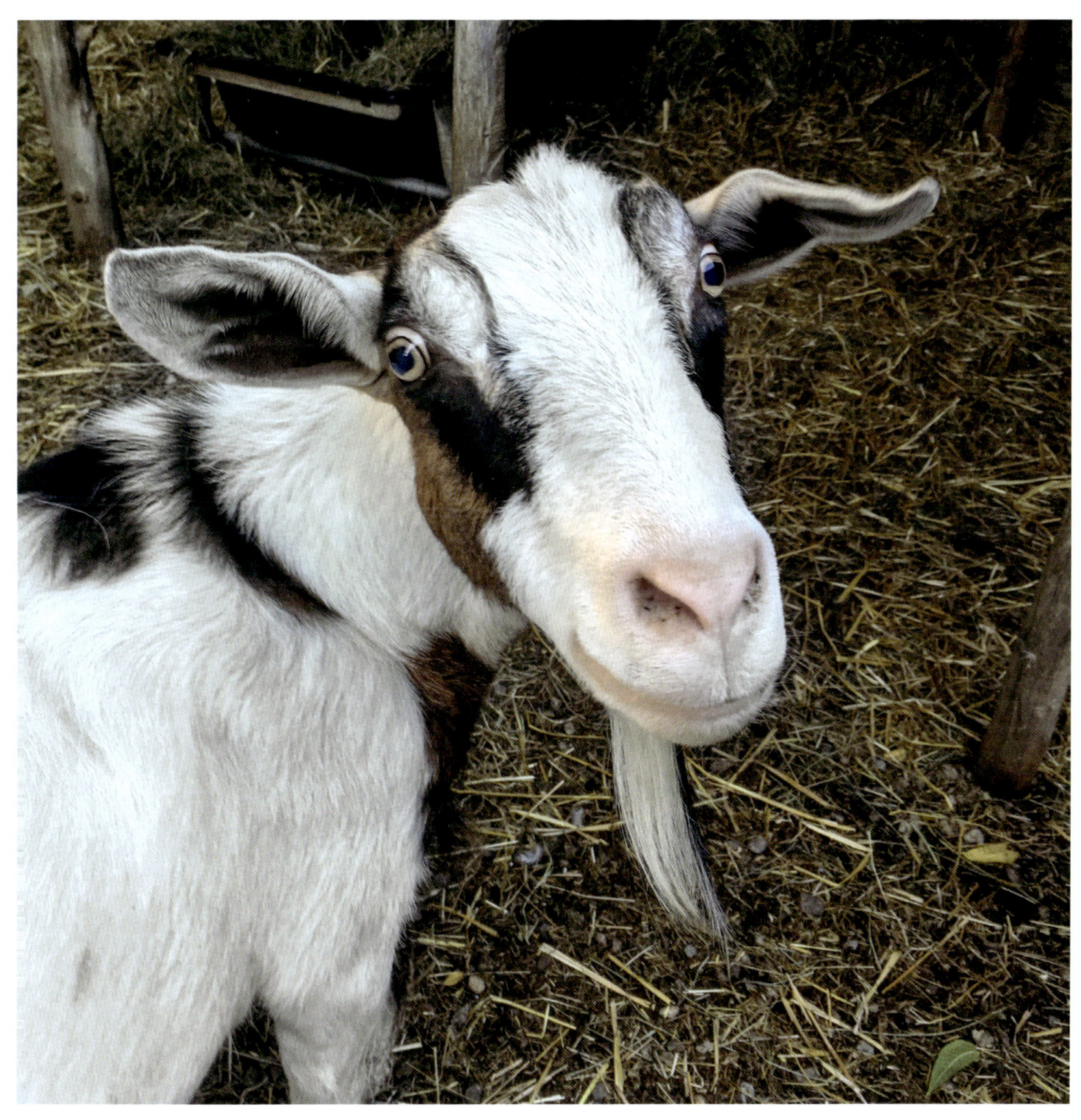

Zaza, Tivoli, New York. 2005

Ziggy, Tivoli, New York, October 31, 2004. 2004

Zelda, Hollow Road, Clinton Corners, New York, September 11, 2016. 2016

A Photographic Chronology
Selected Exhibition History
Selected Bibliography
Checklist of the Exhibition
Acknowledgments
Committee on Photography / Trustees of The Museum of Modern Art

A Photographic Chronology
Kristen Gaylord

This chronology relies heavily on Shore's notebooks, which he kept from 1969 through the 1990s (less carefully in the later years), but also makes use of publications and archival research as well as studio records. Although some significant biographical information is included, the emphasis is on an accounting of Shore's photographing.

Each entry includes whatever is known of the following: date, camera type and format, location, and, for large-format images, the number of shots (indicated in brackets). Publications are listed only when they were the impetus for the photographs or are otherwise especially significant, and titles are listed only for Conceptual works and others that differ from Shore's usual titling convention of location and date. When images of a photograph or publication are included in this book, page numbers are indicated.

Commissions cover all of the dates listed beneath each heading, but not all photographs taken on those days were necessarily part of that commission, especially in the 1970s, when the line between "commissioned" and "personal" work was more porous. Often the phrase "commission by" merely indicates that there was a sponsor or funding source for Shore's travel and/or equipment.

1947 8 October. Born in New York

1953 October. Receives Kodak darkroom equipment for his sixth birthday from his uncle, which he uses to make prints from the family's Hawkeye Brownie negatives

1956 July. Receives Ricoh 35mm rangefinder camera
Ricoh 35mm: New York

1957 Shore family moves to 25 Sutton Place South, New York
Ricoh 35mm: New York
October. Receives Walker Evans's *American Photographs* for his tenth birthday from a neighbor
October. Ricoh 35mm: New York (opposite)

1959 Ricoh 35mm: Unknown locations and Tarrytown and New York, N.Y.
August. Ricoh 35mm: New York

1960 Nikon F 35mm: Unknown locations and New York
March. Nikon F 35mm: New York
June. Nikon F 35mm: New York
August. Nikon F 35mm: New York

1961 Nikon F 35mm: Unknown locations and New York
June 11. Nikon F 35mm: Brandeis University, Waltham, Mass.
September. Nikon F 35mm: New York (page 226)
Studies with Lisette Model

1962 Nikon F 35mm: Unknown locations and New York (pages 227 and 281)
June. Meets with Edward Steichen at MoMA, who buys three prints

1963 Nikon F 35mm and Leica M2 35mm: Unknown locations and New York (pages 223–25)
January. Nikon F 35mm and Leica M2 35mm: New York
June. Article on Shore called "Angry Young Man with a Camera" published in *U.S. Camera* (page 281)
October. Photograph of Jane Kramer published on the cover of *The Book Buyer's Guide* 55, no. 821
Meets Lee Lockwood and becomes involved with the Heliography Gallery, New York

1964 Nikon F 35mm and Leica M2 35mm: Unknown locations and New York (pages 56 and 224–27)
January 26. Shoots *Elevator* on 16mm film, New York
At the request of John Szarkowski, exchanges two 1964 works for two in the MoMA collection
Becomes staff photographer for the Festival Orchestra of New York. Photographs of Thomas Dunn (founder and conductor, Festival Orchestra), Hermann Scherchen (guest conductor, Philadelphia Orchestra), and Luigi Dallapiccola (pianist) are published in advertisements and articles including in *Cue* magazine, the *New York Herald Tribune*, the *New York Times*, and *Newsweek*.

1965 March 22. *Elevator* screens at Film-Makers' Cinematheque in New York. Andy Warhol premieres *The Life of Juanita Castro* at the same event, and the two artists meet.
May. Shore drops out of high school and starts photographing the people and events of Warhol's Factory. He also assists on films and works on lighting for Velvet Underground performances.
Leica M2 35mm, Leica M3 35mm, and Nikon F 35mm: The Factory and around New York (pages 95–98, 100–101, 225, and 275–77)

1966 Leica M2 35mm, Leica M3 35mm, and Nikon F 35mm: The Factory and around New York (pages 95–97, 99–101, 275, and 277)

1967 Leica M2 35mm, Leica M3 35mm, and Nikon F 35mm: The Factory and around New York (pages 95–97, 99–100, 275, and 277)

1968 Moves to 2 Sutton Place South, New York
Summer. Leica 35mm: Madrid, Seville, Cordoba, Rome, and London
Early December. Leica 35mm: Los Angeles

1969 Leica M2 35mm and Leica M3 35mm: Ulster County, N.Y.
February 4. Leica M2 35mm: Los Angeles (pages 79 and 198)
February 11. Leica M2 35mm: New York (for the unrealized *The Official Personal Vibrator Manual*)
February 19. Leica M2 35mm: New York (for the unrealized *The Official Personal Vibrator Manual*)
Travels to London with John Chamberlain
Nikon F 35mm and Leica 35mm: Photographs John Chamberlain, London
March 25. Kodak Instamatic: Photographs Robert Fraser (Warhol's art dealer), 10:30 a.m. to 4:30 p.m., London [13]
March 26. Kodak Instamatic: Photographs Christopher Gibbs, 11:00 a.m. to 5:00 p.m., London [13]
April. Kodak Instamatic: Photographs David Hockney, London
July. Leica M2 35mm: Amarillo and Canyon, Tex. (*4-Part Variation, July 1969*, page 83; *Circle No. 1, July 1969*, page 81; and *KT Ranch, July 1969*, page 157)
July 22. Hasselblad 500EL 2¼-by-2¼: Photographs Michael Marsh, midnight to midnight, Amarillo, Tex. [49] (*July 22–23, 1969*, page 82)

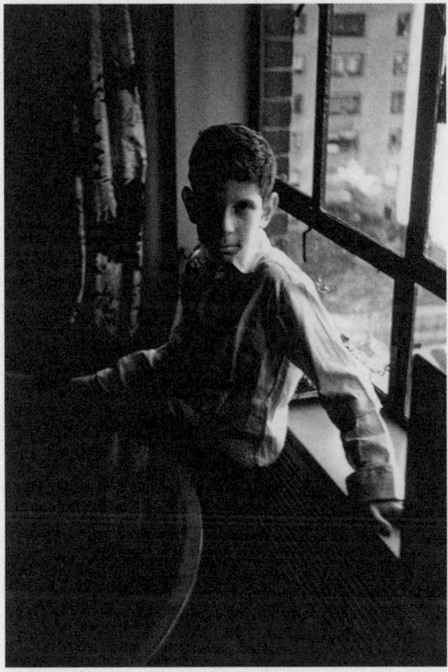

Self-portrait, New York, October 1957

1970 January 9. Hasselblad 500EL $2^{1}/_{4}$-by-$2^{1}/_{4}$: Photographs Sandy Kirkland, noon to midnight, New York [25]

January 18. Hasselblad 500EL $2^{1}/_{4}$-by-$2^{1}/_{4}$: Photographs Fred Shore, noon to midnight, New York [25]

January 27. Hasselblad 500EL $2^{1}/_{4}$-by-$2^{1}/_{4}$: Photographs Fred Shore, 4:22 to 4:46 p.m., New York [25]

March. Leica M2 35mm: Amarillo, Tex. (one image of *Over England, May 1970 and Amarillo, Texas, March 1970*)

April 6. Hasselblad 500EL $2^{1}/_{4}$-by-$2^{1}/_{4}$: Photographs Fred and Ruth Shore, New York (page 177)

May. Leica M2 35mm: In an airplane over England (*Over England, May 1970* and one image of *Over England, May 1970 and Amarillo, Texas, March 1970*)

June. Takes photography workshop with Minor White

June 17. Leica M2 35mm: Sixth Avenue, New York (*Avenue of the Americas*, page 228)

June 25. Leica M2 35mm: Lakeville, Conn. (*The Institute for General Semantics, Lakeville, Connecticut, June 25, 1970*, page 127)

July 31. Leica M2 35mm: New York (one image of *Manhood of Humanity*, page 80)

August. Leica M2 35mm: In an airplane between Denver, Colo., and New York (*Between Denver and New York, August 1970*)

September 5. Makes 400 copies of "Get Rich Quick" to hand out

October 18. Leica M2 35mm: Kingston, New York (*Kingston, New York, October 18, 1970*)

Spends one month at Centro Intercultural de Documentación (CIDOC) in Cuernavaca, Mexico; while there attends a workshop on organic versus arbitrary order led by educational theorist George Dennison

Leica 35mm: San Blas Islands, Panama

1971 Throughout the year uses a Mick-a-Matic camera in New York, Amarillo, Tex., etc. (pages 158–59)

June 24. Leica 35mm: Endicott Hotel, Concord, N.H.

June 25–26. Leica 35mm: Concord, N.H.

June 27. Leica 35mm: Lookout Hotel, Ogunquit, Maine

June 28–30. Leica 35mm: Camden, Maine

July 1. Leica 35mm: Camden, Maine

July 2. Leica 35mm: Camden and Freeport, Maine

July 3. Leica 35mm: Cambridge, Mass.

July 4. Leica 35mm: Cape Cod, Mass.

July 5–6. Leica 35mm: Bristol, R.I.

July 7–8. Leica 35mm: New York

July 16. Leica 35mm: Chambersburg, Pa., and Martinsburg, W.Va.

July 17. Leica 35mm: Luray to Pulaski, Va.

July 18. Leica 35mm: Pulaski, Va., to Knoxville, Tenn.

July 19. Leica 35mm: Nashville, Tenn.

July 20. Leica 35mm: Nashville to Memphis, Tenn.

July 21. Leica 35mm: Memphis, Tenn., to Little Rock to Russellville, Ark.

July 22. Leica 35mm: Oklahoma City, Okla.

July 23. Leica 35mm: McLean to Amarillo, Tex.

July 24–25. Leica 35mm: Canyon, Tex.

July 26. Leica 35mm: Amarillo, Tex.

July 27–28. Leica 35mm: Canyon, Tex.

July 29. Leica 35mm: Amarillo, Tex.

July 30. Leica 35mm: Canyon, Tex.

July 31. Leica 35mm: Santa Fe, N.Mex.

August 1. Leica 35mm Santa Fe and Albuquerque, N.Mex.

August 5. Leica 35mm: Santa Fe, N.Mex., to Amarillo, Tex.

August 6. Leica 35mm: Amarillo, Tex., to Detroit, Mich.

August 7. Leica 35mm: Detroit, Mich.

August 9. Leica 35mm: Chicago

August 10–14. Leica 35mm: Amarillo, Tex.

August 15. Leica 35mm: Amarillo and Canyon, Tex.

August 18. Leica 35mm: Amarillo, Tex.

August 20–23. Leica 35mm: Amarillo, Tex.

August 24. Leica 35mm: Amarillo, Tex., to New York

September 6. Leica 35mm: New York

September 11–12. Leica 35mm: London

September 16. Leica 35mm: London

September 17–20. Leica 35mm: Lisbon, Portugal

September 23. Leica 35mm: Seville, Spain

September 24. Leica 35mm: Seville to Cordoba, Spain

September 26. Leica 35mm: Algarve, Portugal

September 28–30. Leica 35mm: Algarve, Portugal

November 8–20. *All the Meat You Can Eat*, organized by Shore, is shown at 98 Greene Street Loft, New York (pages 15–17)

November 19. Super 8: New York (*Intersections* film, 1971/2000)

November 21–22. Super 8: New York (*Intersections* film, 1971/2000)

November 24. Super 8: Route 22, N.J. (*Intersections* film, 1971/2000); Leica M2 35mm: Route 22, Union, N.J.

November 25. Super 8: Princeton, N.J. (*Intersections* film, 1971/2000)
December 1. Super 8: Bedford Village, N.Y. (*Intersections* film, 1971/2000)
December 18. Super 8: Santa Fe to Cerrillos, and Madrid, N.Mex. (*Intersections* film, 1971/2000)
December 19. Super 8: Santa Fe to Chimayao, N.Mex. (*Intersections* film, 1971/2000)
December 21. Super 8: Amarillo, Tex. (*Intersections* film, 1971/2000)
December 22. Super 8: Amarillo, Tex. (*Intersections* film, 1971/2000)
December 23. Super 8: Canyon to Amarillo, Tex. (*Intersections* film, 1971/2000)
December 24. Super 8: Mrs. O'Brien, Amarillo, Tex. (*Intersections* film, 1971/2000)
December 26. Super 8: Canyon, Tex. (*Intersections* film, 1971/2000)
December 30. Super 8: Amarillo, Tex. (*Intersections* film, 1971/2000)

1972 March. Rollei 35mm: New York (page 23)
April. Rollei 35mm: New York (page 23) and Queens (page 26), N.Y.; Greenwich, Conn.
June 1. Rollei 35mm: New York and Baltimore
June 2. Rollei 35mm: Woodbridge, Fredericksburg, and Richmond, Va.
June 3. Rollei 35mm: Raleigh, N.C.
June 4. Rollei 35mm: Columbia (page 204) and Aiken, S.C.
June 5. Rollei 35mm: Macon (pages 213 and 235) and Columbus, Ga.
June 6. Rollei 35mm: Montgomery and Selma, Ala.
June 7. Rollei 35mm: Meridian, Miss.
June 8. Rollei 35mm: Monroe, La., and Marshall, Tex.
June 9. Rollei 35mm: Tyler, Tex.
June 10. Rollei 35mm: Dallas and Mineral Wells (page 27), Tex.
June 11. Rollei 35mm: Abilene, Sweetwater, and Lubbock, Tex.
June 12. Rollei 35mm: Clovis (page 26), N.Mex.
June 13–22. Rollei 35mm: Sumner, Santa Rosa, Santa Fe (page 27), Taos, Chimayo, Cerrillos (page 45), Pueblo Bonito (page 213), and Albuquerque, N.Mex.
June 23. Rollei 35mm: N.M. 44 (page 26) and Farmington (pages 26 and 45), N.Mex.
June 24. Rollei 35mm: Mesa Verde and Durango, Colo., and U.S. 89 (page 197), Ariz.
June 25. Rollei 35mm: Kanab (pages 27–28 and 234), Utah
June 26–28. Rollei 35mm: Lake Powell (page 28), Utah
June 29. Rollei 35mm: Grand Canyon, Winslow, and Holbrook (pages 26–27), Ariz.
June 30. Rollei 35mm: Gallup and Albuquerque, N.Mex.
July 1. Rollei 35mm: Tucumcari (pages 32, 45, and 212), N.Mex.
July 2–7. Rollei 35mm: Amarillo (pages 19, 34–35, and 213), Canyon, Alanreed, and Shamrock, Tex.
July 8. Rollei 35mm: Granite (pages 31, 63, and 106) and Clinton, Okla.
July 9. Rollei 35mm: Oklahoma City (page 24), Okla.
July 10. Rollei 35mm: Tulsa and Miami (page 34), Okla., and Joplin (page 65) and Springfield, Mo.
July 11. Rollei 35mm: Rolla (page 32), Mo.
July 12. Rollei 35mm: Saint Louis, Mo., and Springfield, Ill.
July 13. Rollei 35mm: Normal (page 171), Ill.
July 14. Rollei 35mm: Chicago (page 25); Toledo, Ohio
July 15. Rollei 35mm: Sandusky, Ohio
July 16. Rollei 35mm: New York (pages 31–32)
July 24. Rollei 35mm: New York (pages 31–32)
July. Rollei 35mm: Philadelphia; Sneden's Landing, N.Y.; Pontiac (page 25), Rochester (page 32), and Birmingham, Mich.
August. Rollei 35mm: Washington, D.C.; New York (pages 35 and 65); and Dayton (pages 35 and 88), Ohio
August 28. Rollei 35mm: Staten Island and New York, N.Y.
September 7. Rollei 35mm: New York
September. Rollei 35mm: Petersburg, N.Y. (page 66), and Westport, Conn.
September–October. Rollei 35mm: New York (pages 30, 33, 36–37, 67, and 206)
October 31. Rollei 35mm: New York (page 37)
November. Rollei 35mm: New York (page 35); St. John, U.S. Virgin Islands; Washington, D.C. (page 29)
December. Rollei 35mm: West Palm Beach, Fla., and London

1973 January. Rollei 35mm: West Palm Beach, Palm Beach, and Jacksonville (page 28), Fla.; Jacksonville and New Bern, N.C.; Cape May, N.J.; New York
January 8. Rollei 35mm: West Palm Beach, Fla.
February. Rollei 35mm: New York (page 28)
March. Rollei 35mm: West Palm Beach, Palm Beach, and Delray Beach, Fla.; New York
March–April. Rollei 35mm: New York (page 25) and Sneden's Landing, N.Y.
April–May. Rollei 35mm: Palm Beach (page 62), West Palm Beach (page 34), and Cape Kennedy, Fla.
June 16. Crown Graphic 4-by-5: Photographs Michael Marsh, Queens, N.Y. [1]
June 17. Crown Graphic 4-by-5: Queens [4] and New York [4], N.Y.
June 19. Crown Graphic 4-by-5: Photographs David Sulzberger, New York [1]
June 24. Crown Graphic 4-by-5: Sneden's Landing (including of Sandy Kirkland), N.Y. [3]

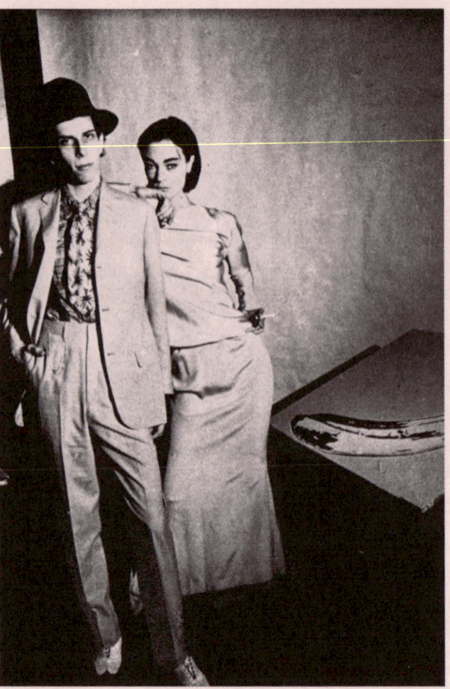

Ivy Nicholson and Stephen Shore at the Factory, New York, 1966. Photograph by Billy Name

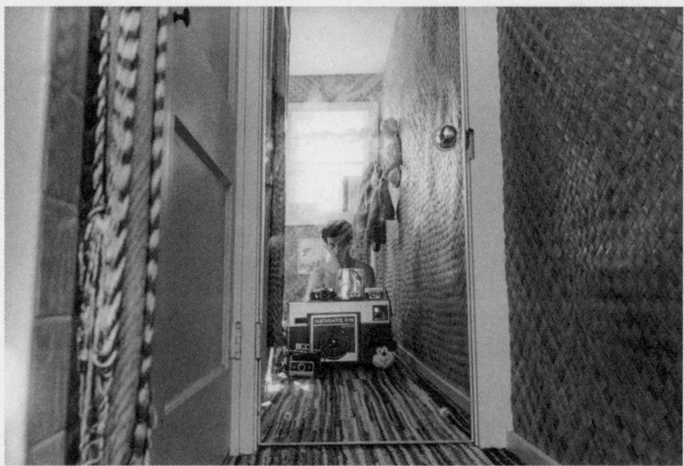

Self-portrait with cameras, New York, c. 1971

June 27. Crown Graphic 4-by-5: Blackamoor, New York [1]
July 1. Crown Graphic 4-by-5: Photographs David McClelland, New York [3]
A Road Trip Journal (published 2008)
July 3. Drives from New York through Easton and Harrisburg, Pa.
July 4. Crown Graphic 4-by-5: Harrisburg [5], Everett [1], and Greensburg [2], Pa.
July 5. Crown Graphic 4-by-5: Pittsburgh, Pa. [2]; Canton [2] and Mansfield [1], Ohio
July 6. Crown Graphic 4-by-5: Lima [2] and Delphos [3], Ohio; Battle Creek [5], Mich. (page 196)
July 7. Crown Graphic 4-by-5: Gaylord, Mich. [9]
July 8. Crown Graphic 4-by-5: Gaylord, along Michigan 123 [3], Paradise [1], Newberry [2], and Manistique [2], Mich. (page 197)
July 9. Crown Graphic 4-by-5: Manistique [4], Norway [2], and Ironwood [1], Mich.; Ashland [9] (page 47), Wis.
July 10. Crown Graphic 4-by-5: Ashland [16], Wis.; Hasselblad 500EL 2¼-by-2¼: Ashland, Wis. [13]
July 11. Mails film to New York. Hasselblad 500EL 2¼-by-2¼: Ashland [2], Wis.; Crown Graphic 4-by-5: Duluth [1] (page 209), Minnesota 210 [2], and Brainerd [1], Minn.
July 12. Crown Graphic 4-by-5: Brainerd [2] and U.S. 10 east of Dilworth [1], Minn.; Fargo [2], Cuba [1], Valley City [1], and Jamestown [1], N.Dak.
July 13. Crown Graphic 4-by-5: Redfield [2], Mt. Vernon [1], and Mitchell [1], S.Dak.; Hasselblad 500EL 2¼-by-2¼: Mitchell [2], S.Dak.
July 14. Crown Graphic 4-by-5: Kadoka [3] and Badlands [5] (page 265), S.Dak.
July 15. Crown Graphic 4-by-5: Custer [2], S.Dak.
July 16. Crown Graphic 4-by-5: Newcastle [1] and Lovell [2], Wyo.
July 17. Crown Graphic 4-by-5: Lovell [1] and Yellowstone National Park [7], Wyo.
July 18. Crown Graphic 4-by-5: Swan Valley [2] and Idaho Falls [1], Idaho
July 19. Crown Graphic 4-by-5: I-15 west of Idaho Falls [1] and Twin Falls [4], Idaho; Ontario [1], Ore.
July 20. Crown Graphic 4-by-5: Bend [4], Ore.; Hasselblad 500EL 2¼-by-2¼: Bend [3], Ore.
July 21. Crown Graphic 4-by-5: U.S. 97 [1] (page 141), Ore., and Weed [2], Calif.
July 22. Crown Graphic 4-by-5: Weed [5] and Sacramento [2], Calif.
July 24. Crown Graphic 4-by-5: Point Lobos [5], Calif.
July 25. Crown Graphic 4-by-5: Big Sur [3], Calif.
July 29. Crown Graphic 4-by-5: Eureka [1], Calif.
July 31. Crown Graphic 4-by-5: Westport [2], Calif.
August 2. Crown Graphic 4-by-5: San Francisco [5]
August 5. Crown Graphic 4-by-5: San Francisco [6]
August 8. Crown Graphic 4-by-5: Wells [1], Nev., and Salt Lake City [3], Utah
August 9. Crown Graphic 4-by-5: U.S. 89 north of Kanab [1] and Kanab [5], Utah
August 10. Crown Graphic 4-by-5: Kanab [3] (page 108), Utah, and Holbrook [9], Ariz.
August 12. Crown Graphic 4-by-5: Albuquerque [2] and Tucumcari [7], N.Mex.
August 14. Crown Graphic 4-by-5: Amarillo [8], Tex.
August 15. Crown Graphic 4-by-5: Amarillo [6], Tex.; Hasselblad 500EL 2¼-by-2¼: Amarillo [4], Tex.
August 16. Crown Graphic 4-by-5: Amarillo [2], Tex.; Hasselblad 500EL 2¼-by-2¼: Amarillo [3], Tex.
August 17. Crown Graphic 4-by-5: Amarillo [14], Tex.; Hasselblad 500EL 2¼-by-2¼: Amarillo [19], Tex.
August 18. Crown Graphic 4-by-5: Amarillo [8] (page 179), Tex. (including of Cyclone Negro, published in "He Knows the Use of Smashes," *The Real World* 1, no. 3, 1974); Hasselblad 500EL 2¼-by-2¼: Amarillo [3], Tex.
August 19. Crown Graphic 4-by-5: Amarillo [3], Tex.
August. Rollei 35mm: Amarillo (pages 31, 36, and 195), Tex.
August 22. Crown Graphic 4-by-5: Harmony [2], Ind.
October 6. Crown Graphic 4-by-5: New York [7]
October 26. Crown Graphic 4-by-5: Palm Beach [7] and West Palm Beach [1], Fla.
October 27. Crown Graphic 4-by-5: Palm Beach [7] and West Palm Beach [9], Fla.
October 28. Crown Graphic 4-by-5: Palm Beach [3], Fla.
November 8. Crown Graphic 4-by-5: New York [1]
November 15. Crown Graphic 4-by-5: Guilford [1], Conn.
Borrows a Calumet 8-by-10 from Weston Naef
November 16. Crown Graphic 4-by-5: Waterford [1], Conn.; Calumet 8-by-10: Old Saybrook [1], Essex [3], and Waterford [2], Conn.
November 17. Crown Graphic 4-by-5: Groton [4], New London [1], and Stonington [1], Conn.; Calumet 8-by-10: New London [3] and Stonington [3], Conn.
November 18. Crown Graphic 4-by-5: Stonington [4], Norwich [2], Andover [1], and Hartford [3], Conn.; Calumet 8-by-10: Hartford [2], Conn.
November 19. Calumet 8-by-10: Waterbury [1], Conn., and Yonkers [1], N.Y.
December 12. Crown Graphic 4-by-5: Riverdale [1], N.Y.
December. Rollei 35mm: Memphis (page 32), Tenn.
December 31. Crown Graphic 4-by-5: West Palm Beach [3], Fla.

1974 January 1. Crown Graphic 4-by-5: Loxahatchee [1], Fla.
January 4. Crown Graphic 4-by-5: Delray Beach [1] and Boca Raton [4], Fla.
January 19. Crown Graphic 4-by-5: Palm Beach [3], Fla.
January 27. Crown Graphic 4-by-5: New York [9]
February 10. Crown Graphic 4-by-5: New York [1]
February 17. Crown Graphic 4-by-5: New York [6]
February 18. Crown Graphic 4-by-5: New York [15]
February 19. Crown Graphic 4-by-5: New York [1]

February 21. Crown Graphic 4-by-5: New York [7] and U.S. 1 [5], N.Y.
February 24. Crown Graphic 4-by-5: New York [12]
March 8. Begins representation with Light Gallery, New York
March 24. Crown Graphic 4-by-5: New York [1]
April 16. Test of Cambo 4-by-5: New York [6]
April 24. Cambo 4-by-5: Union [1] and Plainfield [1], N.J.
April 25. Cambo 4-by-5: Reading [4], Pa., and Washington, D.C. [8]
April 26. Cambo 4-by-5: Washington, D.C. [1]
April 28. Cambo 4-by-5: Front Royal [4], Luray [2], and Harrisonburg [7] (page 262), Va.
April 29. Cambo 4-by-5: Harrisonburg [2], Va.; Fort Seybert [3] (page 87), Bowden [1], Elkins [2], and Buckhannon [2], W.Va.
April 30. Cambo 4-by-5: Weston [8], Clay [3], Nitro [7], and Poca [2], W.Va.
May 1. Cambo 4-by-5: Charleston [2], W.Va.; Grayson [3] (page 260), Owingsville [2], and Louisville [6], Ky.
May 2. Cambo 4-by-5: Brandenburg [3], Ky., and Nashville [7], Tenn.
May 3. Cambo 4-by-5: Nashville [3], Jackson [1], and Brownsville [1], Tenn.
May 4. Cambo 4-by-5: Memphis [5], Tenn., and Sumner (including of William Eggleston) [4], Miss.
May 5. Cambo 4-by-5: Sumner [1], Miss.
May 9. Cambo 4-by-5: New Madrid [2], Mo.
May 10. Cambo 4-by-5: Cairo [9], Ill.
May 11. Cambo 4-by-5: Saint Louis [8], Mo.
May 12. Cambo 4-by-5: Saint Louis [8] (page 255), Mo.
May 13. Cambo 4-by-5: East Saint Louis [2], Ill., and Saint Louis [3], Mo.
May 14. Cambo 4-by-5: French Lick [1], Ind.
May 15. Cambo 4-by-5: Cincinnati [5], Ohio
May 16. Cambo 4-by-5: Parkersburg [3] (page 207), W.Va.
May 17. Cambo 4-by-5: Parkersburg [1] and Sun Valley [2], W.Va.
May 18. Cambo 4-by-5: Martinsburg [4], W.Va.
May 27. Cambo 4-by-5: New York [2]
Again borrows a Calumet 8-by-10 from Weston Naef
June 15. Calumet 8-by-10: New York [1]
June 19. Calumet 8-by-10: Easton [2], Pa.
June 20. Calumet 8-by-10: Easton [7] (page 259) and Bethlehem [1], Pa.
June 21. Calumet 8-by-10: Phillipsburg [4], N.J., and Philadelphia [7] (page 254)
June 22. Calumet 8-by-10: Phillipsburg [3], N.J.; Bethlehem [2] and Easton [2], Pa.
June 23. Calumet 8-by-10: New York [1]
June 24. Calumet 8-by-10: New York [4]
July 11. Arca Swiss 8-by-10: Mt. Kisco [1], N.Y.
July 12. Arca Swiss 8-by-10: Danbury [3], Conn., and Great Barrington [1], Mass.
July 13. Arca Swiss 8-by-10: Great Barrington [1], Lenox [1], Pittsfield [4], and North Adams [3] (page 261), Mass.
July 14. Arca Swiss 8-by-10: North Adams [4] and Florida [6], Mass.
July 15. Arca Swiss 8-by-10: Florida [2], Charlemont [2], and Greenfield [5] (page 167), Mass.
July 16. Arca Swiss 8-by-10: Winchester [2], Keene [1], Henniker [1], and Concord [3], N.H.; Ogunquit [6] (page 61), Maine; Leica M2 35mm: unknown city (page 203), N.H.
July 17. Arca Swiss 8-by-10: Ogunquit [1], Moody [2], Arundel [3], and Rockland [5], Maine
July 18. Arca Swiss 8-by-10: Castine [4] (page 65), Maine
July 20. Arca Swiss 8-by-10: Castine [2] and Orono [1], Maine
July 22. Arca Swiss 8-by-10: Blue Hill [1], Maine
July 23. Arca Swiss 8-by-10: South Blue Hill [1], Brooklin [2], Rockport [2], and Camden [2], Maine
July 24. Arca Swiss 8-by-10: Camden [1], Searsport [1], and Blue Hill [2], Maine
July 25. Arca Swiss 8-by-10: Blue Hill [3], Deer Isle [3], Stonington [1], and Sedgwick [1], Maine
July 26. Arca Swiss 8-by-10: Blue Hill [1], Maine
July 28. Arca Swiss 8-by-10: Blue Hill [1], Maine
July 29. Arca Swiss 8-by-10: Blue Hill (including of Weston Naef) [4], Maine
July 30. Arca Swiss 8-by-10: Farmington [1] and Mexico [2], Maine; Jefferson [3], N.H.; Barre [3], Vt.
July 31. Arca Swiss 8-by-10: Graniteville [3], Vt.; Childwold [1], Natural Bridge [2], and Watertown [4], N.Y.
August 1. Arca Swiss 8-by-10: Watertown [3], N.Y.
August 9. Arca Swiss 8-by-10: Hamilton [1], Ont., Canada
August 10. Arca Swiss 8-by-10: Hamilton [1], Ont., Canada
August 11. Arca Swiss 8-by-10: Parry Sound [1], Ont., Canada
August 12. Arca Swiss 8-by-10: Sudbury [4], Ont., Canada
August 13. Arca Swiss 8-by-10: Nairn Center [1] and Sault Ste. Marie [5], Ont., Canada
August 14. Arca Swiss 8-by-10: Wawa [1] and Terrace Bay [6], Ont., Canada
August 15. Arca Swiss 8-by-10: Dryden [2], Minnitaki [1], and Kenora [6], Ont., Canada
August 16. Arca Swiss 8-by-10: Kenora [3], Ont.; Winnipeg [4] and Brandon [4], Man., Canada
August 17. Arca Swiss 8-by-10: Regina [12], Sask., Canada
August 18. Arca Swiss 8-by-10: Gull Lake [4], Sask., and Medicine Hat [3], Alb., Canada
August 20. Arca Swiss 8-by-10: Banff [3] and Lake Louise [1], Alb., Canada
August 21. Arca Swiss 8-by-10: Coleman [1] and Bellevue [1] (page 43), Alb., Canada
August 22. Arca Swiss 8-by-10: Waterton Park [2], Alb., Canada; St. Mary [1] and Kalispell [6] (page 258), Mont.
August 23. Arca Swiss 8-by-10: Libby [2], Mont., and Sandpoint [3], Idaho
August 24. Arca Swiss 8-by-10: Milan [1] and Spokane [2], Wash.

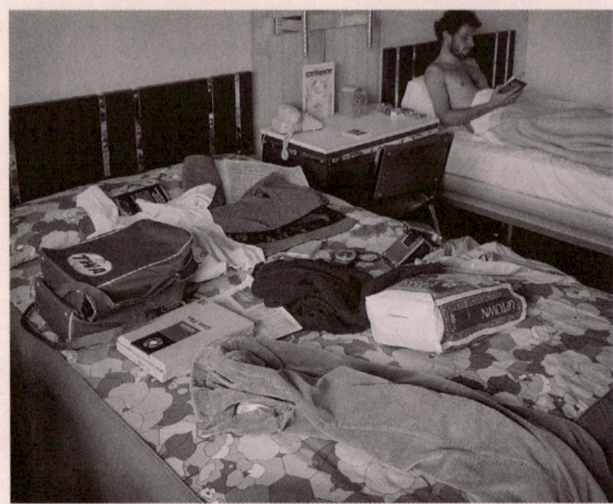

Self-portrait, Holiday Inn, Miami, Florida, November 12, 1977

August 25. Arca Swiss 8-by-10: Spokane [5] (page 255), Wash., and Post Falls [3] (page 266), Idaho

August 27. Arca Swiss 8-by-10: Seattle [3]

August 28. Arca Swiss 8-by-10: Port Angeles [2] and Forks [3], Wash.

August 31. Arca Swiss 8-by-10: Cape Perpetua [3] and Coos Bay [8] (page 180), Ore.

September 1. Arca Swiss 8-by-10: Crescent City [5], Calif.

September 2. Arca Swiss 8-by-10: Eureka [2] and Garberville [3], Calif.

September 4. Arca Swiss 8-by-10: Cazapero [18], Monte Rio [3], Guerneville [27], Forestville [2], Sebastopol [4], and Santa Rosa [7], Calif.

September 5. Arca Swiss 8-by-10: Muir Woods National Monument [4] and San Francisco [4], Calif. (published in "The Story of a Day. Thursday, September 5, 1974," *Life Special Report: One Day in the Life of America*, 1974)

September 6. Arca Swiss 8-by-10: San Francisco [1]

September 7. Arca Swiss 8-by-10: Muir Beach [1], Calif.

September 9. Arca Swiss 8-by-10: Beverly Hills [1]

September 10. Arca Swiss 8-by-10: Beverly Hills [2]

September 23. Arca Swiss 8-by-10: Yuma [2], Ariz.

September 24. Arca Swiss 8-by-10: El Paso [2], Tex.

September 26. Arca Swiss 8-by-10: Roswell [2] and Elida [2], N.Mex.

September 27. Arca Swiss 8-by-10: Amarillo [4] (page 180), Tex.

September 28. Arca Swiss 8-by-10: Amarillo [2], Tex.

September 29. Arca Swiss 8-by-10: Amarillo [3], Tex.

September 30. Arca Swiss 8-by-10: Amarillo [2], Tex.

October 2. Arca Swiss 8-by-10: Amarillo [9] (page 213), Tex.

October 4. Arca Swiss 8-by-10: Shamrock [1], Tex.

October 5. Arca Swiss 8-by-10: Little Rock [3], Ark.

October 7. Arca Swiss 8-by-10: Memphis [2], Tenn.

October 28. Arca Swiss 8-by-10: Queens [5], N.Y.

November–December. Stereo Realist: New York (pages 205 and 218–21)

November 30. Arca Swiss 8-by-10: New York [8]

December 17. Arca Swiss 8-by-10: New York (including of Tony Hiss) [8]

December 19. Arca Swiss 8-by-10: Metropolitan Museum of Art [8], New York

1975 Moves to 47 East 19th Street, New York

January 17. Cambo 4-by-5: New York [12]

January 26. Arca Swiss 8-by-10: New York [7]

February 2. Arca Swiss 8-by-10: New York [2]

February 15. Arca Swiss 8-by-10: Amarillo [2], Tex.

February 16. Arca Swiss 8-by-10: Michael Marsh and Sandy Kirkland's wedding [4], Amarillo, Tex.

February 19. Arca Swiss 8-by-10: Hobbs [6] (page 235) and Carlsbad [4], N.Mex.

February 20. Arca Swiss 8-by-10: Van Horn [4] and Marfa [3], Tex.

February 21. Arca Swiss 8-by-10: Presidio [1] (page 168), Tex.; Ojinaga, Chihuahua, Mexico [10]

April 22. Arca Swiss 8-by-10: Queens [2], North Hempstead [2], Hempstead [2], and Smithtown [4], N.Y.

May 3. Arca Swiss 8-by-10: New York [2]

May 15. Cambo 4-by-5: Long Island [7], N.Y.

May 31. Arca Swiss 8-by-10: Saint Louis [10] (page 179), Mo.

Commission by Venturi & Rauch for *Signs of Life: Symbols in the American City* (pages 49 and 216–17)

June 10. Leica 35mm: Los Angeles, Beverly Hills, and Hollywood

June 11. Arca Swiss 8-by-10: Los Angeles [2]; Leica 35mm: Los Angeles and Santa Monica, Calif.

June 12. Leica 35mm: Disneyland, Anaheim, Long Beach, Chinatown, and Los Angeles, Calif.

June 13. Arca Swiss 8-by-10: Hollywood [3]; Leica 35mm: Hollywood

June 14. Arca Swiss 8-by-10: Hollywood [3]; Leica 35mm: Beverly Hills and Hollywood

June 15. Leica 35mm: Beverly Hills and Los Angeles

June 16. Arca Swiss 8-by-10: Los Angeles [1]; Leica 35mm: Los Angeles and Burbank, Calif.

June 17. Leica 35mm: Los Angeles

June 18. Leica 35mm: Forest Lawn and Los Angeles, Calif.

June 19. Arca Swiss 8-by-10: Los Angeles [3]; Leica 35mm: Los Angeles

June 20. Arca Swiss 8-by-10: Los Angeles [1]; Leica 35mm: Los Angeles

June 21. Arca Swiss 8-by-10: Los Angeles [5] (page 53); Leica 35mm: Hollywood and Los Angeles

June 22. Arca Swiss 8-by-10: Los Angeles [2] (page 269); Leica 35mm: Los Angeles

June 23. Arca Swiss 8-by-10: San Luis Obispo [1], Calif.; Leica 35mm: Santa Barbara and CA-1, Calif.

June 24. Arca Swiss 8-by-10: Carmel [1], Calif.; Leica 35mm: Castroville, CA-1, Pacifica, and San Francisco, Calif.

June 25. Arca Swiss 8-by-10: San Francisco [7]; Leica 35mm: San Francisco

June 26. Arca Swiss 8-by-10: San Francisco [2]; Leica 35mm: San Francisco

June 27. Leica 35mm: Marin County, Calif.

June 28. Leica 35mm: San Francisco and Alameda, Calif.

June 30. Leica 35mm: Las Vegas, Nev.

July 1. Leica 35mm: Las Vegas, Nev.

July 2. Arca Swiss 8-by-10: Kingman [5] (page 257), Ariz.; Leica 35mm: Las Vegas, Nev., and Boulder City, Ariz.

July 3. Leica 35mm: Lake Havasu City, Wittman, Sun City, and Phoenix, Ariz.

July 4. Leica 35mm: Tucson, Ariz.

July 5. Arca Swiss 8-by-10: El Paso [2] (page 91), Tex.; Leica 35mm: Juarez and El Paso, Tex.

July 6. Leica 35mm: Truth or Consequences, N.Mex.

July 7. Leica 35mm: Albuquerque, N.Mex.

July 8. Leica 35mm: Santa Fe, N.Mex.

July 9. Arca Swiss 8-by-10: Chimayo [6], N.Mex.; Leica 35mm: Chimayo, Las Vegas, and Tucumcari, N.Mex.

July 12. Leica 35mm: Amarillo, Tex.

July 13. Arca Swiss 8-by-10: Amarillo [2], Tex.; Leica 35mm: Amarillo, Tex.

July 15. Arca Swiss 8-by-10: Amarillo [2], Tex.; Leica 35mm: Amarillo, Brownwood, and "other Texas towns," Tex.

July 18. Leica 35mm: Austin and Houston, Tex.

July 19. Arca Swiss 8-by-10: Galveston [8], Tex.; Leica 35mm: Galveston, Tex.

July 20. Arca Swiss 8-by-10: Galveston [9], Tex.; Leica 35mm: Galveston, Tex.

July 21. Leica 35mm: Cameron, Creole, and New Orleans, La.

July 24. Arca Swiss 8-by-10: New Orleans [2]; Leica 35mm: Gulf Coast, La.

July 25. Leica 35mm: Panama City and Clearwater, Fla.

July 26. Leica 35mm: Clearwater and Naples, Fla.

July 27. Leica 35mm: Naples, Coral Gables, and Miami, Fla.

July 28. Arca Swiss 8-by-10: Miami [4], Fla.; Leica 35mm: Miami, Fla.

July 29. Leica 35mm: Fort Lauderdale, Fla.

July 30. Arca Swiss 8-by-10: Del Ray Beach [2] and West Palm Beach [2], Fla.; Leica 35mm: Fort Lauderdale, Fla.

July 31. Arca Swiss 8-by-10: Palm Beach [2], Fla.; Leica 35mm: Palm Beach, Fla.

August 1. Arca Swiss 8-by-10: Kennedy Space Center [3], Fla.; Leica 35mm: Kennedy Space Center, Saint Augustine, and Jacksonville, Fla.
August 3. Arca Swiss 8-by-10: Charleston [8] (pages 49 and 259), S.C.; Leica 35mm: Savannah, Ga., and Charleston, S.C.
August 4. Arca Swiss 8-by-10: Charleston [4], S.C.; Leica 35mm: Charleston and Myrtle Beach, S.C.
August 5. Arca Swiss 8-by-10: Richmond [8], Va.
September 30. Unknown 8-by-10: Princeton [4], N.J.
October 4. Unknown 8-by-10: Kingston [2], N.Y.
October 5. Unknown 8-by-10: Marbletown [2] and Accord [2], N.Y.
October 6. Unknown 8-by-10: New York [6]
October 13. Unknown 8-by-10: Princeton [1], New Brunswick [2], and Levittown [1], N.J.
October 14. Unknown 8-by-10: Philadelphia [5]
Commission by Paul Walter
October 21. Unknown 8-by-10: Thermo Electric [14], Saddle Brook, N.J.
October 26. Unknown 8-by-10: Dretzin House [6], Navasky House [1], and Harnick House [2], Hillsdale, N.Y.
October 28. Unknown 8-by-10: Philadelphia [4]
November 5: Unknown 8-by-10: Philadelphia [4]
Commission by Paul Walter
November 11: Unknown 8-by-10: Thermo Electric [12], Saddle Brook, N.J.
November 15: Unknown 8-by-10: New York [4]

1976 Leica 35mm: New York (published in "The Rest of New York," *The Real World* 7, July/August 1976, page 48)
January 6. Unknown 8-by-10: State University of New York [10], Purchase, N.Y.
Commission by Joseph E. Seagram & Sons, Inc., New York, for "The County Courthouse" (published in *Court House: A Photographic Document*, 1978, page 85)
January 21. Deardorff 8-by-10: College Park [1], Md., and Harrisonburg [2], Va.
January 22. Deardorff 8-by-10: Harrisonburg [3] and Staunton [3], Va.
January 23. Deardorff 8-by-10: Chatham [3], Va.; Greensboro [2] and Lexington [3], N.C.
January 24. Deardorff 8-by-10: Gastonia [1], N.C., and Anderson [1], S.C.
January 25. Deardorff 8-by-10: Anderson [7], S.C.
January 28. Deardorff 8-by-10: Athens [3], Watkinsville [2], Greensboro [8] (page 85), Eatonton [1], Milledgeville [2], and Sandersville [2], Ga.
January 29. Deardorff 8-by-10: Lexington [1], Carnesville [5] (page 268), and Lawrenceville [6], Ga.; Arca Swiss 8-by-10 with a 5-by-7 back: Lexington [2], Ga.
January 30. Deardorff 8-by-10: Atlanta [4], Decatur [2], Conyers [2], Jackson [1], and Zebulon [3], Ga.
January 31. Deardorff 8-by-10: Ogelthorpe [2] and Ludowich [1], Ga.
February 2. Deardorff 8-by-10: Brunswick [1], Woodbine [4], and Tifton [2], Ga.
February 3. Deardorff 8-by-10: Moultrie [2], Thomasville [6], Cairo [2], and Bainbridge [4], Ga.; Tallahassee [2], Fla.
February 4. Deardorff 8-by-10: Crawfordville [6], Apalachicola [3] (page 267), and Panama City [3], Fla.
February 5. Deardorff 8-by-10: Bonifay [2] and Marianna [2], Fla.; Dothan [2], Ala.
February 7. Deardorff 8-by-10: Ozark [2], Enterprise [1], and Elba [2], Ala.; De Funiak Springs [1] and Crestview [4], Fla.; Arca Swiss 8-by-10 with a 5-by-7 back: Elba [2], Ala.
February 8. Deardorff 8-by-10: Frisco City [3], Monroeville [2], and Camden [6], Ala.
February 9. Deardorff 8-by-10: Selma [6], Hayneville [5], and Marion [3], Ala.
February 10. Deardorff 8-by-10: Selma [1], Wetumpka [3], Union Springs [4], and Seale [2], Ala.; Arca Swiss 8-by-10 with a 5-by-7 back: Wetumpka [2], Ala.
February 12. Deardorff 8-by-10: Heflin [6], Lafayette [1], and Opelika [2], Ala.; Arca Swiss 8-by-10 with a 5-by-7 back: Opelika [4], Ala.
February 13. Deardorff 8-by-10: Linden [2] and Livingston [3], Ala.
February 14. Deardorff 8-by-10: Sprott [1], Greensboro [1], Eutaw [5], and Carrolton [2], Ala.; Arca Swiss 8-by-10 with a 5-by-7 back: Eutaw [2], Ala.
February 15. Deardorff 8-by-10: Columbiana [3] and Taladega [2], Ala.
February 16. Deardorff 8-by-10: Cullman [1] and Somerville [5], Ala.
February 17. Deardorff 8-by-10: Decatur [2], Huntsville [2], Florence [1], and Tuscumbia [1], Ala.
February 19. Deardorff 8-by-10: Laurens [2] and Newberry [6], S.C.
February 20. Deardorff 8-by-10: Georgetown [3], S.C.
February 21. Deardorff 8-by-10: Dillon [1], S.C., and Lumberton [2], N.C.
February 23. Deardorff 8-by-10: Oxford [4], N.C.; Lunenburg [1], Amelia [5], and Powhatan [2], Va.
February 25. Deardorff 8-by-10: Silver Spring [2] and Ellicott City [2], Md.
February 26. Deardorff 8-by-10: Washington, D.C. [1]; Leesburg [4] and Berryville [2], Va.
February 27. Deardorff 8-by-10: Winchester [2], Va.; Charles Town [2], Martinsburg [3], and Romney [4] (page 85), W.Va.; Cumberland [1], Md.; Arca Swiss 8-by-10 with a 5-by-7 back: Charles Town [2], W.Va.
February 28. Deardorff 8-by-10: Frederick [2], Md.; Arca Swiss 8-by-10 with a 5-by-7 back: Frederick [2], Md.
February 29. Deardorff 8-by-10: Towson [2] and Elkton [2], Md.; Arca Swiss 8-by-10 with a 5-by-7 back: Towson [2], Md.
March 1. Deardorff 8-by-10: Jersey City [1] and Newark [1], N.J.
March 2. Deardorff 8-by-10: Newark [5], N.J.
March 20. Deardorff 8-by-10: Self-portrait, New York
April 6. Deardorff 8-by-10: Purchase [1] and Katonah [10], N.Y.; Arca Swiss 8-by-10 with a 5-by-7 back: Katonah [2], N.Y.
April 7. Deardorff 8-by-10: New York [4]
April 18. Deardorff 8-by-10: New York [2]
Commission by the Polaroid Corporation to test 8-by-10 Polaroid instant film (published in *Faces and Facades*, 1977)
April–May. Sinar 8-by-10: Switzerland, Italy, and France
April–May. Leica M2 35mm: Italy and France
May 26. Deardorff 8-by-10: Renwick Gallery [1], Washington, D.C.
Commission by the Fort Worth Art Museum, funded by the National Endowment for the Arts
June 2. Deardorff 8-by-10: Fort Worth [4], Tex.
June 3. Deardorff 8-by-10: Fort Worth [12] (page 267), Tex.
June 4. Deardorff 8-by-10: Fort Worth [2] and Dallas [4], Tex.
June 5. Deardorff 8-by-10: Dallas [3], Tex.
June 10. Deardorff 8-by-10: Fort Worth [1], Tex.
June 11. Deardorff 8-by-10: Fort Worth [11], Tex.
June 12. Deardorff 8-by-10: Dallas [7], Tex.
June 13. Deardorff 8-by-10: Fort Worth [13], Tex.
June 14. Deardorff 8-by-10: Fort Worth [9], Tex.
June 15. Deardorff 8-by-10: Fort Worth [13], Tex.
June 16. Deardorff 8-by-10: Fort Worth [8], Grand Prairie [2], and Dallas [5], Tex.
June 17. Deardorff 8-by-10: Fort Worth [10], Tex.
June 18. Deardorff 8-by-10: Fort Worth [5], Tex.
June 28. Deardorff 8-by-10: *Signs of Life: Symbols in the American City* [7] (page 215), Renwick Gallery, Washington, D.C.; Pennsylvania Academy of Art [8] and Philadelphia Museum of Art [6], Philadelphia
August 4. Deardorff 8-by-10: Philadelphia Naval Base [5] and Philadelphia [4]

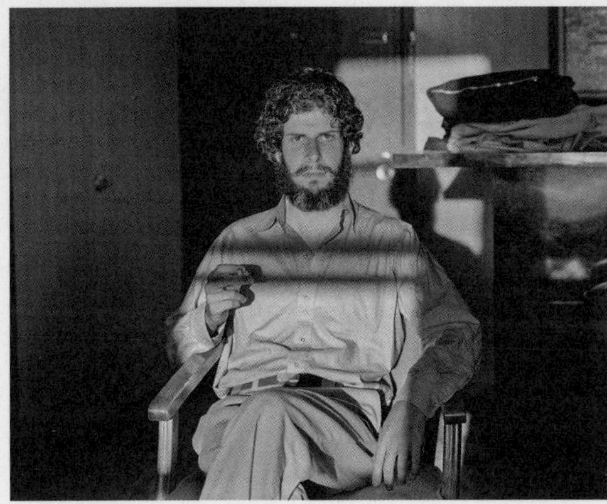

Stephen Shore, Fort Lauderdale, Florida, March 13, 1978. Photograph by Nicholas Nixon

August 9. Deardorff 8-by-10: Whitney Museum of American Art (including of *200 Years of American Sculpture*, page 193) [16], New York
August 15. Deardorff 8-by-10: Pawling [8], N.Y.
August 16. Deardorff 8-by-10: Whitney Museum of American Art (including of *200 Years of American Sculpture*) [18], New York
August 20. Deardorff 8-by-10: Photographs Weston Naef's family [4], New York
September 3. Deardorff 8-by-10: State College [1], Pa.
September 7. Deardorff 8-by-10: New York [2]
September 13. Deardorff 8-by-10: North Bergen [3], N.J.
September 22. Deardorff 8-by-10: New York (including of Sandy Kirkland) [11]
September 24. Deardorff 8-by-10: New York [2]
September 25. Deardorff 8-by-10: Hazleton [4], Pa.
October 18. Deardorff 8-by-10: Maywood [3], N.J.
October 19. Deardorff 8-by-10: Queens [3], N.Y.
November 2. Deardorff 8-by-10: New York (including of Sandy Kirkland) [2]
November 10. Deardorff 8-by-10: Peters Valley [1], N.J.
November 11. Deardorff 8-by-10: Peters Valley [4], N.J., and Milford [7], Pa.
December 6. Deardorff 8-by-10: Tucson [8] (page 260), Ariz.
December 7. Deardorff 8-by-10: Tucson [10], Ariz.
December 8. Deardorff 8-by-10: I-10 [1], Ariz., and Desert Center [2], Calif.
December 10. Deardorff 8-by-10: Berkeley [5], Calif.
December 11. Deardorff 8-by-10: Berkeley [3], Calif.
December 13. Deardorff 8-by-10: Lone Pine [1], Panamint Springs [3], and Death Valley [3], Calif.; Las Vegas, Nev. [1]
December 14. Deardorff 8-by-10: Las Vegas [2], Nev., and Wikieup [3] (page 272), Ariz.
December 15. Deardorff 8-by-10: Tucson [7], Ariz.
December 17. Deardorff 8-by-10: Tucson [8], Ariz.
December 19. Deardorff 8-by-10: Tucson [11], Ariz.

1977 4-by-5 Cambo: Hunan Restaurant, San Francisco (published in ***Henry Chung's Hunan Style Chinese Cookbook***, 1978)
Commission by ***DU*** magazine (published in "New York, Februar 1977," ***DU***, September 1977)
March 1. Leica M2 35mm: Queens (page 207), N.Y.
May. Leica M2 35mm: Las Vegas, Nev.
July 3. Deardorff 8-by-10: Santa Fe [1], N.Mex.
July 4. Deardorff 8-by-10: Santa Fe [1], N.Mex.
July 6. Deardorff 8-by-10: Panguitch [2], Utah
July 22. Cambo 4-by-5: Brooklyn [4], N.Y.
July 23. Cambo 4-by-5: New York [8]
August 8. Deardorff 8-by-10: East Hampton [1], N.Y.
August 11. Deardorff 8-by-10: Ithaca [9], N.Y.
August 12. Deardorff 8-by-10: Rochester [3] and Penfield [2], N.Y.
August 14. Cambo 4-by-5: Photographs Ginger Shore, New York [2]
August 15. Deardorff 8-by-10: New York [5]
August 18. Deardorff 8-by-10: Tampa, Fla.
September 3. Deardorff 8-by-10: New York (including of Weston Naef) [5]
Commission by the Metropolitan Museum of Art (published in "In Monet's Gardens," ***New York Times Magazine***, April 2, 1978, page 74, and ***Monet's House and Garden at Giverny***, a portfolio of fourteen prints, Metropolitan Museum of Art, 1978)
September 23. Deardorff 8-by-10: Giverny [20] (pages 76 and 114), France
September 24. Deardorff 8-by-10: Giverny [2] (pages 76 and 114), France
September 26. Deardorff 8-by-10: Giverny [18] (pages 76 and 114), France
September 30. Deardorff 8-by-10: Giverny [8] (pages 76 and 114) and Vernon [2], France
October 18. Deardorff 8-by-10: New York [6]
Commission by ***Fortune*** magazine (published in "Hard Times Come to Steeltown," ***Fortune***, December 1977, page 72)
October 24. Cambo 4-by-5: Lackawanna [28] (page 87), Pa.
October 25. Cambo 4-by-5: Lackawanna [28], Pa., and South Buffalo [8], N.Y.
October 26. Cambo 4-by-5: South Buffalo [12], N.Y., and Lackawanna [8], Pa.
October 27. Cambo 4-by-5: Boardman [1], Struthers [13] (pages 73, 143, and 179), Campbell [5], and Austintown [9], Ohio
October 28. Cambo 4-by-5: Austintown [13], Struthers [4], and Campbell [10] (page 178), Ohio
October 29. Cambo 4-by-5: Boardman [1], Struthers [4], Youngstown [14], and Lowellville [2], Ohio
October 30. Cambo 4-by-5: Johnstown [9], Pa.
November 5. Deardorff 8-by-10: A1A south of Jacksonville Beach [1], Fla.
November 7. Deardorff 8-by-10: Orlando [3] and Palm Beach [2], Fla.
November 8. Deardorff 8-by-10: Palm Beach [7] (page 106) and West Palm Beach [7], Fla.
November 9. Deardorff 8-by-10: West Palm Beach [10], Lake Worth [1], and Boynton Beach [1], Fla.
November 10. Deardorff 8-by-10: Key Largo [9], Grassy Key [4], and Big Pine Key [4], Fla.
November 11. Deardorff 8-by-10: Vaca Key [2], Key Largo [6] (page 199), and Perrine [2], Fla.
November 12. Deardorff 8-by-10: Miami [17] (page 119), Fla.
November 13. Deardorff 8-by-10: Miami Beach [16] (page 264) and Miami [4], Fla.
November 14. Deardorff 8-by-10: West Palm Beach [5] and Belle Glade [6] (page 273), Fla.; Polaroid SX-70: Belle Glade, Fla.
November 15. Deardorff 8-by-10: South Bay [8], Moore Haven [3] (page 263), Palmdale [3] (page 271), Childs [1], and Winter Haven [3], Fla.

November 16. Deardorff 8-by-10: Winter Haven [1] and Cypress Gardens [13], Fla.
November 17. Deardorff 8-by-10: Tampa [16], Fla.; Polaroid SX-70: Tampa, Fla.
November 18. Deardorff 8-by-10: Tampa [3], Gainesville [3], and Starke [4], Fla.
November 20. Deardorff 8-by-10: Fayetteville [10], N.C.
December 17. Deardorff 8-by-10: New York [2]

1978 Commission by AT&T (published in "Steinbrenner's Yanks," *New York Times Magazine*, April 9, 1978, page 74)
February 26. Deardorff 8-by-10: Fort Lauderdale [11], Fla.
February 27. Deardorff 8-by-10: Fort Lauderdale [26], Fla.
February 28. Deardorff 8-by-10: Fort Lauderdale [9], Fla.
March 1. Deardorff 8-by-10: Fort Lauderdale [17] (page 50), Fla.
March 2. Deardorff 8-by-10: Fort Lauderdale [19], Fla.
March 3. Deardorff 8-by-10: Fort Lauderdale [10], Fla.
March 4. Deardorff 8-by-10: Fort Lauderdale [3], Fla.
March 5. Deardorff 8-by-10: Fort Lauderdale [23] (page 50), Fla.
March 6. Deardorff 8-by-10: Fort Lauderdale [18], Fla.
March 7. Deardorff 8-by-10: Fort Lauderdale [10], Fla.
March 8. Deardorff 8-by-10: Fort Lauderdale [16], Fla.
March 11. Deardorff 8-by-10: Fort Lauderdale [24], Fla.
March 12. Deardorff 8-by-10: Miami [13], Fla.
March 13. Deardorff 8-by-10: Fort Lauderdale (including of Nicholas Nixon) [7], Fla.
March 14. Deardorff 8-by-10: West Palm Beach [17], Fla.
March 15. Deardorff 8-by-10: Fort Lauderdale [11], Fla.
June 20. Deardorff 8-by-10: Basalt [4], Colo.
June 21. Deardorff 8-by-10: Aspen [10], Colo.
June 23. Deardorff 8-by-10: Arches National Park [4], Moab, and Monticello [2], Utah
June 24. Deardorff 8-by-10: Glen Canyon National Recreation Area [2], Utah
June 25. Deardorff 8-by-10: Panguitch [5], Utah
Commission by the *American Institute of Architects Journal* (published in "Selling Fast Food in a More Subdued Setting," July 1978)
June 26. Deardorff 8-by-10: Las Vegas [1], Nev.; Cambo 4-by-5: Las Vegas [17], Nev.
June 27. Cambo 4-by-5: Las Vegas [16], Nev.; Deardorff 8-by-10: Las Vegas [2], Nev.
June 28. Cambo 4-by-5: Las Vegas [16], Nev.
June. Leica M2 35mm: Las Vegas, Nev.
July 3. Deardorff 8-by-10: Amarillo [1], Tex.
July 4. Deardorff 8-by-10: Clarendon [8], Tex.
August 15. Cambo 4-by-5: Frick Collection [26], New York
August 27. Deardorff 8-by-10: Nantucket [4], Mass.
August 28. Deardorff 8-by-10: Nantucket [2], Mass.
August 29. Deardorff 8-by-10: Nantucket [2], Mass.
August 30. Deardorff 8-by-10: Nantucket [2], Mass.

1979 February 16. Renews contract with Light Gallery
Commission by the Library of Congress
May. Cambo 4-by-5: Washington, D.C.
Commission by Geo magazine
June–July. Leica M2 35mm and Leica M3 35mm: Fairfield County (pages 71, 77, and 208), Conn.
Commission by Fuji Film to use 8-by-10 Fujicolor film and Fujinon lenses
July 28. Deardorff 8-by-10: Denver [1], Colo.
July 29. Deardorff 8-by-10: Aspen [6], Colo.
July 30. Deardorff 8-by-10: Aspen 10], Colo.
August 4. Deardorff 8-by-10: Tonopah [4], Nev.
August 5. Deardorff 8-by-10: Mammoth Lakes [6], Calif.

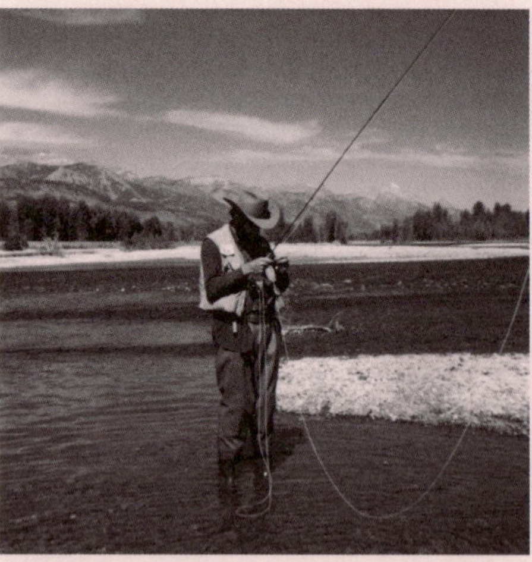

Stephen Shore, Snake River, Jackson, Wyoming, 1979. Photograph by Ginger Shore

August 6. Deardorff 8-by-10: Mammoth Lakes [10], Calif.
August 9. Deardorff 8-by-10: Mammoth Lakes [4], Calif.
August 13. Deardorff 8-by-10: Yosemite National Park [10] (page 153), Calif.
September 2. Deardorff 8-by-10: Jackson [10] (page 142), Wyo.
September 12. Deardorff 8-by-10: West Yellowstone [9], Mont.
September 14. Deardorff 8-by-10: Cameron [6], Mont.
September 18. Deardorff 8-by-10: Wise River [3] (page 270), Mont.
September 20. Deardorff 8-by-10: Wise River [1], Mont.
September 21. Deardorff 8-by-10: Wise River [1], Mont.
September 23. Deardorff 8-by-10: Livingston [5], Mont.
Fall. Moves to 3109 Lewiston Ave, Berkeley, Calif.

1980 Spring. Special Fellowship from the National Endowment for the Arts at the American Academy in Rome
June 22. Marries Ginger in Berkeley, Calif.
December. Moves to 5075 Jackson Creek Road, Bozeman, Mont.

1981 January 12. Deardorff 8-by-10: Livingston [4], Mont.
January 16. Deardorff 8-by-10: Bozeman [6] (page 268), Mont.
January 22. Deardorff 8-by-10: Bozeman [10], Mont.
April 17. Deardorff 8-by-10: Bozeman [1], Mont.
April 18. Deardorff 8-by-10: Bozeman [9] (page 138), Mont.
Commission by Rastar Films to photograph the set of the film *Annie* (published in *Annie on Camera*, 1982, page 75)
August 10–14. Deardorff 8-by-10: Burbank (pages 71 and 93), Calif.
Fall. Commission by the Wallace Foundation to photograph Monet's gardens at Giverny (published in *Monet's Garden*, a portfolio of seven prints, QED Editions, 1984)
October 28. Deardorff 8-by-10: Bozeman [9], Mont.
October 31. Deardorff 8-by-10: Child [4], Mont.

1982 Moves to 1 Cricket Lane, Rhinebeck, N.Y.
January 29. Deardorff 8-by-10: San Clemente [2], Calif.

February 2. Deardorff 8-by-10: Tucson [8], Ariz.
Spring. Commission by the Wallace Foundation to photograph Monet's gardens at Giverny (published in *Monet's Garden*, a portfolio of seven prints, QED Editions, 1984)
July 10. Deardorff 8-by-10: Gallatin County [31] (page 111), Mont.
July 17. Deardorff 8-by-10: Gallatin County [19], Mont.
September. Becomes Director of the Photography Program at Bard College, Annandale-on-Hudson, N.Y.

1983 January 10. Deardorff 8-by-10: Victoria County [3] and Duval County [4], Tex.
January 12. Deardorff 8-by-10: Brewster County [2], Jeff Davis County [4], and Davis Mountain State Park [5], Tex.
January 13. Deardorff 8-by-10: Presidio County [19], Tex.
January 14. Deardorff 8-by-10: Brewster County [2], Tex.
January 15. Deardorff 8-by-10: Big Bend National Park [15], Tex.
January 16. Deardorff 8-by-10: Big Bend National Park [2], Tex.
January 19. Deardorff 8-by-10: Midland County [1] and Conco County [1], Tex.
January 24. Deardorff 8-by-10: Savannah [29], Ga.
January 25. Deardorff 8-by-10: Savannah [22], Ga.
June 6. Deardorff 8-by-10: Bel Air (page 180), Md.
July 6. Deardorff 8-by-10: Gallatin County [17], Mont.
July 19. Deardorff 8-by-10: Gallatin County [3], Mont.
July 27. Deardorff 8-by-10: Flying D Ranch [2], Gallatin County, Mont.
August 2. Deardorff 8-by-10: Flying D Ranch [9] (page 140), Gallatin County, Mont.
August 10. Deardorff 8-by-10: Gallatin County [9], Mont.
August 29. Deardorff 8-by-10: Gallatin County [10], Mont.

1984 Moves to 144 Kripplebush Road, Stone Ridge, N.Y.
January 1. Cambo 4-by-5: New York (published in *Architectural Digest*)
Commission by the Wallace Foundation for "Scenic Hudson" (upstate New York images through 1986)
March 10. Deardorff 8-by-10: Columbia County [2] and Dutchess County [1], N.Y.
March 22. Deardorff 8-by-10: Ulster County [4] (page 137), N.Y.
March 26. Deardorff 8-by-10: Ulster County [2], N.Y.
June 20. Deardorff 8-by-10: Milton [4] and subdivision outside Marlboro [6], N.Y.
June 21. Deardorff 8-by-10: Marlboro [6] and Newburgh [4], N.Y.
July 13. Deardorff 8-by-10: The Rondout, Kingston [10], N.Y.
July 16. Deardorff 8-by-10: Cheviot [4], N.Y.
August 31. Deardorff 8-by-10: Kripplebush [9], N.Y.
September 1. Deardorff 8-by-10: Cornwall-on-Hudson [10], N.Y.
Commission by the Temporary State Commission on the Restoration of the Capitol (published in *The Capitol in Albany*, 1986)
September 7. Deardorff 8-by-10: Capitol building, Albany [10], N.Y.
October 4. Deardorff 8-by-10: Capitol building, Albany [8], N.Y.
October 25. Deardorff 8-by-10: Capitol building, Albany [11], N.Y.
November 8. Deardorff 8-by-10: Capitol building, Albany [9], N.Y.

1985 January 13. Deardorff 8-by-10: Kripplebush [6], N.Y.
August 9. Deardorff 8-by-10: Dutchess County [7] and Cold Spring [3] (page 145), N.Y.
August 12. Deardorff 8-by-10: Kripplebush [10] and Rosendale [6], Ulster County, N.Y.
August 13. Deardorff 8-by-10: Ulster County [3], N.Y.

1986 Commission by Gann Law Books
June 17. Deardorff 8-by-10: Newton [6], Belvidere [5], Flemington [4], and Somerville [4], N.J.
June 18. Deardorff 8-by-10: New Brunswick [3] and Freehold [2], N.J.
June 19. Deardorff 8-by-10: Morristown [4], N.J.
June 25. Deardorff 8-by-10: Patterson [2] and Jersey City [4], N.J.
June 26. Deardorff 8-by-10: Hackensack [5], N.J.
July 10. Deardorff 8-by-10: Highland [1], West Park [3], and Kingston [2], N.Y.
July 14. Deardorff 8-by-10: Trenton [8] and Mt. Holly [5], N.J.
July 15. Deardorff 8-by-10: Camden [2], Woodbury [2], Salem [2], Bridgeton [2], and Cape May [2], N.J.
July 16. Deardorff 8-by-10: Cape May [1], Mays Landing [4], and Toms River [2], N.J.
July 17. Deardorff 8-by-10: Elizabeth [6] and Newark [4], N.J.
July 24. Deardorff 8-by-10: Poughkeepsie [4] and Pawling [2], N.Y.
August 5. Deardorff 8-by-10: Rifton [5], Krumville [5], and Kripplebush [2], N.Y.
August 13. Deardorff 8-by-10: Krumville [7], Lyonsville [4], Stone Ridge [6], and Cottekill [1], N.Y.
August 26. Deardorff 8-by-10: Barrytown [2], Annandale-on-Hudson [6], Tivoli [2], Cheviot [2], North Germantown [2], and Rip Van Winkle Bridge [5], Hudson, N.Y.
October 15. Deardorff 8-by-10: Kripplebush [9] (page 145) and High Falls [4], N.Y.
October 19. Deardorff 8-by-10: High Falls [3], Glasco [3], Saugerties [2], Hurley [2], High Falls [1], and Kripplebush [1], N.Y.
November 1. Deardorff 8-by-10: Lima Locomotive Works [5], Lima, Ohio
November 2. Deardorff 8-by-10: Lima [14], Ohio

1987 January 7. Deardorff 8-by-10: Uvalde County [9], Tex.
January 8. Deardorff 8-by-10: Brewster County [4], Tex.
January 9. Deardorff 8-by-10: Brewster County [17], Tex.
January 10. Deardorff 8-by-10: Brewster County [10], Tex.
January 11. Deardorff 8-by-10: Brewster County [30] (page 143), Tex.
January 12. Deardorff 8-by-10: Brewster County [16], Tex.
January 13. Deardorff 8-by-10: Brewster County [20], Tex.
January 14. Deardorff 8-by-10: Brewster County [8] and Jeff Davis County [6], Tex.
January 18. Deardorff 8-by-10: Las Cruces [3], N.Mex.
January 20. Deardorff 8-by-10: Fredericksburg [4], Tex.
January 21. Deardorff 8-by-10: Gillespie County [1] and Enchanted Rock State Park [6], Tex.
January 22. Deardorff 8-by-10: Gillespie County [2], Bandera County [5], Utopia [2], Uvalde County [6], Real County [2], and Kerr County [1], Tex.
January 23. Deardorff 8-by-10: Fredericksburg [9], Tex.
June 14. Deardorff 8-by-10: Lyonsville [7], N.Y.
June 15. Deardorff 8-by-10: Kripplebush [4], N.Y.
July 5. Deardorff 8-by-10: Keene Valley [6], N.Y.
July 7. Deardorff 8-by-10: Keene Valley [1], N.Y.
July 9. Deardorff 8-by-10: Keene Valley [5], N.Y.
July 12. Deardorff 8-by-10: Keene Valley [4], N.Y.
July 15. Deardorff 8-by-10: South Meadow [8], N.Y.
July 26. Deardorff 8-by-10: Hurley [7] and Marbletown [2], N.Y.
July 27. Deardorff 8-by-10: Hurley [3], N.Y.
July 29. Deardorff 8-by-10: Kripplebush [4], N.Y.
August 12. Deardorff 8-by-10: South Meadow [8], N.Y.
August 18. Deardorff 8-by-10: Marbletown [12], N.Y.
October 15. Deardorff 8-by-10: Catskill [6], N.Y.
October 16. Deardorff 8-by-10: Kerhonkson [1] and New Paltz [6], N.Y.
October 17. Deardorff 8-by-10: Kripplebush [3], N.Y.

October 18. Deardorff 8-by-10: Kripplebush [4], N.Y.
December 31. Deardorff 8-by-10: Jeff Davis County [14], Tex.

1988 January 1. Deardorff 8-by-10: Jeff Davis County [12], Tex.
January 3. Deardorff 8-by-10: Jeff Davis County [19], Tex.
January 4. Deardorff 8-by-10: Jeff Davis County [9], Tex.
January 5. Deardorff 8-by-10: Big Bend National Park [3], Brewster County, Tex.
January 6. Deardorff 8-by-10: Big Bend National Park [5], Brewster County, Tex.
January 7. Deardorff 8-by-10: Big Bend National Park [15] (page 145), Brewster County, Tex.
January 8. Deardorff 8-by-10: Big Bend National Park [9], Brewster County, Tex.
January 9. Deardorff 8-by-10: Big Bend National Park [10], Brewster County, Tex.
January 10. Deardorff 8-by-10: Big Bend National Park [16] (page 147), Brewster County, Tex.
January 11. Deardorff 8-by-10: Big Bend National Park [10], Brewster County, Tex.
January 12. Deardorff 8-by-10: Big Bend National Park [12], Brewster County, Tex.
January 13. Deardorff 8-by-10: Presidio County [2], Tex.
January 15. Deardorff 8-by-10: Las Cruces [2], N.Mex.
February 5. Lens tests in Stone Ridge, N.Y.
March 26. Son Nicholas born
September 5. Deardorff 8-by-10: Muie [8] and road to Langwell [5], Scotland
September 7. Deardorff 8-by-10: road to Unapool [3], north of Unapool [3], and Blackwater [3], Scotland
September 10. Deardorff 8-by-10: north of Scourie [4] and near Unapool [1], Scotland
September 11. Deardorff 8-by-10: north of Scourie [4] and near Foindle [5] (north of Scourie), Scotland
September 12. Deardorff 8-by-10: outside of Lochinier [2], Scotland
September 13. Deardorff 8-by-10: Muie [5], Scotland
September 14. Fishing at Rogart, Scotland
September 15. Deardorff 8-by-10: Rogart [2], Langwell [4], and Craggie [1], Scotland
September 18. Deardorff 8-by-10: Achmeluich [4], Scotland
September 19. Deardorff 8-by-10: near Achmeluich [6], Scotland
September 21. Deardorff 8-by-10: near Achmeluich [8], Scotland
September 22. Deardorff 8-by-10: near Rhiconich [1], south of Scourie [6], and south of Unapool [6], Scotland
September 23. Deardorff 8-by-10: near Achmeluich [9] and Achmeluich [5], Scotland
September 25. Deardorff 8-by-10: Morness [5] and Deardorff 8-by-10: Langwell [1], Scotland
September 27. Deardorff 8-by-10: moors on Rovie Estate [8], Rogart, Scotland
September 28. Deardorff 8-by-10: Loch More [1], Scotland

1989 July 29. Deardorff 8-by-10: Kripplebush [5] and New Paltz [3], N.Y.

1990 January 3. Deardorff 8-by-10: Hoctun [9], Xocchel [9], and Kantunyl [4], Yucatán, Mexico
January 4. Deardorff 8-by-10: Uman [8] and Muna [18], Yucatán, Mexico
January 5. Deardorff 8-by-10: San Pedro [8], Hoctun [3], Kantunyl [15], and Hoctun [2], Yucatán, Mexico
January 6. Deardorff 8-by-10: Hoctun [9] and Izamal [6], Yucatán, Mexico
January 7. Deardorff 8-by-10: Hoctun [23] and Tahmek [1], Yucatán, Mexico
January 8. Deardorff 8-by-10: Xtepen [16], Yucatán, Mexico
January 9. Deardorff 8-by-10: Hoctun [4], Kantunyl [2], Libre Union [6], and Xocchel [1], Yucatán, Mexico
January 10. Deardorff 8-by-10: Dzibilchatun [1] and Xocchel [14], Yucatán, Mexico
January 11. Deardorff 8-by-10: Petentunich [1], Acanceh [5], Tekit [8], and Chumayel [2], Yucatán, Mexico
July 13. Deardorff 8-by-10: Throop [23], Pa.
July 14. Deardorff 8-by-10: Throop [22], Pa.
Commission by J. Paul Getty Museum (published in *Camille Silvy: River Scene, France*, 1992)
July 23. Deardorff 8-by-10: Nogent [18], France
July 23. Deardorff 8-by-10: Gaillard [2], France
July 24. Deardorff 8-by-10: Nogent [26], France
July 25. Deardorff 8-by-10: Nogent [18], France
July 27. Deardorff 8-by-10: Nogent [4], France
December. Moves to Tivoli, N.Y.

1992 Deardorff 8-by-10: Essex County (page 55), N.Y.
Deardorff 8-by-10: Garden in Tivoli, N.Y.

1993 Commission by Linea di Confine per la Fotografia Contemporanea (published in *Stephen Shore: Luzzara*, 1993)
June 4–13. Deardorff 8-by-10: Luzzara (pages 56, 150–51, and 175), Italy

1994 Deardorff 8-by-10: Essex County, N.Y.
Arca Swiss 8-by-10 with a 5-by-7 back: New York

1996 Deardorff 8-by-10: Essex County, N.Y.
September. Becomes Chairman, Arts Division, Bard College (1996–2000)
July 14. Deardorff 8-by-10: Ashkelon [22], Israel
July 15. Deardorff 8-by-10: Ashkelon [22], Israel
July 16. Deardorff 8-by-10: Ashkelon [36], Israel
July 17. Deardorff 8-by-10: Ashkelon [16], Israel
July 22. Deardorff 8-by-10: Hatzor [7], Israel
July 23. Deardorff 8-by-10: Hatzor [24], Israel
July 24. Deardorff 8-by-10: Hatzor [22], Israel
July 25. Deardorff 8-by-10: Hatzor [22], Israel
July 26. Deardorff 8-by-10: Tel Dan and Tel Aviv, Israel [10]

1997 July 29. Deardorff 8-by-10: Aquileia [8], Italy
July 30. Deardorff 8-by-10: Aquileia [10], Italy
July 31. Deardorff 8-by-10: Spilimbergo [12], Italy
August 1. Deardorff 8-by-10: Spilimbergo [4], Italy
August 2. Deardorff 8-by-10: Spilimbergo [9], Italy
August 4. Deardorff 8-by-10: Aquileia [15], Italy
August 5. Deardorff 8-by-10: Aquileia [20], Italy
August 7. Deardorff 8-by-10: Aquileia [18], Italy

1998 Commission by National Millennium Survey (Shore photographs press at major news events)
August 5–6. Pentax 6-by-7: E. Barrett Prettyman Court House, Washington, D.C.
October 29. Pentax 6-by-7: Cape Canaveral, Fla.
November 3. Pentax 6-by-7: Waldorf-Astoria, New York
Commission by the City of Venice (published in *Identificazione di un Paesaggio: Venezia–Marghera*, 2000)
September. Pentax 6-by-7: Porto Marghera, Venice

2000 Deardorff 8-by-10 with a 4-by-10 back: New York (pages 57 and 229)
Commission by *Details* (published in "Farm Hands," *Details*, November 2000)

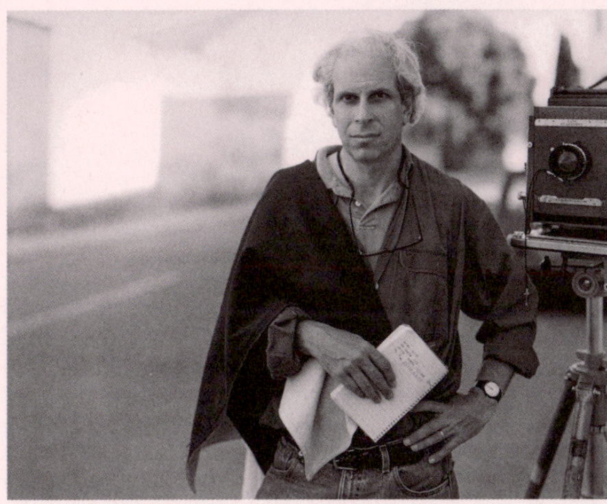

Stephen Shore, Spilimbergo, Italy, August 2, 1997. Photograph by Guido Guidi

Summer. Pentax 6-by-7: Hudson Valley Renegades (page 51), Dutchess Stadium, Fishkill, N.Y.

2001 Deardorff 8-by-10 with a 4-by-10 back: New York (pages 57 and 229)

2002 Deardorff 8-by-10 with a 4-by-10 back: New York (pages 57 and 229)
January 29–30. Cambo 4-by-5 and Olympus E-20: Orlando, Fla. (Titleist advertising campaign, 2002)

2003 February 11. Olympus E-20: Westminster Kennel Club Dog Show, New York (published in *Dog Show*, 2003, page 190)
March 6–9. Pentax 6-by-7: Celebration, Fla. (published in "Suburban Cowboy," *Details*, May 2003)
March. Pentax 6-by-7: Quail Hollow, Winter Park, Fla. (published in *Quail Hollow*, 2003)
March 12. Canon EOS-1DS: New York (Canon advertising campaign, 2003)
March 25. Olympus E-20: New York (published in *3-25-03*, 2003)
June 4. Casio EX-S2: London (published in *Street*, 2003)
July 12. Casio EX-S2: Cap d'Antibes, France (published in *Plage Keller*, 2003)
July 25. Olympus E-20: Tivoli, N.Y. (published in *White Garden*, 2003, page 112)
July 26. Casio EX-S2: Iron Maiden concert, Jones Beach, N.Y. (published in *Fear of the Dark*, 2003)
August 18. Casio EX-S2: Woodstock, N.Y. (published in *A Visit to the Dentist*, 2003)
August 20. Olympus E-20: Dutchess County Fair, Rhinebeck, N.Y. (published in *Fowl*, 2003)
September 6. Casio EX-S2: Chelsea, New York (published in *Chelsea*, 2003)
October 24–25. Canon EOS 1DS: Cawdor, Scotland (published in "High and Mighty," *W* magazine, March 2004, and *Cawdor Moors*, 2003)

2004 January 22. Casio EX-S2: Fairchild Publications, New York (published in *1-22-04*, 2004)
February 2. Casio EX-S2: Heathrow Airport, London, to John F. Kennedy Airport, New York (published in *AA 105*, 2004, page 183)
February 13–19. Olympus E-20 and Casio EX-S2: Sabi Sand Game Reserve, South Africa (published in *African Idyll*, 2004; *The Big Five*, 2004; *Bushveld Walk #1*, 2004; *Bushveld Walk #2*, 2004; *Bushveld Walk #3*, 2004; *The Marula Tree*, 2004; *The Fire Wood Tree*, 2004; and *Bushveld Sky*, 2004)
February 26. Olympus E-20: Paris (published in *2-26-04*, 2004)
March 16–20. Pentax 6-by-7: Wellington, New Zealand (published in "Natural Beauty," *Wallpaper*, October 2005)
March 21. Olympus E-20: Los Angeles (published in *Merrick & Traction*, 2004)
April 17. Olympus E-20: Vienna (published in *Albertina Surfaces*, 2004, and *Flohmarkt*, 2004, pages 184–85)
May–August. Fuji GX680 6-by-8 and rented 4-by-5: Los Angeles and Orange County, Calif.; London; New York; Marseille, France (Orange S.A. advertising campaign)
June 8. Contax SL300RT: Times Square, New York (published in *Times Square No. 1*, 2004)
July 31. Contax SL300RT: Beacon, N.Y. (published in *Union of the Torus and the Sphere*, 2004)
August 23–24. Olympus E-20: Cap d'Antibes, France (published in *Chemin des Mougins*, 2004)
September. Hires first studio assistant, Laura Steele
September 11. Contax SL300RT: Central Park, New York (published in *Central Park*, 2004)
September 12. Sources publicly available security footage of Times Square, New York (published in *Times Square #2*, 2004, page 229)
October 12. Contax SL300RT: Kingston, N.Y. (published in *Heavy Metal Alphabet*, 2004, page 191)
October 16. Olympus E-20: Window Rock, Ariz. (published in *Window Rock, AZ*, 2004)
October 31. Olympus E-20: Tivoli (page 283), N.Y.
November 20. Olympus E-20: Woodstock, Conn. (published in *Season's Greetings*, 2004)

2005 January 16. Olympus E-20: Paris (published in *Colonne de Vendôme*, 2005)
February 24. Contax SL300RT: San Francisco (published in *3323 Washington*, 2005)
March 4–6. Pentax 6-by-7: Surprise, Ariz. (published in "The Soul of the New Exurb," *New York Times Magazine*, March 27, 2005)
August 1. Contax SL300RT: University City, Calif., and Welches, Ore. (published in *City Walk/Salmon River Trail*, 2005)
August 2. Contax SL300RT: Mount Hood, Ore. (published in *Mount Hood*, 2005)
August 31. Olympus E-20: New York (published in *8-31-05*, 2005)
October 29. Canon PowerShot SD450: New York (published in *10-29-05*, 2005)
October 31. Canon PowerShot SD450: Jerónimos Monastery, Belèm, Portugal (published in *Jerónimos Monastery*, 2005)
November 8. Fuji GX680: Long Island, N.Y. (Bottega Veneta advertising campaign, 2006)
November 9. Canon PowerShot SD450: New York (published in *11-9-05*, 2005)
November 30. Canon PowerShot SD450: Los Angeles (published in *11-30-05*, 2005 and *Merry Christmas*, 2005)
December 1–3. Fuji GX680: Los Angeles (published in "In Back of the Real," *Another Magazine*, Spring/Summer 2006, page 103)
December 21. Canon PowerShot SD450: Kingston, N.Y. (published in *12-21-05*, 2005)

2006 January 10–13. Deardorff 8-by-10: Los Angeles
January 18. Canon PowerShot SD450: Lausanne to Geneva, Switzerland (published in *Lausanne–Geneva*, 2006)

February 2. Canon PowerShot SD450: Garmisch, Germany (published in *2-22-06*, 2006)
February 22. Canon PowerShot SD450: Zugspitze, Germany (published in *Zugspitze*, 2006)
March 30. Canon PowerShot SD450: Miami, Fla. (published in *Warehouse*, 2006)
April 19. Canon PowerShot SD450: Metropolitan Museum of Art, New York (published in *Ugolino and His Sons*, 2006)
June 9. Canon PowerShot SD450: Tivoli, N.Y. (published in *6-9-06*, 2006, pages 188–89)
July 25. Canon PowerShot SD450: Milan, Italy (published in *Via Montenapoleone*, 2006)
August 31. Olympus E-2: Tivoli, N.Y. (published in "Marden Manor," *W* magazine, November 2006)
September 3. Olympus E-2: Tivoli, N.Y. (published in "Marden Manor," *W* magazine, November 2006)
September 10. Olympus E-2: Tivoli, N.Y. (published in "Marden Manor," *W* magazine, November 2006)
October 6. Canon PowerShot SD450: Seattle (published in *1223 Spring*, 2006)
November 8. Canon PowerShot SD450: Tivoli, N.Y. (published in *11-8-06*, 2006)
November 9. Canon PowerShot SD450: Tivoli, N.Y. (published in *11-9-06*, 2006)
November 10. Canon PowerShot SD450: Tivoli, N.Y. (published in *11-10-06*, 2006), and Metropolitan Opera, New York (published in *Il Barbiere di Siviglia*, 2006)
November. Rented 4-by-5 with a digital back: New York (Glenfiddich advertising campaign, 2007, page 68)
November 24. Canon PowerShot SD450: Tivoli, N.Y. (published in *Merry Christmas*, 2006, page 115)
December 2. Pentax 6-by-7: Santa Monica, Calif. (published in "The New Age Healers," *W* magazine, February 2007)

2007 February 28. Canon PowerShot SD450: New York (published in *2-28-07*, 2007)
March 1. Canon PowerShot SD450: New York to Baltimore (published in *New York City–Baltimore*, 2007)
March 7. Canon PowerShot SD450 and Motorola phone: New York (published in *3-7-07*, 2007)
April 17. Canon PowerShot SD450: Lausanne, Switzerland (published in *4-17-07*, 2007)
April 21. Canon PowerShot SD450: Visp, Switzerland (published in *EC 123*, 2007)
Commission by Mobile Art
July 3–4. Pentax 6-by-7: Chanel factory, Paris
September 22. Pentax 6-by-7: Ocala, Fla. (published in "A Little Bit Country," *New York Times Style Magazine*, November 18, 2007)
November 1. Canon PowerShot SD450: Amarillo, Tex. (published in *11-1-07*, 2007)
November 2. Canon PowerShot SD450: Amarillo, Tex. (published in *12th Floor*, 2007)
December 12. Canon PowerShot SD450: Tivoli, N.Y. (published in *Joyeux Noël*, 2007)

2008 February 20. Canon PowerShot SD450: Angkor Wat, Cambodia (published in *Bas Relief*, 2008)
February 21. Canon PowerShot SD450: Siem Reap, Cambodia (published in *Market*, 2008, page 109)
February 24. Canon PowerShot SD450: Angkor Thom, Cambodia (published in *Angkor Thom*, 2008)
March 13. Canon PowerShot SD450: Hong Kong to New York (published in *3-13-08*, 2008)
March 16. Canon PowerShot SD450: Hong Kong (published in *Man Mo Temple*, 2008)
March 30. Canon PowerShot SD450: Negev Desert, Israel (published in *Shivta*, 2008, and *Valley of Zin*, 2008)
April 5. Canon Digital IXUS 75: Hebron, West Bank (published in *Hebron Sports Club*, 2008)

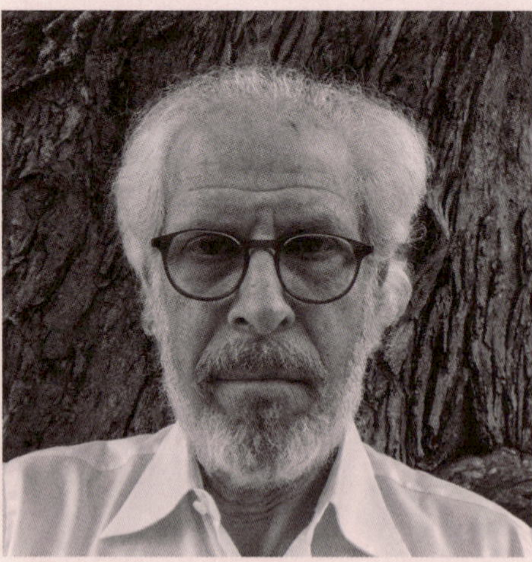

Self-portrait, Tivoli, New York, July 8, 2017

April 24. Hasselblad H1 with Leaf Aptus 75 digital back: Red Hook, N.Y. (published in "Brief Encounter," *Elle*, August 2008, page 102)
April 26. Canon Digital IXUS 75: Kansas City, Mo. (published in *Arthur Bryant's*, 2008, page 109)
June 8–13. Canon Digital IXUS 75: Bali, Indonesia
June 18–28. Pentax 6-by-7: Venice (published in *Mose*, 2011)
June 19. Canon EOS-1Ds Mark III: Venice (published in "A Perfect Stranger," *Elle*, September 2008)
July 13. Canon EOS-1Ds Mark III: Lindsay Lohan, Los Angeles (published in "Hot Child in the City," *Elle*, October 2008)
Commission by Chanel
August. Sinar 4-by-5: Tivoli, N.Y.
September 17. Canon PowerShot SD450: Musée du Louvre, Paris (published in *La Joconde*, 2008, page 191)
September 19. Canon EOS-1Ds Mark III: Paris (published in "City of Light," *Elle*, December 2008)
October 18. Canon PowerShot SD450: Queens, N.Y. (published in *10-18-08*, 2008)
November 6–8. Canon EOS-1Ds Mark III: Apalachicola, Fla. (published in "Forgotten Coast," *Cookie* magazine, March 2009)
November 12. Ricoh GX200: Tivoli, N.Y. (published in *Season's Greetings*, 2008)
December. Rented digital camera: Austin, Tex. (Nike advertising campaign, page 69)

2009 January 10. Canon EOS-1Ds Mark III and Ricoh GX200: Fergie and Josh Duhamel, Malibu, Calif. (published in "All that I Got," *Elle*, March 2009)
March 16. Sinar 4-by-5: Tivoli, N.Y.
April 16. Canon EOS-1Ds Mark III: Bowery Hotel, New York (published in "Room Service," *Details*, June/July 2009)
May 7. Nikon D3X, Nikon D3, and Ricoh GX200: Cavalli Club Dubai, United Arab Emirates (published in "Night at the Oasis," *Elle*, November 2009)
May 8. Nikon D3X: Dubai, United Arab Emirates (published in "A Foreign Affair," *Elle*, November 2009)
July 28. Canon EOS-1Ds Mark III: Former house of Ingmar Bergman, Fårö,

Sweden (published in "The Private World of Ingmar Bergman," *W* magazine, November 2009)
August 9. Sinar 4-by-5: Tivoli, N.Y.
September 10. Deardorff 8-by-10: Nabī Musa [3], West Bank, Wadi Talkid [3], Mount of Beatitudes [1]; Nikon D3X: Tel Aviv
September 11. Deardorff 8-by-10: Near Ariel [7] and Nablus [2], West Bank; Nikon D3X: Mount Gerizim, West Bank
September 12. Deardorff 8-by-10: Wadi Qelt [3], West Bank; Nikon D3X: Jerusalem (page 207)
September 13. Deardorff 8-by-10: Umm el Fahm [6], Israel; Nikon D3X: Haifa, Israel
September 14. Nikon D3X: Southwest of Tel Aviv and Sderot (page 133), Israel
September 15. Deardorff 8-by-10: Nazareth [2] and Bir el Maksūr [1], Israel; Nikon D3X: Jerusalem
September 16. Deardorff 8-by-10: Jerusalem [9]; Neve Daniel [3] and Tel Zif [3], West Bank
September 17. Deardorff 8-by-10: Mount Hebron, West Bank [2]; Lakhish area [1] and Kiryat Gat [5], Israel; Mount Hebron [2], Hebron [2], and Nabī Yakin [2], West Bank; Nikon D3X: Tel Lachish, Israel
September 18. Deardorff 8-by-10: Judean Desert [4], Ein Feshkha [2], Darga Cliffs [2], and Mount Sodom [1], Israel; Nikon D3X: Metzoke Dragot, Israel
September 19. Deardorff 8-by-10: Ma'alé Adummim [2], West Bank
September 20. Deardorff 8-by-10: Judean Desert [11]
September 21. Deardorff 8-by-10: Ramot [2], Abu Ghosh [3], Ein Rafa [2], Ein Naqquba [4], and Ein Karem [2], Israel
September 22. Deardorff 8-by-10: Hurfeish [6], road to Beit Jann [7], and Beit Jann [1], Israel; Nikon D3X: Peqi'in (page 105) and Beit Jann, Israel
September 23. Deardorff 8-by-10: Jerusalem [10]; Nikon D3X: Jerusalem
September 24. Deardorff 8-by-10: Jerusalem [15]
September 25. Nikon D3X: Jerusalem
September 27. Deardorff 8-by-10: Ramat Gan, Israel [4]
September 29. Deardorff 8-by-10: Negev Desert, Israel [5]
September 30. Deardorff 8-by-10 and Nikon D3X: Jaffa, Tel Aviv, and Ben Gurion Airport, Israel
October 1. Deardorff 8-by-10: Nabī Musa [3] and Wadi Og [1], West Bank; Dead Sea [2]; Nikon D3X: Jerusalem
October 3. Nikon D3X: Ramallah, West Bank
October. Nikon D3X: San Francisco and Bay Area (Acorda advertising campaign)
October 23–26. Nikon D3X: Abu Dhabi (page 236)
December 12. Ricoh GX200: Tivoli, N.Y. (published in *Feliz Navidad*, 2009)

2010 January 1. Nikon D3X: Jerusalem (page 133)
January 3. Deardorff 8-by-10: Judean Desert [2] and Negev Desert [3], Israel; Nikon D3X: 'Arad, Israel
January 5. Nikon D3X: Negev Desert, Isarel
January 6. Deardorff 8-by-10: Negev Desert [9], Israel
January 7. Deardorff 8-by-10: Eilat [6], along Road 10 [3], and Eilat Mountains [2], Israel; Nikon D3X: Negev Desert and Eilat, Israel
January 8. Nikon D3X: Negev Desert, Israel
January 9. Nikon D3X: Jerusalem
January 10. Deardorff 8-by-10: Gush Etzion [2], Efrata [1], Umm Dareg [4], Mrara [3], South of Mount Hebron [2], and Suseya [3], West Bank; Nikon D3X: Jerusalem
January 11. Nikon D3X: Hebron (page 129) and Beit Jālā, West Bank; Jerusalem
January 12. Deardorff 8-by-10: Beit Jimāl [4], Israel; Nikon D3X: Eshta'ol, Israel
January 13. Deardorff 8-by-10: Michmash Valley [6] and Beitin [1] (page 130), West Bank; Beit Shemesh [3]; Nikon D3X: Michmash Valley, West Bank
January 14. Deardorff 8-by-10: Umm el Fahm [2], Tiberias [2], and south of Zefat [4] (page 131), Israel
January 15. Deardorff 8-by-10: Metulla [3], Israel; Mount Hermon [5]; Nikon D3X: Metulla and Majdal Shams, Israel
January 17. Deardorff 8-by-10: Sameria [2], northern Jordan Valley [4], and Tiba [1], West Bank
January 19. Deardorff 8-by-10: Nabī Musa [7] (page 163), West Bank, and Jerusalem [4]
January 21. Deardorff 8-by-10: Hebron, West Bank [5]
January 22. Deardorff 8-by-10: Givatayim [4] and Tel Aviv [3], Israel
March 22. Deardorff 8-by-10: Jerusalem [9]
March 23. Deardorff 8-by-10: Nabī Musa [4], West Bank, and Jerusalem [1]
March 24. Deardorff 8-by-10: Jordan Valley [2]
March 25. Deardorff 8-by-10: Jerusalem [16]
April 30–May 2. Nikon D3X: Queens, N.Y. (published in Urban Outfitters Fall Preview, 2010)
June 10. Nikon D3X: Jerusalem
June 11. Nikon D3X: Jerusalem
June 13. Nikon D3X: Jerusalem
June 14. Nikon D3X: Zefat, Israel
June 15. Nikon D3X: Zefat, Israel
June 16. Nikon D3X: Acre, Israel
June 17. Nikon D3X: Tel Aviv, Israel, and the southern coast between Tel Aviv and Gaza
June 18. Nikon D3X: Jerusalem
June 20. Nikon D3X: Netiv HaAsara, Israel, and the Gaza border
July 22–23. Nikon D3X: Crespi d'Adda, Italy (published in "Un Racconto," *Amica*, October 2010, page 102)
September 4. Nikon D3X: Fort Greene, Brooklyn, N.Y. (published in "Double Take," *Details*, November 2010)
December 9. Ricoh GX200: New York (published in *Happy Hanukkah*, 2010)

2011 March 18. Deardorff 8-by-10: Tel Aviv [4] and Harbata [2], Israel
March 22. Deardorff 8-by-10: Jerusalem [10] (page 132)
March 23. Deardorff 8-by-10: Tel Aviv, Israel [8]
March 24. Deardorff 8-by-10: Bethlehem, Israel [4]
March 25. Deardorff 8-by-10: Hebron [9] (page 173), West Bank
Commission by CCA Wattis Institute for Contemporary Arts for *More American Photographs*
July 20. Nikon D3X: East Village, New York
October 28. Nikon D3X: Asbury Park, N.J. (published in "Wish You Were Here," *Lucky*, March 2012)

2012 January. Fuji X10: Beverly Hills
January 8. Nikon D3X: Atwater Village, Los Angeles (published in "Strange Girl in a Strange Land," *Wall Street Journal Magazine*, March 2012)
May 1. Nikon D3X: Tivoli, N.Y. (published in "She's Got Your Eyes," *Telegraph Fashion*, Autumn/Winter 2012)
May 11. Nikon D3X: Tivoli, N.Y. (published in "She's Got Your Eyes," *Telegraph Fashion*, Autumn/Winter 2012)
June. Panasonic DVCPRO P2: New York (published in *A New York Minute*, 2014)
July 18. Nikon D3X: Bucha (pages 106, 244–45, and 249) and Kiev (page 248), Ukraine

July 19. Nikon D3X: Boryspil (pages 242 and 250), Ukraine
July 20. Nikon D3X: Korsun (page 246), Ukraine
July 21. Nikon D3X: Korsun (page 247), Ukraine
July 22. Nikon D3X: Uman (page 249), Ukraine
July 23. Nikon D3X: Mykolayiv (page 243), Ukraine
July 24. Nikon D3X: Bershad (page 239), Ukraine
July 25. Nikon D3X: Tomashpil (page 246), Ukraine
July 27. Nikon D3X: Bazalia (pages 174 and 251), Ukraine
July 28. Nikon D3X: Kiev, Ukraine
July 29. Nikon D3X: Berdychiv (pages 240–41) and Zhytomyr (page 181), Ukraine
July 31. Nikon D3X: Ovruch, Ukraine
December 10. Nikon D3X: Jaipur, India (published in "Indian Summer," *Telegraph Magazine*, June 22, 2013)
December 11. Nikon D3X: Jaipur, India (published in "Indian Summer," *Telegraph Fashion*, Spring 2013)

2013 March 28–29. Nikon D800: Venice, Calif. (published in "California Dreaming," *T* magazine, October 6, 2013)
June 10. Nikon D800: Noguchi Museum, Queens, N.Y. (published in *The Noguchi Museum: A Portrait*, 2015)
June 11. Nikon D800: Jersey City, N.J. (published in "Covered in Glory," *Telegraph Fashion*, Autumn/Winter 2013)
June 25. Nikon D800: Noguchi Museum, Queens, N.Y. (published in *The Noguchi Museum: A Portrait*, 2015)
July 23. Nikon D800: Noguchi Museum, Queens, N.Y. (published in *The Noguchi Museum: A Portrait*, 2015)
September 19. Nikon D800: Winslow (pages 44, 89, 197, 211, and 278–79), Ariz. (published in *Winslow Arizona: September 19th, 2013*, 2014)
October 10. Nikon D800: Budapest, Hungary
October 11. Nikon D800: Uzhgorod, Ukraine
October 12. Nikon D800: Khust (page 181), Kamyamske, Mukachevo, Rakoshyno, and Uzhgorod, Ukraine
October 13. Nikon D800: Rachiv, Dylove, Kosdylyvka, Nyznyi Apsha, Kolomeya, and Teresva, Ukraine
October 14. Nikon D800: Lviv, Ukraine
October 15. Nikon D800: Letychiv, Ozerna, Nemirov, and Bratslav, Ukraine
October 16. Nikon D800: Berdychiv, Nemirov, and Shnuriv Lys (page 201), Ukraine
November 8. Nikon D800: Noguchi Museum, Queens, N.Y. (published in *The Noguchi Museum: A Portrait*, 2015)

2014 May 20. Nikon D800: Hermès executives, New York (published in "A Man with a Clan," *W* magazine, September 2014)
May 21. First Instagram post
May–December. iPhone 5s: New York, Queens, Long Island City, Brooklyn, Bronx, Tivoli (page 114), Rhinebeck, Rhinecliff, Red Hook, Annandale-on-Hudson, and Hudson, N.Y.; Holbrook and Seligman, Ariz.; Gallup, Albuquerque, Santa Rosa, Tucumcari, and Bard, N.Mex.; Weatherford, Okla.; Republic, Mo.; Hebron, Ohio; Des Plaines, Ill.; Bozeman, Gallatin National Forest, McLeod, Big Timber, and Emigrant, Mont.; Yuma County, Colo.; Stellenbosch (page 121) and Cape Town, South Africa; Madrid; Amsterdam; London; and Prague (posted to Instagram)
Summer. Sinar 4-by-5: Tivoli, N.Y.
July 10. Nikon D800: Seligman, Ariz.
July 11. Nikon D800: Holbrook, Ariz., and Gallup, N.Mex.
July 12. Nikon D800: Albuquerque, Santa Rosa, and Tucumcari, N.Mex.
July 13. Nikon D800: Tucumcari and Bard, N.Mex.
July 14. Nikon D800: Brazil, Ind.
July 15. Nikon D800: Hebron, Ohio

2015 January–December. iPhone: Tivoli, Red Hook, Hudson (page 121), Millbrook, Rhinebeck, Rhinecliff, Annandale-on-Hudson, Saugerties, Wyandanch, Kingston, Modena, Germantown, Staatsburg, New York (page 122), Bronx, Queens, and Brooklyn, N.Y.; Englewood Cliffs and Tenafly, N.J.; Great Barrington, Mass.; Big Sky, Bozeman, Gallatin County, Ruby River, Alder, Virginia City, Madison River, Pray, Wilsall (page 213), Yellowstone River, and Park County, Mont.; Los Angeles (page 118), West Hollywood, and Silver Lake, Calif.; Miami Beach, Fla.; New Orleans, La.; London; and Arles and Aix-en-Provence, France (posted to Instagram)
June 15. Sinar 4-by-5: Tivoli (page 114), N.Y.

2016 January–December. iPhone: Tivoli (page 122), Red Hook, Germantown (page 125), Annandale-on-Hudson (page 122), Ghent, Clinton Corners (page 283), Rhinecliff, Rhinebeck, Staatsburg, Millbrook, Poughkeepsie, Barrytown, Woodstock, New York, Bronx, Queens, and Brooklyn, N.Y.; Princeton, Elizabeth, Kearny, Harrison, and Newark, N.J.; Baltimore; Washington, D.C.; Atlanta; Bozeman, Sedan, Bridger Canyon, Missouri Headwaters State Park, Three Forks, Livingston, Ennis, Cameron, Belgrade, and Gallatin County, Mont.; Cache County, Utah; Blue Earth and Worthington, Minn.; Chicago; Ranchester, Wyo.; San Francisco; Bentonville, Ark.; Harbour Island and North Eleuthera, Bahamas; Berlin; Amsterdam; London; Cheltenham and Chipping Campden, Gloucestershire; Admington, Warwickshire; Bath, Wells, and Bruton, Somerset; Stockbridge, Hampshire; Warminster, Salisbury, and Stourhead Gardens (page 113), Wiltshire; Brighton, Northiam, and Rye, East Sussex; Sissinghurst Castle Garden and Benenden, Kent, United Kingdom (posted to Instagram)

Selected Exhibition History
Compiled by Kristen Gaylord

Exhibitions Curated by Shore

1971 *All the Meat You Can Eat.* 98 Greene Street Loft, New York, November 8–15.

1989 *The Friends Focus: On Photography.* Exhibition catalogue. Vassar College Art Gallery, Poughkeepsie, N.Y., December 7, 1989–February 11, 1990.

2011 *Emirati Expressions.* Exhibition catalogue. Manarat Al Saadiyat, Abu Dhabi, October 19, 2011–January 28, 2012.

Solo Exhibitions

1962 Donnell Library Center, New York, March 14–April 16.

1971 *Fifteen Photographs by Stephen Shore.* The Metropolitan Museum of Art, New York, February 23–March 21.

1972 *Amarillo, "Tall in Texas," Photographs by Stephen Shore.* Thomas Gibson Fine Art, London, February 7–25.
American Surfaces: Photographs by Stephen Shore. Light Gallery, New York, September 23–October 21.

1973 *Stephen Shore.* Light Gallery, New York, December 4, 1973–January 5, 1974.

1975 *Stephen Shore.* Light Gallery, New York, February 4–March 1.
Phoenix Gallery, San Francisco, June 3–July 15.
Stephen Shore. Galerie Lichttropfen, Aachen, Germany, November–December.

1976 Deja Vue Gallery, Toronto. January 1–March 30.
Photographs by Stephen Shore. The Museum of Modern Art, New York, October 8, 1976–January 2, 1977.

1977 *Stephen Shore.* Light Gallery, New York, April 6–30.
Stephen Shore: Fotografien. Exhibition catalogue. Städtische Kunsthalle Düsseldorf, April 14–May 22.
Stephen Shore Photographs. Delahunty Gallery, Dallas, October 29–December 2.

1978 *Stephen Shore.* Light Gallery, New York, May 24–June 24.
Stephen Shore. Galerie Nancy Gillespie–Elisabeth de Laage, Paris, June 22–July 13.
Stephen Shore. Photogalerie Lange-Irschl, Munich, September 6–October 14.
Stephen Shore: The Gardens at Giverny. Robert Miller Gallery, New York, September 16–October 7.
Stephen Shore. PPS Galerie F. C. Gundlach, Hamburg, November 9–30.
La Photogaleria, Madrid, November 29–December 31.
Vision Gallery of Photography, Boston.

1979 Cronin Gallery, Houston, March 13–April 14.
Stephen Shore: Color Photographs. Port Washington Public Library, N.Y., April 28–May 31.
Stephen Shore. Kathleen Ewing Gallery, Washington, D.C., June 14–July 28.

1980 *Stephen Shore.* Werkstatt für Photographie der VHS Kreuzberg, Berlin, March 3–April 18.
Color Photographs by Stephen Shore. J. B. Speed Art Museum, Louisville, Ky., July 19–August 31.
Stephen Shore: Monet's Garden at Giverny, France. Light Gallery, Los Angeles, October 10–November 8.
Stephen Shore. Light Gallery, New York, November 6–26.

1981 Artifacts Gallery, Bozeman, Mont., opened August 17.
Stephen Shore: Photographs. Exhibition catalogue. John and Mable Ringling Museum of Art, Sarasota, Fla., September 4–October 11. Traveled to Museum of Arts and Sciences, Daytona Beach, Fla., November 27–December 27; Polk Public Museum, Lakeland, Fla., January 11–February 3, 1982.
Stephen Shore: Photographs 1974–1981. Fraenkel Gallery, San Francisco, December 9, 1981–January 16, 1982.

1982 ARCO Center for Visual Art, Los Angeles, August 22–October 2.

1983 *The Giverny Portfolio.* Pace/MacGill Gallery, New York, December 21, 1983–January 10, 1984.

1984 *Stephen Shore: Gardens at Giverny.* Mattingly-Baker Gallery, Dallas, January 7–February 2.
Sol Mednick Gallery, Philadelphia College of Art, April 11–May 1.
Depot Museum, Lake Wales, Fla., August 16–September 6.
Photographs by Stephen Shore. Art Institute of Chicago, September 29–December 2.

1985 *The Montana Suite.* Center for Creative Photography, Tucson, Ariz., October 13–November 21.

1989 *Stephen Shore: Landscapes of Texas & Scotland.* Pace/MacGill Gallery, New York, June 15–August 31.

1993 Museo Nazionale delle Arti Naives "Cesare Zavattini," Luzzara, Italy, October 23–November 14.

1995 *Stephen Shore: Fotografien 1973 bis 1993.* Exhibition catalogue. Westfälischer Kunstverein, Münster, January 28–March 19. Traveled to Sprengel Museum, Hannover, Germany (*Stephen Shore: Fotografien 1972–1992*), April 11–June 5; Württembergischer Kunstverein, Stuttgart (*Stephen Shore: Fotografien 1973–1993*), September 23–November 19; Amerika Haus, Berlin (*Stephen Shore: Photographs, 1973–1993*), November 29, 1995–January 28, 1996; George Eastman House, Rochester, N.Y. (*Stephen Shore: Photographs 1973–1993*), March 16–June 2, 1996; Spilimbergo Fotografia, CRAF (Centro di Ricerca e Archiviazione della Fotografia), Villa Ciani, Lestans, Italy (*Stephen Shore, Photographs 1973–1993*), July 18–September 13, 1998; Ex-Covento Santa Maria, Gonzaga, Italy, November 7–December 12, 1998; Galeria d'Arte Contemporaneo di Comune di Venezia, Mestre, Italy, February 6–March 7, 1999; Musei Comunali/ Galleria dell'Immagine, Palazzo Gambalunga, Rimini, Italy, April 10–May 8, 1999; Palazzo Civico, Rubiera, Italy, September 25–October 17, 1999; Spazio

Oberdan, Milan (*Seductive Illusion: Stephen Shore, Fotografie 1973/1993*), July 23–September 19, 1999.

The Velvet Years, 1965–1967: Warhol's Factory, Photographs by Stephen Shore. Rock and Roll Hall of Fame, Cleveland, opened September 1995. Traveled to University Art Museum, California State University, Long Beach, March 18–April 27, 1997; Photographic Resource Center, Boston University, May 9–July 3, 1997; George Adams Gallery, Victorian Arts Center, Melbourne, May 12–June 9, 2000; Städtisches Museum Abteiberg Mönchengladbach, Germany (*Andy Warhol's "Factory"—The Velvet Years 1965–67: Fotografien von Stephen Shore*), February 24–April 21, 2002; Sprüth Magers, London (*The Velvet Years: Warhol's Factory 1965–67*), July 26–August 25, 2007; Albin O. Kuhn Library Gallery, Baltimore, August 31–December 12, 2010; Foundry Art Center, Saint Charles, Mo., September 21–December 14, 2012.

Stephen Shore: Old and New. Pace Wildenstein/MacGill, New York, November 22, 1995–January 6, 1996.

1997 *(Un)Common Places. Stephen Shore: Photographs 1975–1982*. Exhibition catalogue. Nederlands Foto Instituut, Rotterdam, March 11–May 22.

1998 *Stephen Shore: Luzzara*. Linea di Confine della Provincia di Reggio Emilia, Rubiera, Italy, February 21–March 5.

1999 *Stephen Shore: American Surfaces 1972*. Exhibition catalogue. Photographische Sammlung/SK Stiftung Kultur, Cologne, July 16–September 5. Traveled to Fotografie Forum, Frankfurt, October 23–December 5.

2000 *American Surfaces*. Schirmer/Mosel, Munich, February 10–March 16.
Stephen Shore. 303 Gallery, New York, May 6–June 3.

2001 *Stephen Shore: Uncommon Places*. Galerie Conrads, Düsseldorf, March 24–May 12.

2002 *Stephen Shore*. Galerie Rodolphe Janssen, Brussels, January 25–March 16.
Stephen Shore: Uncommon Places, 50 Unpublished Photographs, 1973–1978. Exhibition catalogue. Galerie Conrads, Düsseldorf, September 6–October 20; Galerie Kamel Mennour, Paris, September 7–October 21.

2003 *Stephen Shore*. 303 Gallery, New York, September 13–October 25.
Stephen Shore. Sprüth Magers Lee, London, December 4, 2003–January 20, 2004.

2004 *Stephen Shore*. Galerie Rodolphe Janssen, Brussels, October 12–November 13.
The Biographical Landscape: The Photography of Stephen Shore 1968–1993. Organized by the Aperture Foundation. Traveled to Akademie der Bildenden Künste, Vienna, November 12–December 4; Hôtel de Sully, Jeu de Paume, Paris (*Stephen Shore: paysage biographique, photographies 1968–1993*), January 14–March 20, 2005; Hammer Museum, Los Angeles, June 25–October 16, 2005; Presentation House Gallery, North Vancouver, B.C., November 12, 2005–January 15, 2006; Worcester Art Museum, Mass., March 26–June 25, 2006; Henry Art Gallery, University of Washington, Seattle, October 7–December 31, 2006; International Center of Photography, New York (*Biographical Landscape: The Photography of Stephen Shore, 1969–79*), May 11–September 9, 2007; Amarillo Museum of Art, Tex., November 1, 2007–January 6, 2008; Kemper Museum, Kansas City, Mo., February 22–May 18, 2008; Haggerty Museum of Art, Milwaukee (*Biographical Landscapes: The Photography of Stephen Shore, 1969–1979*), July 24–September 28, 2008; Museet for Fotokunst, Odense, Denmark, October 1–December 13, 2009; Museo di Roma in Trastevere, Rome (*Biographical Landscape: Fotografie di Stephen Shore 1969–1979*), February 26–May 23, 2010; NRW-Forum Düsseldorf, September 11, 2010–January 16, 2011.

2005 *American Surfaces*. Galerie Kamel Mennour, Paris, January 13–February 23.
Stephen Shore, Uncommon Places 1973–1979: Vintage Prints. Edwynn Houk Gallery, New York, March 8–April 16.
Stephen Shore: American Surfaces. Sprüth Magers, Cologne, September 6–October 15.
Stephen Shore: American Surfaces. P.S. 1 Contemporary Art Center, Long Island City, N.Y., October 23, 2005–January 23, 2006.

2006 *Stephen Shore: Color Landscapes from the 1970s*. Franklin Parrasch Gallery, New York, January 7–February 25.
American Surfaces. Sprüth Magers, Munich, February 23–April 29.
Artist's Books by Stephen Shore. The Century Association, New York, March 15–April 7.
Stephen Shore. Galerie Kicken Berlin, April 28–June 24.
Stephen Shore. 303 Gallery, New York, May–July.

2008 *Stephen Shore: Colouring American Photography*. Organized by the Roger Ballen Foundation. Iziko South African National Gallery, Cape Town, September 24–November 23.

2009 *Stephen Shore (The Velvet Years)*. 303 Gallery, New York, May 28–July 17.
Stephen Shore: Print-on-Demand. G/P Gallery, Tokyo, September 29–October 25.

2010 *Stephen Shore*. Exhibition catalogue. Douglas Hyde Gallery, Dublin, May 21–July 7.
Der Rote Bulli: Stephen Shore und die Neue Düsseldorfer Fotografie. Exhibition catalogue. NRW-Forum Düsseldorf, September 11, 2010–January 16, 2011.
Uncommon Places. Sprüth Magers, Berlin, November 12, 2010–January 8, 2011.

2011 *Stephen Shore: Uncommon Places*. Autostadt ZeitHaus, Wolfsburg, Germany, July 2–August 28.
Stephen Shore: Abu Dhabi. Aspen Art Museum, Colo., July 29–October 9.

2012 *Uncommon Places*. Photobiennale 2012, Manege Hall, Moscow, March 30–May 9.

2013 *Stephen Shore*. Rose Gallery, Los Angeles, November 2, 2013–January 18, 2014.
Stephen Shore: Something + Nothing. Sprüth Magers, London, November 26, 2013–January 11, 2014.

2014 *Stephen Shore*. 303 Gallery, New York, September 11–November 1.
Stephen Shore. Exhibition catalogue. Fundación MAPFRE, Madrid, September 19–November 24. Traveled to Centro de Cultura Antiguo Instituto de Gijón, Spain, March 26–June 14, 2015; Espace Van Gogh, Les Rencontres d'Arles, France, July 6–September 20, 2015; C/O Berlin, February 6–May 22, 2016; Huis Marseille, Amsterdam (*Stephen Shore: Retrospective*), June 10–September 4, 2016.

2016 *Stephen Shore: Uncommon Places*. Edwynn Houk Gallery, Zurich, February 11–May 7.

Group Exhibitions

1964 *Photo Workshop*. Donnell Library Center, New York, October 1–30.

1968 Andy Warhol. Exhibition catalogue. Moderna Museet, Stockholm, February 10–March 17.

1970 *Foto-Portret*. Exhibition catalogue. Haags Gemeentemuseum, The Hague, February 6–May 3.

1972 *Four Young Photographers*. The Photographers' Gallery, London, February 8–March 1.
Summer Light. Light Gallery, New York. June 27–August 18.
Sequences. Photokina, Cologne. September 23–October 1.

1973 *Sharp Focus Realism: A New Perspective*. Pace Editions, New York, May 5–June 9.
Color Photography. Light Gallery, New York, July 6–31.
Landscape/Cityscape: A Selection of Twentieth-Century American Photographs. The Metropolitan Museum of Art, New York, November 13, 1973–January 6, 1974.

1974 *Ten American Photographers*. The Photographers' Gallery, London, February 1–March 3.
Variety Show 2. Main Gallery, Department of Art, Humboldt State University, Arcata, Calif., February 25–March 15.
New Images in Photography: Object and Illusion. Lowe Art Museum, University of Miami, Coral Gables, Fla., March 24–April 21.
Art Now 74: A Celebration of the American Arts. Exhibition catalogue. John F. Kennedy Center for the Performing Arts, Washington, D.C., May 30–June 16.
Light at Lunn. Lunn Gallery/Graphics International Ltd. (in collaboration with Light Gallery), Washington, D.C., September 7–29.

1975 *Harry Callahan, Duane Michals, Steven [sic] Shore*. Harcus Krakow Rosen Sonnabend Gallery, Boston, July 8–August 31.
Young American Photographers. Kalamazoo Institute of Arts, Mich., September 2–28. Traveled to Flint Institute of Arts, Mich., October 1–November 2; University of Notre Dame Art Gallery, South Bend, Ind., November 16–December 16; Grand Rapids Art Museum, Mich., January 6–February 8, 1976; Kresge Art Center Gallery, Michigan State University, East Lansing, February 22–March 14, 1976.
Color Photography Now. Wellesley College Museum, Mass., September 29–October 27.
New Topographics: Photographs of a Man-Altered Landscape. Exhibition catalogue. International Museum of Photography, George Eastman House, Rochester, N.Y., October 14, 1975–February 2, 1976. Traveled to Otis Art Institute, Los Angeles, March 3–April 4, 1976; The Art Museum, Princeton University, N.J., June 22–September 3, 1976.
Color Photography: Inventors and Innovators, 1850–1975. Exhibition catalogue. Yale University Art Gallery, New Haven, Conn., November 11, 1975–January 11, 1976.

1976 *Signs of Life: Symbols in the American City*. Exhibition catalogue. Renwick Gallery, Smithsonian Institution, Washington, D.C., February 26–October 31.
American Photography: Past into Present: Prints from the Monsen Collection of American Photography. Exhibition catalogue. Seattle Art Museum, March 4–April 11. Traveled to J. B. Speed Art Museum, Louisville, Ky.
100 Master Photographs from the Collection of The Museum of Modern Art. Organized by The Museum of Modern Art. Traveled to Cincinnati Art Museum, Ohio, March 10–May 2; Saint Louis Art Museum, May 28–July 18; Toledo Art Museum, Ohio, September 12–October 24; Handshake, Inc. Gallery, Atlanta, December 5, 1976–January 16, 1977; Museum of South Texas, Corpus Christi, March 4–April 17, 1977; Baltimore Museum of Art, July 12–September 4, 1977; Krannert Art Museum, Champaign, Ill., October 16–November 13, 1977.
Photography for Collectors: Art Lending Service Penthouse Exhibition. The Museum of Modern Art, New York, March 16–June 15.
200 Years of American Sculpture. Whitney Museum of American Art, New York. March 16–September 26.
Aspects of American Photography 1976. Exhibition catalogue. Gallery 210, University of Missouri–Saint Louis, April 1–30.
The County Courthouse: Photographs by Tod Papageorge and Stephen Shore. Seagram Building, 4th Floor Gallery, New York, April–May.
Photography: Recent Acquisitions 1974–1976. The Museum of Modern Art, New York, May 6–July 18.
Harry Callahan, Danny Lyons, Stephen Shore, Aaron Siskind. Silver Image Gallery, Tacoma, Wash., May 13–June 6.
The County Courthouse in the United States. Seagram House, New York, before July 18–August 27.
Photographs from the Delaware Collections. Delaware Art Museum, Wilmington, June 18–July 18.
Six American Photographers: Robert Adams, Harry Callahan, Frank Gohlke, Nicholas Nixon, Tod Papageorge, Stephen Shore. Exhibition catalogue. Thomas Gibson Fine Art, London, July 19–August 31.
Photography Invitational Exhibition. Exhibition catalogue. J. B. Speed Art Museum, Louisville, Ky., October 4–31.
The Fifth Anniversary Show. Light Gallery, New York, October 6–30.
New Portfolios. Exhibition catalogue. Montgomery Art Gallery, Pomona College, Claremont, Calif., November 4–December 12. Traveled to Friends of Photography Sunset Center, Carmel, Calif., January 15–February 20, 1977.
Color Photographs 1976. Broxton Gallery, Los Angeles, December 1976–January 1977.

1977 *8 x 10 x 10*. Vision Gallery of Photography, Boston, January 4–February 4.
10 Photographes Américains Contemporains: Tendances Actuelles aux Etats-Unis. Galerie Zabriskie, Paris, January 29–March 5.
Grant Mudford / Stephen Shore: New Directions in American Landscapes. Silver Image Gallery, Tacoma, Wash., February 5–27.
The American Landscape: Harry Callahan, Walker Evans, Stephen Shore. Nova Gallery, Vancouver, B.C., February 15–March 12.
Nicholas Nixon, Tod Papageorge, Stephen Shore. Longwood Gallery, Massachusetts College of Art, Boston, March 22–April 1.
Courthouse. The Museum of Modern Art, New York, April 12–July 10. An expanded exhibition under the auspices of the American Federation of Arts and the National Trust for Historic Preservation traveled to Art Institute of Chicago, March 4–April 30, 1978; Fred Jones Jr. Museum of Art, University of Oklahoma, Norman, July 5–July 30, 1978; Old Courthouse, Saint Louis (*The County Courthouse: A Photographic Document*).
Some Color Photographs. Castelli Uptown, New York, June 4–July 2.
Documenta 6. Exhibition catalogue. Kassel, Germany, June 24–October 2.
Kress-Sonora Gallery, Taos, N.Mex, opened June 25.
Seven Photographers: The Delaware Valley. Exhibition catalogue. The Gallery, Peters Valley Craftsmen, Layton, N.J., July 23–August 14, 1977.
Contemporary Color Photography. Indiana University Art Museum, Bloomington, September 4–October 8.
Portfolios. Light Gallery, New York, September 7–October 1.
The Great West: Real/Ideal. Exhibition catalogue. University of Colorado at Boulder, September 9–October 15. Traveled to International Center of Photography, New York, July 14–September 3, 1978.
Center: Photographs from the Collection of the Center for Creative Photography.

University of Arizona Museum of Art, Tucson, September 25–October 30.
American Photographers. Forum Stadtpark, Graz, Austria, October 24–November 11. Traveled to Galerie im Taxispalais, Innsbruck, Austria, November 22–December 3; Museum des 20 Jahrhunderts, Vienna, December 7, 1977–January 8, 1978.
Faces and Facades. Exhibition catalogue. Clarence Kennedy Gallery, Cambridge, Mass., November 7–December 30.

1978 *New York.* Light Gallery, New York, January 4–28.
Monet's Years at Giverny: Beyond Impressionism. The Metropolitan Museum of Art, New York, April 22–July 9. Traveled to Saint Louis Art Museum, August 1–October 8.
Photography Since 1955 (Fotografia: correnti dal 1955). Lunn Gallery, Bologna Arts Fair, Italy, June 1–6.
Amerikanische Landschaftsphotographie: 1860–1978. Exhibition catalogue. Neue Sammlung, Munich, June 9–August 13.
Mirrors and Windows: American Photography since 1960. Exhibition catalogue. The Museum of Modern Art, New York, July 28–October 2. Traveled to Cleveland Museum of Art, November 15–December 31; Walker Art Center, Minneapolis, January 27–March 11, 1979; J. B. Speed Art Museum, Louisville, Ky., April 3–May 13, 1979; San Francisco Museum of Modern Art, June 8–July 29, 1979; Krannert Art Museum, University of Illinois, Champaign, August 19–September 23, 1979; Virginia Museum of Fine Arts, Richmond, November 13–December 23, 1979; Milwaukee Art Center, January 10–March 2, 1980.

1979 *Industrial Sights.* Whitney Museum of American Art, New York, January 25–February 28.
American Photography of the 70's. Art Institute of Chicago, February 3–March 25.
Selections of Modern Photography. John Berggruen Gallery, San Francisco, February 14–March 10.
New Acquisitions: Photographs from the Collection of the Center for Creative Photography. Center for Creative Photography, Tucson, Ariz., March 28–May 3.
Attitudes: Photography in the 1970s. Santa Barbara Museum of Art, Calif., May 12–August 5.
Harry Callahan, Stephen Shore. Susan Spiritus Gallery, Newport Beach, Calif., June 22–August 4.
American Images: New Work by Twenty Contemporary Photographers. Exhibition catalogue. Organized by Independent Curators, Inc. Traveled to Corcoran Gallery of Art, Washington, D.C., October 13–December 2; International Center of Photography, New York, January 12–February 10, 1980; Museum of Fine Arts, Houston, March 14–May 18, 1980; Minneapolis Institute of Arts, July 18–September 14, 1980; University of Arizona Museum of Art, Tucson, December 14, 1980–January 25, 1981; Newark Museum, N.J., April 15–July 12, 1981.
Corroborations and Constructions. Chicago Center for Contemporary Photography, October 21–December 5.

1980 *Recent Color Photography.* Sewall Art Gallery, Rice University, Houston, January 16–February 13.
Urban/Suburban: Photographs in Color. Addison Gallery of American Art, Phillips Academy, Andover, Mass., January 18–March 9.
New California Views: Selected Works from the Mills College Collection. Mills College Art Gallery, Oakland, Calif., January 29–March 9. Traveled to Silver Image Gallery, Seattle, April 9–May 11.
Color Photographs in the Collection. Art Institute of Chicago, April 19–June 22.
Farbwerke: Eine neue Generation von Farbphotographen. Kunsthaus Zürich, Siftung für die Photographie, Zurich, July 19–September 14, 1980.
Visitors to Arizona 1846 to 1890. Exhibition catalogue. Phoenix Art Museum, Ariz., September 5–October 12. Traveled to Tucson Museum of Art, Ariz., October 19–November 30, 1980.
Aspects of American Color Photography. Spectrum Photogalerie in Kunstmuseum, Hannover, Germany, December 9, 1980–January 12, 1981.

1981 *Selection.* Light Gallery, New York, February 5–28.
The New Color: A Decade of Color Photography. International Center of Photography, New York, February 27–March 29. Traveled to Everson Museum of Art, Syracuse, N.Y., May 15–July 26.
Acquisitions 1973–1980. George Eastman House, Rochester, N.Y., June 12–September 20.
Summer Light. Light Gallery, New York, July 9–September 5.
Photography: A Sense of Order. Exhibition catalogue. Institute of Contemporary Art, University of Pennsylvania, Philadelphia, December 11, 1981–January 27, 1982.
Light: Tenth Anniversary/Photographers' Selections. Light Gallery, New York, December 17, 1981–January 23, 1982.

1982 *Slices of Time: California Landscapes 1860–1880 and 1960–1980.* Oakland Museum, Calif., January 20–March 14.
Counterparts: Form and Emotion in Photographs. The Metropolitan Museum of Art, New York, February 26–May 9. Traveled to Contemporary Arts Center, Cincinnati, May 20–July 2; Dallas Museum of Fine Arts, August 4–September 13; San Francisco Museum of Modern Art, November 19, 1982–January 9, 1983; Corcoran Gallery of Art, Washington, D.C., February 22–April 18, 1983.
Photography in Color. Art Gallery, Stockton State College, Pomona, N.J., March 2–18.
Color Photographs from the Permanent Collection. Museum of Fine Arts, Houston, April 6–June 20.
Color as Form: A History of Color Photography. Exhibition catalogue. Organized by George Eastman House. Traveled to Corcoran Gallery, Washington, D.C., April 10–June 6; International Museum of Photography, George Eastman House, Rochester, N.Y., July 2–September 5; Creative Photography Lab, Massachusetts Institute of Technology, Cambridge.
Four Art and Photography Portfolios. City Gallery, New York, April 12–16.
Visions of Reality: Color Photography–A Contemporary Art. Goddard-Riverside Community Center, New York, April 29–May 16.
International Photography 1920–1980. Exhibition catalogue. Australian National Gallery, Canberra, November 10, 1982–January 30, 1983.

1983 *Stephen Shore and Richard Pare.* Camera Obscura, Stockholm, March 20–April 17.
Bay Area Collects: A Diverse Sampling. San Francisco Museum of Modern Art, April 21–June 26, 1983.
Summer 1983. Light Gallery, New York.

1984 *Automobile and Culture.* Exhibition catalogue. Museum of Contemporary Art, Los Angeles, July 21, 1984–January 6, 1985. Traveled to Detroit Institute of the Arts, June 12–September 8, 1985.
The Lens in the Garden. Hudson River Museum, Yonkers, N.Y., July 29–September 16.
Photographs from the Museum's Collection. The Metropolitan Museum of Art, New York, December 5, 1984–March 17, 1985.

1985 *David Husom and Steven [sic] Shore.* Film in the Cities Gallery, Saint Paul, Minn., February 6–27.
Western Spaces. Burden Gallery, Aperture Foundation for the Visual Arts, New York, March 14–April 27.

Stephen Shore and Joel Meyerowitz. Chapter Arts Centre, Cardiff, Wales, April 28–May 25.
American Images: Photography 1945–1980. Exhibition catalogue. Barbican Art Gallery, London, May 10–June 30.
Illuminating Color: Four Approaches in Contemporary Painting and Photography. Pratt Manhattan Center Gallery, New York, September 9–October 5; Pratt Institute Gallery, Brooklyn, N.Y., October 16–November 7.

1986 *Competition*. Light Gallery, New York, June–August.
The Capitol in Albany. Exhibition catalogue. Burden Gallery, Aperture Foundation for the Visual Arts, New York, September 3–September 26.

1987 *Images of Excellence. Photographs from the George Eastman House Collection*. George Eastman House, Rochester, N.Y., January–April.
Nuovo paesaggio americano: Dialectical Landscapes. Exhibition catalogue. Palazzo Fortuny, Venice, April 11–July 19.
Diamonds Are Forever: Artists and Writers on Baseball. New York State Museum, Albany, September 16–November 15. Traveled to Norton Gallery of Art, West Palm Beach, Fla., January 23–March 27, 1988; Museum of Art and History, San Juan, Puerto Rico, before April 25–June 12, 1988; Contemporary Arts Center, Cincinnati, July 2–August 21, 1988; Utah Museum of Fine Arts, Salt Lake City, September 10–October 30, 1988; Museum of Fine Arts, Houston, January 15–April 9, 1989; Baltimore Museum of Art, May 13–June 25, 1989; Chicago Public Library Cultural Center, July 8–September 9, 1989; Oakland Museum, Calif., September 30, 1989–January 7, 1990; New York Public Library, February 3–April 15, 1990; Institute of Contemporary Arts, Boston, June 2–July 14, 1990; San Diego Museum of Contemporary Art, La Jolla, Calif., August 18–October 21, 1990; Southeastern Center for Contemporary Arts, Winston-Salem, N.C., November 17, 1990–February 3, 1991; Scottsdale Center for the Arts, Ariz., February 28–April 26, 1992; Albright-Knox Art Gallery, Buffalo, N.Y., May 16–July 5, 1992.
Diverse Secrecies: The Garden Photographed. Exhibition catalogue. Presentation House Gallery, Vancouver, B.C., October 2–25.

1988 *Evocative Presence: Twentieth Century Photographs in the Museum Collection*. Museum of Fine Arts, Houston, February 27–May 1.

1989 *Suburban Home Life: Tracking the American Dream*. Whitney Museum, Downtown at Federal Reserve Plaza, New York, May 3–June 28. Traveled to Whitney Museum of American Art at Champion, Stamford, Conn., July 13–September 6.
On the Art of Fixing a Shadow: One Hundred and Fifty Years of Photography. Exhibition catalogue. Organized by the Art Institute of Chicago and the National Gallery of Art. National Gallery of Art, Washington, D.C., May 7–July 30; Art Institute of Chicago, September 16–November 26; Los Angeles County Museum of Art, December 21, 1989–February 25, 1990.
Picturing California: A Century of Photographic Genius. Exhibition catalogue. Oakland Museum, Calif., August 26–November 5.
Symbol and Surrogate: The Picture Within. Exhibition catalogue. University of Hawaii Art Gallery, Honolulu, November 19–December 22. Traveled to Galleries of the Claremont Colleges, Calif., March 4–April 8, 1990.

1990 *Andy Warhol System: Pub, Pop, Rock*. Exhibition catalogue. Fondation Cartier pour l'art contemporain, Jouy-en-Josas, France, June 14–September 8.

1991 *Poetics of the Real: American Landscape Photography*. Columbus Museum of Art, Ohio, January 13–March 3.
Quick Takes: Approaches to the Snapshot. Davison Art Center, Wesleyan University, Middletown, Conn., March 26–June 9.
Photographing L.A. Architecture. Turner/Krull Gallery, Los Angeles, June 8–July 5.
Who's on First? Lieberman & Saul, New York, June 22–August 2.
The Pleasures and Terrors of Domestic Comfort. Exhibition catalogue. The Museum of Modern Art, New York, September 26–December 31. Traveled to Baltimore Museum of Art, August 26–October 4, 1992; Los Angeles County Museum of Art, November 12, 1992–January 23, 1993; Cincinnati Contemporary Arts Center, April 3–May 29, 1993.

1992 *General Motoring: The Car in the American Scene*. Davison Art Center, Wesleyan University, Middletown, Conn., January 22–March 6.
This Sporting Life, 1878–1991. High Museum of Art, Atlanta, May 16–September 13.
Edward Hopper und die Fotografie. Exhibition catalogue. Museum Essen Folkswang, Germany, June 21–September 27.
Flora Photographica: Masterpieces of Flower Photography. Serpentine Gallery, London, August 18–September 20. Traveled to Royal Botanic Garden, Edinburgh, October 3–November 22; Manchester City Art Galleries, November 28–January 16, 1993; Mead Gallery, Coventry, January 23–March 7, 1993.
Silvy's River Scene, France: The Story of a Photograph. J. Paul Getty Museum, Malibu, December 15, 1992–February 28, 1993.

1993 *Please Observe: Contemporary Photography*. Bard College, Annandale-on-Hudson, N.Y., March 15–April 15.

1994 *Photography Now: Facts and Fantasies*. Rye Arts Center, N.Y., January 16–March 31.
Flesh & Blood: Photographers' Images of Their Own Families. Organized by the American Federation of Arts. Friends of Photography, Ansel Adams Center, San Francisco, January 19–March 6.
Mai de la Photo, Reims, France, May 2–June 5.
Portraits & Memories. Suzan Cooper Fine Art, Woodstock, N Y., August 6–September 5.
Where Have You Gone, Joe DiMaggio? Galveston Arts Center, Tex., October 15–November 20.
After Art: Rethinking 150 Years of Photography. Henry Gallery, Seattle, December 4, 1994–March 5, 1995.
American Studies: Dokumentarische Fotokunst in den USA, 1930 bis 1980. Aktionsforum Praterinsel, Munich, December 9, 1994–January 29, 1995.

1995 *Picturing Modernity: Photographs from the Permanent Collection*. San Francisco Museum of Modern Art, January 18–December 31.
Of Time and the River. Gallery at Hastings-on-Hudson, Municipal Building, N.Y., March 19–May 7.

1996 *Summer in America*. Candace Perich Gallery, Katonah, N.Y., July 13–September 8.
Breuer's Whitney: An Anniversary Exhibition. Whitney Museum of American Art, New York, September 11–December 8.
a/drift: Scenes from the Penetrable Culture. Center for Curatorial Studies Museum, Bard College, Annandale-on-Hudson, N.Y., October 26, 1996–January 5, 1997.

1997 *160 Years of Photography: Masterworks from the San Francisco Museum of Modern Art*. San Francisco Museum of Modern Art, July 10–September 7.
A Sharp Lookout. Center for Photography at Woodstock, N.Y., July 26–September 14.

The Warhol Look/Glamour Style Fashion. Whitney Museum of American Art, New York, November 8, 1997–January 18, 1998.

Capturing Time: A Celebration of Photographs. J. Paul Getty Museum, Los Angeles, December 1, 1997–March 1, 1998.

1998 *The Photographic Era: Highlights from the Permanent Collection*. San Francisco Museum of Modern Art, February 13–June 23.

Andy Warhol: A Factory. Exhibition catalogue. Kunstmuseum Wolfsburg, Germany, October 3, 1998–January 10, 1999. Traveled to Kunsthalle Wien, Vienna, February 5–March 2, 1999; Palais des Beaux-Arts, Brussels, June 1–September 19, 1999; Guggenheim Museum Bilbao, Spain, October 19, 1999–January 16, 2000; Museu de Arte Contemporânea de Serralves, Porto, Portugal, February 11–April 30, 2000.

1999 *Views from the Edge of the World: Landscape Photography*. Marlborough Chelsea, New York, March 6–April 3.

The American Century: Art & Culture, 1900–2000. Exhibition catalogue. Whitney Museum of American Art, New York. Part I, 1900–1950: April 23–August 22; Part II, 1950–2000: September 26, 1999–February 13, 2000.

Andy Warhol: Photography. Exhibition catalogue. Hamburger Kunsthalle, Hamburg, Germany, May 13–August 22. Traveled to Andy Warhol Museum, Pittsburgh, November 6, 1999–February 15, 2000.

Andy Warhol Drawings, 1942–1987. Walker Art Center, Minneapolis, August 8–November 28.

The Promise of Photography: Selections from the DG Bank Collection. P.S. 1 Contemporary Art Center, Long Island City, N.Y., September 12–October 24.

Photographic Innovators: 1840s–1990s. Victoria and Albert Museum, London, September 16, 1999–January 30, 2000.

2000 *Looking into the Collection: Arizona*. Center for Creative Photography, Tucson, Ariz., February 19–April 9.

Walker Evans & Company. Exhibition catalogue. The Museum of Modern Art, New York, March 16–July 26. Traveled to J. Paul Getty Museum, Los Angeles (*Walker Evans & Company: Works from The Museum of Modern Art*), July 10–September 16, 2001.

How You Look at It: Fotografien des 20. Jahrhunderts / Photographs of the 20th Century. Exhibition catalogue. Sprengel Museum, Hannover, Germany, May 14–August 6. Traveled to Städelsches Kunstinstitut and Städelsche Galerie, Frankfurt, August 23–November 12.

Nature & Urbanisme II. Gabrielle Salomon–Art Conseil, Paris, May 31–July 20.

Expanding Horizons: Landscape Photographs from the Whitney Museum of American Art. Whitney Museum of American Art, New York, July 21–October 6.

Identificazione di un Paesaggio: Venezia–Marghera, fotografia e trasformazioni nella città contemporanea. Exhibition catalogue. VEGA Parco Scientifico Tecnologico, Marghera, Italy, September 9–October 29.

Places as Landscape. Uffizi Gallery, Florence, October 20, 2000–January 6, 2001. Traveled to Palazzo Reale, Naples, October 19–November 25, 2001.

Collector's Choice. Exit Art, New York, November 10, 2000–January 6, 2001.

2001 *Revisited: Aspects of American Color Photography*. Galerie Kicken Berlin, January 20–March 16.

Capturing Light: Masterpieces of California Photography, 1850 to the Present. Oakland Museum, Calif., March 3–May 26.

Settings and Players: Theatrical Ambiguity in American Photography. Exhibition catalogue. White Cube, London, March 9–April 14. Traveled to City Gallery, Prague, June 21–September 16.

Where are we? Questions of Landscape. Victoria and Albert Museum, London, April 5–August 28.

Overnight to Many Cities: Travel and Tourism at Home and Away. 303 Gallery, New York, May 31–July 13. Traveled to The Photographers' Gallery, London, April 12–June 4, 2002.

Amerikanische Fotografie ca. 1970. Mai 36 Galerie, Zurich, August 24–October 6.

Pia Fries, Stephen Shore. Galerie Rodolphe Janssen, Brussels, September 8–October 3.

The Natural Environment: Hopelessly Unstrung or Pausing to Rewind? Fine Arts Center Galleries, University of Rhode Island, Kingston, November 6–December 16.

2002 *Pictures*. Greene Naftali, New York, January 18–February 23.

Photographers, Writers, and the American Scene: Visions of Passage. Museum of Photographic Arts, San Diego, Calif., March 24–June 2. Traveled to High Museum of Art, Atlanta, April 2–August 7, 2004.

Gravity Over Time. Gallery 1000 Eventi, Milan, June 6–September 2.

American Standard: (Para)Normality and Everyday Life. Exhibition catalogue. Barbara Gladstone Gallery, New York, June 26–August 16.

Visions from America: Photographs from the Whitney Museum of American Art, 1940–2001. Whitney Museum of American Art, New York, June 27–September 22. Traveled to University of Kentucky Art Gallery, Lexington, November 16, 2003–January 25, 2004; Wexner Center for the Arts, Columbus, Ohio, May 22–August 15, 2004; Rochester Art Center, Minn., January 15–March 13, 2005.

Constellation. Center for Photography at Woodstock, N.Y., August 10–October 20.

A Proposal for an Exhibition. Monte Clark Gallery, Vancouver, B.C., November 30, 2002–January 18, 2003.

International Landscape. Galerie Rodolphe Janssen, Brussels, December 14, 2002–March 8, 2003.

2003 *Yet Untitled: Die Sammlung Bernd F. Künne*. Exhibition catalogue. Städtische Galerie Wolfsburg, Germany, January 18–March 30. Traveled to Suermondt-Ludwig-Museum, Aachen, Germany, July 5–September 28; Det Kongelige Bibliotek, Copenhagen, February 20–May 1, 2004; Kunsthalle Nürnberg, Germany, May 13–July 4, 2004; Galerie Nei Liicht, Dudelange, Luxembourg.

Picturing Modernity: Photographs from the Permanent Collection. San Francisco Museum of Modern Art, January 18, 2003–January 27, 2004.

Affinities . . . Now and Then. H&R Block Artspace at the Kansas City Art Institute, Mo., February 1–March 23.

Best of: Blick in die Sammlung. Akademie der Bildenden Künste, Vienna. Traveled to Photographische Sammlung/SK Stiftung Kultur, Cologne, February 27–April 25.

The Eye and the Camera: A History of Photography. The Albertina, Vienna, March 14–June 8. Traveled to Fotomuseum Winterthur, Switzerland (*The Eye and the Camera: A History of Photography from the Collections of the Albertina in Vienna*), June 26–November 7, 2004.

Cruel and Tender: The Real in the Twentieth-Century Photograph. Exhibition catalogue. Tate Modern, London, June 5–September 7. Traveled to Museum Ludwig, Cologne, November 29, 2003–February 18, 2004.

Within Hours We Would Be in the Middle of Nowhere. 303 Gallery, New York, July 19–August 29.

Sea. Jen Bekman Gallery, New York, August 5–September 13.

Photoforum 2003. Museum of Fine Arts, Houston, September 15–December 1.

Jede Fotografie ein Bild: Siemens Fotosammlung. Exhibition catalogue. Pinakothek der Moderne, Sammlung Moderne Kunst, Munich, December 18, 2003–March 7, 2004.

Pirkle Jones and the Changing California Landscape. San Francisco Museum of Modern Art, December 20, 2003–April 18, 2004.

2004 *Seventies Color Photography*. Marianne Boesky Gallery, New York, January 3–31.
Inside Out: Portrait Photographs from the Permanent Collection. Whitney Museum of American Art, New York, February 7–May 23.
Social Creatures: How Body Becomes Art / Soziale Kreaturen: wie Körper Kunst wird. Exhibition catalogue. Sprengel Museum Hannover, Germany, February 29–June 13.
In the Center of Things: A Tribute to Harold Jones. Center for Creative Photography, Tucson, Ariz., April 3–July 18.
Stephen Shore / Thomas Struth: A Selection of Photographic Works. Pinakothek der Moderne, Munich, May 8–September 12.
Residents. Gallery Luisotti, Bergamot Station, Santa Monica, Calif., May 22–July 3.
Cakewalk. Ambrosino Gallery, Miami, May 28–July 3.
Evidence of Impact: Art and Photography 1963–1978. Whitney Museum of American Art, New York, May 29–October 10.
Subway Series: The New York Yankees and the American Dream. Bronx Museum of the Arts, N.Y., June 2–December 31.
William Eggleston: Los Alamos. San Francisco Museum of Modern Art, August 21, 2004–January 4, 2005.
Super Hits of the '70s: Photographs from the Collection. Milwaukee Art Museum, October 8, 2004–January 2, 2005.
American Pictures. Whitney Museum of American Art, New York, October 16, 2004–February 27, 2005.
Arti & Architettura 1900–2000. Palazzo Ducale, Genoa, October 25, 2004–February 13, 2005.
Stephen Shore, Ed Ruscha. Galerie Trabant, Vienna, November 2–December 18.

2005 *Boxed Sets: Portfolios of the Seventies*. Center for Creative Photography, Tucson, Ariz., March 12–May 22.
Deutsche Börse Photography Prize 2005: Luc Delahaye, J. H. Engström, Jörg Sasse, Stephen Shore. The Photographers' Gallery, London, April 8–June 5.
Calle Mayor: Fotografía urbana en América: Walter Rosenblum, Bill Owens, Stephen Shore. Exhibition catalogue. PhotoEspaña 2005, Centro Cultural de la Villa, Madrid, June 1–July 17.
Safe and Warm in L.A. Franklin Parrasch Gallery, New York, September 8–October 8.
The American Dream. Kunsthalle Mannheim, Germany, September 17–December 30.
Trans Emilia–Sammlung Linea di Confine: Territoriales Erkunden der Emilia-Romagna. Fotomuseum Winterthur, Switzerland, October 22, 2005–February 12, 2006.

2006 *Portraits of Artists*. Luhring Augustine, New York, January 6–February 10.
Middle Ground: Photographs from the Whitney Museum of American Art. Miriam & Ira D. Wallach Art Gallery, Columbia University, New York, January 24–February 11.
Picturing Modernity: Photographs from the Permanent Collection. San Francisco Museum of Modern Art, January 28–April 16.
Photography Collection: Rotation 3. The Museum of Modern Art, New York, March 15–November 27.
A Complex Eden: Photographs of the American West. Museum of Fine Arts, Saint Petersburg, Fla., April 29–August 9.
Mystic River. Exhibition catalogue. Southfirst: Art, Brooklyn, N.Y., May 5–June 18. Traveled to Arcadia University Art Gallery, Glenside, Pa., September 8–October 22.
On Photography: A Tribute to Susan Sontag. The Metropolitan Museum of Art, New York, June 6–September 4.
Full House: Views of the Whitney's Collection at 75. Whitney Museum of American Art, New York, June 29–December 3.
In the Woods: Nineteenth-Century and Contemporary Keene Valley Artists. Skylight Gallery, Keene Valley, N.Y., July 1–September 9.
Die Liebe zum Licht. Kunstmuseum Celle (with Sammlung Robert Simon), Germany, July 19–September 27.
Making Panhandle Pictures. Amarillo Museum of Art, Tex., September 7–October 22.
The Office: In and Out of the Box. Exhibition catalogue. Dorsky Gallery, Long Island City, N.Y., September 10–November 13.
Strange Drugs. Galerie Rodolphe Janssen, Brussels, September 15–October 28.
Where We Live: Photographs of America from the Berman Collection. Exhibition catalogue. J. Paul Getty Museum, Los Angeles, October 24, 2006–February 25, 2007.
Target Collection of American Photography: A Century in Pictures. Museum of Fine Arts, Houston, December 3, 2006–February 25, 2007. Traveled to Austin Museum of Art, Tex., May 19–August 12, 2007.
Photography Collection: Rotation 4. The Museum of Modern Art, New York, December 13, 2006–April 16, 2007.

2007 *Not For Sale*. P.S. 1 Contemporary Art Center, Long Island City, N.Y., February 11–April 30.
When Color Was New. Art Institute of Chicago, February 24–April 29.
Second View: Amerikanische Fotografie in der Sammlung Niedersächsische Sparkassenstiftung Hannover. Kunstmuseum Kloster unser lieben Frauen Magdeburg, Germany, April 1–June 24.
Hidden in Plain Sight: Contemporary Photographs from the Collection. The Metropolitan Museum of Art, New York, May 15–September 3.
Views—*In Passing—From 1930 Until Today: From the Albertina's Photographic Collection*. The Albertina, Vienna, May 16–September 16.
Stephen Shore, Louise Lawler, Jacques De Backer. Maison de la Culture de la Province de Namur, Belgium, June 29–August 14.
Easy Rider: Road Trips through America. Yancey Richardson Gallery, New York, July11–September 8.
People Take Pictures of Each Other. . . La Montagne Gallery, Boston, September 6–October 13.
The Eternal Now: Warhol and the Factory '63–'68. The Model Arts and Niland Gallery, Sligo, Ireland, October 6–December 22. Traveled to Lewis Glucksman Gallery, Cork, Ireland, February 22–June 8, 2008.
Warhol on Warhol. La Casa Encendida, Madrid, November 23, 2007–January 20, 2008.

2008 *Philip-Lorca diCorcia, Mitch Epstein, Stephen Shore*. Galerie Rodolphe Janssen, Brussels, January 11–February 9.
Mobile Art. Central, Hong Kong, February–April; Yoyogi Olympic Plaza, Tokyo, May–July; Central Park, New York, October–November 9.
A Shared Vision: The Fred and Laura Ruth Bidwell Photography Collection. Akron Art Museum, Ohio, February 23–May 25.
When Color Was New: *Vintage Photographs from around the 1970s*. Exhibition catalogue. Julie Saul Gallery, New York, July 7–September 6.
Vik Muniz, Stephen Shore and Janaina Tschäpe. Johannesburg Art Gallery, South Africa, July 26–November 1.
The Greenroom: Reconsidering the Documentary and Contemporary Art. Center for Curatorial Studies and Hessel Museum of Art, Bard College, Annandale-on-Hudson, N.Y., September 27, 2008–February 1, 2009.
Reality Check: Truth and Illusion in Contemporary Photography. The Metropolitan Museum of Art, New York, November 4, 2008–March 22, 2009.

2009 *Edward Hopper & Company*. Exhibition catalogue. Fraenkel Gallery, San Francisco, March 5–May 2.

Into the Sunset: Photography's Image of the West. Exhibition catalogue. The Museum of Modern Art, New York, March 29–June 8.

Inaugural Modern Wing Exhibition. Art Institute of Chicago, May 16–September 7.

Visions of Our Time. Deutsche Börse AG and C/O Berlin, Berlin, May 29–July 19.

Summer Exhibition: A Selection of Works by Gallery Artists. Edwynn Houk Gallery, New York, May 31–July 31.

New Topographics: Photographs of a Man-Altered Landscape. Exhibition catalogue. George Eastman House, Rochester, N.Y., June 13–October 4. Traveled to Los Angeles County Museum of Art, October 25, 2009–January 3, 2010; Center for Creative Photography, Tucson, Ariz., February 19–May 16, 2010; San Francisco Museum of Modern Art, July 17–October 3, 2010; Landesgalerie Linz, Austria, November 10, 2010–January 9, 2011; Photographische Sammlung Stiftung Kultur, Cologne, January 27–April 3, 2011; Jeu de Paume, Paris, April 11–June 12, 2011; Nederlands Fotomuseum, Rotterdam, July 2–September 11, 2011; Bilbao Fine Arts Museum, Spain, October 17, 2011–January 8, 2012.

Glitz & Grime: Photographs of Times Square. Yancey Richardson Gallery, New York, July 9–September 12.

10 Printemps en Automne. Galerie Kamel Mennour, Paris, September 12–October 13.

Stadt, Land, Fluss: Fotografien aus den Sammlungen des Sprengel Museum Hannover. Sprengel Museum Hannover, Germany, September 13, 2009–January 10, 2010.

In the Darkroom: Photographic Processes before the Digital Age. National Gallery of Art, Washington, D.C., October 25, 2009–March 14, 2010.

Shoot: Photography of the Moment. Parco Factory, Tokyo, November 26–December 14.

2010 *In the Vernacular*. Art Institute of Chicago, February 6–May 31.

Starburst: Color Photography in America, 1970–1980. Exhibition catalogue. Cincinnati Museum of Art, February 13–May 9, 2010. Traveled to Princeton Art Museum, N.J., July 10–September 26.

Pioneers of Color. Edwynn Houk Gallery, New York, February 25–April 24. Traveled to Galerie Edwynn Houk, Zurich (*American Pioneers of Color*), September 23–December 18.

Pier 24: The Inaugural Exhibition. Pier 24 Photography, San Francisco, March 16–June 16.

On the Road: A Legacy of Walker Evans. Exhibition catalogue. Robert Lehman Art Center, Brooks School, North Andover, Mass., April 2–June 12.

On the Road. Artpace, San Antonio, Tex., May 13–September 5.

Item. Mitchell-Innes and Nash, New York, June 30–August 13.

The La Brea Matrix. Kaune, Sudendorf Gallery, Cologne, November 14, 2009–January 16, 2010.

2011 *American Dreams*. Bendigo Art Gallery, Victoria, Australia, April 16–July 10.

You Are Here. Vrac/l'Escaut, Brussels, April 22–May 14.

Photography Collection: Rotation 8. The Museum of Modern Art, New York, May 13, 2011–February 12, 2012.

Here. Pier 24 Photography, San Francisco, May 23, 2011–January 31, 2012.

More American Photographs. CCA Wattis Institute for Contemporary Arts, San Francisco, October 4–December 17. Traveled to Museum of Contemporary Art, Denver, March 1–June 3, 2012; Wexner Center for the Arts, Columbus, Ohio, January 27–April 7, 2013; California Museum of Photography at the University of California, Riverside, September 28, 2013–January 11, 2014.

Picturing Modernity: Photographs from the Permanent Collection. San Francisco Museum of Modern Art, November 3, 2011–March 4, 2012.

Danser Sa Vie. Centre Pompidou, Paris, November 23, 2011–April 2, 2012.

Light Years: Conceptual Art and the Photograph, 1964–1977. Art Institute of Chicago, December 13, 2011–March 11, 2012.

2012 *The Dwelling Life of Man: Masterpieces by American and European Photographers from the Martin Z. Margulies Collection, Miami*. Fundació Foto Colectania and Fundació Suñol, Barcelona, February 22–June 16. Traveled to Kunsthal KAdE, Amersfoort, The Netherlands, September 22, 2012–January 6, 2013.

True Stories: Amerikanische Fotografie aus der Sammlung Moderne Kunst. Exhibition catalogue. Pinakothek der Moderne, Munich, March 2–September 30.

Color Pictures. Exhibition catalogue. Art Galleries at Texas Christian University, Fort Worth, March 3–April 14.

2012 Invitational Exhibition of Visual Arts. American Academy of Arts and Letters, New York, March 8–April 15.

Objects in Mirror: The Imagination of the American Landscape. Exhibition catalogue. Centraal Museum, Utrecht, The Netherlands, March 11–April 8.

The Shaping of New Visions: Photography, Film, Photobook (Photography Collection: Rotation 9). The Museum of Modern Art, New York, April 16, 2012–April 21, 2013.

About Face. Pier 24 Photography, San Francisco, May 15, 2012–April 30, 2013.

From the Factory to the World: Photography and the Warhol Community. PhotoEspaña 2012, Theatro Fernan Gomez Centro de Arte, Madrid, June 6–July 22.

DIY: Photographers & Books. Exhibition catalogue. Cleveland Museum of Art, August 11–December 30.

Made in Arizona: Photographs from the Collection. Center for Creative Photography, Tucson, Ariz., August 18–November 25.

UR Feeling. Camden Arts Centre, London, September 27–December 2.

Lost & Found: Anonymous Photography in Reflection. Ambach & Rice, Los Angeles, December 1, 2012–January 12, 2013.

When Collecting Was New: Photographs from the Robert A. Taub Collection. Art Institute of Chicago, December 15, 2012–May 12, 2013.

2013 *Color Rush: 75 Years of Color Photography in America*. Exhibition catalogue (*Color Rush: American Color Photography from Stieglitz to Sherman*). Milwaukee Art Museum, February 22–May 19.

Car Culture: Art and the Automobile. Heckscher Museum of Art, Huntington, N.Y., April 27–August 11.

XL: 19 New Acquisitions in Photography. The Museum of Modern Art, New York, May 10, 2013–January 6, 2014.

Everyday Epiphanies: Photography and Daily Life since 1969. The Metropolitan Museum of Art, New York, June 25, 2013–January 26, 2014.

Lens Drawings. Marian Goodman Gallery, Paris, June 28–August 2.

A Sense of Place. Pier 24 Photography, San Francisco, July 1, 2013–May 30, 2014.

Station to Station by Doug Aitken. Exhibition catalogue. New York; Pittsburgh; Chicago; Minneapolis; Santa Fe, N.Mex.; Winslow, Ariz.; Barstow, Calif.; Los Angeles; and Oakland/San Francisco, September 6–28. Traveled to Barbican Centre, London, June 27–July 26, 2015.

2014 *Only The Good Ones: The Snapshot Aesthetic Revisited*. Galerie Rudolfinum, Prague, January 24–April 6.

Edward Hopper and Photography. Whitney Museum of American Art, New York, July 17–October 19.

Constructing Worlds: Photography and Architecture in the Modern Age. Exhibition catalogue. Barbican Art Gallery, Barbican Centre, London, September 25, 2014–January 11, 2015. Traveled to Swedish Centre for Architecture and Design, Stockholm, February 20–May 17, 2015; Fundación Ico, Madrid, June 3–September 6, 2015.

This Place. Exhibition catalogue. Organized by Chronicle of a People Foundation, Inc. Traveled to DOX Center for Contemporary Art, Prague, October 24, 2014–March 2, 2015; Tel Aviv Museum of Art, May 14–September 6, 2015; Norton Museum of Art, West Palm Beach, Fla., October 15, 2015–January 17, 2016; Brooklyn Museum, N.Y., February 12–June 5, 2016.

Conflict, Time, Photography. Exhibition catalogue. Tate Modern, London, November 26, 2014–March 15, 2015. Traveled to Museum Folkwang, Essen, Germany, April 10–July 5, 2015.

2015 *HyperAmerica: Landscape–Image–Reality*. Kunsthaus, Graz, Austria, April 10–August 30.

In the Garden. George Eastman House, Rochester, N.Y., May 9–September 6.

The Order of Things. Walther Collection, Neu-Ulm, Germany, May 17–October 10.

Warhol Underground. Centre Pompidou Metz, France, July 1–November 23.

Photographier les jardins de Monet: cinq regards contemporains. Musée des impressionismes Giverny, France, July 31–November 1.

The La Brea Matrix—Extended. Organized by The PhotoBookMuseum. Gallery of Photography, Dublin, September 4–October 18.

The Lives of Pictures: Forty Years of Collecting at the Center for Creative Photography. Center for Creative Photography, Tucson, Ariz., October 10, 2015–March 20, 2016.

2016 *The Open Road: Photography and the American Road Trip*. Exhibition catalogue. Organized by the Aperture Foundation. Traveled to Crystal Bridges Museum of American Art, Bentonville, Ark., February 27–May 30; Detroit Institute of Arts, June 17–September 11; Museum of Fine Arts, Saint Petersburg, Fla., February 11–June 4, 2017; Amarillo Museum of Art, Tex., November 4, 2016–January 1, 2017.

Ordinary Pictures. Walker Art Center, Minneapolis, February 27–October 2.

Magical Surfaces: The Uncanny in Contemporary Photography. Parasol Unit Foundation for Contemporary Art, London, April 13–June 19.

California and the West: Photography from the Campaign for Art. San Francisco Museum of Modern Art, May 14–September 5.

An Agreeable State of Uncertainty. Vancouver Art Gallery, B.C., June 11–October 30.

Invisible Adversaries. Center for Curatorial Studies, Hessel Museum of Art, Bard College, Annandale-on-Hudson, N.Y., June 25–September 18, 2016.

Selected Bibliography
Compiled by Gianna Furia

Writings by Shore

1989 *The Friends Focus: On Photography*. Poughkeepsie, N.Y.: Vassar College Art Gallery, 1989.

1993 "The Fractal Geometry of Experience." *Annandale* (Bard College), Winter 1993–94, 13–19.

2005 "Questionnaire: Stephen Shore." *Frieze* 95 (November–December 2005): 148.

2006 "Dear Young Artist." In Peter Nesbett, Shelly Bancroft, and Sarah Andress, eds., *Letters to a Young Artist*, 35–37. New York: Darte Publishing, 2006.
"Photography and Architecture." In *Sze Tsung Leong: History Images*, 142. Göttingen: Steidl, 2006.

2008 "Memorial for John Szarkowski." *Century Association Yearbook*. New York: Century Association, 2008.

2009 "Snapshots." In Ken Miller, *Shoot: Photography of the Moment*, 5. New York: Rizzoli, 2009.
"Stephen Shore." In Lewis Blackwell, ed., *Photo-wisdom: Master Photographers on Their Art*, 190. Sydney: PQ Blackwell/Chronicle Books, 2009.
"Stephen Shore and the Factory." *Time Out New York*, June 11–17, 2009, 2.

2011 "Form and Pressure." *Aperture* 205 (Winter 2011): 44–49.

2013 "No Filter: How I Captured Winslow, Arizona in 180 Images." *Huffington Post* blog post, September 25, 2013, http://www.huffingtonpost.com/stephen-shore/no-filter-how-i-captured-_b_3991291.html.

2014 "Stephen Shore: Intentionality." In Jason Fulford and Gregory Halpern, eds., *The Photographer's Playbook: 307 Assignments and Ideas*, 317. New York: Aperture, 2014.

2016 "Brooklyn: This Place, Stephen Shore." *L'Oeil de la Photographie*, February 25, 2016, www.loeildelaphotographie.com/en/2016/02/25/article/159892100/brooklyn-this-place-stephen-shore/.
"Photographer Stephen Shore on How Andy Warhol Taught Him to Be an Interesting Artist." *Artspace*, October 13, 2016, http://www.artspace.com/magazine/interviews_features/book_report/stephen-shore-andy-warhol-54264.

Books by Shore

1982 *Uncommon Places*. New York: Aperture, 1982.

1983 *The Gardens at Giverny: A View of Monet's World*. Introduction by John Rewald. New York: Aperture, 1983.

1993 *Stephen Shore: Luzzara*, Laboratorio di Fotografia 6. Rubiera, Italy: Arcadia Edizioni, 1993.

1995 *The Velvet Years: Warhol's Factory, 1965–67*. Photographs by Stephen Shore; text by Lynne Tillman. New York: Thunder's Mouth Press, 1995.

1998 *The Nature of Photographs*. Baltimore: Johns Hopkins University Press, 1998.

1999 *American Surfaces 1972*. Munich: Schirmer/Mosel, 1999.

2002 *Essex County*. Tucson, Ariz.: Nazraeli Press, 2002.
Stephen Shore: Uncommon Places, 50 Unpublished Photographs 1973–1978. Düsseldorf: Galerie Conrads; Paris: Galerie Kamel Mennour, 2002.

2004 *Uncommon Places: The Complete Works*. Essay by Stephan Schmidt-Wulffen; conversation with Lynne Tillman. New York: Aperture, 2004.

2005 *American Surfaces*. London and New York: Phaidon Press, 2005.

2006 *Witness Number One*. New York: Joy of Giving Something, 2006.

2007 *Merced River: Yosemite National Park, California 8/13/79*. Portland, Ore.: Nazraeli Press, 2007.
The Nature of Photographs: A Primer. Revised ed. London and New York: Phaidon Press, 2007.

2008 *A Road Trip Journal*. London and New York: Phaidon Press, 2008.
Surfaces américaines. London and New York: Phaidon Press, 2008.

2011 *Ashkelon* (Six by Six, set 2, vol. 4). Portland, Ore.: Nazraeli Press, 2011.
The Hudson Valley. Essay by Laurie Dahlberg. Annandale-on-Hudson, N.Y.: Blind Spot, 2011.
Mose: A Preliminary Report. London: Koenig Books, 2011.

2012 *Pet Pictures*. Portland, Ore.: Nazraeli Press, 2012.
Stephen Shore: The Book of Books. Essay by Jeff Rosenheim. London and New York: Phaidon Press, 2012.

2013 *A New York Minute*. London and New York: Phaidon Press, 2013.

2014 *From Galilee to the Negev*. London and New York: Phaidon Press, 2014.
Winslow Arizona: September 19th, 2013. Tokyo: Amana, 2014.

2015 *Instagram*. Selected by Hans Ulrich Obrist. London: Mörel, 2015.
The Noguchi Museum: A Portrait. Photographs by Stephen Shore and Tina Barney. London and New York: Phaidon Press, 2015.
Survivors in Ukraine. London and New York: Phaidon Press, 2015.

2016 *Factory: Andy Warhol*. London and New York: Phaidon Press, 2016.
Granger Bay, Cape Town, South Africa, June 2014. Brooklyn, N.Y.: Shandaken Project, 2016.
Luzzara. London: Stanley/Barker, 2016.

2017 *Stephen Shore: Selected Works, 1973–1981*. New York: Aperture, 2017.

Publications with Photographs by Shore

1963 *The Book Buyer's Guide* 55, no. 821 (October 1963): cover.

1964 "A Job for that 'Second' Orchestra." *Herald Tribune*, September 27, 1964, 55.
"Macy's and All New York Welcome the Festival Orchestra." *New York Times*, September 30, 1964, 24.
"Music This Fall." *Cue*, September 5, 1964, 12.
"Music's Faust." *Newsweek*, November 16, 1964, 90.

1967 *Art in America* 55, no. 6 (November/December 1967): 90.
Warhol, Andy. *Andy Warhol's Index*. New York: Random House, 1967.

1972 "Stephen E. Shore." *Fox* 1, no. 1 (January 30, 1972): n.p.
"Stephen Shore." *Camera* (Switzerland), October 1972, 19.

1973 "The Once-Whirling Other World of Andy Warhol." *Saturday Review World*, September 25, 1973, 20–24.

1974 "The Story of a Day. Thursday, September 5, 1974." *Life Special Report: One Day in the Life of America*, September 5, 1974, 58.
Blackburn, Rip. "He Knows the Use of Smashes." *The Real World* 1, no. 3 (1974): 1–3.

1975 "Architectural Photography." *Journal of Architectural Education*, November 1975, 10–15.
"Panopticon II: Photography and Architecture." *Camera* (Switzerland), December 1975, 16–17.

1976 "Documentary Photography USA. American Structures: County Courthouses." *Popular Photography*, December 1976, 91–92.
Exposure 14, no. 3 (1976): cover.
"The Rest of New York." *The Real World* 7 (July/August 1976): 26–27.

1977 *Avenue*, October 1977, cover.
"Biographies." *Camera* (Switzerland), July 1977, 27.
"New York, Februar 1977." *DU–Europäische Kunstzeitschrift*, September 1977, 30–31, 42–45.
Smith, Lee. "Hard Times Come to Steeltown." *Fortune*, December 1977, 86–93.
"Stephen Shore." *Camera* (Switzerland), January 1977, cover.

1978 *Avenue*, September 1978, cover.
Chung, Henry. *Henry Chung's Hunan Style Chinese Cookbook*. Photographs by Stephen Shore; edited and with an introduction by Tony Hiss. New York: Harmony Books, 1978.
Goldberger, Paul. "The Age of Philip Johnson." *Eastern Review*, August 1978, 32–33.
——. "The Man Who Designed a Chippendale Skyscraper." *Observer*, December 17, 1978, 56–59.
"In Monet's Gardens." *New York Times Magazine*, April 2, 1978, 30–34.
Pastier, John. "The Architecture of Escapism." *AIA Journal* 67, no. 14 (December 1978): 26–37.
Peters, Paulhans. "Aspekte einer neuen Freiheit in der Architketur." *Baumeister*, no. 12 (December 1978): 1106.
Pizzazz Visits Joey Travolta." *Pizzazz*, August 1978, 27.
Richter, Nora. "Selling Fast Food in a More Subdued Setting." *AIA Journal* 67, no. 8 (July 1978): 60–63.
"Steinbrenner's Yanks." *New York Times Magazine*, April 9, 1978, 38–39.
"Stephen Shore." *Camera Mainichi*, November 1, 1978, 85–92.
"TV Watchers Kit." *Pizzazz*, June 1978, 16–17.

1979 "Neighborhood." *Avenue*, April 1979, 54–59.

1980 "In the Gardens of Monet." *Camera 35*, September 1980, 28–31.
"Monet." *Photo*, no. 153 (June 1980): 70–79.

1982 "Exact Terms: Photographs." *Perspecta* 18 (1982): 128–33.

1990 "The Gardens at Giverny." *The Subaru*, January 1, 1990, n.p.
"Heroes." *Les Inrockuptibles*, July/August 1990, 58–84.

1991 Clendinen, Dudley. "A Natural Passage." *Lear's*, October 1991, 71.

1992 "White People." *Esquire*, February 1992, 70–71.

1993 Lazell, Barry. "Black Angels and Death Songs." *Vox*, no. 34 (July 1993): 4–5.

1994 Brown, Mick. "Saints, Sinners and Neil Jordan." *Telegraph Magazine*, December 1994, 40–41.

1995 Grant, Richard. "Jane Smiley: Homebody Makes Good." *Telegraph Magazine*, May 20, 1995, 36–37.

1996 *American Photo*, May/June 1996, 70–71.
Camus, Renaud. "Tricks." *Frieze* 29 (June/July/August 1996): 54–55.

1998 Hiss, Tony. "The Experience of Place." *Aperture* 150 (Winter 1998): 59.

2000 "Farm Hands." *Details*, November 2000, 136–47.

2001 Gates, David. "George Lassos Moon." *GQ*, December 2001, 180–88.

2003 Gordinier, Jeff. "Suburban Cowboy." *Details*, May 2003, 150–55.
McGuane, Thomas. "Gallatin Canyon." *New Yorker*, January 13, 2003, 72.
"Portfolio: Stephen Shore." Text by Walead Beshty. *Artforum* 41, no. 9 (May 2003): 147–53.
"Real Life: Stephen Shore's America Circa 1972." *Index* 41 (November 2003).
Wall, Jeff. "Frames of Reference." *Artforum* 42, no. 1 (September 2003): 188–92.

2004 Conti, Samantha. "High and Mighty." *W*, March 2004, 386–401.
"A Fluttering Knuckleball: Lunch with Stephen Shore and Tim Davis." *Blind Spot*, no. 26 (2004): n.p.
"The Golden Greek." *W*, October 2004.
"Uncommon Places." *Dwell*, October/November 2004, 120–21.
Wharton, Edith. *The Age of Innocence*. Introduction by Diane Johnson; thirty-two color photographs by Stephen Shore. San Francisco: Arion, 2004.

2005 Christopher, Tom. "The Ghost Forest." *House & Garden*, February 2005, 112–19.
"Flohmarkt, Vienna, Austria, 2004 by Stephen Shore." *Draft*, no. 1 (Spring 2005): 10–23.

Mahler, Jonathan. "The Soul of the New Exurb." *New York Times Magazine*, March 27, 2005, 30–37.
"Natural Beauty." *Wallpaper*, October 2005, 372–83.

2006 "In Back of the Real." *Another Magazine*, Spring/Summer 2006, 258–73.
Reginato, James. "Marden Manor." *W*, November 2006, 362–65.

2007 "A Little Bit Country." *New York Times Style Magazine*, November 18, 2007, 166–71.
"Portfolio: Stephen Shore, 11-09-06." *Foam* 13 (Winter 2007): 23–39.
Snyder, Gabriel. "The New Age Healers." *W*, February 2007, 192–94.
"Warehouse." *Canteen*, no. 2, 36–47.

2008 "Brief Encounter." *Elle*, August 2008, 258–65.
"City of Light." *Elle*, December 2008.
"Hot Child in the City." *Elle*, October 2008.
"A Perfect Stranger." *Elle*, September 2008, 580–87.
"Stephen Shore." *Interview*, February 2008, 74.
"Warhol Wäre 80." *Vanity Fair* (Germany).

2009 "All That I Got." *Elle*, March 2009, 410–15.
"A Foreign Affair." *Elle*, November 209, 307–10.
"Forgotten Coast." *Cookie*, March 2009, 106–13.
"Night at the Oasis." *Elle*, November 2009, 312–13.
"Room Service." *Details*, June/July 2009, 106–13.
Solway, Diane. "The Private World of Ingmar Bergman." *W*, November 2009, 176–87.
Watson, Brad. "Visitation." *New Yorker*, April 6, 2009, 62–63.

2010 "Double Take." *Details*, November 2010.
"Portfolio: Stephen Shore: Abu Dhabi." *Monopol*, September 2010, n.p.
"Un Racconto." *Amica*, October 2010, n.p.

2012 "She's Got Your Eyes." *Telegraph Fashion*, Autumn/Winter 2012, 70–75.
"Strange Girl in a Strange Land." *Wall Street Journal Magazine*, March 2012, 76–79.
"Wish You Were Here." *Lucky*, March 2012, 160–61.

2013 "Covered in Glory." *Telegraph Fashion*, Autumn/Winter 2013, 70–71.
"Gallery: Stephen Shore," *House*, Winter 2013, n.p.
"Indian Summer." *Telegraph Fashion*, Spring/Summer 2013, 50–53.
"Indian Summer." *Telegraph Magazine*, June 22, 2013, 48–49.
Prickett, Sarah Nicole. "California Dreaming." *T* magazine, October 6, 2013, 122–27.

2014 Bagley, Christopher. "A Man with a Clan." *W*, September 2014, https://www.wmagazine.com/story/axel-dumas-hermes-ceo.
"Stephen Shore." *IMA* 7 (Spring 2014): n.p.
"Unassuming Observations." *Aesthetica*, October 2014, 38–49.

2015 "Stephen Shore's Bygone Americana." *OutOfOrder*, no. 6 (Summer 2015): 128–45.

2016 "Washington by Stephen Shore." *Mastermind* 1 (October 2016).

Articles, Essays, Reviews, and Interviews

1963 "Angry Young Man with a Camera." *U.S. Camera*, June 1963, 52–53.

1971 Coleman, A. D. "Latent Image: Little Seen, Less Said." *Village Voice*, April 1, 1971, 24, 26.
——. "Latent Image: Lights On & Chin Up." *Village Voice*, November 18, 1971, 32.
Shirey, David. L. "Prints and Photographs On View at Metropolitan." *New York Times*, February 24, 1971, 34.
Thornton, Gene. "From Fine Art to Plain Junk," *New York Times*, November 14, 1971, D38.
——. "Is It Necessary To Ask What They Mean?" *New York Times*, March 7, 1971, D30.

1972 Coleman, A. D. "Latent Image: A Smattering of Visions." *Village Voice*, August 17, 1972, 26.
——. "Latent Image: American Yawn, Irish Wail." *Village Voice*, October 5, 1972, 31.
Rosenheck, Natalie. "Light Gallery Opens; Room at the Top?" *Popular Photography* 70, no. 3 (March 1972): 106, 109, 110.
Thornton, Gene. "Time-Travel, Other Trips." *New York Times*, August 6, 1972, D14.

1973 Marvel, Bill. "Photos Become 'Art.'" *National Observer*, April 28, 1973, 20.

1974 Collins, James. "Stephen Shore, Light Gallery." *Artforum* 12, no. 6 (March 1974): 75–76.

1975 Kozloff, Max. "Photography: The Coming of Age of Color." *Artforum* 13, no. 5 (January 1975): 30–35.
Parson, Ann. "Harry Callahan, Duane Michals, Steven [*sic*] Shore." *New Boston Review*, Fall 1975, 22.
Russell, John. "Stephen Shore / Frank Gohlke." *New York Times*, February 22, 1975, 23.
Stersic, Tom. "Photography Takes Over." *Kalamazoo Gazette*, September 7, 1975.

1976 Davis, Douglas. "The Ten Toughest Photographs of 1975." *Esquire*, February 1976, 108–15.
——, and Mary Rourke. "New Frontiers in Color." *Newsweek*, April 19, 1976, 56–61.
"Everyday Color." *Newsday*, October 17, 1976.
Huxtable, Ada Louise. "The Pop World of the Strip and the Sprawl." *New York Times*, March 21, 1976, D28.
Ianco-Starrels, Josine. "Otis Gallery to Show 'New Topographics.'" *Los Angeles Times*, February 29, 1976, 63.
Kramer, Hilton. "Celebrating Formalism in Photography." *New York Times*, December 12, 1976, D29.
Negroponte, George. "Stephen Shore." *Art/World*, December 11, 1976.
"New Generation." *Connecticut Advocate*, December 30, 1976.
"New Yorkers Whose Work Invigorates the Avant-Garde." *Village Voice*, December 20, 1976, 73.
Quinn, Jim. "Learning from Our Living Rooms: In the Language of Interiors, One Sofa Is Worth a Thousand Words." *Philadelphia*, October 1976, 160–66.
Ratcliff, Carter. "Route 66 Revisited: The New Landscape Photography." *Art in America* 64, no. 1 (January/February 1976): 86–91.
Scully, Julia, and Andy Grundberg. "U.S.A.: Pushing the Limits." *Modern Photography*, July 1976, 80–81.
"Symbols." *New Yorker*, March 15, 1976, 27.
Thornton, Gene. "Formalists Who Flirt with Banality." *New York Times*, November 14, 1976, D34.
——. "A Strong Sense of Grass-Roots America." *New York Times*, July 18, 1976, D22.
Venturi and Rauch. "Signs of Life: Symbols in the American City." *Aperture* 77 (1976): 49–65.
Wilson, William. "Camera Artists: Truth in Focus." *Los Angeles Times*, March 15, 1976, E10.
Woolard, Robert W. "Man-Shaped Landscapes." *Artweek*, March 27, 1976, 12.

1977 Fondilla, Harvey. "Shows We've Seen." *Popular Photography*, March 1977.
Goldberger, Paul. "Design Notebook: Courthouse as Symbol." *New York Times*, April 21, 1977, C13.
"Miracle on 57th Street." *Modern Photography*, February 1977.
Morris, Maria. "Stephen Shore." *Camera* (Switzerland), January 1977, 14–15, 22–23, 35.
Pare, Richard. "Court Houses: County Symbols." *Historic Preservation*, October/December 1977, 31–37.
Rice, Shelley. "Stephen Shore: Banal Landscapes Revisioned." *Village Voice*, May 2, 1977, 87.
Skoggard, Ross. "Stephen Shore, Museum of Modern Art." *Artforum* 15, no. 5 (January 1977): 65.

1978 Grundberg, Andy, and Julia Scully. "Currents: American Photography Today." *Modern Photography*, September 1978, 82–87.
"Interviews." In Klaus-Jürgen Sembach, *Amerikanische Landschaftsfotografie 1860–1978*, 12–19. Munich: Die Neue Sammlung, 1978.
Kramer, Hilton. "When the City Sits for the Camera." *New York Times*, January 6, 1978, C1, C16.
Lifson, Ben. "'New York, New York': Mostly Applesauce." *Village Voice*, January 23, 1978, 66.
——. "Taking All the Way." *Village Voice*, June 19, 1978, 76.
Loercher, Diana. "Monet at the Met: Horticultural Delight." *Christian Science Monitor*, May 22, 1978, 22.
"Mirrors and Windows: American Photography since 1960." *MoMA*, no. 7 (Summer 1978): 1–3, 6.
Squiers, Carol. "Color Photography: The Walker Evans Legacy and the Commercial Tradition." *Artforum* 17, no. 3 (November 1978): 64–67.
"Thema Photokina." *Bunte Wochen-Zeitung*, September 16–22, 1978, 8–9.
Thornton, Gene. "The New Photography: Turning Traditional Standards Upside Down." *Art News*, April 1978, 74–78.
Zito, Tom. "Supporting Visual Arts by Corporate Largess." *Washington Post*, July 8, 1978, E1.

1979 "Gunilla Alshtröm Hos Stephen Shore i New York." *Aktuell Fotografi*, no. 9 (September 1979): 26–33.
Hiss, Tony. "The Framing of Stephen Shore." *American Photographer*, February 1979, 26–37.
Lewis, Jo Ann. "Galleries." *Washington Post*, July 14, 1979, D8.
Spaid, Gregory Preston. "'Mirrors and Windows' Photo Exhibit Opens at Speed Museum on Tuesday." *Courier Journal*, April 1, 1979, 14.

1980 Crane, Tricia. "Photography Sees the Light. Through the Lens with Light: Photographers and Works." *Daily News*, October 10, 1980, 5, 10–11, 21.
Johnstone, M. "Harry Callahan and Stephen Shore Open New Gallery." *Artweek*, November 1, 1980, 13.
"Light Opening: Photographic Art Gallery." *Beverly Hills People*, October 22, 1980, 6.
Wilson, William. "The Galleries: La Cienega." *Los Angeles Times*, October 17, 1980, VI4.

1981 Allison, Sue. "Gallery View: The Light." *Amateur Photographer*, June 20, 1981, 136–38.
Auping, Michael. "An Interview with Stephen Shore." In *Stephen Shore: Photographs*, 9–15. Sarasota, Fla.: John and Mable Ringling Museum of Art Foundation, 1981.
Haines, Joan. "Valley Draws Celebrated Photographer." *Bozeman Daily Chronicle*, August 5, 1981, 19.
Hedgpeth, Ted. "Saturated with Actuality." *Artweek*, January 9, 1982, 11.
Huisking, Charlie. "What Makes a Photographer Click?" *Sarasota Herald Tribune*, September 20–26, 1981, 16–17.
Schad, Tennyson. "Collecting Photographs for Love and Money." *Camera Arts*, March/April 1981, 24–28.
Shirey, David L. "A Photographic Tour of the U.S., in All Its Diversity." *New York Times*, April 19, 1981, 22.
Thornton, Gene. "Is the New Color Work So Different from the Old?" *New York Times*, November 8, 1981, D27.

1982 Campbell, E. "A Careful Seeing: Stephen Shore." *Artweek*, November 20, 1982, 14.
Grundberg, Andy. "Uncommon Places by Stephen Shore." *New York Times Book Review*, December 5, 1982, 59.
Steinbach, Alice. "Color as Form: Color Looms Small in Art of Photography." *Baltimore Sun*, May 1, 1982, A9.

1983 Squiers, Carol. "Photography: Tradition and Decline." *Aperture* 91 (Summer 1983): 72–76.

1984 Rewald, John. "Looking at Art: Monet's Enchanted Garden." *Art News*, January 1984, 104–8.

1985 "Callahan, Shore and Meyerowitz in Cardiff." *Creative Camera*, May 1985, 9.
Glueck, Grace. "Illuminating Color." *New York Times*, September 20, 1985, C20.

1986 Giovannini, Joseph. "Architecture: Photos of Capitol in Albany." *New York Times*, September 18, 1986, C24.
Grundberg, Andy. "Critics' Choices." *New York Times*, The Guide, July 13, 1986, 2.

1989 Raynor, Vivien. "Life in Suburbia, as Artists Dream of It." *New York Times*, August 20, 1989, WC23.

1990 Handy, Ellen. "The Curvature of the Earth and the Smell of the Air: Photographs from the Yucatán by Stephen Shore." *Annandale* (Bard College), Spring 1990, 39–49.

1991 Arrouye, Jean. "L'imaginaire de la route américaine." *Revue française d'études américaines*, April–July 1991, 321–28.
Raynor, Vivien. "Wesleyan Shows Span Styles and Eras." *New York Times*, June 2, 1991, CN22.

1992 Jones, Malcolm, Jr. "All in the Family." *Newsweek*, October 26, 1992, 62–63.
Raynor, Vivien. "Wesleyan Highlights Its Photo Collection." *New York Times*, February 9, 1992, CN22.

1994 "Abgesang auf einen Traum: 'American Studies' im Aktionsforum Praterinsel." *TZ*, December 12, 1994, 8.
Charles, Eleanor. "Westchester Guide." *New York Times*, January 16, 1994, WC5.
Goetz, Joachim. "Fotografie als Mittel zur Dokumentation: 'American Studies' im Zollgewölbe des Aktionsforums Praterinsel in München." *Straubinger Tagblatt*, December 30, 1994, 10.
"Incontri sulla linea di confine." *Foto Pratica Immagini*, no. 295 (1994): 68–69.
Reitter, Barbara. "American Dream Ausgeträmt." *Mittelbayerische Zeitung*, December 24, 1994, 12.

Teibler, Claudia. "Formale Harmonie: Dokumentarfotografie auf der Praterinsel." *Münchner Merkur*, December 16, 1994, 8.

1995 Godau, Jana. "Sprengel Museum: Ein amerikanisches Tagebuch in Bildern." *Bild Zeitung*, April 12, 1995.

"His pictures have the quality of a first encounter." Bernd and Hilla Becher in conversation with Heinz Liesbrock. In Heinz Liesbrock, ed., *Stephen Shore: Photographs 1973–1993*, 27–33. Munich: Schirmer/Mosel, 1995.

Janzen, Thomas. "Intensität des Alltags: Farbfotografien des Amerikaners Stephen Shore im Westfälischen Kunstverein Münster." *Frankfurter Rundschau*, March 2, 1995.

Karmel, Pepe. "Stephen Shore." *New York Times*, December 22, 1995, 30.

"Land der Unbegrenzten Scheusslichkeiten." *Süddeutsche Zeitung*, January 2, 1995, 12–13.

"Photography View Master." *New York*, December 18, 1995, 76.

Schjeldahl, Peter. "Clouds of Seeing." *Village Voice*, December 26, 1995, 87.

Stöckmann, Jochen. "Wie man Fische und Bilder fängt." *Leipziger Zeitung*, April 26, 1995.

"This Not That: John Baldessari und Stephen Shore im Württembergischen Kunstverein Stuttgart, bis 19. November 1995." *Zeitschrift für Neue Kunst*, October/November 1995.

Trübi, Stephan. "Die Infrastruktur des Alltäglichen. Im Kuppelsaal des Württembergischen Kunstvereins: Fotografien von Stephen Shore." *Esslinger Zeitung*, October 7, 1995, 33.

"Und die Zeit steht still: Fotografien von Stephen Shore im Württembergischen Kunstverein." *Stuttgarter Zeitung*, September 26, 1995, 34.

Wagner, Thomas. "Amerika durchs Beifahrerfenster. Farbe des Gewöhnlichen: Der Fotograf Stephen Shore im Westfälischen Kunstverein Münster." *Frankfurter Allgemeine Zeitung*, March 4, 1995, 33.

Zee, Hartmut. "Plädoyer für den gesunden Verstand." *Stuttgarter Nachrichten*, September 26, 1995, 13.

"Zwei Amerikaner: John Baldessari und Stephen Shore im Kunstverein." *Kritische Blätter für Neugierige*, November 1995, 14.

1996 Raynor, Vivien. "'Summer in America' Gathers 21 Photographic Exhibitors." *New York Times*, August 4, 1996, WC12.

Robins, Carol Peace. "Notes from Underground." *New York Times Book Review*, April 21, 1996, 27.

Smith, Marielle. "Open House." *Boston Book Review*, March 1996.

Smith, Roberta. "Finding Art in the Artifacts of the Masses." *New York Times*, December 1, 1996, H43.

"The Velvet Years: Warhol's Factory 1965–67." *Interview*, April 1996.

1997 Gottlieb, Shirle. "An Inside Look at the World of Andy Warhol." *Press-Telegram*, April 7, 1997, D1, D2.

Knight, Christopher. "Andy Warhol, Properly Labeled." *Los Angeles Times*, Calendar, April 13, 1997, 3, 71.

Lemons, Stephen. "He Shot Andy Warhol: Photographer Stephen Shore Takes Us through the Looking Glass to Warhol's 'Velvet Years'." *Entertainment Today*, April 18–24, 1997, 6–7.

Schoenkopf, Rebecca. "Randy Andy: Photos from Warhol's Factory Inspire a Game of Spot the Cameo." *Orange County Weekly*, April 11–17, 1997, 14.

"'A Sharp Lookout' at the Center for Photography at Woodstock." *Almanac*, September 11, 1997.

Sizgorich, Thomas. "Shore Tops UAM Exhibit List." *Long Beach Union*, January 27, 1997, 3.

Wilson, William. "Photography Exhibition Captures Getty's Spirit." *Los Angeles Times*, December 22, 1997, F4.

——. "The '60s Unite Contrasting Exhibitions." *Los Angeles Times*, March 29, 1997, F4.

1998 Kaufmann, James. "*The Nature of Photographs* by Stephen Shore." *Photographer's Forum*, September 1998, 4.

1999 Imdahl, Georg. "Spiegelei auf Fettgrund: Frühe Fotografien von Stephen Shore in Köln." *Frankfurter Allgemeine Zeitung*, August 4, 1999.

Nathan, Jean. "For 82 Artists, Immortality Is Worth Rising Early." *New York Times*, September 26, 1999, ST2.

"Photographische Sammlung: Blick das Vagabunden." *Kölner Stadt-Anzeiger*, July 30, 1999, 33.

Prior, Ingeborg. "Künstler-Augen sehen anders. Das Ergebnis präsentieren die Top-Fotografen Candida Höfer und Stephen Shore in Köln." *NRW Kultur*, July 18, 1999.

Schroeder, Annette. "Fotografie von Candida Höfer und Stephen Shore: Wo die Flaschen stramm stehen." *Photographische Rundschau*, July 17, 1999.

Smith, Roberta. "Gazing in a Mirror: The Omnipresent Camera." *New York Times*, September 10, 1999, E33.

2000 Aletti, Vince. "Stephen Shore & Company." *Artforum* 39, no. 4 (December 2000): 130.

Belcove, Julie L. "Lenscrafters." *W*, May 2000, 186–88.

Haworth-Booth, Mark. "Amarillo—'Tall in Texas,' A Project by Stephen Shore, 1971." *Art on Paper* 5, no. 1 (September/October 2000): 44–47.

Jones, Kristin M. "Stephen Shore, 303 Gallery, New York." *Frieze* 54 (September/October 2000): 117.

"Photo: Stephen Shore," *Village Voice*, May 23, 2000.

"Photography: Shore Thing." *New York*, May 23, 2000.

"Stephen Shore with Peter Halley." *Index* 23 (April 2000): 26–36.

2001 Coomer, Martin. *Time Out* (London), April 4–11, 2001, 53.

Denes, Melissa. "America Caught Off-Balance." *Sunday Telegraph Magazine*, February 25, 2001, 38–40.

Morris, Renay E. "Urban Legend." *Picture Magazine*, January/February 2001, 29–32.

Schmerler, Sarah. *Time Out New York*, June 1–8, 2001, 91.

2002 Lafreniere, Steve. "Top Ten." *Artforum* 40, no. 9 (May 2002): 47.

Lange, Susanne. "A Conversation with Stephen Shore." In *Bernd und Hilla Becher Festschrift*, 47–50. Munich: Schirmer/Mosel, 2002.

Macel, Christine. "Zoe Leonard Rencontre Stephen Shore." *Beaux Arts Magazine* 222 (November 2002): 14–17.

"Katz und Maus im Atelier: Die Düsseldorfer Galerien offerieren ihr Herbstprogram." *Frankfurter Allgemeine Zeitung*, September 7, 2002.

Meister, Helga. "Katz und Maus, Schädel und Hermelin." *Westdeutsche Zeitung*, September 10, 2002.

——. "Lichtmagie am Highway." *Westdeutsche Zeitung*, October 14, 2002.

2003 Aletti, Vince. "Show World." *Village Voice*, October 8–14, 2003, 160.

Beshty, Walead. "The City Without Qualities: Photography, Cinema, and the Postapocalyptic Ruin." *Influence* 1 (2003): 50–61.

Dorment, Richard. "Shots of the Century." *Daily Telegraph*, June 4, 2003.

Douglas, Sarah. *Art Newspaper*, no. 139 (September 2003): 5.

"Highlights." *Time Out New York*, September, 4–11, 2003.
Kimmelman, Michael. "Around the City, Images from Around the World." *New York Times*, July 15, 2003, E1.
Mackenzie, Suzie. "The Beauty of the Disregarded," *The Guardian*, May 16, 2003, https://www.theguardian.com/artanddesign/2003/may/17/photography.artsfeatures.
Ratner, Megan. *Art on Paper* 8, no. 2 (November/December 2003): 68.
Ribas, Joao. "Stephen Shore: 303." *Flash Art*, October 2003, 117.
Schjeldahl, Peter. "Alone with Baseball: Stephen Shore's Minor Leagues." *Aperture* 172 (Fall 2003): 19–23, 79.
Scott, Andrea. "The Color of Money: A Flourishing Photography Market Boosts the Profile of Stephen Shore's Groundbreaking Work." *Time Out New York*, October 2–9, 2003, 62.
Searle, Adrian. "A Life More Ordinary." *The Guardian*, June 3, 2003, 11.
"Stephen Shore." *New Yorker*, September 29, 2003, 26–28.

2004 Aletti, Vince. "Flashback." *Art+Auction*, February 2004, 66–76.
Baker, Kenneth. "Wave of Attention Rushes Back to Stephen Shore's Photography." *San Francisco Chronicle*, May 31, 2004, E1, E4, E5.
Beem, Edgar Allen. "A Distanced Delight: The World Is Falling in Love with Stephen Shore All Over Again." *Photo District News*, July 2004, 68–72.
Dougherty, Michael. "Uncommon Road Trip." *BlackBook*, Summer 2004, 52.
"A Fluttering Knuckleball: Lunch with Stephen Shore and Tim Davis." *Blind Spot*, no. 26 (2004): n.p.
Gefter, Philip. "Travels with Walker, Robert and Andy." *New York Times*, July 4, 2004, AR28.
Hodgson, Francis. "Primary Colours." *Art Review*, March 2004, 46.
Jamieson, Teddy. "The Real America Exposed." *Herald Magazine*, June 26, 2004, 16–21.
Leffingwell, Edward. "Stephen Shore at 303." *Art in America* 92, no. 3 (March 2004): 124.
Parker, Ian. "American Splendour." *Telegraph* Magazine, July 3, 2004, 45–50.
Pitman, Joanna. "Requiem for a Lost America." *London Times*, January 6, 2004, 21.
Schuman, Aaron. "An Autobiography of Seeing." *Modern Painters*, Spring 2004, 76–79.
——. "*Uncommon Places*: An Interview with Stephen Shore." *Seesaw*, Summer 2004, http://seesawmagazine.com/shore_pages/shore_interview.html.
"Stephen Shore in a Conversation with Lynne Tillman." In *Uncommon Places: The Complete Works*, 173–83. New York: Aperture, 2004.

2005 Aletti, Vince. "Critic's Notebook: Shore Leave." *New Yorker*, November 7, 2005, 12.
Bellenbaum, Rainer. "Crossroad Strategy: Fotografien von Stephen Shore in der Akademie der bildenden Künste, Wien." *Texte zur Kunst* 15, no. 57 (March 2005): 183–85.
Beshty, Walead. "Stephen Shore." *Artforum* 44, no. 1 (September 2005): 120.
Camhi, Leslie. "The Unlikely Beauty of Club Sandwiches Served on Formica." *Village Voice*, November 2–8, 2005, 74.
Cooper, Bernard. "On the Road." *Los Angeles Magazine*, September 2005, 146–48.
Dillon, Brian. "Visual Homages to Things and Stuff." *Financial Times*, November 19–20, 2005, W5.
Dykstra, Jean. "Stephen Shore: Up Close and Impersonal." *Art + Auction*, October 2005, 140–45.
Guerrin, Michel. "Stephen Shore, Luigi Ghirri: et la couleur fut." *Le Monde*, January 21, 2005, 24.
"Interview: Stephen Shore." *Réponses Photo*, April 2005, 10–11.
"Jede Stadt, in die ich kam." *Süddeutsche Zeitung*, December 9, 2005, 14.
Kempf, Jean. "La couleur du réel." *Revue française d'études américaines*, September 2005, 110–24.
Kimmelman, Michael. "Agitprop to Arcadian: Gently Turning a Kaleidoscope of Visions." *New York Times*, November 11, 2005, http://www.nytimes.com/2005/11/11/arts/design/agitprop-to-arcadian-gently-turning-a-kaleidoscope-of-visions.html.
Myers, Terry. "The Biographical Landscape: The Photography of Stephen Shore, 1968–1993." *Modern Painters*, October 2005, 119.
O'Hagan, Sean. "That Was Then." *The Observer* (U.K.), November 13, 2005, 7.
Pagel, David. "Plight of the Comet." *Los Angeles Times*, July 13, 2005, 3.
Ratner, Megan. "Stephen Shore." *Frieze* 94 (October 2005): 208.
Remy, Patrick. "Stephen Shore: voyage au coeur de l'amérique." *L'Oeil* 566 (February 2005): 64–69.
Smith-Littlefield, Cary. "That '70s Show." *Art + Auction*, October 2005, 144.
Wolinski, Natacha. "Stephen Shore: une Odyssée Américaine." *Beaux Arts Magazine* 248 (February 2005): 58–63.

2006 Alemani, Cecilia. "Critic's Picks: Mystic River." *Artforum*, May 16, 2006, https://www.artforum.com/picks/id=11100.
Brayshaw, Christopher. "An Interview with Stephen Shore." *Doppelganger*, no. 5 (March 2006): http://www.doppelgangermagazine.com/march/chris_brayshaw_march.html.
Feeney, Mark. "Finding Minor Miracles in Ordinary Places." *Boston Globe*, April 13, 2006, http://archive.boston.com/ae/theater_arts/articles/2006/04/13/finding_minor_miracles_in_ordinary_places/.
Johnson, Ken. "Stephen Shore." *New York Times*, June 30, 2006, E22.
O'Brien, Glenn. "American Landscape." *Tokion*, 2006, 42–48.
Olson, Christopher. "Stephen Shore." *Border Crossings* 97 (March 2006): 107–8.
Richard, Frances. "Stephen Shore at P.S.1 Contemporary Art Center." *Artforum* 44, no. 5 (January 2006): 222.
Saltz, Jerry. "Seeing It All." *Village Voice*, June 12, 2006, 80.
Shore, Stephen, and Jeff L. Rosenheim. "The Books: A Conversation." In *Witness Number One*, n.p. New York: Joy of Giving Something, 2006.
"Stephen Shore." *New Yorker*, July 3, 2006, 13.
Zamudio, Raul. *Flash Art*, March/April 2006, 109–10.

2007 Barliant, Claire. "Stephen Shore, International Center of Photography." *Modern Painters*, October 2007, 9–93.
Bucarelli, Viviana. "Il ragazzo prodigio Stephen Shore." *Giornale dell'Arte* 25, no. 266 (June 2007): 64.
Colberg, Joerg. "A Conversation with Stephen Shore." *Conscientious Extended*, September 24, 2007, http://jmcolberg.com/weblog/extended/archives/a_conversation_with_stephen_shore/.
"Essential on Every Level." *Eye Magazine*, Winter 2007, http://www.eyemagazine.com/review/article/essential-on-every-level.
Fraenkel, Jeffrey, and Robert Adams. "The Difference a Painter Makes." *Aperture* 195 (Summer 2007): 20–27.
Gefter, Philip. "Sometimes One Thing Has Everything To Do with the Other." *Foam* 13 (Winter 2007): 52–54.
"A Ground Neutral and Replete: Stephen Shore and Gil Blank in Conversation." *Whitewall*, no. 7 (Fall 2007): 92–107.

Jiang, Rong. "An Interview with Stephen Shore: The Apparent Is the Bridge to the Real." *American Suburb X*, January 2, 2012, http://www.americansuburbx.com/2012/01/interview-stephen-shore-the-apparent-is-the-bridge-to-the-real-2007.html.

Kimmelman, Michael. "Passing Mile Markers, Snapping Pictures." *New York Times*, May 18, 2007, E27.

Kunitz, Daniel. "Wish Hue Were Here." *Village Voice*, June 20, 2007, 46.

Lewis, Angharad. "USA Today." *Grafik*, June 2007, 65–69.

"Michael Fried in Conversation with Stephen Shore." In Christy Lange, Michael Fried, and Joel Sternfeld, *Stephen Shore*, 7–37. London and New York: Phaidon Press, 2007.

Schwendener, Martha. "Seen on the Street: Photographers' 'Everyday Epiphanies.'" *New York Times*, June 22, 2007, E30.

"Stephen Shore and Luc Sante, 'The Nature of Photographs.'" *Aperture* 186 (Spring 2007): 72–81.

Tillman, Lynne. "'Accounting for Days,' On Stephen Shore's Road Trip Journal." *Artforum* 45, no. 10 (Summer 2007): 460–67.

Turner-Yamamoto, Judith Bell. "Stephen Shore." *Photographer's Forum* 30, no. 1 (Winter 2007): 28–32.

Ure-Smith, Jane. "I Never Got On with Edie." *Financial Times*, August 4, 2007, 13.

van Grondel, Annemiek. "Stephen Shore: Op Afstand in Opstand." *Identity Matters* 5 (2007): 64–69.

Vanderbilt, Tom. "Best of 2007: Biographical Landscape: The Photography of Stephen Shore, 1969–79 at the ICP." *Artforum* 46, no. 4 (December 2007): 340.

2008 Beem, Edgar Allen. "A Shore Bet: The Wunderkind of the New Topographics Embraces the Digital Age." *Photo District News*, January 2008, 44–46.

Himes, Darius. "Highways, Hamlet, and Pancakes." *Book Forum* 15, no. 2 (Summer 2008): 50–51, 67.

"In Depth: Stephen Shore." *Image* (U.K.) 388 (January 2008): 25–28.

"Stephen Shore." *Esquire* (Japan), November 2008, 55–66.

"Stephen Shore." *Interview*, February 2008, 74.

Yablonsky, Linda. "Road Scholar." *New York Times Travel Magazine*, May 18, 2008, 26.

2009 Decter, Joshua. "Stephen Shore, 303 Gallery." *Artforum*, October 2009, 238–39.

Edkins, Diana. "Stephen Shore." *Katalog* 21, no. 2 (2009): 22–39.

Gartenfeld, Alex. "A Shore Thing," *Interview*, June 11, 2009, http://www.interviewmagazine.com/art/stephen-shore.

Johnson, Ken. "Mythic West of Dreams and Nightmares." *New York Times*, March 27, 2009, C25, C32.

Lafreniere, Steve. "Stephen Shore." *Vice*: The Photo Issue, 2009, 168–73.

Leslie, Richard. "A Conversation with Stephen Shore about What Seeing Looks Like." *Foam* 20 (Fall 2009): 22–26.

Ollman, Leah. "Banality, in Black and White; Exploring the Rise of Photography's New Topographics Movement, Whatever It May Mean." *Los Angeles Times*, November 15, 2009, http://articles.latimes.com/2009/nov/15/entertainment/ca-photos15.

2010 Golden, Reuel. "Shore Thing." *British Journal of Photography*, November 2010, 60–65.

Guadagnini, Walter. "Paesaggi Biografici." *Giornale dell'Arte*, March 2010, 61.

Häntzschel, Jörg. "Die Bilder so komplex wie möglich machen." *Süddeutsche Zeitung*, August 26, 2010, 13.

Honickel, Thomas. "Die Echoräume des Stephen Shore." *Photonews: Zeitung für Fotografie* 9 (September 2010): 8–9.

"'Ich wollte richtige Postkarten'. Wie die Fotokunst die Herrschaft des Schwarzweißen überwand: Ein Gespräch mit Stephen Shore." *Die Welt*, September 13, 2010, 23.

"Interview: Stephen Shore." *Fotomagazin* 11 (November 2010): 116.

"James Welling Puts Five Questions to Stephen Shore." *Blouin ArtInfo*, February 5, 2010, http://blouinartinfo.com/news/story/276009/james-welling-puts-five-questions-to-stephen-shore#.

Langer, Freddy. "Auftanken in Los Angeles." *Frankfurter Allgemeine Zeitung*, April 8, 2010, 8.

Lugon, Olivier. "Before the Tableau Form: Large Photographic Formats in the Exhibition *Signs of Life*, 1976." *Études photographiques* 25 (May 2010): 6–41.

Malvoisin, Armelle. "Le casse-tête des restaurateurs d'art contemporain." *L'Oeil*, October 2010, 48–49.

Packer, Matt. "Hyperreal Fragments. Stephen Shore at the Douglas Hyde Gallery." *Source* 63 (June 2010): 58–59.

Schaden, Christoph. "*Der Rote Bulli* (The Red VW Bus): On the Reception of Stephen Shore's Work in Germany 1972–1995." *American Suburb X*, September 13, 2010, http://www.americansuburbx.com/2010/09/der-rote-bulli-on-reception-of-stephen_09.html.

——. "La Brea Matrix: Six German Photographers and a New Color Icon by Stephen Shore." *Foam* 25 (Winter 2010): 171–90.

Schwendener, Samantha. "Tracking the Rise of Color on Film." *New York Times*, August 8, 2010, NJ8.

"Stephen Shore." *Sunday Times* (London), June 13, 2010, 29.

"Unmediated Moments: David Land Speaks to Colour Pioneer Stephen Shore." *Royal Photographic Society Journal*, October 2010, 458–63.

2011 Cheng, Wendy. "'New Topographics': Locating Epistemological Concerns in the American Landscape." *American Quarterly*, March 2011, 151–62.

Curtis, Elissa. "Stephen Shore: Happy 235th, America." *New Yorker*, July 1, 2011, http://www.newyorker.com/culture/photo-booth/stephen-shore-happy-235th-america.

Gonçalves Filho, Antonio. "O homem que viu a América." *Estadão*, September 15, 2011, 10.

Harder, Matthias. "Der Rote Bulli: Stephen Shore and Düsseldorf." *Aperture* 203 (Summer 2011): 10–11.

"Heroes & Mentors: Stephen Shore and Gregory Crewdson." *Photo District News*, July 20, 2011, https://www.pdnonline.com/features/heroes-mentors-stephen-shore-and-gregory-crewdson/.

Kershner, Isabel. "Top Photographers Looking at Israel from New Angles." *New York Times*, December 15, 2011, A14.

Nicholls, Jemma. "Life Lessons." *National Magazine* (Abu Dhabi), October 15, 2011, 42.

Prince, Mark. "Stephen Shore, Sprüth Magers—Berlin." *Flash Art*, March/April 2011, 127.

"Shifting Focus—The Decade Interview: Stephen Shore." Phaidon.com, February 4, 2011, http://www.phaidon.com/agenda/photography/picture-galleries/2011/february/04/shifting-focus-the-decade-interview-stephen-shore/.

"Stephen Shore with Noah Sheldon and Roger White (2005)." *American Suburb X*, December 2, 2011, http://www.americansuburbx.com/2011/12/interview-stephen-shore-with-noah.html.

Taft, Catherine. "Stephen Shore, Aspen Art Museum." *Artforum* 50, no. 3 (November 2011): 278–79.

Wolff, Rachel. "An American Eye on Abu Dhabi." *Wall Street Journal*, July 23, 2011.

2012 Bosco, Roberta. "Margulies, el gran coleccionista." *El País*, February 22, 2012, 5.

Hughes, Holly. "PPE 2012: Stephen Shore on Challenging Photography's Conventions." PDN Pulse, October 25, 2012, https://pdnpulse.pdnonline.com/2012/10/ppe-2012-pstephen-shore-on-challenging-photographys-conventions.html.

"La Morada del hombre." *La Fotografia*, February 6, 2012, 29–32.
Ribas Tur, Antoni. "El món vist per 50 grans fotògrafs del segle XX." *Ara*, March 5, 2012, 26.
Sesé, Teresa. "Las Huellas del hombre." *La Vanguardia*, February 26, 2012, 53.
Tannenbaum, Barbara. "Stephen Shore." *Aperture* supplement, The Photobook Review, December 2012, 2.
Vidal Oliveras, Jaume. "En el exilio del mundo." *El Cultural*, March 23, 2012, 32.
Yale, Madeline. "Stephen Shore and Tarek Al-Ghoussein." *Spot* magazine (Houston Center for Photography), Spring 2012, 22–29.

2013 Allende, Monica. "American Sheen." *Sunday Times* (London), November 10, 2013, 46–49.
Crair, Ben. "Then I Found Myself Seeing Pictures All the Time." *New Republic*, October 22, 2013, https://newrepublic.com/article/115243/stephen-shore-photography-american-surfaces-uncommon-places.
Hodgson, Francis. "Stephen Shore: Something & Nothing, Sprüth Magers, London." *Financial Times*, December 2, 2013, https://www.ft.com/content/42423636-5b42-11e3-848e-00144feabdc0.
Kuipers, Dean. "Stephen Shore: Photos as Performance for 'Station to Station.'" *Huffington Post*, December 23, 2013, http://www.huffingtonpost.com/dean-kuipers/stephen-shore-photos-as-p_b_3970314.html.

2014 Campany, David. "Ways of Making Pictures." In *Stephen Shore* (Madrid: Fundación MAPFRE; New York: Aperture, 2014).
Cuénin, Jonas. "New York 303 Gallery: Stephen Shore." *L'Oeil de la Photographie*, October 16, 2014, http://www.loeildelaphotographie.com/en/2014/10/16/article/26374/new-york-303-gallery-stephen-shore/.
Frankel, David. "Stephen Shore." *Artforum* 53, no. 4 (December 2014): 304.
Grow, Krystal. "Stephen Shore: Defacto Photographer of Andy Warhol's Factory." *Time Lightbox*, September 2014, http://time.com/3811975/stephen-shore-at-the-factory/.
Heyward, Anna. "Stephen Shore and Peter Schjeldahl Debate Art School and Instagram at Aperture Bookstore." *Art News*, October 9, 2014, http://www.artnews.com/2014/10/09/stephen-shore-and-peter-schjeldahl-debate-art-school-and-instagram-at-aperture-bookstore/.
Kelsey, Colleen. "Shore to Shore." *Interview*, September 2014, http://www.interviewmagazine.com/art/shore-to-shore/#_.
Kunz, Anne. "Sehen, um zu Verstehen." *Zeit Magazin*, no. 44 (October 23, 2014): 34–44.
Li, Lucy. "Stephen Shore." *Brooklyn Rail*, November 2014, 59.
McWhorter, Melanie. "Interview: Stephen Shore on *A New York Minute* and *From Galilee to the Negev*." *Photo-eye*, March 28, 2014, http://blog.photoeye.com/2014/03/interview-stephen-shore-on-new-york.html.
Reznik, Eugene. "Stephen Shore Looks for Everyday Color in Conflict Zones." *American Photo*, September 12, 2014, http://www.americanphotomag.com/stephen-shore-looks-everyday-color-conflict-zones.
"Stephen Shore." *Apollo*, September 4, 2014, 39–40.
"Stephen Shore in Conversation with Charlotte Cotton." *This Place*, Summer 2014, http://www.this-place.org/photographers/stephen-shore/.
"Stephen Shore 'Likes' Instagram." *American Suburb X*, December 29, 2014, http://www.americansuburbx.com/2014/12/stephen-shore-likes-instagram.html.
Vassallo, Jesús. "Documentary Photography and Preservation, or the Problem of Truth and Beauty." *Future Anterior* 11, no. 1 (Summer 2014): 14–33.
Wrigley, Tish. "Ten Things You Might Not Know about Stephen Shore." *Another Magazine*, October 10, 2014, http://www.anothermag.com/art-photography/3982/ten-things-you-might-not-know-about-stephen-shore.

2015 "The Auction Market for Stephen Shore." *L'Oeil de la Photographie*, October 29, 2015, http://www.loeildelaphotographie.com/en/2015/10/29/article/159875020/auction-market-for-stephen-shore/.
Cole, Teju. "Serious Play." *New York Times Magazine*, December 9, 2015, 28–34.
Corty, Axelle. "Les jardins de Monet sans clichés." *Connaissance des Arts* 739 (July/August 2015): 52–55.
Dahan, Alexis. "Stephen Shore on Photography vs Instagram." *Purple Magazine* 24 (Fall/Winter 2015–16): http://purple.fr/magazine/fw-2015-issue-24/stephen-shore/.
Delaury, Vincent. "Quelle photographie peut-on voir à la FIAC?" *L'Oeil* 683 (October 2015): 55.
Farrell, Aimee. "Stephen Shore Loves Instagram (and Thinks Warhol Would Have, Too)." *T Magazine*, May 20, 2015, http://tmagazine.blogs.nytimes.com/2015/05/20/stephen-shore-instagram-photo-london-somerset-house/.
Häntzschel, Jörg. "Grossformat: Die Leichtigkeit, mit der Stephen Shore fotografiert, war immer hart erarbeitet. Bis er Instagram entdeckte." *Süddeutsche Zeitung*, January 24–25, 2015, 22.
Heinz, Lauren. "Wearable Art." *British Journal of Photography* 162, no. 7840 (October 2015): 50–55.
O'Hagan, Sean. "Shady Character: How Stephen Shore Taught America to See in Living Colour." *The Guardian*, July 9, 2015, https://www.theguardian.com/artanddesign/2015/jul/09/stephen-shore-america-colour-photography-1970s.
——. "Survivors in Ukraine: Unearthing the Hidden Stories of Holocaust Survivors." *The Guardian*, September 30, 2015, https://www.theguardian.com/artanddesign/photography-blog/2015/sep/30/survivors-ukraine-stephen-shore-holocaust.
"Photographing Monet's Gardens: Five Contemporary Visions." *L'Oeil de la Photographie*, September 29, 2015, http://www.loeildelaphotographie.com/en/2015/09/29/article/159871768/photographing-monet-s-gardens-five-contemporary-visions/.
Rajagopal, Avinash. "The Noguchi Museum: A Portrait." *Metropolis*, September 2015, 127.
Ryan, Meg. "The Venerable Stephen Shore Shares Wisdom Through the Lens of His Latest Project." *American Photo*, April 4, 2015, http://www.americanphotomag.com/venerable-stephen-shore-shares-wisdom-through-lens-his-latest-project.
Sante, Luc. "Stephen Shore: A Look Back Through the Lens." *Bardian* (Bard College), Spring 2015, 18–19.
"Stephen Shore: 'Ce sont les voitures qui datent les photos.'" *Le Monde*, July 9, 2015, http://www.lemonde.fr/arts/article/2015/07/09/stephen-shore-ce-sont-les-voitures-qui-datent-les-photos_4676765_1655012.html.
Stolz, George. "Stephen Shore." *Art Review* 67, no. 1 (January/February 2015): 145.
Tanenbaum, Barry. "Communication Breakthrough: Legendary Photographer Stephen Shore Makes an Instagram Connection." *Shutterbug*, October 2015, 28–31.
Woodward, Richard B. "Surface to Air." *Artforum* supplement, *Book Forum* 21, no. 4 (December 2014–January 2015): 42–43.
Wychowanok, Thibaut. "Master Photographer Stephen Shore is Celebrated in Arles." *Numero Magazine*, July 17, 2015, 62–70.

2016 Alison, Irene. "Instagram Conquista Stephen Shore: dagli scatti con la macchina fotografica al cellulare." *Corriere della Sera*, July 1, 2016, http://www.corriere.it/foto-gallery/la-lettura/orizzonti/16_luglio_01/instagram-arte-stephen-shore-fotografia-a99470d4-3f6e-11e6-83d3-27b43c152609.shtml.

"Andy Warhol's Factory by Stephen Shore." *L'Oeil de la Photographie*, December 12, 2016, http://www.loeildelaphotographie.com/en/2016/12/12/article/159930053/stephen-shore-factory-andy-warhol/.

"Andy Warhol's Infamous Factory through the Eyes of a Teenage Photographer." CNN, November 11, 2016, http://www.cnn.com/2016/11/08/arts/andy-warhol-factory-stephen-shore/.

"Berlin: Stephen Shore, Retrospective." *L'Oeil de la Photographie*, February 24, 2016, http://www.loeildelaphotographie.com/en/2016/02/24/article/159891879/berlin-stephen-shore-retrospective/.

Blaustein, Jonathan. "Turning Instagram Images into Analog." Lens Blog, *New York Times*, March 15, 2016, https://lens.blogs.nytimes.com/2016/03/15/documentum-instagram-newspaper-stephen-shore-william-boling/.

Gopnik, Blake. "Stephen Shore: Andy Warhol's Factory, More Work Space than Party Place." *Artnet News*, October 21, 2016, https://news.artnet.com/opinion/stephen-shore-warhol-factory-phaidon-711836.

——. "Stephen Shore Gets at Israel's Rocky Past." *Artnet*, April 28, 2016, https://news.artnet.com/exhibitions/stephen-shore-this-place-brooklyn-museum-st-sabas-483500.

Grieve, Michael. "Master and Servant." *British Journal of Photography*, August 2016, 52–66.

"Interview: Stephen Shore / Retrospective." Huis Marseille website, Summer 2016, https://www.huismarseille.nl/en/nieuws/interview-stephen-shore/.

Jobey, Liz. "A Light on History: Modern Berlin Photography." *Financial Times*, February 12, 2016, https://www.ft.com/content/2178945c-d009-11e5-831d-09f7778e7377.

Jones, Jonathan. "From Ansel Adams to Stephen Shore: Famous Photographers Shoot Their Favourite Food." *The Guardian*, March 26, 2016, https://www.theguardian.com/lifeandstyle/2016/mar/26/ansel-adams-stephen-shore-famous-photographers-cookbook-favourite-food.

Judah, Hettie. "Portraits of an Italian Town That Time (Almost) Left Behind." *New York Times*, June 14, 2016, http://www.nytimes.com/2016/06/13/t-magazine/art/stephen-shore-italy-photography-book.html.

——. "Bookshelf; Back in Time." *New York Times*, June 19, 2016, 3.

Klingelfuss, Jessica. "Village People: Stephen Shore Reveals Unseen Photographs of Luzzara." *Wallpaper*, June 24, 2016, http://www.wallpaper.com/art/stephen-shore-publishes-never-before-seen-photographs-from-luzzara-series-in-new-book.

McGrath, Erica. "Factory Andy Warhol by Stephen Shore." *Musée Magazine*, October 31, 2016, http://museemagazine.com/culture/2016/10/31/review-factory-andy-warhol-by-stephen-shore.

Nataf, Natacha. "Stephen Shore: portraitiste des derniers juifs d'Ukraine." *Beaux Arts Magazine* 380 (February 2016): 36.

Neilson, Laura. "Stephen Shore's Key Lime Pie Supreme." *New York Times*, May 24, 2016, https://www.nytimes.com/2016/05/24/t-magazine/food/photographers-cookbook-key-lime-pie-stephen-shore.html.

Oktober Matthews, Katherine. "What Looking Looks Like: An Interview with Stephen Shore." *GUP*, no. 50 (August 2016): http://www.gupmagazine.com/articles/what-looking-looks-like-an-interview-with-stephen-shore.

"Picture Special: I Shot Andy Warhol." *Sunday Times* (London), November 6, 2016, 30.

Prince, Mark. "Stephen Shore: Retrospective." *Art Review* 68, no. 4 (May 2016): 100.

Seymour, Tom. "Unseen Images of Stephen Shore's Hidden Italian Commune." *British Journal of Photography*, June 13, 2016, http://www.bjp-online.com/2016/06/stephen-shores-italy/.

Simmons, William J. "Stephen Shore: Shore to Shore." *Musée* 15 (July 2016): 146–59.

Slenske, Michael. "Stephen Shore's Never Before Seen Photos of Andy Warhol's Factory." *Wall Street Journal*, September 28, 2016, https://www.wsj.com/articles/stephen-shores-never-before-seen-photos-of-andy-warhols-factory-1475075231.

"Stephen Shore, photographe insider à la Factory." *Beaux Arts Magazine* 390 (December 2016): 50.

Books and Exhibition Catalogues

1968 König, Kasper, ed. *Andy Warhol*. Stockholm: Moderna Museet, 1968.

1970 *Foto-Portret*. The Hague: Haags Gemeentemuseum, 1970.

1973 Massar, Phyllis Dearborn. *Landscape/Cityscape: A Selection of Twentieth-Century American Photographs*. New York: The Metropolitan Museum of Art, 1973.

1974 Hirshorn, Anne Sue. *Art Now 74: A Celebration of the American Arts*. Washington, D.C.: Artrend Foundation, 1974.

1975 Geringer, Laura. *Color Photography: Inventors and Innovators, 1850–1975*. New Haven, Conn.: Yale University Art Gallery, 1975.

Jenkins, William. *New Topographics: Photographs of a Man-Altered Landscape*. Rochester, N.Y.: International Museum of Photography, 1975.

1976 *Aspects of American Photography 1976*. Saint Louis: University of Missouri, 1976.

Catalogue of the J. B. Speed Art Museum's 1976 Photography Invitational Exhibit. Louisville, Ky.: J. B. Speed Art Museum, 1976.

New Portfolios. Claremont, Calif.: Pomona College Art Gallery, 1976.

Six American Photographers: Robert Adams, Harry Callahan, Frank Gohlke, Nicholas Nixon, Tod Papageorge, Stephen Shore. London: Thomas Gibson Fine Art, 1976.

Ventura Mozley, Anita. *American Photography: Past into Present. Prints from the Monsen Collection of American Photography*. Seattle: Seattle Art Museum, 1976.

Venturi and Rauch. *Signs of Life: Symbols in the American City*. New York: Aperture, 1976.

1977 *Documenta 6*. 3 vols. Kassel: P. Dierichs, 1977.

Hume, Sandy, and Nathan Lyons. *The Great West: Real/Ideal*. Boulder: University of Colorado, 1977.

Stephen Shore: Fotografien. Düsseldorf: Städtische Kunsthalle Düsseldorf, 1977.

Wolf, Eelco, ed. *Faces and Facades*. Cambridge, Mass.: Polaroid Corporation, 1977.

1978 *Amerikanische Landschaftsphotographie: 1860–1978*. Munich: Neue Sammlung, Staatliches Museum für Angewandte Kunst, 1978.

Pare, Richard, ed. *Court House: A Photographic Document*. New York: Horizon Press, 1978.

Szarkowski, John. *Mirrors and Windows: American Photography since 1960*. New York: The Museum of Modern Art, 1978.

1979 Danese, Renato, ed. *American Images: New Work by Twenty Contemporary Photographers*. New York: McGraw-Hill, 1979.

Holmes, Wendy. *Seven Photographers: The Delaware Valley*. Layton, N.J.: Peters Valley, 1979.

1980 Ballinger, James K., and Andrea D. Rubinstein. *Visitors to Arizona 1846 to 1890*. Phoenix: Phoenix Art Museum, 1980.

1981 Eauclaire, Sally. *The New Color Photography*. New York: Abbeville Press, 1981.
Heyman, Therese Thau, ed. *Slices of Time: California Landscapes 1860–1880 and 1960–1980*. Oakland, Calif.: Oakland Museum, 1981.
Kardon, Janet. *Photography: A Sense of Order*. Philadelphia: Institute of Contemporary Art, University of Pennsylvania, 1981.
Stephen Shore: Photographs. Sarasota, Fla.: John and Mable Ringling Museum of Art Foundation, 1981.

1982 *Annie on Camera: Nine Photographers*. Text by Anne H. Hoy. New York: Abbeville Press, 1982.
Naef, Weston J. *Counterparts: Form and Emotion in Photographs*. New York: The Metropolitan Museum of Art, 1982.
North, Ian, ed. *International Photography 1920–1980*. Canberra: Australian National Gallery, 1982.
Sobieszek, Robert. *Color as Form: A History of Color Photography*. Rochester, N.Y.: George Eastman House, 1982.

1983 Holme, Bryan. *Photography as Fine Art*. Introduction by Douglas Davis. New York: E. P. Dutton, 1983.

1984 Eauclaire, Sally. *New Color/New Work: Eighteen Photographic Essays*. New York: Abbeville Press, 1984.
Silk, Gerald. *Automobile and Culture*. New York: Harry N. Abrams, 1984.
Wester, Rick. *The Lens in the Garden*. Yonkers, N.Y.: Hudson River Museum, 1984.

1985 Turner, Peter, ed. *American Images: Photography 1945–1980*. London: Barbican Art Gallery; New York: Viking Penguin, 1985.

1986 Kennedy, William. *The Capitol in Albany*. New York: Aperture, 1986.

1987 Costantini, Paolo, Silvio Fuso, and Sandro Mescola. *Nuovo paesaggio americano: Dialectical Landscapes*. Milan: Electa, 1987.
Eauclaire, Sally. *American Independents: Eighteen Color Photographers*. New York: Abbeville Press, 1987.
Gordon, Peter H., ed. *Diamonds are Forever: Artists and Writers on Baseball*. San Francisco: Chronicle Books, 1987.
Love, Karen, and E. Theodore Lindberg. *Diverse Secrecies: The Garden Photographed*. Vancouver: Presentation House Gallery, 1987.

1989 Greenough, Sarah, Joel Snyder, David Travis, and Colin Westerbeck. *On the Art of Fixing a Shadow: One Hundred and Fifty Years of Photography*. Boston: Bulfinch Press, 1989.
Heyman, Therese, ed. *Picturing California: A Century of Photographic Genius*. San Francisco: Chronicle Books, 1989.
Schoenfeld, Diana. *Symbol and Surrogate: The Picture Within*. Honolulu: University of Hawaii Art Gallery, 1989.

1990 *Andy Warhol System: Pub, Pop, Rock*. Jouy-en-Josas, France: Fondation Cartier pour l'art contemporain, 1990.

1991 Galassi, Peter. *The Pleasures and Terrors of Domestic Comfort*. New York: The Museum of Modern Art, 1991.

1992 George, Alice Rose, Abigail Heyman, and Ethan Hoffman, eds. *Flesh & Blood: Photographers' Images of Their Own Families*. New York: Picture Project, 1992.
Haworth-Booth, Mark. *Camille Silvy: River Scene, France*. Malibu: J. Paul Getty Museum, 1992.
Koltzsch, George W., and Heinz Liesbrock. *Edward Hopper und die Fotografie*. Cologne: DuMont, 1992.

1995 Liesbrock, Heinz, ed. *Stephen Shore: Photographs 1973–1993*. With texts by Hilla and Bernd Becher, James L. Enyeart, Thomas Weski, Heinz Liesbrock, and Stephen Shore. Munich: Schirmer/Mosel, 1995.

1997 *(Un)common Places: Stephen Shore, Korrie Besems, Eugène Atget*. Rotterdam: Nederlands Foto Instituut, 1997.

1998 Celant, Germano. *Andy Warhol: A Factory*. Ostfildern: Hatje, 1998.

1999 Davis, Keith F. *An American Century of Photography*. Kansas City, Mo.: Hallmark Cards, 1999.
Heinrich, Christoph. *Andy Warhol: Photography*. Hamburg: Hamburger Kunsthalle; Pittsburgh: Andy Warhol Museum, 1999.
Phillips, Lisa. *The American Century: Art & Culture, 1950–2000*. New York: Whitney Museum of American Art and W. W. Norton, 1999.
Stephen Shore: American Surfaces 1972. Cologne: Photographische Sammlung/SK Stiftung Kultur; Munich: Schirmer/Mosel, 1999.

2000 Galassi, Peter. *Walker Evans & Company*. New York: The Museum of Modern Art, 2000.
Mescola, Sandro. *Identificazione di un Paesaggio: Venezia–Marghera, fotografia e trasformazioni nella città contemporanea*. Cinisello Balsamo (Milan): Silvana, 2000.
Weski, Thomas, and Heinz Liesbrock, eds. *How You Look at It: Photographs of the 20th Century*. Essays by Thomas Weski, Heinz Liesbrock, Gerry Badger, Thomas Wagner, and Peter Waterhouse. New York: D.A.P./Distributed Art Publishers, 2000.

2001 Joping, Jay. *Settings and Players: Theatrical Ambiguity in American Photography*. London: White Cube, 2001.

2002 Alms, Barbara, ed. *Die Stadt: Stadtbilder in Zeiten der Transformationsprozesse*. Bremen: Hauschild, 2002.
Tolkin, Michael, and Gregory Crewdson. *American Standard: (Para)Normality and Everyday Life*. New York: Barbara Gladstone Gallery, 2002.
Uncommon Places: 50 Unpublished Photographs, 1973–1978. Düsseldorf: Verlag der Galerie Conrads; Paris: Ediiton Mennour, 2002.

2003 Dexter, Emma, and Thomas Weski, eds. *Cruel and Tender: The Real in the Twentieth-Century Photograph*. London: Tate Publishing, 2003.
Yet Untitled: Die Sammlung Bernd F. Künne. Ostfildern: Hatje Cantz, 2003.

2004 Bischoff, Ulrich, Inka Graeve Ingelmann, and Thomas Weski. *Jede Fotografie ein Bild: Siemens Fotosammlung*. Munich: Pinakothek–DuMont, 2004.
Drück, Patricia, and Inka Schube, eds. *Soziale Kreaturen: wie Körper Kunst wird*. Hannover: Sprengel Museum Hannover; Ostfildern: Hatje Cantz, 2004.

2005 Braun, Stephanie, ed. *Deutsche Börse Photography Prize 2005: Luc Delahaye, J. H. Engström, Jörg Sasse, Stephen Shore*. London: The Photographers' Gallery, 2005.
Rosenblum, Walter. *Calle Mayor: Fotografía urbana en América: Walter Rosenblum,*

Bill Owens, Stephen Shore. Madrid: La Fábrica, 2005.
Seelig, Thomas, and Urs Stahel. *Trans Emilia–Sammlung Linea di Confine: Territoriales Erkunden der Emilia-Romagna*. Basel: Christoph Merian, 2005.

2006 Keller, Judith, and Anne Lacoste, eds. *Where We Live: Photographs of America from the Berman Collection*. Los Angeles: J. Paul Getty Museum, 2006.
Marks, Lee, and Alice Rose George. *The Office: In and Out of the Box*. Long Island City, N.Y.: Dorsky Gallery, 2006.
Sheldon, Noah, and David Griffin. *Mystic River*. N.p.: Books & Tapes, 2006.

2007 Lange, Christy, Michael Fried, and Joel Sternfeld. *Stephen Shore*. London and New York: Phaidon Press, 2007.

2008 Ruf, Beatrix, ed. *Blasted Allegories: Works from the Ringier Collection*. Zurich: JRP/Ringier, 2008.
Yablonsky, Linda, and William Hutnick. *When Color Was New: Vintage Photographs from around the 1970s*. New York: Julie Saul Gallery, 2008.

2009 Fraenkel, Jeffrey, and Frish Brand, eds. *Edward Hopper & Company*. San Francisco: Fraenkel Gallery, 2009.
Respini, Eva, ed. *Into the Sunset: Photography's Image of the American West*. New York: The Museum of Modern Art, 2009.
Salvesen, Brett, and Alison Nordström, eds. *New Topographics: Robert Adams, Lewis Baltz, Bernd and Hilla Becher, Joe Deal, Frank Gohlke, Nicholas Nixon, John Schott, Stephen Shore, Henry Wessel, Jr.* Tucson: Center for Creative Photography, University of Arizona; Rochester, N.Y.: George Eastman House; Göttingen: Steidl, 2009.

2010 Haworth-Booth, Mark. *Stephen Shore*. Dublin: Douglas Hyde Gallery, 2010.
Lippert, Werner, and Christoph Schaden, eds. *Der Rote Bulli: Stephen Shore und die Neue Düsseldorfer Fotografie*. Düsseldorf: NRW–Forum Düsseldorf, 2010.
Moore, Kevin D. *Starburst: Color Photography in America, 1970–1980*. Ostfildern: Hatje Cantz, 2010.
On the Road: A Legacy of Walker Evans. North Andover, Mass.: Robert Lehman Art Center, Brooks School, 2010.

2011 *Emirati Expressions*. Saadiyat, Abu Dhabi: Manarat Al Saadiyat, 2011.
Stephen Shore: Abu Dhabi. Aspen, Colo.: Aspen Art Museum, 2011.

2012 Bosma, Rixt A., and Hans Gremmen. *Objects in Mirror: The Imagination of the American Landscape*. Utrecht: Fotodok; Amsterdam: Fw:Books, 2012.
Colpitt, Frances. *Color Pictures*. Fort Worth: The Art Galleries at TCU, 2012.
Tannenbaum, Barbara. *DIY: Photographers & Books*. Cleveland: Cleveland Museum of Art, 2012.
True Stories: Amerikanische Fotografie aus der Sammlung Moderne Kunst. Munich: Pinakothek der Moderne, 2012.

2013 Foster-Rice, Greg, and John Rohrbach, eds. *Reframing the New Topographics*. Chicago: Center for American Places at Columbia College Chicago, 2013.

2014 Baker, Simon, and Shoair Mavlian, eds. *Conflict, Time, Photography*. London: Tate Publishing, 2014.
Bussard, Katherine, and Lisa Hostetler. *Color Rush: 75 Years of Color Photography in America*. New York: Aperture; Milwaukee: Milwaukee Art Museum, 2014.
Campany, David. *The Open Road: Photography and the American Road Trip*. New York: Aperture, 2014.
Dahó, Marta, ed. *Stephen Shore*. Texts by David Campany, Horacio Fernandez, and Sandra Philips. Madrid: Fundación MAPFRE; New York: Aperture, 2014.
Pardo, Alona, and Elias Redstone, eds. *Constructing Worlds: Photography and Architecture in the Modern Age*. Munich: Prestel, 2014.
Scott, Izabella, and Shela Sheikh, eds. *This Place = Maḳom zeh = Hādhā al-makān*. London: Mack, 2014.

2015 Ferretti, Marina, Jeanne Fouchet-Nahas, and Vanessa Lecomte. *Photographier les jardins de Monet: cinq regards contemporains: Elger Esser, Stephen Shore, Bernard Plossu, Darren Almond, Henri Foucault*. Trézélan, France: Filigranes; Giverny, France: Musée des impressionismes Giverny, 2015.
Karp-Evans, Elizabeth. *Station to Station by Doug Aitken*. Munich: Delmonico Books/Prestel, 2015.

2016 Allen, Jamie M. *Picturing America's National Parks*. New York: Aperture, 2016.
Cornell, Lauren, and Tom Eccles, eds. *Invisible Adversaries*. Annandale-on-Hudson, N.Y.: Center for Curatorial Studies, Hessel Museum of Art, Bard College, 2016.

Checklist of the Exhibition

Unless otherwise specified, all works are by Stephen Shore, and prints are courtesy the artist and 303 Gallery, New York.

Early Street Photography

Untitled. September 1961. Chromogenic color print, printed 2017, 13 1/2 × 9" (34.3 × 22.9 cm)
Page 226

Untitled. 1962. Gelatin silver print, 6 3/4 × 4 3/4" (17.1 × 12.1 cm)
Page 227

Untitled. January 1963. Chromogenic color print, printed 2017, 13 1/2 × 9" (34.3 × 22.9 cm)

New York, New York. 1963. Gelatin silver print, 11 5/8 × 13 1/2" (29.5 × 34.3 cm)
Page 225

Untitled. 1963. Gelatin silver print, 13 1/2 × 10 1/2" (34.3 × 26.7 cm)
Page 224

Untitled. 1963. Gelatin silver print, 9 × 13 1/2" (22.9 × 34.3 cm)
Page 224

Untitled. 1963. Gelatin silver print, 13 3/4 × 10 3/4" (34.9 × 27.3 cm)
Page 223

Elevator. 1964. 16mm film transferred to video: black and white

New York, New York. 1964. Gelatin silver print, 9 × 13 1/2" (22.9 × 34.3 cm)
Page 56

New York, New York. 1964. Gelatin silver print, 9 × 13 1/2" (22.9 × 34.3 cm)
Page 226

Untitled. 1964. Gelatin silver print, 9 1/2 × 6 1/2" (24.1 × 16.5 cm)

Untitled. 1964. Gelatin silver print, 9 1/2 × 13 1/2" (24.1 × 34.3 cm)

Untitled. 1964. Gelatin silver print, 12 × 8" (30.5 × 20.3 cm)
Page 225

Untitled. 1964. Gelatin silver print, 4 1/2 × 6 1/2" (11.4 × 16.5 cm)

Untitled. 1964. Gelatin silver print, 6 3/4 × 4 1/2" (17.1 × 11.4 cm)
Page 224

Untitled. 1964. Gelatin silver print, 9 3/4 × 6 1/2" (24.8 × 16.5 cm)
Page 227

Untitled. 1964. Gelatin silver print, 9 1/4 × 13 1/2" (23.5 × 34.3 cm)
Page 226

Untitled. 1964. Gelatin silver print, 10 3/4 × 13 3/4" (27.3 × 34.9 cm)
Page 56

Untitled. 1965. Gelatin silver print, 6 1/4 × 9 1/2" (15.9 × 24.1 cm)
Page 225

Untitled. 1965. Gelatin silver print, 5 1/2 × 8" (14 × 20.3 cm)

The Factory

Andy Warhol and Edie Sedgwick, New York, New York. 1965. Gelatin silver print, 4 5/8 × 6 5/8" (11.7 × 16.8 cm). The Andy Warhol Museum, Pittsburgh; Founding Collection, Contribution The Andy Warhol Foundation for the Visual Arts, Inc.
Page 98

Andy Warhol, the Factory, New York, New York. 1965. Gelatin silver print, 4 5/8 × 6 7/8" (11.7 × 17.5 cm). The Andy Warhol Museum, Pittsburgh; Founding Collection, Contribution The Andy Warhol Foundation for the Visual Arts, Inc.
Page 97

Andy Warhol, the Factory, New York, New York. 1965. Gelatin silver print, 7 × 4 5/8" (17.8 × 11.7 cm). The Andy Warhol Museum, Pittsburgh; Founding Collection, Contribution The Andy Warhol Foundation for the Visual Arts, Inc.
Page 101

Andy Warhol, the Factory, New York, New York. 1965. Gelatin silver print, 6 × 4" (15.2 × 10.2 cm)
Page 276

Andy Warhol, Fire Island, New York. 1965. Gelatin silver print, 6 1/2 × 9 1/2" (16.5 × 24.1 cm)
Page 276

Andy Warhol, Gerard Malanga, and Stephen Shore, the Factory, New York, New York. 1965. Gelatin silver print, 4 5/8 × 6 7/8" (11.7 × 17.5 cm). The Andy Warhol Museum, Pittsburgh; Founding Collection, Contribution The Andy Warhol Foundation for the Visual Arts, Inc.

Bibbe Hansen and Pat Hartley, the Factory, New York, New York. 1965. Gelatin silver print, 4 5/8 × 7" (11.7 × 17.8 cm). The Andy Warhol Museum, Pittsburgh; Founding Collection, Contribution The Andy Warhol Foundation for the Visual Arts, Inc.

Chuck Wein and Andy Warhol, the Factory, New York, New York. 1965. Gelatin silver print, 4 5/8 × 6 7/8" (11.7 × 17.5 cm). The Andy Warhol Museum, Pittsburgh; Founding Collection, Contribution The Andy Warhol Foundation for the Visual Arts, Inc.

Edie Sedgwick, the Factory, New York, New York. 1965. Gelatin silver print, 4 5/8 × 6 3/4" (11.7 × 17.1 cm). The Andy Warhol Museum, Pittsburgh; Founding Collection, Contribution The Andy Warhol Foundation for the Visual Arts, Inc.

Gino Piserchio, the Factory, New York, New York. 1965. Gelatin silver print, 6 1/2 × 9 1/2" (16.5 × 24.1 cm)

Stephen Shore and Andy Warhol, the Factory, New York, New York. 1965. Gelatin silver print, 4 5/8 × 6 7/8" (11.7 × 17.5 cm). The Andy Warhol Museum, Pittsburgh; Founding Collection, Contribution The Andy Warhol Foundation for the Visual Arts, Inc.
Page 276

Andy Warhol, the Factory, New York, New York. 1965–66. Gelatin silver print, 8 1/2 × 12 1/2" (21.6 × 31.8 cm)
Page 277

1:35 a.m., in Chinatown Restaurant, New York, New York. 1965–67. Gelatin silver print, printed c. 1995, 9 × 13 1/2" (22.9 × 34.3 cm)
Page 275

Andy Warhol and Gerard Malanga, the Factory, New York, New York. 1965–67. Gelatin silver print, printed c. 1995, 6 × 8 3/4" (15.2 × 22.2 cm)
Page 96

Andy Warhol and Ingrid Superstar, the Factory, New York, New York. 1965–67. Gelatin silver print, 4 × 6" (10.2 × 15.2 cm)
Page 97

Billy Name and Chuck Wein, the Factory, New York, New York. 1965–67. Gelatin silver print, 6 1/4 × 9 1/4" (15.9 × 23.5 cm)
Page 100

The Factory, New York, New York. 1965–67. Gelatin silver print, printed c. 1995, 6 × 9" (15.2 × 22.9 cm)

The Factory, New York, New York. 1965–67. Gelatin silver print, 7 1/2 × 9 1/2" (19.1 × 24.1 cm)

Ivy Nicholson, Chuck Wein, Peter Knoll, Danny Fields, and Andy Warhol, the Factory, New York, New York. 1965–67. Gelatin silver print, 7 1/2 × 11" (19.1 × 27.9 cm)

Ivy Nicholson, Factory Party, New York, New York. 1965–67. Gelatin silver print, 4 5/8 × 6 5/8" (11.7 × 16.8 cm). The Andy Warhol Museum, Pittsburgh; Founding Collection, Contribution The Andy Warhol Foundation for the Visual Arts, Inc.
Page 95

Ivy Nicholson and Andy Warhol, the Factory, New York, New York. 1965–67. Gelatin silver print, printed c. 1995, 6 × 8¾" (15.2 × 22.2 cm)
Page 97

John Cale, Jan Cramer, Paul Morrissey, Nico, and Gerard Malanga, New York, New York. 1965–67. Gelatin silver print, 6½ × 9¾" (16.5 × 24.8 cm)

Jonas Mekas and Andy Warhol, the Factory, New York, New York. 1965–67. Gelatin silver print, 6¼ × 9½" (15.9 × 24.1 cm)

Rene Ricard, New York, New York. 1965–67. Gelatin silver print, 9 × 13½" (22.9 × 34.3 cm)

Rene Ricard, New York, New York. 1965–67. Gelatin silver print, 9 × 13½" (22.9 × 34.3 cm)
Page 100

Untitled. 1965–67. Gelatin silver print, 9 × 13½" (22.9 × 34.3 cm)

Marcel Duchamp, New York, New York. 1966. Gelatin silver print, printed c. 1995, 8¾ × 6" (22.2 × 15.2 cm)
Page 100

Nico and Andy Warhol, Rutgers University, New Jersey. 1966. Gelatin silver print, 6⅜ × 9½" (16.2 × 24.1 cm)
Page 101

Rene Ricard with Silver Clouds, the Factory, New York, New York. 1966. Gelatin silver print, 11½ × 9¾" (29.2 × 24.8 cm)

John Cale, the Factory, New York, New York. 1966–67. Gelatin silver print, 9½ × 7½" (24.1 × 19.1 cm)
Page 99

Lou Reed and Andy Warhol, the Factory, New York, New York. 1966–67. Gelatin silver print, 9½ × 6½" (24.1 × 16.5 cm)
Page 96

Lou Reed, the Factory, New York, New York. 1966–67. Gelatin silver print, 9½ × 6½" (24.1 × 16.5 cm)

Lou Reed, the Factory, New York, New York. 1966–67. Gelatin silver print, 6½ × 9½" (16.5 × 24.1 cm)

Lou Reed, John Cale, and Sterling Morrison, the Factory, New York, New York. 1966–67. Gelatin silver print, 6⅜ × 9½"(16.2 × 24.1 cm)

Rod LaRod, Andy Warhol, and Paul Morrissey, New York, New York. 1966–67. Gelatin silver print, 9 × 13½" (22.9 × 34.3 cm)
Page 277

Conceptual Sequences

Los Angeles, California, February 4, 1969. 1969. Twelve gelatin silver prints, each 4½ × 6½" (11.4 × 16.5 cm)
Pages 79 and 198

4-Part Variation, July 1969. 1969. Thirty-two gelatin silver prints, each 5 × 7" (12.7 × 17.8 cm). Tate: purchased with funds provided by the Photography Acquisitions Committee 2012
Page 83

Circle No. 1, July 1969. 1969. Eight gelatin silver prints, printed 2013, each 5 × 7" (12.7 × 17.8 cm). The Museum of Modern Art, New York. Acquired through the generosity of Robert B. Menschel
Page 81

KT Ranch, July 1969. 1969. Ten gelatin silver prints, each 4$\frac{7}{16}$ × 6$\frac{9}{16}$" (11.3 × 16.7 cm). Lent by The Metropolitan Museum of Art, New York. The Elisha Whittelsey Collection, The Elisha Whittelsey Fund, 1971
Page 157

July 22–23, 1969. 1969. Forty-nine gelatin silver prints, each 4 × 4" (10.2 × 10.2 cm). Walther Collection
Page 82

Avenue of the Americas, June 17, 1970. 1970. Sixteen gelatin silver prints, each 5 × 7" (12.7 × 17.8 cm)
Page 228

The Institute for General Semantics, Lakeville, Connecticut, June 25, 1970. 1970. Four gelatin silver prints, each 9⅜ × 7" (23.8 × 17.8 cm). Lent by The Metropolitan Museum of Art, New York. The Elisha Whittelsey Collection, The Elisha Whittelsey Fund, 1971
Page 127

Fred Shore. 1970. Gelatin silver print, 5 × 7⅞" (12.7 × 20 cm)
Page 177

Ruth Shore. 1970. Gelatin silver print, 5 × 7⅞" (12.7 × 20 cm)
Page 177

Manhood of Humanity. 1970. Gelatin silver print, 8 × 6" (20.3 × 15.2 cm)
Page 80

All the Meat You Can Eat

Stephen Shore and others. Material from *All the Meat You Can Eat*, 98 Greene Street Loft, New York, November 8–20, 1971. One hundred forty-seven chromogenic color prints, gelatin silver prints, postcards, and posters, dimensions variable
Pages 15–17 and 158–59

American Surfaces

Get Rich Quick! 1970. Paper, 11 × 8½" (27.9 × 21.6 cm)

The Daily Word. 1970. Paper, 11 × 8½" (27.9 × 21.6 cm)

Absolute Elsewhere. 1970. Paper, 11 × 8½" (27.9 × 21.6 cm)

Greetings from Amarillo, "Tall in Texas." 1971. Ten offset lithographs, each 3½ × 5½" (8.9 × 14 cm). The Museum of Modern Art, New York. Gift of the artist
Pages 19–21

Prints from *American Surfaces*. March 1972–December 1973. Two hundred nineteen chromogenic color prints, printed 2017, each 3$\frac{1}{16}$ × 4⅝" (7.8 × 11.7 cm)
Pages 19, 23–37, 45, 62–63, 65–67, 88, 106, 171, 195, 197, 204, 206, 212–13, and 234–35

Uncommon Places

A Road Trip Journal. 1973. Artist's book, cover 14 × 11" (35.6 × 27.9 cm), spread 14 × 21¾" (35.6 × 55.2 cm)
Pages 196–97

2nd Street, Ashland, Wisconsin, July 9, 1973. 1973. Chromogenic color print, printed 2017, 17 × 21¾" (43.2 × 55.2 cm)
Page 47

J. J. Summers Agency, 1st Street, Duluth, Minnesota, July 11, 1973. 1973. Chromogenic color print, printed 2017, 17 × 21¾" (43.2 × 55.2 cm)
Page 209

Badlands National Monument, South Dakota, July 14, 1973. 1973. Chromogenic color print, printed 2017, 17 × 21¾" (43.2 × 55.2 cm)
Page 265

U.S. 97, South of Klamath Falls, Oregon, July 21, 1973. 1973. Chromogenic color print, printed 2002, 17¾ × 21$\frac{15}{16}$" (45.1 × 55.7 cm). The Museum of Modern Art, New York. The Photography Council Fund
Page 141

Breakfast, Trail's End Restaurant, Kanab, Utah, August 10, 1973. 1973. Chromogenic color print, printed 2013, 16⅞ × 21¼" (42.8 × 54 cm). The Museum of Modern Art, New York. Purchase
Page 108

Elizabeth Street, Harrisonburg, Virginia, April 28, 1974. 1974. Chromogenic color print, 8 × 10¾" (20.3 × 27.3 cm)
Page 262

Fort Seybert, West Virginia, April 29, 1974. 1974. Chromogenic color print, 8 1/2 × 12" (21.6 × 30.5 cm)
Page 87

Grayson, Kentucky, May 1, 1974. 1974. Chromogenic color print, 8 × 10 1/4" (20.3 × 26 cm)
Page 260

11th Street, St. Louis, Missouri, May 12, 1974. 1974. Chromogenic color print, 8 × 10" (20.3 × 25.4 cm)
Page 255

West 3rd Street, Parkersburg, West Virginia, May 16, 1974. 1974. Chromogenic color print, 8 × 10 1/2" (20.3 × 26.7 cm)
Page 207

Church and 2nd Streets, Easton, Pennsylvania, June 20, 1974. 1974. Chromogenic color print, 12 1/4 × 15 1/4" (31.1 × 38.7 cm)
Page 259

21st and Spruce Streets, Philadelphia, Pennsylvania, June 21, 1974. 1974. Chromogenic color print, 8 × 10" (20.3 × 25.4 cm)
Page 254

Holden Street, North Adams, Massachusetts, July 13, 1974. 1974. Chromogenic color print, 12 × 15 1/8" (30.5 × 38.4 cm). The Museum of Modern Art, New York. Gift of Joseph G. Mayer Fund

Holden Street, North Adams, Massachusetts, July 13, 1974. 1974. Chromogenic color print, 7 5/8 × 9 5/8" (19.4 × 24.5 cm). The Museum of Modern Art, New York. Gift of Barbara Schwartz in memory of Eugene M. Schwartz

Holden Street, North Adams, Massachusetts, July 13, 1974. 1974. Chromogenic color print, printed 1987, 14 × 18" (35.6 × 45.7 cm)

Holden Street, North Adams, Massachusetts, July 13, 1974. 1974. Chromogenic color print, printed 2013, 16 7/8 × 21 1/4" (42.8 × 54 cm). The Museum of Modern Art, New York. Purchase
Page 261

Deerfield Street, Greenfield, Massachusetts, July 15, 1974. 1974. Chromogenic color print, printed 2013, 16 7/8 × 21 1/4" (42.8 × 54 cm). The Museum of Modern Art, New York. Purchase
Page 167

Lookout Hotel, Ogunquit, Maine, July 16, 1974. 1974. Chromogenic color print, printed 2013, 17 × 21 3/4" (43.2 × 55.2 cm). The Museum of Modern Art, New York. Acquired through the generosity of an anonymous donor
Page 61

New Hampshire, July 16, 1974. 1974. Chromogenic color print, printed 2017, 15 1/2 × 23 1/4" (39.4 × 59.1 cm)
Page 203

Castine, Maine, July 18, 1974. 1974. Chromogenic color print, printed 2013, 16 7/8 × 21 1/4" (42.8 × 54 cm). The Museum of Modern Art, New York. Purchase
Page 65

Alexandra and Vincent Crapanzano, Castine, Maine, July 20, 1974. 1974. Chromogenic color print, 8 × 10" (20.3 × 25.4 cm)

Bellevue, Alberta, August 21, 1974. 1974. Chromogenic color print, printed 2017, 17 × 21 3/4" (43.2 × 55.2 cm)
Page 43

2nd Street East and South Main Street, Kalispell, Montana, August 22, 1974. 1974. Chromogenic color print, printed 2013, 16 7/8 × 21 1/4" (42.8 × 54 cm). The Museum of Modern Art, New York. Purchase
Page 258

Lincoln Street and Riverside Street, Spokane, Washington, August 25, 1974. 1974. Chromogenic color print, 7 5/8 × 9 5/8" (19.4 × 24.5 cm). The Museum of Modern Art, New York. Gift of Barbara Schwartz in memory of Eugene M. Schwartz
Page 255

U.S. 10, Post Falls, Idaho, August 25, 1974. 1974. Chromogenic color print, 7 1/2 × 9 1/2" (19 × 24.2 cm). The Museum of Modern Art, New York. Gift of the artist
Page 266

Robert and Lucille Wehrly, Coos Bay, Oregon, August 31, 1974. 1974. Chromogenic color print, printed 2017, 17 × 21 3/4" (43.2 × 55.2 cm)
Page 180

Michael and Sandy Marsh, Amarillo, Texas, September 27, 1974. 1974. Chromogenic color print, 7 1/2 × 9 1/2" (19.1 × 24.1 cm). The Museum of Modern Art, New York. Gift of David H. McAlpin Fund
Page 180

San Francisco, California, September 1974. 1974. Chromogenic color print, printed 2017, 15 1/2 × 23 1/4" (39.4 × 59.1 cm)
Page 253

West 9th Avenue, Amarillo, Texas, October 2, 1974. 1974. Chromogenic color print, printed 2013, 17 × 21 3/4" (43.2 × 55.2 cm). The Museum of Modern Art, New York. Acquired through the generosity of an anonymous donor
Page 213

New York, New York, 1974. 1974. Thirty stereo slides, each 1 5/8 × 4" (4.1 × 10.2 cm)
Pages 205 and 218–21

Presidio, Texas, February 21, 1975. 1975. Chromogenic color print, 7 3/4 × 9 3/4" (19.7 × 24.8 cm)
Page 168

Beverly Boulevard and La Brea Avenue, Los Angeles, California, June 21, 1975. 1975. Chromogenic color print, printed 2013, 17 × 21 3/4" (43.2 × 55.2 cm). The Museum of Modern Art, New York. Acquired through the generosity of Thomas and Susan Dunn
Page 53

Alley off Sunset Strip, Hollywood, California, June 22, 1975. 1975. Chromogenic color print, printed 2013, 16 7/8 × 21 1/4" (42.8 × 54 cm). The Museum of Modern Art, New York. Purchase
Page 269

U.S. 93, Kingman, Arizona, July 2, 1975. 1975. Chromogenic color print, printed 2013, 16 7/8 × 21 1/4" (42.8 × 54 cm). The Museum of Modern Art, New York. Purchase
Page 257

Cumberland Street, Charleston, South Carolina, August 3, 1975. 1975. Chromogenic color print, printed 1981, 8 × 10" (20.3 × 25.4 cm)
Page 259

Meeting Street, Charleston, South Carolina, August 3, 1975. 1975. Chromogenic color print, printed 2013, 16 7/8 × 21 1/4" (42.8 × 54 cm). The Museum of Modern Art, New York. Purchase
Page 49

Untitled. 1975. Chromogenic color print, printed 2017, 15 1/2 × 23 1/4" (39.4 × 59.1 cm)
Page 271

Carnesville, Georgia, January 29, 1976. 1976. Chromogenic color print, 12 × 15 1/2" (30.5 × 39.4 cm)
Page 268

Backyard off U.S. 98, Apalachicola, Florida, February 4, 1976. 1976. Chromogenic color print, printed 2013, 16 7/8 × 21 1/4" (42.8 × 54 cm). The Museum of Modern Art, New York. Purchase
Page 267

Sutter Street and Crestline Road, Fort Worth, Texas, June 3, 1976. 1976. Chromogenic color print, printed 2013, 16⅞ × 21¼" (42.8 × 54 cm). The Museum of Modern Art, New York. Purchase
Page 267

Hoff Avenue, Tucson, Arizona, December 6, 1976. 1976. Chromogenic color print, 12 × 15¼" (30.5 × 38.7 cm)
Page 260

U.S. 93, Wikieup, Arizona, December 14, 1976. 1976. Chromogenic color print, printed 2013, 17 × 21¾" (43.2 × 55.2 cm). The Museum of Modern Art, New York. Acquired through the generosity of Thomas and Susan Dunn
Page 272

Queens, New York, March 1, 1977. 1977. Chromogenic color print, printed 2017, 15½ × 23¼" (39.4 × 59.1 cm)
Page 207

Palm Beach, Florida, November 8, 1977. 1977. Chromogenic color print, 12 × 15" (30.5 × 38.1 cm)
Page 106

Ginger Shore, Flagler Street, Miami, Florida, November 12, 1977. 1977. Chromogenic color print, 7¾ × 9¾" (19.7 × 24.8 cm)
Page 119

Miami Beach, Florida, November 13, 1977. 1977. Chromogenic color print, 8 × 10" (20.3 × 25.4 cm)
Page 264

Room 115, Holiday Inn, Belle Glade, Florida, November 14, 1977. 1977. Chromogenic color print, 8 × 10" (20.3 × 25.4 cm)
Page 273

U.S. 27, Moore Haven, Florida, November 15, 1977. 1977. Chromogenic color print, 8 × 10" (20.3 × 25.4 cm)
Page 263

U.S. 27, Palmdale, Florida, November 15, 1977. 1977. Chromogenic color print, 8 × 10" (20.3 × 25.4 cm)
Page 271

North Black Avenue, Bozeman, Montana, January 16, 1981. 1981. Chromogenic color print, printed 2017, 17 × 21¾" (43.2 × 55.2 cm)
Page 268

Commissions and Editorial Work

Robert Venturi, Steven Izenour, and Denise Scott Brown (conception); Stephen Shore and others (photographs). *Little Building / Building as Sign*. 1976. Silver dye bleach, 6' 11¾" × 35" (212.7 × 88.9 cm). The Architectural Archives, University of Pennsylvania by the Gift of Robert Venturi and Denise Scott Brown
Page 217

Robert Venturi, Steven Izenour, and Denise Scott Brown (conception); Stephen Shore and others (photographs). *The Bungalow*. 1976. Silver dye bleach, 48 × 44½" (121.9 × 113 cm). The Architectural Archives, University of Pennsylvania by the Gift of Robert Venturi and Denise Scott Brown
Page 49

Robert Venturi, Steven Izenour, and Denise Scott Brown (conception); Stephen Shore and others (photographs). *Gas Stations / Motels*. 1976. Silver dye bleach, 6' 11¾" × 35" (212.7 × 88.9 cm). The Architectural Archives, University of Pennsylvania by the Gift of Robert Venturi and Denise Scott Brown
Page 216

Greene County, Greensboro, Georgia, January 28, 1976. 1976. Chromogenic color print, 9 11/16 × 7 11/16" (24.6 × 19.5 cm). The Museum of Modern Art, New York. Gift of Joseph E. Seagram & Sons, Inc., Seagram County Court House Archives
Page 85

Georgetown County, Georgetown, South Carolina, February 20, 1976. 1976. Chromogenic color print, 7 11/16 × 9 11/16" (19.5 × 24.6 cm). The Museum of Modern Art, New York. Gift of Joseph E. Seagram & Sons, Inc., Seagram County Court House Archives

Frederick County, Winchester, Virginia, February 27, 1976. 1976. Chromogenic color print, 7 11/16 × 9 11/16" (19.5 × 24.6 cm). The Museum of Modern Art, New York. Gift of Joseph E. Seagram & Sons, Inc., Seagram County Court House Archives

Hampshire County, Romney, West Virginia, February 27, 1976. 1976. Chromogenic color print, 7 11/16 × 9 11/16" (19.5 × 24.6 cm). The Museum of Modern Art, New York. Gift of Joseph E. Seagram & Sons, Inc., Seagram County Court House Archives
Page 85

Gilbride Street and Sixth Street, Lackawanna, New York, October 24, 1977. 1977. Chromogenic color print, printed 2017, 8 × 10" (20.3 × 25.4 cm)
Page 87

Mrs. Evans, 17 Teresa Place, South Buffalo, New York, October 25, 1977. 1977. Chromogenic color print, printed 2017, 8 × 10" (20.3 × 25.4 cm)

Eddie's Wagon Wheel, Bridge Street, Struthers, Ohio, October 27, 1977. 1977. Chromogenic color print, printed 2017, 8 × 10" (20.3 × 25.4 cm)
Page 179

Washington Street, Struthers, Ohio, October 27, 1977. 1977. Chromogenic color print, printed 2017, 8 × 10" (20.3 × 25.4 cm)
Page 73

Washington Street, Struthers, Ohio, October 27, 1977. 1977. Chromogenic color print, printed 2017, 8 × 10" (20.3 × 25.4 cm)
Page 143

Wilson Avenue, Campbell, Ohio, October 27, 1977. 1977. Chromogenic color print, printed 2017, 8 × 10" (20.3 × 25.4 cm)

James Murphy and Solomon Felder, Campbell, Ohio, October 27, 1977. 1977. Chromogenic color print, printed 2017, 8 × 10" (20.3 × 25.4 cm)

Raphael Rentas, Louis Olivera, and Herminio Cadona, Campbell, Ohio, October 28, 1977. 1977. Chromogenic color print, printed 2017, 8 × 10" (20.3 × 25.4 cm)
Page 178

Giverny, France, 1977. 1977. Chromogenic color print, 7 11/16 × 9⅝" (19.5 × 24.5 cm). The Museum of Modern Art, New York. Gift of the Estate of Lila Acheson Wallace
Page 114

Giverny, France, 1977. 1977. Chromogenic color print, 7 11/16 × 9⅝" (19.5 × 24.5 cm). The Museum of Modern Art, New York. Gift of the Estate of Lila Acheson Wallace
Page 114

Giverny, France, 1977. 1977. Chromogenic color print, 7 11/16 × 9⅝" (19.5 × 24.5 cm). The Museum of Modern Art, New York. Gift of the Estate of Lila Acheson Wallace
Page 114

Giverny, France, 1977. 1977. Chromogenic color print, 7 11/16 × 9⅝" (19.5 × 24.5 cm). The Museum of Modern Art, New York. Gift of the Estate of Lila Acheson Wallace

Giverny, France, 1977. 1977. Chromogenic color print, 7 11/16 × 9⅝" (19.5 × 24.5 cm). The Museum of Modern Art, New York. Gift of the Estate of Lila Acheson Wallace

Giverny, France, 1977. 1977. Chromogenic color print, 7 11/16 × 9⅝" (19.5 × 24.5 cm). The Museum of Modern Art, New York. Gift of the Estate of Lila Acheson Wallace
Page 76

Graig Nettles, Fort Lauderdale, Florida, March 1, 1978. 1978. Chromogenic color print, 7 11/16 × 9 11/16" (19.5 × 24.6 cm). The Museum of Modern Art, New York. Acquired with matching funds from Blanchette Hooker Rockefeller and the National Endowment for the Arts, 1978
Page 50

Fort Lauderdale, Florida, March 5, 1978. 1978. Chromogenic color print, printed 2017, 8 × 10" (20.3 × 25.4 cm)
Page 50

West Palm Beach, Florida, March 14, 1978. 1978. Chromogenic color print, printed 2017, 8 × 10" (20.3 × 25.4 cm)

Fairfield County, Connecticut, June 1979. 1979. Chromogenic color print, printed 2017, 12 × 8" (30.5 × 20.3 cm)
Page 71

Fairfield County, Connecticut, June 1979. 1979. Chromogenic color print, printed 2017, 12 × 8" (30.5 × 20.3 cm)
Page 208

Fairfield County, Connecticut, June 1979. 1979. Chromogenic color print, printed 2017, 12 × 8" (30.5 × 20.3 cm)

Fairfield County, Connecticut, June 1979. 1979. Chromogenic color print, printed 2017, 8 × 12" (20.3 × 30.5 cm)
Page 77

Fairfield County, Connecticut, June 1979. 1979. Chromogenic color print, printed 2017, 8 × 12" (20.3 × 30.5 cm)

Fairfield County, Connecticut, June 1979. 1979. Chromogenic color print, printed 2017, 12 × 8" (30.5 × 20.3 cm)

Fairfield County, Connecticut, June 1979. 1979. Chromogenic color print, printed 2017, 8 × 12" (20.3 × 30.5 cm)

Fairfield County, Connecticut, July 1979. 1979. Chromogenic color print, printed 2017, 12 × 8" (30.5 × 20.3 cm)

Burbank, California, August 10, 1981. 1981. Chromogenic color print, printed 2017, 10 × 8" (25.4 × 20.3 cm)

Burbank, California, August 11, 1981. 1981. Chromogenic color print, printed 2017, 10 × 8" (25.4 × 20.3 cm)

Burbank, California, August 11, 1981. 1981. Chromogenic color print, printed 2017, 10 × 8" (25.4 × 20.3 cm)
Page 71

Burbank, California, August 11, 1981. 1981. Chromogenic color print, printed 2017, 10 × 8" (25.4 × 20.3 cm)
Page 93

"Hard Times Come to Steeltown," *Fortune*, December 1977
Page 72

"In Monet's Gardens," *New York Times Magazine*, April 2, 1978
Page 74

"Steinbrenner's Yanks," *New York Times Magazine*, April 9, 1978
Page 74

Richard Pare, ed., *Court House: A Photographic Document*, Horizon Press, 1978
Page 85

"In the Gardens of Monet," *Camera 35*, September 1980
Page 74

Annie on Camera: Nine Photographers, Abbeville Press, 1982
Page 75

The Nature of Photographs

Thomas Annan. *Close No. 61 Saltmarket*. 1868. Photogravure, 8 1/4 × 6 1/2" (21.0 × 16.5 cm). The Museum of Modern Art, New York. Purchase

Peter Henry Emerson. *During the Reed-Harvest*. c. 1885. Platinum print, 8 9/16 × 11 5/16" (21.7 × 28.7 cm). The Museum of Modern Art, New York. Gift of William A. Grigsby

André Kertész. *Dubo, Dubon, Dubonnet, Paris*. 1934. Gelatin silver print, 13 3/4 × 10 5/16" (34.9 x 26.2 cm). The Museum of Modern Art, New York. Gift of the artist

Walker Evans. *Mining Town, West Virginia*. 1936. Gelatin silver print, 7 9/16 × 9 9/16" (19.2 × 24.3 cm). The Museum of Modern Art, New York. Purchase

Robert Frank. *View from Hotel Window—Butte, Montana*. 1956. Gelatin silver print, 9 1/8 x 13 7/16" (23.1 x 34.2 cm). The Museum of Modern Art, New York. Acquired through the generosity of Marti Meyerson Hooper

Garry Winogrand. *Texas State Fair, Dallas*. 1964. Gelatin silver print, printed 1974, 8 9/16 × 12 13/16" (21.7 × 32.6 cm). The Museum of Modern Art, New York. Gift of N. Carol Lipis

Garry Winogrand. *World's Fair, New York City*. 1964. Gelatin silver print, printed 1974, 8 9/16 × 12 15/16" (21.8 × 32.8 cm). The Museum of Modern Art, New York. Gift of N. Carol Lipis

Lee Friedlander. *Knoxville, Tennessee*. 1971. Gelatin silver print, 6 5/16 × 9 1/2" (16 × 24.2 cm). The Museum of Modern Art, New York. Purchase

El Paso Street, El Paso, Texas, July 5, 1975. 1975. Chromogenic color print, 7 11/16 × 9 11/16" (19.5 × 24.6 cm). The Museum of Modern Art, New York. Gift of the artist
Page 91

Larry Fink. *Studio 54, New York City*. May 1977. Gelatin silver print, 14 1/16 × 13 7/8" (35.7 x 35.2 cm). The Museum of Modern Art, New York. Gift of the artist

Jan Groover. Untitled. 1985. Gelatin silver print, 11 7/8 × 15" (30.2 × 38 cm). The Museum of Modern Art, New York. Robert and Joyce Menschel Fund

Judith Joy Ross. Untitled from *Easton Portraits*. 1988. Gelatin silver print, 9 5/8 × 7 11/16" (24.5 × 19.6 cm). The Museum of Modern Art, New York. E. T. Harmax Foundation Fund

Thomas Struth. *Pantheon, Rome*. 1990. Chromogenic color print, 54 1/8 × 76 3/8" (137.5 × 194 cm). The Museum of Modern Art, New York. Gift of Werner and Elaine Dannheisser

Yucatán, Mexico, 1990. 1990. Chromogenic color print, printed 2017, 24 × 30" (61 × 76.2 cm)
Page 144

Landscapes

Merced River, Yosemite National Park, California, August 13, 1979. 1979. Chromogenic color print, printed 2013, 35 7/8 × 44 15/16" (91.2 × 114.2 cm). The Museum of Modern Art, New York. Gift of the artist
Page 153

Gallatin County, Montana, April 18, 1981. 1981. Chromogenic color print, printed 2017, 36 × 45" (91.4 × 114.3 cm)
Page 138

Gallatin County, Montana, July 10, 1982. 1982. Chromogenic color print, printed 2017, 36 × 45" (91.4 × 114.3 cm)
Page 111

Gallatin County, Montana, August 2, 1983. 1983. Chromogenic color print, printed 2017, 36 × 45" (91.4 × 114.3 cm)
Page 140

Ulster County, New York, 1984. 1984. Chromogenic color print, printed 2017, 36 × 45" (91.4 × 114.3 cm)
Page 137

Putnam County, New York, 1985. 1985. Chromogenic color print, printed 2017, 36 × 45" (91.4 × 114.3 cm)
Page 145

Ulster County, New York, 1986. 1986. Chromogenic color print, printed 2017, 36 × 45" (91.4 × 114.3 cm)
Page 145

Brewster County, Texas, 1987. 1987. Chromogenic color print, printed 2017, 36 × 45" (91.4 × 114.3 cm)
Page 143

Brewster County, Texas, 1988. 1988. Chromogenic color print, printed 2017, 36 × 45" (91.4 × 114.3 cm)
Page 145

Brewster County, Texas, 1988. 1988. Chromogenic color print, printed 2017, 36 × 45" (91.4 × 114.3 cm)
Page 147

County of Sutherland, Scotland, 1988. 1988. Chromogenic color print, 35 1/2 × 45 1/2" (90.2 × 115.6 cm). The Museum of Modern Art, New York. Gift of Susan and Arthur Fleischer, Jr.
Page 139

County of Sutherland, Scotland, 1988. 1988. Chromogenic color print, printed 2017, 36 × 45" (91.4 × 114.3 cm)
Page 146

County of Sutherland, Scotland, 1988. 1988. Chromogenic color print, printed 2017, 36 × 45" (91.4 × 114.3 cm)
Page 140

Yucatán, Mexico, 1990. 1990. Chromogenic color print, printed 2017, 24 × 30" (61 × 76.2 cm)
Page 172

Yucatán, Mexico, 1990. 1990. Chromogenic color print, printed 2017, 24 × 30" (61 × 76.2 cm)

Yucatán, Mexico, 1990. 1990. Chromogenic color print, printed 2017, 24 × 30" (61 × 76.2 cm)
Page 233

Yucatán, Mexico, 1990. 1990. Chromogenic color print, printed 2017, 24 × 30" (61 × 76.2 cm)
Page 237

Essex County. 1992. Inkjet print, printed 2017, 30 × 38" (76.2 × 96.5 cm)
Page 55

Luzzara, Italy, 1993. 1993. Gelatin silver print, 8 × 10" (20.3 × 25.4 cm)

Luzzara, Italy, 1993. 1993. Gelatin silver print, 8 × 10" (20.3 × 25.4 cm)
Page 175

Luzzara, Italy, 1993. 1993. Gelatin silver print, 8 × 10" (20.3 × 25.4 cm)

Luzzara, Italy, 1993. 1993. Gelatin silver print, 8 × 10" (20.3 × 25.4 cm)
Page 150

Luzzara, Italy, 1993. 1993. Gelatin silver print, 8 × 10" (20.3 × 25.4 cm)
Page 151

Luzzara, Italy, 1993. 1993. Gelatin silver print, 8 × 10" (20.3 × 25.4 cm)

Luzzara, Italy, 1993. 1993. Gelatin silver print, 8 × 10" (20.3 × 25.4 cm)
Page 151

Luzzara, Italy, 1993. 1993. Gelatin silver print, 8 × 10" (20.3 × 25.4 cm)
Page 56

Instant Photography

Dog Show: The 127th Westminster Kennel Club Dog Show. 2003. Thirty-four-page book, printed 2017, 8 5/8 × 11" (21.9 × 27.9 cm)
Page 190

3-25-03. 2003. Forty-page book, printed 2017, 8 5/8 × 11" (21.9 × 27.9 cm)

Jigsaw Puzzle: Lookout Hotel, Ogunquit, Maine 7/16/74. 2003. Twenty-page book, printed 2017, 8 5/8 × 11" (21.9 × 27.9 cm)
Page 135

Merced River: Yosemite National Park, California 8/13/79. 2003. Twenty-two-page book, printed 2017, 8 5/8 × 11" (21.9 × 27.9 cm)
Page 191

White Garden. 2003. Twenty-four-page book, printed 2017, 8 5/8 × 11" (21.9 × 27.9 cm)
Page 112

AA 105: 2-2-04. 2004. Thirty-six-page book, printed 2017, 8 5/8 × 11" (21.9 × 27.9 cm)
Page 183

The Marula Tree. 2004. Twenty-two-page book, printed 2017, 8 5/8 × 11" (21.9 × 27.9 cm)

The Fire Wood Tree. 2004. Twenty-two-page book, printed 2017, 8 5/8 × 11" (21.9 × 27.9 cm)

Merrick & Traction. 2004. Thirty-page book, printed 2017, 8 5/8 × 11" (21.9 × 27.9 cm)

Flohmarkt. 2004. Twenty-eight-page book, printed 2017, 8 5/8 × 11" (21.9 × 27.9 cm)
Pages 184–85

Central Park. 2004. Forty-four-page book, printed 2017, 8 5/8 × 11" (21.9 × 27.9 cm)

Times Square #2. 2004. Twenty-page book, printed 2017, 8 5/8 × 11" (21.9 × 27.9 cm)
Page 229

Heavy Metal Alphabet. 2004. Fifty-four-page book, printed 2017, 8 5/8 × 11" (21.9 × 27.9 cm)
Page 191

Window Rock, AZ. 2004. Thirty-page book, printed 2017, 8 5/8 × 11" (21.9 × 27.9 cm)

Civic Architecture: Postcard Series. 2005. Twenty-six-page book, printed 2017, 8 5/8 × 11" (21.9 × 27.9 cm)
Pages 186–87

Union of the Torus and the Sphere. 2004. Thirty-four-page book, printed 2017, 8 5/8 × 11" (21.9 × 27.9 cm)

11-9-05. 2005. Twenty-eight-page book, printed 2017, 8 5/8 × 11" (21.9 × 27.9 cm)

11-30-05. 2005. Eighteen-page book, printed 2017, 8 5/8 × 11" (21.9 × 27.9 cm)

6-9-06. 2006. Sixty-page book, printed 2017, 8 5/8 × 11" (21.9 × 27.9 cm)
Pages 188–89

La Joconde. 2008. Twenty-two-page book, printed 2017, 8 5/8 × 11" (21.9 × 27.9 cm)
Page 191

Winslow, Arizona, September 19, 2013. 2013. Digital slideshow, one hundred eighty-three images
Pages 44, 89, 197, 211, and 278–79

Images posted by Stephen Shore to his Instagram account. 2014–ongoing
Pages 113, 118, 121–25, 213, and 283

Israel and the West Bank

Ashkelon, Israel, 1996. 1996. Inkjet print, 30 × 38" (76.2 × 96.5 cm)
Page 38

Ashkelon, Israel, 1996. 1996. Inkjet print, 30 × 38" (76.2 × 96.5 cm)
Page 41

Hatzor, Israel, 1996. 1996. Inkjet print, 30 × 38" (76.2 × 96.5 cm)
Page 40

Hatzor, Israel, 1996. 1996. Inkjet print, 30 × 38" (76.2 × 96.5 cm)
Page 39

Hatzor, Israel, 1996. 1996. Inkjet print, 30 × 38" (76.2 × 96.5 cm)
Page 131

Jerusalem, Israel, September 12, 2009. 2009. Chromogenic color print, printed 2017, 16 × 20" (40.6 × 50.8 cm)
Page 207

Sderot, Israel, September 14, 2009. 2009. Chromogenic color print, 16 × 20" (40.6 × 50.8 cm). The Museum of Modern Art, New York. Gift of the artist
Page 133

Peqi'in, Israel, September 22, 2009. 2009. Chromogenic color print, 16 × 20" (40.6 × 50.8 cm). The Museum of Modern Art, New York. Gift of the artist
Page 105

Jerusalem, Israel, January 1, 2010. 2010. Chromogenic color print, 16 × 20" (40.6 × 50.8 cm). The Museum of Modern Art, New York. Gift of the artist
Page 133

Hebron, West Bank, January 11, 2010. 2010. Chromogenic color print, 16 × 20" (40.6 × 50.8 cm). The Museum of Modern Art, New York. Gift of the artist
Page 129

Beitin, West Bank, January 13, 2010. 2010. Chromogenic color print, 36×45" (91.4×114.3 cm). The Museum of Modern Art, New York. Gift of the artist
Page 130

South of Zefat, Israel, January 14, 2010. 2010. Chromogenic color print, printed 2017, 36×45" (91.4×114.3 cm)
Page 131

Nabī Musa, West Bank, January 19, 2010. 2010. Chromogenic color print, printed 2017, 36×45" (91.4×114.3 cm)
Page 163

Beit Safāfā, Jerusalem, Israel, March 22, 2011. 2011. Chromogenic color print, 36×45" (91.4×114.3 cm). The Museum of Modern Art, New York. Gift of the artist
Page 132

Ukraine

Bucha, Kyivska Province, Ukraine, July 18, 2012. 2012. Chromogenic color print, printed 2017, 16×20" (40.6×50.8 cm)
Page 249

Room 509, Dnipro Hotel, Kiev, Kyivska Province, Ukraine, July 18, 2012. 2012. Chromogenic color print, 16×20" (40.6×50.8 cm). The Museum of Modern Art, New York. Gift of the artist
Page 248

Tzylia Bederman, Bucha, Kyivska Province, Ukraine, July 18, 2012. 2012. Chromogenic color print, printed 2017, 20×16" (50.8×40.6 cm)

Tzylia Bederman, Bucha, Kyivska Province, Ukraine, July 18, 2012. 2012. Chromogenic color print, printed 2017, 16×20" (40.6×50.8 cm)
Page 245

Home of Tzylia Bederman, Bucha, Kyivska Province, Ukraine, July 18, 2012. 2012. Chromogenic color print, printed 2017, 16×20" (40.6×50.8 cm)
Page 245

Home of Tzylia Bederman, Bucha, Kyivska Province, Ukraine, July 18, 2012. 2012. Chromogenic color print, printed 2017, 16×20" (40.6×50.8 cm)
Page 106

Home of Tzylia Bederman, Bucha, Kyivska Province, Ukraine, July 18, 2012. 2012. Chromogenic color print, printed 2017, 16×20" (40.6×50.8 cm)
Page 106

Home of Tzylia Bederman, Bucha, Kyivska Province, Ukraine, July 18, 2012. 2012. Chromogenic color print, printed 2017, 16×20" (40.6×50.8 cm)
Page 244

Home of Tzylia Bederman, Bucha, Kyivska Province, Ukraine, July 18, 2012. 2012. Chromogenic color print, printed 2017, 16×20" (40.6×50.8 cm)

Boryspil, Kyivska Province, Ukraine, July 19, 2012. 2012. Chromogenic color print, printed 2017, 16×20" (40.6×50.8 cm)
Page 250

Lyubov Brenman, Boryspil, Kyivska Province, Ukraine, July 19, 2012. 2012. Chromogenic color print, printed 2017, 16×20" (40.6×50.8 cm)
Page 242

Home of Lyubov Brenman, Boryspil, Kyivska Province, Ukraine, July 19, 2012. 2012. Chromogenic color print, printed 2017, 16×20" (40.6×50.8 cm)

Home of Lyubov Brenman, Boryspil, Kyivska Province, Ukraine, July 19, 2012. 2012. Chromogenic color print, printed 2017, 16×20" (40.6×50.8 cm)
Page 242

Home of Lyubov Brenman, Boryspil, Kyivska Province, Ukraine, July 19, 2012. 2012. Chromogenic color print, printed 2017, 16×20" (40.6×50.8 cm)

Home of Lyubov Brenman, Boryspil, Kyivska Province, Ukraine, July 19, 2012. 2012. Chromogenic color print, printed 2017, 16×20" (40.6×50.8 cm)

Home of Lyubov Brenman, Boryspil, Kyivska Province, Ukraine, July 19, 2012. 2012. Chromogenic color print, printed 2017, 16×20" (40.6×50.8 cm)
Page 242

Home of Lyubov Brenman, Boryspil, Kyivska Province, Ukraine, July 19, 2012. 2012. Chromogenic color print, printed 2017, 16×20" (40.6×50.8 cm)

Home of Lyubov Brenman, Boryspil, Kyivska Province, Ukraine, July 19, 2012. 2012. Chromogenic color print, printed 2017, 16×20" (40.6×50.8 cm)
Page 242

Tsal Groisman, Korsun, Cherkaska Province, Ukraine, July 20, 2012. 2012. Chromogenic color print, printed 2017, 20×16" (50.8×40.6 cm)
Page 246

Korsun, Cherkaska Province, Ukraine, July 21, 2012. 2012. Chromogenic color print, printed 2017, 16×20" (40.6×50.8 cm)
Page 247

Uman, Cherkaska Province, Ukraine, July 22, 2012. 2012. Chromogenic color print, printed 2017, 16×20" (40.6×50.8 cm)
Page 249

Mira and Beba Pasek, Mykolayiv, Mykolayivska Province, Ukraine, July 23, 2012. 2012. Chromogenic color print, printed 2017, 20×16" (50.8×40.6 cm)
Page 243

Bershad, Vinnytska Province, Ukraine, July 24, 2012. 2012. Chromogenic color print, printed 2017, 16×20" (40.6×50.8 cm)

Bershad, Vinnytska Province, Ukraine, July 24, 2012. 2012. Chromogenic color print, printed 2017, 16×20" (40.6×50.8 cm)

Bershad, Vinnytska Province, Ukraine, July 24, 2012. 2012. Chromogenic color print, printed 2017, 16×20" (40.6×50.8 cm)
Page 239

Bershad, Vinnytska Province, Ukraine, July 24, 2012. 2012. Chromogenic color print, printed 2017, 16×20" (40.6×50.8 cm)
Page 239

Galina Karpenko, Tomashpil, Vinnytska Province, Ukraine, July 25, 2012. 2012. Chromogenic color print, printed 2017, 16×20" (40.6×50.8 cm)
Page 246

Bazaliya, Khmelnytska Province, Ukraine, July 27, 2012. 2012. Chromogenic color print, printed 2017, 16×20" (40.6×50.8 cm)
Page 251

Isaak Nibulskiy, Zhytomyr, Zhytomyrska Province, Ukraine, July 29, 2012. 2012. Chromogenic color print, printed 2017, 16×20" (40.6×50.8 cm)
Page 181

Home of Isaak Nibulskiy, Zhytomyr, Zhytomyrska Province, Ukraine, July 29, 2012. 2012. Chromogenic color print, printed 2017, 16×20" (40.6×50.8 cm)

Home of Isaak Nibulskiy, Zhytomyr, Zhytomyrska Province, Ukraine, July 29, 2012. 2012. Chromogenic color print, printed 2017, 16×20" (40.6×50.8 cm)

Home of Isaak Nibulskiy, Zhytomyr, Zhytomyrska Province, Ukraine, July 29, 2012. 2012. Chromogenic color print, printed 2017, 16×20" (40.6×50.8 cm)

Isaak Bakmayev, Berdychiv, Zhytomyrska Province, Ukraine, July 29, 2012. 2012. Chromogenic color print, printed 2017, 16×20" (40.6×50.8 cm)
Page 240

Isaak Bakmayev's Medals, Berdychiv, Zhytomyrska Province, Ukraine, July 29, 2012. 2012. Chromogenic color print, 16×20" (40.6×50.8 cm). The Museum of Modern Art, New York. Gift of the artist
Page 241

Vera Katz and Her Son, Khust, Zakarpatska Province, Ukraine, October 12, 2013. 2013. Chromogenic color print, printed 2017, 16×20" (40.6×50.8 cm)
Page 181

Shnuriv Lys, Kyivska Province, Ukraine, October 16, 2013. 2013. Chromogenic color print, printed 2017, 16×20" (40.6 × 50.8 cm)
Page 201

Shore's World

Stephen Shore. Self-portrait, New York, October 1957. Chromogenic color print, printed 2017, 10×8" (25.4 × 20.3 cm)
Page 287

Grace Mayer's notes from Stephen Shore's meeting with Edward Steichen, 1962. The Museum of Modern Art Library, New York
Page 161

Stephen Shore's artist record, 1962. The Museum of Modern Art Library, New York
Page 161

"Angry Young Man with a Camera," *U.S. Camera*, June 1963
Page 281

The Book Buyer's Guide, October 1963

Promotion for the Exploding Plastic Inevitable at the Balloon Farm in the *East Village Other*, October 1–15, 1966
Page 277

Kasper König, ed., *Andy Warhol*, Moderna Museet, 1968
Page 99

Stephen Shore, mock-up for *The Official Personal Vibrator Manual*, 1969

Mick-a-Matic camera, 1971. Mfr.: Child Guidance Products
Page 159

Rollei 35 camera, 1972. Mfr.: Rollei

Invitation to *American Surfaces*, Light Gallery, New York, 1972
Page 149

Crown Graphic 4-by-5 camera, 1973. Mfr.: Graflex

Western Union Telegram from William Eggleston to Stephen Shore, April 4, 1975

Invitation to *New Topographics: Photographs of a Man-Altered Landscape*, George Eastman House, Rochester, N.Y., 1975

Light Gallery calendar, 1975
Page 149

"U.S.A.: Pushing the Limits," *Modern Photography*, July 1976
Page 64

Stephen Shore, *Uncommon Places*, Aperture, 1982

Poster for French re-release of *Getaway* (1972), 1985

Stephen Shore's notebook, 1988

Invitation to *Stephen Shore: Fotografien 1973 bis 1993*, Westfälischer Kunstverein, Münster, 1995

Poster for *Stephen Shore: American Surfaces 1972*, Photographische Sammlung/SK Stiftung Kultur, Cologne, 1999

Olympus E-20 camera, 2002. Mfr.: Olympus Corporation

"In Back of the Real," *Another Magazine*, Spring/Summer 2006
Page 103

Stephen Shore, *The Nature of Photographs: A Primer*, revised edition, Phaidon Press, 2007
Page 165

Disposable placemats, 2007. Paper, each 11 × 17" (27.9×43.2 cm). Mfr.: Bob's Your Uncle, New York
Page 154

"Bard College," *Esquire* (Japan), April 2009
Page 231

Nike advertisement, 2009
Page 69

J. Crew catalogue, October 2009
Page 59

iPhone 5s, 2014. Mfr: Apple

IMA Concept Store iPhone 6 case, 2015. Mfr.: IMA Books
Page 155

Acknowledgments

Museum exhibitions, even those that are monographic, are always collective ventures. My sincere thanks go first to Glenn D. Lowry, who enthusiastically supported this endeavor from the very beginning. I am also grateful to my brilliant colleagues among the senior staff at MoMA: Kathy Halbreich, Associate Director and Laurenz Foundation Curator; Ramona Bronkar Bannayan, Senior Deputy Director of Exhibitions and Collections; Todd Bishop, Senior Deputy Director of External Affairs; Peter Reed, Senior Deputy Director for Curatorial Affairs; Wendy Woon, The Edward John Noble Foundation Deputy Director for Education; and James Gara, Chief Operating Officer and Assistant Treasurer.

For decades The Committee on Photography has unfailingly provided financial support and good counsel to the Department of Photography. In recent years, a number of Committee members have supported acquisitions of Stephen Shore's works, and I want to express particular appreciation to Tom and Susan Dunn, Charles Heilbronn, and Bob Menschel. I owe thanks to the Jo Carole Lauder Publications Fund, which made this book possible, and to all those who generously funded the exhibition, including Allianz, The William Randolph Hearst Endowment Fund, The International Council of The Museum of Modern Art, and our Committe Chairman, David Dechman, and Michel Mercure.

An undertaking of this scale relies on the contributions of many individuals, only a few of whom can be named here. Cate Griffin, Exhibition Manager, handled myriad details with efficiency and good nature, and Victoria Manning, Assistant Registrar, oversaw the transportation and installation of hundreds of objects with great care. Aimee Keefer, Exhibition Designer, developed an exhibition space that is both lively and elegant, complemented by the designs of Derek Flynn, Art Director, and Olga Domoradova, Senior Graphic Designer. Lee Ann Daffner, Andrew W. Mellon Foundation Conservator of Photographs, ensured the safety of Shore's art and restored the three *Signs of Life* transparencies, while Peter Perez and his team framed and installed prints with inspired expertise. One-Year Intern Gianna Furia worked on many aspects of the exhibition and publication, including compiling an extensive body of research, and Curatorial Intern Olga Lemagnen assisted with the final stages of the book.

I further extend my thanks to extraordinarily dedicated staff members in the departments of Archives, Audio Visual, Communications, Development, Digital Media, Education, General Counsel, Imaging and Visual Resources, Information Technology, Library, Marketing, Retail, Security, Special Programming and Events, and Visitor Services. I feel particularly honored to work alongside my colleagues in the Department of Photography. Megan Feingold and Marion Tandé tirelessly manage the department, and Dana Bell and Tasha Lutek care for the collection with consummate skill. Finally, I rely on the initiative, creativity, and experience of three extremely talented curators: Lucy Gallun, Roxana Marcoci, and Sarah Meister.

Many generous lenders—institutions, private collections, and commercial galleries—helped to make this ambitious exhibition a reality. Very special thanks go to Jeff Rosenheim at The Metropolitan Museum of Art, Simon Baker at Tate, Artur Walther at The Walther Collection, and Patrick Moore at The Andy Warhol Museum for entrusting us with vintage prints from their collections. Expert craftspeople ensured that Shore's work was produced to his high standards, and I appreciate the skill of Laura Major and A. J. Rohner at ColorLab, Doug Gillespie at GHP, Oleg Baburin at Chicago Albumen Works, and particularly Alison Brashaw and Stephanie Houde at Laumont Photographics. At 303 Gallery, Cristian Alexa, Senior Director, and Anabel Wold, Artist Liaison, gave unsparingly of their time and energy.

Editor Kate Norment and Production Manager Matthew Pimm applied their good judgment and patience to every aspect of the book, and it has benefited from their guidance as well as the support of Christopher Hudson, Chul R. Kim, Rebecca Roberts, Marc Sapir, and Don McMahon in the Department of Publications. Henrik Nygren and his team, especially Jonas Bard and Petter Dybvig, created a dynamic yet graceful design for this publication. Author and curator David Campany and Martino Stierli, The Philip Johnson Chief Curator of Architecture and Design, contributed illuminating texts to the catalogue that reflect their decades of engagement with Shore's photography. And we all owe a debt to Weston Naef, one of Shore's earliest supporters and a curator who has changed the landscape of American photography.

At Shore's studio, Laura Steele was essential to the realization of this project; I warmly thank her for her hard work, unwavering attention, and diligent organization. And at MoMA, nothing would have been possible without Kristen Gaylord, Beaumont and Nancy Newhall Curatorial Fellow, who from the very beginning assisted me with the project. Her unflagging energy, sharp intelligence, consistent enthusiasm, and deep knowledge of Shore's work made her contributions to both the exhibition and this catalogue invaluable.

Finally, my deepest gratitude is reserved for Stephen Shore, a true collaborator in this endeavor. As a European, I first engaged with Stephen's photographs through books in the early nineties. Gradually I discovered how wide-ranging, complex, independent, and demanding his work is, and eventually had the additional privilege of discovering the man: his generosity, intelligence, and vision have only furthered the honor of presenting his work in this exhibition and publication.

Quentin Bajac

This exhibition and book were conceived of and organized by Quentin Bajac. My respect and appreciation for him, his insight, and his imagination cannot be fully expressed. Kristen Gaylord was closely involved with the exhibition and the book from their inception, and her efforts were truly invaluable. I'm grateful to David Campany and Martino Stierli for their perceptive essays in the catalogue and to Matthew Pimm, who brought his infallible instincts to the book's production. I'd also like to express my appreciation to Kate Norment, who edited the catalogue; Aimee Keefer, who designed the exhibition; and Gianna Furia, who assisted Quentin and Kristen.

I'm indebted to Lisa Spellman and Cristian Alexa of 303 Gallery for their continued support of my work, and to Anabel Wold, who was extremely helpful in the organization and identification of material. I'd like to thank Becky Lewis of Art + Commerce for her efforts on my behalf. The contemporary prints were made, under my supervision, by Alison Brashaw and Valerie Sullo at Laumont Photographics, whom I've worked with for almost twenty years—I consistently depend on their fine craftsmanship. I'm also grateful to Philippe Laumont for his support and friendship. At my studio, the involvement of Laura Steele, assisted by Harriette Slagle, was crucial, and I relied upon her at every turn. Weston Naef has been a friend since 1970, and for this exhibition he put much effort into locating material from *All the Meat You Can Eat* that has been in his personal archive for more than forty-five years.

The exhibition covers about six decades of my life and work. Of these years, I've spent the last forty with my wife, Ginger. Her visual acuity and honesty have always pushed me forward. Spending my life with her, my son, Nick, and my stepson, Alex, has been my greatest pleasure.

Finally, I'd like to express my gratitude to you, the reader, for your interest in my work.

Stephen Shore

Photograph Credits

Courtesy Architectural Archives, University of Pennsylvania: 49, 215–17; Photo © Billy Name Estate, Courtesy Dagon James: 288; Courtesy Frances Mulhall Achilles Library, Whitney Museum of American Art: 193; Courtesy George Eastman Museum: 169; © Guido Guidi: 297; Courtesy IMA, Amana Inc.: 154–55; © 2017 Ken Josephson: 165; Courtesy Lisa Kereszi and Yancey Richardson Gallery: 165; © 2017 Andrew L. Moore / courtesy Yancey Richardson Gallery: 165; © 2017 The New York Times: 74, 157; © 2017 Nicholas Nixon: 293; NRW-Forum Düsseldorf / Ed. Werner Lippert & Christoph Schaden: 117; © 2007 Phaidon Press Limited: 165; Courtesy Seagram County Court House Archives, Library of Congress (LC-537-5521-1, LC-537-5522-2, LC-537-5526-3, LC-537-5546-1): 85; © Ginger Shore: 294; Courtesy UNIQLO / 2014: 155; © 2017 Walker Evans Archive, The Metropolitan Museum of Art: 93; © 2017 Henry Wessel: 169

© The Museum of Modern Art, New York: photo David Allison: 161, 192; photo Peter Butler: 154, 155, 159; photo John Wronn: 15, 19–21, 48, 59, 64, 72, 74–75, 85, 99, 102, 103, 117, 149, 154, 161, 165, 169, 217, 231, 277, 281

Published in conjunction with the exhibition *Stephen Shore*, organized by Quentin Bajac, The Joel and Anne Ehrenkranz Chief Curator of Photography, with Kristen Gaylord, Beaumont and Nancy Newhall Curatorial Fellow, Department of Photography, at The Museum of Modern Art, New York, November 19, 2017–May 28, 2018.

Allianz

Allianz is a partner of contemporary art at MoMA.

Major support for the exhibition *Stephen Shore* is provided by The William Randolph Hearst Endowment Fund, The International Council of The Museum of Modern Art, and David Dechman and Michel Mercure.

Additional support is provided by the Annual Exhibition Fund.

Support for this publication is provided by the John Szarkowski Publications Fund and by the Jo Carole Lauder Publications Fund of The International Council of The Museum of Modern Art.

Produced by the Department of Publications, The Museum of Modern Art, New York.
Christopher Hudson, Publisher
Chul R. Kim, Associate Publisher
Don McMahon, Editorial Director
Marc Sapir, Production Director

Edited by Kate Norment
Designed by Henrik Nygren Design, Stockholm
Production by Matthew Pimm
Printed and bound by Brizzolis, S.A., Madrid
Duotone and color separations by Brizzolis, S.A., Madrid

This book is typeset in Sabon LT Pro and Futura EF. The paper is 115gsm Sirio Color Perla, 150gsm Perigord, and 115gsm Sirio Color Nude.

Published by The Museum of Modern Art
11 West 53 Street
New York, New York
10019-5497
www.moma.org

Library of Congress Control Number: 2017952660
ISBN: 978-1-63345-048-6

Distributed in the United States and Canada by Artbook | D.A.P.
75 Broad Street, Suite 630
New York, New York 10004
www.artbook.com

Published outside the United States and Canada by Thames & Hudson Ltd
181A High Holborn, London WC1V 7QX
www.thamesandhudson.com

Printed in Spain

Front cover: Stephen Shore. *U.S. 93, Wikieup, Arizona, December 14, 1976*. 1976. Chromogenic color print, printed 2013, 17 × 21 3/4" (43.2 × 55.2 cm). The Museum of Modern Art, New York. Acquired through the generosity of Thomas and Susan Dunn